an introduction to theories of personality

Canadian edition

B.R. Hergenhahn
Professor Emeritus
Hamline University

Matthew H. Olson
Hamline University

Ken Cramer
University of Windsor

Prentice
Hall

Toronto

National Library of Canada Cataloguing in Publication

Hergenhahn, B. R., 1934–
    An introduction to theories of personality / B.R. Hergenhahn, Matthew H. Olson,
Ken Cramer—Canadian ed.

Includes bibliographical references and index.
ISBN 0-13-035842-8

    1. Personality. I. Olson, Matthew H. II. Cramer, Kenneth M. (Kenneth Michael),
1967–III. Title.

BF81.H39 2002   155.2   C2002-903187-7

ISBN 0-13-035842-8

Vice President, Editorial Director: Michael J. Young
Signing Representative: Carine Pierzchalski
Senior Acquisitions Editor: Jessica Mosher
Senior Developmental Editor: Lise Dupont
Marketing Manager: Judith Allen
Production Editor: Cheryl Jackson
Copy Editor: Gilda Mekler
Proofreader: Imogen Brian
Permissions Manager: Susan Wallace-Cox
Photo Researcher: Christina Beamish
Production Manager: Wendy Moran
Formatter: Debbie Kumpf
Creative Director: Mary Opper
Cover Design: Zena Denchik
Cover Image: Melissa Hayden/Photonica

16 17 18 CP 15 14 13
Printed and bound in Canada.

Dedicated to Linda J. Samson
with love and appreciation — B.R.H.

and

to Marce Soderman-Olson
with love and appreciation — M.H.O.

and

to Zachary, Jillian, and Alexander
and their unique personalities — K.C.

and

to the memory of
Edward L. Walker
(1914–1997)

Contents

5   *Karen Horney   103*

6   *Erik H. Erikson   127*

7   *Gordon Allport*   *153*

8   *Raymond B. Cattell and Hans J. Eysenck*   *181*

9   *B. F. Skinner*   *218*

10   *John Dollard and Neal Miller*   *246*

11   *Albert Bandura and Walter Mischel*   *275*

12   *Edward O. Wilson and David P. Barash*   *305*

15   *Abraham Maslow*   400

17   *A Final Word*   *451*

Preface

This text reflects our contention that it is in an Introduction to Theories of Personality course that the student experiences the full richness of psychology. In such a course, the student experiences everything from psychology's most rigorous scientists to its most mystical nonscientific thinkers. It is in such a course that the student reviews answers to questions such as: What, if anything, do all human beings have in common? What accounts for individual differences among people? How are the mind and the body related? How much of what we call personality is inherited and how much results from experience? And, how much of human behaviour is determined and how much of it is a function of free will? In such a course, the major theories of human motivation are reviewed and the major schools, paradigms, or "isms" within psychology are sampled: for example, psychoanalysis, behaviourism, humanism, and existentialism. It is in such a course that the student is exposed to the history of psychology, from Freud to the modern theorists, including Erikson, Allport, Cattell, Eysenck, Skinner, Bandura, Mischel, Wilson, Barash, Kelly, Rogers, and May. It is also in such a course that students encounter information that helps them make sense out of their own lives and their relationships with other people. Finally, in such a course, the nature of psychopathology and its treatment are explored. What other psychology course covers as much territory? Our answer is none, and therefore it is our belief that if a student were to take only one psychology course beyond the introductory course, it should be an Introduction to Theories of Personality course.

Although this text covers all of the topics already mentioned, its main purpose is to summarize the major theories of personality. The text is built around the belief that it is misleading to search for *the* correct theory of personality. Rather, we assume that the best understanding of personality is derived from a variety of viewpoints. Thus, theories representing the psychoanalytic, sociocultural, trait, learning, sociobiological, and existential-humanistic paradigms are offered as different—yet equally valid—ways of approaching the study of personality.

This Canadian edition was designed to show how the various personality theories can help us better understand the challenges we face as Canadians, but also to foster an appreciation for the richness and diversity of Canadian life. References to Canadian sports, politics, crime, language, music, and culture are included to illustrate the concepts and theories. For example, Adler's concept of overcompensating is discussed with reference to athletic heroes Terry Fox and Rick Hansen. Erikson's stages of development are applied to Ontario's investment in early childhood programs, the current concern with teen violence and bullying, and the transition of university students to adult roles. Canadian identification with Olympic medal-winners is cited as an illustration of Allport's concept of self-extension.

But equally important is the consideration of the enormous contributions made by Canadian researchers to the field of personality. Investigators at universities and research institutions across the country have made remarkable discoveries in recent years, opening up new avenues for both theory and application. New sections on research cover:

- dream analysis and defence mechanisms (p. 45);
- Myers-Briggs testing as it relates to Jung's theories (p. 74);
- religion (p. 74–75);

- cultural psychology and exposure to feminist philosophy (p. 123–124);
- identity formation and life transitions in early adulthood (p. 149);
- self-theory with respect to both self-esteem and self-deception (p. 176);
- the Five Factor model of personality and extroversion (p. 208);
- the role of self-talk in self-awareness and self-understanding (p. 270);
- the person-situation debate (p. 300);
- mate selection criteria and artificial insemination (p. 337);
- the prediction and control of important life events (p. 367);
- perfectionism in the context of self-actualization, depression, and eating disorders (p. 394–395);
- self-help books, self-actualization inventories, and the struggles of Ernest Hemingway and Nirvana's Curt Cobain with success (p. 423); and
- the nature of loneliness in the college population (p. 446).

While we cannot include all interesting and relevant research, this book represents our effort to capture a significant slice of it, sufficient, we think, to stimulate the interests of the student with a curiosity for personality.

Acknowledgments

We would like to thank a number of academics, including a few not listed here because they wish to remain anonymous, for agreeing to review the Canadian chapters and make suggestions for improvement. These reviewers include Susan Butt, University of British Columbia; Mike Condra, Queen's University; Helene Fung, University of Alberta; Ralph Howlett, Fanshawe College; Robert J. Konopasky, Saint Mary's University; Han Li, University of Northern British Columbia; Jennifer Out, University of Windsor; Terry J. Prociuk, University of Calgary; Janet Waters, Capilano College; and Suzanne Weld, University of Ottawa.

Sincere and warm thanks are also extended to Kandice Collins, Michelle Langlois, Marcy Peterson, and Ryan Stanga—graduate and undergraduate assistants who conducted exhaustive library and Internet searches on the personality research in Canada.

Finally, our thanks to the capable team at Pearson Education Canada, including Lise Dupont, Senior Developmental Editor; Tracy Bordian, Managing Editor; Cheryl Jackson, Production Editor; Gilda Mekler, Copy Editor; and Imogen Brian, Proofreader.

B. R. Hergenhahn
Professor Emeritus
Hamline University

Matthew H. Olson
Hamline University

Ken Cramer
University of Windsor

1 What Is Personality?

The term *personality* comes from the Latin word **persona**, which means mask. Those defining personality as a mask view personality as one's public self. It is that aspect of ourselves we select to display to the world. This definition of personality implies that important aspects of a person remain concealed for some reason. Other definitions of personality range from the popular notion that personality allows a person to be socially effective (a person may be viewed as having a wonderful personality, a terrible personality, or no personality at all), to highly technical definitions involving mathematical formulations. Therefore, several definitions of personality exist. In fact, every theory of personality can be viewed as an attempt to define personality and these definitions differ markedly from one another.

Three Concerns of Personality Theory

Kluckhohn and Murray (1953, p. 53) observed that every human being is (1) like every other human being; (2) like some other human beings; and (3) like no other human being. We are like all other human beings insofar as there is a **human nature** that describes "humanness." One task of the personality theorist is to describe what all human beings have in common, what we come equipped with at birth—that is, to describe human nature. Next we are like *some* other human beings insofar as we share a common culture. For example, it may be part of human nature to adorn one's body, to attempt to make sense of the universe and one's place in it, to seek a mate and produce offspring, to care for one's offspring, and to live cooperatively with one's fellow humans. It is culture, however, that determines how these things are done. In our culture, for example, if we want to marry, we must have only one wife or husband at a time. Lastly, each human is unique, with his or her own particular cluster of genes and his or her own particular cluster of personal experiences.

In describing personality, the personality theorist attempts to show how we are the same as other humans and how we are different from them. The former issue concerns human nature, and the latter concerns individual differences. It is one achievement to *describe* the components of human nature and the characteristics on which humans differ; it is another to explain their origins, how they interact, how they change over time, and their functional significance. The goals of personality theory are to describe what humans are like and to explain why we are like that—to describe and explain both human nature and individual differences. This is a large order and no single theory has been completely successful at doing either. Rather, different theories emphasize different aspects of human nature and individual differences, and offer different descriptions, explanations, and methods for studying them. For this reason, perhaps, the best understanding of personality is provided by the composite of many theories of personality as opposed to any single theory.

Proposed Determinants of Personality

In this section we review some of the factors stressed by various personality theorists in their attempts to explain personality. We see that one theorist may emphasize one or more of the following factors, whereas other theorists minimize them or ignore them altogether.

Genetics.   Probably the most common lay explanation of personality is based on genetics. If asked, people on the street tend to express the belief that personality characteristics are present for the same reasons that eye colour, hair colour, or physique are present. To ask why a person is shy is basically the same as asking why he or she is tall. Both characteristics, according to this viewpoint, are genetically determined. Common statements such as "He has an Irish temper," "She takes after her father," or "He has his uncle's artistic tendencies," imply a genetic explanation of personality because they all have an "It's in the blood" tone to them.

You should not be left with the impression that only nonprofessionals view personality characteristics as being influenced by heredity. Recent research suggests that heredity plays a far greater role in determining personality than was previously suspected. For example, for the past several years, Thomas J. Bouchard, Jr., has been studying identical twins separated at birth and reared apart. Bouchard consistently finds great similarity in the personalities of identical twins even when they had no contact with each other and were reared by distinctly different families. Bouchard (1984) concludes, "Both the twin studies and adoption studies . . . converge on the surprising finding that common family environmental influences play only a minor role in the determination of personality" (pp. 174–175). In other words, if children reared in the same family have similar personality characteristics, that fact seems to be explained more by their common genes than by their shared family experiences. Using the Multidimensional Personality Questionnaire to investigate the heritability of 11 personality traits, Tellegen, Lykken, Bouchard, Wilcox, Segal, and Rich (1988) found that genetics was the single most influential variable in determining the extent to which a person possesses such personality traits as well-being, social potency, achievement, aggression, and traditionalism. Perhaps most surprising is the fact that religiosity was also found to be highly heritable (Waller, Kojetin, Bouchard, Lykken,

& Tellegen, 1990). The authors of the latter study concluded, "Social scientists will have to discard the a priori assumption that individual differences in religious and other social attitudes are solely influenced by environmental factors" (1990, p.141). After reviewing the work of Bouchard and others, Holden (1987) concluded the following:

> Although behavioural geneticists quibble about each others' methodologies, most appear to be in accord with the conclusion that the common environment seems to have a negligible role in creating personality similarities among family members. From the standpoint of the organism, it seems, there may be no such thing as a common environment for two given individuals unless those individuals also have all their genes in common. (p. 600)

The field of sociobiology (chapter 12) also stresses the role of genetics in its explanation of personality. In fact, all theories of personality are built on an inherited quality whether it be physiological needs, described, for example, by Freud (chapter 2), Skinner (chapter 9), Dollard and Miller (chapter 10), and Maslow (chapter 15); the tendency toward self-actualization, described, for example, by Jung (chapter 3), Horney (chapter 5), Rogers (chapter 14), and Maslow (chapter 15); or social interest, as discussed by Adler (chapter 4). Thus the question is not whether genes influence personality, but rather to what degree and in what manner.

The question of how much personality is influenced by inheritance is as old as psychology itself. The **nativism-empiricism controversy** (also called the nature-nurture controversy) exists in every major category within psychology, and personality is no exception. In general, **nativism** claims that an important attribute, such as intelligence, is largely genetically determined. The nativist would say, for example, that the maximum level of intelligence that people can attain is determined at conception, and life's circumstances, at best, can help people to realize this genetically determined intellectual potential. The empiricist, conversely, believes that people's major attributes are largely created by experience. Intelligence, to the empiricist, is determined more by people's experiences than by their genetic endowment. To the empiricist, the upper limit of a person's intelligence is found in the environment, not in the genes.

The nativism-empiricism controversy manifests itself in many ways in personality theory, and we confront it several times in this text.

Traits.   Several personality theorists believe that what distinguishes people from one another are the traits they possess. Some traits, it is assumed, are learned (for example, food preferences), and others are genetically determined (for example, one's emotional makeup); some exert a powerful influence in one's life (for example, intelligence), and others have only a minor influence (for example, fashion preferences). Trait theorists believe the traits one possesses remain relatively constant throughout one's life and, therefore, they believe one's behaviour will tend to remain consistent across time and similar situations. The theories of Allport (chapter 7) and Cattell and Eysenck (chapter 8) stress the importance of traits in their explanations of personality.

Sociocultural Determinants.   To a large extent, one's culture determines what are considered proper dating practices, marital arrangements, child-rearing practices, political and religious institutions, education, justice, and views of other cultures. These, and other cultural variables, have a significant impact on one's personality. These cultural variables explain many important individual differences among humans, that is, differences among people of different cultures.

More specifically, some theorists say that one's personality can be viewed as a combination of the many roles one plays. If you were asked to start a blank sheet of paper with the words "I am" and then to list all of your qualities, you would have a rather extensive list. For example, you may be female, 20 years old, a university student, an Anglican, from Manitoba, 5 feet 4 inches, a member of several organizations, a New Democrat, attractive, a Virgo, a psychology major, and so on. Each entry on your list has a prescribed role associated with it, and for each role, society has defined what is an acceptable range of behaviour (norms). If you deviate from that range, you will confront social pressure of some type. Indeed, what is considered normal behaviour and what is considered abnormal is, to a large extent, determined by societal expectations.

Other sociocultural determinants of personality include the socioeconomic level of one's family, one's family size, birth order, ethnic identification, religion, the region of the country in which one was raised, the educational level attained by one's parents, and the like. One simply does not have the same experiences in a financially secure home as one would have in an impoverished home. These fortuitous circumstances into which a person is born (for example, culture, society, and family) certainly have a major impact on personality. Again, this point is one that all personality theorists accept; it is just a matter of how much each one emphasizes it. The theories of Adler (chapter 4), Horney (chapter 5), and Erikson (chapter 6) stress the importance of sociocultural determinants of personality.

Learning.   Those accepting a genetic explanation of personality represent the nativistic side of the nativism-empiricism controversy. Those emphasizing the learning process in their explanations of personality represent the empiricistic side. An example is the learning theorist's contention that we are what we have been rewarded for being; therefore, if our history of reward had been different, our personalities would be different. The difference between a successful person and an unsuccessful one, according to some learning theorists, is found in patterns of reward, not in the genes.

A powerful implication of this theoretical position is that one can control personality development by controlling the circumstances under which rewards are dispensed or withheld. Theoretically, according to this perspective, it is possible to create any type of personality by systematically manipulating reward. Those emphasizing the genetic basis of personality deny that personality is as pliable as the learning theorist suggests. The theories of Skinner (chapter 9), and Dollard and Miller (chapter 10) emphasize the importance of reward in the learning process. Bandura and Mischel (chapter 11) also stress the learning process but deny the importance of reward in that process.

Considerable compatibility exists between those stressing sociocultural determinants in their explanations of personality and those stressing the learning process. Both accept **environmentalism.** One's personality is shaped by cultural expectations but it is through patterns of reward and punishment that those expectations are conveyed to children. That is, they both believe that personality results from one's life experiences.

Existential-Humanistic Considerations.   Theories emphasizing existential-humanistic principles ask such questions as the following: What does it mean to be aware of the fact that ultimately you must die? What are the sources of meaning in human existence or in an individual's existence? According to what values is it best to live one's life and how are those values determined? How do the human needs for predictability and security relate to the human needs for adventure and freedom?

Such theories stress the importance of free will. Humans may be thrown by circumstance beyond their control into certain conditions of life, but how they value, interpret, and respond to those conditions is a matter of personal choice. For example, you may be born male or female, rich or poor, during peace or war, during famine or bountiful times. You may have been abused as a child, or you may have been raised under loving conditions. No matter what conditions you find yourself in or what experiences you have had, it is you who give those conditions or experiences whatever meaning they have for you. It is you who are in charge of your life; therefore, you alone are responsible for the type of person you become. The theories of Kelly (chapter 13), Rogers (chapter 14), Maslow (chapter 15), and May (chapter 16) fall into this category.

Unconscious Mechanisms. In many important respects, theories that emphasize unconscious mechanisms are the opposite of existential-humanistic theories. The primary concern of these so-called depth theories is to discover the underlying causes of behaviour. According to this viewpoint, because the ultimate causes of behaviour are unconscious and typically have their origins in childhood, the search for them is extremely complicated. Complex tools are needed in the search, tools such as dream and symbol analysis, free association, hypnosis, and the analysis of lapses of memory. According to this viewpoint, because what characterizes the unconscious mind can manifest itself in consciousness in any number of ways, one cannot really understand much about a person by studying his or her conscious experience. To understand personality, one must somehow get beneath the arbitrary manifestations of the unconscious mind to the unconscious mind itself. In other words, one must get beneath a person's mask. A personality theorist embracing this perspective does not ask a person why he or she acts in a particular way because the real causes of the behaviour are typically not known to that person. The theories of Freud (chapter 2) , Jung (chapter 3), and Horney (chapter 5) stress unconscious mechanisms in their analysis of personality.

Cognitive Processes. Currently there is considerable interest in cognitive processes within the realm of personality theory. Such processes determine how information from the environment is perceived, retained, transformed, and acted on by a person. Those theories stressing cognitive processes are typically interested in self-regulated behaviour and focus on the importance of self-reward, which comes from goal attainment, rather than on rewards that come from sources outside the person. Cognitively oriented theories also tend to emphasize the importance of present experience and future goals in determining behaviour and de-emphasize the importance of the past. Theories featuring cognitive processes include those of Bandura and Mischel (chapter 11) and Kelly (chapter 13).

Personality as a Composite of Factors. Because almost every theory of personality contains elements of all of the explanations just reviewed, perhaps it is safe to say that personality is a function of all of them. The elements emphasized depend on which theory of personality one considers. Assuming that, the situation can be summarized as follows:

Genetics	
Traits	
Culture–society	
Learning	Personality
Personal choice	
Unconscious mechanisms	
Cognitive Processes	

Questions Confronting the Personality Theorist

Personality theorists are in the unique position in psychology of studying the entire person. Most other psychologists are concerned with only one aspect of humans such as child development, old age, perception, intelligence, learning, motivation, memory, or pathology. It is only the personality theorist who tries to present a complete picture of the human being.

The task is monumental and is related not only to developments in other aspects of psychology but to developments in other disciplines as well: for example, medicine, neurophysiology, biology, sociology, anthropology, philosophy, and computer science. The personality theorists attempt to synthesize the best information from diverse portions of psychology and other disciplines into a coherent, holistic configuration. As personality theorists have attempted this synthesis through the years, they have addressed several questions related to human nature and individual differences. These are questions for which very diverse answers exist; no matter what the answer, however, each personality theory addresses them directly or indirectly. We have already discussed the nativism-empiricism controversy that reflects one such question. Other important questions addressed by personality theorists follow.

What Is the Relative Importance of the Past, the Present, and the Future? One question here is how childhood experiences are related to adult personality characteristics. A related question is, Are there critical irreversible stages of personality development? Freud, for example, said that personality was essentially fully developed by the end of the fifth year of life. Other theorists stress the importance of future goals for human behaviour. Goal-directed or future-oriented behaviour is also called **teleological behaviour**, and it plays a prominent role in the theories of Jung (chapter 3), Allport (chapter 7), and Bandura and Mischel (chapter 11). Both the learning theorists, such as Skinner (chapter 9), and the existential-humanists, such as May (chapter 16), tend to stress the importance of the present in their explanations of personality.

What Motivates Human Behaviour? Almost all theorists postulate a "master" motive for human behaviour. That is, they specify what they believe is the major driving force behind most human behaviour. Freud, Skinner, and Dollard and Miller postulate **hedonism,** or the tendency to seek pleasure and avoid pain. Jung, Horney, Maslow, and Rogers postulate **self-actualization,** or the impulse to realize one's full potential. Adler postulates striving for superiority. May and Kelly postulate a search for meaning and the reduction of uncertainty. Wilson and Barash postulate the desire to perpetuate copies of one's genes into the next generation. Bandura and Mischel postulate the need to develop cognitive processes that are effective in dealing with the world.

How Important Is the Concept of Self? Those theories that view human behaviour as smooth running, consistent, and well organized need somehow to account for these characteristics of behaviour. Several theories postulate the **self** as the organizing agent of personality. Also, it is often the self that is postulated as the mechanism providing individual consistency over time and across situations. The theories of Horney (chapter 5), Allport (chapter 7), and Rogers (chapter 14) rely heavily on the concept of self. Other theorists claim that employing the concept of self simply switches all of the questions we have about the person to questions about the self. In other words, the self is viewed as a homunculus (that is, a little person) inside the person who causes the person's actions. According to the opponents of the self concept, exactly how the self causes a person's actions remains a mystery. The concept of ego is often used in the same way as the concept of self and is criticized for the same reason. Skinner (chapter 9) was a theorist who was highly critical of self theories.

How Important Are Unconscious Mechanisms?   The depth theories, such as those of Freud and Jung, focus on the unconscious mind. Theories that emphasize unconscious mechanisms confront questions such as, What is the relationship between the conscious and unconscious minds? How can the unconscious be investigated? Can people ever become aware of their own unconscious motives and, if so, how?

Unconscious mechanisms are also important to many theorists stressing socio-cultural determinants of personality (for example, Adler, Horney, and Erikson) and to the sociobiologists (for example, Wilson and Barash). Conversely, trait theorists (such as Allport, Cattell, and Eysenck), learning theorists (such as Skinner, Dollard and Miller, and Bandura and Mischel), and existential-humanistic theorists (such as Kelly, Rogers, Maslow, and May), either deny or minimize the importance of unconscious determinants of personality.

Is Human Behaviour Freely Chosen or Is It Determined?   If all the influences acting on a person at any given time were known, would it be possible to predict that person's behaviour with complete accuracy? If your answer is yes, you are a determinist. If your answer is no, you probably believe in free will. Notice this question assumes we could know all the factors influencing a person's behaviour, and that is impossible. For example, imagine it is your task to determine what caused a person to commit a burglary. The possible causes would be numerous indeed and would include biological, social, and personal factors. More likely the cause of this, or any behaviour, would be a combination of these and other factors. For this reason, even strict determinists realize their predictions about behaviour must be probabilistic. Most personality theorists are determinists but, as we have seen, they stress different determinants of behaviour.

The only theorists who reject the doctrine of **determinism** are the existential-humanists, who believe that human behaviour is freely chosen. For them, we are masters of our destiny. We are not necessarily the victims of our biography, culture, genes, traits, patterns of reward, or any other factors.

What Can Be Learned by Asking People about Themselves?   Examining the contents of one's mind is called **introspection.** This question concerns the extent to which introspective reports can be trusted. Answers to this question run the gamut from existentialists, who claim that introspection is the most valuable tool available for studying personality, to some learning theorists who claim that introspection is not only invalid but unnecessary. In between the two extremes are the theories of Freud and Jung, according to which introspective reports are useful only if they are interpreted by a trained analyst.

Uniqueness versus Commonality.   We saw earlier that each person is unique because no cluster of genes or environmental experiences is the same for any two people. It is also true that all human beings have a great deal in common. The fact that we share similar brains and sensory apparatuses and a culture with other humans means we respond as others do to many situations. To a large extent, what we find aesthetically pleasing, what makes us laugh or cry, and our beliefs concerning the supernatural are culturally determined. Thus it is possible to emphasize either the fact that each human being is unique or the fact that each human has much in common with other humans.

Both emphases are found in personality theories. The study of a single individual is called **idiographic research**, and the study of groups of individuals is called **nomothetic research.** Theorists such as Allport (chapter 7), Skinner (chapter 9), and Kelly (chapter 13) use the idiographic approach because they emphasize the uniqueness of each individual. Theorists such as Cattell and Eysenck (chapter 8) emphasize the nomothetic approach because they stress traits that many individuals have in common.

Are People Controlled Internally or Externally?   Where is the locus of control for human behaviour? Some theorists stress internal mechanisms such as traits and self-regulatory systems, for example, Allport (chapter 7), Cattell and Eysenck (chapter 8), Horney (chapter 5), Rogers (chapter 14), and Maslow (chapter 15); others stress external factors such as environmental stimuli and patterns of reward, for example, Skinner (chapter 9) and Dollard and Miller (chapter 10); still others emphasize the importance of both internal and external controls, for example, Bandura and Mischel (chapter 11). Variables controlling a person's behaviour internally are called **person variables**; those controlling externally are called **situation variables.** The determination of the relative importance of person and situation variables for human behaviour is one of the primary concerns of current personality theorists. The question concerning internal versus external control is often posed in terms of subjective versus objective reality. A person variable would include a person's subjective awareness (consciousness) and the term situation variable is just another way of referring to the objective environmental circumstances a person experiences.

How Are the Mind and Body Related?   The question here is how something purely mental such as the mind, thoughts, or consciousness can influence something purely physical such as the brain, the body, or behaviour, and vice versa. The question is as old as psychology itself and still very much alive. One proposed answer is that no problem really exists because no mind exists; what we refer to as mental states are nothing more than subtle bodily responses. This position is called **physical monism** (materialism). Another answer is that mental events are merely the byproducts of bodily responses and, therefore can be ignored in the analysis of human behaviour. This position is called **epiphenomenalism.** Another proposed solution claims that an external event causes both bodily and mental events at the same time, but the two types of events are independent of each other. This position is called **parallelism.** Finally, some maintain that the mind influences the body and that the body influences the mind (such as when Freud maintains that pathogenic ideas can cause bodily ailments). This position is called **interactionism.** We will see that virtually all positions on the **mind-body problem** are represented among the various personality theorists.

What Is the Nature of Human Nature?   How a personality theorist answers this question determines the major thrust of his or her theory. Some answers include the following: The *empirical theory* states that people become what they experience, and the *rational theory* states that human behaviour is, or can be, under the control of thoughtful, logical, rational thought processes. The *animalistic theory* states that humans possess the same impulses and instincts as other animals, particularly other primates. The *sociobiological theory* claims that humans inherit behavioural tendencies from our evolutionary past but that these tendencies can be modified by rational thought or cultural influence. The *existential theory* states that the most important point about humans is our ability to choose courses of action and to assign meaning to the events in our lives. The *humanistic theory* claims humans are born basically good; if we engage in undesirable behaviour it is because cultural, societal, or familial conditions have forced us to do so. The *mechanistic theory* states that humans are automatons who respond automatically to environmental events. The automatic response may be a simple response to an environmental stimulus or a response given after information from the environment has been processed through several information-processing systems. In either case the response is automatic and machinelike. In the latter case, the mechanistic theory of human nature likens humans to computers. Again, virtually all assumptions about human nature are found among the various theories of personality.

How Consistent Is Human Behaviour?   Those theorists who stress traits, habits, genetics, or unconscious mechanisms in their explanations of personality assume a person's behaviour should be consistent in similar situations and over time. For example, it is assumed a person who possesses the trait of honesty would be honest in most situations in which honesty or dishonesty is possible. Likewise, an aggressive person would be aggressive in a wide variety of situations. Traditionally most personality theorists assumed a person's behaviour is consistent, and they saw their task as accounting for that consistency. More recently, however, it has been discovered that human behaviour may not be so consistent. For example, after a careful review of studies investigating the consistency of behaviour across time and across similar situations, Mischel (1968) concluded that human behaviour is too inconsistent to be explained in terms of such things as traits. Evidence suggests that some people are consistent in some ways but not in others, and these areas of consistency vary from person to person. The questions that personality theorists must now confront are, How consistent is human behaviour? What constitutes consistency? What accounts for individual differences in consistency? What variables account for consistency and inconsistency? Efforts to answer these questions usually involve a discussion of the relative importance of person (internal) versus situation (external) variables and the interaction between them. We will address the question of behavioural consistency in chapter 11.

How Do We Find the Answers?

Epistemology.   **Epistemology** is the study of knowledge. It attempts to answer questions such as, What does it mean to know? What are the limits of knowledge? What are the origins of knowledge? Because science, at least in part, is a method of gaining knowledge, it can be considered an epistemological pursuit.

Science.   **Science** combines two ancient philosophical positions on the origins of knowledge. One of these positions, called **rationalism**, contends that one gains knowledge by exercising the mind, in other words, by thinking, reasoning, and using logic. According to the rationalist, information must be sorted out by the mind before reasonable conclusions can be drawn. The other philosophical position, called **empiricism**, contends that sensory experience is the basis of all knowledge. In its extreme form, empiricism states that we know only what we experience. Thus the rationalist emphasizes mental operations whereas the empiricist equates knowledge with experience. Science combines the two positions thereby creating an extremely powerful epistemological tool.

Scientific Theory.   In the realm of science, rationalism and empiricism meet in **scientific theory**. Note this marriage of philosophical schools in the following quotation by S.S. Stevens: "Science seeks to generate confirmable propositions by fitting a formal system of symbols (language, mathematics, logic) to empirical observations" (1951, p. 22).

The first step in utilizing scientific theory involves making a number of empirical observations concerning some problem or phenomenon of interest. Next, one attempts to make sense out of these observations by thinking about, grouping, and synthesizing them. This attempt to make observations more constructive by thinking about them in various ways is a rational endeavour.

Thus, in science, observations are made (empiricism) and then they are organized in some meaningful way (rationalism). Next, the scientist must verify whether the groupings are, in fact, meaningful. If they are, they should indicate where to look for additional information. In other words, if the concepts used to organize the original observations are to be useful, they must do two things: (1) synthesize observations, and (2) generate new research. This process can be represented schematically as follows:

We can see that a scientific theory comes into existence to explain several observations (its **synthesizing function**), and when it exists, it must be able to suggest other places where the researcher may seek additional information. A theory's ability to generate new research is called its **heuristic function**.

As an example of the foregoing, let us say young Freud is talking with a friend when the friend realizes he has missed his dental appointment. This incident registers in Freud's sensitive mind. Later, Freud observes his friend's other lapses of memory and notes they all have something in common: painful or anxiety-related experiences. Freud speculates that many disturbing thoughts are repressed; that is, they are held in the unconscious mind thereby preventing the discomfort that would be caused by their conscious recognition. The theoretical notion of the repression of disturbing thoughts serves two purposes. It helps to make sense out of previously disjointed observations, and it aids in discovering other truths. For example, if disturbing thoughts are repressed, the unconscious mind will be a veritable storehouse of such thoughts, which could be released under the appropriate circumstances. In other words, if one could tap the contents of the unconscious mind with such devices as hypnotism, dream analysis, or free association, one should find an abundance of repressed memories.

Principle of Verification.   The feature of scientific explanations that most differentiates them from nonscientific explanations is the **principle of verification.** All scientific explanations must be capable of being tested by objective, empirical methods, for example, by experimentation. Furthermore, this test must be available to any interested person. That is, scientific propositions must be capable of public verification. No matter how interesting a theory may be, without the potential for public empirical validation it is not a scientific theory. Marx and Goodson (1976) make this point: "If there is no way of testing a theory it is scientifically worthless, no matter how plausible, imaginative, or innovative it may be" (p. 249).

History has been plagued by pseudoscientific explanations of personality. At one time or another all of the following have had wide popular appeal: astrology, numerology, palmistry, phrenology, physiognomy, and graphology. Although popular, all of these "explanations" of personality violate the principle of verification. That is, their claims are so general and nebulous that no test is available to clearly demonstrate their truth or falsity.

Optimally, scientific theories, in addition to being able to synthesize (explain) observations, should be internally consistent, precise, testable, heuristic, and as simple as possible. Few, if any, personality theories meet all these criteria, but this does not necessarily render such theories useless. Even personality theories containing terms and propositions too general to verify directly often generate research hypotheses that are capable of empirical verification. Hall and Lindzey (1978) make this point:

> However vague and poorly developed the theory, and however inadequate its syntax and empirical definitions, if it can be shown to have had a generative effect upon significant areas of research we would have to conclude that it passes the crucial test. Thus, the payoff question that overrides, and actually makes trivial, all questions of formal adequacy is the matter of how much important research the theory has produced. (p. 20)

It is this ultimate concern with the empirical verification of its terms and propositions that differentiates the efforts of the personality theorists from those of pseudo-scientists.

Science and Personality Theory

Scientific theories differ in their rigour. In such sciences as physics or chemistry, theories are highly developed. The terms used in them are precisely defined, and a high correspondence exists among the words, signs, and symbols in the theory and the empirical events it purports to explain. The use of complex mathematics is common in such theories. In psychology, theories exist in almost all stages of development. In areas such as psychophysics, cognition, and learning, psychology has theories that rival those in the physical sciences in terms of rigour. Many theories in psychology are in their infant stages, however, containing terms that are not precisely defined. Also, the relationship between their terms and empirical events is not a tight one. Most personality theories are in the latter category. In fact, some theories of personality make no claim to being scientific in the sense that they can be tested under highly controlled conditions. Such theories claim that their verification comes either from everyday experience or from clinical practice.

As we have seen, to say that most personality theories lack scientific rigour is not the same thing as concluding that they are not useful. Each personality theory provides us with a different viewpoint. In the final analysis, we may learn more about some topic by viewing it from a variety of angles than we would by burrowing in deeply from one angle.

Kuhn's View of Science. Thomas Kuhn (1922–1996) in his influential book, *The Structure of Scientific Revolutions* (1973), indicated that most scientists accept a "viewpoint" concerning their subject matter as they carry out their research. This viewpoint guides their research activities and to a large extent determines what is studied and how it is studied. Kuhn called a viewpoint shared by many scientists a **paradigm.** For example, years ago most physicists accepted a Newtonian viewpoint regarding their work but now most follow an Einsteinian viewpoint. The dominant paradigm in physics shifted from Newton's theory to Einstein's theory.

In psychology, no one paradigm ever guided all psychological research; rather, several paradigms have always existed simultaneously. In addition, the term *paradigm*, as it applies to psychology, corresponds to groups of interrelated theories commonly called a "school of thought" or an "ism" instead of to a single theory, as is the case in physics. In either case, a paradigm can be considered a way of looking at and investigating a certain subject. Therefore, different scientists exploring the same subject matter go about their work differently, depending on which paradigm guides their research activities.

The most important point regarding paradigms is that it is not necessary to consider one correct and the others incorrect; they all simply generate different research methodologies.

How do these ideas relate to personality theory? Personality is a complex topic, and many approaches to its study exist. In fact, these approaches are paradigms, and everything that has been said applies to them. In the remainder of this text, we sample paradigms that guide research in the area of personality. These six paradigms are listed along with the theorists who have been chosen to represent them.

Psychoanalytic Paradigm
> Sigmund Freud
> Carl Jung

Sociocultural Paradigm
> Alfred Adler
> Karen Horney
> Erik Erikson

Trait Paradigm
> Gordon Allport
> Raymond B. Cattell and Hans J. Eysenck

Learning Paradigm
> B. F. Skinner
> John Dollard and Neal Miller
> Albert Bandura and Walter Mischel

Sociobiological Paradigm
> Edward Wilson and David Barash

Existential-Humanistic Paradigm
> George Kelly
> Carl Rogers
> Abraham Maslow
> Rollo May

Note that each paradigm is named for its central theme. The psychoanalytic paradigm focuses on the analysis of the psyche, and the sociocultural paradigm focuses on the study of societal-cultural factors influencing personality. The trait paradigm emphasizes the importance of the various traits that people possess, and the learning paradigm focuses on the importance of learning for personality development. The sociobiological paradigm emphasizes the inherited tendency to engage in certain social behaviours, and the existential-humanistic paradigm focuses on free choice and personal responsibility.

Again, do not attempt to find the paradigm that is most correct. All paradigms provide useful information about personality; the information generated by one paradigm is just different from that generated by others. To attempt to build a house with only one tool such as a hammer, a saw, or a screwdriver would be ineffective. Likewise, attempting to understand personality using only one theoretical orientation would leave huge gaps in one's understanding. This text offers a variety of theories that collectively may provide a far greater understanding of personality than any one of them taken alone could do.

Popper's View of Science. We have just reviewed Kuhn's philosophy of science with his emphasis on the concept of paradigm. It is also important to examine Karl Popper's philosophy of science because it has special relevance to personality theory. According to Popper (1902–1994), if a theory can account for everything that could possibly happen, the theory cannot be considered scientific. Such a theory explains everything and, therefore, it explains nothing. To be scientific, a theory must make **risky predictions.** That is, it must make predictions that have a chance of being incorrect. If a theory does generate predictions (hypotheses) that are not confirmed, the theory is considered invalid and should be revised or abandoned. So, to be scientific, a theory must generate hypotheses that could invalidate the theory if they are not confirmed; this is what is meant by making risky predictions. If, conversely, a theory makes predictions so general that anything that happens can be considered in accordance with the theory, no conceivable observation could be made that would falsify or refute the theory. Thus, according to Popper's **principle of falsifiability** (also called the principle of refutability), all scientific theories must be falsifiable. Astrology, for example, cannot be considered scientific because each horoscope is so general as to apply to almost anyone. If astrology made highly specific, potentially false predictions about the major events in the lives of individuals, then the predictions could be objectively evaluated, but it does not do so. Marx and Goodson (1976) describe the implications of Popper's principle of falsifiability.

> In real scientific life theories typically contribute not by being right but by being wrong. In other words, scientific advance in theory as well as experiment tends to be built upon the successive correction of many errors, both small and large. Thus the popular notion that a theory must be right to be useful is incorrect. (p. 249)

Popper's principle of falsification is especially important in the realm of personality theory. Many theories of personality are extremely difficult, if not impossible to falsify. Hergenhahn and Olson (1997) give an example:

> Freud's theory . . . . makes no risky predictions. Everything that a person does can be "explained" by Freud's theory. If, for example, Freud's theory predicts that on the basis of early experience a man should hate women but is found to love them, the Freudian can say that he is displaying a "reaction formation." That is, he really does hate women on the unconscious level, and he is simply going overboard in the opposite direction to reduce the anxiety that his recognition of his true hatred of women would cause. Astrology suffers the same fate since there is no conceivable observation that could be made that would refute its claims. Contrary to common belief, if every conceivable observation agrees with a theory, the theory is weak, not strong. (p. 25)

Obviously, a theory's ability to generate predictions (hypotheses) is vitally important in Popper's philosophy of science; without predictions falsification would not be possible. Unfortunately, in the realm of personality theory the concern is often with postdiction rather than prediction. Hall and Lindzey (1978) say, "Most personality theorists have been oriented toward after-the-fact explanations rather than toward the generation of new predictions concerning behaviour" (p.16).

Many theories of personality cannot pass the test of falsifiability and, therefore, according to Popper, are not scientific. Remember, however, that personality is enormously complex and has many subjective components that cannot be observed or measured directly. Also, the systematic, objective study of personality is relatively new compared to the subject matters of the older, more established sciences. Finally, to say that a theory is not scientific is not to say that it is useless. Popper (1963) made the following observation:

> Historically speaking all—or nearly all—scientific theories originate from myths, and. . . a myth may contain important anticipations of scientific theories. . . . I thus [believe] that if a theory is found to be non-scientific, or "metaphysical". . . it is not thereby found to be unimportant, or insignificant, or "meaningless," or "nonsensical." (p. 38)

We believe that although the theories that follow vary in terms of their scientific rigour, all of them contribute to our understanding of personality.

SUMMARY

1. The definition of personality varies with the assumptions and beliefs of those studying it. Thus, there are at least as many definitions of personality as there are theories of personality. The personality theorist attempts to describe what all humans have in common (human nature), what some have in common, and the uniqueness of each individual (individual differences).

2. The authors of the present text assume that a comprehensive explanation of personality would specify the relative importance of genetics, traits, sociocultural determinants, learning, existential-humanistic considerations, unconscious mechanisms, and cognitive processes. Each personality theorist must implicitly or explicitly address a number of basic questions such as: What is the relative importance of the past, present, and future? What motivates human behaviour? How important is the concept of self? How important are unconscious mechanisms? Is human behaviour freely chosen or is it determined? What can be learned by asking people about themselves? What should be emphasized, human uniqueness or commonality? Are people controlled internally or externally? How are the mind and body related? What is the nature of human nature? How consistent is human behaviour?

3. The most objective way to answer questions such as those above is to employ scientific method. Scientific theory combines empiricism and rationalism by insisting that first empirical observations be made of the phenomena of interest, and then precise explanations be formulated that attempt to explain the observations. In addition to explaining observations, a good scientific theory will generate additional research (its heuristic function). In the realm of science, all terms and propositions must be capable of public, empirical verification. The principle of verification is what differentiates scientific from pseudoscientific explanations.

4. Kuhn observed that most scientists embrace a general paradigm that determines their research topics and methodologies. The physical sciences are usually dominated by a single paradigm but in psychology several paradigms have always existed simultaneously. The paradigms that have guided research on personality include the psychoanalytic, sociocultural, trait, learning, sociobiological, and existential-humanistic.

5. Popper's philosophy of science features the principle of falsifiability. According to this principle, in order for a theory to be considered scientific, it must generate predictions that run a real risk of being disconfirmed. If the predictions

generated by a theory are so general that most any outcome confirms them, the theory, according to Popper, is not scientific. Many theories of personality fail Popper's test of falsifiability and therefore, according to his definition, are not scientific. However, Popper observed that non-scientific theories often precede scientific theories and, therefore, nonscientific theories can be useful.

EXPERIENTIAL EXERCISES

1. Place the words "I am" at the top of a blank sheet of paper and proceed to list the characteristics that are true about you at the moment. For example, I am a woman, a Christian, a psychology major, a mother, a waitress. Briefly describe the culturally prescribed role associated with each item on your list. Do you believe a person who either refuses to play a socially prescribed role, or is incapable of doing so, will experience social pressure of some type? Explain.

2. To demonstrate the difficulty in determining the cause of any behaviour, list the factors that led you to enrol in the university you are now attending (for example, your decision to go to university, the proximity of the university to your residence, the fact that you applied and were admitted, friends or relatives attending the same university, and so forth). Do the same thing for your choices of major and your significant other.

3. Formulate your own theory of personality. Indicate what your theory stresses. For example, what assumption about human nature does it make? Does it stress the importance of the past, the present, or the future? Unconscious mechanisms? Would you place it within the existential-humanistic paradigm? If not, which one? Is your theory falsifiable? Save your theory and compare it to the one you will be asked to formulate at the end of this book.

4. List several of your most important personality characteristics and also those of someone with whom you are very familiar. Note that the adjectives you use in this exercise will suggest the types of personality characteristics that you think are most important and, therefore, might suggest which of the theories covered in this text will appeal to you the most.

5. How does the consistency-inconsistency controversy apply to your personality? Are there some aspects of your personality that you consider consistent over time and across situations and some you consider inconsistent? Give examples of each. Attempt to account for both the consistent and inconsistent aspects of your personality.

6. We typically identify a person as a specific individual at birth, and claim that he or she remains the same individual until death. Specify what you believe makes a person the same person throughout his or her lifetime. What, for example, justifies punishing a person for a crime committed 20 or more years ago? Another way to approach this problem is to specify what would need to change about a person before you would be willing to conclude that he or she is no longer the same person. His or her physical appearance? Beliefs? Memories? Gender? A combination of these characteristics? Something else?

DISCUSSION QUESTIONS

1. Give an example of how each of the following might influence a person's personality: genetics, traits, sociocultural determinants, learning, existential-humanistic considerations, unconscious mechanisms, and cognitive processes.

2. What is determinism? Give examples of the types of determinism represented among the personality theories. What is the alternative to believing that human behaviour is determined?

3. Briefly discuss each of the following theories of human nature: empirical, rational, animalistic, sociobiological, existential, humanistic, and mechanistic.

4. Describe Popper's principle of falsifiability and explain why, in terms of this principle, astrology and Freud's theory of personality cannot be considered scientific.

KEY TERMS

Determinism, p. 7
Empiricism, p. 9
Environmentalism, p. 4
Epiphenomenalism, p. 8
Epistemology, p. 9
Hedonism, p. 6
Heuristic function of a theory, p. 10
Human nature, p. 1
Idiographic research, p. 8
Interactionism, p. 8
Introspection, p. 7
Mind-body problem, p. 8
Nativism, p. 3
Nativism-empiricism controversy (also called the nature-nurture controversy), p. 3
Nomothetic research, p. 8
Paradigm, p. 11

Parallelism, p. 8
Person variables, p. 8
Persona, p. 1
Physical monism (also called materialism), p. 8
Principle of falsifiability (also called principle of refutability), p. 13
Principle of verification, p. 10
Rationalism, p. 9
Risky predictions, p. 13
Science, p. 9
Scientific theory, p. 10
Self, p. 6
Self-actualization, p. 6
Situation variables, p. 8
Synthesizing function of a theory, p. 10
Teleological behaviour, p. 6

2 Sigmund Freud

Chapter Outline

Freud (1917/1966, pp. 284–285) observed that humans have had three major blows to their self-esteem. The first came from Copernicus, who demonstrated that the earth was not the centre of the universe, as humans had so egotistically believed. In fact, Copernicus demonstrated that the earth was not even the centre of our solar system, a fact that was not easily digested.

The second blow came from the work of Charles Darwin, who demonstrated that humans were not the product of "special creation" but were descended from and continuous with the so-called lower animals.

As the dust caused by Darwin's revelations was settling, our self-esteem was salvaged by the belief that humans were rational animals. Although we descended from lower animals, somewhere in the process of evolution we became qualitatively different from them by becoming dependent on our intellect. Animals were driven by instinct; only human behaviour was rationally determined.

It was Freud who dealt the third blow to human self-esteem by demonstrating that human behaviour is primarily instinctive and motivated mainly by unconscious processes. In other words, according to Freud, most humans are anything but rational animals. Whether we agree with Freud's theory or not, Freudian concepts have completely revised the way we view human nature.

Biographical Sketch

Sigmund Freud

Sigmund Freud was born on May 6, 1856, in Freiberg, Austria (now Pribor, Czech Republic). As we see shortly, however, it is possible that Freud was born on March 6 instead of May 6. When Freud was four years old, he and his family moved to Vienna, where he continued to live for nearly 80 years. His father, Jakob, was a not-too-successful wool merchant and a strict authoritarian father. At the time of Freud's birth, his father was 40 years old, and his mother, who was his father's third wife, was a youthful 20. Freud was the first of eight children born to his mother, Amalie Nathansohn Freud, in the course of 10 years. One son, however, died at the age of seven months when Sigmund was two years old. It is interesting to note that Amalie was Jakob Freud's third wife, not his second as has been commonly believed. Examination of the town records of Freiberg in 1968 revealed that Jakob's second wife was a woman named Rebecca, about whom practically nothing is known. Years earlier it was also discovered by examining the birth register of Freiberg that Sigmund Freud's official birthday was March 6, 1856, not May 6 as is commonly reported. Ernest Jones, Freud's official biographer, suggests that the discrepancy reflects only a clerical error, but others see it as more significant. For example, Balmary (1979) believed that Freud's parents reported the birthdate of May 6 to conceal the fact that Freud's mother (Amalie) was pregnant with Sigmund when she married Jakob. In her book, *Psychoanalyzing Psychoanalysis: Freud and the Hidden Fault of the Father* (1979), Balmary speculated that both "family secrets" (the fact that Amalie was Jakob's third, not his second wife, and that Freud's mother was pregnant when she married) had a significant influence on Freud and his subsequent theorizing. Jakob had two sons by his first wife (Sally Kanner) and was a grandfather when Sigmund was born. It is interesting to note that Jakob Freud's sons by his first marriage were about the same age as Sigmund's mother. In fact, one of Freud's first playmates was the son of his half-brother. This playmate, Freud's nephew, was a year older than Freud. Sigmund and his mother had a strong relationship, the effects of which Freud felt throughout his life. In fact, Freud attributed much of his success to his mother's faith in him. Freud's mother died on September 12, 1930, at the age of 95, only nine years before her son's own death.

Sigmund Freud, age 16, with his Mother, Amalie Nathansohn Freud, in 1872.

Freud was an outstanding student and graduated at the head of his high school class. At home, his brothers and sisters were not allowed to study musical instruments because doing so disturbed his studies. He entered medical school at the University of Vienna when he was 17 years old, but it took him almost eight years to finish a four-year medical program, mainly because he pursued many interests outside of medicine. Freud chose medical school because medicine was one of the few careers open to a Jew in Austria at that time. Although not interested in becoming a physician, he saw the study of medicine as a vehicle for engaging in scientific research.

Freud hoped to become a professor of neurology and published several highly regarded articles on the topic. He soon discovered, however, that advancement within the academic ranks would be extremely slow for a Jew, and this realization, along with the fact that he needed money, prompted him to enter private practice as a clinical neurologist on April 25, 1886. About five months later, on September 13, 1886, he was finally able to marry Martha Bernays, to whom he had been engaged since 1882. During their five-year engagement, Freud wrote more than 400 letters to his fiancée. They remained married until Freud's death. They had six children, three daughters and three sons. One daughter, Anna, became a famous child psychiatrist in London. It is generally agreed by Freud's biographers that his relationship with Martha was the only intimate relationship he ever had.

The Cocaine Incident.   In 1884, Freud began experimenting with cocaine after hearing from a German army physician that the drug enhanced the endurance of soldiers. Taking the drug himself, Freud found it relieved depression and increased his ability to concentrate; furthermore, it appeared to have no negative side effects. Impressed with the drug, Freud took it freely himself and gave it to Martha, his sisters, his friends, and colleagues. Eventually Freud published six articles on cocaine, recommending it as a stimulant, local anesthetic, cure for indigestion, and harmless substitute for morphine. One of Freud's associates, Carl Koller, learned from Freud that cocaine could be used as an anesthetic during eye operations, and Koller presented a paper describing an experiment in which it was successfully used as such. Koller's paper caused a sensation and brought him worldwide fame almost overnight. Freud wished he had received this professional recognition himself.

Although cocaine was of value in eye surgery, Freud's other beliefs concerning the "magical substance" were soon proven false. Freud treated one of his close friends with cocaine to terminate his addiction to morphine, and the friend became addicted to cocaine instead. Reports of cocaine addiction began to pour in from all over the world, and cocaine came under heavy attack from the medical community. Because Freud was closely associated with the harmful drug, his medical reputation suffered considerably. To a large extent, it was this cocaine episode that created the skepticism with which Freud's later ideas were met by his medical colleagues. Although Freud avoided addiction to cocaine, he did become addicted to nicotine. For most of his adult life he smoked an average of 20 cigars a day.

Early Influences on Freud's Theory

Freud's Visit with Charcot.   In 1885, Freud received a small grant that allowed him to study with the famous French neurologist Jean-Martin Charcot (1825–1893), who was experimenting with hypnotism. At that time, Charcot was at the peak of his career and in French medicine was considered second in prominence only to Louis Pasteur.

Jean-Martin Charcot Demonstrating Hypnotism
(Culver Pictures, Inc.)

By endorsing the use of hypnotism, Charcot dramatically reversed the negative attitude toward the phenomenon held by members of the medical community since, in the 1770s, Franz Anton Mesmer (1734–1815) had claimed it resulted from the rearrangement of animal spirits within the body. After hypnotizing a patient, Charcot demonstrated that various types of paralyses could be created and removed artificially through the inducement of the hypnotist. Thus he demonstrated that physical symptoms could have a psychological origin as well as a physical or organic origin. Charcot was so impressed by the mind's ability to create and remove physical symptoms that he wondered if his discovery could eventually explain faith healing (Sulloway, 1979, p. 30).

Charcot's observations had clear implications for the treatment of **hysteria.** Hysteria is a term used to describe a wide variety of symptoms such as paralysis, loss of sensation, and disturbances of sight and speech. Originally, it was assumed that hysteria was exclusively a female disorder (*hystera* is the Greek word for uterus). Because it was often impossible to find anything organically wrong with hysteric patients, the medical community tended to view them as malingerers, and the physicians who agreed to treat them were typically discredited. Charcot's research indicated that the physical symptoms of hysteric patients could be psychogenic, and therefore the disease must be taken seriously even if symptoms could not be explained in terms of organic dysfunction. Thus Charcot did much to make the treatment of hysteria respectable. Charcot also convincingly demonstrated that, contrary to what most physicians had believed, hysteria was not an exclusively female disorder. By showing the psychogenic nature of bodily symptoms, Charcot provided a new approach to studying hysteria, an ailment that had puzzled the medical community for centuries. Freud soon explored the implications of this approach. Freud was so impressed by Charcot that he named his first son, Jean-Martin, after him.

Freud's Visit with Bernheim.   After Freud returned from his visit with Charcot, he attempted to use hypnotism in his private practice but was only partially successful. In an effort to improve his skills as a hypnotist, Freud returned to France in 1889. This time, however, he visited Hippolyte Bernheim (1840–1919) in Nancy, France. Like Charcot and his colleagues, members of the "Nancy School" were experimenting with hypnosis as a means of treating hysteria. Freud learned information from this visit that profoundly influenced both his later theorizing and his therapeutic method. Bernheim hypnotized people, and while they were under hypnosis he had them perform various acts. While still under hypnosis, he instructed them not to remember what they had done under hypnosis when they awoke. This created **posthypnotic amnesia;** that is, the person was unable to recall what he or she had done while hypnotized. Bernheim demonstrated that the amnesia was not complete, however. He showed that if the hypnotist insisted strongly and convincingly that the memory would return, it would do so. To facilitate this recall Bernheim placed his hand on the forehead of the awake person as he insisted the events that occurred during the hypnotic session be remembered. Freud learned from Bernheim that persons can have memories they are not aware of; however, under pressure these memories can be retrieved.

A second important lesson that Freud learned from Bernheim involved **posthypnotic suggestion.** To exemplify this phenomenon, Bernheim hypnotized a woman and told her that after waking and a specified period of time had expired, she would walk over to the corner of the room, pick up the umbrella that was found there, and open it. After being aroused from the hypnotic trance and after the designated period of time had expired, she did exactly that. When questioned as to why she had opened the umbrella, the woman said she wanted to see if it belonged to her. Freud learned from this that behaviour can be caused by ideas of which a person is totally unaware. Thus Freud learned from his visit with Bernheim that behaviour can be caused by unconscious ideas, and that these ideas can be brought into consciousness under the right circumstances.

Freud got many of the ideas that were later to characterize psychoanalysis from Charcot and Bernheim; many others he got from Josef Breuer.

Josef Breuer and the Case of Anna O.   Freud first met Josef Breuer (1842–1925) at the University of Vienna when both men were engaged in neurological research in the late 1870s. Breuer was 14 years older than Freud and, like Charcot, was a highly regarded physician and researcher. Breuer gave Freud advice and friendship, and loaned him money. Breuer's wife also became a good friend of Freud and his wife, and they named their first daughter, Mathilde, after her. Most important for the development of psychoanalysis, however, was Breuer's treatment of a young woman anonymously referred to as Fräulein Anna O.

Anna O. was 21 years old when Breuer began treating her in December 1880, and her treatment continued until June 1882. Anna O.'s symptoms included paralysis of various parts of her body, problems with vision, periodic deafness, a nervous cough, periodic aversion to nourishment and liquids, suicidal impulses, an occasional inability to speak in her native German language while retaining an ability to speak in English, and various hallucinations. Anna O.'s condition was diagnosed as hysteria.

Much to his amazement, Breuer found that if Anna O. traced a symptom to its original occurrence it disappeared either temporarily or permanently. Breuer found that Anna O. was able to discuss the origins of her various symptoms while she was either hypnotized or very relaxed. Working several hours each day for more than a year, Breuer systematically removed each of Anna O.'s symptoms in this manner. Anna O. herself called this laborious procedure the "talking cure" or "chimney sweeping";

Breuer called it **catharsis.** Aristotle had originally used this term to describe the emotional release and feeling of purification that an audience experiences while viewing a drama. It turned out that most of Anna O.'s symptoms originated from a series of traumatic experiences she had had as she was nursing her dying father.

Several important facts were learned from Breuer's treatment of Anna O. Perhaps most important was that her condition improved when she openly expressed her feelings. Breuer also observed that as treatment continued, Anna O. began transferring to him the feelings she had toward her father. This phenomenon, in which a patient responds to the analyst as if he or she were an important person in the patient's life, is called **transference.** Freud considered transference a vital part of effective psychoanalysis. Likewise, Breuer was becoming emotionally involved with Anna O. The phenomenon of an analyst forming an emotional attachment to a patient was later called **countertransference.**

The Development of Free Association.   Influenced by what he had observed during his visits with Charcot and Bernheim, Freud tried hypnosis in his practice but was not satisfied with the results. Freud eventually gave up hypnosis because he found that not all his patients could be hypnotized. One of his patients, Frau Emmy Von N., became furious with him over his constant interruptions while trying to hypnotize her. She expressed the desire simply to be allowed to speak her mind without being interrupted.

Next, Freud tried hand pressure, a technique he learned from Bernheim, instead of hypnosis. He would place his hand on his patients' foreheads and instruct them to begin talking when he released the pressure. Although this technique was somewhat successful, he eventually abandoned it and settled on **free association,** which he called "the fundamental rule of psychoanalysis."

Freud's experiences with hypnosis and hand pressure and his recollection of an essay by Ludwig Borne, which had been given to him when he was 14, gradually evolved into the technique of free association. The following quotation from Borne's essay entitled, "The Art of Becoming an Original Writer in Three Days," contains the seeds of what later became the technique of free association:

> Take a few sheets of paper and for three days on end write down, without fabrication or hypocrisy, everything that comes into your head. Write down what you think of yourself, of your wife, of the Turkish War, of Goethe, of Fonk's trial, of the Last Judgment, of your superiors—and when three days have passed you will be quite out of your sense with astonishment at the new and unheard-of thoughts you have had. (quoted in Freud 1920b/1955, p. 265)

Breuer and Freud worked on several cases of hysteria and in 1895 published the book *Studies on Hysteria,* which is usually considered the beginning of the psychoanalytic movement. Although their book is now regarded as having monumental significance, it then was met with negative reviews, and it took 13 years to sell 626 copies. Breuer and Freud, who had been extremely close friends, soon parted company because of Freud's insistence that sexual conflicts were the cause of hysteria. Breuer agreed that sexual conflicts were often the cause of mental disorders, but disagreed with Freud's contention they were the only cause.

Freud began his highly influential self-analysis in 1897. He began this self-analysis for both theoretical and personal reasons; for example, he had a dread of railroad travel and was preoccupied by thoughts of his own death. The main vehicle in his self-analysis was the interpretation of his dreams. This analysis finally resulted in what many consider Freud's greatest work, *The Interpretation of Dreams,* published in 1900. As with his earlier book, written with Breuer, this one also met with considerable criticism; it was eight years before 600 copies were sold, for which Freud received the equivalent of $209. Eventually, however, the importance of the book was realized, and it was translated and published throughout the world.

It was after the publication of *The Interpretation of Dreams* that the psychoanalytic movement began to gain momentum. International recognition finally came when Freud and a few of his close followers were invited by G. Stanley Hall to give a series of lectures at Clark University in 1909. Although Freud did not care much for the United States and never returned, he looked on his visit to Clark University as significant in the development of the psychoanalytic movement.

In 1923, Freud was diagnosed with cancer of the mouth, which was linked to his smoking 20 cigars a day, a habit he did not abandon even after his cancer was detected. From 1923 to his death in 1939, he underwent 33 operations. Although in constant pain because of his refusal to accept pain-reducing drugs, his mind remained alert and he worked on his theory until the end of his life.

When the Nazis came to power in 1933, they publicly burned Freud's books in Berlin as a Nazi spokesman shouted, "Against the soul-destroying overestimation of the sex life—and on behalf of the nobility of the human soul—I offer to the flames the writings of one Sigmund Freud!" (Schur, 1972, p. 446). About this event Freud commented, "What progress we are making. In the Middle Ages they would have burnt me; nowadays they are content with burning my books" (Jones, 1957, p. 182). Freud resisted leaving Vienna even after it was invaded in 1938. Finally, after his daughter Anna had been arrested and interrogated by the Nazis, he agreed to go to London. Four of his sisters were later killed by the Nazis in Austria.

In London, the Freuds took up residence at 20 Maresfield Gardens in Hampstead, North London. Here, in great pain, Freud continued to write, see patients, and occasionally attend meetings of the London Psychoanalytic Society.

Freud had reached an agreement with his physician, Max Schur, that when Freud's condition became hopeless, Schur would assist him in dying. Peter Gay (1988) describes Freud's final days:

> Schur was on the point of tears as he witnessed Freud facing death with dignity and without self-pity. He had never seen anyone die like that. On September 21, Schur injected Freud with three centigrams of morphine—the normal dose for sedation was two centigrams—and Freud sank into a peaceful sleep. Schur repeated the injection, when he became restless, and administered a final one the next day, September 22. Freud lapsed into a coma from which he did not awake. He died at three in the morning, September 23, 1939. (p. 651)

Instincts and Their Characteristics

For Freud, all aspects of the human personality are derived from biological instincts. This point cannot be stressed too much. No matter how lofty the thought or the accomplishment—discovering the principles of physics, comforting the bereaved, writing the great Canadian novel, risking your life to defend your country or on a peacekeeping mission—it ultimately relates to the satisfaction of a physiological need. For example, the soldier who is ostensibly defending peace may be actually acting out of a deeply buried instinctual urge to aggression. This may explain why ostensibly

These protesters in Windsor, Ontario, are fiercely opposed to global trade expansion. Although these people are engaged in a seemingly worthy cause of action, Freud's theory suggests a less than noble motivation: These aggressive acts reside in a deeply buried reservoir of instinctual biological urges and desires.

altruistic military missions can sometimes go so terribly wrong, as was the case when Canadian soldiers supposed to be defending Somali citizens tortured a teenaged boy.

Freud's theory is a hedonistic one: It assumes that humans, like other animals, continually seek pleasure and avoid pain. When all the bodily needs are satisfied, one experiences pleasure; when one or more needs are not satisfied, one experiences discomfort. The main motive for humans, then, is to obtain the steady state that one experiences when all of one's biological needs are satisfied.

An **instinct** has four characteristics: (1) a source, which is a bodily deficiency of some kind; (2) an aim, which is to remove the bodily deficiency, thereby re-establishing an internal balance; (3) an object, which is those experiences or objects that reduce or remove the bodily deficiency; and (4) an impetus, which is determined by the magnitude of the bodily deficiency. For example, a person experiencing the hunger instinct will need food (source), will want to eliminate the need for food (aim), and will seek and ingest food (object). The intensity with which these activities occur will depend on how long the person has gone without food (impetus).

Life and Death Instincts.   All the instincts associated with the preservation of life are called the *life instincts*, and the psychic energy associated with them collectively is called the **libido.** Some people overflow in libidinal or life energy—they appear to be 'full of life,' while others seem to just drag themselves through their daily routine. In Freud's earlier writings, he equated libido with sexual energy but in light of increased evidence to the contrary and because of severe criticism from even his closest colleagues, he expanded the notion to include the energy associated with all of the life instincts including sex, hunger, and thirst. Freud's final position was that libidinal energy is expended to prolong life. Freud also referred to the life instincts collectively as **eros.**

The death instinct, named **thanatos,** stimulates a person to return to the inorganic state that preceded life. Death is the ultimate steady state because there is no longer a struggle to satisfy biological needs. Quoting Schopenhauer, Freud claimed "the aim of all life is death" (1920a/1955, p. 38). The most important derivative of the death instinct, or the death wish as it is sometimes called, is aggression, which, according to Freud, is the need for self-destruction turned outward to objects other than the self. Cruelty, suicide, murder, as well as aggression, were thought by Freud to derive from the death instinct. Our growing interest in television "shockumentaries" about natural disasters, accidents, even serial murderers stems from this instinct. We may enjoy weekend monster truck rallies or powerboat races not merely because of their speed but perhaps in hopes of witnessing an accident. Even though Freud never developed thanatos as fully as eros, it is nonetheless an important part of his theory.

Divisions of the Mind

THE ID

The mature adult mind has three divisions: an **id,** an **ego,** and a **superego.** At birth, however, the entire mind consists of only the id (from the German *das es,* meaning "the it"). The id consists of pure, unadulterated, instinctual energy and exists completely on the unconscious level. The id cannot tolerate the tension associated with a bodily need and therefore demands the immediate removal of that tension. In other words, the id demands immediate gratification of bodily needs and is said to be governed by the **pleasure principle.**

The id has two means of satisfying bodily needs: **reflex action** and **wish fulfillment.** Reflex action is responding automatically to a source of irritation. For example, an infant may sneeze in response to an irritant in the nose or reflexively move a confined limb thereby freeing it. In both cases, reflex action effectively reduces tension. Coughing and blinking are also examples of reflex action.

Wish fulfillment is more complicated. In addition to the characteristics of instincts described earlier, instincts can be considered mental representations of physiological needs. It is within the id and via the concept of instinct that Freud came to grips with the mind-body question. The mind-body question asks how physiological events and psychological events are related to each other. It is a question which every theory with a cognitive component eventually must address.

Freud's answer to the mind-body question was as follows. A biological deficiency (a need) triggers in the id an attempt to reduce the tension associated with that need by imagining an object or event that will satisfy the need. For example, the need for food will automatically trigger in the id a food-related image that has the effect of temporarily reducing the tension associated with the need for food; this is called wish fulfillment. At this point, Freud becomes quite mystical. What images does the entirely unconscious id conjure in response to the various needs? Certainly, it cannot conjure a hamburger in response to the hunger drive because it never experienced a hamburger or anything else that is directly related to the reduction of the hunger drive. The alternative seems to be that the id has available to it the inherited residuals of experience from preceding generations. If so, it has available to it the images of things that consistently satisfied the needs of humans through many past generations. Freud accepted this view, thus embracing Lamarck's notion of the **inheritance of acquired characteristics,** about which we say more later.

Because wish fulfillment can never really satisfy a bodily need except on a temporary basis, another component of the personality must develop to make real satisfaction possible. That component is the ego. As we have seen, the id attempts to reduce needs through hallucinations (mental pictures of objects that could satisfy a need). These, along with reflex actions, are called the **primary processes.** The primary processes of the id, however, are ineffective in ultimately alleviating the need. The id cannot distinguish between its images and external reality. In fact, for the id, its images are the only reality.

THE EGO

Eventually, the ego (from the German *das ich*, meaning "the I") develops and attempts to match the images of the id with objects and events in the real world. Freud called this matching process **identification.** The ego is governed by the **reality principle** and operates in the service of the id. In other words, the ego comes into existence to bring the person into contact with experiences that truly satisfy his or her needs. When the person is hungry, the ego finds food; when the person is sexually aroused, the ego finds appropriate sexual objects; and when the person is thirsty, the ego finds liquid. The ego goes through the process of **reality testing** to find appropriate objects. Because the ego is aware of both the images of the id and external reality, it operates on both the conscious and unconscious level. The realistic efforts of the ego that bring about true biological satisfaction are called **secondary processes,** which contrast with the ineffective primary processes of the id. The relationship between the id and the ego is summarized in the diagram below.

Within Freudian theory, it is important to realize that the ego operates in the service of the id.

> The ego must on the whole carry out the id's intentions, it fulfils its task by finding out the circumstances in which those intentions can best be achieved. The ego's relation to the id might be compared with that of a rider to his horse. The horse supplies the locomotive energy, while the rider has the privilege of deciding on the goal and of guiding the powerful animal's movement. But only too often there arises between the ego and the id the not precisely ideal situation of the rider being obliged to guide the horse along the path by which it itself wants to go. (Freud, 1933/1966, p. 541)

THE SUPEREGO

If the only two components of the personality were the id and the ego, we would have a hedonistic, animalistic person who, when in a need state, would seek immediate gratification of needs (id) from appropriate environmental objects (ego). The superego, a third component of the personality, makes this process more complicated, however. The superego (from the German *das überich*, meaning "the over I") is the moral arm of the personality. It develops primarily from the internalized patterns of reward and punishment that the young child experiences. That is, depending on the values of the parents, certain things the child does or says are rewarded and thereby encouraged; other things the child does or says are punished and thereby discouraged. Those experiences that bring reward and punishment are gradually internalized, and the superego is said to be fully developed when self-control replaces environmental or direct parental control.

The fully developed superego has two subdivisions. The **conscience** is the internalized experience of behaviours for which the child had been consistently punished—for example, stealing another child's toy. Engaging in these behaviours now, or even thinking about engaging in them, makes the child feel guilty or "naughty." The second subdivision of the superego is the **ego ideal**: the internalized experience of behaviours for which the child had been consistently rewarded—for example, listening to instructions, cleaning, working hard. Engaging in these behaviours now, or even thinking about engaging in them, makes the child feel successful or proud. Although Freud believed the superego was strongly influenced by internalized personal experiences, he also believed it was influenced by historical or phylogenetic experiences. We see examples of the latter later.

The superego constantly strives for perfection and is, therefore, as unrealistic as the id. For the superego, there is no time in the day for eating or sleeping or having sex; time is better spent in a church or library. Any experience that violates the internalized values of the child is not tolerated by the superego; now, the job of the ego becomes more complicated. Not only must the ego find objects and events that satisfy the needs of the id, it also must find objects and events that do not violate the values of the superego. If, for example, a boy felt the need to urinate while on a city bus, the id would demand immediate gratification through urination. The ego would allow this to happen by causing the pants to be unzipped and so on. Urinating on a city bus, however, would in all likelihood violate an internalized value of the superego and lead to considerable guilt or anxiety. The ego, aware of the needs of both the id and the superego, would probably cause the boy to get off the bus at the next stop and enter a washroom in which urination would satisfy all the components of the personality. It is no wonder the ego is called the executive of the personality. Freud (1933/1966) described the enormous task of the ego.

> We are warned by a proverb against serving two masters at the same time. The poor ego has things even worse: it serves three severe masters and does what it can to bring their claims and demands into harmony with one another . . . . Its three tyrannical masters are the external world, the super-ego and the id . . . . [On the one hand it] attempts to mediate between the id and reality . . . . On the other hand it is observed at every step it takes by the strict super-ego, which lays down definite standards for its conduct . . . and . . . if those standards are not obeyed, punishes it with tense feelings of inferiority and of guilt. Thus the ego, driven by the id, confined by the super-ego, repulsed by reality, struggles to master its economic task of bringing about harmony among the forces and influences working in and upon it; and we can understand how it is that so often we cannot suppress a cry: 'Life is not easy!' (pp. 541–542)

Cathexis and Anticathexis

Freud's most influential teacher at the University of Vienna was the renowned physiologist Ernst Brücke (1819–1892), who, along with Hermann Von Helmholtz (1821–1894) and a few other physiologists, had revolutionized the field of physiology by purging it of all subjective, nonscientific concepts and terminology. Their goal was to explain all physiological events in terms of known, measurable, verifiable physical events. That is, living systems were viewed as dynamic energy systems that obey the laws of the physical universe. **Vitalism,** or the belief that life consists of some vital force that cannot be reduced to physical events, was strongly opposed by these individuals. For them, there was no "ghost in the machine" that existed independently of physiological events and the laws that governed them. It was in this "Helmholtzian school of medicine" that Freud received his early training; this positivistic training had a strong and lasting influence on him. In fact, one of Freud's first endeavours in psychology was entitled *Project for a Scientific Psychology.* This was an effort to explain psychological phenomena entirely in terms of neurophysical processes. Although the *Project* was completed in 1895 (the same year Freud published *Studies on Hysteria* with Breuer), Freud considered it a failure, and it was not published in his lifetime (it was first published in 1950 in German, and 1954 in English). Although Freud later employed subjective (nonphysiological) terminology in his theory of personality, the positivism of the Helmholtzian school remained highly influential in that he continued to avoid vitalistic and teleological concepts in explaining human behaviour.

Following his practice of naming his children after individuals who had deeply impressed him, Freud named his fourth son Ernst after Brücke.

One Helmholtzian concept that Freud adopted was the **principle of conservation of energy.** This principle states that within a system, energy is never created or lost but only rearranged or transformed from one place or form to another. The principle did not originate with Helmholtz, but he was the first to apply it to living organisms. For example, Helmholtz demonstrated that the total energy expended by an organism equalled the amount of energy associated with the food and oxygen it consumed.

Freud applied the principle of conservation of energy to the human mind. According to Freud, each person is born with more or less the same amount of **psychic energy** and that amount remains more or less the same from birth to death. This energy, however, can be transformed and rearranged, and it is how the energy is distributed at any given time that determines a person's personality characteristics.

Freud used the term **cathexis** (from the Greek *kathexo,* meaning to occupy) to describe the investment of psychic energy in the thoughts of objects or processes that will satisfy a need. The energy itself never leaves the body, but if considerable energy is invested in the image of an object, an intense longing occurs for it in the form of thoughts, images, and fantasies. For example, one may think for long periods about a special person, or alternatively about germs and the likelihood of contamination. These thoughts and feelings continue until the need is satisfied, at which point the energy dissipates and is available for other cathexes. Again, if only the id and the ego existed, humans would be animalistic. That is, a need would arise, an image (wish) of an object that would satisfy that need would form, and that wish would be endowed with energy, thereby creating a tension that continues until the need is satisfied. There would be no regard for other people and no differentiation between acceptable and unacceptable objects with which to satisfy needs. As we have seen, however, with the development of the superego comes the need to inhibit certain primitive desires. This requires the expenditure of energy to prevent unacceptable cathexes. Freud called the energy expended to prevent undesirable cathexes an **anticathexis.** Because the emergence of an unacceptable cathexis would cause anxiety, the ego and the superego often team up to create an anticathexis powerful enough to inhibit the strong primitive cathexes of the id. In such cases, the original need does not disappear. Instead, the original cathexis is displaced to other, safer objects.

Anxiety

According to Freud, our most overwhelming experience of anxiety occurs when we are separated from our mother at birth. Freud called this experience the *birth trauma* because we suddenly go from an environment of complete security and satisfaction to one in which the satisfaction of our needs is far less predictable. The feeling of helplessness following birth is, according to Freud, the basis of all subsequent feelings of anxiety.

The function of anxiety is to warn us that if we continue thinking or behaving in a certain way, we will be in danger. Because anxiety is not pleasant, we will do what is necessary to reduce it. That is, we will tend to terminate those thoughts or actions that cause anxiety. Freud distinguished three types of anxiety: **Reality anxiety** is caused by real, objective sources of danger in the environment and is the easiest type of anxiety to reduce because doing so requires solving a problem objectively, for example, leaving a building that is on fire. **Neurotic anxiety** is the fear that the impulses of the id will overwhelm the ego and cause the person to do something for which he or she will be punished. Examples include becoming overly aggressive or giving in to one's sexual desires. Generally, this fear is one of becoming animal-like. **Moral anxiety** is fear that the person will do something contrary to the superego and thus experience guilt. For example, if one has learned that being honest is good, then even thinking of being dishonest would cause moral anxiety. Neurotic anxiety is the fear that one will be punished externally (by other people) for impulsive actions, whereas moral anxiety is the fear that one will be punished internally (by feelings of guilt) if the dictates of one's superego are violated. Thus anxiety controls our behaviour by causing us to avoid threatening experiences in the environment, to inhibit the impulses of the id, and to act in accordance with our internalized values.

One of the ego's biggest tasks is to avoid or reduce anxiety. In addition to anticathexis, the ego has several other processes available to it for use in its battle against anxiety; these processes are referred to collectively as the ego-defence mechanisms.

Ego-Defence Mechanisms

If normal, rational approaches of the ego to reduce or remove anxiety are ineffective, the ego may revert to irrational methods called **ego-defence mechanisms.** All ego-defence mechanisms have two things in common: (1) They are unconscious; that is, the person is unaware that he or she is using them, and (2) they falsify or distort reality. Freud's daughter Anna (1936/1966) was mainly responsible for elaborating the ego-defence mechanisms, and we consider several of them.

Repression.   This is the most basic defence mechanism because for any of the other defence mechanisms to occur, **repression** must occur first. Freud said, "The theory of repression is the corner-stone on which the whole structure of psycho-analysis rests" (1914/1966, p.14). Repression is the mechanism by which the ego prevents anxiety-provoking thoughts from being entertained on the conscious level. These thoughts can be either those innately part of the id, in which case their repression is referred to as **primal repression,** or they can be memories of painful experiences from one's lifetime, in which case their repression is referred to as **repression proper.** For example, abuse at the hands of an adult, whether in a reform school or hockey arena, may be so traumatic for young children that they cannot remember the incident. In either case, the ego keeps the potentially anxiety-provoking thought in the unconscious with an anticathexis whenever it threatens to reach consciousness. It is important to realize what Freud considered to be innately part of the id. The primary drives that we share with other animals are inherited as part of the id but, according to Freud, more is contained in the id than physiological needs. As we mentioned earlier, Freud was an ardent Lamarckian. That is, he believed we inherit memories of what our ancestors had learned from their experiences. Freud believed our id comes well stocked with inherited prohibitions because of the punishment our ancestors received for engaging in certain behaviours. Many of the events that cause anxiety in our lifetimes do so because of the experiences of our ancestors. Thus we can fear castration, believe we have been sexually attacked as children by an adult, and avoid incest not necessarily because we have learned to do so in our lifetimes but because these thoughts are part of our **phylogenetically inherited endowment.**

Consider the following quotation:

> The experiences of the ego seem at first to be lost for inheritance; but when they have been repeated often enough and with sufficient strength in many individuals in successive generations, they transform themselves, so to say, into experiences of the id, the impressions of which are preserved by heredity. Thus in the id, which is capable of being inherited, are harboured residues of the existence of countless egos. (Freud, 1923/1961, p. 38)

Thus, if our ancestors were consistently punished for certain activities, we are born with the tendency to inhibit those activities. The impulse to engage in those tendencies (for example, incest or violence) continues to exist in the id, however, and energy must be expended to inhibit them and related impulses. Another way to state Freud's position is to say that he believed at least part of human morality is inherited. In *Totem and Taboo* (1913/1958) Freud said, "I have supposed that the sense of guilt for an action has persisted for many thousands of years and has remained operative in generations which can have no knowledge of that action" (pp. 157–158). Freud's belief in Lamarck's concept of the inheritance of acquired characteristics is also stated in his last book, *Moses and Monotheism* (1939/1964):

> We become aware of the probability that what may be operative in an individual's psychical life may include not only what he has experienced himself but also things that were innately present in him at his birth, elements with a phylogenetic origin— an archaic heritage. (p. 98)

For Freud, the mechanism of repression was of vital importance because repressed thoughts do not stop having an influence on our personality; they simply are not readily available in consciousness. The whole purpose of procedures such as dream analysis, free association, hypnosis, and the analysis of slips of the tongue or memory lapses (which we discuss later) is to attempt to discover repressed thoughts so their effects on one's personality can be determined. Not all material in the unconscious mind is repressed, however. An abundance of information exists that is simply not relevant to a person at any given moment, such as names, telephone numbers, or dates. Although the person is not usually aware of this kind of information, he or she can easily become aware of it when needed. Such information is said to exist in the **preconscious.**

Displacement.   As we saw earlier, **displacement** is the substitution of one need satisfier for another. For example, the ego may substitute an available object for one that is not available, or it may substitute a non-theatening object or activity for one that provokes anxiety. With displacement, what a person truly desires is repressed and is replaced by something safer.

In his book *Civilization and Its Discontents* (1930/1961), Freud indicated that civilization itself depends on the displacement of libidinal energy from one object to another. When a displacement results in something advantageous to civilization, it is called **sublimation**, such as when sexual impulses are displaced into such activities as painting, writing, building, or just plain hard work. "Sublimation of instinct," wrote Freud, "is an especially conspicuous feature of cultural development; it is what makes it possible for higher psychical activities, scientific, artistic or ideological, to play such an important part in civilized life" (1930/1961, p. 63).

All impulses can be displaced, even those associated with the death instinct. For example, the impulse toward self-destruction can be displaced to the destruction of others, and an aggressive impulse directed toward a threatening person such as a boss or a parent can be displaced to less threatening objects such as other cars on the street while driving home, children, household pets or, quite commonly, to athletic teams opposing the hometown team. These are examples of **displaced aggression,** one of Freud's most influential concepts.

Identification.   Freud used the term **identification** in two ways. The one we have already covered is the process by which the ego attempts to match objects and events in the environment to the subjective wishes of the id. The term *identification* is also used to describe the tendency to increase personal feelings of worth by affiliating oneself psychologically with a person, group, or institution perceived as illustrious. The feelings of pride when the home team wins a game or when one's country wins a gold medal in the Olympics are examples. Choices of fashion, music collection, reading material, and even mannerisms can also exemplify identification if they bring a person closer psychologically to individuals perceived as successful, powerful, or attractive. Wearing T-shirts or jackets with team, business, or institutional logos also exemplifies identification.

The child also identifies with his or her parents (accepts their values) thereby eliminating the punishment that comes from having contrary values. This is primarily how the superego develops.

Denial of Reality.   This mechanism involves the denial of some fact in one's life despite abundant evidence of its reality. Examples include the refusal to believe a loved one has died; the refusal to acknowledge the negative attributes of a loved one; the refusal to believe that one's poor driving was the cause of an accident; the tendency for some severely overweight and underweight individuals to deny they have a weight problem; and the tendency for people addicted to substances such as alcohol, nicotine, or cocaine to believe such substances will not harm them or that they could easily quit their habits. By definition a person using the mechanism of **denial of reality** is not in touch with at least some aspect of reality and this could impair normal functioning.

Projection.   This mechanism is the one by which something that is true of the person and would cause anxiety if it were recognized is repressed and projected onto someone or something else instead. For example, the statement "I want to go to bed with him" may be true, but because it causes anxiety it is converted into "He wants to go to bed with me." Also, the statement, "I failed the test because I was unprepared," although perhaps true, is converted into statements such as "Our textbook is terrible," "She's the worst teacher I've ever had," or "The test had trick items."

In general, **projection** is repressing anxiety-provoking truths about oneself and seeing them in others instead, or excusing one's shortcomings by blaming them on environmental or life circumstances.

Undoing.   Here a person performs an unacceptable act, or thinks about doing so, and then engages in ritualistic activities designed to atone for or "undo" the unacceptable act or thought. With **undoing,** it is as if the person is attempting to magically undo one act with another, "It is a kind of negative magic in which the individual's second act abrogates or nullifies the first" (A. Freud, 1936/1966 p. 33). For example, after colluding in the murder of Duncan, Lady Macbeth compulsively washes her hands as if to absolve herself of the heinous act. Likewise, a man, after physically abusing his wife, may attempt to undo the abuse by profusely apologizing to her, expressing his true love for her, or by buying her flowers.

Reaction Formation.   This mechanism is the one by which objectionable thoughts are repressed and their opposites expressed. For example, the person who is most attracted to sexual materials may become the town censor, or the mother who really does not care much for her child may become overprotective. Freud believed that the clue in determining the difference between a **reaction formation** and true feelings is the degree to which the feelings are emphasized. People displaying a reaction formation tend to be more intense and extravagant in their emotions as when a boyfriend insists, "I love you, I love you, I love you more than anything in the world," or when someone says, "You should meet my mother. She is absolutely wonderful beyond belief." In Shakespeare's *Hamlet,* the lady doth protest too much, and in so doing reveals her guilt.

Finally, crimes against gays and lesbians (called "gay bashing") have increased in Canada, the United States, and around the world. In December 1996, a prominent

In December, 1996, Duncan Wilson, a prominent Vancouver politician, was viciously attacked by teenagers, leaving him with an ugly scar and a broken cheekbone. The Freudian perspective on gay bashing is that deep hatred for homosexual lifestyles stems from a struggle with one's own homosexual thoughts and impulses.

Vancouver politician, Duncan Wilson, received an ugly scar and a broken cheekbone in an attack one night by roaming teenagers. Two years later, the public outcry against the 1998 beating death of Matthew Shepard in Wyoming led to widespread legislation making gay bashing a hate crime. The Freudian perspective on gay bashing is that the deep hatred for this lifestyle actually represents a struggle with one's own homosexual thoughts and impulses. In fact, this explanation helps us understand extreme reactions to members of any distinct group: intense hatred of individuals for their skin colour or beliefs can be seen as a reaction formation for affiliation to these groups, while overly affectionate considerations of other individuals would be a reaction formation for latent hatred.

Rationalization.   Through this mechanism, the person rationally explains or justifies behaviours or thoughts that may otherwise be anxiety provoking. The ego excuses through faulty logic outcomes that would be disturbing if they were not explained in some way. The so-called sour grapes **rationalization** is quite common. Aesop, in about 500 B.C., told of a fox who saw clusters of grapes hanging from a trellised vine. It tried everything in its power to reach them but nothing worked. Finally, it turned away saying, "The grapes were probably sour anyhow." Likewise, something that at first was not overly attractive may be glorified after it is obtained. This has been called a "sweet lemon" rationalization. Finally, people may rationalize failing to help others. For example, they may drive right past someone whose car is stuck in the snow, convincing themselves that it would take too much time or that another driver will surely stop.

Intellectualization (also called isolation of affect).   Here an idea that would otherwise cause distress is stripped of its emotional content by intellectual analysis. Thus, a disturbing thought is not denied consciousness but is denied the accompanying negative emotion. Using **intellectualization,** it is possible to ponder topics such as death, separation from a loved one, severe illness, or personal loss without the negative emotions typically associated with such events. For example, attempting to understand the medical nature of cancer in a logical, detached manner can minimize the emotional impact of a loved one having the disease. Likewise, the negative emotions associated with the death of a loved one can be minimized by emphasizing the thought that death is the inevitable consequence of life. Finally, a person whose house has burned down may intellectually stress the futility of becoming emotionally attached to material things.

Regression.   With this mechanism, the person returns to an earlier stage of development when he or she experiences stress. For example, a child may revert to bed-wetting or thumb-sucking when a new sibling is born. We have more to say about **regression** in our discussion of the psychosexual stages of development, to which we turn shortly.

The ego-defence mechanisms described above were those described by Freud and his colleagues and were summarized by his daughter Anna in her book *The Ego and the Mechanisms of Defence* (1936/1966).

It should be made clear that everyone uses ego-defence mechanisms and doing so in moderation often facilitates normal functioning. Using one or more of them extensively, however, can be dysfunctional.

Psychosexual Stages of Development

Freud believed every child goes through a sequence of developmental stages, and the child's experiences during these stages determine adult personality characteristics. In fact, Freud believed that for all practical purposes, the adult personality is formed by the end of the fifth year of life.

Each stage has an **erogenous zone** associated with it, which is the greatest source of stimulation and pleasure during that particular stage of development.

To make a smooth transition from one psychosexual stage to the next, the child must be neither undergratified nor overgratified, either of which cause the child to be fixated at that stage. A **fixation** occurs when a substantial amount of psychic energy remains cathected in images of objects that can satisfy the needs corresponding to a particular stage of development. Again, a fixation can occur either because the needs corresponding to a stage are consistently frustrated (undergratified) or are satisfied too often and too easily (overgratified). An example of the latter is an infant who is breast-fed whenever she shows the least sign of hunger or discomfort. Fixation and regression go hand in hand, because, in regressing, a person tends to go back to the stage at which he or she had been fixated. In addition, a person who is fixated at a certain stage will, as an adult, display personality characteristics corresponding to that stage. We see examples of this next.

Oral Stage.   The **oral stage** occurs during about the first year of life, and the erogenous zone during this stage is the mouth. During the early oral stage (less than eight months old) pleasure comes mainly from the mouth, lips, and tongue through the activities of sucking and swallowing. According to Freud, an adult who is fixated at the early oral stage engages in an abundance of oral activities such as eating, drinking, smoking, and kissing. This person also engages in activities that are symbolically equivalent to those oral activities, such as collecting things, being a good listener (taking in knowledge), or being gullible, that is, "swallowing" anything he or she hears. Such a person is called an **oral-incorporative character.**

In the later oral stage (from eight months to about one year) experience is concentrated on the teeth, gums, and jaws, and pleasure comes from activities such as biting and devouring. An adult fixated at the late oral stage may be a fingernail biter and also would like eating. This person also would engage in activities symbolically equivalent to biting, such as sarcasm, cynicism, and ridicule. Such a person is called an **oral-sadistic character.**

Anal Stage.   The **anal stage** occurs during about the second year of life, and the erogenous zone is the anus-buttocks region. During this stage, the child must learn to control his or her physiological processes so they function in accordance with the demands of society. That is, the child must be toilet trained.

In the first part of the anal stage, pleasure derives from feces expulsion. Fixation at this level may result in an adult having physical problems such as a lack of sphincter control or enuresis. Symbolically, the person would be overly generous, wanting to give away nearly everything he or she owns and may also tend to be creative. Such a person is called an **anal-expulsive character.**

In the later anal stage, pleasure comes from feces possession. Fixation here may manifest itself physically, in a problem with constipation, or symbolically in stinginess, parsimony, orderliness, and a tendency toward perfectionism. Such a person is called an **anal-retentive character.**

Phallic Stage.   This stage occurs from about the third year of life to about the fifth year, and the erogenous zone is the phallus or penis. Although the phallus is a male organ, Freud believed the phallic stage described the development of both male and female children. Freud believed the clitoris was a small penis and, therefore, activity related to it such as clitoral masturbation was viewed as masculine in nature. The

phallic stage is one of the most complicated and controversial of Freud's stages. It is during this stage when our subsequent adjustments to members of the opposite sex are determined. The phallic stage is the scene of the Oedipus complex, the resolution of which has a profound influence on adult life.

The **Oedipus complex** is named after an ancient play by Sophocles entitled *Oedipus Rex,* in which King Oedipus kills his father and marries his mother. According to Freud, both male and female children develop strong, positive feelings toward the mother because she satisfies their needs. For example, because of breast-feeding and sexual contact from bathing and grooming, both male and female children develop erotic feelings toward their mother. These feelings persist in the boy but typically change in the girl.

The boy begins to fear the father as the dominant rival for his mother's affection and this fear becomes **castration anxiety.** That is, the boy develops the fear of losing his sex organs because they are assumed to be responsible for the conflict between him and his father. According to Freud, it is not necessary for a male child to be overtly threatened with castration to develop castration anxiety. Boys may have the opportunity to observe that girls do not possess penises and assume that they once did. That is, boys may believe that girls lost their penises because their penises, like their own, were the source of trouble with their father. Also, according to Freud, castration anxiety could result from the phylogenetic memory of actual castrations that occurred in the distant past.

No matter what its source, castration anxiety causes a repression of the sexual desire for the mother and creates hostility toward the father. Next, the boy identifies with his father, thereby gaining vicarious satisfaction of his sexual impulses toward his mother. In a sense, the boy becomes the father and thereby shares the mother. By identifying with his father, the male child also accepts his father's notions of right and wrong as his own, thereby completing the development of his superego. That is, his father's morality becomes his morality. This process exemplifies what Anna Freud called identification with the aggressor and describes what was for Freud the healthy resolution of the Oedipus complex.

The female version of the Oedipus complex is more complicated. Freud pondered calling the female version of the Oedipus complex the Electra complex after another play by Sophocles entitled *Electra,* in which Electra causes her brother to kill her mother, who had killed Electra's father. Freud rejected the idea, however, choosing instead to refer to the male and female Oedipal complexes.

As we have seen, female children also start life with a strong attraction to their mothers. This attraction is reduced, however, when the girl discovers she does not possess a penis. Whereas a male child assumes that female children once had penises and had lost them, the female child assumes that all other children possess penises but for some reason she was deprived of one. The female child holds the mother responsible for purposely depriving her of this valued organ. The rejection of the mother is coupled with an attraction to the father, whom she knows possesses the valued organ which she wants to share. Her positive feelings toward the father, however, are mixed with envy because he has something that she does not and she is said to have **penis envy.** Freud leaves the girl suspended between the mother and father, with positive and negative feelings toward both.

Unlike castration anxiety in boys, which is quickly repressed, Freud believed penis envy, in one form or another, could last for years. According to Freud, the female's sexuality changes from masculine to feminine when she fantasizes about having her father's baby. It is this fantasy, rather than any maternal instinct, that explains the female impulse to reproduce. Of course, this impulse symbolically generalizes to other men and represents the healthy resolution of the female Oedipal complex. For Freud, the final resolution of the female Oedipal complex occurs when the female eventually has a baby, especially a male baby.

The phallic stage is further complicated by the fact that both male and female children are bisexual. As we have seen, both male and female children begin with a strong sexual attraction to their mother. This attraction typically persists in males and results in heterosexual development. However, because of his strong attraction toward his mother, the male child also imagines his father as a love object and has erotic fantasies about him. Likewise, although penis envy causes the female child to turn from the mother to the father, the strong positive feelings she has toward her mother are not completely abandoned. Because male and female children identify with both their mothers and fathers, they possess both masculine and feminine characteristics; that is, they are bisexual. Freud considered bisexuality to be universal and normal. It is when life's circumstances cause these natural impulses to become exaggerated that homosexuality results. According to Freud, all humans have the potential to become homosexual.

Regression to the phallic stage for the male may include displaying many of the father's characteristics and, also typically, brashness and an overconcern with masculinity and virility. Regression to the phallic stage for the girl may exemplify penis-envy-related activities. These activities may include seeking to share a penis—for example, promiscuity or seductiveness—or activities that symbolically castrate men, such as embarrassing, deceiving, or hurting them.

Latency Stage.   The **latency stage** lasts from about the sixth year to about the twelfth year. This is a time when sexual interests are repressed and displaced to substitute activities such as learning, athletics, and peer group activities. That is, during this stage, libidinal energy is sublimated.

Genital Stage.   The **genital stage** is the final stage of development and begins at puberty. At this time, the person emerges from the pregenital stages as the adult he or she is destined to become. The child is sometimes transformed from a selfish, pleasure-seeking child to a realistic, socialized adult—typically with heterosexual interests leading to marriage and perhaps child rearing. If, however, the experiences during the pregenital stages cause fixations, they will manifest themselves throughout the person's adult life. Only psychoanalysis can dredge up the remnants of these early experiences, which otherwise would remain repressed in the unconscious, and cause the individual to face them, thereby reducing their influence.

In fact, the process of psychoanalysis can be viewed as a means of discovering repressed thoughts that are having a negative influence on one's life. The question is, How does one gain access to thoughts that have been actively held in the unconscious mind all one's life? It is to this question that we turn, after summarizing Freud's views on feminine psychology.

Summary of Freud's Views on Feminine Psychology

There is no doubt that Freud considered the psychology of women more enigmatic than that of men. He once commented to his friend Marie Bonaparte, "The great question that has never been answered and which I have not yet been able to answer, despite my thirty years of research into the feminine soul, is 'What does a woman want?'" (quoted in Jones, 1955, p. 421). But Freud tried strenuously to understand women via many approaches. At times his proposed explanations emphasized the role of society in determining gender differences, saying that women are inferior to males because society oppresses them. Most consistently, however, he claimed that "anatomy is destiny"; that is, gender differences have a biological origin.

Freud persisted in viewing women as failed or inferior men. The cornerstone of his psychology of women remained penis envy. For males, the Oedipal complex is terminated by castration anxiety, causing them to identify with their fathers and to seek female partners in their adult lives. For females, penis envy commences the Oedipal complex, causing them to turn (partially) away from their mothers and toward their fathers as sex objects. This switch of affiliation causes the female erogenous zone to change from the clitoris to the vagina because of the latter organ's involvement in reproduction. According to Freud, it is only after the erogenous zone changes from the clitoris to the vagina that true feminine sexuality begins.

Freud believed that women could respond to their "castration" in three ways: (1) they could later withdraw from sexual activity altogether, becoming frigid; (2) they could cling to their masculinity and become homosexual or embrace feminism (which he believed is characterized by masculine aggressiveness); or (3) they could symbolically take their father as a sex object, leading to heterosexuality and child bearing.

Freud believed that because penis envy is not as intense as castration anxiety, females do not have the same need to engage in defensive identification as males. Remember, it is the defensive identification with their fathers that completes the development of the male superego. But what about the female? Freud believed the female does identify somewhat with her mother (mainly because of the fear of losing her love), but the identification is not nearly as intense and complete as it is for the male. The result, according to Freud, is that the female superego tends to be weaker than that of the male; that is, she is morally inferior.

Even as Freud expressed his views on feminine psychology, he had many supporters and detractors. It is interesting to note that many of his supporters were female psychoanalysts (for example, Jeanne Lampl-de Groot and Helene Deutsch). Likewise, many of his critics were male psychoanalysts (for example, Ernest Jones). This is not to say, however, that all female analysts agreed with him and all male analysts disagreed with him. One of his most outspoken critics was Karen Horney, whose theory of personality we review in chapter 5.

In the end, Freud essentially admitted defeat in his attempt to understand women. Following are his last words on the subject:

> That is all I [have] to say to you about femininity. It is certainly incomplete and fragmentary and does not always sound friendly. . . . If you want to know more about femininity, enquire from your own experiences of life, or turn to the poets, or wait until science can give you deeper and more coherent information. (1933/1966, p. 599)

Freud's views on feminine psychology have been harshly criticized for reflecting only the thought processes of his disturbed patients, the Victorian culture in which he practised, and his own personal biases, or for being scientifically incorrect. As valid as these and other criticisms may be, Freud has often been criticized for things he never said. Also, he sometimes held the same views as his critics, for example, the view that it is often the societal oppression of women that contributes to their apparent inferiority to men. In order to provide a more objective appraisal of Freud's views on feminine psychology, Young-Bruehl (1990) collected all of his writings on the topic. She arranged these writings in chronological order so it can be observed how Freud's views on feminine psychology changed over the course of his career.

Tapping the Unconscious Mind

If repressed anxiety-provoking thoughts are effectively anticathected by the ego or superego, how can we come to know what they are? To say the least, it is not easy, but it is the business of psychoanalysis to attempt to do so. Freud employed several methods of determining the contents of the unconscious mind, and we examine a few of them.

Free Association.   Earlier in this chapter we showed how the technique of free association gradually evolved. To stimulate free association (the fundamental rule of psychoanalysis), Freud instructed his patients as follows:

> You will notice that as you relate things various thoughts will occur to you which you would like to put aside on the ground of certain criticisms and objections. You will be tempted to say to yourself that this or that is irrelevant here, or is quite unimportant, or nonsensical, so that there is no need to say it. You must never give in to these criticisms, but must say it in spite of them—indeed, you must say it precisely *because* you feel an aversion to doing so. . . . Finally, never forget that you have promised to be absolutely honest, and never leave anything out because, for some reason or other, it is unpleasant to tell it. (1913/1958, pp. 134–135)

The idea was that even in conscious expressions, there are hints as to the contents of the unconscious mind that the trained observer can detect. What is not said is as important as, if not more important than, what is said. Topics to which patients offer strong **resistance** provide the analyst with useful hints to problem areas in the unconscious mind. One reason that Freud abandoned hypnosis is because a hypnotized patient does not display revealing resistances. During the course of free association resistance can take the form of telling carefully structured stories, long periods of silence, refusing to say something considered (by the patient) silly or embarrassing, avoiding certain topics, the tendency to report events in a highly intellectual, unemotional manner, "forgetting" important insights that had been gained from previous therapeutic sessions, and hiding important thoughts behind excessive emotion. In addition, if the therapeutic process appears dangerously close to revealing anxiety-provoking material, the patient may be late for an appointment or not show up at all.

Revealing the contents of the unconscious mind is difficult and requires a great deal of time. Typically a patient undergoing psychoanalysis is in therapy for four to six 50-minute sessions per week for several years. To facilitate the flow of ideas Freud had his patients lie on a couch in a dim room while he sat out of the patient's view. Freud remained out of sight for two reasons: (1) He did not want his gestures and expressions to influence the patient's thoughts, and (2) he could not tolerate being stared at for hours on end. At times Freud demonstrated a rather cavalier attitude toward his therapeutic sessions. Early in his career, he wrote a letter to his friend Wilhelm Fliess while one of his patients was under hypnosis (Masson, 1985, p. 21). Later, he confessed to taking naps during his afternoon sessions, presumably as his patients free associated (Masson, 1985, p. 303).

It should be realized that although Freud referred to his major therapeutic technique as "free association," he believed the reported associations to be anything but "free" in the sense of being random or accidental. Rather, the patient's associations reflect the complex ways that unacceptable impulses are repressed, displaced, and in other ways disguised. Thus a patient's associations may seem free, but to the trained analyst they reflect the complex interactions between the conscious and unconscious levels of the mind.

Dream Analysis.   Freud considered his book *The Interpretation of Dreams* (1900/1965) to be his most important contribution, and it was this book that finally brought Freud the professional recognition he had been seeking. Freud believed it was in dreams that the contents of the unconscious are most available, still hidden or distorted, but available. Indeed, Freud thought "The interpretation of dreams is the royal road to knowledge of the unconscious activities of the mind" (1900/1965, p. 608).

According to Freud, a dream is caused when the events of the day activate unacceptable impulses in the unconscious mind, causing them to seek conscious expression. At night, as the person sleeps, these impulses continue to seek conscious expression, but the ego realizes that if the contents of a dream are too threatening, they will cause the dreamer to awake prematurely. The ego, therefore, censors the impulses by driving them back into the unconscious. If these unacceptable impulses are ever to be consciously recognized they must be at least partially camouflaged. Freud referred to the various mechanisms that make impulses more acceptable by distorting their true meaning collectively as **dream work.** The two most important types of dream work are condensation and displacement.

Condensation occurs when a dream element represents several ideas at the same time. For example, one person in a dream can represent several people in the dreamer's waking life. **Displacement** occurs when an unacceptable dream-thought is replaced by a thought that is symbolically equivalent but is acceptable such as when penises become objects such as baseball bats or flagpoles; breasts become mountains, balloons, or cantaloupes; and sexual intercourse becomes dancing or horseback riding, to give but a few examples. Freud believed most of the symbols that occur in a particular person's dream are derived from the events in that person's life. Freud did believe, however, that some dream symbols were universal. For example, kings and queens symbolize mothers and fathers; boxes, chests, and cupboards symbolize the womb; walking up or down staircases, ladders, or steps symbolizes sexual intercourse; haircutting, baldness, and decapitation symbolize castration; small animals symbolize children; and long, stiff objects symbolize the penis. The symbols that occur in a person's dream can come from events in the person's waking life, from his or her childhood, or from the phylogenetic heritage of the human species.

The dream work creates several disjointed symbols that have little meaning to the dreamer, and thus they are allowed past the censor and enter consciousness. The dream symbols no longer cause anxiety because they represent unacceptable wishes, but they do cause anxiety for another reason. Because the rational (secondary) processes of the ego seek to interact with the physical world in a logical, intelligible manner, the meaningless symbols attempting to enter consciousness cannot be tolerated. To make the material acceptable, the ego engages in what Freud called **secondary revision** (sometimes called secondary elaboration). That is, the ego synthesizes the symbols in some coherent fashion. It is this secondary revision that we recall as a dream. When we recall a dream, we describe its **manifest content**, or what it appeared to be about. More important is the dream's **latent content**, which consists of the repressed thoughts seeking expression.

Dream work and secondary revision act on a dream to make its content more acceptable, but still the latent meaning is always there for the trained observer to discover. Because dreams always contain at least some threatening material, the patient and therapist must work quickly before their contents are repressed again. The nature of dreams and the process of repression explain why the memory of dreams is so short-lived.

Everyday Life.   In 1901, Freud wrote a book entitled *The Psychopathology of Everyday Life*, in which he gave numerous examples of **parapraxes,** that is, the manifestation of repressed thoughts in the course of everyday living. Being a determinist, Freud believed all human behaviour had a cause, that nothing happened simply by chance—not even "accidents." Freud believed little "mistakes" such as temporary lapses of memory provided information about the unconscious mind. For example, one may forget a potentially painful visit to the dentist or psychoanalyst. One may forget a date altogether or show up on Saturday instead of on Friday. One may stop at a green light on the way to his or her mother-in-law's house.

Slips of the tongue, which have come to be known as **Freudian slips**, are also thought to reveal unconscious motives. Legend has it that once Freud was introduced as Dr. Sigmund Fraud. Zimbardo and Ruch (1977, p. 416) reported that a radio announcer reading a commercial for Barbara Ann Bread instead of saying "Barbara Ann for the best bread" read "Barbara Ann for the breast in bed."

Even actual accidents were thought by Freud to have meaning. After all, an automobile accident is a socially acceptable way of not getting somewhere. The main point here is that just because a thought is repressed does not mean it goes away; it is always there striving for expression, and these manifestations in everyday life are another way of getting a glimpse into the unconscious.

Humour.   According to Freud, humour allows the expression of repressed thoughts in a socially approved manner. In his book *Jokes and Their Relation to the Unconscious* (1905/1960) Freud indicated that through humour a person can express aggressiveness (for example, practical jokes) or sexual desires without the fear of retaliation by either the ego or the superego. Jokes, then, are like dreams in that both allow the compromise expression of unacceptable impulses and both employ condensation, displacement, and symbolization. The purpose of both jokes and dreams is to satisfy unacceptable impulses indirectly that would be shocking if expressed directly.

Hostile jokes are typically directed towards members of a distinct group. In Canada, many people have become the target of this humour because of their Aboriginal status, geographical region, language, religion, gender, skin colour, etc. Newfoundlanders or "Newfies" have been the brunt of more than their share of jokes, just as people from New Jersey or Poland have been in other parts of the world. More common today in Canada are jokes about people from the big city, Toronto. According to Freudian theory, making fun of people from particular groups is a socially acceptable way to defeat or conquer them. Hostility hidden behind a joke can easily be disclaimed as "only a joke."

A joke that is too blatant fails to be humourous, just as a nightmare fails to preserve the sleep of the dreamer. In both cases, the impulses involved were not disguised enough. In fact, for a joke to be "funny," it must contain anxiety-provoking material. According to Freud, we laugh only at jokes that bother us. An examination of North American humour shows sex, elimination, and death to be favourite topics, and this would indicate to a Freudian that they contain an abundance of repressed thoughts. In fact, say the Freudians, one way to discover what has been repressed in a person's unconscious mind is to examine what he or she finds humorous.

Freud's View of Religion

When our ancestors were children they turned to their fathers for protection and guidance. Fathers tended to be revered, feared, and relied on. According to Freud, it is understandable that our ancestors created a God with the same characteristics as real fathers. According to Freud, these infantile conceptions of the father were generalized to an image of a deity who had to be blindly obeyed, just like a real father. This God protects his children from natural disasters such as earthquakes, storms, floods, volcanic eruptions, and disease. God, and the religions based on his existence, protect humans from feeling helpless and from feeling confused in light of the many apparent contradictions in life. Typically, religions teach that life continues after death; life after death can be perfect even if life on earth is not; good people will eventually be rewarded and bad ones punished; the difficulties one may experience in his or her life serve a higher purpose, and therefore no need for despair exists; and, in general, the world is being governed by a providence of superior wisdom and infinite goodness who relates to humans with the intimacy of a loving father. Religions also teach it is God's will that humans inhibit their sexual and aggressive tendencies to live in harmony with their fellow humans. About the role of religion in the lives of so many humans, Freud said: "The whole thing is so patently infantile, so foreign to reality, that to anyone with a friendly attitude to humanity it is painful to think that the great majority of mortals will never be able to rise above this view of life" (1930/1961, p. 22).

Perhaps, according to Freud, the uneducated masses will always need the illusions of religion to cause them to restrain their passions but educated, intelligent persons should live their lives according to scientific facts, not illusions. It is time, said Freud, to admit that our ancestors were wrong about religion; miracles never existed; natural disasters kill both believers and nonbelievers; no life after death occurs; and the course of human history is explained by evolutionary principles rather than the unfolding of a divine plan. Furthermore, although civilization does require rules, regulations, and inhibitions, these should be justified on rational grounds rather than claiming that they are the will of a deity. In other words, humans should be shown how various sanctions ultimately work to their own self-interests and, for that reason, should strive to preserve them.

Freud hoped that religion would eventually be replaced by rational, scientific principles. Just as Freud took no pain-killing drugs during his 16-year bout with cancer, he believed that humans could and should confront reality without the aid of illusions:

> No belittlement of science can in any way alter the fact that it is attempting to take account of our dependence on the real external world, while religion is an illusion and it derives its strength from its readiness to fit in with our instinctual wishful impulses. (1933/1966, pp. 638–639)

Freud concluded his book *The Future of an Illusion* (1927/1961) saying, "Our science is no illusion. But an illusion it would be to suppose that what science cannot give us we can get elsewhere" (p. 71).

Freud's View of Human Nature

To Freud, humans were mainly biological organisms whose master motive was the satisfaction of bodily needs. Cultural achievements in the sciences, arts, and religion were regarded mainly as displacements away from the more direct (and natural) ways of satisfying our biological needs in general and our sexual needs in particular. Freud viewed humans as hedonistic creatures driven by the same impulses that drive nonhuman animals. Religion and civilization developed either because of our fear of the unknown or because we needed protection against our own inborn aggressive tendencies.

Although pessimistic, Freud believed humans could, and should, live more rational lives, and the information that his theory provided could help them do so. To live rationally one must come to understand the workings of his or her own mind. Freud (1917/1955) said:

The news that reaches your consciousness is incomplete and often not to be relied on. . . . Even if you are not ill, who can tell all that is stirring in your mind of which you know nothing or are falsely informed? You behave like an absolute ruler who is content with the information supplied him by his highest officials and never goes among the people to hear their voice. Turn your eyes inward, look into your own depths, learn first to know yourself! (p. 143)

Modifications of the Freudian Legend

Few would doubt that Freud was one of the most influential figures in human history. Recently, however, several researchers have provided information that requires rather substantial changes in the traditional view of Freud and his ideas.

Freud's Revision of His Seduction Theory.   In April 1896, Freud delivered a paper entitled "The Aetiology of Hysteria" in which he concluded that hysteria is caused by a sexual seduction that had been experienced by the patient in childhood. At this time, Freud reported the seducers as nursemaids, governesses, domestic servants, adult strangers, tutors, and in most cases brothers who were slightly older than the sisters they supposedly seduced; no mention was made of parents as seducers. Freud's address to his colleagues was met with total silence, and he was urged not to publish his findings because doing so would damage his professional reputation beyond repair. Despite the warnings, however, Freud published his article in 1896 (reprinted in Masson, 1984) and he continued to experience professional, emotional, and intellectual isolation. Even Wilheim Fliess (1858–1928), Freud's closest friend at the time, was not supportive of Freud's seduction theory.

Freud abandoned his **seduction theory** in September 1897, although it was never scientifically refuted. The reasons for this abandonment are still a matter of speculation. In any case, Freud acknowledged that he had made a mistake in believing his patients that a *real* seduction had occurred in their childhoods. His revised position was that the seductions were often imaginary. Freud later claimed that this change from real to imagined seductions marked the beginning of psychoanalysis as a science, therapy, and profession. It was only at this time that Freud claimed his patients reported parents, usually the father, as their seducers. It is now believed that this change was designed to make Freud's clinical "observations" compatible with his newly proposed Oedipal theory. This exemplifies Freud's tendency to find support for whatever theoretical notions he was entertaining at the time. About this tendency, Esterson (1993) says, "It is difficult to escape the conclusion that both self-deception and dishonesty play a role in this story though at times it is scarcely possible to distinguish one from the other" (p. 31).

Jeffrey Masson in his book *The Assault on Truth: Freud's Suppression of the Seduction Theory* (1984) explored possible reasons why Freud changed his belief from real to imaginary seductions and concludes he did so mainly because he lacked personal courage, not for any clinical or theoretical reasons. Masson, the former projects director of the Sigmund Freud Archives, bases his conclusion on several previously unpublished or newly discovered letters and other documents. Masson, himself a psychoanalyst, also concludes that psychoanalysis would be better off today had Freud not revised his seduction theory:

By shifting the emphasis from an actual world of sadness, misery, and cruelty to an internal stage on which actors performed invented dramas for an invisible audience of their own creation, Freud began a trend away from the real world that, it seems to me, is at the root of the present day sterility of psychoanalysis and psychiatry throughout the world. (p. 144)

Masson (1984) provided a number of personal reasons that may have caused Freud to revise his seduction theory, reasons that are most unflattering to Freud in particular and to psychoanalysis in general. Masson believes that Freud's basic mistake was not accepting recovered memories of children's sexual seduction as reflecting actual events. But what if there were no recovered memories of any kind? There is now convincing evidence that Freud entered into the therapeutic situation with the strong conviction that repressed memories of infantile abuse existed in his patients, and he manipulated events during therapy in ways that caused his conviction to be confirmed. Furthermore, evidence indicates that it was Freud's interpretations and reconstructions of his patient's responses that were offered as evidence for his beliefs, rather than anything his patients actually said. For example, Esterson (1993) says, "A consideration of all the evidence . . . points to the conclusion that Freud's early patients, in general, did not recount stories of infantile seductions, these stories were actually analytic reconstructions which he foisted on them" (pp. 28–29). Esterson (1998) provides further evidence that none of Freud's patients during the time he was formulating his seduction theory reported that they had been sexually seduced in childhood. Similarly, Webster (1995) concludes, "There is no evidence that any of the patients who came to Freud without memories of sexual abuse had ever suffered from such abuse" (p. 517).

Others supporting the conclusions reached by Esterson (1993, 1998) and Webster (1995) include: Cioffi, 1974; Eissler, 2001; Gelfand and Kerr, 1992; Israëls and Schatzman, 1993; Powell and Boer, 1994; Schatzman, 1992; and Wilcocks, 1994. Given the fact that Freud described the concept of repression as the "cornerstone" of psychoanalysis, these, and other, researchers are attacking the very foundation of psychoanalysis.

Obviously, concern about the reality of repressed memories is not only of historical interest. A number of contemporary researchers are concerned about the widespread search for repressed memories by current therapists. Elizabeth Loftus (1993), for example, wonders why so many individuals enter therapy without memories of abuse but leave with them. She speculates that often it is the suggestions made by therapists that make the difference.

> If therapists ask questions that tend to elicit behaviors and experiences thought to be characteristic of someone who had been a victim of childhood trauma, might they too be creating this social reality?
>
> Whatever the good intentions of therapists, the documented examples of rampant suggestion should force us to at least ponder whether some therapists might be suggesting illusory memories to their clients rather than unlocking distant memories. . . . What is considered to be present in the client's unconscious mind might actually be present solely in the therapist's conscious mind. (p. 530)

Researchers such as Loftus do not deny that many children are sexually abused or that therapy can help them deal effectively with such experiences. It is the notion of repression and the techniques used to recover "repressed memories" that are being questioned.

> Many tortured individuals live for years with the dark secret of their abusive past and only find the courage to discuss their childhood traumas in the supportive and empathic environment of therapy. We are not disputing those memories. We are only questioning the memories commonly referred to as "repressed"—memories that did not exist until someone went looking for them. (Loftus & Ketcham, 1994, p. 141)

In recent times, allegations of childhood sexual abuse based on recovered memories have become so widespread that the False Memory Syndrome Foundation (FMSF) was created in 1992 to investigate and assess such charges (see, for example, False Memory Syndrome Foundation, 1992). The American Psychological Association (APA) approved the FMSF as a provider of information concerning so-called recovered memories of abuse (American Psychological Association, 1995).

Correcting Other Freudian Myths.   The Freudians have been accused of distorting their history to make it more interesting or flattering. In the same vein, Freud and his followers tended to paint Freud as a lonely, heroic figure who suffered discrimination because he was a Jew and because of the difficulty others had in accepting his bold, creative, original ideas. Henri Ellenberger has done much to demythologize the Freudian legend. According to Ellenberger (1970), the Freudian legend has two main features:

> The first is the theme of the solitary hero struggling against a host of enemies, suffering "the slings and arrows of outrageous fortune" but triumphing in the end. The legend considerably exaggerates the extent and role of anti-Semitism, of the hostility of the academic world, and of alleged Victorian prejudices. The second feature of the Freudian legend is the blotting out of the greatest part of the scientific and cultural context in which psychoanalysis developed, hence the theme of the absolute originality of the achievements, in which the hero is credited with the achievements of his predecessors, associates, disciples, rivals, and contemporaries. (p. 547)

According to Ellenberger a careful reading of the facts indicates that Freud's career was only slightly hampered by anti-Semitism; that Freud experienced no more than the normal amount of hostility from his fellow physicians and not nearly as much as several more prominent physicians did; and that most of Freud's ideas concerning dreams, the unconscious mind, and sexual pathology were not original. Ellenberger (1970) said, "Much of what is credited to Freud was diffuse current lore, and his role was to crystallize these ideas and give them an original shape" (p. 548).

Freud and his early followers had a low tolerance for criticism and usually attributed it to a lack of understanding, resistance, or bigotry. Frank Sulloway in his book *Freud, Biologist of the Mind: Beyond the Psychoanalytic Legend* (1979), however, concluded that most of the criticisms directed at psychoanalysis as it began to become popular were rational and justified. Sulloway (1979) summarizes those criticisms:

> In addition to the criticisms that had already been raised before Freud acquired a substantial following, common objections against psychoanalysis now began to include: (1) that psychoanalysts were continually introducing their assertions with the statement, "We know from psychoanalytic experience that. . . ," and then leaving the burden of proof to others; (2) that Freud's disciples refused to listen to opinions that did not coincide with their own; (3) that they never published statistics on the success of their method; (4) that they persisted in claiming that only those who had used the psychoanalytic method had the right to challenge Freud; (5) that they saw all criticism as a form of "neurotic resistance"; (6) that psychoanalysts tended to ignore all work that had been done before them and then proceeded to make unwarranted claims about their own originality; (7) that they frequently addressed themselves to the wider lay audience as if their theories were already a proven fact, thus making their opponents seem narrow-minded and ignorant; (8) that so-called wild analysts, or individuals without proper training, were analyzing patients in irresponsible ways; and (9) that Freud's followers were becoming a sect, with all of the prominent features of one, including a fanatical degree of faith, a special jargon, a sense of moral superiority, and a predilection for marked intolerance of opponents. In their contemporary context, such criticisms were considerably more rational and had far more merit than traditional psychoanalytic historians have been willing to admit. (p. 460)

Evaluation

EMPIRICAL RESEARCH

The many attempts to validate Freudian ideas experimentally have produced mixed results. In his review of numerous studies, J. McVicker Hunt (1979) found support for Freud's contention that early experience is important in moulding adult personality but little support for the influence of specific psychosexual stages as Freud described them (Frank, 2000). In his review, Maddi (1996) found considerable support for the various mechanisms of defence postulated by Freud, especially repression (see Cicchetti, Laor, & Wolmer, 2001; Cramer, 2001; and Kahn, 2002). Maddi (1996) also found evidence that boys experience more castration anxiety than do girls (see also Albert, 1999 and Myers, 2001). Silverman (1976), Blum (1962), and Hall and Van de Castle (1965) also found more castration anxiety in boys relative to girls and the reverse for penis envy. Kline (1972) reviewed more than 700 studies designed to test Freudian notions and concluded that Freudian theory could not be rejected on the basis of the research designed to test it because "Too much that is distinctively Freudian has been verified [and] there are few good experiments which actually refute the theory" (p. 350). Fisher and Greenberg (1977) reached a similar conclusion: "Scanning the spectrum of tests we have applied to Freud's theories, we are generally impressed with how often the results have borne out his expectations" (p. 393). Also, responding to the frequently made assertion that Freudian notions are too nebulous to be tested, Fisher and Greenberg (1977) said, "We have actually not been able to find a single systematic psychological theory that has been as frequently evaluated scientifically as have Freud's concepts!" (p. 396). Masling (1983) and more recently Cabre and Candioti (1996) and DeSwart (2001) also reported numerous experiments that verify several Freudian notions.

Given that the crux of Freudian theory lies in the assumption of unconscious thoughts and impulses, the challenge is to convince readers, clients, and skeptics that there are unconscious processes at work, and that those processes influence behaviour in various areas in a number of ways. Researchers have explored many connections between unconscious processing and behaviour, specifically in the domain of dream analysis and defence mechanisms. Daniel Bernstein of Simon Fraser University and Kathryn Belicki of Brock investigated the relationship between dream content and personality characteristics (Bernstein & Belicki, 1996). To categorize dreams, they used the Dream Content Questionnaire (Bernstein & Roberts, 1995), which breaks dreams down by characters, settings, social interactions, and the dreamer's emotions. They found a relationship between bizarre dream content and bizarre personality characteristics and between aggressive dreams and aggressive personalities. However, other aspects of personality, such as emotional states and patterns of social interaction, did not relate to dream content. In other words, even if you know someone especially well (even yourself), you cannot reliably predict what that person will dream about; nor will dreams give you a complete picture of someone's personality.

Defence mechanisms are regarded by many as one of the most significant and solidly supported areas of Freudian theory. It is through these mechanisms that we get a glimpse of the underlying dynamic of the id, ego, and superego. The source of individual differences lies in what defences a person uses, how often, and in what circumstances. Freud suggested that defensive processes play a major role in character formation. If so, we would expect a relation between personality characteristics and the use of certain defence mechanisms; highly creative individuals, for example, may use sublimation or displacement more often than less creative individuals. Many researchers, including Delroy Paulhus from the University of British Columbia, have attempted to link defence mechanisms to major personality traits (Paulhus, Fridhandler, & Hayes, 1997; Paulhus & John, 1998; Yik, Bond, & Paulhus, 1998). They categorized defences into two principal tendencies. The first, called impression management, involves purposefully tailoring your responses to impress an audience. For example, you might refuse to admit that you ever feel like smashing things, or ever took something that didn't belong to you. That is, you may portray yourself as more altruistic and dependable than others would see you. The second category, called self-deceptive enhancement, involves unconsciously thinking of yourself in a positive light. For example, you might believe that compared to the average person, you are a better driver, and more intelligent and attractive. Analysis of a large number of self- and peer-report personality ratings did support the idea that people tend to use one type or another of defence mechanism and that this pattern was related to their personality.

CRITICISMS

Earlier we reviewed several criticisms of psychoanalytic theory that were made in Freud's day just as his theory was gaining widespread recognition. Many current critics of Freudian theory believe that those early criticisms are still valid. In addition, say the critics, Freudian theory can be criticized for being internally inconsistent; demonstrating male chauvinism (for example, assuming that girls long to have a penis); overemphasizing sexual motivation; overemphasizing unconscious motivation; being too pessimistic about human nature (for example, asserting that humans are basically aggressive and irrational); and equating the ultimate state of happiness with the tension-free state that results when all of one's biological needs are satisfied.

Critics also claim that, although a few Freudian concepts have been supported by empirical research, most of his more important notions remain untestable. For example, how would one design an experiment to verify if the mind is a closed energy system or if the death instinct exists? Many important aspects of Freud's theory are not formulated precisely enough to generate risky predictions. As we saw in Chapter 1, if a theory does not generate risky predictions it cannot be falsified and, therefore, according to Popper, it is not scientific. From what has preceded, then, we can conclude that some aspects of Freud's theory are scientific (testable) but many others are not.

CONTRIBUTIONS

Despite the many criticisms of Freud's theory, most would agree that its overall value is positive. Freud contributed to our understanding of personality by demonstrating the importance of anxiety as a determinant of human behaviour; by showing that physical and physiological disorders can have psychological as well as physiological origins; by showing that conflicts originating in childhood have lifelong consequences; by showing the importance of childhood sexuality in personality development; by showing the many ways that people defend themselves against unbearable anxiety; by showing that much "normal" behaviour is determined by the same processes that determine "abnormal" behaviour; by showing that many human problems result from the clash between the selfish, biological nature of humans and our need to live harmoniously with other humans in society; and by developing a technique for treating unbearable anxiety. Freud has provided us with a general framework with which to study personality. Although portions of Freud's theory may be incorrect or vague and difficult to test, it has raised questions that researchers have attempted to answer ever since.

As we pointed out at the beginning of this chapter, few people in history have had the impact on human thought that Freud has had. No major category of human existence has been untouched by his ideas. For example, he has influenced religion, philosophy, education, literature, art, and all of the social sciences.

What follows in this text can be understood mainly as a reaction to Freud. Some theories support and extend his thoughts, and others refute them, but it was Freud who was first to establish a formal theory of personality, and first is always the most difficult to be.

SUMMARY

1. From his visit with Charcot, Freud learned that physical disorders could have psychological as well as organic origins, and therefore concluded that hysteria should be viewed as a serious, treatable disorder. From Bernheim, Freud learned that behaviour can be caused by ideas of which individuals are unaware, but also that unconscious ideas can be made conscious if certain procedures are followed. From Breuer, Freud learned that when a patient openly discusses his or her problems, a release of tension (catharsis) often occurs. Sometimes a patient responds to a therapist as if he or she were an important person in the patient's life, a process called transference. With much experimentation, Freud arrived at free association as a major therapeutic technique for studying the unconscious.

2. According to Freud, instincts constitute the driving force behind personality. Instincts have a source, an aim, an object, and an impetus. Freud referred to the life instincts collectively as eros and to the associated energy as libido. The death instinct (thanatos) is responsible for aggression, believed to be an impulse toward self-destruction turned outward.

3. The mind, in Freud's theory, is divided into the id (which is shared with lower animals and seeks ultimate pleasure), the ego (the personality executive, which must reckon with reality) and the superego (the moral component, made up of the conscience and ego ideal). When a physiological need arises, the id creates a mental image of an object (a wish) that will satisfy that need. Because wishes cannot satisfy needs, the ego must seek out real objects in the environment to actually satisfy the need.

4. The investment of psychic energy in the image of an object to satisfy a need is called cathexis. If a desired object conflicts with the values of the superego, anxiety will be experienced, and the ego will resist the id's attempt to invest energy in its image. Freud distinguished between

three types of anxiety: reality anxiety (fear of actual dangers), neurotic anxiety (fear of punishment), and moral anxiety (experienced when one of the superego's values is violated). Ego-defence mechanisms are unconscious processes that reduce anxiety by distorting or falsifying reality; they include repression, displacement, sublimation, identification, denial, projection, undoing, reaction formation, rationalization, intellectualization, and regression.

5. Each child, in Freud's theory, goes through certain psychosexual stages of development, and the child's experiences during these stages determine what type of personality he or she will possess as an adult. During each psychosexual stage, one area of the body (called an erogenous zone) is associated with maximum pleasure. Either too much or too little gratification during any stage can result in fixation, meaning that characteristics of that stage persist into adulthood. Fixation at the oral stage results in either an oral-incorporative or oral-sadistic character. Fixation at the anal stage results in either an anal-expulsive or anal-retentive character. The third or phallic stage largely determines adult sexual preferences. During this stage, the Oedipus complex arises, wherein boys experience castration anxiety and girls experience penis envy. A latency period follows that marks a dormancy (repression and displacement) of sexual interests in place of school, learning, and peer groups. Beginning at puberty, the final (genital) stage marks the passage to adulthood. Despite several theoretical approaches to understanding women, Freud most consistently claimed that "anatomy is destiny," and that gender differences are ultimately biological in origin.

6. Freud's major tools for investigating the unconscious mind were free association, analysis of dreams and everyday experiences, and humour. During free association, patients resisted pondering certain ideas and Freud assumed those ideas were especially anxiety-

provoking. In dream analysis, Freud differentiated between the manifest or apparent content and latent or true content. In everyday life, Freud noted that people tend to forget anxiety-provoking experiences, sometimes have "accidents" on purpose, and sometimes reveal their true (unconscious) feelings through "slips of the tongue." Like dreams, jokes allow indirect expression of thoughts that, if expressed directly, would cause unbearable anxiety.

7. Freud believed that the helplessness that our ancestors felt when confronting the power of nature and the uncertainties of life caused them to create a God that had the characteristics of a powerful, all-knowing, and benevolent father. Freud believed it was dangerous for contemporary humans to go on basing their lives on the irrational wish fulfillments that constitute religion. It is better to live in accordance with the objective facts provided by science.

8. Recently the Freudian legend has been modified in several important ways. The reasons for Freud's abandonment of his seduction theory have been questioned. It has also been discovered that Freud did not experience as much anti-Semitism nor rejection from the medical community as has been claimed. Finally, many of the ideas that were attributed to Freud were not original.

9. Many attempts to validate Freud's ideas empirically have produced equivocal results. Critics say that many of Freud's most basic notions are incapable of falsification. Other criticisms include internal inconsistency, male chauvinism, overemphasis on sexual and unconscious motivation, being too pessimistic about human nature, and equating true happiness with the tension-free condition that occurs when all of one's biological needs are satisfied.

EXPERIENTIAL EXERCISES

1. Keep track of your dreams for about a week. As soon as possible following each dream, write down as much of it as you can remember. Analyze the dreams as Freud would have. In other words, analyze the manifest content of each dream, assuming that a more basic latent content exists. Also, free-associate to your dreams, again assuming that the associations triggered by the dream's manifest content will reveal something about the dream's latent content. Summarize what you think your dreams reveal about the content of your unconscious mind.

2. Although, according to Freud, the ego-defence mechanisms function on the unconscious level, it is sometimes possible to detect one's own use of them by carefully observing one's behaviour. Make a list of the ego-defence mechanisms you use and describe how you use them.

3. Observe your own behaviour for about a week and note the following: appointments you were late for or missed altogether, slips of the tongue, memory lapses, any "accidents" that you had, and any jokes you heard and found amusing. Analyze these everyday experiences with the idea they may reflect the contents of your unconscious mind. Summarize your conclusions.

4. Freud believed that to a large extent anatomy is destiny. That is, whether one is born a boy or a girl will determine many of the personality characteristics that one will possess as an adult. Drawing on your own life's experiences give the reasons why you either accept or reject Freud's assertion.

5. Try your hand at free association. While in a relaxed mood, write down on a piece of paper any thoughts, feelings, or memories that come to mind. Do not inhibit your responses in any way and do not eliminate a response because it seems unimportant. Analyze this free flow of ideas with the intent of discovering any deep, underlying memories that may be present but cannot be expressed openly. Be especially attentive to any signs of resistance. Describe what you think a psychoanalyst would conclude about your free associations.

DISCUSSION QUESTIONS

1. Discuss the ego-defence mechanism of repression and explain why it is so important to Freud's theory.
2. Define and give an example of the following ego-defence mechanisms: denial of reality, projection, reaction formation, undoing, rationalization, and intellectualization.
3. Discuss the psychosexual stages of development. Include in your answer the major experiences that occur within each stage and their possible influences on adult behaviour. Pay special attention to the male and female Oedipal complexes.
4. Jeffrey Masson believes Freud's mistake was not accepting as real the instances of childhood sexual abuse told to him by his patients. According to researchers such as Esterson and Webster, Freud's mistake was more basic. What, according to them, was it?
5. Choose a field other than psychology (for example, art, literature, or philosophy) and show how Freudian concepts have influenced that field.

KEY TERMS

Anal-expulsive character, p. 34
Anal-retentive character, p. 34
Anal stage, p. 34
Anticathexis, p. 28
Castration anxiety, p. 35
Catharsis, p. 22
Cathexis, p. 28
Condensation, p. 39
Conscience, p. 27
Countertransference, p. 22
Denial of reality, p. 31
Displaced aggression, p. 31
Displacement, p. 30
Dream work, p. 39
Ego, p. 25
Ego-defence mechanisms, p. 29
Ego ideal, p. 27
Erogenous zone, p. 34
Eros, p. 24
Fixation, p. 34
Free association, p. 22
Freudian slip, p. 40
Genital stage, p. 36
Hysteria, p. 20
Id, p. 25
Identification, p. 31
Inheritance of acquired characteristics, p. 25

Instinct, p. 24
Intellectualization (also called isolation of affect), p. 33
Latency stage, p. 36
Latent content of a dream, p. 39
Libido, p. 24
Manifest content of a dream, p. 39
Moral anxiety, p. 29
Neurotic anxiety, p. 29
Oedipus complex, p. 35
Oral-incorporative character, p. 34
Oral-sadistic character, p. 34
Oral stage, p. 34
Parapraxes, p. 39
Penis envy, p. 35
Phallic stage, p. 35
Phylogenetically inherited endowment, p. 30
Pleasure principle, p. 25
Posthypnotic amnesia, p. 21
Posthypnotic suggestion, p. 21
Preconscious, p. 30
Primal repression, p. 29
Primary processes, p. 26

Principle of conservation of energy, p. 28
Projection, p. 32
Psychic energy, p. 28
Rationalization, p. 33
Reaction formation, p. 32
Reality anxiety, p. 29
Reality principle, p. 26
Reality testing, p. 26
Reflex action, p. 25
Regression, p. 33
Repression, p. 29
Repression proper, p. 29
Resistance, p. 38
Secondary processes, p. 26
Secondary revision (also called secondary elaboration), p. 39
Seduction theory, p. 42
Sublimation, p. 31
Superego, p. 25
Thanatos, p. 24
Transference, p. 22
Undoing, p. 32
Vitalism, p. 28
Wish fulfillment, p. 25

3 Carl Jung

As we see in this chapter, Jung's theory of personality is complex. In fact, the picture of human nature that he portrays may be the most complicated developed by any personality theorist. As might be expected, Jung himself was a complicated person. The details of his life often appear to be contradictory. For example, Stern (1976) portrayed Jung as a prepsychotic (if not psychotic), opportunistic person with anti-Semitic and pro-Nazi leanings. On the other hand, Hannah (1976), a Jungian herself and a close friend of Jung's, portrayed him as a brilliant, sensitive humanitarian who was anything but an anti-Semite or pro-Nazi. The Jung whom Hannah describes is indeed an uncommon, sometimes troubled, person with many idiosyncrasies but these, in her opinion, are attributes of a genius, not of a madman. Jung's autobiography (1961) does not help much because it is, Jung confessed, a combination of myth and fact.

It appears that many truths about Jung's personal life, if they are ever to be known at all, will need to unfold in the future. What follows is a summary of those facts about Jung over which there is little or no disagreement. As far as Jung's theoretical notions are concerned, as with any other personality theorist, either his ideas are valid and useful or they are not. The personal experiences that gave rise to those ideas may be interesting in themselves but they are scientifically irrelevant.

Biographical Sketch

Carl Jung

Carl Gustav Jung was born on July 26, 1875, in the Swiss village of Kesswyl but grew up in the university town of Basel. Religion was a strong theme running through Jung's early years. His father, Paul Jung, was a pastor in the Swiss Reformed Church, and his mother, Emilie Preiswerk Jung, was the daughter of a theologian. Jung's father viewed himself as a failure, and his religion was little comfort to him. As a child, Jung often asked his father penetrating questions concerning religion and life but was unable to obtain satisfactory answers. It became clear to Jung that his father accepted church dogma completely on faith and was never really personally touched by real religious experience. According to Jung, these fruitless theological discussions alienated him from his father. Later in Jung's life, religion became a vital part of his theory, but it was the kind of religion that touched individuals emotionally and had little to do with specific churches or religious dogma.

Jung considered his mother to be the dominant member of the family, although he saw her as terribly inconsistent, which caused him to suspect that she was really two persons in one body. One person was kindly and extremely hospitable, with a great sense of humour; the other was uncanny, archaic, and ruthless. Jung described how he reacted when his mother's second personality emerged: "[I was] usually struck to the core of my being, so that I was stunned into silence" (1961, p. 49). It is interesting that the young Jung thought that he, like his mother, was really two different people. One person he labelled number one (the schoolboy), the other number two (the wise old man). Later, Jung realized that his number one self represented his ego or conscious mind, and his number two self represented his more powerful unconscious mind. Thus, as a boy, Jung experienced what he later considered the very essence of human existence: the interaction between the conscious and unconscious mind.

Perhaps because of the constant bickering of his parents, Jung began to isolate himself from his family in particular and the world in general. Increasingly his dreams, visions, and fantasies became his primary reality, and he developed the belief that this inner reality was furnishing him with secret knowledge that only a select few persons were given, and therefore it could not easily be shared with others.

Jung's Early Dreams, Visions, and Fantasies

Stone.   When Jung was about seven years old, he discovered a large stone with which he began to play an imaginary game. First he would perceive himself as sitting on the stone, which he was. Then, however, he would assume the perspective of the stone. Jung imagined himself to be the stone being sat on by a boy. Jung found that he could switch perspectives with ease. In fact, it was difficult for Jung to tell if he was sitting on the stone or if he was the stone being sat on: "The answer remained totally unclear, and my uncertainty was accompanied by a feeling of curious and fascinating darkness. But there was no doubt whatsoever that this stone stood in some secret relationship to me. I could sit on it for hours, fascinated by the puzzle it set me" (Jung, 1961, p. 20).

When Jung returned to this stone 30 years later, as a married, professionally successful man, the magic of the stone returned immediately: "The pull of that other world was so strong that I had to tear myself violently from the spot in order not to lose hold of my future" (1961, p. 20).

Manikin.   When Jung was 10 years old, he carved a wooden figure of a man from a ruler and kept it in a little wooden case. Jung dressed the figure in a coat, black boots, and a top hat and gave it a little stone of its own. This figure became a refuge for Jung and whenever he was troubled he would visit his secret friend. At school Jung would write in a secret language on little scrolls of paper, which he would later place in the pencil case containing the manikin. The addition of each scroll required a solemn ceremonial act. Jung never worried about explaining these actions because they provided him with a sense of security. "It was an inviolable secret which must never be betrayed, for the safety of my life depended on it. Why that was so I did not ask myself. It simply was so" (1961, p. 22). Jung's "relationship" with his manikin lasted for about a year.

Phallus Dream.   Although strange, the manikin and stone experiences were not frightening to Jung. In fact, as we have seen, the manikin provided him with an element of peace and security. Other mystical experiences of the young Jung were not as tranquil, however. A dream that Jung had when he was about four years old was terrifying to him. In this dream, Jung discovered a stone-lined hole in the ground, peered down, and saw a stone stairway leading downward. Jung descended and at the bottom found a round arch closed off by a lush green curtain. Pushing the curtain aside, Jung observed a rectangular chamber about 30 feet long. In the chamber was a platform on which was a rich, magnificent king's golden throne. Standing on the throne was an object 12 to 15 feet high and about 2 feet thick. The object consisted of skin and naked flesh, and on the top was a rounded head with no face or hair. On the top of the object was a single eye staring upward. This was obviously a giant phallus. Although the object did not move, it gave the appearance of being able to. Within his dream Jung was paralyzed with terror and he dreamed he heard his mother saying, "Yes, just look at him. That is the man-eater!" (1961, p. 12). Jung's fear intensified, and he awoke sweating and terrified. For many nights following, Jung could not go to sleep for fear of having that or a similar dream again.

The phallus dream haunted Jung for years and it influenced his view of Christianity for many years. From his dream, Jung concluded that the giant phallus was the underground counterpart of the Lord Jesus:

> At all events, the phallus of this dream seems to be a subterranean God "not to be named," and such it remained throughout my youth, reappearing whenever anyone spoke too emphatically about Lord Jesus. Lord Jesus never became quite real for me, never quite acceptable, never quite lovable, for again and again I would think of his underground counterpart, a frightful revelation which had been accorded me without my seeking it. (1961, p. 13)

Jung was so shaken by the phallus dream that he did not mention it to anyone until he was 65 years old.

Throne Vision.   One day, when Jung was about 12 years old he left school on a warm summer day. The new, brightly glazed tiles on the roof of a nearby cathedral sparkled in the radiant sunshine. Jung was struck with the notion that God made that beautiful day and that beautiful church and was viewing his creations from his golden throne high above in the blue sky. Suddenly Jung was struck with the idea that if he did not stop thinking, a terrible thought would enter his mind. He was convinced that if he continued thinking he would commit the most terrible sin, and his soul would be damned for all eternity. The next few days were torture for Jung as he tried desperately to fend off the forbidden thought. Finally, Jung allowed himself to experience the forbidden thought:

I saw before me the cathedral, the blue sky. God sits on His golden throne, high above the world—and from under the throne an enormous turd falls upon the sparkling new roof, shatters it, and breaks the walls of the cathedral asunder.

So that was it! I felt an enormous, an indescribable relief. Instead of the expected damnation, grace had come upon me, and with it an unutterable bliss such as I had never known. I wept for happiness and gratitude. (1961, pp. 39–40)

This vision had a profound effect on Jung. He now believed he knew what his father had not known about God. By taking the Bible's commandments as his guide, Jung's father had never directly experienced the will of God.

Personal experiences, such as those just described, convinced Jung there are aspects of the human psyche that are independent of any individual's personal experience. Jung (1961) summarized what he had learned from his fantasies:

My fantasies brought home to me the crucial insight that there are things in the psyche which I do not produce, but which produce themselves and have their own life. . . . I understood that there is something in me which can say things that I do not know and do not intend, things which may even be directed against me. (p. 183)

Jung eventually dedicated his professional life to understanding the nature and origins of the many extraordinary psychological experiences he had had as a child.

Jung's Early Professional Life

Jung first wanted to study archaeology but a dream convinced him to follow in his paternal grandfather's footsteps and become a physician. Jung became aware of the new field of psychiatry during his medical studies at the University of Basel, where he attained his medical degree in 1900. In psychiatry, Jung believed he had found his true calling. Jung's interest in unusual psychic phenomena never wavered and his dissertation for his medical degree, published in 1902, was entitled "On the Psychopathology of So-Called Occult Phenomena." At this time, Jung was almost totally absorbed with the study of the occult. He attended séances, participated in experiments with mediums, and devoured books on parapsychology. In addition to his visions and his readings in parapsychology, personal experience also seemed to confirm the existence of the supernatural. For example, as Jung was at home studying in his room, he and his mother heard a loud noise and observed that a solid table had split from the rim to the centre, not along the joints as would be expected. Two weeks later, after another loud blast, it was discovered that the blade of a butter knife had shattered into pieces. Examination by a cutler revealed no fault in the steel that would explain the explosion. On another occasion, Jung was entertaining a group by telling an imaginary story about a person he did not know, only to learn that he was clairvoyantly revealing true facts about the man. Lastly, Jung awoke one night with an extremely painful headache only to learn that one of his patients had shot himself in the head that very night.

Jung's first professional appointment was at the noted Burghölzli psychiatric hospital in Zurich, where he worked under the supervision of Eugen Bleuler, who coined the term *schizophrenia*. Bleuler was interested in psychological tests and he encouraged Jung to experiment with the word-association test that had been used previously by Francis Galton (Darwin's cousin) and Wilhelm Wundt (the founder of the school of voluntarism). We have more to say about Jung's extensive use of the word-association test when we discuss complexes later in this chapter. In 1905, Jung was given a lectureship at the University of Zurich, where he lectured on psychopathology, psychoanalysis, and hypnosis. Also, Jung became clinical director of Burghölzli Hospital and head of the outpatient clinic. Jung resigned his positions at the Burghölzli in 1909 and his lectureship in 1914 to devote his time to his growing private practice, research, and writing.

On February 14, 1903, Jung married Emma Rauschenbach, the daughter of a rich industrialist, and they raised four daughters and a son. Emma herself became a practitioner of her husband's theory. During middle age Jung began a lengthy affair with a woman 13 years his junior. Her name was Toni Wolfe, and she was an attractive, well-educated former patient of Jung's. At first Jung's wife Emma was deeply upset but their situation eventually worked out. (Stern, 1976).

Jung's Relationship with Freud

Jung first became interested in Freud after reading *The Interpretation of Dreams*. Jung began to apply Freud's ideas to his own practice and eventually wrote a monograph entitled *The Psychology of Dementia Praecox* (1907/1960) summarizing their effectiveness. Jung had found considerable support for Freud's notion of repression in his own word-association studies, and he reported this fact in his book and in several articles. In 1906, Jung initiated correspondence with Freud, and in February of the following year, the two met in Freud's home in Vienna. Their first face-to-face meeting was intense and lasted 13 hours. The two became extremely close friends, and when Jung returned to Zurich, a correspondence began that lasted about seven years. Freud decided that Jung would become his successor. In 1911, Freud nominated Jung as the first president of the International Psychoanalytic Association and, despite considerable opposition from the members, Jung was elected.

Even at this early stage in their relationship, differences appeared in the two men's views of the libido, as shown in this 1907 exchange of letters:

> Is it not conceivable, in view of the limited conception of sexuality that prevails nowadays, that the sexual terminology should be reserved only for the most extreme forms of your "libido," and that a less offensive collective term should be established for *all* the libidinal manifestations? (quoted in McGuire, 1974, p. 25)

Freud responded:

> I appreciate your motives in trying to sweeten the sour apple, but I do not think you will be successful. Even if we call the unconscious "psychoid," it will still be the unconscious, and even if we do not call the driving force in the broadened conception of sexuality "libido," it will still be libido. . . . We cannot avoid resistances, why not face up to them from the start? (quoted in McGuire, 1974, p. 28)

Jung travelled with Freud to America in 1909 to give a series of lectures at Clark University. Jung was invited primarily because of his experimentation with the word-association test. Aboard ship, Jung and Freud spent considerable time analyzing each others' dreams. Jung was surprised at the inability of Freud, the master of dream interpretation, to analyze several dreams. More surprising, however, was that Freud would not share the private aspects of his life that might explain the symbolism of his dreams, saying instead, "I cannot risk my authority." Jung (1961) described his reaction to Freud's assertion, "At that moment he lost it altogether. That sentence burned itself into my memory; and in it the end of our relationship was already foreshadowed. Freud

Photograph Taken During the Visit of Freud and Jung to Clark University, 1909. Top row, from left to right: Sandor Ferenczi, Ernest Jones (Freud's biographer), and A. A. Brill. Bottom row, from left to right: Carl Jung, G. Stanley Hall (then president of Clark University), and Sigmund Freud.

was placing personal authority above truth" (p. 158). It was also during this trip to the United States that Jung first began to entertain doubts about the emphasis on sexual motivation in Freud's theory. He did not express these doubts strongly, however, and the two remained close friends. Jung simply suggested to Freud that his theory might be more palatable to American audiences if he played down the role of sex. Freud viewed this suggestion as a departure from scientific ethics.

It was not until about 1911 that Jung openly expressed doubts about Freud's interpretation of libidinal energy as primarily sexual. Jung's book *The Psychology of the Unconscious* (1912/1953) and a series of lectures he gave at Fordham University entitled *The Theory of Psychoanalysis* (1913/1961) amplified the differences between Jung's conception of the libido and Freud's.

The relationship between Jung and Freud became so strained that they agreed to stop their personal correspondence in 1912, and in 1914 Jung completely terminated the relationship when he resigned his presidency of the International Psychoanalytic Association and also withdrew as a member. The break was especially disturbing to Jung, who was then almost 40 years old. The separation from Freud caused Jung to enter what he called the "dark years," a period of about four years during which he explored in depth his own dreams and fantasies, an activity that brought him, in the opinion of many, to the brink of madness.

Jung's Creative Illness.   Jung said, "After the parting of the ways with Freud, a period of inner uncertainty began for me. It would be no exaggeration to call it a state of disorientation. I felt totally suspended in mid-air, for I had not yet found my own footing" (1961, p. 170). According to Ellenberger (1970), what Jung experienced during the "dark years" following the collapse of his relationship with Freud was a **creative illness** that Ellenberger (1970, p. 447) defined as "a period of intense preoccupation with an idea and search for a certain truth. It is a polymorphous condition that can take the shape of depression, neurosis, psychosomatic ailments, or even psychosis. . . ."

Some believe that Jung went on a voluntary voyage of self-exploration during his creative illness (see, for example, Van der Post, 1975); others see his journey as a series of full-fledged psychotic episodes (see, for example, Stern, 1976). In any case, Jung continued to maintain his psychiatric practice and his home life during his illness. In fact, according to Jung, it was his family and his patients that kept him sane during his illness. It was during his "confrontation with the unconscious" that Jung developed his previously described relationship with Toni Wolfe.

How strange it must have been for Jung to be engaged in this intense self-exploration at a time when he was treating psychotic patients. Strange or not, however, Jung appears to have learned a great deal about the human psyche from both sources.

Jung emerged from his creative illness with his own theory of personality, a theory that bore only a remote resemblance to that of his mentor, Freud. The results of the long, agonizing search of his own psyche are to be found everywhere in his theory of personality.

Jung continued to develop his theory up to the time of his death, at the age of 86, on June 6, 1961, at his tower home in Bollingen, Switzerland. A prolific writer for six decades, Jung's *Collected Works* consists of 20 volumes. Among his many honors are eight honorary doctorates from institutions such as Harvard (1936), Oxford (1938), and the University of Geneva (1945). In 1938, he was named Honorary Fellow of the Royal Society of Medicine and in 1943 he became an Honorary Member of the Swiss Academy of Sciences. In 1944, the University of Basel established the Chair of Medical Psychology in his name. In 1948, the first C. G. Jung Institute was founded in Zurich and was soon followed by the founding of the International Analytical Psychology Association. Today Jungian training institutes exist in several countries including Denmark, England, France, Germany, Israel, Italy, the Netherlands, Sweden, Switzerland, and the United States.

Libido and the Principles of Equivalence, Entropy, and Opposites

Libido.   Freud and Jung disagreed about the nature of the **libido**. At the time of his collaboration with Jung, Freud saw libido mainly as sexual energy. Jung believed this view was too narrow and instead defined the libido as general biological life energy that is concentrated on different problems as they arise. For Jung, libido was a creative life force that could be applied to the continuous psychological growth of the person. Life can be enjoyed across a host of domains, not just through sex, but also through family and friends, work, art, science, etc. In essence, more libido meant more life in whatever domain. In the early years of life, according to Jung, libidinal energy is expended mainly on eating, elimination, and sex, but as the person becomes more proficient at satisfying these needs or as these needs become less important, libidinal energy is applied to the solution of more philosophical and spiritual needs. Thus for Jung, libido is the driving force behind the **psyche** (Jung's term for personality), which is focused on various needs, whether biological or spiritual. Those components of the personality in which considerable libidinal energy is invested are said to be valued more than others. Thus, according to Jung, the **value** of something is determined by how much libidinal energy is invested in it.

Principle of Equivalence.   Like Freud, Jung drew heavily on the physics of his day for his theory of personality. His use of the principles of equivalence, entropy, and opposites demonstrates this orientation. The **principle of equivalence** is the first law of thermodynamics, which states that the amount of energy in a system is essentially fixed (conservation of energy), and if it is removed from one part of a system it will show up in another. Applied to the psyche, this means that only so much psychic energy (libido) is available, and if one component of the psyche is overvalued, it is at the expense of the other components. If, for example, psychic energy is concentrated on conscious activities, then unconscious activities will suffer and vice versa. Likewise, spending a good deal of time in one domain, such as studying for final exams, necessarily means that the time must be drawn from some other domain, such as relationships.

Principle of Entropy.   The **principle of entropy** is the second law of thermodynamics and states that a constant tendency exists towards equalizing the energy within a system. If, for example, a hot object and a cold one are placed side by side, heat will flow from the hot object to the cold one until their temperatures are equalized. Likewise, according to Jung, a tendency exists for all components of the psyche to have equal energy. For example, the conscious and unconscious aspects of the psyche would have equal energy and thus equal representation in one's personality. The psychic balance, however, is extremely hard to achieve and must be actively sought. If the balance is not sought, the person's psychic energy will not be balanced and thus personality development will be uneven. That is, certain aspects of the psyche will be more highly valued than others. For example, to invest considerable time in school at the expense of relationships is to watch one's relationships suffer. The resulting tension is an effort to return the imbalance to a state of balance.

Principle of Opposites.   The **principle of opposites** is found almost everywhere in Jung's writings. This principle is similar to Newton's contention that "for every action there is an equal and opposite reaction" or Hegel's statement that "everything carries within itself its own negation." Every concept in Jung's theory has its polar opposite. The unconscious is contrasted with the conscious, the rational with the irrational, feminine with masculine, the animalistic with the spiritual, causality with teleology, progression with regression, introversion with extroversion, thinking with feeling, and sensing with intuiting. When one aspect of the personality is developed, it is usually at the expense of its polar opposite; for instance, as one becomes more masculine, one necessarily becomes less feminine. For Jung the goal of life, in accordance with the principle of entropy, is to seek a balance between these polar opposites, thereby giving both expression in one's personality. Such a synthesis is constantly aspired to but seldom accomplished.

Components of the Personality

Ego.   According to Jung, the **ego** is everything of which we are conscious. It is concerned with thinking, feeling, remembering, and perceiving. It is responsible for seeing that the functions of everyday life are carried out. It is also responsible for our sense of identity and our sense of continuity in time. It is important not to equate the ego with the psyche. The conscious experience of the ego represents only a small portion of the personality; the psyche refers to both the conscious and the more substantial unconscious aspects of personality. Considerable similarity exists between Jung's concept of ego and Freud's.

Personal Unconscious.   The **personal unconscious** consists of material that was once conscious but was repressed or forgotten, or was not vivid enough to make a conscious impression at first. The personal unconscious contains clusters of emotionally loaded (highly valued) thoughts that Jung called complexes. More specifically, a **complex** is a personally disturbing constellation of ideas connected by common feeling tone (Jung, 1913/1973, p. 599). A complex has a disproportionate influence on one's behaviour, in the sense that the theme around which the complex is organized recurs over again in one's life. A person with a mother complex will spend a considerable amount of time on activities that are either directly or symbolically related to the idea of mother. A person similarly may have a father, sex, power, money, or any other kind of complex.

Jung's early claim to fame was a technique he used to study complexes. He took the **word-association test** developed earlier by Francis Galton and Wilhelm Wundt, and redesigned it as a tool to tap the personal unconscious in search of complexes. Jung's technique consisted of reading to a patient a list of 100 words, one at a time, and instructing the patient to respond as quickly as possible with the first word that came to mind. Words such as *child, green, water, sing, death, long,* and *stupid* were used. How long it took the patient to respond to each word was measured with a stopwatch. Breathing rate was also measured, as was the electroconductivity of the patient's skin.

The following were used by Jung as "complex indicators," that is, factors that indicated the presence of a complex:

1. displaying a longer-than-average reaction time to a stimulus word
2. repeating the stimulus word back as a response
3. failing to respond at all
4. using expressive bodily reactions, such as laughing, increased breathing rate, or increased conductivity of the skin
5. stammering
6. continuing to respond to a previously used stimulus word
7. reacting meaninglessly, for example, with made-up words
8. reacting superficially with a word that sounds like the stimulus word (die–lie), for example
9. responding with more than one word
10. misunderstanding the stimulus word as some other word

Jung used his word-association test in many ways. For example, he found that male subjects tended to respond faster to stimulus words than female subjects did, and that educated people tended to respond faster than uneducated people. In addition, he found that members of the same family had remarkably similar reactions to stimulus words. The following shows the reaction of a mother and her daughter to several stimulus words (Jung, 1909/1973, p. 469):

Stimulus Word	**Mother**	**Daughter**
law	God's commandment	Moses
potato	tuber	tuber
stranger	traveler	travelers
brother	dear to me	dear
to kiss	mother	mother
merry	happy child	little children

Jung believed it was important to discover and deal with complexes because they require the expenditure of so much psychic energy and therefore inhibit balanced psychological growth.

With his use of the word-association test, Jung demonstrated that it was possible to investigate the unconscious mind systematically. This accomplishment alone would have given Jung a prominent place in psychology's history.

Collective Unconscious.   To understand the **collective unconscious,** Jung's boldest, most mystical, and most controversial concept, is to understand the heart of Jung's theory. The collective unconscious reflects the collective experiences that humans have had in their evolutionary past, or in Jung's own words, it is the "deposit of ancestral experience from untold millions of years, the echo of prehistoric world events to which each century adds an infinitesimally small amount of variation and differentiation" (Jung, 1928, p. 162). Not only are fragments of all human history found in the collective unconscious but traces of our prehuman or animal ancestry are found there as well. Because the collective unconscious results from *common* experiences that all humans have, or have had, the contents of the collective unconscious are essentially the same for all humans. Put another way, it means that despite the tremendous range of backgrounds and cultural differences that make up the Canadian population, Jung's theory implies that we all share a collective unconscious of similar experiences, motivations, fear, and even myths. This may be more meaningful when you consider that for several decades, Canadians have struggled to achieve a sense of national unity, and to define what it means to be Canadian. In Jung's view, the characteristics that link all Canadians remain largely unconscious and, more importantly, link all peoples—past, present, and future. Jung said it is "detached from anything personal and is common to all men, since its contents can be found everywhere" (Jung, 1917/1966, p. 66). For Jung, the terms collective unconscious and transpersonal unconscious were synonymous.

These ancestral experiences that are registered in the psyche have been called at various times racial memories, primordial images, or more commonly, archetypes. An **archetype** can be defined as an inherited predisposition to respond to certain aspects of the world. Just as the eye and the ear have evolved to be maximally responsive to certain aspects of the environment, so has the psyche evolved to cause the person to be maximally responsive to certain categories of experience that humans have encountered over and over again through countless generations. An archetype exists for whatever experiences are universal, those that each member of each generation must experience. You can generate a list of archetypes yourself by simply answering the question, What must every human experience in his or her lifetime? Your answer must include such experiences as birth, death, the sun, darkness, power, women, men, sex, water, magic, mother, heroes, and pain. Humans have an inherited predisposition to react to these and other universal categories of experience. Specific responses and ideas are not inherited; what is inherited is the tendency to respond to categories of common human experience in terms of emotionally charged myths. For example, when our ancestors experienced a bolt of lightning or a clap of thunder, it stimulated in them emotional responses that immediately took the form of myths. Jung (1917/1966) explained:

> One of the commonest and at the same time most impressive experiences is the apparent movement of the sun every day. We certainly cannot discover anything of the kind in the unconscious, so far as the known physical process is concerned. What we do find, on the other hand, is the myth of the sun-hero in all its countless variations. It is this myth, and not the physical process, that forms the sun archetype. The same can be said of the phases of the moon. The archetype is a kind of readiness to produce

over and over again the same or similar mythical ideas. Hence it seems as though what is impressed upon the unconscious were exclusively the subjective fantasy-ideas aroused by the physical process. We may therefore assume that the archetypes are recurrent impressions made by subjective reactions. (p. 69)

Primitive humans responded to all of their emotional experiences in terms of myths, and it is this tendency toward myth making that is registered in the collective unconscious and passed on to future generations. What we inherit, then, is the tendency to reexperience some manifestation of these primordial myths as we encounter events that have been associated with those myths for eons. Each archetype can be viewed as an inherited tendency to respond emotionally and mythologically to certain kinds of experience—for example, when a child, a mother, a lover, a nightmare, a death, a birth, an earthquake, or a stranger is encountered. Consider the great ice storm of 1998. The ordeal of people in Quebec and Eastern Ontario struck a chord with Canadians everywhere. To even lightly contemplate urban living in Canada without heat or electricity is to confront scores of archetypes: dark, light, cold, fire, shelter, food, communication. In fact, any major disaster that challenges one's way of life will return the focus to basic necessities and survival, and responses naturally prewired in the human organism.

The collective unconscious is by far the most important and influential part of the psyche and its inherited predispositions seek outward manifestation. When the contents of the collective unconscious are not recognized in consciousness, they are

When an ice storm hit eastern Canada in 1998, people across Canada sympathized with those who had no electricity for weeks. For most Canadians, the thought of living without electricity during the winter requires them to confront scores of archetypes such as darkness, cold, and isolation.

manifested in dreams, fantasies, images, and symbols. Because few people fully recognize the contents of their collective unconscious, most can learn about themselves by studying the contents of their dreams and fantasies. In fact, according to Jung, humans can learn a great deal about their future by studying these dreams because they symbolize basic human nature. In that sense, the collective unconscious knows more than any single human or generation of humans knows. Jung gathered information about the archetypes from a wide variety of sources including his own dreams and fantasies, primitive tribes, art, religion, literature, language, and the hallucinations of psychotic patients.

Although Jung recognized the existence of many archetypes, he wrote extensively on only a few. These were the persona, the anima, the animus, the shadow, and the self. We consider each of these next.

Persona, Anima, Animus, Shadow, and Self

PERSONA

Persona is the Latin word for mask, and Jung used this term to describe one's public self. The persona archetype develops because of humans' need to play a role in society. Although all humans share the same collective unconscious, individuals exist at a particular time and in a particular place. Archetypes must manifest themselves within these social and cultural circumstances. That is, the expression given to the archetypes is influenced by social conventions and by the unique circumstances of a person's life. Thus the persona is the outward manifestation of the psyche that is allowed by a person's unique circumstances. The changing face of some politicians, who may espouse the virtues of education and health care reform at one time but change their promises at a later time or for a different audience, is frustrating to Canadians. The persona is the part of the psyche by which we are known by other people. Jung pointed out that some people equate their persona with their entire psyche and this is a mistake. In a sense, the persona is supposed to deceive other people, because it presents to them only a small part of one's psyche, but if people believe that they are what they pretend to be, they are deceiving themselves, and that is unfortunate. Jung said,

> The construction of a collectively suitable persona means a formidable concession to the external world, a genuine self-sacrifice which drives the ego straight into identification with the persona, so that people really do exist who believe they are what they pretend to be. [However] . . . these identifications with a social role are a very fruitful source of neuroses. A man cannot get rid of himself in favour of an artificial personality without punishment. Even the attempt to do so brings on, in all ordinary cases, unconscious reactions in the form of bad moods, affects, phobias, obsessive ideas, back-slidings, vices, etc. The social "strong man" is in his private life often a mere child where his own states of feeling are concerned; his discipline in public (which he demands quite particularly of others) goes miserably to pieces in private. His "happiness in his work" assumes a woeful countenance at home; his "spotless" public morality looks strange indeed behind the mask—we will not mention deeds, but only fantasies, and the wives of such men would have a pretty tale to tell. As to his selfless altruism, his children have decided views about that. (1917/1966, pp. 193–194)

Jung described the situation in which the persona is valued too highly as **inflation of the persona.** As with all components of the psyche, if the persona is valued too highly, it develops at the expense of other components.

ANIMA

The **anima** is the female component of the male psyche that results from the experiences men have had with women through the eons. This archetype serves two purposes. First, it causes men to have feminine traits. "No man," said Jung, "is so entirely masculine that he has nothing feminine in him" (1917/1966, p. 189). These feminine traits include intuition, tenderness, sentimentality, and gregariousness. Leo Buscaglia, well known for his mainstream books on loving relationships and communication, exemplifies this archetype. Second, it provides a framework within which men interact with women. "An inherited collective image of woman exists in a man's unconscious, with the help of which he apprehends the nature of woman" (Jung, 1917/1966, p. 190). Because men's collective experiences with women have involved interactions with them as mothers, daughters, sisters, loved ones, and perhaps as heavenly goddesses, all of these elements are reflected in the anima, and together they form a complex, idealized image of women. This image portrays women at once as perilous, loyal, seductive, dangerous, and challenging. Women are viewed as the source of good and evil, hope and despair, and success and failure. It is within this idealized framework that men form their interactions with women in their lifetimes. Also, according to Jung, this complex image of women has inspired the portrayal of women by artists, poets, and novelists through the years.

ANIMUS

The **animus** is the masculine component of the female psyche. It furnishes the woman with masculine traits such as independence, aggression, competitiveness, and adventuresomeness. The animus also provides a framework that guides a woman's relationships with men. Consider, for example, Canada's Chief Justice Beverley McLachlin, television celebrity Oprah Winfrey, and the CEOs of major corporations such as Carly Fiorina of Hewlett-Packard. As the anima furnishes men with an ideal of the woman, the animus furnishes women with an ideal of the man. This ideal comes from women's experience with men through the eons as fathers, sons, brothers, loved ones, warriors, and perhaps as gods. As with the anima, the complex animus with its many conflicting images is projected onto actual men in a woman's lifetime.

The anima provides males with female traits and with a basis for understanding women. The animus provides females with masculine traits and with a basis for understanding men. It is best, according to Jung, when both genders recognize and give expression to their characteristics of the other sex. The male who gives little or no expression to his feminine characteristics lacks sensitivity, feeling, intuition, and creativity. The female who gives little or no expression to her male characteristics is overly passive. Also, if a component of the psyche is not given adequate, conscious expression it is forced to manifest itself unconsciously, making its influence uncontrolled and irrational. Thus if a woman denies expression to her masculine traits or a man his feminine traits, those traits will manifest themselves in indirect ways such as through dreams and fantasies.

According to Jung, for a man to give too much expression to his feminine traits or for a female to give too much expression to her masculine traits is also undesirable. Jung said, "A woman possessed by the animus is always in danger of losing her femininity, her adapted feminine persona, just as a man in like circumstances runs the risk of effeminacy" (1917/1966, p. 209). As everywhere in Jung's theory, a balance should be sought.

SHADOW

The **shadow** is the darkest, deepest part of the psyche. It is the part of the collective unconscious that we inherit from our prehuman ancestors and contains all of the animal instincts. Because of the shadow, we have a strong tendency to be immoral, aggressive, and passionate. People often contemplate someone like Paul Bernardo, infamous for raping, torturing, and murdering two teenage girls, with horrified (or fascinated) incomprehension. They consider him a monster, saying no human being could do such things. To Jung, violence and criminal behaviour have their roots in the shadow; the impulses that led to Bernardo's elaborate cruelty arise in a part of the psyche common to us all. It is perhaps the underdevelopment or poor integration of other parts of his psyche that led Bernardo to act on such impulses.

As with all of the archetypes, the shadow seeks outward manifestation and is projected onto the world symbolically as devils, monsters, or evil spirits. It can even be projected onto a person, as Jung found out when he asked one of his young patients the following question:

> "How do I seem to you when you are not with me?" . . . She said, "Sometimes you seem rather dangerous, sinister, like an evil magician or a demon. I don't know how I ever got such ideas—you are not a bit like that." (1917/1966, p. 91)

Not only does the preceding quotation describe the projection of the shadow, it also exemplifies Jung's approach to psychotherapy. Jung's goal was to introduce his patient to the various components of his or her psyche, and when the components were known, to synthesize them into an interrelated configuration resulting in a deeper, more creative person. Unlike Freud, who thought the unconscious, irrational mind had to be made increasingly conscious and rational if humans were to become truly civilized, Jung believed the archetypes, for example, the shadow, should be recognized and then used rather than overcome. The animal nature of the shadow was, to Jung, a source of spontaneity and creativity. This is not to say that works of art are inspired by underlying evil, but rather that the capricious and boundless nature of the shadow contributes to new and exciting expressions of shape, form, and movement as never before seen. The person who does not use his or her shadow, according to Jung, tends to be dull and lifeless.

SELF

The **self** is the component of the psyche that attempts to harmonize all the other components. It represents the human striving for unity, wholeness, and integration of the total personality. When this integration has been achieved, the person is said to be self-realized. We have more to say about the self when we consider "life's goal" later in this chapter.

Psychological Types

Attitudes.   Jung thought there were two general orientations the psyche could take. One was inward, toward the subjective world of the individual; and the other was outward, toward the external environment. Jung called these orientations **attitudes;** the former he labelled **introversion,** and the latter he labelled **extroversion.** The introvert tends to be quiet, imaginative, and more interested in ideas than in other people. The extrovert tends to be sociable, outgoing, and interested in people and environmental events.

The attitudes of introversion and extroversion were first presented by Jung at the International Psychoanalytic Congress at Munich in 1913. They were later elaborated in his book *Psychological Types* (1921/1971). Jung even applied the concepts of introversion and extroversion to explain why different personality theorists create different kinds of personality theories. For example, Freud was an extrovert and thus developed a theory that stressed the importance of external events, such as sex objects. Adler's theory (as we see in chapter 4) stressed the importance of internal feelings because Adler was an introvert (Jung, 1917/1966, pp. 41–43). Jung could easily have given his own theory as an example of one created by an introvert.

Functions of Thought. In addition to the attitudes or general orientations, the four **functions of thought** pertain to how a person perceives the world and deals with information and experience.

Sensing. Detects the presence of objects. It indicates that something is there but does not indicate what it is.

Thinking. Tells what an object is. It gives names to objects that are sensed.

Feeling. Determines what an object is worth to the person. Pertains to liking and disliking.

Intuiting. Provides hunches when factual information is not available. Jung said, "Whenever you have to deal with strange conditions where you have no established values or established concepts, you will depend upon the faculty of intuition" (Jung, 1968, p. 14).

Examples of the functions of thought are detecting the presence of an object in the environment (sensing), noting that the object is a stranger who is a member of the opposite sex (thinking), experiencing an attraction toward the person (feeling), and believing that a long-term relationship with the person is possible (intuiting).

Thinking and feeling are called **rational functions** because they make judgements and evaluations about experiences. In addition, thinking and feeling are considered polar opposites, because, as Jung said, "When you think you must exclude feeling, just as when you feel you must exclude thinking" (1968, p. 16). Likewise, sensing and intuiting, the **irrational functions,** are thought to be polar opposites. Sensing and intuiting are considered irrational because they both occur independently of logical thought processes. Sensing occurs automatically because of the sensory mechanisms of the body, and intuiting involves a prediction made in the absence of factual information.

Ideally, the attitudes and functions would be equally developed and all would work in harmony; this, however, is seldom the case. Usually, one attitude and one function become dominant, and the other attitude and the other three functions remain underdeveloped and unconscious. For the functions, the one opposite the dominant conscious one is the least developed, but the other two functions are subservient to the dominant function and in that way may become somewhat developed. For example, in a person whose thinking function is highly developed, the other three functions, especially feeling (the opposite of thinking) will be relatively undeveloped on the unconscious level and may be expressed in dreams and fantasies or in odd and disturbing ways.

Eight Personality Types. By combining the two attitudes and the four functions, Jung described eight different types of people. Note, however, that these eight types probably never exist in pure form because each person possesses both attitudes and all four functions, and which is conscious and which is unconscious is a matter of personal development. The eight pure types are listed here with a brief description of each type's tendencies (summarized from Jung, 1921/1971, pp. 330–405).

Thinking Extrovert.   Objective reality dominates, as does the thinking function of thought. Feeling, sensing, and intuiting are repressed. Intellectual analysis of objective experience is of utmost importance. The truth exists "out there" and everyone must follow it. Activities dependent on feelings such as aesthetics, development of close friendships, and introspective religious and philosophical experiences are minimized. This person lives according to fixed rules and expects everyone else to do the same. He or she is dogmatic and cold. Personal matters such as health, social position, family interests, and finances are neglected. Jung believed many scientists are thinking extroverts.

Feeling Extrovert.   Objective reality dominates, as does the feeling function of thought. Thinking, sensing, and intuiting are repressed. This type responds emotionally to objective reality. Because the feelings experienced are externally determined, they tend to be appropriate to the situation, such as those elicited at the theatre, at concerts, or at church. Such people are respectful of authority and tradition. They always attempt to adjust their feelings to those appropriate to the situation and, therefore, their feelings seem feigned. For example, the choice of a "loved one" will be determined more by a person's age, social position, income, and family status than by their subjective feelings about that person. That is, love is the expected feeling to have toward that person under the circumstances.

Sensing Extrovert.   Objective reality dominates, as does the sensing function of thought. Intuiting, thinking, and feeling are repressed. This type is buffeted about by sensory experience. He or she is a realist and is concerned only with objective facts. Because the life of this type is governed by just what happens, he or she makes an entertaining companion. There is little inclination to analyze situations or to dominate them. Once an experience has been sensed, there is little additional concern with it. Only the tangible, the concrete has value. He or she rejects subjective thoughts or feelings as guides for living for himself or herself and for others.

Intuiting Extrovert.   Objective reality dominates, as does the intuiting function of thought. Sensing, thinking, and feeling are repressed. This type sees in external reality a multitude of possibilities. New experiences are sought with enthusiasm, pondered until their implications are understood, and then abandoned. There is little concern with the convictions and the morality of others and, therefore, this type is often viewed as immoral and unscrupulous. Careers are sought that allow the exploitation of new possibilities such as being an entrepreneur, stockbroker, or politician. Although socially useful, this type may waste considerable time moving from one project to another. Like the sensing extrovert, this type is irrational and is little concerned with logic. Meaningful communication with individuals in which the rational functions (thinking or feeling) dominate is very difficult for these types.

Thinking Introvert.   Subjective reality dominates, as does the thinking function of thought. Feeling, sensing, and intuiting are repressed. Because the life of this type is determined by subjective rather than objective reality, he or she appears to others to be inflexible, cold, arbitrary, and even ruthless. Such individuals will follow their own thoughts regardless of how unconventional and dangerous to others they may be. Support and understanding from others are of little value.

They value only the few friends who understand their internal frame of reference. For this type, subjective truth is the only truth, and criticism, regardless of its validity, is rejected. Logical thought is applied only to one's own subjective experience. Jung described himself as a thinking introvert.

Feeling Introvert.   Subjective reality dominates, as does the feeling function of thought. Thinking, sensing, and intuiting are repressed. Rather than directing intellectual processes toward subjective experience, as is the case with the thinking introvert, this type emphasizes the feelings that such experience provides. Objective reality is important only insofar as it elicits subjective images that can be privately experienced and valued. Communication with others is difficult because it requires at least two individuals to have the same subjective reality and its associated feelings. Such a person is considered egotistical and unsympathetic. The basic motives of this type are inaccessible to others, and they are therefore viewed as cold and indifferent. For this type there is no need to impress or influence others. Like all introverts, all that is important is internal rather than external.

Sensing Introvert.   Subjective experience dominates, as does the sensing function of thought. Intuiting, feeling, and thinking are repressed. As is the case with many artists, this type gives his or her own meaning to sensory experience. Because this type embellishes his or her sensory experiences with subjective evaluations, interactions with objective reality are unpredictable. Sensory experience is important only insofar as it elicits subjective images.

Intuiting Introvert.   Subjective experience dominates, as does the intuiting function of thought. Sensing, feeling, and thinking are repressed. Here the implications of internal images are explored thoroughly. Such a person, often a mystic, a seer, or a daydreamer, produces new and strange ideas. Of all the types, this type is most aloof, distant, and misunderstood. He or she is often viewed as an eccentric genius. Important philosophical and religious insights are often produced by this type.

In Jung's typology, we see the principles of equivalence, opposites, and entropy in operation. Because only so much libidinal energy is available to a person, little will be left for the other components (principle of equivalence) if an abundance of this energy is invested in a particular component of the psyche. When something is conscious, its opposite is unconscious and vice versa (principle of opposites). A constant tendency exists for the libidinal energy to equalize itself across all components and levels of the psyche (principle of entropy). The components of the psyche that we have discussed in this section can be summarized as follows:

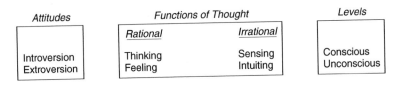

Attitudes	Functions of Thought		Levels
	Rational	*Irrational*	
Introversion	Thinking	Sensing	Conscious
Extroversion	Feeling	Intuiting	Unconscious

Stages of Development

Stages of development were not as important to Jung as they were to Freud, but he did talk about them in general terms. Jung's stages were defined in terms of the focus of libidinal energy. We saw earlier that Jung disagreed with Freud about the nature of the libido. Freud believed the libido was mainly sexual in nature and how it was invested within the first five years of life determined, to a large extent, what a person's adult personality would be like. Jung, conversely, thought that libidinal energy was directed simply toward whatever was important to the person at the time and what was important changed as a function of maturation. Jung's stages of development can be summarized as follows:

> *Childhood* (from birth to adolescence).   During the early portion of this period, libidinal energy is expended on learning how to walk, talk, and other skills necessary for survival. After the fifth year, more and more libidinal energy is directed toward sexual activities and this focus of libidinal energy reaches its peak during adolescence.
>
> *Young Adulthood* (from adolescence to about age 40).   During this stage, libidinal energy is directed toward learning a vocation, getting married, raising children, and relating in some way to community life. During this stage the individual tends to be outgoing, energetic, impulsive, and passionate.
>
> *Middle Age* (from about age 40 to the later years of life).   This stage of development was the most important for Jung. The person is transformed from an energetic, extroverted, and biologically oriented person to one with more cultural, philosophical, and spiritual values. The person is now much more concerned with wisdom and with life's meaning. The needs that must be satisfied during this stage are just as important as those of the preceding stages, but they are different kinds of needs.

> Our life is like the course of the sun. In the morning it gains continually in strength until it reaches the zenith-heat of high noon. Then . . . the steady forward movement no longer denotes an increase, but a decrease, in strength. . . . But it is a great mistake to suppose that the meaning of life is exhausted with the period of youth and expansion. . . . The afternoon of life is just as full of meaning as the morning; only, its meaning and purpose are different. . . . What youth found and must find outside, the man of life's afternoon must find within himself. (1917/1966, pp. 74–75)

Because it is during middle age that a person begins to determine the meaning of life, it is a time when religion becomes important. Jung believed every person possesses a spiritual need that must be satisfied, just as the need for food must be satisfied. Jung's definition of religion, however, included any systematic attempt to deal with God, spirits, demons, laws, or ideals. We saw earlier that Jung did not have much patience with the kind of religion that involved religious denominations and dogma that was to be taken on faith.

Jung believed that the general decline of the religious life among modern people was causing a disorientation in worldview. More specifically, he found that the absence of the meaning, or spiritual equilibrium, once provided by a religious worldview caused the neurotic complaints of his middle-aged patients.

> Of all my patients past middle life, that is, past thirty-five, there is not one whose ultimate problem is not one of religious attitude. Indeed, in the end every one suffered from having lost that which living religions of every age have given to their believers, and none is really cured who has not regained his religious attitude, which naturally has nothing to do with creeds or belonging to a church. (quoted in Wehr, 1987, p. 292)

Life's Goal

According to Jung, life's primary goal is to achieve **self-realization,** or a harmonious blending of the many components and forces within the psyche. Although self-realization is never completely achieved, approximating it involves a long, complex journey of self-discovery.

Self-realization and individuation go hand in hand. **Individuation** refers to the lifelong process of psychological maturity by which components of the psyche are recognized and given expression by a particular individual. Jung believed that individuation, or the tendency toward self-realization, is inherent in all living organisms: "Individuation is an expression of that biological process—simple or complicated as the case may be—by which every living being becomes what it was destined to become from the beginning" (quoted in Stevens, 1994, p. 62). The process of individuation describes a personal journey toward self-realization, but the process provides an important connection among all humans. Jung (1917/1966) said:

> The more we become conscious of ourselves through self-knowledge, and act accordingly, the more the layer of the personal unconscious that is superimposed on the collective unconscious will be diminished. In this way there arises a consciousness which is no longer imprisoned in the petty, oversensitive, personal world of ego, but participates freely in the wider world of objective interests. . . . The complications . . . are no longer egotistic wish-conflicts, but difficulties that concern others as much as oneself. . . . We can now see that the unconscious produces contents which are valid not only for the person concerned, but for others as well, in fact for a great many people and possibly for all. (p. 178)

Elsewhere, Jung (1931/1969) said:

> This process is, in fact, the spontaneous realization of the whole man. . . . The more he is merely "I," the more he splits himself off from the collective man, of whom he is also a part, and may even find himself in opposition to him. But since everything living strives for wholeness, the inevitable one-sidedness of our conscious life is continually being corrected and compensated by the universal human being in us, whose goal is the ultimate integration of conscious and unconscious, or better, the assimilation of the ego to a wider personality. (p. 292)

As self-realization is approximated, the self becomes the new centre of the personality and is experienced as being suspended among the opposing forces of the psyche. Jung believed the self was symbolized by a **mandala,** which is the Sanskrit word meaning circle. The self is perceived as the centre of the circle, or midway among the many polarities that make up the psyche. Jung found variations of the mandala in different cultures all over the world, indicating to him its universality. As with all archetypes, the self creates a sensitivity to certain experiences, which in this particular case is a sensitivity to symbols of balance, perfection, and harmony like the circle. Here is an example of a mandala:

Where does that leave all of us who are not self-realized? According to Jung, we are in various degrees of trouble. The degree of our problem depends on how lopsided our development has been:

> Modern man does not understand how much his "rationalism" (which has destroyed his capacity to respond to numinous symbols and ideas) has put him at the mercy of the psychic "underworld." He has freed himself from "superstition" (or so he believes), but in the process he has lost his spiritual values to a positively dangerous degree. His moral and spiritual tradition has disintegrated, and he is now paying the price for this break-up in world-wide disorientation and dissociation. . . . As scientific understanding has grown, so our world has become dehumanized. Man feels himself isolated in the cosmos, because he is no longer involved in nature and has lost his emotional "unconscious identity" with natural phenomena. These have slowly lost their symbolic implications. Thunder is no longer the voice of an angry god, nor is lightning his avenging missile. No river contains a spirit, no tree is the life principle of a man, no snake the embodiment of wisdom, no mountain cave the home of a great demon. No voices now speak to man from stones, plants, and animals, nor does he speak to them believing they can hear. His contact with nature has gone, and with it has gone the profound emotional energy that this symbolic connection supplied. (Jung, 1964, pp. 84–85)

Aboriginal peoples will point out that too many Canadians have left behind their connections with Mother Earth in the search for income, success, and status. The rise of the environmental movement across Canada involves more than a practical concern for safe air and water; it also embodies a desire for reunion with nature, a step toward restoring the balance between nature and society. In fact, Canada itself is defined by its foundation in nature, as seen in the maple leaf in the national flag, or the blue and white (symbolizing water and ice) in the provincial flag of Newfoundland and Labrador.

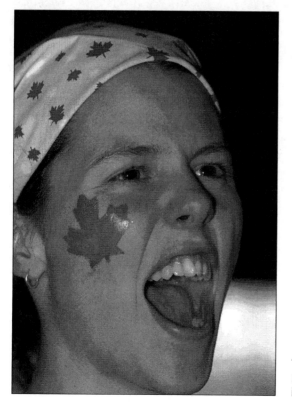

The symbols that define Canada represent the country's foundation in nature.

Jung believed more to life existed than merely being rational. In fact, he believed that ignoring the irrational part of the psyche has caused many of our current problems:

> [Contemporary man] is blind to the fact that, with all his rationality and efficiency, he is possessed by "powers" that are beyond his control. His gods and demons have not disappeared at all; they have merely got new names. They keep him on the run with restlessness, vague apprehensions, psychological complications, an insatiable need for pills, alcohol, tobacco, food—and, above all, a large array of neuroses. (Jung, 1964, p. 71)

Despite the current emphasis on rationality and science, archetypes continue to manifest themselves. They do so, however, within the technological context of modern times. An example is the phenomenon of flying saucers. Writing during the Cold War, Jung said the following about flying saucers:

> A psychic phenomenon of this kind would, like a rumour, have a compensatory significance, since it would be a spontaneous answer of the unconscious to the present conscious situation, i.e., to fears created by an apparently insoluble political situation which might at any moment lead to a universal catastrophe. At such times men's eyes turn to heaven for help, and marvelous signs appear from on high, of a threatening or reassuring nature. (1954/1978, p. 131)

Causality, Teleology, and Synchronicity

Causality.   By **causality**, Jung meant the attempt to explain adult personality in terms of prior experiences, as Freud did. According to Jung, not only is such an attempt incomplete, but it also gives one a feeling of despair and hopelessness. This theory maintains that what a person will become is a function of what the person already has been.

Teleology.   Although Jung did not discount causality altogether, he thought teleology must be added to it to have a complete picture of human motivation. **Teleology** means that human behaviour has a purpose; that is, our behaviour is drawn by the future as much as it is pushed by the past. Jung said, "Causality is only one principle, and psychology cannot be exhausted by causal methods only, because the mind lives by aims as well" (1916/1961, p. 292). In other words, to truly understand a person, one must understand his or her goals and aspirations for future attainment on a personal level. Jung's general view of human motivation can be represented schematically as follows:

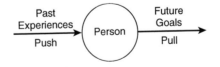

Synchronicity.   Jung referred to **synchronicity** as meaningful coincidence, as when one dreams of a person and shortly thereafter the person appears, or when one fantasizes about an event and the event occurs. According to Jung, such events are of great importance to one's life, and they must be more clearly understood. Synchronicity is one of Jung's more complex concepts, and we discuss it only briefly here. For synchronicity to take place, two events must occur independently of each other. That is, the two events have their own causality but are not causally related to each other. Then, at some point, an individual experiences them together, and in combination they have meaning to that person, whereas if they were experienced separately, they would not. It is this coming together in a meaningful way of two otherwise meaningless events that defines synchronicity.

The following is a personal example of this meaningful coincidence. When my son was six years old, he and I attended a festival featuring decorated trees, holiday music, and a candy house contest. My son went off to look at the houses. After looking at the trees, I too went to see the candy houses, looking for the one entered by one of my students, Karen. When I got to the candy house exhibit, an older woman was poised to take a picture of Karen's house, and noticed my son staring wide-eyed at that very house. "What a great picture this would make!" she thought, and snapped the shutter. Coincidentally, the photographer was Karen's mother (who had never met me or my son). Karen had asked her to photograph her candy house entry because she was unable to attend the exhibit. Karen's mother later admitted that she had bypassed several other children in favour of one boy who took a keen interest in Karen's house. When Karen later saw the photograph, she remarked "I know that boy." Indeed, she had met my son previously.

As Jung indicates, synchronicity involves not simply a coincidence, but a meaningful one. The meaning, as perceived by at least one of the participants, is derived from deeply influential forces buried in the collective unconscious. For this particular example, Karen's mother could have taken the photo of any child who happened to notice her daughter's house, but selected this child. My son could have stared longingly at any of 30 unique candy houses at the exhibit, but he selected that house. The Jungian interpretation resides in the interaction between a mother-daughter relationship on one side and a father-son relationship on the other. That is, Karen's mother's choice to photograph my son is traced back to the original relationship between me and my honours student. More symbolically, it was Karen taking my photograph.

In a more complex way, the concept of synchronicity can be applied to the relationship between the collective unconscious and various experiences we have. As we have seen, each archetype can be regarded as a predisposition to respond emotionally to a certain class of environmental events. In fact, an archetype can be considered a *need* to have certain kinds of experiences. Under these circumstances, when we have an experience that gives symbolic expression to an archetype, the experience is as satisfying as finding food is to a hungry person. This explains why humans react emotionally to certain music, art forms, and various symbols in their lives. According to Jung, we all have archetypes, and when our experiences give them expression, the result is emotionally satisfying. Because the archetypes have one causal heritage and the environmental events that give them symbolic expression have another, their coming together is an example of synchronicity.

Research Techniques

We have already viewed Jung's research using his word-association test; this research was his most scientifically orthodox. The other sources of evidence he used to support his theory were more controversial. For example, he studied in depth his own dreams and visions. He studied the contents of the hallucinations of psychotic patients. He travelled to such places as Arizona, New Mexico, Tunis, Uganda, India, and Kenya to study the religions, rituals, myths, and symbols of various cultures. He studied theology, philosophy, history, mythology, literature, and poetry. He studied all forms of art and language. In short, he studied every major category of human existence, and everywhere he found support for his contention that humans are born with predispositions to respond to the world in certain ways. He believed that he found symbols corresponding to the content of the collective unconscious everywhere; symbols with powerful influences, yet not completely understood by those responding to them.

Psychotic Patients.   It was during his years at Burghölzli that Jung realized that much could be learned about the psyche by studying psychotic patients. Jung (1961) reflected:

> Through my work with the patients I realized that paranoid ideas and hallucinations contain a germ of meaning. A personality, a life history, a pattern of hopes and desires lie behind the psychosis. The fault is ours if we do not understand them. It dawned upon me then for the first time that a general psychology of the personality lies concealed within psychosis, and that even here we come upon the old human conflicts. Although patients may appear dull and apathetic, or totally imbecilic, there is more going on in their minds, and more that is meaningful, than there seems to be. At the bottom we discover nothing new and unknown in the mentally ill; rather, we encounter the substratum of our own natures. (p. 127)

Jung's encounter with a psychotic patient in 1906 exemplifies how we can learn about the psyche from mentally ill persons. Looking out the window, a patient called Jung over and told him that if he half-closed his eyes and looked at the sun, Jung would be able to see a phallus hanging from it. Furthermore, the patient told Jung that if he moved his head, from side to side, the sun's phallus would swing back and forth. Finally, the patient asserted that it was the swinging of the sun's phallus that caused the wind (Jung, 1931/1969, pp. 151–152). It was not until four years later that Jung discovered that the patient's hallucination may have reflected the contents of the unconscious mind. In 1910, Jung was reading a book about the rituals and visions of an ancient Greek religious cult. One of the visions described was that of the sun with a tube hanging from it, and the direction of the bending tube was determined by the direction of the wind. Because the patient could not have been aware of the ancient vision, Jung was startled by the similarity between the two visions. In subsequent years, Jung learned that the sun-phallus or the divine phallus was a common theme in many primitive cultures. Because the many cultures displaying such a myth could not have communicated with each other it must be, concluded Jung, a manifestation of the collective unconscious.

Analysis of Dreams.   Like Freud, Jung viewed dreams as one of the most important sources of information about the unconscious mind. But Jung interpreted dreams differently than Freud. First, Jung disagreed with Freud's distinction between manifest and latent contents of a dream. To Jung, the content of a dream is just what it appears to be:

> I have long maintained that we have no right to accuse the dream of, so to speak, a deliberate [maneuver] calculated to deceive. Nature is often obscure or impenetrable, but she is not, like man, deceitful. We must therefore take it that the dream is just what it pretends to be, neither more nor less. (Jung, 1917/1966, p. 100)

Later Jung stated:

The dream comes in as the expression of an involuntary, unconscious psychic process beyond the control of the conscious mind. It shows the inner truth and reality of the patient as it really is: Not as I conjecture it to be, and not as he would like it to be, but *as it is.* (1931/1969, p. 139)

Jung's statements are a bit misleading, however, because the contents of dreams can include fragments of ancient symbols and myths and may require considerable knowledge of history, religion, and anthropology to comprehend them.

One of the most important functions of the dream, according to Jung, is to compensate for neglected parts of the psyche. For example, if the shadow is not given an opportunity to express itself consciously, it will manifest itself in dream content and the person's dreams will be characterized by demons, devils, monsters, and passionate, immoral impulses. In other words, the person will have an abundance of nightmares. One way, therefore, to detect undeveloped portions of the psyche is to analyze the contents of dreams.

Jung was not restricted by ordinary methods of science, and he felt no need to apologize because he believed traditional methods of science could not be applied to the richness of the human psyche. He thought one's methods had to be as complex and flexible as what was being studied, and the methods of laboratory science did not qualify. According to Jung, the arena of human experience, not the laboratory, is the proper place to study the human psyche. Jung gave the student of the psyche the following advice:

Anyone who wants to know the human psyche will learn next to nothing from experimental psychology. He would be better advised to abandon exact science, put away his scholar's gown, bid farewell to his study, and wander with human heart through the world. There, in the horrors of prisons, lunatic asylums and hospitals, in drab suburban pubs, in brothels and gambling-hells, in the salons of the elegant, the Stock Exchanges, Socialist meetings, churches, revivalist gatherings and ecstatic sects, through love and hate, through the experience of passion in every form in his own body, he would reap richer stores of knowledge than text-books a foot thick could give him, and he will know how to doctor the sick with real knowledge of the human soul. (Jung, 1917/1966, pp. 246–247)

Jung's View of Human Nature

Certainly Jung's view of human nature is among the most complex ever described. The human psyche is embedded in the past, present, and future; it consists of conscious and unconscious elements, masculine and feminine traits, rational and irrational impulses, spiritualistic and animalistic desires, and a tendency to bring all these contradictory components and impulses into harmony with each other. Self-realization is achieved when such harmony is approximated but self-realization must be sought; it does not occur automatically.

To Jung, the spiritual need must be satisfied, which usually happens during middle age, when the person discovers many of the components of the psyche. As we have seen, religion, broadly defined, was to Jung a major vehicle in the journey toward self-realization. If Freud was pessimistic about human destiny, Jung was optimistic. Jung's optimism, however, was contingent on humans coming to grips with their unconscious mind; if they did not, the projections of the unconscious mind, such as the shadow, would continue to cause gross irrationality in our lives and perhaps even a third world war (Jung, 1958).

Evaluation

EMPIRICAL RESEARCH

Jung's theory does not have the kind of precision that easily lends itself to testing; it is difficult to test such theoretical concepts as archetypes and collective unconscious. However, researchers have empirically evaluated several of Jung's concepts, focusing mainly on the eight psychological types (Deanna, Evans, & Salter, 1997; Karner, Kubinger, & Menghin, 1999; Kline & Saggino, 1996). This area is especially interesting to students because they can readily see their own characteristics and those of their friends and family.

Questionnaires and scales have been developed to determine a person's type. The typical instrument is the **Myers-Briggs Type Indicator** (MBTI) (Myers, 1962): a standardized pencil-paper test that measures where individuals fall along four bipolar dimensions adapted from those Jung described. Myers-Briggs's scales measure introversion versus extroversion, thinking versus feeling, sensing versus intuiting, and perceiving versus judging. The MBTI has proved fruitful in evaluating Jung's type theory across a host of domains. For instance, Robert Baudouin and Norman Uhl (1998) from the University of Moncton examined the relation between Jung's psychological types and constructs thought to predict whether a student will stick with university, namely initial commitment, academic integration, social integration, and subsequent commitment. Several hundred full-time university students completed the MBTI at the beginning of the school year, then the Institutional Integration Scales at the end of the year. Students' files were then checked to determine who had returned and who had dropped out. In line with expectations, students who dropped out were more likely to be classified as either sensing, sensing-feeling, or extroverted-sensing-feeling-perceiving types. As Jung suggested, extroverted-sensing types were more apt to change and grow bored with sameness. Similarly, a study at the University of Western Ontario (Rosati, 1997) showed that students who had a successful first year of engineering were more likely to be categorized as introverted, feeling, and perceiving types. Overall, these results should prove useful in screening student reaction to the first year experience. Specifically, will the adjustment to course demands and new social networks be easier for students with a particular personality type?

Does culture influence personality? Yes, according to a study by Anastassios Stalikas and Lazarus Fitopoulos (1998) from McGill University, who translated the MBTI into Greek and compared the profiles of almost 30 000 Greek, French-Canadian, and American university students. Greek students were routinely classified as thinking and perceiving types, and gender differences in thinking and feeling were observed in all three samples. Analysis of scores from Anglophones in Ontario and Francophones in Quebec and Ontario uncovered significant linguistic-cultural differences. English students were more likely to be classified as feeling, intuitive, and perceiving types, whereas French students were more likely to be classified as introverted, sensing, thinking, and judging types. Further studies will be needed to show whether this method is relevant in other cross-cultural comparisons, such as between Aboriginal and non-Aboriginal samples.

Empirical research has also provided support for some of Jung's views on religion. Researchers have explored the extent to which religious affiliation is associated with life satisfaction, itself tied to self-realization (Altemeyer & Hunsberger, 1992, 1997; Hunsberger, 1985, 1992). In addition, Douglas MacDonald from the University of Windsor (MacDonald, 2000; Taylor & MacDonald, 1999) considered how religious affiliation, orientation, and involvement were related to a comprehensive personality inventory. More than a thousand Canadian university students completed a personality inventory plus a scale of religious orientation. Interestingly, respondents with strong religious convictions were more agreeable and conscientious. However, contrary to expectations, religion was not related (at least among females) to extroversion, emotional stability, or openness to experience. In part, this supports Jung's notion that the road to self-realization is paved with personal conviction, though formal religion is not necessarily the vehicle to get us there.

CRITICISMS

Jung's theory, like all theories covered in this text, has not gone uncriticized. He has been accused of being friendly toward occultism, spirituality, mysticism, and religion, all areas thought by many to emphasize the irrational. Jung believed that he was vastly misunderstood on this issue, however, and insisted that studying these topics in no way implied a belief in them. Rather, he studied them to gain information about the collective unconscious. He, like many personality theorists of his time, believed that if a scientific method could not be applied to the study of a complex topic, the method should be discarded, not the topic. He thought personality was an example of such a topic.

Jung's theory has also been criticized for being incomprehensible, unclear, inconsistent, and even contradictory. Also, his concept of self-realization has been labelled elitist because it is possible for only highly intelligent, well-educated people with an abundance of leisure time to arrive at the degree of self-insight necessary for self-realization. This restriction omits most people.

Finally, Jung's theory, like Freud's, has been criticized for being nonfalsifiable and therefore unscientific. Except for some research on psychological types and the functions of thought, little empirical research has been performed in an effort to validate the major components of Jung's theory. Jungian concepts such as the principles of equivalence, entropy, and opposites, as well as his notions of the collective unconscious and self-realization, go untested. Because Jung's theory makes few risky predictions, it runs little risk of being proved incorrect. Jung would not be distressed by this observation, however. Except for his research using the word-association test, Jung sought validation for his theory not within controlled laboratory conditions but rather in the vast arena of human experience and within human intuition.

CONTRIBUTIONS

On the positive side, Jung's theory can be credited with many original concepts in personality theory. His was the first modern theory to discuss the process of self-realization, which is currently so popular among personality theorists. His was the first modern theory to emphasize the importance of the future in determining human behaviour. Related to this idea was his emphasis on the importance of purpose and meaning in one's life. This theme is now emphasized in the existential-humanistic theories of personality. Jung's theory was optimistic about human destiny. Jung's theory stressed the attainment of selfhood as a master motive in human behaviour, rather than the sexual impulses and early experiences that Freud stressed.

Somehow Jung's theory creates an image of the psyche that is believable in light of the times in which we live. He leaves us with an image of a psyche that is pushed by the past, pulled by the future, and attempts to make sense of itself in the present. It is a complex psyche struggling to give expression to its various components. Such a psyche causes a wide range of behaviours and interests, some of which might even be considered bizarre. Despite criticisms, Jungian theory remains popular in contemporary psychology (see, for example, DeAngelis, 1994).

SUMMARY

1. Jung was a complex person who had a troubled childhood. Although when they first met, Freud and Jung became close friends, theoretical differences (e.g., different interpretations of libido) eventually caused them to terminate their association.

2. Drawing on the physics of the time, Jung conceptualized psychic energy in terms of three principles: equivalence, entropy, and opposites. The psyche consists of an ego and a self (representing a striving toward wholeness and harmony) and both a personal unconscious (a deposit of one's own repressed memories) and a collective unconscious (or phylogenetic memory). The collective unconscious also contains archetypes, or inherited predispositions to respond emotionally to certain categories of experiences, including the persona (the mask we wear in public), the shadow (what we share with nonhuman animals), and the anima (the female part of the male psyche) and animus (the male part of the female psyche).

3. Jung postulated two major attitudes a psyche could manifest. The introvert tends to be internally oriented whereas the extrovert tends to be externally oriented. In addition to the attitudes, Jung discussed four functions of thought: sensing (detects the presence of objects), thinking (tells us what an object is), feeling (tells us whether an object is acceptable), and intuiting (allows us to make guesses about objects or events in the absence of facts). Thinking and feeling are rational functions; sensing and intuiting irrational functions. Combining two attitudes with four functions yields eight personality types.

4. There are three stages of development according to Jung: childhood (birth to adolescence) is a time to learn necessary survival skills; young adulthood (adolescence to about 40 years) is a time to learn a vocation, get married, and raise children; and middle age (about 40 years to later years), considered most important by Jung, is a time to reflect on philosophical and spiritual values.

5. For Jung, individuation denoted the lifelong process by which the components of the personality are discovered and given expression within the context of an individual's life. The primary goal in life is to approach self-realization (the fully integrated and harmonious psyche).

6. Jung accepted both causality (personality is determined by past experiences) and teleology (what we do is determined by our anticipation of the future). He accepted synchronicity, or meaningful coincidence, as a major influence in a person's life. For Jung, dreams compensated for an unevenly developed psyche by giving expression to those portions of the psyche that are unable to manifest themselves more directly. Finally, Jung argued that the techniques used to study humans had to reflect human complexity and uniqueness—the scientific method was of limited value in studying and understanding humans. Empirical research has verified Jungian predictions concerning psychological types and the functions of thought, but most of Jung's major concepts have not been empirically tested.

7. Jung's theory has been criticized for not being falsifiable; many also see it as mystical, inconsistent, unclear, and contradictory. Conversely, Jung's theory has been praised for accounting for the multitude of human attributes, emphasizing the importance of the future for human behaviour, describing the self-realization process, being optimistic, and recognizing the importance of meaning for human existence.

EXPERIENTIAL EXERCISES

1. The following 20 items are from Jung's word-association test:

death	pity	unjust	anxiety
to sin	stupid	family	to abuse
money	book	friend	ridicule
pride	sad	happiness	pure
journey	to marry	lie	to beat

Respond to each word as quickly as you can. Using as many criteria specified in the chapter as possible, do you find any indication of a complex? If so, how would you describe that complex? Next, give the test to a close relative and see if you can detect a similar pattern of responding. Finally, give the test to a close friend and compare his or her reactions to your own and those of your relative. How do you explain the individual differences in responses to these words? Do you agree with Jung that a test such as this one can supply information concerning an individual's unconscious mind? Explain why you do or do not agree.

2. Describe how synchronicity has played a role in your life.

3. Assuming that Jung was correct in believing that dreams are compensatory, what do your dreams tell you about those aspects of your personality that are undeveloped? Jung thought that recurring dreams were of special relevance, so you may want to be especially attentive to such dreams in doing this exercise.

4. According to Jung, for humans to live together in social groups they must be willing to play social roles and conform to social mores. Jung refers to the innate tendency to have a public self as the persona. Assuming that Jung is correct in distinguishing between a superficial,

public self and a basic underlying, private self, describe the difference between the two as it applies to you. Give a few examples of how the public image that you project is different from your private self.

5. According to Jung, primitive humans responded to their world in terms of myths and it is these myth-making tendencies that we inherit as archetypes. Explain the role that myth plays in your life. If, in your opinion, myth plays no role in your life, what would Jung say about you?

6. Ponder the eight pure personality types postulated by Jung. Which type best describes your personality? Which type best describes the person you are emotionally closest to? Without sharing your conclusion, have that person choose the type that he or she believes best describes himself or herself, and which type best describes your personality. Compare your choices. Discuss the implications of what you have learned.

DISCUSSION QUESTIONS

1. Explain the principles of equivalence, entropy, and opposites.
2. Describe Jung's concept of the collective unconscious. Be sure to include in your answer a description of the most fully developed archetypes.
3. Describe how the attitudes of introversion and extroversion combine with the four functions of thought to create eight personality types.
4. Summarize the kinds of evidence used by Jung to validate his theory.
5. Compare and contrast Freud and Jung on each of the following: methodology, the nature of the unconscious mind, motivation, and religion.

KEY TERMS

Anima, p. 62
Animus, p. 62
Archetype, p. 59
Attitudes, p. 63
Causality, p. 70
Collective unconscious, p. 59
Complex, p. 58
Creative illness, p. 56
Ego, p. 57
Extroversion, p. 63
Feeling, p. 64
Functions of thought, p. 64
Individuation, p. 68

Inflation of the persona, p. 61
Introversion, p. 63
Intuiting, p. 64
Irrational functions, p. 64
Libido, p. 56
Mandala, p. 68
Myers-Briggs
    Type Indicator, p. 74
Persona, p. 61
Personal unconscious, p. 58
Principle of entropy, p. 57
Principle of equivalence, p. 57
Principle of opposites, p. 57

Psyche, p. 56
Rational functions, p. 64
Self, p. 63
Self-realization, p. 68
Sensing, p. 64
Shadow, p. 63
Synchronicity, p. 70
Teleology, p. 70
Thinking, p. 64
Value, p. 56
Word-association test, p. 58

4 Alfred Adler

Biographical Sketch

Alfred Adler was born in a suburb of Vienna, Austria, on February 7, 1870. His father, Leopold, was a moderately successful grain merchant. Adler grew up under comfortable physical circumstances and was able to enjoy open spaces, relative freedom from want, and the rich culture of Vienna, which was one of the great centres of Europe. In addition, he was able to share his love of music with his entire family.

Despite apparent physical comfort, however, Adler looked on his childhood as miserable. He thought of himself as undersized and ugly. He was the third of seven children and had a major rivalry with his older brother, who apparently was very athletic and a model child. Adler's mother seemed to prefer his older brother to him, but Adler got along very well with his father.

Adler's views of himself were not without foundation. He was a sickly child who was unable to walk until he was four years old. He suffered from rickets, which prevented him from engaging in any strenuous physical activity.

> One of my earliest recollections is of sitting on a bench bandaged up on account of rickets, with my healthy elder brother sitting opposite me. He could run, jump, and move about quite effortlessly, while for me, movement of any sort was a strain and an effort. Everyone went to great pains to help me and my mother and father did all that was in their power to do. (quoted in Bottome, 1957, pp. 30–31)

Alfred Adler

At the age of three, Adler witnessed the death of a younger brother in a bed next to his. At five, he caught pneumonia and almost died. In fact, he heard the doctor say to his parents, "Your boy is lost" (Orgler, 1963). He was also run over twice. These experiences gave him an awareness and a fear of death. He decided to become a physician when he grew up, believing that such a profession would provide a means of conquering death.

Yet Adler remained a friendly, sociable child with a genuine love for people (traits he retained all his life). His unhappiness continued in school, where he began as a poor student (especially in mathematics). One of his teachers counselled his parents to train him as a shoemaker because he apparently was not capable of anything else. Eventually, however, Adler became one of the best students in his class.

Adler's childhood ambition was realized when he obtained his medical degree from the University of Vienna (Freud's alma mater) in 1895. He first specialized in ophthalmology (diseases of the eye) and later changed to general practice and finally to psychiatry. Two years after his graduation from medical school, he married Raissa Epstein, a rich Russian girl who came to Vienna to study. Raissa was a particularly liberated, domineering woman who was a militant socialist. Perhaps it was Raissa's influence that led to Adler's first publication the year after his marriage; it concerned the terrible working conditions of independent tailors and the need for socialized medicine for the poor. Marxism remained an influence in Adler's life and influenced his theory of personality. From Marx, Adler learned that the social context within which one lives can significantly influence one's personality. Marx's philosophy also supported Adler's deep concern for common people.

The Adlers had four children. One daughter (Alexandra) and his only son (Kurt) became psychiatrists and continued their father's work in individual psychology (individual psychology is discussed shortly). Adler's wife died on April 21, 1962, at the age of 89 in New York City.

Adler read Freud's book *The Interpretation of Dreams* and wrote an article defending Freud's theoretical position. On the basis of this defence, Adler was invited by Freud to join the Vienna Psychoanalytic Society in 1902. Adler accepted Freud's invitation, becoming one of Freud's earliest colleagues. Adler became president of the society in 1910, just a year before his official break from the Freudian group. It appears now that joining the group may have been a mistake from the beginning because Adler had little in common with Freud. This incompatibility became increasingly obvious and, in 1911, while still president of the Vienna Psychoanalytic Society, he resigned from the society. Adler and Freud never met again. The differences that caused this separation were numerous and are reviewed at the end of this chapter, but the following quotation from Freud's biographer, Ernest Jones, lists a few of Adler's beliefs that were contrary to Freud's.

> Sexual factors, particularly those of childhood, were reduced to a minimum: a boy's incestuous desire for intimacy with his mother was interpreted as the male wish to conquer a female masquerading as sexual desire. The concepts of repression, infantile sexuality, and even that of the unconscious itself were discarded so little was left of psychoanalysis. (1955, p. 131)

Freud characteristically had a low tolerance for "defectors," and he remained hostile to Adler all his life. Adler was the pigmy in Freud's statement, "I made a pigmy great" (Wittels, 1924, p. 225). Adler said of Freud's theory that it was founded on the mythology of sex and that psychoanalysis was stimulated by the selfishness of a pampered child. Freud, who could not understand the grief a friend was suffering over the death of Adler, said, "I don't understand your sympathy for Adler. For a Jewish boy out of a Viennese suburb a death in Aberdeen is an unheard of career in itself and a proof of how far he had got on. The world really rewarded him richly for his service in having contradicted psychoanalysis" (quoted in Jones, 1957, p. 208). Fiebert (1997) provides interesting details concerning Adler's initial professional involvement with Freud, the sources of dissension between Adler and Freud, and the nature of the relationship between the two following Adler's "excommunication."

After breaking with the Freudians, Adler and his followers formed a group first called the Society of Free Psychoanalytic Research to express their contempt for the restrictive nature of the Freudian organization. However, they soon changed their name to Society for Individual Psychology because they did not want to be perceived as simply rebels against psychoanalysis. Because the term *individual psychology* can be easily misunderstood, the next section in this chapter clarifies its meaning.

Adler served as a physician in the Austrian Army during World War I and, following his release, was asked by the government to open several child-guidance clinics in Vienna. This was one of Adler's early efforts to apply his theory to the problems of child rearing, education, and other everyday problems. Many of his books, articles, and lectures (of which there were hundreds) were directed either toward teachers or toward the general public. Adler's fame quickly spread and, in Vienna, he was surrounded by many students, friends, and admirers. Freud, disturbed by all this, proclaimed (incorrectly) that Adler's theory was actually nothing but psychoanalytic knowledge that Adler had labelled his own by changing its terminology.

In 1926, Adler first visited the United States and was warmly received by educators. In 1927, he was appointed lecturer at Columbia University, and in 1932 he became a professor of medical psychology at the Long Island College of Medicine in New York. In 1935, partly because of the Nazi takeover in Europe, Adler made the United States his permanent home. He died of a heart attack on May 28, 1937, in Aberdeen, Scotland, while on a lecture tour there.

One peak in the popularity of Adlerian psychology was in 1930, when 2000 people attended the fifth International Congress of Individual Psychology in Berlin (Ansbacher, 1983). Another peak is more recent. According to Ansbacher:

> The Adlerian movement today numbers several thousand members in the United States, Canada, and European countries, especially Germany. It is composed of psychiatrists, psychologists, social workers, counselors, and educators, as well as lay people who accept the theory and apply the method of Adlerian psychology to family life and personal development. (1983, p. 76)

Adler's theory continues to be promoted today by the *American Journal of Individual Psychology* and by the American Society of Individual Psychology. Heinz and Rowena Ansbacher summarized many of Adler's ideas in two volumes (1956, 1979). Adler was a strong believer in bringing his ideas to nonprofessionals, a task perpetuated by Rudolf Dreikurs (1957, 1964).

Individual Psychology

In many ways, Adler's theory of personality is the opposite of Freud's. Freud viewed individuals as constantly in conflict with one another and with society, whereas Adler viewed them as seeking companionship and harmony. Freud ignored questions concerning life's meaning and the effects of aspirations on one's life, whereas Adler made these questions a central part of his theory. Freud saw the mind as consisting of different components, often in conflict with one another, whereas Adler viewed the mind as an integrated whole working to help attain the future goals of the person. So by choosing the term **individual psychology** for his theory, Adler by no means intended to imply that people are selfishly motivated to satisfy their own biological drives. Rather, he meant that although individuals are unique, they are characterized by inner harmony and a striving to cooperate with fellow humans.

Adler's theory is related to humanism because of its concern with the positive relationships among humans. His theory is related to existentialism because of its concern with questions about the meaning of human existence. Adler shared with the existentialists the belief that humans are future-oriented (a belief also shared by Jung), free to determine their own fate, and concerned with the meaning of life. Clearly, little similarity exists between Adler's individual psychology and Freud's psychoanalysis.

Organ Inferiority and Compensation

In 1907/1917, Adler published his now famous essay entitled "Study of Organ Inferiority and Its Physical Compensation." In this essay, Adler put forth the idea that people are especially vulnerable to disease in organs that are less developed or "inferior" to other organs. For example, some people are born with weak eyes, others with weak stomachs, others with weak hearts, and still others with damaged limbs. These biological deficiencies cause problems in the person's life because of the stresses put on them by the environment. These organic weaknesses inhibit the person from functioning normally and, therefore, must be dealt with in some way. At this early stage in the development of his theory, Adler emphasized biological inferiority, compensation, and over-compensation.

Because the body acts as an integrated unit, a person can **compensate** for a weakness either by concentrating on its development or by emphasizing other functions that make up for the weakness. For example, someone with a frail body may work hard to overcome this frailty. Likewise, a blind person may concentrate on developing auditory skills.

In some cases, a person may **overcompensate** by converting a biological weakness into a strength. For example, Teddy Roosevelt was an extremely frail child who became a hardy outdoorsman. Likewise, Terry Fox, Canadian hero and poster boy for the fight against cancer, achieved athletic greatness in spite of physical disabilities. The same can be said for Rick (the "Man in Motion") Hansen, who travelled 40 000 km around the world in his wheelchair to show the potential of people with physical disabilities.

Feelings of Inferiority

In 1910, Adler shifted his emphasis from actual **organ inferiority** to subjective inferiority, also called **feelings of inferiority**. Now compensation or overcompensation was directed toward either real or imagined inferiorities. At this point in his theorizing, Adler left the biological sciences and entered psychology. Anything that caused inferiority feelings was worthy of study.

According to Adler, athletes like Rick Hansen over-compensate for their physical disabilities by converting a biological weakness into a strength.

Adler pointed out that all humans start life with feelings of inferiority because we are completely dependent on adults for survival. Children feel completely helpless compared to the powerful adults on whom they depend. This feeling of being weak, impotent, and inferior stimulates in the child an intense desire to seek power, thereby overcoming feelings of inferiority. At this point in the evolution of Adler's theory, he stressed aggression and power as a means of overcoming feelings of inferiority.

Unfortunately, but mainly because of cultural conditions at the time that Adler was writing, he equated power and strength with masculinity and inferiority with femininity:

> Any form of uninhibited aggression, activity, potency, power, and the traits of being brave, free, rich, aggressive or sadistic can be considered masculine. All inhibitions and deficiencies, as well as cowardliness, obedience, poverty, and similar traits, can be considered as feminine. (Adler, 1910/1956, p. 47)

According to Adler, every person has feelings of weakness (femininity) and an impulse to become strong (masculinity) and, in that sense, all humans are bisexual. For Adler, however, bisexuality was primarily psychological, whereas for Freud it was primarily biological. That is, Adler did not believe that anatomy is destiny; rather he believed that attitudes toward one's self and toward others are destiny.

In any case, at this stage in Adler's theorizing, to become more powerful meant to become more masculine and, consequently, less feminine. He referred to this striving to become more masculine as the **masculine protest.** Because both men and women seek to become powerful enough to overcome inferiority feelings, both attempt to approximate the cultural ideal of masculinity. In other words, both men and women engage in the masculine protest. Adler believed, however, that the cultural overvaluation of masculinity over femininity was not positive for either men or women:

What I have said concerning the hatreds and jealousies between nations and groups also holds good of the bitter struggle between the sexes, a struggle that is poisoning love and marriage and is ever born anew out of the inferior valuation of woman. The idealized picture of overestimated masculinity imposes both on the boy and the grown-up man the obligation of appearing, if not being, superior to woman. This causes him to distrust himself, to exaggerate his demands on life and his expectations from it, and increases his sense of insecurity. On the other hand, a girl feels that she is valued less than a boy, and this may stimulate her either to exaggerated efforts to make up for her inadequacy and to fight real or apparent depreciation on all sides, or else may cause her to resign herself to her supposed inferiority. (Adler, 1956, p. 452)

The masculine protest occurs in any culture where power is associated with males and weakness with females. In any culture where females are perceived as powerful, the situation is reversed and there is a feminine protest. For Adler, then, sexuality was important because of what it symbolized within a culture rather than because of biological gender differences.

Feelings of Inferiority as Motivational

Are feelings of inferiority bad? No, said Adler. In fact, being human means feeling inferior. It is a condition common to all humans and, therefore, is not a sign of weakness or abnormality. In fact, such feelings are the primary motivating force behind all personal accomplishments. One feels inferior and is therefore driven to accomplish something. A short-lived feeling of success exists after such an accomplishment but in light of the accomplishments of others, one again feels inferior and again is motivated to accomplish more, and on it goes without end.

However, even though feelings of inferiority act as a stimulus for all positive growth, they also can create neurosis. A person can become overwhelmed by feelings of inferiority, at which point he or she is prevented from accomplishing anything. Under these circumstances, feelings of inferiority act as a barrier rather than as a stimulus for positive accomplishment. Such a person is said to have an **inferiority complex**. According to Adler, all humans experience the feeling of being inferior but in some it stimulates neurosis and in others it creates a need to succeed. We have something to say about what makes the difference later in this chapter.

Striving for Superiority

Adler modified his theoretical position to state that it is not more aggression, power, or masculinity that we seek but superiority or perfection. Adler now referred to striving for superiority as the **fundamental fact of life.** Adler's theory, which had started by emphasizing compensation for organ inferiority, evolved to focus on compensation for subjective inferiority through aggression and power and later on human striving for superiority-perfection as the fundamental fact of life. What is the origin of this striving for perfection? According to Adler, it is innate to all humans:

It runs parallel to physical growth. It is an intrinsic necessity of life itself. . . . All our functions follow its direction; rightly or wrongly they strive for conquest, surety, increase. The impetus from minus to plus is never-ending. The urge from "below" to "above" never ceases. Whatever premises all our philosophers and psychologists dream of—self-preservation, pleasure principle, equalization—all these are but vague representations, attempts to express the great upward drive . . . a fundamental category of thought, the structure of our reason . . . *the fundamental fact of our life.* (Adler, 1930, pp. 398–399)

In his final theoretical position, Adler retained striving for superiority as the master motive but he changed from striving for individual superiority to striving for a superior or perfect society. Adler also believed that striving for superiority could be beneficial or harmful. If a person concentrates exclusively on his or her own superiority while ignoring the needs of others and of society, he or she may develop a **superiority complex.** A person with a superiority complex tends to be domineering, vain, boastful, arrogant, and depreciative of others. According to Adler, such a person lacks social interest (discussed in a later section) and is, indeed, undesirable. Take for example the attitude change that occurs in many professional athletes after receiving public recognition and a large salary contract (e.g., professional basketball's Dennis Rodman). They overvalue their personal contribution not only to their team, but to the world in general. In 2000, public outrage at a proposed federal bailout of Canadian hockey teams made it clear that most Canadians did not accept players at their own valuation.

Fictional Goals and Lifestyles

In 1911, Hans Vaihinger (1852–1933) wrote *The Philosophy of "As If": A System of the Theoretical, Practical and Religious Fictions of Mankind* (1911/1952). Vaihinger's major premises were: (1) We can only be certain of sensations, that is, the subjective conscious elements provided by sensory stimulation and the relationships among them because we experience the physical world only indirectly through sensations; and (2) in order to make sense of our sensations we invent terms, concepts, and theories that give them meaning. According to Vaihinger, such inventions, or "fictions," make all of civilized life possible.

Adler embraced Vaihinger's philosophy enthusiastically and made it an important part of his theory. However, whereas Vaihinger was primarily interested in demonstrating how the use of fictions in science, mathematics, religion, philosophy, and jurisprudence made complex societal life possible, Adler applied the idea of fiction to the lives of individuals. From the interpretation of early experience, various worldviews can result. For example, the world can be perceived as an evil or dangerous place to be avoided, or as a pleasant or loving place to be embraced. It is important to emphasize that for Adler subjective reality was more important than physical reality. That is, it is the child's *perception* of the major events in his or her life that determines the child's worldview, not actual reality. If the child perceives the world to be a harsh, unpredictable place, he or she will adjust by creating life goals that incorporate those facts. If the child perceives the world as a warm, loving, predictable place, then those perceptions will be important in his or her adjustments to life. Because the important early experiences that mould a child's personality are those most vividly remembered through the years, they are the ones most likely to be reported as the person's earliest recollections. Thus Adler believed that one's earliest memories provide important information about one's life goals and one's lifestyle. We have more to say about the importance of first memories later in this chapter.

Coupled with feelings of inferiority, a child's worldview will determine his or her final goal, or **fictional finalism,** and his or her **lifestyle.** If a negative worldview develops, the child will believe that he or she must do battle with the world or escape from it in order to gain superiority. Here the goal will be to dominate, to defeat, to destroy, or to withdraw. If a positive worldview develops, the child will believe that he or she must participate in the world in order to gain superiority. Here the goal will be to join in, to create, to love, or to cooperate. Either type of worldview can manifest itself in a number of lifestyles. In turn, these lifestyles can manifest themselves in a number of professions. For example, a person with a negative worldview may become a ruthless businessperson or politician, a criminal, a hermit, or a domineering parent, teacher, or spouse. A person with a positive worldview may become a loving parent, spouse, teacher, physician, social worker, artist, writer, philosopher, or theologian, or a politician whose goal is to improve the human condition. Sometimes, a person's entire life can be dominated by a positive worldview, spilling into both professional and casual interactions, thought processes, memories, and identity. Consider, for example, the altruism of the late Mother Teresa.

The concept of fictional finalism, which Adler later called "a guiding self-ideal," or simply a "guiding fiction," gave Adler's theory a strong teleological (future-oriented) component but it did not ignore the past altogether. Now we can view the person as pushed by feelings of inferiority or imperfection toward perfection, using his or her unique lifestyle as a means of attaining some future goal.

Adler emphasized that these future goals or ideals are convenient fictions invented to make life more significant than it otherwise would be. Healthy people, according to Adler, change fictions when circumstances warrant it. Neurotic people, conversely, cling to their fictions at all costs. In other words, according to Adler, healthy individuals use fictional goals or ideals as tools in dealing with life. Life is unbearable without meaning, and chaotic without a plan, so they invent meaning and a plan. For healthy people, such goals, ideals, or plans are a means of living a more effective, constructive life. For the neurotic, the idea that these are only tools is lost. The goals, ideals, or plans become ends in themselves, rather than means to an end; they are retained even when they have become ineffective in dealing with reality. Thus, for Adler, an important difference between the healthy person and the neurotic is the ease with which fictional tools can be dispensed with if circumstances warrant it. The healthy or normal person seldom loses sight of reality whereas for neurotic persons the fictional life plan becomes reality. For example, a person might decide that communism will bring a better world; another might set a life goal of becoming a solo violinist. But if events show that communism in action does not produce the desired results, a healthy person will shift politics or turn to some other form of community work. An aspiring violinist who does not have the talent for a solo career may become a successful music teacher. A neurotic person, on the other hand will spend a lifetime championing lost causes and pursuing hopeless careers.

We are reminded once again why Adler's theory is called individual psychology. The individual invents a worldview and derives a final goal or guiding self-ideal from that worldview. The individual then invents a lifestyle as a means of achieving that goal. All of this invention implies a great deal of personal freedom, an implication we explore further when we discuss the creative self later in this chapter.

Social Interest

Adler's earlier theory had been criticized because it portrayed humans as selfishly motivated to strive for personal superiority. With his concept of **social interest,** Adler put such criticism to rest. Social interest was, according to Adler, an innate need of all humans to live in harmony and friendship with others and to aspire toward the development of the perfect society. As we have seen, the attainment of the perfect society replaced perfection of the individual as the primary motive in Adler's theory. A well-developed social interest relates to almost all aspects of one's life:

> It is almost impossible to exaggerate the value of an increase in social feeling. The mind improves, for intelligence is a communal function. The feeling of worth and value is heightened, giving courage and an optimistic view, and there is a sense of acquiescence in the common advantages and drawbacks of our lot. The individual feels at home in life and feels his existence to be worthwhile just as far as he is useful to others and is overcoming common, instead of private, feelings of inferiority. Not only the ethical nature, but the right attitude in aesthetics, the best understanding of the beautiful and the ugly, will always be founded upon the truest social feeling. (Adler, 1956, p. 155)

However, what a person inherits, according to Adler, is the potential for social interest. If that potential is not realized, the person will live a most unfortunate life. Simply put, those without well-developed social interest are neurotic or worse. "In all human failure, in the waywardness of children, in neurosis and neuropsychosis, in crime, suicide, alcoholism, morphinism, cocainism, in sexual perversion, in fact in all nervous symptoms, we may read lack of proper degree of *social feeling*" (Adler, 1930, p. 401).

According to Adler, each individual must solve three major problems in life, all of which require a well-developed social interest: (1) *occupational tasks*—through constructive work the person helps to advance society; (2) *societal tasks*—this requires cooperation with fellow humans. Adler said, "It was only because man learned to cooperate that the great discovery of the division of labor was made, a discovery which is the chief security for the welfare of mankind" (1933/1964, p. 132); (3) *love and marriage tasks*—the relationship between this task and the continuance of society is clear. Adler said, "On his approach to the other sex and on the fulfillment of his sexual role depends his part in the continuance of mankind" (1956, p. 132).

What determines whether a person will have a well-developed social interest or not? Primarily the mother. According to Adler, the first major social situation the child encounters is in relation to the mother. The mother-child relationship acts as a model for subsequent social relationships. If the mother maintains a positive, cooperative atmosphere, the child will tend to develop social interest. If, however, the mother binds the child exclusively to herself, the child will learn to exclude other people from his or her life and will develop low social interest. For Adler, it is the nature of the mother's early interactions with her child that primarily determines whether or not the child will have a healthy, open attitude toward other people.

In the final version of Adler's theory, a person's fictional goal and lifestyle must take the improvement of society into consideration. If they do not, the person will be neurotic. For Adler, then, social interest was the index of normality.

MISTAKEN LIFESTYLES

Any lifestyle that is not aimed at socially useful goals is a **mistaken lifestyle.** We already have encountered two examples, the person who seeks personal superiority (superiority complex) and the person who is so overwhelmed by feelings of inferiority as to accomplish nothing (inferiority complex). Both individuals lack social interest and, therefore, their lifestyles are mistaken or incorrect.

Adler delineated four types of people, who were labelled according to their degree of social interest: (1) the **ruling-dominant type**, who attempts to dominate or rule people; (2) the **getting-leaning type**, who expects everything from others and gets everything he or she can from them; (3) the **avoiding type**, who "succeeds" in life by avoiding problems (such a person avoids failure by never attempting anything); and (4) the **socially useful type**, who confronts problems and attempts to solve them in a socially useful way. The first three types have faulty or mistaken lifestyles because they lack proper social interest. Only "the socially useful type" can hope to live a rich, purposeful life.

Where do faulty lifestyles originate? Adler said they begin in childhood at the same time that a healthy lifestyle originates. Adler described three childhood conditions that tend to create a faulty lifestyle. The first is **physical inferiority**, which can either stimulate healthy compensation or overcompensation, or can result in an inferiority complex. The second is spoiling or pampering, which makes a child believe it is up to others to satisfy his or her every need. Such a child is the centre of attention and grows up to be selfish, with little, if any, social interest. Neglecting, the third condition, causes the child to feel worthless and angry and to look on everyone with distrust. Adler considered pampering as the most serious of parental errors:

> The most frequent difficulty is that the mother excuses the child from giving her any help or cooperation; heaps caresses and affection on him; and constantly acts, thinks and speaks for him, curtailing every possibility of development. Thus she pampers the child and accustoms him to an imaginary world which is not ours and in which everything is done for the child by others. (Adler, 1956, pp. 373–374)

Adler elaborated on how pampered children (and adults) view the world:

> The pampered child is trained to expect that his wishes will be treated as laws. . . . When he comes into circumstances where he is not the center of attention and where other people do not make it their chief aim to consider his feelings, he will be very much at a loss: he will feel that his world has failed him. He has been trained to expect and not to give. . . . When he has difficulties before him, he has only one method of meeting them—to make demands on other people. . . . Grown-up pampered children are perhaps the most dangerous class in our community. (1931/1958, p. 16)

According to Adler, pampering creates the Oedipus complex. "We could probably induce an [Oedipus] complex in any child. All we would need is for its mother to spoil it, and refuse to spread its interest to other people, and for its father to be comparatively indifferent or cold" (1931/1958, p. 54). It is interesting to note that Adler viewed Freud's theory of personality as the creation of a pampered child:

> And, indeed, if we look closely we shall find that the Freudian theory is the consistent psychology of the pampered child, who feels that his instincts must never be denied, who looks on it as unfair that other people should exist, who asks always, "Why should I love my neighbor? Does my neighbor love me?" (Adler, 1931/1958, p. 97)

The opposite of pampering is neglect, and it too gives the child an erroneous worldview. In the case of neglect, the child develops the impression that the world is a cold and unsympathetic place, and it is on this impression that the child formulates his or her life's goal and lifestyle. According to Adler (1931/1958) the neglected child:

> has never known what love and cooperation can be: he makes up an interpretation of life which does not include these friendly forces. . . . He will overrate [the difficulties of life] and will underrate his own capacity to meet them . . . [and] will not see that he can win affection and esteem by actions which are useful to others. (p. 17)

Family experiences other than pampering and neglect can lead children to have distorted worldviews and, therefore, faulty lifestyles. According to Adler, other negative family experiences include ridiculing sentiment or failing to express a normal amount of tenderness; using punishment excessively, especially corporal punishment; setting unattainable standards or goals; criticizing other people excessively; and considering one parent as superior to the other.

It is important to remember when considering the factors that may lead to a mistaken lifestyle that it is the child's perceptions that determine his or her personality, not reality. A pampered child who feels neglected will develop the worldview of a neglected child and vice versa. Adler said, "It is not the child's experiences which dictate his actions; it is the conclusions which he draws from his experiences" (1931/1958, p. 123).

Creative Self

Hall and Lindzey called Adler's concept of the **creative self** his "crowning achievement as a personality theorist." They went on to say, "Here at last was the prime mover, the philosopher's stone, the elixir of life, the first cause of everything human for which Adler had been searching" (1978, pp. 165–166).

With his concept of the creative self, Adler stated that humans are not simply passive recipients of environmental or genetic influences. Rather, each person is free to act on these influences and combine them as he or she wishes. Thus no two people are ever the same even if the ingredients of their personalities are similar. We saw earlier that some people with physical inferiorities compensate and become socially useful. Others develop an inferiority complex and accomplish nothing. To Adler, the difference is largely a matter of choice. According to Adler, heredity and environment provide a person only the "bricks which he uses in his own 'creative' way in building up his attitude toward life. It is his individual way of using these bricks—or in other words, it is his attitude toward life—which determines his relationship to the outside world" (1935/1956, p. 206). Elsewhere Adler said:

> We concede that every child is born with potentialities different from those of any other child. Our objection to the teachings of the hereditarians and every other tendency to overstress the significance of constitutional disposition, is that the important thing is not what one is born with, but what use one makes of that equipment. . . . As to the influence of the environment, who can say that the same environmental influences are apprehended, worked over, digested, and responded to by any two individuals in the same way? To understand this fact we find it necessary to assume the existence of still another force: the creative power of the individual. (Adler, 1932/1979, pp. 86–87)

For Adler, then, personality is essentially self-created. People assign meaning to their lives according to their perceptions of the world, themselves, and others. This is essentially an existential viewpoint.

Safeguarding Strategies

All neurotics have in common a self-centredness, a concern with their own sense of security and superiority. That is, they lack social interest. According to Adler, neurotics know (or feel) that their goal of *personal* perfection is a mistaken one and may be exposed. Such public exposure would heighten the neurotic's already intense feelings of inferiority. Adler believed that neurotics use **safeguarding strategies** to protect what little self-esteem and illusions of superiority a mistaken lifestyle can generate. The feelings of self-esteem and superiority experienced by healthy persons are real because they are based on social interest and, therefore, they do not need to be supported by deceptive strategies. Adler's safeguarding strategies are similar to Freud's ego-defence mechanisms except, unlike ego-defence mechanisms, safeguarding strategies are used only by neurotics, can operate either on the conscious or unconscious levels, and protect persons from outside threats and the problems of life. Adler discussed three categories of safeguarding strategies: excuses, aggression, and distancing.

EXCUSES

The neurotic develops symptoms and uses them as **excuses** for his or her shortcomings:

> The patient . . . selects certain symptoms and develops them until they impress him . . . as real obstacles. Behind his barricade of symptoms the patient feels hidden and secure. To the question, "What use are you making of your talents?" he answers, "This thing stops me; I cannot go ahead," and points to his self-erected barricade. We must never neglect the patient's own use of his symptoms. . . . The patient declares that he is unable to solve his task "on account of the symptoms, and only on account of these." He expects from the others the solution of his problems, or the excuse from all demands, or, at least, the granting of "extenuating circumstances." (Adler, 1956, pp. 265–266)

This safeguarding strategy consists of the "yes, but . . ." and "if only" excuses that protect a weak sense of worth and deceive neurotics, and those around them, into believing they are more worthy than they really are.

Freud too was well aware that patients often use their symptoms to gain attention and to rationalize ineffective behaviour. Freud referred to these "benefits" of illness as *pleasurable secondary gains.*

AGGRESSION

According to Adler, neurotics may also use **aggression** to protect their exaggerated sense of superiority and self-esteem. Neurotic aggression can take three forms: depreciation, accusation, and self-accusation. **Depreciation** is the tendency to overvalue one's own accomplishments and to undervalue the accomplishments of others. There are two common types of depreciation. The first is *idealization*, or judging people by standards so high that no real person could possibly live up to them. Teen idols, for example, may set a standard so high that new relationships, especially with the opposite sex, may struggle by comparison to get off the ground.

Adler (1956) gave the following examples of idealization:

> A short girl prefers tall men; or a girl falls in love only when the parents have forbidden it, while treating the attainable [partner] with open disdain and hostility. In the conversation and thoughts of such girls the limiting word "only" always crops up. They want only an educated man, only a rich man, only a real he-man, only platonic love, only a childless marriage, only a man who will grant his wife complete freedom. Here one sees the depreciation tendency so strongly at work that, in the end, hardly a man is left who would satisfy their requirements. Usually they have a ready-made, often unconscious, ideal to which traits of the father, a brother, a fairy-tale hero, a literary or historical character are admired. The more we become familiar with these ideals, the greater becomes our conviction that they have been posited as a fictional measure by which to depreciate reality. (p. 268)

A second type of depreciation is *solicitude*, which is exemplified when neurotics act as if other people are incapable of caring for themselves. Using this strategy, neurotics constantly offer advice, demonstrate concern, and generally treat other people as children. Neurotics thereby safeguard their vulnerable feelings of self-esteem by convincing themselves that other people could not get along without them.

The second type of neurotic aggression discussed by Adler was **accusation**, or the neurotic's tendency to blame others for his or her shortcomings and to seek revenge against them. Adler believed that an element of revenge exists in all neuroses and that neurotic symptoms are often designed to make others suffer. Adler (1956) said:

> In the investigation of a neurotic style of life we must always suspect an opponent, and note who suffers most because of the patient's condition. Usually this is a member of the family. There is always this element of concealed accusation in neurosis, the patient feeling as though he were deprived of his right—that is, of the center of attention—and wanting to fix the responsibility and blame upon someone. (p. 270)

Thus, according to Adler, a major goal of neurotics is to make those thought to be responsible for their misfortunes suffer more than they do.

The third type of neurotic aggression discussed by Adler is **self-accusation**, which involves:

> cursing oneself, reproaching oneself, self-torture, and suicide. This may seem strange, until we realize that the whole arrangement of the neurosis follows the trait of self-torture, that the neurosis is a self-torturing device for the purpose of enhancing the self and depreciating the immediate environment. And indeed the first stirrings of the aggression drive directed against one's own person originate from a situation in which the child wants to hurt the parents or wants to attract their attention more effectively. (Adler, 1956, p. 271)

Thus, in injuring themselves, neurotics really attempt to hurt or at least get the attention of other people. Also, guilt-inspired confessions are often used to inflict misery on other people. Adler gives the example of a domineering woman who confessed to her husband that she had deceived him with another man 25 years before. She accused herself of being unworthy and attributed the confession to guilt. Adler asked, "Who is so simple as to think that [this] is a case of the majesty of the truth vindicating itself after a quarter of a century?" (1956, p. 272). According to Adler, the facts of the case show that the woman was attempting to hurt her husband by her confession and self-accusation because he no longer obeyed her.

DISTANCING

According to Adler, neurotics often escape from life's problems by **distancing** themselves from their problems. Adler discussed several ways in which neurotics distance themselves from the problems of life: moving backward, standing still, hesitating, constructing obstacles, experiencing anxiety, and using the exclusion tendency. *Moving backward* involves safeguarding a faulty lifestyle by reverting to a more secure, less complicated time of life. This form of distancing often involves the use of disorders such as attempted suicide, fainting, migraines, refusal to take food, alcoholism, and crime to obtain the attention of others, to gain some control over them, and to avoid social responsibility. This roughly corresponds to Freud's concept of regression.

About *standing still* Adler (1956) said, "It is as if a witches' circle had been drawn around the patient, which prevents him from moving closer toward the reality of life, from facing the truth, from taking a stand, from permitting a test or a decision regarding his value" (p. 274). The disorders that Adler thought facilitate standing still include insomnia (with subsequent incapacity for work), a weak memory, masturbation, and impotence. *Hesitating* involves vacillating when faced with difficult problems.

Adler believed most compulsions serve the purpose of occupying the neurotic long enough so that he or she is finally able to say, It's too late now. Adler (1956) gave the following examples: "Washing compulsion, . . . coming too late, retracing one's steps, destroying work begun . . . or always leaving something unfinished are found very often. Equally often one sees that the patient, under an 'irresistible' compulsion toward some unimportant activity or amusement, delays a piece of work or a decision until it is too late" (p. 275).

Constructing obstacles creates distance so that it can be overcome, whereas other forms of distancing remove the neurotic from the problems of life. According to Adler, neurotics can create minor obstacles in their lives (distance) through such things as mild anxiety, certain compulsions, fatigue, sleeplessness, constipation, stomach and intestinal disorders, and headaches. These and other types of obstacles create a no-lose situation for the neurotic: "The patient's self-esteem is protected in his own judgment, and usually also his prestige in the estimation of others. If [he is unsuccessful] he can refer to his difficulties and to the proof of his illness which he has himself constructed. If he [is] victorious, what could he not have done if he were well, when, as a sick man, he achieved so much—one-handed so to speak!" (1956, p. 276). Likewise, it is not uncommon for students to avoid studying before a midterm in an effort to fashion a ready excuse in the event that they fail.

Experiencing anxiety amplifies all of the distancing strategies. Neurotics are often fearful of undertakings such as leaving home, separating from a friend, applying for a job, or developing opportunities for relationships with members of the opposite sex. Insofar as these and other experiences cause anxiety, neurotics will attempt to distance themselves from them. The greater the amount of anxiety, the greater the distance sought. Using the *exclusion tendency* to avoid life's problems, the neurotic lives within narrow limits. "He tries to keep at a distance the real confronting problems of life and confines himself to circumstances in which he feels able to dominate. In this way he builds for himself a narrow stable, closes the door, and spends his life away from the wind, the sunlight, and the fresh air" (Adler, 1956, p. 278). Living in a "narrow stable" would include being habitually unemployed as an adult, indefinitely postponing marriage, doing poorly in school, and maintaining close social ties only with one's family members. The various types of safeguarding strategies are summarized in Figure 4–1.

Figure 4–1
Safeguarding Strategies

A summary of the various safeguarding strategies used by neurotics to protect their fragile and false sense of superiority and self-esteem.

Excuses	Distancing
Aggression	Moving backward
Depreciation	Standing still
Idealization	Hesitating
Solicitude	Constructing obstacles
Accusation	Experiencing anxiety
Self-accusation	Using the exclusion tendency

Goal of Psychotherapy

Healthy people have well-developed social interest; unhealthy people do not. Those with faulty lifestyles, however, are likely to continue having them because lifestyles tend to be self-perpetuating. As we saw earlier, a lifestyle focuses a person on one way of looking at things, and this mode of perception persists unless the person runs into major problems or is made to understand his or her lifestyle through education or psychotherapy:

> Individual psychology considers the essence of therapy to lie in making the patient aware of his lack of cooperative power, and to convince him of the origin of this lack in early childhood maladjustments. What passes during this process is no small matter; his power of cooperation is enhanced by collaboration with the doctor. His "inferiority complex" is revealed as erroneous. Courage and optimism are awakened. And the "meaning of life" dawns upon him as the fact that proper meaning must be given to life. (Adler, 1930, pp. 403–404)

By using an analysis of birth order, first memories, dreams, and mannerisms (all discussed shortly), Adlerians trace the development and manifestation of a mistaken lifestyle, one that necessitates therapy because it is ineffective in dealing with life's problems. The patient, with the therapist's help, seeks a new lifestyle that contains social interest and therefore will be more functional.

The Adlerian approach to therapy avoided criticism, blame, punishment, and an authoritarian atmosphere because these things typically amplified the patient's already strong feelings of inferiority. The therapist sits face to face with the patient and is informal and good-humoured. Patients are not allowed to use their neuroses, however, to gain the sympathy of the therapist as they once may have done with their parents or other persons. Although the therapist avoids pampering, he or she also avoids the opposite error of neglect. The Adlerian therapist believes that any insights gained should be explained with such clarity that they will be understood and accepted by the patient both intellectually and emotionally. The Adlerian therapist expects to see some improvement in the patient in about three months (with sessions once or twice a week); rarely does the entire therapeutic process take more than a year.

Adler was always interested in common people and a high percentage of his clientele were from the lower and middle classes, a rarity among psychiatrists of his time. Also extremely unusual was the fact that Adler worked directly with children. Adler typically treated children in the natural setting of their homes and insisted that their parents participate in the therapeutic process. As a result of his approach to treating children, Adler is considered one of the founders of group and family psychotherapy. Also, Adler insisted on treating problem children in front of a public audience in mental health clinics to help the child realize that his or her difficulty is a community problem.

Strongly as he believed in the effectiveness of psychotherapy, Adler always insisted that it would be far easier and less costly to prevent disorders through proper child rearing and education than to treat them later in life.

Adler's View of the Unconscious

With his concept of the creative self, Adler denied the very foundation of Freudian psychoanalysis, that is, the importance of repressed traumatic experiences. Adler said, "We do not suffer the shock of [traumatic experiences] we make out of them just what suits our purposes" (1931/1958, p. 14). As we have seen, once a worldview, a final goal, and a lifestyle are formulated by an individual, all experiences are interpreted relative to them. Experiences compatible with a person's personality can be consciously pondered; those experiences incompatible are simply *not understood*. Thus, for Adler, compatibility with one's personality determined the difference between conscious and unconscious experience. If a person's personality changes, as is hoped will happen in therapy, many experiences previously not understood become understandable. We can only be aware of those experiences that make sense to us; all others are simply incomprehensible. We see in chapter 13 that George Kelly explained the "unconscious" in essentially the same way that Adler did.

Methods of Research

Adler referred to birth order, first memories, and dreams as the three "entrance gates" to mental life, and he studied them extensively to discover the origins of a person's life goal and lifestyle.

BIRTH ORDER

Adler contended that each child is treated differently within a family depending on the child's *birth order* and that this differential treatment influences the child's worldview and thus his or her choice of a life goal and lifestyle. "Above all," said Adler, "we must rid ourselves of the superstition that the situation within the family is the same for each individual child" (Adler, 1933/1964, p. 229).

Adler concentrated his research on the firstborn, secondborn, youngest, and the only child. The firstborn child is the focus of attention until the next child is born, at which time he or she is "dethroned." According to Adler, the loss caused by the birth of a sibling is deeply felt by the firstborn, because now the attention of the mother and father must be shared with a rival. Adler said, "Sometimes a child who has lost his power, the small kingdom he ruled, understands better than others the importance of power and authority" (1956, pp. 378–379). The age of the firstborn when the second child is born can make a substantial difference, however. If the firstborn is old enough to have already developed a lifestyle and if that lifestyle is a cooperative one, then the firstborn may develop a cooperative attitude toward the new sibling. If not, the resentment toward the new sibling may last a lifetime.

The secondborn child has to be extremely ambitious because he or she is constantly attempting to catch up and surpass the older sibling. Of all the birth orders, Adler thought the secondborn was the most fortunate. According to Adler, the secondborn child behaves as if in a race, as if someone were a step or two in front, and he or she must rush to get ahead. Secondborns, Adler said, are "rarely able to endure the strict leadership of others" (1956, p. 380).

The youngest child is, according to Adler, in the second worst position after the firstborn. Adler stated that the reason for this

> generally lies in the way in which all the family spoils him. A spoiled child can never be independent. He loses courage to succeed by his own effort. Youngest children are always ambitious; but the most ambitious children of all are the lazy children. Laziness is a sign of ambition joined with discouragement; ambition so high that the individual sees no hope of realizing it. (1931/1958, p. 151)

The youngest child, according to Adler, is the one most likely to seek a unique identity within a family, such as becoming a musician in a family of scientists or vice versa.

The only child is like a firstborn child who is never dethroned, at least by a sibling. The shock for the only child usually comes later (for example, in school) on learning that he or she cannot remain the centre of attention. The only child often develops an exaggerated sense of superiority and a sense that the world is a dangerous place. The latter results if the parents are overly concerned with the child's health. The only child is likely to lack well-developed social interest and display a parasitic attitude, expecting others to offer pampering and protection:

> Only children are often very sweet and affectionate, and later in life they may develop charming manners in order to appeal to others, as they train themselves in this way, both in early life and later. . . . We do not regard the only child's situation as dangerous, but we find that, in the absence of the best educational methods, very bad results occur which would have been avoided if there had been brothers and sisters. (Adler, 1929/1964, pp. 168–169)

Many factors can interact with the effects of birth order, bringing about results contrary to those generally expected. Such factors include the sex of older or younger siblings; the number of years separating them; and, most important, the way the child views his or her relations with other members of the family. For many reasons, then, all of Adler's remarks concerning the effects of birth order must be interpreted as describing only general tendencies; Adler intended them to be viewed this way.

FIRST MEMORIES

For Adler, the best way to identify a person's lifestyle is to obtain the person's earliest recollections of infancy or early childhood. These memories represent one's subjective starting point in life. It is irrelevant whether these memories are accurate or not. In either case, they reflect the person's interpretation of early experiences, and it is this interpretation of experience that shapes the child's worldview, life's goal, and lifestyle. It is these *interpretations* of experience that are recalled as *first memories*. Adler (1956) explained:

> A depressed individual could not remain depressed if he remembered his good moments and his successes. He must say to himself, "All my life I was unfortunate," and select only those events which he can interpret as instances of his unhappy fate. Memories can never run counter to the style of life. If an individual's goal of superiority demands that he should feel, "Other people always humiliate me," he will choose for remembrance incidents which he can interpret as humiliations. Insofar as his style of life alters, his memories also will alter; he will remember different incidents, or he will put a different interpretation on the incidents he remembers.
>
> Most illuminating of all is the way the individual begins his story, the earliest incident he can recall. The first memory will show his fundamental view of life, his first satisfactory crystallization of his attitude. It offers us an opportunity to see at one glance what he has taken as the starting point for his development. (p. 351)

As we have seen, Adler's own first memories were of illness and death, and it was his concern about these matters that steered him in the direction of a medical career. Hertha Orgler (1963), Adler's friend and biographer, reported that Adler gave up his general medical practice after the death of several of his diabetic patients (before the discovery of insulin). Apparently his first memories of helplessness in the face of death were rekindled. Adler then turned to psychiatry, in which psychological death (of a mistaken lifestyle) and rebirth (the attaining of a new lifestyle with a healthy amount of social interest) were possible. Adler asked more than 100 medical physicians for their earliest memories, and most of them were of either serious illness or a death in the family.

DREAM ANALYSIS

Adler agreed with Freud on the importance of dreams but disagreed with Freud's interpretation of them. According to Freud, dreams allowed partial satisfaction of a wish that would be impossible to satisfy directly in a waking state. For Adler, dreams are always an expression of one's lifestyle and must be consistent with it. To Adler, however, dreams offer emotional support for mistaken lifestyles; therefore, their occurrence almost always suggests that the dreamer has a mistaken lifestyle. "Dreaming is the adversary of common sense. We shall probably find that people who do not like to be deluded by their feelings, who prefer to proceed in a scientific way, do not dream often or do not dream at all. Others, who are further away from common sense . . . have very frequent dreams" (Adler, 1931/1958, p. 101). Typically, dreams support a faulty lifestyle by creating an emotional state that will carry over into waking life and will justify actions compatible with the dreamer's faulty lifestyle. For example, if a student unconsciously wants to create a distance between himself or herself and an important examination, he or she may dream of being chased by criminals, fighting a losing war, or of being forced to attempt to solve insoluble problems. The student awakens from the dream experiencing such emotions as fear, discouragement, or helplessness—the very emotions that will support a decision to delay or avoid the forthcoming examination.

Adler (1931/1958) said:

> The purpose of dreams must be in the feelings they arouse. The dream is only the means, the instrument, to stir up feelings. The goal of the dream is the feeling it leaves behind. . . . The style of life is the master of dreams. It will always arouse the feelings that the individual needs. We can find nothing in a dream that we shall not find in all the other symptoms and characteristics of the individual. We would approach problems in the same way whether we dreamed or not; but the dream offers a support and justification for the style of life. (pp. 98, 101)

Adler emphasized the self-deceptive and therefore the unhealthy nature of dreams. "In dreams we are fooling ourselves. Every dream is an auto-intoxication, a self-hypnosis. Its whole purpose is to excite the mood in which we are prepared to meet the situation" (Adler, 1931/1958, p. 101).

In summary, Adler believed that most dreams provide the self-deception necessary to maintain a mistaken lifestyle. Healthy people do not require the irrational, emotional support provided by dreams and therefore dream little if at all.

BEHAVIOURAL MANNERISMS

In addition to analyzing birth order, first memories, and dreams, Adler also observed a client's characteristic ways of behaving in order to gain an understanding of his or her lifestyle. He observed how a client walked, spoke, and dressed, and where and how he or she sat. He also observed if a client was constantly leaning on something, the distance maintained between the client and other people, and eye contact or the lack of it. The goal was always to understand how the client viewed the world and himself or herself.

Summary of the Differences Between Adler and Freud

The major differences between Adler and Freud can be summarized as follows:

ADLER	FREUD
Mind viewed as integrated whole	Mind viewed as consisting of warring factions
Emphasized conscious mind	Emphasized unconscious mind
Future goals important source of motivation	Future goals unimportant
Social motives primary	Biological motives primary
Optimistic about human existence	Pessimistic about human existence
Dreams analyzed to learn about lifestyles	Dreams analyzed to detect contents of unconscious mind
Humans free to determine their own personality	Personality completely determined by heredity and environmental factors
Minimized importance of sex	Maximized importance of sex
Goal of therapy to encourage lifestyle incorporating social interest	Goal of therapy to discover repressed early memories

Evaluation

EMPIRICAL RESEARCH

Most of the research generated by Adler's theory has explored the relationship between birth order and various personality characteristics (see Eckstein, 2000; Gaylor, Gih, Hurtung, & Leong, 2001). Many studies have found that firstborn and only children have higher levels of educational aspiration and achievement than laterborn children and are also more intelligent (for example, Falbo, 1981). Generally it is found that firstborns are more responsible and achievement oriented and laterborns are more socially successful (for example, Steelman & Powell, 1985). The proposed explanation for these results is that firstborn and only children receive greater parental attention and are the objects of greater parental expectations. Falbo (1981) also found that lastborn children typically have lower self-esteem than firstborn children. This result was explained by the fact that lastborn children typically have competent older siblings with whom to compare themselves. Zajonc and Markus (1975) studied the relationships among birth order, family spacing, and family size and intellectual development. It was found that the fewer the number of children in a family and the greater the spacing between children, the more intelligent each child is likely to be. Also it was found that, within a family, older children tend to be more intelligent than younger ones.

Caution is necessary when interpreting birth order studies because results are often contradictory. For this reason, some researchers are highly skeptical about birth order research in general. For example, Ernst and Angst (1983) reviewed the studies on birth order between 1946 and 1980. The hundreds of studies reviewed investigated the relationship between birth order and such variables as intelligence, school and occupational achievement, aggressiveness, self-esteem, empathy, creativity, and various types of mental illness. Ernst and Angst (1983) concluded that research on birth order has been characterized by numerous methodological flaws and is, therefore, "*a sheer waste of time and money* " (p. xi).

Dunn and Plomin (1990) do not agree that birth order research is useless but they do say birth order "plays only a bit-part in the drama of sibling differences" (p. 85). Somit, Arwine, and Peterson (1996) reach a similar conclusion.

Developmental experts agree that many birth order studies overlook a key problem. Most investigations use a between-family design—that is, personality comparisons are made between individuals from different families. This approach invites any of a number of confounds with birth order, including socioeconomic status, parental personality, number of siblings, but most importantly genetics. The solution: within-family research that compares individuals from the same family, thus naturally controlling all between-family differences. Using four within-family data sets, researchers at the University of British Columbia investigated whether firstborns tend to be achievers and laterborns tend to be rebels (Paulhus, Trapnell, & Chen, 1999). Participants nominated "achievers" and "rebels" among family members, and rated personality variables drawn from a comprehensive personality inventory, the Five-Factor Model (discussed further in chapter 8). Firstborns were indeed overrepresented among achievers, and laterborns were overrepresented among rebels. Firstborns were more often nominated as conscientious and dependable, laterborns as liberal, agreeable or pleasant, and rebellious.

Sulloway (1996) agrees with Ernst and Angst (1983) that much birth order research has been poorly controlled and involved hypotheses too nebulous to be objectively tested. When these problems are attended to, however, the effects of birth order on personality can be dramatic. As part of his massive historical undertaking, Sulloway (1996) studied how 3890 scientists reacted to 28 scientific innovations when they were first reported (16 considered revolutionary, such as those of Copernicus, Darwin, and Freud, and 12 somewhat less radical). He found that those scientists who rejected the innovation in question were typically firstborns and those accepting it were typically laterborns. Sulloway (1996) says, "For the 28 innovations included in my survey, the odds are 2.0 to 1 in favor of laterborn adoption. The likelihood of this difference arising by chance is substantially less than one in a billion" (p. 42). Furthermore, as is shown in Figures 4–2 and 4–3, Sulloway found that this birth order effect was independent of number of siblings ("sibship size") and socioeconomic class.

How does the eldest child's personality differ from the youngest's? New research that compares members of the same family suggests that birth order does make a difference.

Figure 4–2

Receptivity to Scientific Innovation by Birth Order and Sibship Size.

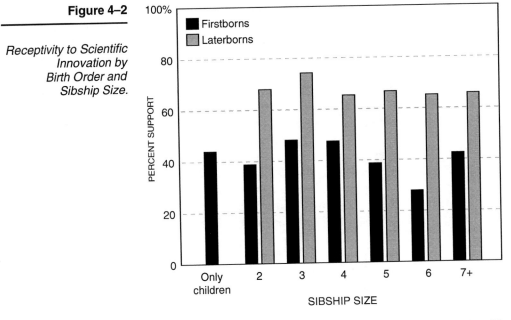

(From Sulloway, 1996, p. 48)

Figure 4–3

Receptivity to Scientific Innovation by Birth Order and Socioeconomic Class.

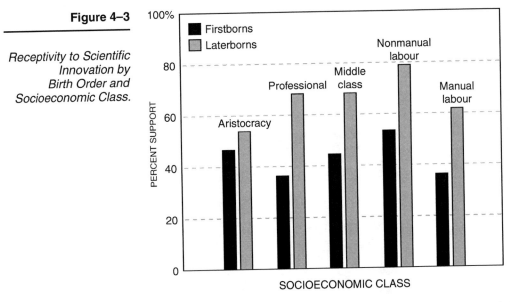

(From Sulloway, 1996, p. 49)

Sulloway (1996) found similar results when religious and social innovations were considered. In general, laterborns are much more receptive to innovation than firstborns. Of laterborns Sulloway says, "From their ranks have come bold explorers, the iconoclasts, and the heretics of history" (1996, p. xiv).

This finding has been consistent over time and across a wide variety of groups.

For the past five centuries, the most consistent predictor of revolutionary allegiances turns out to be *birth order*. Compared with firstborns, laterborns are more likely to identify with the underdog and to challenge the established order. Because they identify with parents and authority, firstborns are more likely to defend the status quo. The effects of birth order transcend gender, social class, race, nationality, and—for the last five centuries—time. (Sulloway, 1996, p. 356)

Sulloway's research confirms the rather puzzling observation consistently made over the last two decades that, "siblings who grow up together are almost as different in their personalities as people plucked randomly from the general population" (1996, p. 352). The question is why this is so, and Sulloway offers a Darwinian answer. Within a family, siblings compete for parental resources, including affection. Without siblings to compete with, firstborns have everything to themselves and usually identify with parents and authority and grow up defending the status quo. The challenge of the laterborn "is to find a valued family niche that avoids duplicating the one already staked out by the parent-identified firstborn" (Sulloway, 1996, p. 353). This search is facilitated by an openness to experience, or versatility, which, once developed, lasts a lifetime. Sulloway (1996) concludes, "From a Darwinian point of view, personality is the repertoire of strategies that each child develops in an effort to survive childhood" (1996, p.86).

Although Sulloway explained the effects of birth order within a Darwinian framework, the conclusion he reached was very much within the spirit of Adlerian analysis, "Families are best seen as containing an array of diverse niches, each occupied by a different individual and each presenting different vantage points of life. From these differing perspectives, family members experience the same events differently" (1996, p. 352).

Several attempts have been made to make other Adlerian concepts more measurable and thus more useful in counselling and therapeutic situations. Crandall (1980, 1981, 1982) devised a scale for measuring level of social interest and found that social interest indeed varies with one's level of social adjustment, among other things. Thorne (1975) devised a 200-item questionnaire called The Life Style Analysis, which is designed to determine a person's lifestyle. Rule (1972) and Rule and Traver (1982) devised and used an Early Recollection Questionnaire, and Altman (1973) created the Early Recollection Ratings Scale of Social Interest. Olson (1979) presented a collection of papers showing how early memories are used in clinical diagnosis and psychotherapy. Hafner, Fakouri, and Labrentz (1982) found that more alcoholics than nonalcoholics described their earliest memories as threatening.

CRITICISMS

Difficult to Falsify.   Like the theories of Freud and Jung, many of the terms in Adler's theory are not defined precisely enough to validate. Because they lack clear definition it is difficult, if not impossible, to determine the impact of such concepts as inferiority, superiority, social interest, and creative power on a person's personality. Adler's contention that "everything can also be different" (1956, p. 194) makes it practically impossible to make a falsifiable prediction using his theory. As we have seen, Adler believed it was subjective, not objective, reality that determines behaviour. Therefore, if a person develops a personality unlike the one that is supposed to characterize, for example, his or her birth order, it can always be attributed to the person's unique perceptions of the situation. Also, Adler claimed that heredity and experience provide only the raw materials of personality and the creative self acts on those materials to mould a unique personality. The concept of creative self, then, makes it impossible to predict adult personality characteristics on the basis of either heredity or environmental experience.

Overly Simplistic.   Adler claimed that it is often a few early experiences that determine adult personality, and that if a person's interpretations of the world based on those experiences could be changed, an unhealthy lifestyle could be changed into a healthy one. Also, Adler relied almost exclusively on social factors in explaining personality, minimizing biological, hereditary factors. Finally, Adler contends that in the final analysis personality is, or could be, freely chosen by each person. Many modern personality theorists consider all of these Adlerian assumptions to be overly optimistic. Also, with his belief that all humans are born with the innate potential for social interest, Adler had trouble explaining the widespread occurrence of war, murder, rape, crime, and other human acts of violence. Many believe that the theories of Freud and Jung are far better able to explain the more unseemly aspects of human behaviour.

CONTRIBUTIONS

The Importance of Social Variables.   Although some consider Adler's emphasis on social variables a drawback to his theory, others consider that emphasis as Adler's most significant contribution. Adler vividly pointed out that the world each person lives in is a world of his or her own creation. Furthermore, the most important factor in formulating that worldview is the person's relationships with other people. For example, a person's family constellation is one variable that can influence his or her worldview. The importance of social variables for personality development were minimized by Freud and Jung.

Widely Influential.   Adler's terms "lifestyle" and "inferiority complex" have become part of everyday language. In the realms of personality theory and psychotherapy, we see Adler's influence in the contemporary emphasis on self-selected goals as determinants of behaviour; social determinants of personality; family therapy, group therapy, and community psychiatry; the importance of subjective reality as opposed to objective reality; and personal freedom and responsibility in living one's life.

Several influential theorists regard Adler's contribution to psychology as greater than Freud's. For example, Albert Ellis says:

> Alfred Adler, more even than Freud, is probably the true father of modern psychotherapy. Some of the reasons are: He founded ego psychology, which Freudians only recently rediscovered. He was one of the first humanistic psychologists. . . . He stressed holism, goal-seeking, and the enormous importance of values in human thinking, emoting, and acting. He correctly saw that sexual drives and behavior, while having great importance in human affairs, are largely the result rather than the cause of man's non-sexual philosophies. . . .
>
> It is difficult to find any leading therapist today who in some respect does not owe a great debt to the Individual Psychology of Alfred Adler. (1970, p. 11)

Viktor Frankl stated that Adler's opposition to Freud

> was no less than a Copernican switch. No longer could man be considered as the product, pawn, and victim of drives and instincts; on the contrary, drives and instincts form the material that serves man in expression and action.
>
> Beyond this, Alfred Adler may well be regarded as an existential thinker and as a forerunner of the existential-psychiatric movement. (1970, p. 12)

SUMMARY

1. Adler spent much of his childhood suffering from physical ailments and feelings of inferiority. He felt he was in a losing competition with his older brother. He was one of Freud's earliest associates, but numerous differences caused them to terminate their relationship. Adler's viewpoint (Individual Psychology) stresses the wholeness and uniqueness of each person as he or she struggles to overcome feelings of inferiority by aspiring toward some future goal. Adler's theory is compatible with both existentialism and humanism.

2. Adler believed that people were motivated to compensate for actual physical weaknesses by emphasizing other qualities. He thought a person could overcompensate and convert a weakness into a strength. He extended his theory to include not only actual physical weaknesses but imagined ones.

3. Earlier, Adler equated inferiority with femininity and superiority with masculinity; the striving to become more masculine in order to become more powerful was called masculine protest. Feeling inferior was not necessarily bad; such feelings are the motivating force behind most personal accomplishments. Some individuals, however, are overcome by feelings of inferiority. When such feelings become a barrier to personal growth they are called an inferiority complex.

4. Humans are primarily motivated to seek superiority or perfection. A healthy person seeks not a selfish individual superiority but one compatible with society. A person who selfishly seeks personal superiority while ignoring the needs of others and society is said to have a superiority complex.

5. Adler believed that people must insert meaning into their lives by inventing ideals or fictional goals (called fictional finalisms or guiding fictions) that give them something for which to live and around which to organize their lives. Healthy people use such fictions as tools for living a more significant, effective life. Healthy people can easily discard these fictions if circumstances warrant. Neurotics confuse fictions with reality and cling to them at all costs. The means of attaining a fictional goal is called a lifestyle.

6. All people, according to Adler, have an innate potential to live in harmony with others, called social interest. Each person must solve three major problems in life: (a) occupational tasks, (b) societal tasks, and (c) love and marriage tasks. Adler believed the nature of a child's interaction with the mother determines to what extent the child develops social interest. Mistaken lifestyles were characterized by low social interest, and include the ruling-dominant type, getting-leaning type, and avoiding type. Three childhood conditions can cause mistaken lifestyles: physical inferiority, spoiling or pampering, and neglecting. Adler did not believe that personality is fully determined by biological inheritance, early experiences, or the environment. With the creative self, he believed each person is free to interpret or create life in any number of ways—it allows us to be what we choose to be.

7. Because the feelings of self-esteem generated by a mistaken lifestyle are deceptive, they must be safeguarded. Adler listed several strategies: excuses, aggression (accusation, depreciation, self-accusation), and distancing (moving backward, standing still, hesitating, constructing obstacles, experiencing anxiety, using the exclusion tendency). The major goal of psychotherapy is to replace a mistaken lifestyle with one containing a healthy level of social interest. Adler's research methods included the study of birth order, first memories, and dream analysis.

8. Adler's theory differed from Freud's in many significant ways: Adler emphasized the conscious integrated mind, social motives, future goals, personal freedom, and dreams supporting faulty lifestyles; he de-emphasized sexual motivation.

9. Adler's theory is criticized for containing terms too nebulous to measure (making them nonfalsifiable), being too simplistic, and overlooking the baser side of human beings. Adler's theory has been praised for noting the importance of social variables in personality development, introducing new terms, concepts, and methodologies, and understanding personality and the therapeutic process. Despite considerable research on the effects of birth order on various personality characteristics, results are equivocal.

EXPERIENTIAL EXERCISES

1. Adler believed that one's earliest memories provide the subjective starting point in one's life. List your earliest memories and discuss their possible relationship to your major goals in life.

2. Adler identified four basic types of people: the ruling type, the getting type, the avoiding type, and the socially useful type. Indicate which of the four types characterizes you best and give evidence supporting your conclusion.

3. According to Adler, each child is treated differently within a family depending on the child's birth order. Given your birth order, describe how your experiences may have been different than a child with a different birth order. Discuss how the experiences caused by your birth order may have influenced your adult personality. By interviewing acquaintances, determine whether or not people with the same birth order have similar personality characteristics.

4. According to Adler, the main source of meaning in one's life is provided by one's fictional final goal. It is around this goal that one's psychic life is integrated and all more immediate, concrete goals are steps toward the attainment of the fictional final goal. A glimpse of your fictional goal can be provided by responding to the following questions: What is it that you value most highly? What is it that you see yourself striving for? How would you describe an ideal future for yourself? Answer these questions and, based on your answers, describe what appears to be your fictional final goal. Discuss how this goal influences your beliefs, choices, and actions.

5. Discuss the safeguarding strategies as they apply to your life. If you think you do not employ such strategies, discuss a person that you know who does.

DISCUSSION QUESTIONS

1. Trace the evolution of Adler's theory from its concern with organ inferiority to its concern with social interest.

2. According to Adler, what is a lifestyle?

3. Discuss Adler's concept of the creative self.

4. Give an example of each of the following safeguarding strategies: excuses, aggression, and distancing.

5. List the major differences between Adler's theory of personality and Freud's theory.

KEY TERMS

Accusation, p. 90
Aggression, p. 89
Avoiding type person, p. 87
Compensation, p. 81
Creative self, p. 88
Depreciation, p. 89
Distancing, p. 90
Excuses, p. 89
Feelings of inferiority, p. 81
Fictional finalism, p. 85
Fundamental fact of life, p. 83
Getting-leaning type person, p. 87
Individual psychology, p. 81

Inferiority complex, p. 83
Lifestyle, p. 85
Masculine protest, p. 82
Mistaken lifestyle, p. 86
Organ inferiority, p. 81
Overcompensation, p. 81
Physical inferiority, p. 87
Ruling-dominant type person, p. 87
Safeguarding strategies, p. 89
Self-accusation, p. 90
Social interest, p. 85
Socially useful type person, p. 87
Superiority complex, p. 84

5 Karen Horney

Biographical Sketch

Karen Horney (pronounced "Horn-eye") was born Karen Danielson in a small village near Hamburg, Germany, on September 15, 1885 (the year Freud was studying hypnotism with Jean Charcot in Paris). Her father, Berndt Henrik Wackles Danielson, was a Norwegian sea captain, and her mother, Clotilde Marie van Ronzelen, was a member of a prominent Dutch-German family. Horney's mother was 18 years younger than the captain and was his second wife. The family consisted of four children from the captain's previous marriage and Horney's older biological brother, Berndt, who was considered the darling of the family. Horney's father was a tall, dashing, stern, God-fearing, fundamentalist who strongly believed that women were inferior to men and were the source of evil in the world. He often clashed with Horney's mother, who was proud, beautiful, intelligent, and free thinking. Horney had mixed feelings about her father. On the one hand, she felt intimidated by his stern, self-righteous manner and by his derogatory statements about her appearance and intelligence. Conversely, he added adventure to her life by taking her along on at least three lengthy sea voyages and by bringing her exotic gifts from around the world. Perhaps it was because of these fond memories that Horney began wearing a captain's cap when she was in her thirties. As an example of her father's negative side, Horney recalled that after reading the Bible at length, he sometimes exploded in a fit of anger and threw the Bible at his wife. The children referred to him as the "Bible thrower" (Rubins, 1978, p. 11). It is little wonder

Karen Horney

that Horney developed a negative attitude toward religion and a skepticism toward authority figures. After she was treated by a physician when she was 12, Horney decided to become a physician herself—a decision that was strongly supported by her mother and opposed by her father.

In 1906, when Karen was 21, she entered medical school at Freiberg, Germany, one of the few medical schools that accepted women. Shortly afterward she met Oskar Horney, an economics major on vacation from another institution, and was attracted to him because he was stern, intelligent, independent, and physically and emotionally strong. Karen married Oskar on October 31, 1909 (the year Freud and Jung gave a series of lectures at Clark University in the United States), and the union produced three daughters. By the time they married, Oskar had become a lawyer (as had Karen's brother). By 1910 Horney was pregnant with Brigitte, the first of their three daughters. Shortly before the birth of Brigitte, Horney's mother died of a stroke. It was also about this time that Horney underwent her own psychoanalysis in preparation for a career as a psychoanalyst. Needless to say, these were tense times in Horney's life. Within the space of just a few years she experienced marriage, the death of her mother, childbirth, and psychoanalysis.

Horney's marriage to Oskar was never very happy:

> By early 1912, Oskar had ceased to play an important role in Karen's life. She felt that the great tensions and emotions were missing in their marriage and sought satisfaction of her needs elsewhere. . . . Within two years of their wedding, Karen and Oskar appear to have agreed on an open marriage, in which each pursued other relationships without concealment or deceit. . . . Karen and Oskar continued their liaisons discreetly and maintained the appearance of being a conventional family as their three daughters were growing up, but the vitality went out of their relationship within a year after Brigitte's birth. (Paris, 1994, p. 49)

Through the years Horney's lovers, who were almost always younger men, included her colleagues (sometimes married) and her students. There is evidence that Horney's sexual appetites extended to women (Paris, 1994). About her numerous relationships, Paris says, "They were not . . . the main focus of Horney's life; her need for men was compulsive but not all-consuming. It did not interfere with her creative work but rather fueled her continuing search for psychological insight" (pp. 149–150).

Although Horney felt essentially unwanted and unloved as a child, she was viewed by her own children as having a laissez-faire attitude toward them. Rubins (1978, p. 51) reported that during a Christmas dinner, the middle daughter, Marianne, leaned back too far in her chair. In an attempt to catch herself from falling she grabbed the tablecloth and took to the floor with her the entire Christmas dinner. Marianne's father (Oskar) beat her with a dog whip while the two other daughters cried, and Horney looked on without displaying any emotion.

The Horney marriage, such as it was, began to disintegrate in 1923, about the time that Karen's brother died of pneumonia at the age of 40. Shortly after her brother's death, the Horney family went on vacation. Karen went swimming alone and when she did not return for more than an hour, family members went looking for her. She was found clinging to a piling pondering whether to continue living or to take her own life. After much pleading she agreed to swim back to shore. This bout was but one of the many with deep depression that Karen experienced throughout her life. Also, about this time, Oskar's life was becoming extremely difficult. The firm that he worked for went bankrupt, his investments failed, and he borrowed heavily to survive financially. After a near-fatal attack of meningitis, the formerly successful Oskar was himself bankrupt, morose, and withdrawn. He became increasingly difficult to live with, and in 1926 Horney and her three girls moved into a small apartment. It was not until 1936 that Horney officially filed for a divorce, and the divorce did not become final until 1938.

Horney completed her medical studies in 1913 at the University of Berlin. She was an excellent student throughout her academic career and was often first in her class. From 1914 to 1918, she received psychoanalytic training at the Berlin Psychoanalytic Institute. In 1919, at age 33, she became a practising psychoanalyst. From 1918 to 1932, she taught at the Berlin Psychoanalytic Institute, besides having a private practice.

In 1932, she accepted an invitation from Franz Alexander to come to the United States and become an associate director of the Chicago Institute of Psychoanalysis. Two years later, she moved to New York, where she established a private practice and trained analysts at the New York Psychoanalytic Institute. It was while she was at the Institute that Horney re-established a relationship with her old friend Erich Fromm. She had originally met Fromm at the Berlin Institute for Psychoanalytic Training in 1922 and there was a mutual attraction. Fromm was married at the time, however, and nothing romantic occurred. The two were together for a while at the Chicago Institute of Psychoanalysis but apparently their intimate relationship did not begin until they both moved to New York in 1934. Rubins (1978) observes that the relationship was mutually beneficial because Horney "learned sociology from Fromm and he psychoanalysis from her" (p. 195). Fromm, who was 15 years Horney's junior, became highly successful and authored several influential books including *Escape From Freedom* (1941). The intimate relationship with Fromm lasted several years and even when it ended a social and professional relationship continued for several more years. After Fromm, Horney's next romantic relationship was with Hans Baumgartner. Torn between marrying Hans or getting a cocker spaniel, Horney opted for the cocker spaniel (Paris, 1994, p. 145).

At the New York Psychoanalytic Institute, major differences between Horney and the traditional Freudians became apparent. Eventually the theses submitted by her students were routinely rejected because they reflected ideas contrary to traditional Freudian doctrine. Opposition to her ideas became so strong that her teaching was curtailed and she was barred as a training analyst. Under such pressure Horney resigned from the Institute in 1941; soon thereafter she founded her own organization, called the American Institute for Psychoanalysis, where she continued to develop her own ideas and which she headed until her death on December 4, 1952.

Disagreements with Freudian Theory

Horney was trained in the Freudian tradition, and all her work was influenced by that training. In fact, while at the Berlin Psychoanalytic Institute, she was psychoanalyzed by Karl Abraham and Hans Sachs, two of the most prominent Freudian analysts at that time. As time went on, however, Horney found it more and more difficult to apply Freudian notions to her work. She completely disagreed with Freud's notions of the Oedipal complex and his division of the mind into the id, ego, and superego. She thought Freud's theory reflected a different country and a different time. To state it simply, Horney found that Freud's theory did not fit the problems people were having during the Great Depression in the United States. Sexual problems were secondary to several other problems that those special environmental conditions had created. Instead of sexual problems, people were worried about losing their jobs and not having enough money to pay the rent, buy food, or provide their children with needed medical care.

Horney reasoned that because such major differences exist in the types of problems that people experience from one country to another or from one time in history to another, they must be culturally rather than biologically determined, as Freud had assumed. So Horney's theory ended up being quite different from Freud's. To Horney, what a person experiences socially influences the development of personality and determines whether or not he or she will have psychological problems and, if so, what type they will be. The conflict is caused by environmental conditions, not by opposing components of the mind.

As we shall see, Horney did not abandon Freud's theory completely but her viewpoint is much more compatible with Adler's than with Freud's.

Basic Evil, Hostility, and Anxiety

In her book *The Neurotic Personality of Our Time* (1937), Horney elaborated her contention that neuroses are caused by disturbed human relationships. More specifically, she maintained that the rudiments of neurotic behaviour are found in the relationship between parent and child. This point agrees with Freud's theory because Horney also stressed the importance of early childhood experience in personality development. Horney, however, did not accept Freud's notion of the psychosexual stages of development. Like Adler, Horney believed the child starts life with a feeling of helplessness relative to the powerful parents. She believed the two basic needs in childhood are *safety* and *satisfaction*, and that the child is completely dependent on the parents for satisfaction. The need for **satisfaction** refers to the child's needs for food, water, and sleep. At least minimal satisfaction of such physiological needs is necessary for survival. According to Horney, however, the satisfaction of physiological needs is less important for personality development than the satisfaction of the need for **safety**— that is, security and freedom from fear.

Although all children are helpless and dependent on the parents during the early years, this need not necessarily create a psychological problem. Horney did not agree with Adler's earlier view that all children feel helpless and inferior and spend the rest of their lives compensating or overcompensating for this feeling. She believed the condition of helplessness is a necessary but not a sufficient condition for the development of neurosis. Two possibilities exist: (1) The parents can demonstrate genuine affection and warmth toward the child, thereby satisfying the need for safety; or (2) the parents can demonstrate indifference, hostility, or even hatred toward the child, thereby frustrating the need for safety. The former condition leads to normal development, and the latter neurotic development.

Horney called parental behaviour that undermines a child's security the **basic evil.** Here is a sample list of such behaviours:

Indifference toward the child

Rejection of the child

Hostility toward the child

Obvious preference for a sibling

Unfair punishment

Ridicule

Humiliation

Erratic behaviour

Unkept promises

Isolation of the child from others

A child who is abused by the parents in one or more of the preceding ways experiences **basic hostility** toward his or her parents. The child is now caught between dependence on the parents and hostility toward them, a most unfortunate situation. Because the child is in no position to change the situation, he or she must repress the hostile feelings toward the parents to survive. This repression of the child's basic hostility is motivated by feelings of helplessness, fear, love, or guilt (Horney, 1937). The child who represses basic hostility because of feelings of helplessness seems to be saying, "I have to repress my hostility because I need you" (Horney, 1937). The child who represses basic hostility because of fear seems to be saying, "I have to repress my hostility because I am afraid of you" (Horney, 1937).

In some homes, real love for a child may be lacking but at least there is some effort to make the child seem wanted. For example, verbal expressions of love and affection may be substituted for real love and affection. The child, according to Horney, has little trouble telling the difference but clings to the "substitute" love because that is all there is. This child says, "I have to repress my hostility for fear of losing love" (Horney, 1937). The child may also repress basic hostility because of guilt. Such a child feels sinful and unworthy. The motto of this child is, "I have to repress hostility because I would be a bad child if I felt hostile" (Horney, 1937).

Unfortunately the feeling of hostility caused by the parents does not remain isolated; instead, it generalizes to the entire world and all the people in it. The child is now convinced that everything and everyone is potentially dangerous. At this point, the child is said to experience **basic anxiety,** one of Horney's most important concepts. Horney described basic anxiety and its relationship to basic hostility as follows:

> The condition that is fostered or brought about by the factors I have mentioned . . . is an insidiously increasing, all-pervading feeling of being lonely and helpless in a hostile world. . . . This attitude as such does not constitute a neurosis but it is the nutritive soil out of which a definite neurosis may develop at any time. Because of the fundamental role this attitude plays in neuroses I have given it a special designation: the basic anxiety; it is inseparably interwoven with a basic hostility. (1937, pp. 76–77)

According to Horney, the origins of neurotic behaviour are found in parent-child relationships. If the child experiences love and warmth, he or she will feel secure and probably develop normally. In fact, Horney thought that if a child were truly loved, he or she could survive a variety of bad experiences without ill effects: "A child can stand a great deal of what is often regarded as traumatic—such as sudden weaning, occasional beating, sex experiences—as long as inwardly he feels wanted and loved" (Horney, 1937, pp. 68–69). If, however, the child did not feel loved there would be hostility toward the parents, and this hostility would eventually be projected onto everything and everyone and become basic anxiety. According to Horney, a child with basic anxiety is well on the way to becoming a neurotic adult.

Anxieties with roots in childhood can come to the fore in adult life when we are torn between the inborn desire to affiliate and bond with other human beings and the cultural expectation of competition to maximize our personal worth and success. We feel

Anxiety can result when our inborn desire to affiliate and bond with people clashes with cultural expectations to compete and achieve economic success.

compelled to work long hours to afford a large house, several cars, and elaborate vacations; but this comes at the price of losing contact with family and friends. In the end, we find ourselves unsatisfied and starving for human contact. Though we may have success and achievement through our jobs, we feel empty and alone.

Adjustments to Basic Anxiety

Because basic anxiety causes feelings of helplessness and loneliness, the person experiencing it must find ways to keep it to a minimum. Originally, Horney (1942) described 10 strategies for minimizing basic anxiety that she called **neurotic trends** or neurotic needs. As you read through these neurotic needs, you will note they are needs that almost everyone has, which is an important point. The normal person, in fact, has many or all of these needs and pursues their satisfaction freely. In other words, when the need for affection arises, one attempts to satisfy it. When the need for personal admiration arises, one attempts to satisfy that need, and so forth. The neurotic person, however, does not pass easily from one need to another as conditions change. Rather, the neurotic person focuses on one of the needs to the exclusion of all the others. The neurotic person makes one of these needs the focal point of life. The approach to satisfying the need is out of proportion to reality, disproportionate in intensity, and indiscriminate in application, and when the need goes unsatisfied, it stimulates intense anxiety. "If it is affection that a person must have, he must receive it from friend and enemy, from employer and bootblack" (Horney, 1942, p. 39).

The 10 neurotic trends or needs are as follows (Horney, 1942, pp. 51–56):

1. Need for Affection and Approval. A person emphasizing this need lives to be loved and admired by others. "Center of gravity in others and not in self, with their wishes and opinions the only thing that counts; dread of self-assertion; dread of hostility on the part of others or of hostile feelings within self" (1942, p. 51). Consider the individual who jumps immediately from one relationship to another.

2. Need for a Partner Who Will Run One's Life. A person emphasizing this need must be affiliated with someone who will protect him or her from all danger and fulfill all of his or her needs. "Overevaluation of 'love' because 'love' is supposed to solve all problems; dread of desertion; dread of being alone" (1942, pp. 51–52). For example, such a person may gladly relinquish key decisions on childrearing or finances to his or her partner.

3. Need to Live One's Life Within Narrow Limits. A person emphasizing this need is very conservative, avoiding defeat by attempting very little. Such individuals may seem to fear success. "Necessity to be undemanding and contented with little, and to restrict ambitions and wishes for material things; necessity to remain inconspicuous and to take second place; belittling of existing faculties and potentialities, with modesty the supreme value" (1942, p. 52).

4. Need for Power. A person emphasizing this need glorifies strength and despises weakness. "Domination over others craved for its own sake; . . . essential disrespect for others, their individuality, their dignity, their feelings, the only concern being their subordination; . . . indiscriminate adoration of strength and contempt for weakness; dread of uncontrollable situations; dread of helplessness" (1942, pp. 52–53).

5. Need to Exploit Others. A person emphasizing this need dreads being taken advantage of by others but thinks nothing of taking advantage of them. "Others evaluated primarily according to whether or not they can be exploited or made use of; . . . pride in exploitative skill; dread of being exploited and thus of being 'stupid'" (1942, p. 54).

6. Need for Social Recognition and Prestige. A person emphasizing this need lives to be recognized—for example, to have his or her name in the newspaper. The highest goal is to gain prestige. For example, some people feel compelled to get the latest technology, the newest automobile, and the largest house, not so much to enjoy them as to "keep up with the Joneses." "All things—inanimate objects, money, persons, one's own qualities, activities, and feelings—evaluated only according to their prestige value" (1942, p. 54).

7. Need for Personal Admiration. A person emphasizing this need lives to be flattered and complimented. This person wants others to see him or her in accordance with the idealized image he or she has of himself or herself. "Need to be admired not for what one possesses or presents in the public eye but for the imagined self; self-evaluation dependent on living up to this image and on admiration of it by others" (1942, p. 54).

8. Need for Ambition and Personal Achievement. A person emphasizing this need has an intense interest in becoming famous, rich, or important, regardless of the costs. "Need to surpass others not through what one presents or is but through one's activities; self-evaluation dependent on being the very best—lover, sportsman, writer, worker—particularly in one's own mind, recognition by others being vital too, however, and its absence resented" (1942, p. 55).

9. Need for Self-Sufficiency and Independence. A person emphasizing this need goes to great extremes to avoid being obligated to anyone and does not want to be tied down to anything or anyone. Enslavement is to be avoided at all costs. "Necessity never to need anybody, or to yield to any influence, or to be tied down to anything, any closeness involving the danger of enslavement; distance and separateness the only source of security; dread of needing others, of ties, of closeness, of love" (1942, p. 55).

10. Need for Perfection and Unassailability. A person emphasizing this need attempts to be flawless because of hypersensitivity to criticism. An example of this can be found in the perfectionism typically associated with both anorexia and bulimia nervosa. "Relentless driving for perfection; . . . feelings of superiority over others because of being perfect; dread of finding flaws within self or of making mistakes; dread of criticism or reproaches" (1942, pp. 55–56).

Again, normal people experience most, if not all, of the 10 needs, and, when they do, put them in proper perspective. For example, normal people's need for power is not intense enough to cause a conflict with other needs, such as the need for affection. Normal people are able to satisfy all their needs because they do not have an intense emotional investment in any one of them. The neurotic, conversely, has made *one* of the needs a way of life. The neurotic's whole life is spent attempting to satisfy just one of the needs at the expense of all the others. Because it is important that many of the other needs be satisfied, the neurotic is locked into a vicious circle. The more one neurotic need is emphasized as a means of coping with basic anxiety, the more other important needs go unsatisfied. The more these other needs go unsatisfied, the more basic anxiety the neurotic feels, and the more anxious this person feels, the deeper he or she burrows into a single strategy to cope with the anxiety. And on it goes.

MOVING TOWARD, AGAINST, OR AWAY FROM PEOPLE

In her book *Our Inner Conflicts* (1945), Horney summarized her list of 10 neurotic needs into three major adjustment patterns describing the neurotic's adjustment to other people. These patterns of adjustment are considered by many to be Horney's most significant contribution to personality theory.

Moving Toward People. This adjustment pattern includes the neurotic needs for affection and approval, for a dominant partner to control one's life, and to live one's life within narrow limits. This person, whom Horney called the **compliant type,** seems to say, "If I give in, I shall not be hurt" (Horney, 1937, p. 83):

> In sum, this type needs to be liked, wanted, desired, loved; to feel accepted, welcomed, approved of, appreciated; to be needed, to be of importance to others, especially to one particular person; to be helped, protected, taken care of, guided. (Horney, 1945, p. 51)

It should be noted that, like the 10 neurotic needs, these adjustments to other people also are based on basic anxiety that is, in turn, based on basic hostility. So, although a person may adjust to basic anxiety by **moving toward people** and by apparently seeking love and affection, the person is still basically hostile. Thus the compliant person's friendliness is superficial and is based on repressed aggressiveness.

Moving Against People. In most ways, this person is the opposite of the compliant type. This adjustment pattern combines the neurotic needs for power, for exploitation of others, for prestige, and for personal achievement. This person, whom Horney called the **hostile type,** seems to say, "If I have power, no one can hurt me" (Horney, 1937, p. 84):

> Any situation or relationship is looked at from the standpoint of "What can I get out of it?"—whether it has to do with money, prestige, contacts, or ideas. The person himself is consciously or semiconsciously convinced that everyone acts this way, and so what counts is to do it more efficiently than the rest. (Horney, 1945, p. 65)

The hostile type is capable of acting polite and friendly, but it is always a means to an end. Many people would consider newspaper mogul Conrad Black typical of this adjustment pattern. When Black ran the Southam newspaper chain, it was criticized for swallowing up smaller newspapers in its growth.

Moving Away from People.   This adjustment pattern includes the neurotic needs for self-sufficiency, independence, perfection, and unassailability. This person, whom Horney called the **detached type,** seems to be saying, "If I withdraw, nothing can hurt me" (Horney, 1937, p. 85):

> What is crucial is their inner need to put emotional distance between themselves and others. More accurately, it is their conscious and unconscious determination not to get emotionally involved with others in any way, whether in love, fight, co-operation, or competition. They draw around themselves a kind of magic circle which no one may penetrate. (Horney, 1945, p. 75)

As with the 10 neurotic needs, the normal person uses all three adjustments to other people, depending on which one is appropriate at the time. Neurotic people cannot. They emphasize one of the three adjustments at the expense of the other two. This causes further anxiety because all humans at various times need to be aggressive, to be compliant, and to be detached or withdrawn. The lopsided development of the neurotic causes further anxiety, which in turn causes further lopsided development. Thus we have the vicious circle again.

Note that the three adjustment patterns are basically incompatible. For example, one cannot move toward people and away from people at the same time. For both the neurotic and the normal person, the three adjustment patterns are in conflict with each other. For the normal person, however, the conflict is not as emotionally charged as it is for the neurotic. Therefore, the normal person has far greater flexibility, being able to move from one adjustment mode to another as conditions change. The neurotic person must meet all of life's problems using only one of the three adjustment patterns whether that pattern is appropriate or not. It follows that the neurotic person is far less flexible and is therefore less effective in dealing with life's problems than the normal person is.

Real and Idealized Self

According to Horney, each human is born with a healthy **real self** that is conducive to normal personality growth. If people live in accordance with their real selves, they are on the road to **self-realization,** which means they will approximate their full potential and live in harmony with their fellow humans:

> You need not, and in fact cannot, teach an acorn to grow into an oak tree, but when given a chance, its intrinsic potentialities will develop. Similarly, the human individual, given a chance, tends to develop his particular human potentialities. He will develop then the unique alive forces of his real self: the clarity and depth of his own feelings, thoughts, wishes, interests; the ability to tap his own resources, the strength of his will power; the special capacities or gifts he may have; the faculty to express himself, and to relate himself to others with his spontaneous feelings. All this will in time enable him to find his set of values and his aims in life. In short, he will grow, substantially undiverted, toward *self-realization*. And that is why I speak . . . of the *real self* as that central inner force, common to all human beings and yet unique in each, which is the deep source of growth. (Horney, 1950, p. 17)

If children experience loving satisfaction of their biological and security needs, they develop in accordance with their real selves and become normal, flexible, productive adults. If, however, the basic evil is experienced, children become alienated from their real selves. Such children view themselves as lowly and despicable; why else would they have suffered the abuse they did? This distorted view of one's self as unworthy displaces the real self as a frame of reference for living. Such a person creates an **idealized self** that has little relationship to the real self.

According to Horney, when a person lives in accordance with an illusionary, idealized self instead of the real self, he or she is neurotic. The neurotic uses his or her idealized self as an escape from his or her real self, which is viewed negatively. Unlike the real self, the idealized self is an unrealistic, immutable dream.

When a person's life is directed by an unrealistic self-image, that person is driven by what *should be,* rather than what is. For example, the increase in the incidence of eating disorders has been attributed in part to the change in society's image of the ideal female body—athletic, beautiful, and slim. Due to pervasive media portrayals, many young women have struggled with their weight in an effort to live up to these ideals, an image they believe they *should* achieve and fiercely maintain. A study of more than 1700 Ontario schoolgirls suggests that a disturbingly large number of adolescent girls are on the path toward the development of an eating disorder such as anorexia or bulimia nervosa (Jones, Bennet, Olmstead, Lawson, & Rodin, 2001). Horney referred to the drive for perfection as the **tyranny of the should:**

> Forget about the disgraceful creature you actually are; this is how you should be; and to be this idealized self is all that matters. You should be able to endure everything, to understand everything, to like everybody, to be always productive—to mention only a few of these inner dictates. Since they are inexorable, I call them "the tyranny of the should." (1950, pp. 64–65)

This young woman keeps herself thin in a struggle to live up to an idealized self-image; Horney would say she is driven by the "tyranny of the should."

The neurotic is locked into the illusion of the ideal self, an illusion that does not reflect reality and one that tends to be unchanging. The more intensely the neurotic chases the ideal, the further the person is driven from the real self and the more intense the neurosis becomes. Horney (1945) explained:

> A person builds up an idealized image of himself because he cannot tolerate himself as he actually is. The image apparently counteracts this calamity; but having placed himself on a pedestal, he can tolerate his real self still less and starts to rage against it, to despise himself and to chafe under the yoke of his own unattainable demands upon himself. He wavers then between self-adoration and self-contempt, between his idealized image and his despised image, with no solid middle ground to fall back on. (p. 112)

For such a person, the only hope is a well-trained analyst or a highly disciplined self-analysis. (Horney's procedures for self-analysis are discussed later in this chapter.)

Normal people, conversely, have dreams, but they are realistic and changeable. Normal people experience both success and failure and both influence changes in their aspirations. Neurotic people experience mainly failure, because their ideals tend to be incompatible with their real selves. The feelings that neurotics experience cannot provide meaningful feedback concerning the effectiveness of their interactions with the environment and with people because those feelings are not genuine. The neurotic "feels what he *should* feel, wishes what he *should* wish, likes what he *should* like" (Horney, 1950, p. 159).

> When discrepancies between the actual self and the idealized one reach a point where tensions become unbearable, [the person] can no longer resort to anything within himself. The only thing left then is to run away from himself entirely and see everything as if it lay outside. (Horney, 1945, pp. 115–116)

Horney referred to this tendency to view everything of importance occurring outside oneself as **externalization,** defined as "the tendency to experience internal processes as if they occurred outside oneself and, as a rule, to hold these external factors responsible for one's difficulties. It has in common with idealization the purpose of getting away from the real self" (1945, p. 115).

Auxiliary Approaches to Artificial Harmony

According to Horney, neurotic people lie to themselves when they attempt to live their lives according to their idealized self-images and all of the "shoulds" associated with those images. To support that lie they need to externalize whatever real feelings they may have, another lie. To support those lies, or to control the damage done by them, neurotics need to employ other lies, and on it goes. For instance, a man may convince himself that he needs to work long hours to give his family a large house and exotic vacations. He creates a self-image of a devoted father sacrificing for his family, and denies any behaviours that do not fit this image. However, since he rarely sees his children, he is not close to them. He externalizes his feelings by saying his children reject him. But since this contradicts the picture of a loving father, he attributes his children's response to bad companions. When his wife does not agree with him, he accuses her of lax parenting. When his long hours of work do not bring him the satisfaction he is not receiving from his family, he concludes that he is treated badly at work. By now he is alienated from both family and workmates, but does not acknowledge any responsibility for his isolation. Horney (1945) explained:

> It is a commonplace that one lie usually leads to another, the second takes a third to bolster it, and so on till one is caught in a tangled web. Something of the sort is bound to happen in any situation in the life of an individual or group where a determination to go to the root of the matter is lacking. The patchwork may be of some help, but it will generate new problems which in turn require a new makeshift. So it is with neurotic attempts to solve the basic conflict; and here as elsewhere, nothing is of any real avail but a radical change in the conditions out of which the original difficulty arose. What the neurotic does instead—and cannot help doing—is to pile one pseudo solution upon another. (p. 131)

Horney described seven unconscious devices neurotics use to deal with the inevitable conflicts that arise when one displaces one's real self with an idealized self. Horney viewed these devices as additional lies that neurotics use in attempting to live an illusionary life.

There is a similarity among what Freud called ego-defence mechanisms, what Adler called safeguarding strategies, and what Horney called auxiliary approaches to artificial harmony.

BLIND SPOTS

This approach involves denying or ignoring certain aspects of experience because they are not in accordance with one's idealized self. For example, if one views oneself as extremely intelligent, one tends to overlook experiences that suggest one is not. Also, people who view themselves as Christlike will remain oblivious to any blatant acts of aggression in which they engage. Horney (1945) gave the following example:

> A patient . . . who had all the characteristics of the compliant type and thought of himself as Christlike, told me quite casually that at staff meetings he would often shoot one colleague after another with a little flick of his thumb. True enough, the destructive craving that prompted these figurative killings was at the time unconscious; but the point here is that shooting, which he dubbed "play," did not in the least disturb his Christlike image. (p. 132)

Horney's concept of **blind spots** is similar to Freud's ego-defence mechanism of denial of reality.

COMPARTMENTALIZATION

This involves dividing one's life into various components with different rules applying to each. For example, one set of rules applies to one's family life and another set to one's business life. Thus one can act in accordance with Christian principles at home and be ruthless in one's business dealings. The neurotic sees no conflict here because the situations are different. Horney (1945) elaborated on **compartmentalization:**

> There is a section for friends and one for enemies, one for the family and one for outsiders, one for professional and one for personal life, one for social equals and one for inferiors. Hence what happens in one compartment does not appear to the neurotic to contradict what happens in another. It is possible for a person to live that way only when, by reason of his conflicts, he has lost his sense of unity. (pp. 133–134)

RATIONALIZATION

According to Horney, **rationalization** is the type of self-deception that involves giving logical, plausible but inaccurate excuses to justify one's perceived weaknesses, failures, or inconsistencies. Compliant types must offer such excuses for acts of aggression, and hostile types must offer them for acts of kindness.

EXCESSIVE SELF-CONTROL

This is guarding against anxiety by controlling any expression of emotion. The goal here is to maintain rigid self-control at all costs. Horney (1945) elaborated:

> Persons who exert such control will not allow themselves to be carried away, whether by enthusiasm, sexual excitement, self-pity, or rage. In analysis they have the greatest difficulty in associating freely; they will not permit alcohol to lift their spirits and frequently prefer to endure pain rather than undergo anesthesia. In short, they seek to check all spontaneity. (p. 136)

ARBITRARY RIGHTNESS

Often the life of a neurotic is characterized by indecision, ambiguity, and doubt but the feelings generated by these characteristics are intolerable. By using **arbitrary rightness** as a protective device in ambiguous situations, the neurotic chooses one solution, one answer, one position and dogmatically declares that the problem is solved and the debate is over. The position taken by the neurotic becomes the "truth" and therefore cannot be challenged. The neurotic no longer needs to worry about what is right and wrong, or what is certain and uncertain. A mild version of arbitrary rightness may be responsible for the curious but consistent finding that people often learn more about an automobile or major appliance brand *after* their purchase. In other words, they are gathering information not to guide their choice but to prove to themselves that their decision was right.

ELUSIVENESS

Elusiveness is the opposite of arbitrary rightness. The elusive neurotic seldom makes a decision about anything. If one is not committed to anything, one cannot be wrong, and if one is not wrong, one cannot be criticized. Horney (1945) described the characteristics of the elusive neurotic:

> They are vicious one moment, sympathetic the next; at times overconsiderate, ruthlessly inconsiderate at others; domineering in some respects, self-effacing in others. They reach out for a dominating partner, only to change to a "doormat," then back to the former variety. After treating someone badly, they will be overcome by remorse, attempt to make amends, then feel like a "sucker" and turn to being abusive all over again. Nothing is quite real to them. (pp. 138–139)

CYNICISM

The elusive neurotic postpones making decisions, whereas the cynic does not believe in anything. Cynics take pleasure in pointing out the meaninglessness of the beliefs of others. Horney believed that this technique probably grew out of repeated failures associated with previous beliefs. By not believing anything, cynics are immune to the disappointment that comes from being committed to something shown to be false. Also, they are spared the difficult task of arriving at their own system of beliefs. They simply say *nothing* is worth believing. Also, by not accepting any moral values these neurotics justify their Machiavellian approach to interpersonal relationships. Horney (1945) said of the cynical neurotic, "All that counts is appearance. You can do as you please as long as you don't get caught. Everyone is a hypocrite who isn't fundamentally stupid" (p. 140).

Again, the difference between normal people and neurotics is one of degree. Normal people will undoubtedly use each of these secondary adjustment techniques at one time or another. Neurotics, however, will overuse one or more of them, thus reducing their flexibility and efficiency in solving life's inevitable problems.

The Psychology of Sex and Gender

Horney was trained as a Freudian psychoanalyst. It is not surprising, then, that her early work closely followed Freud's teaching. For example, in an address entitled "The Problem of the Monogamous Ideal" given in 1927, Horney analyzed the problems inherent in monogamous marriage from a strictly Freudian perspective. Her major point was that because males symbolically marry their mothers and females symbolically marry their fathers, the Oedipal complex necessarily manifests itself within marriage. On this point Horney quoted Freud: "The husband or the wife is always a substitute" (1967, p. 85). Insofar as a child learned to inhibit his or her incestuous desires for his or her parent, those inhibitions will manifest themselves in marriage:

> The manner and degree in which the influence of the early [Oedipal] situation will show itself [in marriage] will depend on the extent to which the incest prohibition still makes itself felt as a living force in the mind of the individual concerned. (Horney, 1967, p. 86)

According to Horney, the incest prohibition typically has the same result in marriage as it does in parent-child relationships. That is, "direct sexual aims give place to an affectionate attitude in which the sexual aim is inhibited" (Horney, 1967, p. 86). Thus Horney reached the conclusion that because maintaining a sexual relationship with one's spouse is symbolically the same as maintaining such a relationship with one's parent, the sexual aspect of marriage soon diminishes:

> I know personally of only one case in which this development [the transition from a sexual relationship to an affectionate one] has not supervened, the wife remaining permanently in love with her husband as a sexual object, and in this case the woman had, at the age of twelve, enjoyed actual sexual gratification with her father. (1967, p. 86)

According to Horney, the damage done by the resurrected Oedipal complex in marriage can be minimized by seeking a marital partner as different from one's mother or father as possible:

> It may be that the woman selected as wife must in no way recall the mother; in race or social origin, intellectual calibre or appearance she must present a certain contrast to the mother. This helps to explain why marriages prompted by prudence or contracted through the intervention of a third party tend to turn out relatively better than genuine

love matches. . . . We can perceive that there was a certain psychological wisdom in the institution of an intermediary to arrange marriages, such as obtains among the Eastern Jews. (1967, p. 87)

Thus perhaps the problems of monogamous marriage can be reduced but they cannot be eliminated: "It never has been and never will be possible to find any principle that will solve these conflicts of married life" (Horney, 1967, p. 98). For example, the possessiveness often displayed toward one's partner in marriage is "plainly [the] revival of the infantile wish to monopolize the mother or father" (1967, p. 91).

Horney's early analysis of marriage reflected many of the orthodox Freudian views of the male and female Oedipal complexes and therefore a belief that anatomy is destiny. Increasingly, however, Horney disagreed with Freud's contention that women are destined to possess certain personality traits simply because of their anatomy. She gradually developed the belief that cultural factors are more important than biological factors in explaining the personality characteristics of both men and women. Horney began writing articles on issues of special interest to women in 1923 and continued to do so until 1937. These articles, which also reflect Horney's transition from biological to cultural determinism, were compiled in *Feminine Psychology* (1967).

Arguably, Horney's "feminine psychology" was a founding influence in feminist thinking. According to recent research (Smith & De Man, 1996), Canadian men with conservative values were more likely than other men to hold negative views of feminism (as measured by their assessment of the attractiveness of the photograph of an unknown woman and the likelihood that she was a feminist). Among women, those with high trait anxiety are more likely to feel negatively about feminism. Mere exposure also makes a difference; subjects who had read feminist philosophy were more likely to have positive attitudes towards it.

Horney's Explanation of Penis Envy.   According to Freud, one of the most traumatic experiences in the psychological development of girls is their discovery that they do not possess penises, although boys do. They react to this discovery by wishing to have a penis and being envious of more fortunate males. In this biological area, females must settle only for symbols, thus they wish to have male children who will finally furnish them (symbolically) with their own penises. According to Freud, *anatomy is destiny* and women are destined to be inferior to men (or at least *feel* inferior) and have a contempt for their own sex because they lack penises.

Horney rejected the Freudian notion of penis envy and said instead that women often feel inferior to men because they are, indeed, *culturally* inferior. Because men control the power in culture, women may appear to wish to be masculine (to have a penis) when in reality they are merely attempting to participate in those desirable experiences over which men have control. Horney said, "Our whole civilization is a masculine civilization. The State, the laws, morality, religion, and the sciences are the creation of men" (1967, p. 55). Horney (1939) also said:

> The wish to be a man, as Alfred Adler has pointed out, may be the expression of a wish for all those qualities or privileges which in our culture are regarded as masculine, such as strength, courage, independence, success, sexual freedom, right to choose a partner. (p. 108)

Thus it is not penises that woman envy and desire but the ability to influence and to participate in their culture freely. Furthermore, Horney found that male patients often displayed an envy of motherhood at least as strong as women's supposed penis envy.

From the biological point of view woman has in motherhood, or in the capacity for motherhood, a quite indisputable and by no means negligible physiological superiority. This is most clearly reflected in the unconscious of the male psyche in the boy's intense envy of motherhood. . . . When one begins, as I did, to analyze men only after a fairly long experience of analyzing women, one receives a most surprising impression of the intensity of this envy of pregnancy, childbirth, and motherhood, as well as of the breasts and of the act of suckling. (Horney, 1967, pp. 60–61)

Why does psychoanalysis seem to understand men better than women and to paint a more favourable picture of men than women? Horney answered, "The reason for this is obvious. Psychoanalysis is the creation of a male genius, and almost all those who have developed his ideas have been men. It is only right and reasonable that they should evolve more easily a masculine psychology and understand more of the development of men than of women" (1967, p. 54). Horney (1967) continued:

Like all sciences and all valuations, the psychology of women has hitherto been considered only from the point of view of men. It is inevitable that the man's position of advantage should cause objective validity to be attributed to his subjective, affective relations to the woman . . . the psychology of women hitherto actually represents a deposit of the desires and disappointments of men. (p. 56)

Horney (1939) believed that Freud was a genius with limited intellectual vision:

It is one of the characteristics of a genius to have the power of vision and the courage to recognize current prejudices as such. In this sense as in others Freud certainly deserves to be called a genius. It is almost incredible how often he freed himself from venerable ways of thinking and looked upon psychic connections in a new light. It sounds like a banality to add that on the other hand no one, not even a genius, can entirely step out of his time, that despite his keenness of vision his thinking is in many ways bound to be influenced by the mentality of his time. (p. 37)

Psychotherapy

As far as psychotherapeutic techniques are concerned, Horney borrowed much from Freud. She commonly used dream analysis and free association. She used them, however, to discover which major adjustment technique a patient was using (moving toward, against, or away from people). She also believed strongly in Freud's concept of transference. "Were someone to ask me," she said, "which of Freud's discoveries I value most highly, I should say without any hesitation: it is his finding that one can utilize for therapy the patient's emotional reactions to the analyst and to the analytical situation" (1939, p. 154). For Horney, what was revealed through transference was, once again, the patient's major adjustment technique. Thus hostile types attempted to dominate the therapist; the detached type waited like a bystander while the therapist provided a miraculous cure; and the compliant type attempted to use his or her pain and suffering to gain sympathy and help from the therapist.

Horney saw the tendency for neurotics to externalize as a major obstacle in psychotherapy.

A patient with a general tendency to externalize offers peculiar difficulties in analysis. He comes to it as he would go to a dentist, expecting the analyst to perform a job that does not really concern him. He is interested in the neurosis of his wife, friend, brother, but not in his own. He talks about the difficult circumstances under which he lives and is reluctant to examine his share in them. If his wife were not so neurotic or his work so upsetting, he would be quite all right. For a considerable period he has no realization whatever that any emotional forces could possibly be operating within himself; he is afraid of ghosts, burglars, thunderstorms, of vindictive persons around him, of the political situation, but never of himself. He is at best interested in his problems for the intellectual or artistic pleasure they afford him. But as long as he is, so to speak, psychically nonexistent, he cannot possibly apply any insight he may gain to his actual living, and therefore in spite of his greater knowledge about himself can change very little. (Horney, 1945, pp. 129–130)

Goal of Psychotherapy

Like Adler, Horney believed that humans are born with a tendency toward positive growth but that this tendency may be interfered with by social forces. According to Horney, we strive toward *self-realization,* which involves being productive, truthful, and relating to fellow humans in a spirit of mutuality. If nothing interferes with this innate tendency, humans develop as normal, healthy persons. Horney (1945) compared her optimistic view of humans with Freud's pessimistic view:

> Freud's pessimism as regards neuroses and their treatment arose from the depths of his disbelief in human goodness and human growth. Man, he postulated, is doomed to suffer or to destroy. The instincts which drive him can only be controlled, or at best "sublimated." My own belief is that man has the capacity as well as the desire to develop his potentialities and become a decent human being, and that these deteriorate if his relationship to others and hence to himself is, and continues to be, disturbed. I believe that man can change and go on changing as long as he lives. (p. 19)

The goal of psychotherapy, then, is to bring the patient back in touch with his or her real self, that is, his or her capacity for positive growth and for warm, productive relationships with his or her fellow humans. The patient must first be convinced that he or she has been living in accordance with an illusion (idealized self) and that doing so made life more frustrating than it needed to be. Gradually patients must be steered in the direction of self-realization by showing them their capacity for cooperative human relations, their true talents and creative powers, and their responsibilities. It is not enough that patients come to understand these qualities intellectually; they must understand them *emotionally* as well. The insights gained must become a living truth within the patient.

Horney described the characteristics she hoped would emerge in patients if psychotherapy were effective (1945, pp. 241–242): *responsibility,* to make decisions in one's life, accept the consequences of those decisions, and recognize obligations to other people; *inner independence,* to live in accordance with one's own values and respect the right of others to do likewise; *spontaneity of feeling,* to be able to honestly experience one's own love, hate, happiness, sadness, fear, or desire; and *wholeheartedness,* "To be without pretense, to be emotionally sincere, to be able to put the whole of oneself into one's feelings, one's work, one's beliefs" (Horney, 1945, p. 242). When a person displays these characteristics, he or she is on the road to self-realization.

The goal of psychotherapy is not to create perfect human beings; rather, it is to help people who have been diverted from their self-realization process to become "real" people again. Real people have real problems, real anxiety, real failures, and real successes. Horney (1939) said, "The aim of analysis is not to render life devoid of risks and conflicts, but to enable an individual eventually to solve his problems himself" (p. 305).

Self-Analysis

Freud believed that to become an effective psychoanalyst one had to have intense training in psychoanalytic theory and then be psychoanalyzed oneself. With her book *Self-Analysis* (1942) Horney radically departed from Freudian tradition by claiming that individuals could engage in **self-analysis** if they were provided with proper knowledge and skills. Horney believed such knowledge could be partially acquired by reading the works of Freud and other analysts, such philosophers as Nietzsche and Schopenhauer, and such literary figures as Ibsen, Goethe, Shakespeare, and Dostoevsky. To assist in self-analysis, Horney (1942) presented her own theory concerning the origin of neuroses and the 10 neurotic trends or needs. She also provided numerous case studies in order to show how psychoanalysis typically proceeds and the complexities involved.

According to Horney, three main tasks confront patients engaged in either professional psychoanalysis or self-analysis:

> The first is to express himself as completely and frankly as possible. The second is to become aware of his unconscious driving forces and their influence on his life. And the third is to develop the capacity to change those attitudes that are disturbing his relations with himself and the world around him. (1942, p. 93)

The success of therapy is determined by the extent to which these difficult tasks are accomplished. Therefore, effective therapy requires from the patient "a good deal of determination, self-discipline, and active struggle" (1942, p. 112).

For both self- and professional analysis, honest, free association is vital: "The process of free association, of frank and unresolved self-expression, is the starting point and continuous basis of all analytic work—self-analysis as well as professional analysis" (1942, p. 225). Closely associated with the use of free association is the problem of resistance.

> Can a person overcome his own resistances? This is the real question upon the answer to which hinges the feasibility of self-analysis. . . . Whether the job can be done depends, of course, on the intensity of the resistances as well as on the strength of the incentive to overcome them. But the important question . . . is to what extent it can be done rather than whether it can be done at all. (1942, pp. 134–135)

And what about transference, the phenomenon so important in professional analysis? In self-analysis the professional analyst is absent and therefore cannot be responded to as if he or she were a significant figure in the patient's life. Horney believed similar information could be gained by a person engaged in self-analysis if he or she would carefully observe his or her social interactions:

> There remains the fact that the analyst is not merely an interpreting voice. He is a human being, and the human relationship between him and the patient is an important factor in the therapeutic process. [The analyst-patient relationship] presents a unique and specific opportunity for the patient to study, by observing his behavior with the analyst, what his typical behavior is toward other people in general. This advantage can be fully replaced if he learns to watch himself in his customary relationships. The expectations, wishes, fears, vulnerabilities, and inhibitions that he displays in his work with the analyst are not essentially different from those he displays in his relations with friends, lover, wife, children, employer, colleagues, or servants. If he is seriously intent upon recognizing the ways in which his peculiarities enter into all these relationships, ample opportunities for self-scrutiny are provided him by the mere fact that he is a social being. (1942, p. 135)

Freud, too, was aware that transference occurs in all human relationships: "Transference arises spontaneously in all human relationships just as it does between the patient and the physician" (Freud, 1910/1977, p. 51).

For Horney, then, effective self-analysis is certainly possible. How effective such analysis is, however, depends on the self-discipline and self-determination of the individual involved.

Comparison of Horney and Freud

EARLY CHILDHOOD EXPERIENCE

Both Freud and Horney thought early childhood experiences are extremely important—but for different reasons. Freud believed there are universal stages of development, and fixation at any particular stage strongly influences one's adult personality. For Horney, it is the child's relationship to the parents that is important, because it determines whether the child will develop basic anxiety.

UNCONSCIOUS MOTIVATION

Both Horney and Freud emphasized the importance of unconscious motivation. For Horney, it is repressed hostility that leads to basic anxiety, which leads to neurosis. Thus the basis of all neurotic behaviour is repressed basic hostility, which, of course, is unconscious.

BIOLOGICAL MOTIVATION

Freud emphasized biological motivation. To him, all conflicts are derived from attempts to satisfy biological drives—especially the sex drive. Horney de-emphasized biological motivation by stressing the importance of the child's need for a feeling of security. Thus we say that Freud's theory is biological and Horney's theory is social. For example, here is Horney's explanation of the Oedipus complex:

> If a child, in addition to being dependent on his parents, is grossly or subtly intimidated by them and hence feels that any expression of hostile impulses against them endangers his security, then the existence of such hostile impulses is bound to create anxiety. . . . The resulting picture may look exactly like what Freud describes as the Oedipus complex: passionate clinging to one parent and jealousy toward the other or toward anyone interfering with the claim of exclusive possession. . . . But the dynamic structure of these attachments is entirely different from what Freud conceives as the Oedipus complex. They are an early manifestation of neurotic conflicts rather than a primarily sexual phenomenon. (1939, pp. 83–84)

PSYCHOTHERAPY

Horney used Freud's methods of free association and dream analysis, and agreed with Freud on the importance of transference. Freud, however, used all of these concepts to uncover repressed traumatic memories whereas Horney used them to discover a neurotic's major adjustment technique. Also, whereas Freud discouraged analysis by individuals not professionally trained in psychoanalytic theory and technique, Horney actively encouraged self-analysis.

IS ANATOMY DESTINY?

Yes for Freud, no for Horney.

PROGNOSIS FOR PERSONALITY CHANGE

Freud believed that personality is formulated early in life, and major changes thereafter are extremely difficult to make. Horney agreed that personality is strongly influenced by early experiences but maintained that it remains changeable throughout life. Thus, she was more optimistic than Freud. "Our daring to name such high goals rests upon the belief that the human personality can change. It is not only the young child who is pliable. All of us retain the capacity to change, even to change in fundamental ways, as long as we live" (Horney, 1945, p. 242). Elsewhere Horney said:

> Albert Schweitzer uses the terms "optimistic" and "pessimistic" in the sense of "world and life affirmation" and "world and life negation." Freud's philosophy, in this deep sense, is a pessimistic one. Ours, with all its cognizance of the tragic elements in neurosis, is an optimistic one. (1950, p. 378)

Evaluation

EMPIRICAL RESEARCH

Most of the research supporting Horney's theory is indirect. Horney believed that behaviour disorders result when people attempt to live their lives in accordance with their idealized selves. Such people believe they are brilliant, great lovers, paragons of virtue, unselfish, or courageous. They also see the source of everything important in their lives as external to themselves (externalization). In other words, Horney believed a correlation exists between the irrational beliefs people have about themselves and psychopathology. Horney's suspicion has been confirmed in several areas (Ingram, 2001; Mitchell, 1998). For example, people with several irrational beliefs about themselves are more likely to be depressed (Dobson & Breiter, 1983); to be socially ineffective (Hayden & Nasby, 1977); to have unhappy marriages (Eidelson & Epstein, 1982); and to be ineffective problem solvers (Schill, Monroe, Evans, & Ramanaiah, 1978). Furthermore, the rational-emotive therapy developed by Albert Ellis is based on the assumption that psychopathology results from the irrational beliefs held by patients. The rational-emotive therapist actively challenges the patient's erroneous beliefs and replaces them with more realistic thoughts and feelings. Considerable evidence exists that such therapy is effective (Ellis & Greiger, 1977; Smith, 1983).

Horney believed that culture plays a major role in determining the types of problems people experience and, indeed, their personalities. Canada's multicultural population offers fertile ground for evaluating the influence of culture on personality. Canadian researchers have taken up the challenge, with investigations into many aspects of this question, including cross-cultural personality assessment (Paunonen & Ashton, 1998), a comparison of European Canadian and First Nations' ethnic identity and group attitudes (Corenblum & Stephan, 2001), and context-bound measurement of orientation toward the self or toward others (Lay et al., 1998).

Cultural psychologists believe that the self is born from the interaction between the person and a set of culturally derived beliefs, values, institutions, customs, and practices. Because self inherently contains cultural meaning, self and culture remain intertwined. Horney, along with other personality theorists, emphasized the discrepancies between people's real and idealized selves, and between their view of themselves and their real selves. What role does culture play in shaping people's concepts both of what they are and of what they should be? Will people of different cultures show a different degree of self-discrepancy: that is, the gap between a person's self-assessment and his or her ideal?

To explore this question, Darrin Lehman of the University of British Columbia and his colleagues compared self-discrepancies among undergraduates who were European-Canadian, Japanese, or Canadian-born of Asian ancestry. (Heine & Lehman, 1997, 1999; Heine, Takata, & Lehman, 2000). Students first completed a general personality test, and indicated how important they thought each personality trait was. European-Canadians rated themselves higher than Japanese students; the differences were greater on traits that the students considered important. Canadian-born Asian students fell in between. Japanese students showed the greatest discrepancy between their actual selves and their ideal self-images; they were more likely to focus on their perceived inadequacies. The study confirmed that impression that Japanese people view themselves less positively than Westerners. In contrast, positive self-distortions (that is, having an unrealistically favourable self-image) may be more common among Westerners. For a Westerner, large discrepancies between the way one is and the way one wants to be may be debilitating; a self-enhancing bias is protective. However, Japanese culture, with its greater emphasis on interdependence, seems to encourage such discrepancies. These findings support the importance of culture in personality development.

CRITICISMS

Unoriginal Contributions.   Like Freud, Horney emphasized the importance of early childhood experience, unconscious motivation, and defence mechanisms. Also like Freud, she used free association, dream analysis, and the analysis of transference in her approach to psychoanalysis. Like Adler, Horney de-emphasized the biological origins of behaviour disorders and instead emphasized their social origins. Adler's notion of safeguarding strategies is similar to Horney's auxiliary approaches to artificial harmony; both mask the person's real self. Both Horney and Adler believed that when a culture is male dominated, women will often attempt to become more masculine in order to gain power. Finally, both Jung and Horney employed the concept of self-realization, which in both cases meant the natural impulse toward healthy personality development. One way to view Horney's theory, then, is as a blending of the theories of Freud, Jung, and Adler.

Little Empirical Support.   Often a personality theory contains language and concepts that are too nebulous to verify empirically. Furthermore, those personality theorists who were also clinicians claim that the true value of their theories is determined by subsequent enhancement of the therapeutic process. For them, empirical verification using controlled experimental procedures is irrelevant. Both of the preceding statements are true for Horney's theory although, as we have seen, some indirect empirical verification of the theory exists.

Disregard of Healthy People.   Although Horney did discuss the natural tendency toward self-realization, she concentrated almost exclusively on understanding people whose tendency toward self-realization had been disrupted, namely, neurotics. Paris

(1994) disagrees with this criticism, however, saying instead that Horney's mature theory had much in common with the humanistic theories of Rogers (see chapter 14) and Maslow (see chapter 15), which are primarily concerned with normal, healthy individuals.

CONTRIBUTIONS

Original Ideas.   Although some have criticized Horney for borrowing too heavily from Freud, Jung, and Adler, others see her blending of these (and other) theories as a highly original and important contribution to the understanding of personality. For example, her notions of the tyranny of the should and the major neurotic adjustment techniques, as well as her discussion of what happens when one becomes alienated from his or her real self, have had a significant influence on modern personality theory and therapeutic techniques (see, for example, Carl Rogers, chapter 14).

Self-Analysis.   Directly contrary to Freud and the other psychoanalysts of the time, Horney believed that many people could and should analyze themselves, and she hoped her writings would help them to do so. Horney's book *Self-Analysis* (1942) was one of the first self-help books in psychology, and it created quite a controversy. Now it is generally believed many troubled people can improve their situations if given the proper information. However, most therapists believe, as Horney did, that severely disturbed people must receive professional treatment.

The Psychology of Sex and Gender.   Horney's thoughts on feminine psychology were among the first in an area that is popular today. Although Horney was strongly influenced by Freudian theory and agreed with much of it, she disagreed with almost every conclusion that Freud reached about women. For a psychoanalyst of the time, departing from Freudian dogma was no easy matter. Horney, and others who dared to contradict the master, were excommunicated from the psychoanalytic community, just as if they had violated religious canons. Perhaps it was her observations as a child of the effects on her father of blind belief in religious dogma that made her willing to challenge Freud.

SUMMARY

1. Though trained as a Freudian, Karen Horney departed from Freudian tradition in several significant ways. Horney stressed early parent-child relationships, and suggested children would experience basic hostility toward the parents if they react to the child with indifference, superficiality, or aggression. The child's repressed hostility toward parents is projected onto the world in general, becoming basic anxiety or feelings of being alone and helpless in a hostile world.

2. To combat basic anxiety, people adopt one of three major adjustment patterns relative to others—they move toward, against, or away from them. Normal people display all these patterns at times, depending on the circumstances. Neurotic people are dominated by one pattern; the other two go unfulfilled, generating more conflict and anxiety. For neurotics, the real self is replaced by the idealized self, and their lives are governed by a list of unrealistic "shoulds" instead of goals based on their own experiences.

3. Horney also postulated the following secondary adjustment techniques: blind spots (ignoring inconsistencies in one's life), compartmentalization (applying different values to different situations), rationalization (giving logical but erroneous explanations for wrongdoings or shortcomings), excessive self-control (minimizing

failure by living with a narrow and predictable range of events), arbitrary rightness (taking a stand equated with truth and unchallengeable), elusiveness (avoiding failure by postponing decisions), and cynicism (believing nothing is worth commitment).

4. Horney said that what had been written about the female personality to date largely reflected male biases and misunderstandings. Women often do aspire to be more masculine, not because of penis envy, but rather because masculinity in a male-dominated society is the only way to gain power. Thus, psychological differences between men and women result from cultural pressures rather than biological destiny.

5. Psychotherapy is intended to confront the patient with the fact that he or she is attempting to live an illusion (the idealized self). Once this is accomplished, the therapist can help the patient to discover his or her real self, beginning the road to self-realization. Though Horney agreed with Freud that much behaviour is unconsciously motivated, she disagreed on the importance of biological motivation—she saw the social need for security as much more important than the need for biological satisfaction.

6. Horney's theory is supported by the positive correlation between the number of people's irrational beliefs about themselves and their tendency to be depressed and socially ineffective, to be poor problem solvers, and to have unhappy marriages. Albert Ellis' rational-emotive therapy has demonstrated that patients show improvement when their irrational beliefs are actively challenged and replaced by more realistic beliefs and feelings. Research on self-discrepancies among Canadian and Japanese students highlight the adaptiveness of self-enhancement in some and self-effacement in others, depending upon cultural expectations.

7. Horney's theory has been criticized for being unoriginal, for stimulating little empirical research, and for ignoring the personality development of healthy people. Others praise Horney's creative blending of Freudian, Jungian, and Adlerian theory, her encouragement of self-analysis, and her elaboration of feminine psychology.

EXPERIENTIAL EXERCISES

1. Describe your personality in terms of Horney's major adjustment techniques. Do you move toward, against, or away from people with about equal frequency? If not, which of the three do you emphasize? Using Horney's theory, attempt to explain why you use the major adjustment techniques the way you do.

2. Horney said that each person is born with a tendency toward self-realization, that is, toward normal, healthy growth. The tendency toward self-realization, however, can be disrupted by basic evil, in which case the real self is displaced by an idealized self. The person living in accordance with an idealized self is, according to Horney, living an illusion. Are you living in accordance with your tendency toward self-realization or is your life governed by an idealized self? Explain.

3. Give an example of your use of externalization. Also, give examples of how you have used blind spots, compartmentalization, rationalization, excessive self-control, arbitrary rightness, elusiveness, and cynicism.

4. Respond to Freud's contention that "anatomy is destiny" from Horney's viewpoint and then from your own.

DISCUSSION QUESTIONS

1. List a few examples of what Horney called the neurotic needs or trends, and describe the difference between the normal person's adjustment to these needs and that of the neurotic individual.

2. Describe the difference between the real and the idealized self. Explain the difference in the relationship between the real and the idealized selves for the normal person versus the neurotic person. Include in your answer a discussion of Horney's concept of the tyranny of the should.

3. Give a brief definition and an example of each of the following secondary adjustment techniques: blind spots, compartmentalization, rationalization, excessive self-control, externalization, arbitrary rightness, elusiveness, and cynicism.

4. Summarize Horney's reaction to the Freudian contention that women experience penis envy.

5. Compare Horney's theory of personality with Freud's theory.

KEY TERMS

Arbitrary rightness, p. 115
Basic anxiety, p. 107
Basic evil, p. 106
Basic hostility, p. 107
Blind spots, p. 114
Compartmentalization, p. 114
Compliant type person, p. 110
Detached type person, p. 111
Elusiveness, p. 115
Externalization, p. 113
Hostile type person, p. 110

Idealized self, p. 112
Moving toward people, p. 110
Neurotic trends, p. 108
Rationalization, p. 115
Real self, p. 111
Safety, p. 106
Satisfaction, p. 106
Self-analysis, p. 120
Self-realization, p. 111
Tyranny of the should, p. 112

6 Erik H. Erikson

Biographical Sketch

Erik Erikson was born near Frankfurt, Germany, on June 15, 1902. His father abandoned his mother before Erikson was born, and three years later she married Erikson's pediatrician, Dr. Theodore Homburger. The fact that Dr. Homburger was not Erik's biological father was kept a secret throughout his childhood, but he still developed the feeling that somehow he did not belong to his parents and fantasized about being the son of "much better parents." Erikson used his stepfather's surname for many years and wrote his first articles using the name Erik Homburger. It was only when he became a U.S. citizen in 1939 that he changed his last name to Erikson. The circumstances of Erikson's birth created a problem in adopting an appropriate last name: "Erik's birth had resulted from an extramarital liaison of his mother's, and Erikson kept her secret until he was 68" (Hopkins, 1995, p. 796) Because "Erikson" was not the name of his biological father, his reason for choosing this name is a matter of speculation:

> One story has it that his children were troubled by the American tendency to confuse "Homburger" with "hamburger," and that he asked one of his sons for an alternative; being Erik's son, he proposed Erikson. For Erikson's children such a name would be in accord with Scandinavian custom; but for Erikson it connoted that he was his own father, self-created. The name also harked back to his identifying with the Danish father who had abandoned him. (Roazen, 1976, pp. 98–99)

In any case, "Homburger" was reduced to the middle initial of the name that Erikson then used to identify his works.

Erikson's sense of not belonging to his family was amplified by the fact that his mother, Karla Abrahamsen Homburger, was Lutheran and Danish and his stepfather, Theodore Homburger, was Jewish. Erikson himself was tall, with blue eyes and blond

Erik H. Erikson

hair. In school he was referred to as a Jew, whereas at his stepfather's temple, he was called a "goy" (the Yiddish word for gentile). Is it any wonder that the concept of *identity crisis* later became one of Erikson's most important theoretical concerns? Erikson was well aware of this influence on his later work: "No doubt my best friends will insist that I needed to name [the identity] crisis and to see it in everybody else in order to really come to terms with it in myself" (1975b, p. 26).

After graduating from a gymnasium (roughly equivalent to a Canadian high school), he rebelled against his stepfather's desire for him to become a physician by studying art and roaming freely around Europe. Generally, Erikson was not a good student in school but did have artistic ability. Erikson (1964) said, "I was an artist then, which can be a European euphemism for a young man with some talent, but nowhere to go" (p. 20).

The year 1927 was a turning point in Erikson's life. In that year, at the age of 25, he was invited to Vienna by an old school friend, Peter Blos, to work at a small school attended by the children of Freud's patients and friends. He was hired first as an artist, then as a tutor, and finally, he was asked by Anna Freud if he would like to be trained as a child analyst. Erikson accepted the offer and received his psychoanalytic training under Anna Freud, for which she charged him $7 per month. The training lasted three years and was conducted almost daily. Anna Freud's particular brand of psychoanalytic theory, which differed in several ways from her father's, had a profound influence on Erikson, and in 1964 he showed his appreciation by dedicating his book *Insight and Responsibility* to her.

When Erikson joined the Freudian circle, Freud was 71 years old, and Erikson knew him only informally. It was only gradually that Erikson came to appreciate Freud's accomplishments. At the time, however, Erikson deeply appreciated the warm reception given to him by those associated with the psychoanalytic movement. The situation was perfectly suited to Erikson. He was asked to join a group of people who were still considered to be outside the medical establishment. By joining this group of "outcasts," he could maintain his identity as the "outsider." Conversely, because the group's function was to help disturbed people, he could at least indirectly satisfy his stepfather's desire for him to become a physician.

His graduation from the gymnasium, a Montessori diploma, and his training as a child analyst are the only formal training Erikson ever had. Because Erikson earned no advanced degrees, he is a clear example of Freud's contention that one need not be trained as a physician to become a psychoanalyst. Erikson graduated from the Vienna Psychoanalytic Institute in 1933. The fact that Erikson was granted full (rather than associate) membership in the Vienna Psychoanalytic Institute also made him a member of the International Psychoanalytic Association.

In 1929, Erikson met Joan Serson, a Canadian-born American student with a master's degree in sociology from the University of Pennsylvania. Joan was in Europe collecting data for her doctoral dissertation on the origins of modern dance. She was also being psychoanalyzed by Ludwig Jekels, one of Freud's early followers. Erikson and Serson married on April 1, 1930, and Joan became Erikson's intellectual partner for the remainder of his long life. In 1933, in response to the increasing Nazi threat, the Eriksons (now with two sons) moved first to Denmark and then to Boston, Massachusetts, where he entered private practice as a child analyst.

Besides his private practice, Erikson was a research fellow under the supervision of Henry Murray in the Department of Neuropsychiatry at Harvard Medical School. Erikson enrolled at Harvard as a Ph.D. candidate in psychology but dropped out of the program within a few months. Perhaps because he had already been voted a full member of the Vienna Psychoanalytic Institute, he considered further formal education unnecessary.

Between 1936 and 1939, Erikson held a position in the Department of Psychiatry at the Yale University Medical School, where he worked with both normal and emotionally disturbed children. At this time Erikson came in contact with anthropologists Ruth Benedict and Margaret Mead, and in 1938 he went on a field trip to the Pine Ridge Reservation in South Dakota to observe the child-rearing practices of the Sioux Indians. Anthropological studies such as this one increased Erikson's awareness of the importance of social and cultural variables to personality development—an awareness that ultimately permeated his entire theory of personality.

In 1939, Erikson moved to California, where he became a research associate at the Institute of Child Welfare at the University of California. By 1942, he was a professor of psychology but lost his professorship in 1950 when he refused to sign a loyalty oath. Later, when the University of California found him "politically reliable," he was offered his job back but refused to accept it because other professors had been dismissed for the same "crime."

In 1950, the same year he left the University of California, Erikson published his well-known book *Childhood and Society,* which strongly emphasized the importance of social and cultural factors to human development. This book also greatly elaborated the functions of the ego, launching what is now called *ego psychology*. We have more to say about ego psychology later in this chapter.

Between 1951 and 1960, Erikson lived in Stockbridge, Massachusetts, where he was both a senior staff consultant at the Austen Riggs Center (a treatment centre for disturbed adolescents) and a professor in the Department of Psychiatry at the University of Pittsburgh Medical School.

In 1960, Erikson returned to the Harvard Medical School, where he was a professor of human development and taught "The Human Life Cycle," an extremely popular undergraduate course. According to Erikson, his students renamed this course "from womb to tomb." At Harvard, Erikson also led a seminar in which the lives of famous people and historical figures were analyzed. By now, colleges and universities throughout the world were inviting him to lecture. In 1962, he travelled to India to conduct a seminar on the life cycle. While there he became intensely interested in Mahatma Gandhi, whose nonviolent protest against British imperialism dramatically changed the British Empire.

As we see in this chapter, Erikson made several notable contributions to psychology. One is the application of his theory of development to the study of major historical figures. Such an endeavour has been labelled **psychohistory**. Erikson has analyzed such historical figures as Adolf Hitler, Maxim Gorky, Martin Luther, and Mahatma Gandhi. Erikson's book *Gandhi's Truth* (1969) was awarded both a Pulitzer Prize and a National Book Award in philosophy and religion.

Throughout most of his writings, Erikson insisted that a strong relationship exists between his theory and Freud's, but one gets the impression this is mostly a tribute to Freud. Although it is true there are some similarities between the theories, the differences between the two are more important. Erikson's theory, for example, is more optimistic about the human capacity for positive growth. We compare Erikson's theory to Freud's throughout this chapter, but for now we point out one feature common to both theories. Both have transcended the bounds of psychology and have influenced a variety of other fields such as religion, philosophy, sociology, anthropology, and history.

In 1970, Erikson retired from Harvard and the Erikson family divided its time between Marin County, California and Cape Cod, Massachusetts. In 1987, Erikson moved back to Cambridge after the founding of the Erik Erikson Center, which was associated with Cambridge Hospital and the Harvard Medical School. Erikson died on May 12, 1994 in Harwich, Massachusetts. He was survived by his wife Joan and three children (Kai Erikson, Jon Erikson, and Sue Erikson Bloland).

Anatomy and Destiny

The closest Erikson came to traditional Freudian theory is in the chapter "The Theory of Infantile Sexuality" in his book *Childhood and Society* (1950/1985). In this chapter, Erikson summarized his research on 10-, 11-, and 12-year-old boys and girls in California. The children were instructed by Erikson to "construct on the table an exciting scene out of an imaginary moving picture" (p. 98). The children were to use toy figures and various-shaped blocks. Much to Erikson's surprise, in over a year and a half, about 150 children constructed about 450 scenes, and not more than about six were scenes from a movie. For example, only a few of the toy figures were given names of actors or actresses. But if the children were not following Erikson's suggestion in creating their scenes, what was guiding their activities? The answer to this question came when Erikson noted that the common themes or elements in the scenes created by boys were quite different from those created by girls.

Erikson observed, for example, that the scenes created by girls typically included an enclosure that sometimes had an elaborate entrance and contained such elements as people and animals. The scenes created by girls tended to be static and peaceful, although often their scenes were interrupted by animals or dangerous men. The scenes created by boys often had high walls around them and had many objects such as high towers or cannons protruding from them. The scenes created by boys also had relatively more people and animals outside the enclosure. The boys' scenes were dynamic and included fantasies about the collapse or downfall of their creation.

Erikson concluded that the scenes created by the children were outward manifestations of their genital apparatus. This tendency was so reliable that Erikson was surprised and uneasy when a departure from it occurred. For example, Erikson stated:

> One day, a boy arranged . . . a "feminine" scene, with wild animals as intruders, and I felt that uneasiness which I assume often betrays to an experimenter what his innermost expectations are. And, indeed, on departure and already at the door, the boy exclaimed, "There is something wrong here," came back, and with an air of relief arranged the animals along a tangent to the circle of furniture. Only one boy built and left such a configuration, and this twice. He was of obese and effeminate build. As thyroid treatment began to take effect, he built, in his third construction (a year and a half after the first) the highest and most slender of all towers—as was to be expected of a boy. (1950/1985, p. 101)

It should be emphasized, however, that Erikson never said that biology was the *only* factor that determines how a person perceives and acts on the world. Social factors are also important. We are instructed by our culture how boys and girls are expected to act and think, and these cultural dictates obviously influence our outlook:

> Am I saying, then, that "anatomy is destiny"? Yes, it is destiny, insofar as it determines not only the range and configuration of physiological functioning and its limitations but also, to an extent, personality configurations. The basic modalities of woman's commitment and involvement naturally also reflect the ground plan of her body. . . . [But] a human being, in addition to having a body, is *somebody,* which means an indivisible personality and a defined member of a group. . . . In other words, anatomy, history, and personality are our combined destiny. (Erikson, 1968, p. 285)

Needless to say, Erikson's views of male-female differences have not gone uncriticized. One reaction came from Naomi Weisstein (1975) in her article, "Psychology Constructs the Female, or the Fantasy Life of the Male Psychologist (with Some Attention to the Fantasies of His Friends, the Male Biologist and the Male Anthropologist)." Weisstein argued that psychology does not know what either men or women are really like because it deals only with the cultural stereotypes of both. She insisted that what have been called biologically determined differences in behaviour between the sexes are really better explained as the result of social expectations. She concluded that insofar as there are behavioural differences between the sexes, they are the result of cultural expectations and the prejudices of male social scientists.

Paula Caplan (1979) also criticized Erikson's contention that the type of sex organs one possesses influences how one interacts with the world. She was especially critical of Erikson's assertion that a woman's kinesthetic experience of her own "inner space," that is, of her own uterus, determines even partially her personality characteristics. It was Erikson's belief that it is the girl's experience of this "inner space" that leads to the kinds of configurations shown during his play experiments. Caplan (1979) pointed out that Erikson's claim is impossible:

> The most important physiological factor to take into account is that there is no inner space. The walls of the uterus touch each other, as do the walls of the vagina. They are open only when separated by and filled with substances, as in intercourse or pregnancy. If girls' play constructions were to represent their uteri, they should look more like folded flapjacks than enclosures. Further, although the penis is external and erectable, so is the clitoris, although to a lesser degree. The movement of the ovum is as important for fertilization as that of the sperm, and although not as highly mobile as the sperm, both ovum and uterus move (the uterus contracts often in orgasm and delivery and certainly expands in pregnancy). So differences in play constructions should, if biologically based, be different in degree rather than in kind. (pp. 101–102)

Caplan repeated much of Erikson's research on play constructions; however, she used preschool children as her subjects. She justified using children who were younger than those used by Erikson because of Erikson's claim that gender differences in personality manifest themselves throughout the life span. Caplan (1979) summarized her results: "No sex differences were found in the frequency of constructions of simple enclosures, enclosures only in conjunction with elaborate structures or traffic lanes, height of structures, construction of a tower, or construction of a structure, building, tower, or street—all categories in which Erikson had reported sex differences" (p. 105). Caplan interpreted her results as indicating that there are no sex-determined personality characteristics. If these characteristics exist, they would be evident in her young subjects. Rather, she said, the personality differences between men and women that emerge later are due exclusively to differential socialization practices. Therefore, anatomy is definitely *not* destiny.

Erikson reacted to criticisms such as those just discussed in his essay entitled "Once More the Inner Space" (1975a). Essentially he said that (1) psychoanalytic truths are often disturbing and he can understand people being upset by them, and (2) biology is only one strong determinant of personality; culture is another.

Another important point should be made about Erikson's view of sexual differences. He did not say that males are better than females or vice versa. Rather, he said that there are important differences between males and females and that male traits and female traits complement each other. In some cultures, such as ours, the male role has been glorified relative to the female role but Erikson found this unfortunate. He believed that both men and women are hurt by current cultural stereotypes. Erikson stated that "only a renewal of social creativity can liberate both men and women from reciprocal roles which, in fact, have exploited both" (1975a, p. 237).

Ego Psychology

Erikson's view of the relationship between biology and personality exemplifies a point on which he was in close agreement with Freud. In this section, we review the part of Erikson's theory that most disagrees with Freud's theory.

According to Freud, the job of the ego is to find realistic ways of satisfying the impulses of the id while not offending the moral demands of the superego. Freud viewed the ego as operating "in the service of the id" and as the "helpless rider of the id horse." The ego, according to this view, has no needs of its own. The id is the energizer of the entire personality, and everything a person does is ultimately reduced to its demands. As we saw in chapter 2, Freud viewed enterprises such as art, science, and religion as mere displacements or sublimations of basic desires of the id.

The first shift away from Freud's position came from his daughter Anna in her book *The Ego and the Mechanisms of Defense* (1936/1966). Anna Freud suggested that instead of emphasizing the importance of the id, psychoanalysis should "acquire the fullest possible knowledge of all the three institutions [that is, id, ego, and superego] of which we believe the psychic personality to be constituted and to learn what are their relations to one another and to the outside world" (1936/1966, pp. 4–5). Erikson was obviously influenced by his teacher, Anna Freud, but he believed she did not go far enough.

Erikson gave the ego properties and needs of its own. The ego, according to Erikson, may have started out in the service of the id but, in the process of serving it, developed its own functions. For example, it is the ego's job to organize one's life and to assure continuous harmony with one's physical and social environment. The ego is the source of self-awareness and identity. This conception emphasizes the influence of the ego on healthy growth and adjustment. This contrasts sharply with the Freudian view that the ego's sole job is to minimize the id's discomfort. Because Erikson stressed the autonomy of the ego, his theory exemplifies what has come to be called **ego psychology**. Although, as we saw in chapter 4, there are those who credit Alfred Adler with the founding of ego psychology, it is an honour generally given to Erikson, perhaps because he actually emphasized the term *ego* in his theory. Indeed, Erikson's entire theory can be viewed as a description of how the ego gains or loses strength as a function of developmental experiences.

Epigenetic Principle, Crises, Ritualizations, and Ritualisms

EPIGENETIC PRINCIPLE

Erikson saw life as consisting of eight stages, which stretch from birth to death. According to Erikson, the *sequence* of the eight stages is genetically determined and is unalterable. Such a genetically determined sequence of development is said to follow the **epigenetic principle,** a term Erikson borrowed from biology. Erikson described this principle as follows:

> Whenever we try to understand growth, it is well to remember the *epigenetic principle* which is derived from the growth of organisms *in utero*. Somewhat generalized, this principle states that anything that grows has a ground plan, and that out of this ground plan the parts arise, each part having its special ascendancy, until all parts have arisen to form a functioning whole. (1968, p. 92)

Although, according to Erikson, personality unfolds across eight stages of development, all eight developmental stages are present in rudimentary form at birth. As each personality characteristic unfolds, it is incorporated into characteristics that developed during previous stages, thus creating a new configuration of personality characteristics. In other words, each stage, as it unfolds, builds on those that preceded it. Erikson (1950/1985) said, "The strength acquired at any stage is tested by the necessity to transcend it in such a way that the individual can take chances in the next stage with what was more vulnerably precious in the previous one" (p. 263). According to the epigenetic principle, the personality characteristics that become salient during any particular stage of development exist before that stage and continue to exist after that stage. For social and biological reasons, however, the development of a certain personality characteristic becomes the focus of one stage as opposed to other stages.

CRISES

Each stage of development is characterized by a **crisis.** Erikson used the word *crisis* in its medical sense, that is, an important turning point. Thus the crisis characterizing each stage of development has a possible positive resolution or a negative one. A positive resolution contributes to a strengthening of the ego and therefore to greater adaptation. A negative resolution weakens the ego and inhibits adaptation. Furthermore, a positive crisis resolution in one stage increases the likelihood that the crisis characterizing the next stage will be resolved positively. A negative resolution in one stage lowers the probability that the next crisis will be resolved positively. Erikson did not believe a solution to a crisis is either completely positive or completely negative. Rather, he said the resolution of a crisis has both positive and negative elements. When the positive elements outweigh the negative, the crisis is said to be resolved positively. We say more about this in our discussion of the first stage of development, to which we turn shortly.

In accordance with the epigenetic principle, a crisis exists in three phases: the *immature phase*, at which it is not the focal point of personality development; the *critical phase, at which,* for a variety of biological, psychological, and social reasons, it is the focal point of personality development; and the *resolution phase*, at which the resolution of the crisis influences subsequent personality development. If the crises associated with the eight stages of development are resolved positively, normal personality development occurs. If one or more crises are resolved negatively, normal development is inhibited. In other words, each crisis must be positively resolved in the stage of development in which it is critical before a person is fully prepared to deal with the crises that dominate subsequent stages.

Although biology determines when the eight stages of personality development will occur, because the maturational process determines when certain experiences become possible, it is the *social* environment that determines whether or not the crisis associated with any given stage is resolved positively. For this reason, the stages proposed by Erikson are called **psychosocial stages of development,** to contrast them with Freud's *psychosexual stages.*

RITUALIZATIONS AND RITUALISMS

For Erikson, it is essential to realize that personality development occurs within a cultural setting. Rather than viewing humans as warring with their culture, as Freud did, Erikson emphasized the compatibility between individuals and their culture. In fact, to a large extent, the job of culture is to provide effective ways of satisfying both biological and psychological human needs. According to Erikson, a person's internal and external experiences must fit together, at least to some degree, if an individual is to develop and function normally in a particular culture. Erikson (1950/1985) said, "Each successive stage and crisis has a special relation to one of the basic elements of society, and this for the simple reason that the human life cycle and man's institutions have evolved together" (p. 250).

The harmonious interplay between unfolding personality requirements and existing social and cultural conditions is made possible by **ritualizations.** According to Erikson (1977), ritualizations are recurring patterns of behaviour that reflect those beliefs, values, customs, and behaviours sanctioned by a particular society or culture. These differ considerably. For example, the different ways that Canadian Aboriginal and Non-Aboriginal groups approach family, religion, work, and the environment lead to different traditions of child rearing and education. Although it is ritualizations that make life meaningful within a particular society or culture, most individuals engage in them without knowing that they are doing so:

> [Each child must] be coaxed and induced to become "speciated" during a prolonged childhood by some form of family: he must be *familiarized by ritualization* with a particular version of human existence. He thus develops a distinct sense of corporate identity. . . . We must realize from the outset that ritualization is an aspect of everyday life which is more clearly seen in a different culture or class or even family than in our own, where, in fact, ritualization is more often than not experienced simply as the only proper way to do things; and the question is only why does not everybody do it our way. (pp. 79–80)

Ritualizations, then, are culturally approved patterns of everyday behaviour that allow a person to become an acceptable member of the culture. They include characteristic ways in which we relate to each other, such as shaking hands, kissing, and hugging. They provide guides that set the boundaries between acceptable and unacceptable behaviour. For example, you may be permitted to make bodily contact with a stranger at a dance but such behaviour may not be tolerated under other circumstances. Likewise, it may be permissible for a woman to wear a bikini on a beach whereas such attire may cause a stir at work or at school. Ritualizations guide almost every aspect of social behaviour and are the mechanisms by which people of a certain culture become "socialized."

Erikson defined **culture** as "a particular version of human existence," suggesting that many equally valid versions exist. The belief in the validity of many cultures underlies Canadian support for multicultural policies that strive to maintain many living cultures. Indeed, Erikson believed that except for the requirement that ritualizations satisfy basic human needs, they are arbitrary. For example, many cultural variations exist for courting, mating, and child-rearing practices, but these differences are less important than the fact that they all encourage reproduction and the perpetuation of the culture in which they occur. Some people lose sight of the arbitrary nature and functional value of ritualizations. For them, ritualizations take on excessive significance. Erikson referred to such exaggerated or otherwise distorted ritualizations as **ritualisms.** Ritualisms are inappropriate or false ritualizations, and they are the causes of much social and psychological pathology. For example, a ritualization within a culture might encourage addressing certain accomplished people with titles to encourage respect for their status. To idolize or worship these dignitaries, however, would be an inappropriate exaggeration of that ritualization. A ritualism, then, is a ritualization that has become mechanical and stereotyped. Such empty ceremonies lack the power to bond people of a culture together, thus subverting the original purpose of the ritualization.

Erikson considered that personality development occurred within a culture. With its customs and rituals, each culture passes on its values and beliefs.

We discuss the ritualizations and the ritualisms associated with each stage of development in the next section.

Eight Stages of Personality Development

The most famous aspects of Erikson's work are his descriptions of the eight developmental stages through which he believes all humans pass and what happens to the ego during each of these stages. The first five stages of personality development proposed by Erikson closely parallel Freud's proposed psychosexual stages of development in the time at which they are supposed to occur. As to what is supposed to occur during these stages, however, little agreement exists between Erikson and Freud. The last three stages are Erikson's own and represent one of his major contributions to psychology. It should be noted that the epigenetic principle determines the exact order in which the stages must occur; however, when they occur cannot be specified exactly. Therefore, the ages associated with each of the following stages should be viewed only as approximations. We label each stage according to the developmental level at which it occurs and according to the crisis it features.

1. INFANCY: BASIC TRUST VERSUS BASIC MISTRUST

This stage lasts from birth through about the first year and corresponds closely to Freud's oral stage of psychosexual development. This is the time when children are most helpless and thus most dependent on adults. If those caring for infants satisfy their needs in a loving and consistent manner, the infants will develop a feeling of **basic trust.** If, however, their parents are rejecting and satisfy their needs in an inconsistent manner, they will develop a feeling of mistrust.

If care is loving and consistent, infants learn they need not worry about a loving, reliable parent and therefore are not overly disturbed when that parent leaves their sight:

> The infant's first social achievement, then, is his willingness to let the mother out of sight without undue anxiety or rage, because she has become an inner certainty as well as an outer predictability. Such consistency, continuity, and sameness of experience provide a rudimentary sense of ego identity which depends, I think, on the cognition that there is an inner population of remembered and anticipated sensations and images which are firmly correlated with the outer population of familiar and predictable things and people. (Erikson, 1950/1985, p. 247)

The basic trust versus **basic mistrust** crisis is resolved positively when the child develops more trust than mistrust. Remember, it is the ratio of the two solutions that is important. A child who trusted everyone and everything would be in trouble. A certain amount of mistrust is healthy and conducive to survival. It is the child with a predominance of trust, however, who has the courage to take risks and who is not overwhelmed by disappointments and setbacks.

Erikson said that when the crisis characterizing a stage is positively resolved, a **virtue** emerges in one's personality. A virtue adds strength to one's ego. In this stage, when the child has more basic trust than basic mistrust, the virtue of *hope* emerges. Erikson defined hope as "the enduring belief in the attainability of fervent wishes, in spite of the dark urges and rages which mark the beginning of existence" (1964, p. 118). Trusting children dare to hope, a process that is future oriented. In contrast, children lacking trust cannot hope; they must worry constantly about whether their needs will be satisfied and therefore are tied to the present.

Numinous versus Idolism. The primary ritualization during this stage is the **numinous.** The numinous involves the various ways that mothers attend to their infants' needs in a particular culture. That is, the ways they "recognize" the infant, through touching, smiling, naming, feeding, and looking. Although personal, these mother-infant interactions also reflect culturally sanctioned child-rearing practices. As a result of these mother-infant interactions, the child develops positive feelings toward the mother and becomes socially responsive. Thus, the mother's warm, predictable caring leads the child to seek interactions with others.

If the infant's normal reverence and respect for the mother become exaggerated, the ritualism of **idolism** results. Idolism occurs when normal respect and deep appreciation for a person becomes excessive admiration and idealization. Idolism steers the developing child in the direction of blind hero worship.

2. EARLY CHILDHOOD: AUTONOMY VERSUS SHAME AND DOUBT

This stage occurs from about the end of the first year to about the end of the third year and corresponds to Freud's anal stage of psychosexual development. During this stage, children rapidly develop a wide variety of skills. They learn to walk, climb, push, pull, and talk. More generally, they learn how to hold on and to let go—not only to physical objects but to feces and urine as well. In other words, children can now willfully decide to do something or not. Thus children are engaged in a battle of wills with their parents.

The parents must perform the delicate task of controlling the child's behaviour in socially acceptable directions without injuring the child's sense of self-control or autonomy. In other words, the parents must be reasonably tolerant but still be firm enough to assure behaviour that is socially approved. If the parents are overly protective or unjust in their use of punishment, the child will be doubtful and experience shame:

> This stage, therefore, becomes decisive for the ratio of love and hate, cooperation and willfulness, freedom of self-expression and its suppression. From a sense of self-control without loss of self-esteem comes a lasting sense of good will and pride; from a sense of loss of self-control and of foreign overcontrol comes a lasting propensity for doubt and shame. (Erikson, 1950/1985, p. 254)

If the child develops more **autonomy** than **shame and doubt** during this stage, the virtue of *will* emerges. Erikson defined will as "the unbroken determination to exercise free choice as well as self-restraint, in spite of the unavoidable experience of shame and doubt in infancy" (1964, p. 119). Again, it is important to note that the positive resolution of the crisis characterizing this stage does not mean the child no longer experiences shame and doubt. Rather, it means the child's ego becomes strong enough to deal adequately with the inevitable experiences of shame and doubt.

Notice that the virtues emerging as the result of positive crisis resolutions are ego functions. For example, the virtues of hope and will have some influence on the quality of one's life but little on survival. Persons without much hope or will do survive;— that is, they are able to satisfy their biological (idinal) needs—but they probably are not as flexible, optimistic, or generally as happy as those with more hope and will.

Judiciousness versus Legalism.   Autonomy is best served when one's will is freely exercised. Because each culture restricts some behaviours and allows others, however, the child must learn to discriminate between right and wrong, between what is acceptable and what is unacceptable. Erikson called **judiciousness** the ritualization by which the child learns what is culturally sanctioned and what is not. Through judiciousness the child learns the laws, rules, honoured practices, and regulations that characterize the child's culture. Before this stage, it was the parents' responsibility to guide the child's behaviour properly. Now, however, as the rules and regulations of a culture are internalized, the child begins to judge his or her own behaviour as well as that of others. Children must learn to judge themselves as others judge them. As the superego develops, it is used by the child to make moral evaluations.

The perversion of the ritualization of judiciousness is the ritualism of **legalism,** which Erikson defined as "the victory of the letter over the spirit of the word and the law. It is expressed in the vain display of righteousness or empty contrition, or in a moralistic insistence on exposing and isolating the culprit whether or not this will be good for him or anybody else" (1977, p. 97). For the legalistic child or adult, the punishment and humiliation of transgressors is more important than the intent of the law that was transgressed.

3. PRESCHOOL AGE: INITIATIVE VERSUS GUILT

This stage occurs from about the fourth year to about the fifth year and corresponds to Freud's phallic stage of psychosexual development. During this stage the child is increasingly capable of detailed motor activity, refined use of language, and vivid use of imagination. These skills allow the child to *initiate* ideas, actions, and fantasies, and to *plan* future events. According to Erikson, the child during this stage "is apt to develop an untiring curiosity about differences in sizes in general, and sexual differences in particular . . . his learning is now eminently intrusive and vigorous: it leads away from his own limitations and into future possibilities" (1959, p. 76).

The importance of these early stages was supported recently by the Early Years Study, commissioned by the Ontario government in 1998. The study endorsed the Freudian and Eriksonian view that events that take place before the age of six are critical to a child's health, learning, and personality development. As a result, with the help of federal funding, Ontario opened in spring 2002 the first of 103 planned Early Years Centres, offering interactive learning activities and resources for children under six and their parents.

In the preceding stages, children learned that they are people. Now they begin to explore what type of person they can become. During this stage, they test limits to learn what is permissible and what is not. If parents encourage children's self-initiated behaviours and fantasies, the children will leave this stage with a healthy sense of **initiative.** If, however, parents ridicule children's self-initiated behaviour and imagination, they will leave this stage lacking self-sufficiency. Instead of taking the initiative, they will tend to experience **guilt** when pondering such behaviour and therefore will tend to live within the narrow limits that others set for them.

If children develop more initiative during this stage than guilt, the virtue of *purpose* will emerge. Erikson defined purpose as "the courage to envisage and pursue valued goals uninhibited by the defeat of infantile fantasies, by guilt and by the foiling fear of punishment" (1964, p. 122). Children who have positively resolved the crises of the first three stages possess the virtues of hope, will, and purpose.

Authenticity versus Impersonation.   In addition to playing with toys, children at this stage typically engage in a great deal of playacting, imitating, wearing costumes, and even pretending to be various types of animals. Such play provides them with an intermediate reality where they can explore the relationship between their inner and outer worlds. Both positive and negative roles are played to reconfirm the limits on behaviour. Through the process of "trying on" various roles and reconfirming what is possible and what is not, children discover the "mix" of roles that is just right for them. Erikson referred to those activities as the ritualization of **authenticity.**

Exaggeration of the ritualization of authenticity results in the ritualism of **impersonation,** which occurs when one confuses one's true self with one or more of the roles that one plays. Rather than a role becoming just a part of the true self or furnishing information about it, the child becomes the role he or she plays, losing the rich blending of personality characteristics that have developed during previous stages into a unique, authentic person.

4. SCHOOL AGE: INDUSTRY VERSUS INFERIORITY

This stage lasts from about the sixth year to about the eleventh year and corresponds to Freud's latency stage of psychosexual development. Most children in our society attend school throughout this stage. It is during this stage that children learn the skills necessary for economic survival, the technological skills that will allow them to become productive members of their culture:

The inner stage seems all set for "entrance into life," except that life must first be school life, whether school is field or jungle or classroom. The child must forget past hopes and wishes, while his exuberant imagination is tamed and harnessed to the laws of impersonal things—even the three R's. For before the child, psychologically already a rudimentary parent, can become a biological parent, he must begin to be a worker and potential provider. (Erikson, 1950/1985, pp. 258–259)

School is the place where children are trained for future employment in and adjustment to their culture. Because survival requires the ability to work cooperatively with others, social skills are among the important lessons taught by the schools. The most important lesson that children learn during this stage is "the pleasure of work completion by steady attention and persevering diligence" (Erikson, 1950/1985, p. 259). From this lesson comes a sense of **industry,** which prepares children to look confidently for productive places in society among other people.

If children do not develop a sense of industry, they will develop a sense of **inferiority** that causes them to lose confidence in their ability to become contributing members of society. Such children are more likely to develop a "negative identity," a concept that is explained in our discussion of the next stage.

Another danger associated with this stage is that children may later overvalue their positions in the workplace. For such people, work is equated with life, and they are blinded to the many other important aspects of human existence. "If he accepts work as his only obligation, and 'what works' as his only criterion of worthwhileness, he may become the conformist and thoughtless slave of his technology and of those who are in a position to exploit it" (Erikson, 1950/1985, p. 261). According to Erikson, the skills necessary for future employment must be encouraged during this stage but not at the expense of other important human attributes.

If children's sense of industry is greater than their sense of inferiority, they will leave this stage with the virtue of *competence.* "Competence . . . is the free exercise of dexterity and intelligence in the completion of tasks, unimpaired by infantile inferiority" (Erikson, 1964, p. 124). Like the virtues discussed earlier, competence comes from loving attention and encouragement. A sense of inferiority comes from ridicule or lack of concern by those most important to the children.

Formality versus Formalism.   During this stage, children learn that to be a productive member of their community they must possess real (not imagined) skills and knowledge. Erikson called the ritualization corresponding to this stage **formality,** and it involves learning the appropriate ways of doing tasks. Whatever the child does, whether it be at school, at home, at work, or on the athletic field, he or she must learn to do it "properly."

The exaggeration of the ritualization of formality results in the ritualism of **formalism:** overconcern with technique and blindness to the purpose and meaning of a task. The student whose only concern is with high grades exemplifies formalism. Erikson (1977) said of formalism:

> Whatever the name, it must express the fact that human striving for method and logic can also lead to that self-enslavement which makes of each man what Marx called a "craft-idiot," that is, one who for the sake of a proficiency will forget and deny the human context within which it has a significant and maybe dangerous function. (p. 106)

5. ADOLESCENCE: IDENTITY VERSUS ROLE CONFUSION

This stage occurs between about 12 and 20 years of age and corresponds roughly to Freud's genital stage of psychosexual development. Erikson is best known for his description of this psychosocial stage, for it contains his well-known concept of **identity crisis.**

Erikson believed that this stage represents the transition period between childhood and adulthood. In the preceding stages, children were learning what they were and what it was possible for them to do, that is, the various roles that were available to them. During this stage, children must ponder the accumulated information about themselves and their society and ultimately commit themselves to some strategy for life. When they have done this, they have gained an identity and have become adults. Gaining a personal **identity** marks the satisfactory end of this stage of development. The stage itself, however, is viewed as a time of searching for an identity but not of having one. Young people often "try on" different selves, expressed in their choice of music and fashions, friends and relationships, groups, ideologies, even future professions. Erikson called the interval between youth and adulthood a **psychosocial moratorium.** Erikson (1964) vividly described what it is like to be in this period between childhood and adulthood:

> Like a trapeze artist, the young person in the middle of vigorous motion must let go of his safe hold on childhood and reach out for a firm grasp on adulthood, depending for a breathless interval on a relatedness between the past and the future, and on the reliability of those he must let go of, and those who will "receive" him. (p. 90)

Erikson used the term *identity* (sometimes called ego identity) in a variety of ways. For example, it is "a feeling of being at home in one's body, a sense of 'knowing where one is going,' and an inner assuredness of anticipated recognition from those who count" (Erikson, 1968, p. 165). Erikson made no apology for using the term identity in a variety of ways. Because it is a complex concept, he thought it must be approached from many angles.

If young adults do not leave this stage with an identity, they leave it with **role confusion** or perhaps with a **negative identity.** Role confusion is characterized by the inability to choose a role in life, thus prolonging the psychological moratorium indefinitely. People stuck at this stage can make only superficial commitments that are soon abandoned. Negative identities are those roles that children are warned not to assume. Erikson defined negative identity as "an identity perversely based on all those identifications and roles which, at critical stages of development, had been presented to the individual as most undesirable or dangerous, and yet also as most real" (1959, p. 131). Erikson gave an example:

> A mother who is filled with unconscious ambivalence toward a brother who disintegrated into alcoholism may again and again respond selectively only to those traits in her son which seem to point to a repetition of her brother's fate, in which case this "negative" identity may take on more reality for the son than all his natural attempts at being good: he may work hard on becoming a drunkard. (1959, p. 131)

For Erikson, the concepts of role confusion and negative identity explained much of the unrest and hostility expressed by adolescents in this country. For example, the adolescent may lash out at those identities that do not fit him or her:

> The loss of a sense of identity often is expressed in a scornful and snobbish hostility toward the roles offered as proper and desirable in one's family or immediate community. Any aspect of the required role, or all parts, be it masculinity or femininity, nationality or class membership, can become the main focus of the young person's acid disdain. (Erikson, 1959, p. 129)

Why should an adolescent choose a negative identity if a positive one is not available? Erikson said because an adolescent would "rather be nobody or somebody bad,

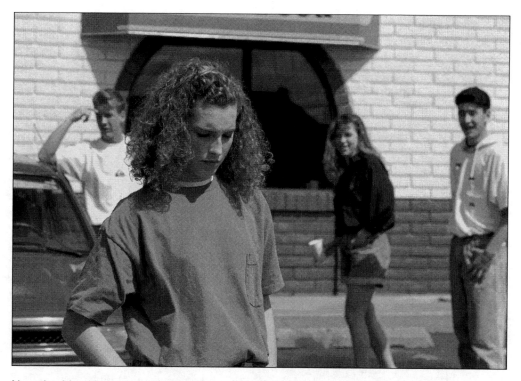

Negative identities or role confusion may contribute to teenage violence and bullying.

or indeed, dead—and this totally, and by free choice—than be not-quite somebody" (1959, p. 132).

Perhaps it is negative identities, sometimes combined with scorn for other teens who are trying awkwardly to find their own roles and identities, that leads to the kind of violence that has grabbed headlines in the last few years. In November 1997, several teenagers, mostly girls, beat and kicked Reena Virk of Saanich, B.C., while others watched. Two of them allegedly returned, kicked her in the head, and drowned her. The attacks apparently originated with a complaint that Virk had tried to steal the boyfriend of one of the girls.

The Virk case was one of several that awakened the public to the struggles of many teenagers who suffer at the hands of bullies. In April 1999, a 14-year-old boy entered W.R. Myers High School in Taber, Alberta, shot and killed a 17-year-old student and badly wounded his 17-year-old friend. The shooter had been an "at home" student, because as everybody's punching bag, he feared going to school. In a third case, Dawn-Marie Wesley, 14, of Mission, B.C., left a suicide note in November 2000 after constant bullying by three schoolgirls. Drawing on Erikson's position on development during the adolescent years, each of these events illuminates a broader issue. What is the effect on the personality characteristics of teenagers, already struggling with their new roles and responsibilities, who experience bullying, whether as a victim, a perpetrator, or a spectator?

If young adults emerge from this stage with a positive identity rather than with role confusion or a negative identity, they also will emerge with the virtue of *fidelity*. Erikson defined fidelity as "the ability to sustain loyalties freely pledged in spite of the inevitable contradictions of value systems" (1964, p. 125). This paves the way for later develop-ment, allowing the person to commit not only to relationships but also to chosen values and institutions such as political movements or the church.

The stages preceding this one provided the child with the qualities from which an identity could be derived. In this stage, the person must synthesize this information. The development of an identity marks the end of childhood and the beginning of adulthood. From this point on, life is a matter of acting out one's identity. Now that the person knows who he or she is, the task of life becomes one of carrying oneself optimally through the remaining stages of life.

Ideology versus Totalism.   The ritualization corresponding to this stage is **ideology**. The adolescent searches for an ideology that synthesizes all of the ego developments from the previous stages. The ideology furnishes a "game plan" for life; it gives life meaning. An identity cannot emerge until all previous ego functions are integrated, and commitment to an ideology allows such integration. A chosen ideology could be religious, political, or philosophical. The only stipulation is that acting in accordance with it furthers both individual and cultural goals.

The exaggeration of the ritualization of ideology results in the ritualism of **totalism**. Totalism involves the unquestioning commitment to overly simplistic ideologies. For example, adolescents may accept the values mouthed by various "heroes" in religious cults, musical groups, drug cultures, athletics, gangs, films, or political groups. According to Erikson, when adolescents overidentify with such groups or individuals it is because they seem to provide answers to life's most difficult questions. The simplistic thinking involved in totalism, then, can make life easier for the troubled adolescent and, if it is temporary, it may not be harmful. It is when totalism lasts beyond the time when an identity should be achieved that it becomes a problem.

It is important to remember that according to the epigenetic principle all crises exist in all stages of development. For example, the identity crisis exists in the young child as it does in the mature adult. However, it does so in the immature and resolution phases of the crisis, respectively. It is only during adolescence that, for biological, psychological, and social reasons, the identity crisis exists in its critical phase.

6. Young Adulthood: Intimacy versus Isolation

This stage lasts from about 20 to about 24 years of age. For this and the remaining psychosocial stages, there is no corresponding Freudian psychosexual stage of development.

According to Erikson, "normalcy" for the young adult consists of, to a large extent, being able to love and work effectively; on this point, he agreed with Freud:

> Freud was once asked what he thought a normal person should be able to do well. The questioner probably expected a complicated answer. But Freud, in the curt way of his old days, is reported to have said: "Lieben und arbeiten" (to love and to work). It pays to ponder on this simple formula; it gets deeper as you think about it. . . . We may ponder, but we cannot improve on "the professor's" formula. (Erikson, 1950/1985, pp. 264–265)

Although Erikson agreed with Freud on the importance of love, he believed only the person with a secure identity can risk entering a loving relationship. The young adult with a strong identity eagerly seeks intimate relationships with others:

> The young adult, emerging from the search for and the insistence on identity, is eager and willing to fuse his identity with that of others. He is ready for intimacy, that is, the capacity to commit himself to concrete affiliations and partnerships and to develop the ethical strength to abide by such commitments, even though they may call for significant sacrifices and compromises. (Erikson, 1950/1985, p. 263)

People who do not develop a capacity for productive work and **intimacy** withdraw into themselves, avoid close contacts, and thus develop a feeling of **isolation.** If individuals develop a greater capacity for intimacy than for isolation during this stage, they will also emerge with the virtue of *love*. Erikson defined love as "the mutuality of devotion forever subduing the antagonisms inherent in divided function" (1964, p. 129).

Affiliation versus Elitism.   Once an identity has been achieved and an ideology has been chosen that allows for the productive manifestation of that identity, a person can affiliate productively with fellow humans in work, friendship, and love. The ritualization characterizing this stage is **affiliation,** the various ways a culture sanctions caring, productive relationships between adults. The marriage ceremony and the subsequent honeymoon are two such sanctioning rituals. The wedding ceremony may involve the exchange of rings and a pledge of fidelity. We see in the wedding ceremony elements of the ritualizations from previous stages. For example, the ceremony casts a numinous (that is, reverent or spiritual) spell; it has a judicious element in that certain rights are bestowed; the ceremony and subsequent marital relationship may reflect earlier experimentation with role playing; formality is reflected in the fact that the ceremony includes elements that must be performed according to accepted practice; and the mutual pledges taken by the man and woman affirm their identities as husband and wife. Affiliation further prepares individuals to live harmoniously with fellow humans within a culture.

The exaggeration of the ritualization of affiliation results in the ritualism of **elitism.** Those individuals who experience a sense of isolation rather than intimacy tend to surround themselves with small groups of like-minded individuals rather than forming deeply emotional relationships with healthy individuals. Their lives tend to be characterized by snobbery, status symbols, and membership in exclusive clubs; because such relationships are not truly intimate, they continue the person's sense of isolation within his or her culture.

7. ADULTHOOD: GENERATIVITY VERSUS STAGNATION

This stage occurs from about age 25 to about 64 and is called middle adulthood. If one has been fortunate enough to develop a positive identity and to live a productive, happy life, one attempts to pass on the circumstances that caused such a life to the next generation. This can be done either by interacting with children directly (they need not be one's own) or by producing or creating experiences that will enhance the lives of those in the next generation. Such productivity can occur within one's job (e.g., writing, research, or building houses), but also in volunteer activities, such as coaching kids' soccer or organizing community activities. The person who does not develop a sense of **generativity** is characterized by "stagnation and interpersonal impoverishment" (Erikson, 1950/1985, p. 267). If generativity outweighs **stagnation**, one leaves this stage with the virtue of *care*, which Erikson defined as "the widening concern for what has been generated by love, necessity, or accident; it overcomes the ambivalence adhering to irreversible obligation" (1964, p. 131).

Generationalism versus Authoritism.   The ritualization characterizing this stage is **generationalism,** which involves the many ways in which older adults transmit cultural values to the next generation. Parents, teachers, physicians, and spiritual leaders are especially influential in conveying cultural values to children. Healthy adults are concerned with providing children with the same types of experiences they were fortunate enough to have, that is, with experiences that both facilitate personality growth and perpetuate cultural values.

The exaggeration of the ritualization of generationalism results in the ritualism of **authoritism**. Authoritism occurs when authority figures in a culture use their power not for the care and instruction of the young but for their own selfish purposes.

8. OLD AGE: EGO INTEGRITY VERSUS DESPAIR

This stage occurs from about the age of 65 to death and is called late adulthood. Erikson defined **ego integrity** as follows:

> Only in him who in some way has taken care of things and people and who has adapted himself to the triumphs and disappointments adherent to being the originator of others or the generator of products and ideas—only in him may gradually ripen the fruit of these seven stages—I know no better word for it than ego integrity. (1950/1985, p. 268)

According to Erikson, the person who can look back on a rich, constructive, happy life does not fear death. Such a person has a feeling of completion and fulfilment. The person who looks back on life with frustration experiences *despair.* As strange as it may seem, the person experiencing despair is not as ready for death as the person with a sense of fulfillment because the former has not yet achieved any major goals in life.

Not only are the eight stages progressively related to each other but the eighth stage is directly related to the first. In other words, the eight stages are interrelated in a circular fashion. For example, the adult's attitude toward death will directly influence the young child's sense of trust. Erikson said, "It seems possible to further paraphrase the relation of adult integrity and infantile trust by saying that healthy children will not fear life if their elders have integrity enough not to fear death" (1950/1985, p. 269). If the person has more ego integrity than despair, his or her life will be characterized by the virtue of *wisdom*, which Erikson defined as "detached concern with life itself, in face of death itself" (1964, p. 133).

Integralism versus Sapientism.   If all has gone well in a person's life, that person realizes how instrumental he or she has been in perpetuating culture. That is, the person has a sense of immortality, knowing that the culture he or she helped sustain will survive his or her own death. The ritualization of **integralism** involves the final unification of previous ritualizations. This last integration of the ritualizations puts life, and therefore death, into perspective:

> We can see now what rituals must accomplish: by combining and renewing the ritualizations of childhood and affirming generative sanction, they help to consolidate adult life once its commitments and investments have led to the creation of new persons and to the production of new things and ideas. And, of course, by tying life cycle and institutions into a meaningful whole, they create a sense of immortality not only for the leaders and the elite but also for every participant. And there can be little doubt that the ritualizations of everyday life permit, and even demand, that adults forget death as the inscrutable background of all life, and give priority to the absolute reality of world views shared with others of the same geography, history, and technology. By means of ritual, in fact, death becomes the meaningful boundary of such reality. (Erikson, 1977, pp. 112–113)

The exaggeration of the ritualization of integralism results in the ritualism of **sapientism**, which Erikson defined as "the unwise pretense of being wise" (1977, p. 112). The older person experiencing despair instead of ego integrity may play the role

Table 6–1

The Eight Stages of Development and Their Associated Crises, Virtues, Ritualizations, and Ritualisms

STAGE	APPROXI-MATE AGE (YEARS)	CRISIS	VIRTUE	RITUALI-ZATION	RITUALISM
Infancy	Birth–1	Basic trust versus basic mistrust	Hope	Numinous	Idolism
Early child-hood	1–3	Autonomy versus shame and doubt	Will	Judicious-ness	Legalism
Preschool age	4–5	Initiative versus guilt	Purpose	Authenticity	Impersona-tion
School age	6–11	Industry versus inferiority	Compe-tence	Formality	Formalism
Adolescence	12–20	Identity versus role confusion	Fidelity	Ideology	Totalism
Young adulthood	20–24	Intimacy versus isolation	Love	Affiliation	Elitism
Adulthood	25–64	Generativity versus stagnation	Care	Generation-alism	Authoritism
Old age	65–Death	Ego integrity versus despair	Wisdom	Integralism	Sapientism

of a person having all the answers, of being absolutely right; however, he or she is unable to place his or her life in the context of continuous cultural evolution. Such a life is viewed as having little meaning.

The eight stages of development and their associated crises, virtues, ritualizations, and ritualisms are summarized in Table 6–1.

Goal of Psychotherapy

Erikson stressed that his psychotherapeutic practices differed from those of traditional psychoanalysis because modern times had created different types of disorders. For example, Erikson explained that "the patient of today suffers most under the problem of what he should believe in and who he should—or, indeed, might—be or become; while the patient of early psychoanalysis suffered most under inhibitions which prevented him from being what and who he thought he knew he was" (1950/1985, p. 279).

For Erikson, the main focus in the therapeutic process is the patient's ego, which must be strengthened to cope with life's problems. "Rehabilitation work can be made more effective and economical if the clinical investigation focuses on the patient's shattered life plan and if advice tends to strengthen the resynthesis of the elements on which the patient's ego identity was based" (1959, p. 43).

Erikson believed the traditional technique of releasing the contents of the unconscious mind may do more harm than good. Erikson said the psychoanalytic method "may make some people sicker than they ever were . . . especially if, in our zealous pursuit of our task of 'making conscious' in the psychotherapeutic situation, we push someone who is leaning out a little too far over the precipice of the unconscious" (1968, p. 164).

Like Adler, Erikson had his patients sit across from him in an armchair rather than lie down on a couch because the former creates a more equitable situation for the patient.

Briefly stated, the healthy person is one whose ego is characterized by the eight virtues resulting from the positive solution of each crisis in the eight stages of development. The purpose of psychotherapy is to encourage the growth of whatever virtues are missing, even if it means going back and helping the person to develop a sense of basic trust. For Erikson, the outcome of every crisis resolution is reversible. For example, the person leaving the first stage of development without basic trust may later gain it, and the person having it may lose it.

Comparison of Erikson and Freud

The major areas in which Erikson and Freud differ are listed next.

DEVELOPMENT

Freud concentrated his studies on the psychosexual stages of development coming before the age of six because he thought that most of what is important to personality development occurs by then. Erikson studied development as it occurs throughout life. Although Jung, too, believed that important developments occurred throughout one's life, Erikson's description of the development process was much more detailed.

ANATOMY AS DESTINY

Freud emphasized the importance of biological differences between males and females for personality development. Erikson agreed that anatomical differences provide patterns of internal stimulation but insisted that such stimulation interacts with the social environment to produce personality characteristics. The term *penis envy* does not appear in Erikson's major work (1950/1985). Elsewhere, Erikson (1968) argued that so-called penis envy, and the behaviours and attitudes supposedly associated with it, was necessitated by Freud's theory and therapeutic methods: "It must always be suspected that a special method bares truths especially true under circumstances created by the method" (p. 275). Erikson's theory and methods generated no support for Freud's concept of penis envy.

EGO PSYCHOLOGY

Under the influence of Anna Freud, Erikson shifted attention away from the id and toward the ego. Rather than viewing the individual as warring with society, Erikson viewed society as a potential source of strength.

As we have seen, Erikson believed that culture must provide ritualizations that help people positively resolve the crises characterizing the various stages of development. The individual serves culture and culture serves the individual.

UNCONSCIOUS MIND

Although Erikson's theory emphasized the conscious ego, he did not neglect unconscious mechanisms completely. In fact, although the ego gains strength from certain social experiences, the experiences themselves are largely unconscious. His use of the term *unconscious*, however, was very different from Freud's.

DREAM ANALYSIS

Although Erikson used little dream analysis in his practice, he did agree with Freud's contention that dreams provide information about the unconscious and that dream work creates dream symbols with more than one meaning. Furthermore, Erikson believed that free association is an effective way of studying dreams. Most important to Erikson, however, was the ego's influence on dreams. Healthy egos remain powerful even during sleep and they make compromises with idinal impulses that produce dreams of success and achievement so that the dreamers can awake with a sense of competence and wholeness. Erikson also believed that dreams often suggest solutions to the dreamer's problems. In fact, during therapy a patient may dream dreams for the sole purpose of being analyzed by the dreamer's analyst, "Once we set out to study our dreams . . . we may well dream them in order to study them" (Erikson, 1977, p. 134). Furthermore, the patient may oblige the therapist by having just the type of dream the therapist is looking for:

> Patients . . . know that they will or should report their dreams, and this in the context of a therapeutic style: wherefore Jungian or Freudian patients, for example, seem to differ radically in their manifest dream imagery. Their dreams, in fact, can be seen to reflect the vision of the respective "schools"—a therapeutic communality, then, maybe seasoned with a bit of obliging "politic"? (Erikson, 1977, p. 134)

Thus, although Erikson agreed with Freud that dreams may provide information about unconscious, idinal desires, he chose to concentrate on the aspects of dreams that are constructive and teleological and therefore useful and refreshing to the dreamer. When Erikson used dream analysis at all, he used it to determine the strength of the dreamer's ego rather than as a way of discovering repressed, traumatic experiences. Erikson's approach to dream analysis was more similar to Adler's than to Freud's.

PSYCHOTHERAPY

We have seen that Erikson considered people healthy if they successfully traverse the eight stages of life, thus acquiring the virtues of hope, will, purpose, competence, fidelity, love, care, and wisdom. If people do not acquire these virtues, their egos will be weaker than they otherwise would be, and it is the job of the therapist to help provide the circumstances under which the virtues can develop. This is in marked contrast to Freud's belief that therapy facilitates the understanding of repressed memories using techniques such as dream analysis and free association.

RELIGION

Freud took a dim view of religion, saying that it is merely a collective neurosis based on infantile fears and desires. Erikson totally disagreed. For him, religion is something that many people truly need. For centuries, humans have used religion to make the events of their lives more understandable and therefore less threatening. Without it, according to Erikson, the lives of millions of people would be filled with uncertainty. In this respect, Erikson agreed with Jung and Adler.

According to Erikson, a key function of religion is to provide a "shared world image. For only a reasonably coherent world provides the faith which is transmitted by the mothers to the infants in a way conducive to the vital strength of *hope*" (Erikson, 1968, p. 106). In other words, for adults to instill hope in their children they must have faith in their world. Erikson did not believe, however, that religion is the only thing that can provide a world image conducive to trust, hope, and faith. Many people, he said, derive faith from such secular areas as science and social action (1950/1985, p. 251).

Although Erikson called himself a Freudian, his theory had little in common with Freud's. In addition, his conception of human nature is in marked contrast to Freud's. Perhaps Erikson's insistence that his theory is closer to Freud's than it really is reflects Erikson's deep appreciation that the Freudians took him into their camp, thus solving his own identity crisis.

Evaluation

EMPIRICAL RESEARCH

Like so many personality theories, Erikson's theory cannot be evaluated on the basis of laboratory investigations alone, at least not yet. Erikson did not create his theory with the researcher in mind. He attempted to classify conceptually several items related to personality development, and one either believes they are clarified or they are not; either his theory is a useful guide to understanding personality or it is not. "The proof lies in the way in which the communication between therapist and patient 'keeps moving,' leading to new and surprising insights and to the patient's greater assumption of responsibility for himself" (Erikson, 1964, p. 75). The point is that Erikson believed there are ways other than laboratory investigations to evaluate a personality theory. Despite Erikson's thoughts about the need to verify his theory scientifically, others have taken it on themselves to do just that (Butler, Culp, Hurlbut, & Jambunathan, 1997). For example, Ciaccio (1971) asked 120 male white children to make up stories about five pictures. The boys were equally divided into three groups consisting of five-, eight-, and eleven-year-old children. Several judges categorized the stories sentence by sentence according to which stage of development they best represented. The percentages of each child's sentences that expressed concern with the first five of Erikson's stages were recorded. The data tended to support Erikson's theory. The five-year-old children showed the greatest number of themes corresponding to stage 2 (46 percent); next was stage 3 (42 percent). The eight-year-old children showed the greatest number of themes corresponding to stage 3 (56 percent), with stage 2 second (20 percent). The eleven-year-old children showed the greatest number of themes corresponding to stage 4 (44 percent), with stage 3 second (26 percent).

By far, most of the research generated by Erikson's theory has involved the concept of identity. Several researchers have devised methods of quantifying the concept of identity so that it can be investigated experimentally (see, for example, Bourne, 1978; Heilman, 1998; Kasser & Sheldon, 2001; Kowaz & Marcia, 1991; Kroger, 2000; Marcia, 1966; 1993; Rosenthal, Gurney, & Moore, 1981). Research using one or more of these objective measures of identity has found that identity achievers choose more difficult academic majors (for example, chemistry, engineering, biology, mathematics) than those chosen by nonachievers (for example, anthropology, education, and physical education) (Marcia & Friedman, 1970); identity achievers have higher grades than nonachievers (Cross & Allen, 1970); identity achievers show greater tolerance for out-groups and higher levels of logical and moral reasoning than nonachievers (Cote & Levine, 1983; Rowe & Marcia, 1980; Waterman, 1982). Studies show that many students achieve both occupational and ideological identities sometime between their freshman and senior years, indicating that adolescence is a time of profound psychosocial growth, just as Erikson had said (Adams & Fitch, 1982; Waterman, Geary, & Waterman, 1974). People are far more likely to attain an identity if they attained a sense of trust, autonomy, initiative, and industry in the earlier stages of development (Waterman, Buebel, & Waterman, 1970). The development of an identity greatly increases the probability of achieving an intimate relationship during middle age (Kahn, Zimmerman, Csikszentmihalyi, & Getzels, 1985; Schiedel & Marcia, 1985; Tesch & Whitbourne, 1982). Moreover, people who experience role confusion are much more affected by peer pressure than are identity achievers (Adams, Ryan, Hoffman, Dobson, & Nielsen, 1985).

Bradley and Marcia (1998) examined the strategies people aged 42 to 64 used in resolving Erikson's seventh stage of normative psychosocial development: Generativity vs. Stagnation. Using several measures of generativity and a comprehensive personality inventory, they confirmed Erikson's view that adult personality depends on how this stage (and each previous stage) is resolved.

Like Jung, Erikson's theory deals with significant life transitions, such as the transition to university. The first year gives opportunities for young people still seeking their identity to try out roles in a new setting; it is also an important time in establishing adult relationships. Increased expectations, homesickness, loneliness, new surroundings, and the sheer volume of schoolwork make the transition stressful for many students. A team of researchers from Wilfrid Laurier University found that some students have realistic expectations of their first year, while others, who subscribe to the "freshman myth," hold a simplistic, rosy picture of university life. To explore the effects of such attitudes, Pancer and his colleagues (Pancer, Hunsberger, Pratt, & Alisat, 2000) surveyed students' knowledge and attitudes before they started university, and later took measures of their perceived stress and adaptation to university. Students who were well informed and had a varied, complex picture of university life reported less stress and better adaptation than those with simplistic expectations.

CRITICISMS

Difficult to Test Empirically.   We have seen that Erikson had little interest in testing his own theory empirically and what research he does report (for example, his research on the play activities of boys and girls) lacks quantification and statistical analysis. Others, however, have had some success in verifying some Eriksonian concepts related to the stages of development and especially that of identity.

Overly Optimistic View of Humans.   Although claiming a close affiliation with Freud's theory, Erikson painted a much rosier picture of humans than did Freud. Little in Erikson's theory describes an intense struggle to keep our animalistic nature in check. By emphasizing and expanding on the functioning of the ego, Erikson concentrated on problems of identity, problem solving, and interpersonal relationships rather than on the taming of powerful sexual and aggressive instincts. To some critics, Erikson's portrayal of humans is too optimistic, unrealistic, and simplistic.

Support of Status Quo.   Essentially Erikson defined a healthy person as one who adjusts to, accepts, and passes on to the next generation the elements of his or her culture. To many critics, this sounds like advocating conformity. Indeed, Erikson insisted that healthy egos require the support of culturally sanctioned roles, and this insistence is taken by many as endorsement of those roles. For those seeing gross injustices, dangerous values, shallowness, and even stupidity in their culture, it makes little sense to define mental health in terms of adjustments to such an abnormal situation.

Excessive Moralizing.   Erikson's definition of the positive adjustments to crises at various stages of development are in accordance with Christian ethics and with existing social institutions. The danger in this (as in all personality theories) is that Erikson may have been describing his own values rather than objective reality. Roazen (1980) elaborated:

> Confusing "ought" and "is" statements can lead to . . . undesirable consequences. . . . There is the danger of conservatism—throwing a mantle of morality over the preexisting world and endorsing everything that already "is" with an ethical sanction. Erikson's message communicates too much of what we want to hear. His hopefulness is too often allied to social conservatism. (p. 339)

Roazen (1976) also commented:

As one reflects on the implications of Erikson's ego psychology, with its deferential attitude toward the benefits of pre-existing social institutions, a consistent ethical mood does emerge; marriage, heterosexuality, and the raising of children are unquestionably part of what he takes the good life to consist of. (p. 171)

The criticism that Erikson's theory is too moralistic is closely related to the criticism that his theory supports the status quo.

Failure to Properly Acknowledge Influences on His Theory.   One criticism here concerns Erikson's insistence on being a "post-Freudian" when, in fact, he has little in common with Freud. It has been suggested that Erikson's motives were pragmatic: to avoid being "excommunicated" from psychoanalytic circles. Conversely, Erikson neglected to properly acknowledge theorists such as Adler and Horney who had earlier stressed the importance of social variables.

CONTRIBUTIONS

Expansion of Psychology's Domain.   Despite Erikson's lack of scientific rigour, his theory is considered by many to be one of the most broadly influential ever developed. Henceforth, when you encounter the terms *psychosocial development, ego strength, psychohistory, identity, identity crisis,* and *life-span psychology,* keep in mind that they are concepts that were first articulated by Erikson and have since become an important part of psychology.

Considerable Applied Value.   Erikson's theory has been successfully used in such areas as child psychology and psychiatry, vocational counselling, marital counselling, education, social work, and business.

Development of Ego Psychology.   By developing and promoting ego psychology, Erikson encouraged the study of healthy people in addition to neurotics and psychotics; encouraged the study of personality development across the entire life span; and painted a dignified picture of humans. Also, by stressing the positive influences of society instead, Erikson promoted the integration of psychology with such disciplines as sociology and anthropology.

SUMMARY

1. Although Erikson had only the equivalent of a high school diploma, an invitation to work in a small daycare introduced him to Anna Freud, who would train him in her growing field of ego psychology, which emphasized the autonomous functions of the ego rather than the importance of the id.

2. Erikson agreed with Freud that one's gender markedly influences one's personality but he believed anatomical differences always interact with societal influence to produce individual differences. Erikson did not believe that masculine traits are better or worse than feminine traits, but that masculine and feminine traits complement each other.

3. The best known aspect of Erikson's theory is his description of the eight stages of personality development. According to the epigenetic principle, the stages unfold in a genetically determined sequence. Each stage is character-

ized by a crisis that can be resolved positively or negatively. The stages and crises characterizing them are: (1) infancy—basic trust versus mistrust, (2) early childhood—autonomy versus shame and doubt, (3) preschool age—initiative versus guilt, (4) school age—industry versus inferiority, (5) adolescence—identity versus role confusion, (6) young adulthood—intimacy versus isolation, (7) adulthood—generativity versus stagnation, (8) old age—ego integrity versus despair.

4. For Erikson, the outcomes of the experiences during the stages of development are reversible; that is, a favourable outcome can become unfavourable, and an unfavourable outcome can become favourable. Erikson viewed the therapeutic process mainly as a means of reversing the negative outcomes of various stages of development. The goal of therapy then was to strengthen the conscious ego, rather than (as Freud saw it) to understand the contents of the unconscious mind. Many other differences exist between Freud and Erikson; for example, Freud viewed religion as a collective neurosis based on infantile desires, fear, and ignorance, while Erikson viewed it as conducive to healthy adjustment.

5. Most research generated by Erikson's theory has focused on the stages of development and on his concept of identity, and generally support the predictions. Erikson's theory has been criticized for being difficult to test empirically, for portraying humans too simplistically and too optimistically, for supporting the status quo, and for being too moralistic. Erikson has also been criticized for not properly acknowledging those who influenced him. His contributions include expanding psychology's domain, developing ego psychology (concerned with healthy people), studying personality development across the entire life span, and stressing the positive role of societal forces. His theory has proved useful in many areas.

EXPERIENTIAL EXERCISES

1. Probably the most significant event in a person's life occurs when he or she gains an identity. Erikson believed this occurs toward the end of the fifth stage of development. The alternative to leaving this stage with an identity is to leave with role confusion. Drawing on the information in this chapter, would you say you have developed an identity or are you experiencing role confusion? Give evidence to support your answer.

2. Erikson asserted that one cannot experience true intimacy with another human until one has gained an identity. That is, two people cannot share themselves in a deep, loving relationship unless they have both gained an identity. Respond to this assertion as it applies to your life and as it applies to the relationship of a close friend.

3. To minimize life's confusion, adolescents often idolize and overidentify with a teacher, a television or movie star, an athlete, or even a friend. Was there someone in your adolescent years you idolized? If so, was this overidentification helpful? Harmful? Explain.

4. How did Erikson characterize those individuals experiencing role confusion or negative identities? Respond to Erikson's characterizations in terms of those you know.

5. Analyze your personality in terms of Erikson's theory. How have you resolved the crises that you have gone through? Which of the Eriksonian virtues do you possess? What stage are you in now? Does Erikson's description of that stage seem valid to you?

DISCUSSION QUESTIONS

1. Compare ego psychology with traditional psychoanalytic theory.
2. Summarize the eight stages of development suggested by Erikson. Include in your summary the crisis that characterizes each stage and the virtue that emerges if the crisis is resolved positively.
3. Define ritualization and ritualism. List the ritualizations and ritualisms for each stage of development and give an example of each.
4. Summarize the major differences between the theories of Erikson and Freud.

KEY TERMS

Affiliation, p. 143
Authenticity, p. 138
Authoritism, p. 144
Autonomy, p. 137
Basic mistrust, p. 136
Basic trust, p. 136
Crisis, p. 133
Culture, p. 134
Ego integrity, p. 144
Ego psychology, p. 132
Elitism, p. 143
Epigenetic principle, p. 132
Formalism, p. 139
Formality, p. 139
Generationalism, p. 143
Generativity, p. 143
Guilt, p. 138
Identity, p. 140
Identity crisis, p. 139
Ideology, p. 142
Idolism, p. 136
Impersonation, p. 138

Industry, p. 139
Inferiority, p. 139
Initiative, p. 138
Integralism, p. 144
Intimacy, p. 143
Isolation, p. 143
Judiciousness, p. 137
Legalism, p. 137
Negative identity, p. 140
Numinous, p. 136
Psychohistory, p. 129
Psychosocial moratorium, p. 140
Psychosocial stages of development, p. 133
Ritualisms, p. 134
Ritualizations, p. 134
Role confusion, p. 140
Sapientism, p. 144
Shame and doubt, p. 137
Stagnation, p. 143
Totalism, p. 142
Virtue, p. 136

7

Gordon Allport

Biographical Sketch

Gordon Allport was born in Montezuma, Indiana, on November 11, 1897, making him the first North American-born personality theorist we discuss. Allport was the youngest of four sons. His father, John Edwards Allport, was a physician, and his mother, Nellie Edith Wise Allport, was a teacher, and both had a strong, positive influence on him. In his brief autobiography, he said:

> My mother had been a school teacher and brought to her sons an eager sense of philosophical questioning and the importance of searching for ultimate religious answers. Since my father lacked adequate hospital facilities for his patients, our household for several years included both patients and nurses. Tending office, washing bottles, and dealing with patients were important aspects of my early training. . . . Dad was no believer in vacations. He followed rather his own rule of life, which he expressed as follows: If every person worked as hard as he could and took only a minimum financial return required by his family's needs, then there would be just enough wealth to go around. Thus it was hard work tempered by trust and affection that marked the home environment. (1967, pp. 4–5)

Allport credited his lifelong concern with human welfare and his strong humanistic psychology to experiences like those just described. Contrast Freud's view of human nature (see chapter 2) with the one embraced by Allport:

Gordon Allport

Normal men everywhere reject, in principle and by preference, the path of war and destruction. They like to live in peace and friendship with their neighbors; they prefer to love and be loved rather than to hate and be hated. (Allport, 1958, pp. ix–x)

Although Allport was born in Indiana, he grew up in Cleveland, Ohio, where he attended public schools. At the urging of his older brother Floyd, a Harvard graduate (who also became a famous psychologist), Gordon Allport entered Harvard in 1915. He barely passed the entrance examination and his early grades were Cs and Ds. He worked hard, however, and finished the year with straight As. He graduated from Harvard in 1919 with a major in economics and philosophy.

Apparently not sure of what to do next and still seeking his personal identity, he spent the next year teaching English and sociology at Robert College in Istanbul, Turkey. Allport enjoyed teaching so much he decided to accept a fellowship offered to him by Harvard to do graduate work in psychology.

On his way back to the United States, Allport stopped in Vienna to visit one of his brothers. While there he had an experience that was to have a profound effect on his later theorizing. He wrote to Freud asking for permission to visit with him and permission was granted. Allport described his brief visit with Freud:

Soon after I had entered the famous red burlap room with pictures of dreams on the wall, he summoned me to his inner office. He did not speak to me but sat in expectant silence for me to state my mission. I was not prepared for silence and had to think fast to find a suitable conversational gambit. I told him of an episode on the tram car on my way to his office. A small boy about four years of age had displayed a conspicuous dirt phobia. He kept saying to his mother, "I don't want to sit there . . . don't let that dirty man sit beside me." To him everything was *schmutzig* [filthy]. His mother was a well-starched *Hausfrau,* so dominant and purposive looking that I thought the cause and effect apparent.

When I finished my story Freud fixed his kindly therapeutic eyes upon me and said, "And was that little boy you?" Flabbergasted and feeling a bit guilty, I contrived to change the subject. While Freud's misunderstanding of my motivation was amusing, it also started a deep train of thought. I realized that he was accustomed to neurotic defenses and that my manifest motivation (a sort of rude curiosity and youthful ambition) escaped him. For therapeutic progress he would have to cut through my defenses, but it so happened that therapeutic progress was not here an issue. (1967, pp. 7–8)

Allport learned from this experience that it is possible for "depth" psychology to dig so deeply that more important truths may be overlooked. Allport believed that he had perfectly valid, conscious reasons for visiting Freud and for telling him his little story, which were completely missed by Freud in his attempt to arrive at a "deeper" truth. About his visit with Freud, Allport (1968) said, "This experience taught me that depth psychology, for all its merits, may plunge too deep, and that psychologists would do well to give full recognition to manifest motives before probing the unconscious" (p. 384). As we see throughout this chapter, Allport believed the best way to discover a person's true motives is to ask the person about them.

Allport returned to Harvard, where he earned his MA in 1921 and his Ph.D. in 1922, at age 24. His early work was indeed indicative of what was to become Allport's own brand of personality theory. His first publication, co-authored with his brother Floyd, was titled "Personality Traits: Their Classification and Measurement" (Allport & Allport, 1921). His Ph.D. dissertation was titled "An Experimental Study of the Traits of Personality."

Allport's interest in personality traits was foreign to the psychology of his day. One dominant school of psychology at the time was structuralism, which sought to study scientifically the elements of conscious thought and the principles by which those elements become associated. The founder and leader of structuralism was the illustrious and authoritarian *Edward Titchener* (1867–1927). Allport described his meeting with Titchener:

> Standing at a frontier was a somewhat alarming business. The climax of my conflict came in connection with my single encounter with Titchener. I had been invited to attend the select gathering of his group of experimentalists, which met at Clark University in May, 1922, just as I was finishing my thesis. After two days of discussing problems in sensory psychology Titchener allotted three minutes to each visiting graduate to describe his own investigations. I reported on traits of personality and was punished by the rebuke of total silence from the group, punctuated by a glare of disapproval from Titchener. Later Titchener demanded of Langfeld [Allport's thesis adviser] "Why did you let him work on that problem?" Back in Cambridge Langfeld again consoled me with the laconic remark, "You don't care what Titchener thinks." And I found that I did not. (1967, p. 9)

Allport viewed his encounter with Titchener as an important growing experience: "The whole experience was a turning point. Never since that time have I been troubled by rebukes or professional slights directed at my maverick interests" (1967, p. 9).

Aided by a travelling fellowship, Allport spent the school year from 1922 to 1923 at the University of Berlin and the University of Hamburg, and the school year from 1923 to 1924 in England at Cambridge University. In 1924, he returned to Harvard, where he taught the first course on personality ever offered in the United States—Personality: Its Psychological and Social Aspects.

On June 30, 1925, Allport married Ada Lufkin Gould, who later became a clinical psychologist. They had one son, Robert Brandlee, who became a pediatrician. Except for a four-year appointment at Dartmouth College from 1926 to 1930, Allport was at Harvard for his entire professional career. He died of lung cancer on October 9, 1967, a month before his 70th birthday.

Allport was truly an eclectic theorist, taking the best from a wide variety of other theories of personality. However, he was the first to criticize what he considered the worst in those theories. At one time or another, Allport took issue with psychoanalysis, behaviourism (stimulus-response [S-R] psychology), animal research designed to provide information about humans, and statistical methods of studying personality, such as factor analysis (see the theories of Cattell and Eysenck in the next chapter).

Allport believed strongly that the principles governing the behaviour of nonhuman animals or of neurotic humans are different from those governing the behaviour of healthy adult humans; therefore, little can be learned about one by studying the other. "Some theories of becoming are based largely upon the behavior of sick and anxious people or upon the antics of captive and desperate rats. Fewer theories have derived from the study of healthy human beings, those who strive not so much to preserve life as to make it worth living" (Allport, 1955, p. 18). We see in this statement a clear anticipation of what would become humanistic or third force psychology (see chapter 15). In fact, according to DeCarvalho (1991), Allport was the first to use the term humanistic psychology.

Clearly, Allport battled with any viewpoint in psychology that obscured human individuality or dignity. If one had to isolate the dominant theme running through all of Allport's works, it is *the importance of the individual*. This theme put Allport in a position contrary to "scientific" psychology because it was considered the job of science to find the general laws governing all behaviour. Science was interested in what is generally true, and Allport was interested in what is specifically true.

Allport believed psychological research should have practical value, and in addition to his books on personality theory, he wrote: *The Individual and His Religion* (1950); *The Nature of Prejudice* (1954/1958); and *The Psychology of Rumor* (1947) with Leo Postman.

What Is Personality?

In his 1937 book *Personality: A Psychological Interpretation,* Allport introduced a unique approach to the study of **personality.** From the very beginning, Allport was opposed to the established viewpoints of psychoanalysis and behaviourism. Allport's early theorizing was influenced mainly by Gestalt psychology, which he encountered in Germany after his graduation from Harvard, and by the strong humanistic tendencies developed early in his life. Gestalt psychology emphasized the wholeness and interrelatedness of conscious experience and also ignored the unconscious mind almost completely. Allport said Gestalt psychology was "the kind of psychology I had been longing for but did not know existed" (1967, p. 10). In fact, Allport distrusted science as a source of information about personality. He was more comfortable with the traditional descriptions of humans found in literature and philosophy. This is not to say that Allport ignored information provided by the scientific method; clearly he did not. He did not want to be restricted, however, to scientific method in his efforts to understand personality. He believed much useful nonscientific information had accumulated through the years, and that it would be foolhardy not to make use of that information. In fact, Allport did not want to be restricted to any particular approach or viewpoint in his attempt to understand personality: "Better to expand and refashion one's theories until they do some measure of justice to the richness and dignity of human personality, than to clip and compress personality until it fits one closed system of thought" (1937, p. vii).

In 1937, Allport reviewed the history of the word *personality,* beginning with its ties to the Latin word *persona,* which means mask. He then reviewed 50 definitions of personality before arriving at his own, now-famous, definition: "Personality is the dynamic organization within the individual of those psychophysical systems that determine his unique adjustments to his environment" (1937, p. 48).

In 1961, Allport changed the phrase "unique adjustments to his environment" to "characteristic behavior and thought" (p. 28). Because Allport's definition of personality acts as a summary of most of his major concepts, we examine its key components more carefully.

DYNAMIC ORGANIZATION

Personality, though always organized, is constantly changing, or dynamic. According to Allport, personality is never something that is; rather, it is something that is *becoming.* Although enough similarity exists within people to maintain their identity from one experience to another, in a sense they never are quite the same people they were before a particular experience. Allport borrowed this idea from the ancient Greek philosopher Heraclitus, who said, "Nothing is, everything is becoming," and "No man can step into the same river twice." It is the same with personality; it has organization and continuity within the person, but it is constantly changing or becoming something different.

PSYCHOPHYSICAL SYSTEMS

According to Allport, "The term 'psychophysical' reminds us that personality is neither exclusively mental nor exclusively neural. The organization entails the operation of both body and mind, inextricably fused into a personal unit" (1937, p. 48).

DETERMINANT

According to Allport, personality is not an abstraction or a convenient fiction; it actually exists: "Personality *is* something and *does* something. . . . It is what lies *behind* specific acts and *within* the individual" (1937, p. 48). Allport believed a person is by no means simply a passive reactor to the environment. Rather, a person's behaviour is generated from within by the personality structure.

CHARACTERISTIC BEHAVIOUR AND THOUGHT

As we mentioned, Allport revised his definition of personality in 1961 by deleting the phrase "unique adjustments to the environment" and replacing it with "characteristic behaviour and thought." He did so because he believed the earlier statement placed too much emphasis on survival and thus on the satisfaction of biological needs. His revised definition covered *all* behaviour and thought whether or not they were related to adaptation to the environment. One's dreams for the future, for example, are just as important as satisfying the hunger drive, but they have little or nothing to do with biological survival.

Both versions of Allport's definition of personality stressed the importance of individuality. In the 1937 definition, the word *unique* was used; in the 1961 definition, the word *characteristic* was used. Indeed, as we have seen, the emphasis on studying individual human beings rather than on the laws governing all human beings was a constant theme running through all of Allport's work. He repeatedly said that no two humans are the same, and therefore the only way to learn about a particular person is to study that particular person.

Character, Temperament, and Type

Allport distinguished among the terms *personality, character, temperament,* and *type.*

CHARACTER

Allport was bothered by the term **character** because it implied the moral judgment of a person, such as when it is said that a person has "a good character." Allport preferred "to define *character* as *personality evaluated,* and *personality* . . . as *character devaluated*" (1961, p. 32).

TEMPERAMENT

Allport referred to temperament, intelligence, and physique as the *raw materials of personality* and all three are genetically determined. **Temperament** is the emotional component of the personality.

TYPE

A **type** is a category in which one person can be placed by another person. In other words, we use the word *type* when we describe other people. Types, therefore, are ways of categorizing people. If a person continually acts aggressively, we may say he or she is the aggressive type, which is to say that his or her behaviour fits into this category. Personality, conversely, is something that is within a person causing him or her to behave in certain ways. We can say personality generates behaviour patterns that can be described as types.

Criteria for an Adequate Theory of Personality

In 1960, Allport described five characteristics that he believed a good theory of personality should possess.

1. Views personality as contained within the person.   According to Allport, those theories that explain personality in terms of the various roles people play or in terms of behaviour patterns elicited by environmental circumstances are inadequate. In other words, personality must be explained not in terms of external mechanisms but in terms of internal mechanisms that persist from situation to situation. This effectively distinguishes personality psychology from social psychology.

2. Views the person as filled with variables that contribute to his or her actions. This statement, related to point 1, was made to show Allport's disdain of those behaviourists who assumed, for methodological reasons, that the human organism was empty. To those psychologists the proper way to study human behaviour was to make a "functional analysis" of stimulating conditions (S) and responses to those conditions (R). Such psychologists prided themselves on studying the *empty organism*. (B. F. Skinner led this group, and his theory is discussed in chapter 9.) In other words, if you could remove within a person all the S-R learning bonds accumulated over the course of a lifetime, Skinnerian learning theorists would picture a shell of a human being—nothing would be left over. Allport believed this position was especially distasteful and dehumanizing. For him, what was left over was the person, the essence of what made us individuals, what made us unique, what made us peculiarly us. "Any theory of personality pretending adequacy must be dynamic and, to be dynamic, must assume a well-stocked organism" (Allport, 1960, p. 26).

3. Seeks motives for behaviour in present instead of past.   Here Allport expressed his dissatisfaction with psychoanalytic theory that traces adult motives to childhood experiences: "People it seems, are busy leading their lives into the future, whereas psychology, for the most part, is busy tracing them into the past" (Allport, 1955, p. 51). According to Allport, neurotics may be prisoners of their past, and psychoanalytic methods may be useful in dealing with them but the motives for healthy, mature adults are found in the present. Furthermore, healthy, normal adults are aware of their motives and can describe them accurately if asked to do so.

We see in our discussion of functional autonomy, later in this chapter, that Allport viewed healthy adult motivation as independent of earlier experiences.

4. Employs units of measure capable of "living synthesis."   According to Allport, the integrity of the total personality must never be lost. People are more than a collection of test scores or conditioned reflexes. Whatever units of measure are used to describe a person, they must be capable of describing the whole, dynamic personality:

To say that John Brown scores in the eightieth percentile of the "masculinity-femininity" variable, in the thirtieth percentile on "need for achievement" and at average on "introversion-extroversion" is only moderately enlightening. Even with a more numerous set of dimensions, with an avalanche of psychometric scores, patterned personality seems to elude the psychodiagnostician. (Allport, 1960, p. 30)

In short, the personality was always greater than the sum of its parts, and Allport's theory never lost sight of the whole person. As we shall see, the unit of measure that he believed made this possible is the "trait."

5. Adequately accounts for self-awareness.   Humans are the only animals possessing self-awareness—that is, the only creatures that see themselves both as living, breathing participants in this world and also as objects influenced by forces around them. This fact must be considered in any adequate account of personality. We explore Allport's attempt to deal with this difficult problem when we discuss the "proprium" later in this chapter.

Allport's Concept of Trait

We have seen that Allport believed an adequate theory of personality would employ units of measure capable of "living synthesis." For Allport, that unit was the **trait.** To help describe the various traits that people may possess, Allport and Odbert (1936) examined 17 953 adjectives that have been used to characterize people. Allport, however, certainly did not equate traits with descriptions. Traits, for Allport, were actual biophysical structures.

Allport defined a trait as "a neuropsychic structure having the capacity to render many stimuli functionally equivalent, and to initiate and guide equivalent (meaningfully consistent) forms of adaptive and expressive behaviour" (1961, p. 347). In other words, a trait causes a person to respond to similar environmental situations in a similar way.

According to Allport, traits develop through a combination of innate needs and learning. He gave the following example:

A young child finding that his mother is nearly always present to satisfy his wants, develops for her an early affective attachment (conditioning). But later other social contacts likewise prove to be conducive to this child's happy and successful adjustment: playmates, for example, or family gatherings, or crowds at the circus. . . . The child gradually comes to seek people, rather than to avoid them. A trait (not an instinct) of gregariousness develops. The child grows eager for social intercourse; he enjoys being with people. When isolated from them for some time, he misses them and becomes restless. The older he grows the more ways he finds of expressing this gregarious interest. He seeks to ally himself with groups of people at the lodge, at the theater, at church; he makes friends and keeps in touch with them, often entertains them, and corresponds with them. . . . Sociability has become a deep and characteristic quality of this individual's personality. Its expression is variable; a wide range of equivalent stimuli arouse it. (1937, pp. 292–293)

Traits account for the consistency in human behaviour. Because no two people possess exactly the same pattern of traits, each confronts environmental experiences differently. A person possessing a strong trait of friendliness will react differently to a stranger than will a person possessing a strong trait of suspiciousness. In both cases, the stimulus is the same but the reactions are different, because different traits are involved. Or, as Allport explained, "The same fire that melts the butter hardens the egg" (1961, p. 72).

People's traits organize experiences because people confront the world in terms of their traits. For example, if people are basically aggressive, they will be aggressive in a wide range of situations. Traits will guide their behaviour because people can respond to the world only in terms of their traits. Traits, therefore, both initiate and guide behaviour. How a trait influences the way one will react to various situations is shown in Figure 7–1.

Traits cannot be observed directly, and therefore their existence must be inferred. Allport suggested the following criteria for assuming the existence of a trait:

> The *frequency* with which a person adopts a certain type of adjustment is one criterion of a trait. A second criterion is the *range of situations* in which he adopts this same mode of acting. A third criterion is the *intensity* of his reactions in keeping with this "preferred pattern" of behavior. (1961, p. 340)

Allport's theory predicts considerable cross-situational consistency in a person's behaviour. The type of consistency displayed is assumed to be determined by the traits a person possesses. Although consistency of behaviour is predicted or assumed by most personality theories, it has recently been found that a person's behaviour is not nearly as consistent from one situation to another as it had been thought to be. We examine this consistency-versus-inconsistency controversy in more detail when we review social cognitive theory in chapter 11.

Interaction of Traits and Situations.   In fairness to Allport, he never said that the possession of a trait or a pattern of traits necessarily caused a person to act the same in *all* similar situations. *Some* consistency in behaviour must exist before a trait or pattern of traits is assumed to exist, but instances of inconsistency do not necessarily suggest such traits do not exist. For Allport, a person's traits create a possible range of responses to a given situation but it is the nature of the situation itself that determines which of the potential behaviours actually occur.

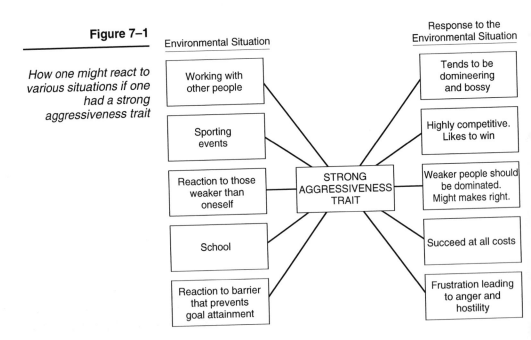

Figure 7–1

How one might react to various situations if one had a strong aggressiveness trait

Environmental Situation

Response to the Environmental Situation

Working with other people

Sporting events

Reaction to those weaker than oneself

School

Reaction to barrier that prevents goal attainment

STRONG AGGRESSIVENESS TRAIT

Tends to be domineering and bossy

Highly competitive. Likes to win

Weaker people should be dominated. Might makes right.

Succeed at all costs

Frustration leading to anger and hostility

Allport (1961) described how he thought traits and situations interacted:

We are forced . . . to the conclusion that while the situation may modify behaviour greatly, it can do so only within the limits of the potential provided by the personality. At the same time, we are forced to concede that traits of personality must not be regarded as fixed and stable, operating mechanically to the same degree on all occasions. Rather we should think of traits as *ranges of possible behaviour*, to be activated at varying points within the range according to the demands of the situation.

It is wrong to say that Jim has *y*-amount of anxiety, or of extroversion, or of aggressiveness. Rather we should say that he has *upper* and *lower limits* of these traits. This would mean that he never shows more than *x*-amount and never less than *z*-amount. His exact location within the range at any given time will depend on what the situational cues bring forth. To put the matter slightly differently, we may conceive of [the] situation as "pulling" a person higher or lower on his scale of potentialities, but always within his particular limits. (pp. 180–181)

Even in the early version of his theory, Allport said, "Perfect consistency [of behaviour] will never be found and must not be expected" (1937, p. 330). In 1961, he gave an example of how traits and situations interact to produce behaviour, "The young teacher is not always 'friendly'; he is not uniformly 'ambitious' in every direction; his 'enthusiasm' surely depends on what and whom he is teaching" (p. 333).

Thus, Allport believed that different situations, although similar, can arouse trait-related behaviour to varying degrees. Because of this belief, Zuroff (1986) concludes that Allport was an early interactionist, instead of a pure trait theorist. An interactionist is one who believes that behaviour always results from the combined influence of person variables (e.g., traits) and situation variables. We will say more about person variables, situation variables, and the interactions between them in chapter 11.

TRAITS ARE NOT HABITS

Habits are more specific than traits. For example, one may have the habits of brushing one's teeth, putting on clean clothing in the morning, brushing one's hair, washing one's hands, and cleaning one's nails. One has all these habits, however, because one has the trait of cleanliness. In other words, a trait synthesizes a number of specific habits.

TRAITS ARE NOT ATTITUDES

Attitudes, like habits, are more specific than traits. A person has an attitude toward something, for instance, a certain person, a make of automobile, or travel. A trait, conversely, is more general. For example, if a person is basically aggressive, he or she will tend to act aggressively toward strangers, acquaintances, animals, world affairs, and the like. A second distinction between attitudes and traits is that attitudes usually imply evaluation; that is, attitudes are usually for or against something; they are either positive or negative; and they imply either acceptance or rejection of something. Traits, conversely, are responsible for all behaviour and cognitions whether or not evaluation is involved.

Types of Traits

First, Allport distinguished between **individual traits** and **common traits.** As their names imply, individual traits are those possessed by a particular individual, and common traits are those shared by several individuals. Any group can be described by its traits. One might, for instance, describe the typical Maritimer according to a definitive set of traits, quite different from the traits used to describe Western Canadians. The same could be true for urban vs. rural Canadians, Anglophone vs. Francophone Canadians, and Aboriginal vs. Immigrant Canadians. In fact, those who travel to different parts of the country may be more sensitive to noticing different traits in different regions. For example, a group can be described as friendly, aggressive, or intelligent. Likewise, any individual can be described by his or her traits; one can be described as friendly, aggressive, or intelligent. When traits are used to describe a group, they are called common traits; when they are used to describe an individual, they are called individual traits. Although recognizing the existence of both types of traits, Allport believed strongly that the personality theorist should focus on individual traits.

The distinction between individual and common traits is often confused by the assumption that an individual trait is one that only a single individual possesses. This assumption is incorrect. It is almost impossible to imagine any individual without some degree of friendliness, honesty, neatness, aggression, or any other trait. What Allport meant by individual uniqueness is the pattern of traits that an individual possesses. That is, one person may have a strong friendliness trait, a weak honesty trait, and a moderate aggressiveness trait. Another person may be moderate in friendliness, honesty, and aggressiveness. When the list of traits is extended and when it is realized that each trait can be possessed to almost any degree, the number of possible trait configurations is extremely large. What Allport meant by individual traits was a unique *pattern* of traits possessed by a particular individual. Furthermore, it is important to remember that a trait specifies a possible range of behaviours. For example, many people are aggressive but no two people are aggressive in exactly the same way and under exactly the same circumstances. It is because any trait can manifest itself in an almost infinite number of ways that Allport (1937) said, "Strictly speaking, no two persons have precisely the same trait" (p. 297). Thus individuals differ not only in the pattern of traits they possess but also in how any particular trait manifests itself in their personalities.

Borrowing his terms from the philosopher Wilhelm Windelband, Allport insisted the personality theorist use the **idiographic method** of research—that is, the intense study of a single case—and avoid the **nomothetic method**, which studies groups of individuals and analyzes averages. Allport believed averages were merely abstractions and really described no single individual accurately. In other words, Allport believed the only way to learn about a particular person is to study that person, because no two people have exactly the same levels or configuration of traits.

Later in the evolution of his theory, Allport came to believe using the term *trait* to describe both group and individual characteristics was confusing. He therefore retained the term *common traits* to describe characteristics of groups but changed the term *individual trait* to **personal disposition**, which he defined as a "generalized neuropsychic structure (peculiar to the individual), with the capacity to render many stimuli functionally equivalent, and to initiate and guide consistent (equivalent) forms of adaptive and stylistic behavior" (1961, p. 373). Note that the definition of personal disposition is essentially the same as the earlier definition of trait.

Having decided on the study of personal dispositions, it was clear to Allport that not all dispositions a person possesses have the same impact on personality. He therefore distinguished among cardinal, central, and secondary dispositions.

CARDINAL DISPOSITIONS

If a person possesses a cardinal disposition, it influences almost everything he or she does. When you think of Don Juan, for example, you think of a man possessed by

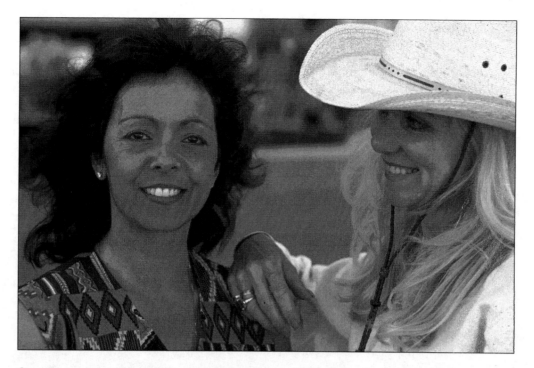

Canadians often attribute different personality traits to people from different regions of the country, language groups, or ethnic backgrounds.

romance, and when you think of Florence Nightingale, you think of a person driven by human compassion. Both individuals exemplify **cardinal dispositions.** Among the adjectives Allport (1937, pp. 302–303) used to describe the cardinal dispositions were: Christlike, Dionysian, Faustian, Machiavellian, Quixotic, and sadistic. Cardinal dispositions are observable in only a small number of people.

CENTRAL DISPOSITIONS

Think of a person you know quite well. Now pretend you have been asked to write an honest letter of recommendation for that person. Jot down the person's characteristics that you would mention in such a letter. Those terms on your list describe that person's **central dispositions** and summarize the consistencies in the person's behaviour. Examples might be punctuality, neatness, creativity, and persistence.

Allport believed each person possesses surprisingly few central dispositions. "When psychology develops adequate diagnostic methods for discovering the major lines along which a particular personality is organized (personal dispositions), it may turn out that the number of such foci will normally vary between five and ten" (1961, p. 367).

SECONDARY DISPOSITIONS

Secondary dispositions apply to a more specific range of behaviours than either cardinal or central dispositions. Secondary dispositions are similar to habits or attitudes but are still more general than either. These include a person's idiosyncrasies, such as preferences for certain types of food or clothing.

The Proprium

Earlier we saw that Allport defined personality as a "dynamic organization." We also saw that Allport believed personality consisted of biological as well as psychological structures such as personal dispositions. The fact that all of the diverse aspects of personality are continuous and are organized implies the existence of an organizing agent. In ancient times, this agent was called the soul. Later it was called the self, mind, or ego. Allport believed that these terms were too nebulous, and he renamed the organizer of the personality the **proprium**. The proprium includes all the facts about a person that make him or her unique.

This inward organization and self-awareness are not present at birth but rather, evolve slowly over time. Allport believed full propriate functioning characterizes only the final stage of an eight-stage developmental sequence that starts at birth and continues until adulthood.

1. Sense of bodily "me" (first year).   Infants learn their bodies exist because of the many sensations they experience. Although the sense of **bodily "me"** is the first aspect of the proprium to evolve, it remains a lifelong anchor of our self-awareness. The sense of bodily "me" is used to distinguish what is part of oneself, and therefore, warm and intimate, and what is foreign to oneself. Allport (1961) vividly demonstrated the difference between what is perceived as belonging to oneself and what is not:

> Think first of swallowing the saliva in your mouth, or do so. Then imagine spitting it into a tumbler and drinking it. What seemed natural and "mine" suddenly becomes disgusting and alien. Or, to continue this unpleasant line of thought for a moment, picture yourself sucking the blood from a prick in your finger; then imagine sucking blood from a bandage around your finger. What you perceive as belonging intimately to your body is warm and welcome; what you perceive as separate becomes instantly cold and foreign. (p. 114)

2. Sense of self-identity (second year).   With this sense comes the realization that there is self-continuity over time. That is, children come to realize they are the same people although there are changes in their size and experiences. The development of language is directly related to the development of **self-identity**. Specifically, children learn their name, which acts as an anchor for their identity through a variety of experiences. "By hearing his name repeatedly the child gradually sees himself as a distinct and recurrent point of reference. The name acquires significance for him in the second year of life. With it comes awareness of independent status in the social group" (Allport, 1961, p. 115).

3. Sense of self-esteem (third year).   **Self-esteem** is the feeling of pride that emerges when children learn they can do things on their own. During this stage, children often seek complete independence from adult supervision. That independence is achieved through children's further mastery of the language, and their acquisition of gross and fine motor skills like running, jumping, and climbing.

4. Sense of self-extension (fourth year).   During this stage children learn the meaning of the word *mine.* Now they realize that not only do their bodies belong to them but so do certain toys, games, parents, pets, sisters, and so on. At this time, the sense of self is extended to external objects. This **self-extension** can reach into organizations later in life, with affiliations to *my* church, *my* community, *my* politics. During the 2002 Olympic Games in Salt Lake City, Canadians celebrated medals in men's and women's curling and ice hockey, not to mention the controversial gold for pairs figure skating. Many Canadians felt a sense of ownership and affiliation to "their" athletes that strengthened their sense of identity as Canadians.

"We won!" Canadians took personal satisfaction in the victory of *our* hockey team at the 2002 Winter Olympics because of a sense of ownership and affiliation—an example of Allport's fourth stage of development, in which the sense of self is extended to external objects.

5. Emergence of self-image (fourth to sixth year).   During this stage, children develop a conscience that acts as a frame of reference for "the good me" and "the bad me." Now children can compare what they do with the expectations others have of them. The **self-image** develops by comparison to others. For example, a child may be "the best" at running, but not "the best" at mathematics. It is also during this stage that children begin to formulate future goals for themselves.

6. Emergence of self as a rational coper (sixth to twelfth year).   At this stage, children recognize thinking as a means of solving life's problems. In a sense, children begin to think about thinking. For example, children may now be flexible enough to alter game rules that earlier they would have rigidly adhered to.

7. Emergence of propriate striving (twelfth year through adolescence).   At this stage, people become almost completely future oriented. Long-term goals are created that give organization and meaning to life. According to Allport, the primary objective in life is not **need reduction,** as so many theorists would have us believe. Rather, it is **need induction** that is important. In other words, healthy adults create problems by formulating future goals that, in many cases, are unattainable:

> Propriate striving confers unity upon personality, but it is never the unity of fulfillment, of repose, or of reduced tension. The devoted parent never loses concern for his child; the devotee of democracy adopts a lifelong assignment in his human relationships. The scientist, by the very nature of his commitment, creates more and more questions, never fewer. Indeed, the measure of our intellectual maturity, one philosopher suggests, is our capacity to feel less and less satisfied with our answers to better and better problems. (Allport, 1955, p. 67)

Table 7-1	PERIOD OF DEVELOPMENT	PROPRIATE DEVELOPMENT
Eight Stages of Development of the Proprium and Functions Associated with Them	1. First year	Infant learns that he or she exists, through the many sensations experienced
	2. Second year	Child learns that identity remains intact although circumstances change
	3. Third year	Feeling of pride results from individual accomplishments
	4. Fourth year	Child extends self-image by recognizing that certain objects belong to him or her
	5. Fourth to sixth year	Child develops a conscience or a superego; now can deal with the concepts of right and wrong
	6. Sixth to twelfth year	Child uses reason and logic to solve complex problems
	7. Twelfth year through adolescence	Child formulates future goals and begins to organize his or her life around them
	8. Adulthood	Individual who has synthesized the preceding stages of development emerges

The possession of long-range goals, regarded as central to one's personal existence, distinguishes the human being from the animal, the adult from the child, and in many cases, the healthy personality from the sick.

8. Emergence of self as knower (adulthood). The final stage of development occurs when the self is aware of, unifies, and transcends the preceding seven aspects of the self. In other words, the **self as knower** synthesizes all of the propriate functions. In our daily experience it is most often the case that several, if not all, aspects of the proprium function simultaneously. Allport (1961) gave the following example:

> Suppose that you are facing a difficult and critical examination. No doubt you are aware of your high pulse rate and of the butterflies in your stomach (bodily self); also of the significance of the exam in terms of your past and future (self-identity); of your prideful involvement (self-esteem); of what success or failure may mean to your family (self-extension); of your hopes and aspirations (self-image); of your role as the solver of problems on the examination (rational agent); and of the relevance of the whole situation to your long-range goals (propriate striving). In actual life, then, a fusion of propriate states is the rule. And behind these experienced states of selfhood you catch indirect glimpses of yourself as "knower." (p. 137)

The term *proprium* refers to all eight aspects of the self. The development of the proprium is summarized in Table 7-1.

CONSCIENCE

According to Allport, the conscience emerges along with several aspects of the proprium, especially self-esteem, self-image, and propriate striving. Allport viewed conscience evolving in two stages. First a **must conscience** exists, which is the only type of conscience a child has. The must conscience evolves out of parental restrictions and prohibitions, which, after becoming internalized, guide behaviour even when the parents are not present. For example, a young child may believe that stealing (under all possible circumstances) is wrong; any single instance is unforgivable and must be punished. On this point, Allport agreed with Freud: "There seems to be no doubt that this early stage of conscience is, as Freud argued, due to the internalization of tribal and parental values. Violation causes anxiety and guilt even though immediate punishment does not threaten" (1961, p. 135).

Gradually must conscience is displaced by **ought conscience.** Must conscience is sustained by fear of punishment whereas ought conscience is tied closely to the person's proprium. For example, the young adult realizes that if certain long-term goals are to be attained certain experiences ought to be sought out and others avoided. Allport (1961) summarized the distinction between must conscience and ought conscience:

> There remain many "musts" in adulthood, but they spring now from a rational recognition of consequences and are seldom felt any longer as matters of conscience: I *must* obey traffic regulations. I must have the electric wiring repaired. I must not show her my true feelings. But, on the other hand, I *ought* to vote. I ought to write that letter. I ought to study harder. I ought to pursue the good as I see it. These are propriate value-judgments. No one will punish me if I fail to live according to my own preferred style. . . . Mature conscience, then, is a sense of duty to keep one's self-image in an acceptable shape, to continue one's chosen lines of propriate striving—in short, to build (and not tear down) one's style of being. Conscience becomes a kind of generic self-guidance. Emphasis has shifted from tribal and parental control to individual control. (p. 136)

Thus Allport agreed with Freud concerning the development of must conscience but disagreed with Freud's contention that the internalized values of authority figures guide a person's moral behaviour throughout his or her life. Allport did agree that the morality of *some* adults is governed by infantile prohibitions and restrictions but considered these adults unhealthy. Normal adult morality is of the *ought* variety and is therefore rational, future oriented, and personal.

Consider the case of Robert Latimer, a Saskatchewan farmer who in October 1993 smothered his 12-year-old daughter Tracy because he could not watch her suffer from a severe form of cerebral palsy. A jury gave Latimer a life sentence for second-degree murder, a ruling upheld in January 2001 by the Supreme Court of Canada. Latimer believes that killing is wrong in general but that his own actions were justified by extreme circumstances. Many Canadians agreed and called for mercy. Disability awareness groups disagreed, asserting that leniency would diminish the perceived value of a disabled person's life. The case involved complex issues of *must* conscience (killing is murder) and *ought* conscience (balancing relief from pain against the value of human life).

Functional Autonomy

Allport had four requirements for an adequate theory of motivation.

1. It must recognize the contemporary nature of motives. As we have seen, Allport did not believe the child is the father to the man, as the psychoanalysts believed. According to Allport, for a motive to be a motive, it must exist in the present. "Whatever moves us," Allport said, "must move us now" (1961, p. 220).

2. It must allow for the existence of several types of motives. Allport believed that to reduce all human motivation to one factor, such as drive reduction or aspiring for superiority, was foolhardy. "Motives are so diverse in type that we find it difficult to discover the common denominator" (1961, p. 221).

3. It must recognize the importance of cognitive processes. To Allport, it was impossible to truly understand a person's motives without knowing his or her plans, values, and intentions. He believed that perhaps the best way to understand a person's personality structure is to ask, What do you want to be doing five years from now?

Like Adler and Erikson, Allport emphasized the importance of conscious, cognitive processes as guides for behaviour.

4. It must recognize that each person's pattern of motivation is unique.   Just as no two people have the same configuration of traits, neither do they have the same configuration of motives. Because Allport believed traits initiated behaviour, they can be equated with motives. Allport asked, "What is the relation between units of motivation and units of personality? I would suggest that all units of motivation are at the same time units of personality" (1960, p. 118).

Allport introduced a motivational concept he believed satisfied the foregoing requirements. This was **functional autonomy,** which he defined as "any acquired system of motivation in which the tensions involved are not of the same kind as the antecedent tensions from which the acquired system developed" (1961, p. 229). Allport believed the concept of functional autonomy to be so important that he referred to it as "a declaration of independence for the psychology of personality" (1937, p. 207).

Functional autonomy, which is probably Allport's most famous concept, simply means that the reasons why an adult now engages in some form of behaviour are not the same reasons that originally caused him or her to engage in that behaviour. In other words, past motives are not functionally related to present motives. Allport offered the following examples:

> An ex-sailor has a craving for the sea, a musician longs to return to his instrument after an enforced absence, a miser continues to build his useless pile. Now the sailor may have first acquired his love for the sea as an incident in his struggle to earn a living. The sea was "secondary reinforcement" for his hunger drive. But now the ex-sailor is perhaps a wealthy banker; the original motive is destroyed and yet the hunger for the sea persists and even increases in intensity. The musician may first have been stung by a slur on his inferior performance into mastering his instrument; but now he is safely beyond these taunts, and finds that he loves his instrument more than anything else in the world. The miser perhaps learned his habit of thrift in dire necessity, but his miserliness persists and becomes stronger with the years even after the necessity has been relieved. (1961, p. 227)

> A student who first undertakes a field of study in college because it is required, because it pleases the parents, or because it comes at a convenient hour may end up finding himself absorbed in the topic, perhaps for life. The original motives may be entirely lost. What was a means to an end becomes an end in itself. (1961, pp. 235–236)

Allport believed that when motives become part of the proprium they are pursued for their own sake and not for external encouragement or reward. Such motives are self-sustaining because they have become part of the person. To say that healthy adults pursue goals because they are rewarded for doing so was, to Allport, ridiculous. For example, Allport commented:

> How hollow to think of Pasteur's concern for reward, or for health, food, sleep, or family, as the root of his devotion to his work. For long periods of time he was oblivious to them all, losing himself in the white heat of research. And the same passion is seen in the histories of geniuses who in their lifetimes received little or no reward for their work. (1961, p. 236)

Allport distinguished between two types of functional autonomy: (1) **Perseverative functional autonomy** refers to repetitious activities in which one blindly engages, and that once served a purpose but no longer do so. These activities occur independently of reward and independently of the past but are low-level activities of little importance. An example is when a man still rises at 7:30 each morning although he has been retired for some time. (2) **Propriate functional autonomy** refers to an individual's interests, values, goals, attitudes, and sentiments.

Allport suggested that propriate functional autonomy was governed by these three principles:

1. **Principle of organizing energy level.**   This principle states that when one no longer needs to be concerned with survival and early adjustments in life, a considerable amount of energy becomes available. Because this energy is no longer needed for basic adaptation, it can be diverted into propriate striving—for instance, future goals.

2. **Principle of mastery and competence.**   Healthy adults have an innate need to increase their efficiency and effectiveness and to aspire to greater mastery. In other words, according to Allport, healthy humans have a need to become better and better at more and more tasks. This is another case of drive *induction,* rather than drive *reduction.*

3. **Principle of propriate patterning.**   The person's proprium is the frame of reference that determines what is pursued in life and what is not. This means that although motives become functionally independent of the past, they do not become independent of the proprium. In other words, all motives must be compatible with the total self (proprium). This assures the consistency and the integration of the personality.

Not all behaviour is caused by functionally autonomous motives. Much human behaviour is stimulated by biological drives, reflex action, reward, and habit. Allport recognized this but believed that behaviour under the control of functionally autonomous motives was characteristically human and therefore should be the personality theorist's focus of study.

The Healthy, Mature Adult Personality

Allport's theory did not grow out of psychoanalysis. In fact, he was not a psychotherapist and was not much interested in emotionally disturbed people. He believed strongly that the principles governing the healthy, adult personality could not be learned by studying animals, children, the past, or neurotics. According to Allport, the difference between a neurotic and a healthy person is that the former's motives lie in the past whereas the latter's lie in the present or future. Allport's humanistic orientation is clearly seen in his following lament:

> We find today many studies of criminals, few of law-abiders; many of fear, few of courage; more on hostility than on affiliation; much on blindness in man, little on his vision; much on his past, little on his outreaching into the future. (1955, p. 18)

Allport's concern with studying healthy humans instead of neurotics is remarkably close to the position taken later by Maslow (see chapter 15). Maslow attempted to correct the situation by exploring the lives of what he called self-actualizing people. The list of characteristics that Maslow found such persons to possess is similar to the following list of attributes Allport believed characterized the normal, healthy adult.

1. Capacity for self-extension. Healthy adults participate in a wide range of events. They have many friends and hobbies and tend to be active politically or religiously.

2. Capacity for warm human interactions. Healthy adults are capable of intimate relationships with others without being possessive or jealous. Such people are compassionate, as evidenced by their ability to tolerate major differences in values and beliefs between themselves and others. In a large and diverse multicultural country like Canada, tolerance for language and cultural differences is especially important for a healthy society.

3. Demonstration of emotional security and self-acceptance. Healthy adults have the tolerance necessary to accept the conflicts and frustrations inevitable in life. They also have a positive image of themselves. This is contrasted with the immature person who is filled with self-pity and has a negative self-image.

4. Demonstration of realistic perceptions. Healthy adults see events as they are, not as they hoped they would be. They display good common sense when appraising a situation and in determining adjustments to it. By this, Allport is suggesting that mental wellness comes when defence mechanisms are not needed.

5. Demonstration of self-objectification. Healthy adults have an accurate picture of their own assets and liabilities. They also have a good sense of humour. Humour necessitates the ability to laugh at what one cherishes, including oneself. People who are not sure of themselves see nothing funny about jokes directed at them or at what they believe.

6. Demonstration of unifying philosophy of life. According to Allport, the lives of healthy adults are "ordered or steered toward some selected goal or goals. Each person has something quite special to live for, a major intention" (1961, pp. 294–295).

Allport, like Jung and Erikson and to a somewhat lesser degree like Adler, placed great importance on religion; and like Jung, Allport believed the importance of religion can be realized only in adulthood. Allport believed all healthy adults have a need for some unifying orientation, and although this orientation is commonly religious it does not need to be:

> Psychologically speaking we should point to the close analogy that exists between a religious orientation and all other high-level schemata that influence the course of becoming. Every man, whether he is religiously inclined or not, has his own ultimate presuppositions. He finds he cannot live his life without them, and for him they are true. Such presuppositions, whether they are called ideologies, philosophies, notions, or merely hunches about life, exert creative pressure upon all conduct that is subsidiary to them (which is to say, upon nearly *all* of a man's conduct). (Allport, 1955, pp. 95–96)

We have more to say about Allport's views on religion later but first we present Allport's view of the unhealthy individual.

Unhealthy People. According to Allport, the healthy person is one who displays the six characteristics listed above and who is in a constant state of becoming. Such a person is future oriented. Unhealthy people are those whose growth has been stifled. Their motives are often found in their past rather than in the present or future. In his explanation of why some children develop into unhealthy adults, Allport essentially accepted Horney's position:

All in all a generous minimum of security seems required in early years for a start toward a productive life-style. Without it the individual develops a pathological craving for security, and is less able than others to tolerate setbacks in maturity. Through his insistent demanding, jealousy, depredations, and egoism he betrays the craving that still haunts him. By contrast, the child who receives adequate gratification of his infant needs is more likely to be prepared to give up his habits of demanding, and to learn tolerance for his later frustrations. Having completed successfully one stage of development he is free to abandon the habits appropriate to this stage and to enter the mature reaches of becoming. Having known acceptance in an affectionate environment he learns more readily to accept himself, to tolerate the ways of the world, and to handle the conflicts of later life in a mature manner. (1955, p. 32)

To overcome his or her difficulties, the unhealthy person must experience the love that he or she missed early in life. This love can be provided by family, friends, or a therapist. In any case, "Love received and love given comprise the best form of therapy" (Allport, 1955, p. 33). This advice was to be echoed in the work of Carl Rogers, with terms such as unconditional positive regard and conditions of worth (see Chapter 14).

It is important to note that, according to Allport, the unhealthy person becomes healthy when he or she begins living in accordance with his or her proprium—that is, in accordance with his or her own personal goals, values, and aspirations. Health, therefore, is not defined in terms of adjustment to societal standards. In fact, conformity to societal standards can cause otherwise healthy people to become unhealthy or make unhealthy people even more unhealthy. Allport explained why:

Society itself is sick. Why then make a patient content with its injustices, hypocrisies, and wars? And to what society shall we adjust the patient? To his social class, thus making him provincial and depriving him of aspiration? To his nation, thus giving him no vision of mankind as a whole? It is doubtful that we can accept society (any society) as a standard for a healthy personality. A head-hunter society demands well-adjusted head-hunters as citizens, but is the deviant in this group who questions the value of decapitation necessarily an immature human being? (1961, p. 305)

Religion

Freud viewed the need for religion as a characteristic of the weak or the neurotic whereas Allport believed a religious orientation often characterizes the healthy adult personality. Allport believed, however, that embracing some forms of religion was beneficial and embracing other forms was harmful. In other words, for Allport, there was healthy religion and unhealthy religion.

EXTRINSIC RELIGION

Extrinsic religion is unhealthy religion. It is immature and is often a carryover from childhood. Such religion constructs a deity who favours the interests of those who believe in him, "like a Santa Claus or an overindulgent father. Or the sentiment may be of a tribal sort: 'My church is better than your church. God prefers my people to your people'" (Allport, 1961, p. 300). Extrinsic religion is often embraced because it is superficially useful. For example, membership in a church can be used to make business contacts or to become a respected member of the community. Extrinsic religion tends to be a divisive factor in a person's life rather than a unifying theme. In fact, embracing extrinsic religion creates an individual who lacks most, if not all, of the criteria of a healthy, mature adult:

> Studies show that ethnic prejudice is more common among churchgoers than among nonchurchgoers. This fact alone shows that religion is often divisive rather than unifying. Extrinsic religion lends support to exclusions, prejudices, hatreds that negate all our criteria of maturity. The self is not extended; there is no warm relating of self to others, no emotional security, no realistic perception, no self-insight or humor. (Allport, 1961, p. 300)

Insofar as Freud criticized extrinsic religion, Allport agreed with him.

INTRINSIC RELIGION

Intrinsic religion is healthy religion. Intrinsic religion motivates a person to seek and follow the value underlying all reality for its own sake and as an end in itself. It directs the course of a person's life and development and facilitates the realization that many important experiences transcend one's own existence. It provides a possible explanation for the many mysteries that characterize human existence, such as the fact that human behaviour appears to be both free and determined, the simultaneous existence of good and evil, and the fact that the innocent often suffer. Furthermore, it creates a perspective within which to evaluate one's self and organize one's life. Intrinsic religion encourages an identification with all of humanity, not just with those who share one's beliefs. By providing a means by which a person can relate meaningfully to the totality of existence, intrinsic religion provides a unifying theme that characterizes the healthy, mature adult personality. With intrinsic religion in mind, Allport (1950) said, "A man's religion is the audacious bid he makes to bind himself to creation and to the Creator. It is his ultimate attempt to enlarge and to complete his own personality by finding the supreme context in which he rightly belongs" (p. 142). Allport himself was a devout Episcopalian and from 1938 to 1966, he offered a series of 33 meditations in the Appleton chapel at Harvard University (Allport, 1978).

In an effort to explore why churchgoers are often more prejudiced than nonchurchgoers Allport and Ross (1967) created the Religious Orientation Scale (ROS). The scale included subscales that differentiated between a tendency toward extrinsic religion as opposed to intrinsic religion. Contrary to their expectations, Allport and Ross (1967) found that not everyone could be categorized as either intrinsically or extrinsically religious. Rather, they found that some people embraced *both* kinds of religion. These people were labelled *indiscriminately proreligious* and were the most prejudiced, followed by those embracing extrinsic religion. Those embracing intrinsic religion were least prejudiced. The ROS has become a popular research tool, and we will discuss some of its recent applications when we evaluate Allport's theory at the end of this chapter.

Letters from Jenny

Given Allport's emphasis on the individual, how does one go about attempting to understand a specific person's personality? Allport believed that one of the best methods was to use personal documents such as diaries, autobiographies, letters, or interviews. Allport's most thorough use of personal documents to describe an individual's personality was a collection of 301 letters written by Jenny Grove Masterson (a pseudonym) during an 11-year period. The final version of this study was published as *Letters from Jenny* in 1965, although Allport had worked on the case for a number of years prior to that time.

Jenny was born in Ireland in 1868 and moved to Canada when she was five. She had five younger sisters and one younger brother, all of whom were very dependent on her because her father had died when she was 18. Jenny outraged her family when she married a divorced railway inspector. She and her husband moved to Chicago, where she described life as boring. Her husband died in 1897, when she was 29 years old. Shortly after her husband's death, Jenny gave birth to her only child, whom she named Ross. She worked hard and devoted herself to Ross. When Ross reached puberty she enrolled him in an expensive boarding school. In order to afford this private school, she took a job as a librarian and lived primarily on cereal and milk in a small, windowless room. Until Ross was 17, he and his mother were very close, but at that time he left home to go to Princeton. In his sophomore year Ross enlisted in the army, in the Ambulance Corps. Before Ross went overseas to France, Jenny visited him at Princeton and met two of his friends, Glenn and Isabel, with whom she later corresponded.

When Ross returned home, he had changed completely and, except for finishing his degree at Princeton, his life was characterized by a series of failures and quarrels with his mother. The most intense quarrel followed Jenny's discovery of Ross's secret marriage. On this Allport commented, "On his first visit to her [Jenny] following her discovery she drove him out of her room with violent denunciations and a threat to have him arrested if he ever tried to see her again" (1965, p. 6). Following this encounter, Jenny contacted Ross's old friends, Glenn and Isabel, who were now married and teaching in an eastern college town. They offered "to keep in touch" with Jenny, and the result was 301 letters. The correspondence started in March 1926, when Jenny was 58, and continued until October 1937, when Jenny died, at the age of 70. She outlived her son Ross by 8 years.

By 1928, Ross had abandoned his wife and begun a relationship with another woman named Marie. In a letter written in 1929, Jenny mentioned Ross's poor health. He suffered from an ear infection and, when they operated, the doctors found a tumour on the inner ear and an abscess on the outer tissue covering of the brain. Ross did not recover from his illness and died shortly afterward. In a letter written toward the end of 1929, Jenny blames Marie, who she refers to as a "chip" (whore) for Ross's death.

> My affairs. Oh, they are all in turmoil. The chip lady (although) all dissolved in tears, and of course heartbroken, is not too liquid to forget that material things count in this mundane sphere, and lo! she claimed Ross's clothes, and Ross's car. [She claims to be Ross's closest relative.] If she is Ross's nearest relative it is she who will receive the [Veteran's Administration's] compensation, and that would be tragic enough to make one die of laughter. She has only known him *6 months*. February was the beginning of their "Great Romance"—dirty and low as they are made—the low contemptible street dog. She killed Ross—morally and physically. (Allport, 1965, pp. 73–74)

Following Ross's funeral and cremation, Jenny was reported to have said, "The body is consumed, now we'll have a good steak dinner" (recollection of Isabel, in Allport, 1965, p.153).

In 1931, Jenny entered a home for women, where she lived until her death. The superintendent of the home reported that she had become unbearably difficult during the year prior to her death. For example, she swept her dinner on the floor if it displeased her, and she hit one of her fellow boarders over the head with a pail. The superintendent considered moving her to an institution for the insane shortly before she died.

Allport had 36 judges read Jenny's letters in sequence and they, along with Allport, used 198 trait names to describe Jenny. But when synonymous traits were lumped together, it was observed that Jenny could be described accurately using eight trait names. They were:

1. Quarrelsome—suspicious
2. Self-centred
3. Independent
4. Dramatic
5. Aesthetic—Artistic
6. Aggressive
7. Cynical—Morbid
8. Sentimental

Using a computer, Jeffrey Paige (1966), one of Allport's students, performed a complex statistical factor analysis of Jenny's letters and isolated eight "factors" characterizing them.

1. Aggression
2. Possessiveness
3. Need for Affiliation
4. Need for Autonomy
5. Need for Familial Acceptance
6. Sexuality
7. Sentience (love of art, literature, etc.)
8. Martyrdom

On reviewing Paige's study, Allport concluded that the automated approach yielded about the same traits as did his "longhand" approach.

There is probably no better example of what Allport meant by idiographic research than his analysis of Jenny's letters. It is because of this type of research that Allport has been accused of being more of an artist than a scientist.

Study of Expressive Behaviour and Values

Besides his studies of religion, prejudice, and rumour, and his extensive idiographic study of Jenny through her letters, Allport also investigated expressive behaviour and values. These studies retained his emphasis on the importance of the individual. His research on expressive behaviour, for example, investigated a person's unique facial expressions, style of walking, speech mannerisms, and handwriting (Allport & Cantril, 1934; Allport & Vernon, 1933). His *Study of Values,* first published with Vernon in 1931, is now in its third edition. To study values, Allport and his collaborators (Allport, Vernon, & Lindzey, 1960) devised a scale that attempted to determine the extent to which a person emphasized certain values in his or her life. Allport observed that the scale of values actually combines nomothetic and idiographic methodologies: "We begin with an instrument that measures six common traits [values], but end with a profile that is strictly personal and individual" (quoted in Evans, 1976, p. 211). The following six values measured by the scale of values were first proposed by Eduard Spranger (1882–1963) in 1913 (Spranger, 1913/1928).

1. *Theoretical.* The person emphasizing this value is primarily concerned with the search for truth. This value might be seen in a scientist or philosopher.
2. *Economic.* The person emphasizing this value is very pragmatic and interested in the relevance of knowledge. They seek applications of theories and ideas.
3. *Aesthetic.* The person emphasizing this value is strongly inclined toward artistic experiences, "as seen in painters like Alex Colville and Jack Shadbolt or musicians like Shauna Ralston and Diana Krall.
4. *Social.* The person emphasizing this value gives high priority to developing and maintaining warm human relationships.
5. *Political.* The person emphasizing this value is primarily interested in attaining power, as shown in New York financier Donald Trump or political leaders including Prime Minister Jean Chrétien.
6. *Religious.* The person emphasizing this value gives great importance to seeking unity and harmony in the universe. An example would be South African freedom fighter and Nobel Peace Prize recipient Nelson Mandela.

Allport, Vernon, and Lindzey (1960) reported that the scale produced the expected results; for example, clergymen scored highest on the religious value, art students scored highest on the aesthetic value, and business students scored highest on the economic value.

Evaluation

EMPIRICAL RESEARCH

Allport was the first to describe the personality in terms of traits, and therefore, the thousands of studies done involving personality traits are directly or indirectly derived from his theory. Also, Allport and his colleagues did more research to test their theoretical notions than any other personality theorists covered thus far in this text. Allport and Ross's (1967) Religious Orientation Scale (ROS) has been refined (Hood, 1970) and used in numerous other studies (Bloomingdale & Reinert, 2000; Donahue, 1985; Genia, 1998; Schiaffino & Zalesk, 2000; Wulff, 1991). For example, performance on the ROS has been found to be related to psychological health. Bergin, Masters, and Richards (1987) found that a high score on the intrinsic religion scale was negatively related to anxiety and positively related to self-control and effective personal functioning. The opposite relationships were found for performance on the extrinsic religion scale. Watson, Morris, and Hood (1990) found that people scoring high on the intrinsic scale had fewer personal problems than those scoring high on the extrinsic scale.

As we have seen, Allport and his colleagues also did extensive research on expressive behaviour and provided one of the few tools by which to study human values. Although Allport's scale of values is more than 50 years old, this simple, straightforward instrument is still being used. For example, Huntley and Davis (1983) found that students who later became physicians scored high on theoretical and social values and students who later became businesspeople scored high on political and economic values. Allport's early interest in expressive behaviour is now reflected in numerous experiments on nonverbal communication and body language. (See Harper, Wiens, & Matarazzo, 1978 for a review of such studies.)

Allport's theory has been evaluated within several domains of self theory. A good deal of research has explored Allport's third stage, development of self-esteem. Although we readily link high self-esteem with all that is good, like academic and vocational success and physical and psychological health, recent work suggests the picture is more complex. For instance, people with high self-esteem are more likely to deceive themselves (Baldwin & Wesley, 1996; Paulhus & Reid, 1991). To help illustrate this, suppose you had always believed you were very smart and especially good at school. But suppose also that you receive a shockingly low mark on a test — will this event prompt you to change your self-assessment? And if you do deceive yourself, will that help or hurt you? Edward Johnson of the University of Manitoba and colleagues believed that self-deceivers would cope better with negative information and perform better in the future (Johnson, 1995; Johnson, Vincent, & Ross, 1997). They tested a large group of undergraduates using measures of self-deception and self-esteem. They then set them up for an initial failure, using IQ-type problems, some of which had no solution. Self-deception was measured in part by how many problems they thought they had solved. Participants were then timed on how long it took to complete 20 solvable anagrams. Contrary to the researchers' expectation, self-deception had an *adverse* rather than a beneficial influence on later performance. That is, self-deception failed to protect respondents' self-esteem from the negative feelings of failure.

Finally, as kind of a belated tribute to Allport, there has been a resurgence of interest in the use of idiographic techniques (e.g., the study of personal documents) in the study of personality (Bem & Allen, 1974; Hermans, 1988; Lamiell, 1981; Pelham, 1993; Runyan, 1983; Stewart, Franz, & Layton, 1988; West, 1983; Wrightman, 1981).

CRITICISMS

Lack of Scientific Rigour.   Allport's theory was often criticized for being unscientific. Because all sciences seek to discover general laws, usually by using nomothetic methods, Allport's emphasis on the idiographic method, in which the single case is studied intensively, seemed unscientific. Furthermore, the study and understanding of *unique* individuals does not produce principles by which human behaviour can be understood in general. For many, Allport's insistence on studying unique individuals is more like art than science. For example, the study of Jenny's letters may be interesting and pleasing but unless it is possible to generalize what is found to other people it has little scientific value.

Circularity.   In Allport's theory, traits are inferred from behaviour and then are used to explain the very behaviour from which they were inferred. For example, if we say that Linda is aggressive because she hit Bud, we cannot then say that Linda hit Bud because she is aggressive. Such circular reasoning tells us nothing about the cause of aggressiveness. Likewise, if a person acts suspiciously in a variety of situations, we conclude that he or she possesses the trait of suspiciousness. When then asked *why* he or she acts suspiciously we say it is *because* he or she possesses the trait of suspiciousness. For Allport traits were used to both describe and explain behaviour, and that is circular.

Absence of Theory.   Some claim that Allport did an admirable job of describing personality but failed to explain it. A person's personality is described in terms of traits or dispositions arranged in a hierarchy, but little is said about how specific traits or dispositions develop or change.

Denial of Important Facts about and Approaches to Study of Personality.   Allport was criticized for assuming a discontinuity between animals and humans, between child and adult, and between normal and abnormal. He was criticized for placing too much emphasis on the conscious mind at the expense of the unconscious mind and for stressing internal causes of behaviour at the expense of external causes. Probably Allport's most severely criticized concept was functional autonomy. When most, if not all, accepted viewpoints in psychology were attempting to determine the relationship between early experience and adult personality, Allport claimed that such a relationship did not exist.

On the matter of unconscious motivation, it is ironic that the very experience that caused Allport to mistrust depth psychology may in fact have supported it. To demonstrate the ineffectiveness of psychoanalysis, Allport often retold the story, related earlier in this chapter, of how Freud had misinterpreted his relating of an incident on the way to the office—told, according to Allport, just to break an awkward silence. Faber (1970), however, suggested that Allport chose that particular story about a child with a strong aversion to dirt (of many that were possible) because of his preconception that Freud liked to hear "dirty" stories. Allport felt "naughty" in presuming to call on Freud, and he manifested this naughtiness by "pulling a dirty trick" on Freud. According to Faber, Freud saw through the entire situation and with his question attempted to put the conversation on a more honest level. Furthermore, Elms (1972) pointed out that Allport was a neat, orderly, punctual, and meticulous person, known as "Mr. Clean Personality." According to Elms, Freud immediately saw Allport's "pathological" concern with dirt, and therefore his question to Allport was not as far off the mark as Allport suggested. Elms claimed Allport tried to change the topic immediately after Freud's question because Allport knew unconsciously that Freud was correct. Such insights demonstrate either that Allport was wrong in rejecting the importance of unconscious motivation, or that nothing exists that psychoanalytic theory cannot explain after the fact.

Inconsistency of Behaviour Precludes Description in Terms of Traits.   As we have seen, Allport deduced the existence of traits or personal dispositions from consistencies in behaviour. Although Allport believed traits or personal dispositions allow a range of behaviours that are situationally determined, he still assumed considerable consistency in behaviour across time and similar situations. Mischel (1968) examined Allport's assumption and concluded, "With the possible exception of intelligence, highly generalized behavioural consistencies have not been demonstrated and the concept of personality traits as broad response predispositions is thus untenable" (p. 146). We say more about Mischel's conclusion and reactions to it in chapter 11.

Behaviouristic Critique.   The behaviourists believe behaviour should be explained in terms of environmental stimuli. The postulating of inner mechanisms such as instincts, an unconscious or conscious mind, or traits just creates additional mysteries that need to be explained. Once it is known that certain environmental conditions tend to produce certain types of behaviour, the explanation is complete. To say that traits (or anything else) intervene between the environment and behaviour is, at best, irrelevant. We say more about the behaviouristic position when we review Skinner's explanation of behaviour in chapter 9.

CONTRIBUTIONS

Original Concepts and Methodologies.   Allport pioneered the social psychological studies of such complex topics as prejudice, religion, rumour, and values. Also, he did more than anyone to define and clarify the concept of trait. Furthermore, Allport showed that a great deal can be learned about a person by using the straightforward methods of self-reports, personal documents, and the observation of expressive behaviour. "Too often," Allport said, "we fail to consult the richest of all sources of data, namely, the subject's own self-knowledge" (1962, p. 413). Allport was willing to use whatever method he believed contributed to an understanding of human behaviour. "Whatever contributes to a knowledge of human nature" he said, "is an admissible method to science" (1942, p. 140). Allport thus facilitated the spirit of eclecticism that characterizes much of contemporary psychology.

Refreshingly New Way of Viewing Personality.   Like Adler's, Allport's theory can be considered a forerunner of the existential-humanistic theories that we review in chapters 13 to 16. All such theories have in common the emphasis on the uniqueness of the individual and the beliefs that human motives are not merely biological in nature, that humans are future oriented, and that psychology should be socially relevant. Allport believed in all of these statements. In fact, Allport resisted many powerful trends in psychology because he believed they caused humans to lose their individuality. The healthy person that Allport envisioned creates tension in his or her life by creating future goals, is rational, possesses an "ought" rather than a "must" conscience, and, if he or she is religious, embraces intrinsic rather than extrinsic religion. Also, the healthy person, while belonging to various groups, ultimately identifies with all humankind. Allport's major concern was with the dignity and uniqueness of each human being.

SUMMARY

1. Allport was the first personality theorist from North America. His 1937 definition of personality emphasized personality as dynamic, organized, and unique. Personality is also real in that it both initiates and guides behaviour. He distinguished between *personality, character, temperament,* and *type. Character* implies evaluation. *Temperament,* intelligence, and physique are the innate "raw materials" of personality. And *type* is a classification used by one person to categorize another person.

2. Allport theorized that traits provided the structure, the uniqueness, and the motivation that characterizes a person's personality. Individual traits refer to those patterns of traits that characterize individuals and also the way in which a particular trait, such as aggressiveness, manifests itself in a particular individual's personality. What Allport originally called individual traits he later renamed personality dispositions to avoid their confusion with common traits (those that characterize groups of individuals).

3. Nomothetic methods are used to examine what people have in common, but Allport's idiographic methods are used to discover what is true about the individual. Because not all personal dispositions have the same influences on one's behaviour, Allport distinguished among cardinal dispositions, which influence almost everything a person does; central dispositions, of which everyone has five to ten; and secondary dispositions, which are only slightly more general than a complex habit. *Letters from Jenny* (1965) summarized Allport's major idiographic research project, in which a woman's dispositions are studied through the 301 letters she wrote during an 11-year period.

4. Allport believed that the mature adult personality developed slowly through eight stages: (1) the bodily "me," (2) self-identity, (3) self-esteem, (4) self-extension, (5) self-image, (6) self as rational coper, (7) propriate striving, and (8) self as knower. Allport mainly studied healthy, adult humans, believed to display the following characteristics: (1) self-extension, (2) warm human interactions, (3) emotional security and self-acceptance, (4) realistic perceptions, (5) self-objectification, and (6) a unifying philosophy of life.

5. Allport distinguished between "must" conscience, which exists when a child's or an unhealthy adult's moral behaviour is guided by the internalized values of authority figures; and an "ought" conscience, which exists when a person's moral behaviour is guided by personal values and propriate strivings. Allport's most controversial concept was functional autonomy—although one set of circumstances originally may have explained the existence of a motive, that motive can exist in an adult independently of those earlier circumstances.

6. Like Horney, Allport believed that the unhealthy person is one whose positive growth has been stifled by a lack of childhood security. To overcome the damage done by the lack of security the person must feel loved by family, friends, or a therapist. A person can also become unhealthy by conforming to the mores of society. Religion can be either healthy or unhealthy. Extrinsic religion is superficial and not conducive to personal growth; intrinsic religion involves the honest quest for meaning and higher purpose in life, and can provide the type of unifying philosophy of life that characterizes the personalities of healthy people.

7. Allport and his colleagues did extensive research on expressive behaviour and created a scale by which human values could be measured. Allport's influence on current research on personality can be seen in the popularity of the concept of trait, a call for greater use of personal documents in assessing personality, a re-emergence of idiographic research in general, and the popularity of experiments on nonverbal communication and body language.

8. Allport's theory has been criticized for being unscientific and circular, ignoring important facts about personality such as unconscious motivation and the importance of early experience, predicting that human behaviour is more consistent than it actually is, and postulating inner mechanisms that confuse rather than clarify our understanding of personality. Allport's theory has been praised for being the first to study such important topics as rumour, prejudice, traits, and values; for showing the benefits of accepting personal reports and documents at face value; for using expressive behaviours in assessing personality; and for doing much to promote what is now called existential-humanistic psychology.

EXPERIENTIAL EXERCISES

1. Apply Allport's criteria for a mature, healthy personality to yourself. First, list the criterion that characterizes you the most, then second most, and so on. Be sure to elaborate on your unifying philosophy of life, if such a philosophy characterizes your life. Using Allport's criteria, do you think you are a mature, healthy person? What, if anything, still needs improvement?

2. Allport distinguished between extrinsic religion and intrinsic religion. Review his distinction and then indicate whether religion plays an important role in your life. If so, is it extrinsic or intrinsic religion?

3. According to Allport, the motives of healthy adults are grounded in the present, not in the past. In other words, their motives have become functionally autonomous or independent from the motivational forces that originally created them. Give an example of a functionally autonomous motive in your life. Describe what originally supported this motive and what supports it now.

4. Describe your personality in terms of cardinal, central, and secondary dispositions. Because having a cardinal disposition is rare, you may need to start your self-description with a list of your central dispositions. According to Allport, the average college student has about seven central dispositions.

5. Allport was interested in all forms of expressive behaviour including handwriting, doodles, gestures, and gait (walking style). He believed such behaviour reflects a person's unique cluster of personal dispositions. Analyze your own body language and other nonverbal behaviour, and also have a close friend observe and record your mannerisms and then compare notes. What consistencies were observed in your expressive behaviour? What do they indicate about your personality?

6. Allport asserted that a qualitative difference exists between healthy, mature adults and neurotics, psychotics, and children. Based on your personal experience, explain why you agree or disagree with Allport's assertion.

DISCUSSION QUESTIONS

1. First state Allport's definition of personality and then discuss each of the definition's major components.
2. Distinguish between nomothetic and idiographic research techniques.
3. List and describe the stages in the development of the proprium.
4. List and describe the six characteristics of a normal, healthy, mature adult.

KEY TERMS

Attitude, p. 161
Bodily "me," p. 164
Cardinal dispositions, p. 163
Central dispositions, p. 163
Character, p. 157
Common traits, p. 161
Extrinsic religion, p. 171
Functional autonomy, p. 168
Habit, p. 161
Idiographic method, p. 162
Individual traits, p. 161
Intrinsic religion, p. 172
Must conscience, p. 166
Need induction, p. 165
Need reduction, p. 165
Nomothetic method, p. 162
Ought conscience, p. 167
Perseverative functional autonomy, p. 168
Personal disposition, p. 162

Personality, p. 156
Principle of mastery and competence, p. 169
Principle of organizing energy level, p. 169
Principle of propriate patterning, p. 169
Propriate functional autonomy, p. 169
Propriate striving, p. 165
Proprium, p. 164
Secondary dispositions, p. 163
Self as rational coper, p. 165
Self as knower, p. 166
Self-esteem, p. 164
Self-extension, p. 164
Self-identity, p. 164
Self-image, p. 165
Self-objectification, p. 170
Temperament, p. 157
Trait, p. 159
Type, p. 158
Unifying philosophy of life, p. 170

8

Raymond B. Cattell
Hans J. Eysenck

Chapter Outline

In this chapter, we explore the theories of Raymond B. Cattell and Hans J. Eysenck, both of whom were educated at the University of London. Both theories are based on sophisticated statistical techniques, and both place great importance on the role of genetic factors in personality. However, it is often the case in science that researchers with similar orientations examine similar sets of data using similar techniques but arrive at very different conclusions. As we will see, there are common ideas in the theories of Cattell and Eysenck, yet the theories differ in several significant ways.

Previous chapters introduced theories that attempted, in part, to improve on the Freudian tradition. These theories shared an interest in development from infancy through the later years, and with the exception of Allport's theory, they also traced many abnormal adult behaviours to problems or conflicts that occurred during childhood. In addition, these theories tended to focus on the idiosyncratic expression of each individual's personality, to de-emphasize average group processes, and to place only minor emphasis—if any—on scientific methods.

The theories of Cattell and Eysenck represent distinct departures from the theories discussed in preceding chapters. Both emphasize the scientific discovery and measurement of basic psychological traits possessed by all people. Both use scientific rather than clinical methodology, and although both devote considerable time to psychopathology, they are primarily concerned with explaining the personality of normal adults. And, as noted above, both are more interested in the contributions of biological and genetic factors than in developmental events.

Biographical Sketches

Raymond B. Cattell

RAYMOND B. CATTELL

Raymond B. Cattell was born in Staffordshire, England, on March 20, 1905. He remembered his childhood as a happy one, with an abundance of activities like exploring caves, swimming, and sailing. He did, however, report considerable competition with his brother, who was three years older. England entered World War I when Cattell was nine years old and the war had a major effect on his life. Seeing hundreds of wounded soldiers treated in a nearby house that had been converted into a hospital taught him life could be short and one should accomplish as much as possible while one could. As we will see, this sense of urgency about work characterized Cattell throughout his academic life.

At 16, Cattell entered the University of London, where he majored in physics and chemistry. He graduated in 1924, at 19, with high honours. Throughout his undergraduate years, Cattell became increasingly concerned with social problems and aware that his background in the natural sciences had not prepared him to deal with those problems. These realizations prompted him to enter graduate school in psychology at the University of London, where he earned his Ph.D. degree in 1929. In 1937, the University of London granted Cattell an honorary doctorate in science in recognition of his many accomplishments. While in graduate school, he worked with the famous psychologist-statistician Charles E. Spearman, who invented the technique of factor analysis and applied it to the study of intelligence. As we shall see, Cattell used factor analysis extensively in his study of personality.

After receiving his Ph.D., Cattell had great difficulty finding work doing what he had been trained to do, so he accepted a number of what he called "fringe" jobs. He was a lecturer at the University of Exeter in England (1927 to 1932), and he was the founder and director of a psychology clinic in the school system in the city of Leicester, England (1932 to 1937). In 1937, he was invited by the prominent American psychologist Edward L. Thorndike to come to America to become his research associate at Columbia University. Cattell accepted Thorndike's invitation and remembered his first year in New York as depressing because he deeply missed England.

From 1938 to 1941, Cattell was the G. Stanley Hall Professor of Genetic Psychology at Clark University in Worcester, Massachusetts. In 1941, Gordon Allport invited Cattell to join the faculty at Harvard where, in the stimulating environment provided by Allport, Henry Murray, and Robert White, Cattell expanded the application of factor analysis from the study of intelligence to the more diverse problems of personality theory. He remained at Harvard as a lecturer until 1944.

Cattell never lost interest in applying the statistical technique of factor analysis to the study of personality. At the age of 40, in 1945, Cattell was offered a position at the University of Illinois as research professor and director of the Laboratory of Personality and Group Analysis. Without teaching responsibilities, Cattell was finally able to pursue his ambition of determining the structure of personality scientifically. Cattell's professional output while he was at the University of Illinois (1945 to 1973) was voluminous. Cattell pursued his goal until at least 11 P.M. every night and observed that his car was easy for him to find in the parking lot because it was the only one left.

Cattell married Monica Rogers on December 1, 1930, and had one son, who is now a surgeon. His wife left him a few years after their marriage because of their poverty and his total dedication to his work. He was married again, on April 2, 1946, to Alberta Karen Schuetter, a mathematician, with whom he eventually had three daughters and a son.

As already mentioned, early in life Cattell developed the belief that one should work hard and not waste time. Throughout his 70-year career, Cattell published more than 450 professional articles and more than 40 books. It is not only the quantity of Cattell's work that is impressive but its quality as well. His work at the Laboratory of Personality and Group Analysis won him worldwide recognition as a personality theorist. Cattell died on February 2, 1998 at his home in Honolulu at the age of 92.

HANS J. EYSENCK

Hans J. Eysenck

Hans Jurgen Eysenck was born in Berlin on March 4, 1916. His father, Eduard, was a celebrated actor and singer, and his mother, Ruth (Werner) Eysenck acted in silent films using her stage name, Helga Molander. His parents divorced when he was two years old, and his father initially wanted Eysenck to carry on the family tradition in the theatre. His acting career was short-lived, however. Eysenck recalled that at "the tender age of five or six," (1980, p. 154) he played a minor role in a film in which his mother starred, but he was not allowed to see his own performance in the adults-only feature (1990b, p. 6). In the film, he helped reconcile his estranged parents, but that role was not played out in his real life. His father remarried and remained in Berlin, and his mother moved to Paris to avoid Nazi persecution after marrying Max Glass, a Jewish filmmaker. Eysenck's father was Catholic and his mother was Protestant (Lutheran), however both were more deeply moved by the theatre and theatre life than by religion. Neither parent encouraged religious study by young Hans. After his parents' divorce, Ruth Glass left Hans to be raised by her mother in Berlin, and the grandmother promised him a new bicycle if he would study to be confirmed a Lutheran. He earned his bicycle, but religious training played no further role in Eysenck's development. For example, he stated that he "never had the slightest interest in religion, other than as a social and literary phenomenon" (Eysenck, 1990b, p. 10). Probably because of his mother's marriage to a Jew, one of Eysenck's college and graduate mentors later accused him of leading a Jewish conspiracy to take control of a psychiatric training facility. There is no evidence that he ever converted to Judaism, however.

Although young Eysenck believed that socialism would provide solutions to many of Germany's problems, he did not embrace Hitler's Nazi party, nor was he interested in joining the communist party nor various underground political movements. After being told that he could not attend college in Germany unless he joined the Nazi secret police, he left Germany permanently in the summer of 1934 to live in France with his mother and her husband. He studied literature and history for approximately one year at the University of Dijon and then moved to England, where he took college prerequisite courses at Pitman College and then enrolled at the University of London.

Eysenck's early life experiences and his year in France convinced him that he did not want to pursue a career in the arts, and he went to London with the intention of studying physics. In his 1980 autobiographical essay, he recalled:

I had, from the beginning of my conscious life, been quite decided that art was for fun, for emotional experiences, for enjoyment, and that my life's work would lie in science. By that I meant physics and astronomy. . . . I was told I could not study physics because I had taken the "wrong" subjects in my matric! I could not wait another year and retake the right subjects, so I asked if there was any scientific subject I could take. Yes, I was told, there was always psychology. "What on earth is that?" I inquired in my ignorance. "You'll like it," they said. And so I enrolled in a subject whose scientific status was perhaps a little more questionable than my advisers realized. (p. 156)

While at the university, Eysenck met and married Margaret Davies, a Canadian student, who was conducting research in aesthetic responses to odours for her master's degree in psychology. Eysenck graduated in 1938 and immediately began his doctoral studies in psychology, which he completed in 1940 with a dissertation on aesthetics. In 1944, Eysenck and his wife had a son, Michael, but soon after his birth, their marriage began to fail. Michael Eysenck went on to earn a Ph.D. in psychology and collaborated numerous times with his father, most notably on the book *Personality and Individual Differences* (1985).

While his marriage to Margaret Davies was in its final stages, Eysenck was introduced to and began a romantic relationship with Sybil Rostal, a psychology student. Although the romance was potentially professionally damaging, Eysenck did not attempt to conceal his relationship with Rostal, and neither career suffered. They were married in 1950 and gave birth to numerous research articles and books, as well as to three sons and a daughter.

During 1949 and 1950, Eysenck travelled to the United States where he held a visiting professorship at the University of Pennsylvania. During that visit, Eysenck studied training programs in clinical psychology and the roles of clinical psychologists in general. Upon his return to England, he campaigned for a more scientific psychological training for clinical psychologists, for more applications of scientific psychological principles in therapy, and for independence from psychiatrists. He became particularly dissatisfied with adherence to Freudian theory, both in psychiatry and clinical psychology. In his work at Maudsley Hospital (a premier British psychiatric facility), he began to develop a new approach to clinical training that focused on behavioural therapy. In 1952, he assessed the effectiveness of Freudian psychotherapy and published evidence that patients experiencing psychoanalytic therapy improved no more than patients who had received no therapy at all. Throughout his life he remained a severe critic of Freudian analysis as well as of projective testing methods (e.g., the Rorschach Ink Blot test).

Beginning with a review of L. L. Thurstone's work in factor analysis, published while he was still an undergraduate, Eysenck published more than 70 books and more than 700 research articles in a career that spanned more than 55 productive years. He founded the journal *Behavior Research and Therapy,* edited the journal *Personality and Individual Differences,* and conducted research in the area of personality until his death from cancer on September 4, 1997.

In 1991, both historians of psychology and departmental chairpersons rated Eysenck among the ten most important contemporary psychologists (Korn, Davis, & Davis, 1991). In 1996, the APA Division of Clinical Psychology, as part of the celebration of the 100th year of Clinical Psychology, presented Eysenck with a special Centennial Award, citing his insistence on scientific rigour, his influential theories, and his thought-provoking stands that stimulated much research by others.

Factor Analysis

Even the naive psychology student has heard something about Freud, Jung, or Skinner before reading this text. Few new students, if asked to name influential psychologists, would come up with the names of Cattell or Eysenck. It also seems fair to say that Cattell's and Eysenck's theories of personality have not become overwhelmingly popular among those studying personality. The lack of wide acceptance can be explained by two facts. First, the sheer bulk of these theorists' contributions has made it impossible for the "outsider" to digest. It would be difficult for any scholar not devoted exclusively to mastering the works of Cattell or Eysenck to understand the breadth of their theoretical work and critique it effectively. All that one could reasonably do with either theory would be to sample parts of it and hope that the most important concepts are included in that sample. Such a sample is offered in this chapter.

Second, both theories rely on **factor analysis.** There is no doubt that the apparent complexities of this technique have caused many to overlook Cattell's and Eysenck's theories. We contend, however, that factor analysis is only *apparently* complex, and the logic behind it is simple and straightforward.

Because, in most important ways, to understand factor analysis is to understand Cattell's, and to a lesser extent Eysenck's, theory of personality, we begin with a rudimentary discussion of this method.

The cornerstone of factor analysis is the concept of **correlation.** When two variables vary together they are said to be correlated, that is, *co-related.* For example, a correlation exists between height and weight because when one increases, the other will also tend to increase. The stronger the tendency is for two variables to vary together, the stronger is the correlation between them. The strength of the relationship between two variables is expressed mathematically by a **correlation coefficient.** A correlation coefficient can vary in magnitude from +1.00 to -1.00. A coefficient of + 1.00 indicates a perfect **positive correlation** between two variables; that is, as measures on one variable increase, so will measures on the second variable. A coefficient of -1.00 indicates a perfect **negative correlation** between two variables; that is, as measures on one variable increase, measures on the other variable decrease. A correlation coefficient of + .80 indicates a strong positive correlation between two variables, but not a perfect one. That is, there is a tendency for the two variables to vary together. For example, a person who is highly talkative is also likely to be highly sociable. A coefficient of –.56 indicates a moderate negative correlation. For example, a person who is highly talkative is *not* likely to be especially shy.

In general, factor analysis begins with a large number of measurements taken from a large sample of people, although one could also begin by taking those same measurements many times from one individual. The data may include many different types of variables. For example, we might record biographical information (birth order, number of siblings, ages of parents, etc.), results of different tests and questionnaires (IQ scores, scores on various personality inventories, etc.), results of different experiments (scores from a learning experiment, reaction times in a decision-making task, etc.), and perhaps even physiological data such as heart rates or EEG recordings. The next step is to intercorrelate all of the data, creating a **correlation matrix.** To simplify matters, we assume the data we are analyzing consists of performance on five tests. A hypothetical outcome of such analysis is shown in Table 8–1.

	TESTS	A	B	C	D	E
Hypothetical	A	—	1.00	1.00	.00	.00
Correlation Matrix	B	1.00	—	1.00	.00	.00
Showing a Complete	C	1.00	1.00	—	.00	.00
Set of Intercorrelations	D	.00	.00	.00	—	1.00
among Five Tests	E	.00	.00	.00	1.00	—

Table 8–1

Next, the following assumptions are made:

1. Two tests that measure the same variable must give similar results. In other words, tests measuring the same ability will tend to be correlated.

2.   The extent of agreement (correlation) between two tests will indicate the extent to which the two tests measure the same thing.

With these assumptions in mind, the correlation matrix is examined to determine which tests are highly correlated with each other. In other words, clusters of correlations are sought. Such a search is called a **cluster analysis.** When a cluster of tests showing high correlation with one another is observed, the tests are considered to measure the same ability or characteristic. An ability discovered in such a way is called a **factor,** and in both Cattell's and Eysenck's theories the term *factor* can be equated with the term **trait.** For Cattell, factor analysis is a method used to discover traits, which he regarded as the building blocks of personality. For Eysenck, factors themselves are subjected to additional analysis to discover what he calls **superfactors** or **types.**

The procedures of factor analysis can be summarized as follows:

1.   Measure many people in a variety of ways.
2.   Correlate performance on each measure with performance on every other measure. This creates a correlation matrix.
3.   Determine how many factors (traits) need to be postulated in order to account for the various intercorrelations (clusters) found in the correlation matrix.

In the hypothetical correlation matrix depicted in Table 8–1, it is clear that tests A, B, and C have a great deal in common with one another because they are perfectly correlated, but they have nothing in common with tests D and E. Conversely, tests D and E have a great deal in common because they are perfectly correlated with each other, but they have nothing in common with Tests A, B, and C. Our correlation matrix has detected two separate factors or traits. One is measured by tests A, B, and C, and the other is measured by tests D and E.

A sample of the ways in which three tests could be related to each other is shown in Figure 8–1. The upper left corner of the figure shows what would happen if the three tests measure separate factors. The upper right corner shows that tests A and B tend to measure a common factor, but Test C measures a different factor. The lower left corner of the figure indicates that all three tests measure a common factor. The lower right corner of the figure shows that test A measures one factor, and Tests B and C measure another factor.

Figure 8–1

Examples of ways in which three tests can be related

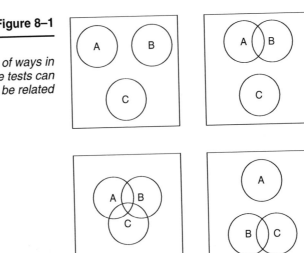

Factor analysis, then, is a technique, based on the methods of correlation, that attempts to account for the interrelationships found among numerous measures. The technique is certainly not confined to the study of personality. As mentioned earlier, Cattell's mentor, Charles Spearman, used factor analysis to study intelligence; and Cattell, in addition to using it to study personality, used factor analysis to study the characteristics of groups, institutions, and even nations.

CATTELL'S APPROACH TO RESEARCH

Cattell's early work is an example of **inductive reasoning** or inductive research. That is, he began without a specific guiding hypothesis, collected a large data set, and generated future hypotheses from patterns that emerged from the data. Cattell's procedure was to measure many people in as many ways as possible. For example, he recorded such everyday behaviour as how many accidents they had, the number of organizations to which they belonged, and the number of social contacts they had. This information could be drawn from medical or police records, school grades and awards, letters, diaries, etc. He called the information gathered by such observations **L-data,** the *L* for life record. He gave his subjects questionnaires on which they rated themselves on various characteristics. He called the information gathered by such a technique **Q-data,** the *Q* for questionnaire. Q-data includes performance on standard self-report inventories and various scales that measure attitudes, opinions, and interests. Cattell realized that Q-data has limitations. First, some people may not know much about themselves and therefore their responses to questionnaires, inventories, and scales may not reflect their true personalities. Second, some subjects falsify or distort their responses to create a desirable image of themselves. For example, an aggressive person may believe that aggressiveness would be frowned on and may try to respond in ways that suggest passivity. To overcome the problems inherent in Q-data, Cattell used a third source of data that he called **T-data,** the *T* for test. T-data is gathered in situations in which examinees cannot know what aspect of their behaviour is being evaluated. Examples include performance on word-association tests, the Rorschach inkblot test, or the thematic apperception test. Cattell referred to such tests as *objective* because they are resistant to faking. Cattell and Warburton (1967) listed more than 400 tests that appear to meet this criterion.

Cattell used factor analysis to search for clusters of measurements or factors that co-occur in stable patterns across a number of situations or over long periods of time. He then attempted to determine the extent to which these factors are, in fact, fundamental personality traits. As we will see below, Cattell claimed to have identified 16 fundamental traits found in the normal personality.

Cattell (1965) provided a colourful summary of his approach to understanding personality that reflects his enthusiasm for factor analysis:

> The problem which baffled psychologists for many years was to find a method which would tease out . . . functionally unitary influences in the chaotic jungle of human behavior. But let us ask how in the literal tropical jungle, the hunter decides whether the dark blobs which he sees are two or three rotting logs or a single alligator? He watches for movement. If they move together—come and disappear together—he infers a single structure. (p. 56)

EYSENCK'S APPROACH TO RESEARCH

Eysenck's approach was characterized by **hypothetico-deductive reasoning** (contrasted with Cattell's inductive reasoning). In this process, one begins with an experimental hypothesis derived from an existing theory, logically deduces testable predictions from the hypothesis, and then gathers data to determine whether the predictions are accurate. If they are, the hypothesis is supported and subjected to additional tests. If the predictions are inaccurate, the hypothesis is refuted and must be either abandoned or modified.

Eysenck's procedure began much like Cattell's in that he gathered a large number of measurements and used factor analysis to identify fundamental personality traits, those traits that, as we will see, are assumed to have genetic and biological bases. While Cattell believed that these primary factors or traits are the appropriate focus for analysis of personality, Eysenck was more interested than Cattell in the *intercorrelations* between the primary traits. He subjected this first set of factors to a second level of factor analysis, thus identifying clusters of primary traits called superfactors or types. Eysenck, therefore, focused on more general factors than those identified by Cattell.

It is important to note that Eysenck used factor analysis, for the most part, at the beginning of his research process. That is, he used the procedure to identify and verify the fundamental components of personality. Of factor analysis and his role as a factor analyst, he said:

> I'm the one who thinks least of it. I regard it as a useful adjunct, a technique that was invaluable under certain circumstances, but one which we must leave behind as soon as possible in order to get a proper causal type of understanding of the factors and to know what they mean. (quoted in Evans, 1976, p. 256)

NOMOTHETIC VERSUS IDIOGRAPHIC TECHNIQUES

Cattell's R- and P-Techniques.   During the early 1940s, when Cattell was a lecturer at Harvard, he often had lunch with Gordon Allport. At the time, Cattell's interest was primarily to discover the basic traits that constitute personality and then to determine how individuals differ in the degree to which they possess those traits. As we have seen, Cattell's approach to discovering traits was to measure many people in many ways and to factor-analyze the results. Allport expressed dismay that Cattell's approach stressed group performance (the nomothetic technique) and ignored the unique individual (idiographic technique). As a result of Allport's influence, Cattell began to investigate how trait strengths differ in the *same* person from time to time. Cattell's early idiographic research was performed on his wife but was soon extended to others.

The type of factor analysis that we described, in which many subjects are measured on many variables and the scores intercorrelated, is called the **R-technique.** The type of factor analysis that traces the strength of several traits over a period of time for the *same person* is called the **P-technique.** Figure 8–2 shows the outcome of one P-technique study. This study measured the same individual 80 times on eight traits over a 44-day period. The person being studied kept a diary during the experiment, and several of his major experiences are indicated along the baseline of Figure 8–2. For example, he had to rehearse for a play in which he was to play the lead role, he had a cold, the play for which he rehearsed was held, his father was in an accident, an aunt criticized him for not helping his family enough, and he was worried because his academic adviser was apparently hostile toward him. We can clearly see from Figure 8–2 that the various traits one possesses will manifest themselves with varying strength as one's life circumstances change.

Eysenck's Nomothetic-Idiographic Compromise.   Eysenck viewed his approach to personality theory as a scientific compromise between a purely idiographic method, like the one advocated by Allport, and the nomothetic method used by most experimental

(From Cattell, 1957, p. 553)

Figure 8-2 *An example of Cattell's P-technique, in which certain traits that a person possesses are measured over time.*

psychologists. He believed that, in the extreme, the former, in which each individual is seen as unique, makes derivation of general scientific laws and principles impossible. The latter, which allows for the scientific derivation of general laws, ignores the unique characteristics of the individual. Eysenck and Eysenck (1985) wrote:

> One of the major arguments against the hypothesis that all organisms are unique, profoundly different from each other, and hence incapable of being studied by the ordinary methods of science appeals to the simple fact that the existence of *differences* implies the existence of *similarities* and that both differences and similarities must be along certain measurable dimensions. . . . We shall not pursue here the debate between ideographic and nomothetic psychologists. . . . From one point of view the debate is a philosophical one and of little practical interest to psychologists. (pp. 5–7)

Taxonomy of Traits

CATTELL'S ANALYSIS OF TRAITS

As noted above, Cattell considered traits the building blocks of personality, and clearly the concept of trait is the most important concept in his theory. Most of his factor-analytic research was a search for personality traits, and that search has uncovered several categories of traits, which we review next.

Surface Traits and Source Traits.   The difference between surface traits and source traits was probably the most important distinction made in Cattell's theory. **Surface traits** are groups of observations that are correlated. For example, people with more formal education may go to the movies less than people with less formal education do. Such observations are superficial in that they explain nothing. They are simply a statement of what type of observed characteristics tend to be grouped together (correlated). Such characteristics can, and probably do, have many causes.

Source traits, conversely, are the causes of behaviour. They constitute the most important part of a person's personality structure and are ultimately responsible for all of a person's consistent behaviour. Thus every surface trait is caused by one or more source traits, and a source trait can influence several surface traits.

Another way to describe the difference between source traits and surface traits is to say that the latter are always manifestations of the former. The source traits can be considered the basic elements of personality, in that everything we do is influenced by them. Cattell concluded that all individuals possess the same source traits but in varying degrees. For example, all people possess intelligence (a source trait), but all people do not possess the same amount of intelligence. The strength of this source trait in a given individual will influence many things about that person, for example, what the person reads, who his or her friends are, what he or she does for a living, and the person's attitude toward a college education. All of these outward manifestations of the source trait of intelligence are surface traits. Our examples are somewhat misleading, however, because, as we have seen, hardly anything that a person does is caused by only one source trait.

Perhaps influenced by his background in chemistry, Cattell's goal was to establish a **personality sphere** that would provide the same function as the periodic table created by Mendeleev in 1869. Whereas the periodic table classifies the basic elements of the physical world, the personality sphere would describe the basic elements of personality. Unlike Mendeleev's effort, however, Cattell's goal has been elusive. The important question as to how many source traits exist is still unanswered. The search for source traits is complex and, at times, frustrating. For example, if a source trait exists, one might expect it to manifest itself in L-, Q-, and T-data, but this is not always the case. Although some source traits do appear when all three sources of data are factor-analyzed, others emerge from only one or two sources. Also, as Cattell's measures became more diverse and sophisticated, additional source traits were being discovered.

Cattell's early factor-analysis of L- and Q-data yielded 16 source traits that characterize the normal personality (see Table 8–2). The first 12 factors listed were discovered by factor-analyzing L-data or L- and Q-data. The last four emerged only from the factor analysis of Q-data. Cattell (with Saunders and Stice) constructed his influential Sixteen Personality Factor Questionnaire (16 PF) (1950) around these 16 factors. In addition to assessing individual personalities, this questionnaire has been used to compare a wide variety of groups. The performance of several groups on the 16 PF is also available for assessing the personality traits of various age groups, for example, ages four to six, six to eight, eight to twelve, and twelve to eighteen. In agreement with Freud, these tests indicate that the major source traits characterizing adult personality appear at about the age of four (Coan, 1966).

Note, for comparison with Eysenck's analysis of traits, that Cattell (1979) recognized the intercorrelations between the 16 "first-order" traits that are identified by the 16 PF. Cattell's analysis of these intercorrelations yields eight "second-order" or more general traits. Unlike Eysenck, however, Cattell felt that the important level of analysis is at the level of the 16 primary traits rather than at the level of higher order factors.

Table 8–2

Cattell's 16 Personality Factors

(Adapted from Cattell, 1965)

FACTOR	HIGH SCORE INDICATES A TENDENCY TOWARD	LOW SCORE INDICATES A A TENDENCY TOWARD
A	*Affectia* Socially adjusted Easygoing Warmhearted Outgoing	*Sizia* Socially hostile Indifferent Reserved
B	*Intelligence* Alert Imaginative Thoughtful Wise	*Unintelligent* Dull Stupid Unimaginative
C	*Ego Strength* Unworried Mature Stoic Patient	*Ego Weakness* Anxious Infantile Worried Impatient
E	*Domination* Confident Boastful Competitive Assertive	*Subordination* Unsure Modest Accommodating Humble
F	*Surgency* Talkative Genial Cheerful Responsive Happy-go-lucky	*Desurgency* Silent Serious Depressed Seclusive
G	*Superego Strength* Conscientious Responsible Persevering Loyal	*Superego Weakness* Unscrupulous Frivolous Irresolute Undependable
H	*Parmia* Carefree Overtly interested in sex Venturesome	*Threctia* Careful Overtly disinterested in sex Shy
I	*Premisia* Introspective Sensitive Sentimental Intuitive	*Harria* Insensitive Practical Logical Self-sufficient
L	*Protension* Suspicious Jealous Skeptical Wary	*Alaxia* Credulous Trustful Unsuspecting Gullible
M	*Autia* Eccentric Imaginative Complacent Self-absorbed	*Praxernia* Practical Conventional Poised Earnest
N	*Shrewdness* Socially alert Insightful regarding others Expedient Calculating	*Artlessness* Socially clumsy Crude Indifferent Apathetic

Table 8–2

(Continued)

FACTOR	HIGH SCORE INDICATES A TENDENCY TOWARD	LOW SCORE INDICATES A A TENDENCY TOWARD
O	*Guilt Proclivity* Timid Worrisome Depressed Moody	*Guilt Rejection* Self-confident Cheerful Without fear Self-sufficient
Q(1)	*Radicalism* Encourages change Rejects convention Freethinking	*Conservatism* Rejects change Disgusted by foul language Traditional
Q(2)	*Self-Sufficiency* Temperamentally independent Prefers working with a few assistants rather than a committee Prefers reading to classes Prefers textbooks to novels	*Group-Adherence* Seeks social approval Group dependent Prefers to travel with others Joiner
Q(3)	*High self-sentiment strength* Controlled Sensitive to uncertainty Does not make promise he cannot keep Does not say things he later regrets	*Low self-sentiment strength* Careless Rapidly changing interests Tries several approaches to the same problem Does not persevere in the face of obstacles
Q(4)	*High ergic tension* Tense Unexpected lapses of memory Suffers frustration because of unsatisfied physiological needs	*Low ergic tension* Relaxed Composed Few periods of depression Disinclined to worry

*Note that each factor is bipolar. A high score on a particular factor indicates a tendency to possess the traits on the left of the diagram, and a low score indicates a tendency to possess the traits listed on the right side of the diagram.

Constitutional and Environmental-Mould Traits. Some source traits are genetically determined and are called **constitutional source traits;** others result from experience and are called **environmental-mould traits.**

> If source traits found by factorizing are pure, independent influences, as present evidence suggests, a source trait could not be due both to heredity and environment but must spring from one or the other. . . . Patterns thus springing from *internal* conditions or influences we may call *constitutional source traits.* . . . On the other hand, a pattern might be imprinted on the personality by something external to it. . . . Such source traits, appearing as factors, we may call *environmental-mold traits,* because they spring from the molding effect of social institutions and physical realities which constitute the cultural pattern. (Cattell, 1950, pp. 33–34)

Thus, for Cattell, some source traits are genetically determined and some are culturally determined.

Ability Traits. Some source traits that a person possesses determine how effectively he or she works toward a desired goal; such traits are called **ability traits.** One of the most important ability traits is intelligence. Cattell distinguished between two types of intelligence, crystallized and fluid. He defined **fluid intelligence** as "that form of general intelligence which is largely innate and which adapts itself to all kinds of material regardless of previous experience with it" (1965, p. 369). Cattell defined **crystallized intelligence** as "a general factor, largely in a type of ability learned at school, representing the effect of past application of fluid intelligence, and amount and intensity of schooling; it appears in such tests as vocabulary and number ability measures" (1965, p. 369).

Cattell believed that too often a person's intelligence is equated with crystallized intelligence, which most traditional IQ tests attempt to measure. To help remedy the situation, Cattell developed the **Culture Free Intelligence Test** (1944), designed to measure fluid intelligence.

Cattell's research led him to conclude that both fluid intelligence and crystallized intelligence are strongly influenced by heredity. His research indicates that fluid intelligence is 65% inherited and crystallized intelligence is 60% inherited (Cattell, 1979, 1980, vol. 2, p. 58). Thus according to Cattell, not only is one's general intelligence (fluid intelligence) strongly influenced by heredity but so is one's ability to benefit from experience and to use what one has learned (crystallized intelligence). This belief, and its implications, is one of the issues that made Cattell a controversial figure. Psychologists continue to debate the relative contributions of genetics and experience to intelligence (one aspect of the nature-nurture problem).

Temperament Traits.   These are genetically determined characteristics that determine a person's general "style and tempo." **Temperament traits** determine the speed, energy, and emotion with which a person responds to a situation. They determine how mild-mannered, irritable, or persistent a person is. Temperament traits, therefore, are constitutional source traits that determine a person's emotionality. Of the source traits measured by the 16 PF, 15 are temperament traits and 1 (factor B, intelligence) is an ability trait.

Dynamic Traits.   Temperament traits determine a person's style of behaving; they determine *how* a person typically responds to situations. Ability traits determine a person's effectiveness in solving problems; they determine *how well* a person typically responds to situations. **Dynamic traits** determine *why* a person responds to situations. Dynamic traits set the person in motion toward some goal; they are the motivational elements of personality. Cattell elaborated two different dynamic or motivational traits: ergs and metaergs.

An **erg** is a dynamic, constitutional source trait, similar to what other theorists have called drives, needs, or instincts. Cattell chose the term *erg* (from the Greek *ergon*, meaning energy) because he thought the other motivational terms were too ambiguous. The ergs provide the energy for all behaviour. Cattell defined erg as

> an innate psycho-physical disposition which permits its possessor to acquire reactivity (attention, recognition) to certain classes of objects more readily than others, to experience a specific emotion in regard to them, and to start on a course of action which ceases more completely at a certain specific goal activity than at any other. (1950, p. 199)

It can be seen from this definition that an erg has four aspects:

1. It causes selective perception; that is, it causes some things to be attended to more than others. For the hungry person, food-related events are attended to more than events unrelated to food.
2. It stimulates an emotional response to certain thoughts or objects. For example, the thought of eating is pleasant.

3. It stimulates goal-directed behaviour. For example, the hungry person will do whatever is necessary to come into contact with food.
4. It results in some sort of consummatory response. That is, when one comes into contact with food, one will eat it.

Of course, ergs can vary in intensity. One can be hungry, sexually aroused, curious, or angry in varying degrees. The level at which an erg exists determines the amount of **ergic tension** present.

It is interesting to note that in claiming all human behaviour is ultimately instinctual, Cattell essentially agreed with Freud. Cattell's list of instincts (ergs), however, was far more extensive than Freud's. Cattell's research has revealed 11 ergs, which are listed on the right side of Figure 8–3.

A **metaerg** is a dynamic source trait with an environmental origin. In other words, a metaerg is an environmental-mould, dynamic source trait. Thus a metaerg is the same as an erg except for its origin. Both ergs and metaergs cause motivational predispositions toward certain environmental objects, however, ergs are innate whereas metaergs are learned. To clarify, the desire to sleep is driven by an innate or ergic tension; the desire to earn money is driven by a learned or metaergic tension. Metaergs are divided into sentiments and attitudes. According to Cattell, **sentiments** are "major acquired dynamic trait structures which cause their possessors to pay attention to certain objects or classes of objects, and to feel and react in a certain way with regard to them" (1950, p. 161). Cattell believed sentiments are usually centred on such things as one's career or profession, sports, religion, one's parents, one's spouse or sweetheart, or oneself. The most powerful sentiment of all, according to Cattell, is the **self-sentiment**, which organizes the entire personality:

> In the first place, the preservation of the self as a physically healthy and intact going concern is obviously a prerequisite for the satisfaction of any sentiment or erg which the individual possesses! So also is the preservation of the social and ethical self as something which the community respects. . . . Dynamically, the sentiment towards maintaining the self correct by certain standards of conduct, satisfactory to community and super-ego, is therefore a *necessary instrumentality* to the satisfaction of most other of our life interests. . . . It contributes to all sentiment and ergic satisfactions, and this accounts also for its dynamic strength in controlling, as the "master sentiment," all other structures. (1965, pp. 272–273)

A sentiment is an acquired predisposition to respond to a class of objects or events in a certain way. An **attitude** is more specific but is derived from a sentiment, which, in turn, is derived from an erg. An attitude, according to Cattell, is a tendency to respond in a particular way in a particular situation to a particular object or event. Cattell (1957, p. 444) described the manifestation of an attitude:

In these circumstances (Stimulus situation)	I (Organism)	want so much (Interest-need of a certain intensity)	to do this (Specific goal, course of action)	with that (Object concerned in action)

Thus an attitude is an interest, of a certain intensity, in doing something with something in a certain situation.

Cattell used the term **subsidiation** to describe the fact that sentiments are subsidiary to ergs (that is, dependent on them) and attitudes are subsidiary to sentiments. Stated

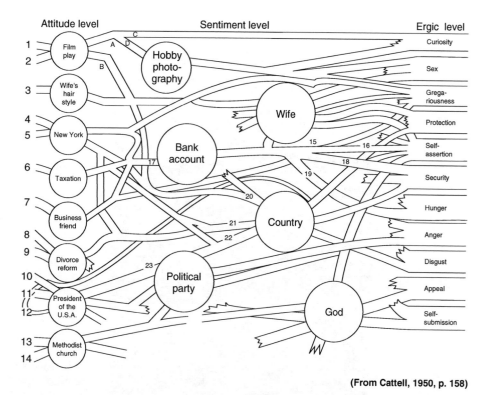

(From Cattell, 1950, p. 158)

Figure 8-3 *A dynamic lattice showing the relationship among ergs, sentiments, and attitudes*

differently, attitudes are studied (factor analyzed) to discover more basic sentiments, and sentiments are studied (factor analyzed) to discover more basic ergs. The relationships among attitudes, sentiments, and ergs are diagrammed in what Cattell called the **dynamic lattice,** shown in Figure 8–3.

It can be seen in Figure 8–3 that ergic desires are seldom satisfied directly. Instead, one usually goes about satisfying a basic need indirectly. For example, one may develop skills to get a job, get married, or satisfy one's sex drive. Cattell called this indirect satisfaction of an ergic impulse **long-circuiting.** Also, it can be seen that each sentiment is a function of, or subsidiary to, a number of ergs. For example, the sentiment toward wife reflects the ergs of sex, gregariousness, protection, and self-assertion. The most important point about the dynamic lattice is that it demonstrates the complexity of human motivation. Attitudes, sentiments, and ergs are constantly interacting and are constantly reflecting not only current circumstances but also an individual's future goals.

EYSENCK'S ANALYSIS OF TRAITS

Eysenck included the concept of intelligence in a general, informal discussion of personality, and he clearly acknowledged the genetic aspects of intelligence. The focus of his formal theory of personality, however, is **temperament,** defined as the emotional, motivational, and non-ability-related cognitive aspects of behaviour. Eysenck did not include intelligence, cognitive ability, or other so-called ability traits in this definition (Eysenck, 1970, Eysenck & Eysenck, 1985), and he often used the terms "personality" and "temperament" interchangeably:

École Polytechnique, the scene of the Montreal Massacre. Do you believe, as Eysenck's theory would suggest, that Marc Lepine was born violent?

The use of the term "personality" is often ambiguous; for some, such as R. B. Cattell, it includes intelligence, while for others it only refers to the non-cognitive aspects of behaviour. I will here continue the more usual habit of referring to non-cognitive aspects under the term "personality," and to the cognitive ones as "intelligence." (1990a, p. 193)

For Eysenck, the most important traits were those that Cattell would categorize as constitutional source traits. Thus, in Eysenck's theory, the important traits are those that are relatively permanent, that have clear biological origins, and that influence what he saw as the secondary behavioural patterns acquired through learning. Although he believed that the environment makes important contributions to overall patterns of behaviour and personality, Eysenck's theory does not have a trait-concept akin to Cattell's environmental-mould trait. For Eysenck, types, and the traits they encompass, are genetically determined; they do not arise from learning.

The implications of this concept can be seen when you consider criminal activity. Consider the Montreal Massacre of Dec. 6, 1989. Marc Lepine walked into École Polytechnique (an engineering school at the University of Montreal) with a semi-automatic rifle, and started firing—at one point shouting "I hate feminists!" He killed 14 women before turning the rifle on himself. Was Lepine born with a violent disposition, even in a rudimentary form? If you think Lepine's way of thinking and criminal behaviour stems from genetic factors, then reconsider the case of Reena Virk's attackers (see chapter 6) or the cases of Eric Harris and Dylan Klebold, the teenagers responsible for the deaths of 12 students and one teacher in Littleton, Colorado. Were they *born* violent, or were they raised to be, influenced by identifiable and changeable factors in their environment?

HISTORICAL ROOTS OF EYSENCK'S THEORY

Jung's Hypothesis.   As we saw in chapter 3, Jung viewed the introvert as an individual who is reflective, basically withdrawn, and oriented toward subjective or internal reality, while the extrovert is outgoing and oriented toward external events. Jung (1921) also speculated that, when introverts experience neurotic disorders, they exhibit internalized symptoms such as anxiety, sensitivity, fatigue, and exhaustion. Eysenck proposed the term **dysthymic** to refer to the severely disordered neurotic introvert. On the other hand, Jung proposed that the extrovert expresses neurotic disorders with hysteric symptoms or in other ways that are externalized and removed from the "inner" self. Eysenck reserved the term **hysteric** to refer to the disordered neurotic extrovert.

In his first book, *Dimensions of Personality* (1947), Eysenck reported that psychiatric patients (and personalities in general) were described by two major *independent* types or superfactors. These were **neuroticism** (vs stability) (N) and **extroversion** (vs introversion) (E). These superfactors appeared to separate the highly neurotic study subjects into two groups. Indeed, the most severe cases seemed to be individuals who expressed either the introverted pattern of anxiety-related symptoms (dysthymia) or the extroverted pattern of hysteric disorders (hysteria), thus confirming the hypothesis suggested by Jung.

In the hierarchical structures shown in Figure 8–4, each higher order type includes a number of correlated traits. Thus, an individual who is highly neurotic expresses this general factor through the traits of anxiety, depression, feelings of guilt, low self-esteem and so on. Similarly, the individual who is highly extroverted tends to be sociable, lively, assertive, and sensation-seeking, among other traits.

Figure 8–4

(a) Traits making up the type concept of extroversion. (b) Traits making up the type concept of psychoticism. (c) Traits making up the type concept of neuroticism.

(From Eysenck & Eysenck, 1985, pp. 14, 15)

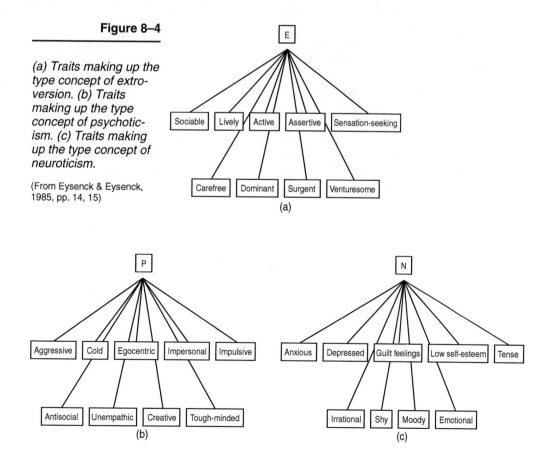

After identifying the first two general types, Eysenck constructed the Maudsley Medical Questionnaire, which could be administered to hospitalized, neurotic subjects as well as to healthy individuals who were neither hospitalized nor complaining of psychological problems. [Questionnaires developed later included the Eysenck Personality Inventory (EPI), the Eysenck Personality Questionnaire (EPQ), and the revised Eysenck Personality Questionnaire (EPQ-R).] In his second book, *The Scientific Study of Personality* (1952), Eysenck paid considerable attention to differences between the hospitalized patients and healthy people. He concluded that a third superfactor, **psychoticism** (P), must be added to N and E to provide a complete description of personality. It should be noted that the final type, P, was included primarily to aid in making distinctions between those subjects with neurotic disorders and those who would be diagnosed with psychotic disorders. Although psychoticism remains part of Eysenck's theoretical scheme, it did not play a major role in his research concerning the personality structures of normal, healthy people. In Figure 8–4, we see that the correlated traits under the superfactor of psychoticism include being aggressive, cold, egocentric, impulsive, and so forth. Despite the order in which these three superfactors were identified, Eysenck and others often use the acronym PEN (psychoticism, extroversion, neuroticism) to refer to the superfactor theory.

Additional Historical Influences. Although their approaches were not scientific by contemporary standards, Eysenck gave credit to Hippocrates (ca. 460–377 B.C) and the Greek physician Galen (ca. 130–200) for their influence on his thinking about personality (Eysenck & Eysenck, 1985). Hippocrates believed that humans consisted of four elements: earth, air, fire, and water. Furthermore, he associated each element with a humour: earth with black bile; air with yellow bile; fire with blood; water with phlegm. It was Galen who extended Hippocrates's thinking to temperaments, thus creating an early theory of personality. If the dominant or excessive body humour is blood, the individual expresses a *sanguine* personality and is warm, optimistic, and easy-going. If black bile dominates, it produces a *melancholic* personality, and the individual is depressed and anxious. An excess of yellow bile produces a choleric personality, which is expressed by excitability, anger, and assertiveness. Finally, if there is excessive phlegm, the individual is *phlegmatic* and therefore slow, lazy or lethargic, and calm.

These embryonic ideas about personality were developed further by the influential philosopher Immanuel Kant (1724–1804) when he included a detailed discussion of temperament in his book *Anthropology From a Pragmatic Point of View* (1798/1912). Like the analyses of Hippocrates and Galen, Kant's analysis of temperament did not allow for combinations of types. For example, one could not be a phlegmatic-melancholic, a person who is anxious and worried as well as reasonable and principled. It was Wilhelm Wundt (1832–1920) founder of the first experimental psychology laboratory, who developed the idea that personality was not a simple issue of *categorical* type. Wundt (1903) pointed out that the categories described by Kant were matters of degree, depending on one's position along the dimensions of *emotional strength* and *emotional changeability*. Choleric and melancholic types, for example, tend to experience intense emotions while sanguine and phlegmatic types tend to have less intense emotional experiences. In addition, choleric and sanguine types supposedly experience very rapid changes in their emotions while melancholic and phlegmatic types are described as more stable, experiencing slower emotional changes.

Eysenck's contribution to this analysis, shown in Figure 8–5, was recognizing that extroversion-introversion was equivalent to the dimension that Wundt called "emotional changeability" and that neuroticism (stability vs instability) was identical to the dimension that Wundt labelled "emotional strength."

Figure 8–5

Relation between the four temperaments and the modern neuroticism–extroversion dimensional system.

(From Eysenck & Eysenck, 1985, p. 50)

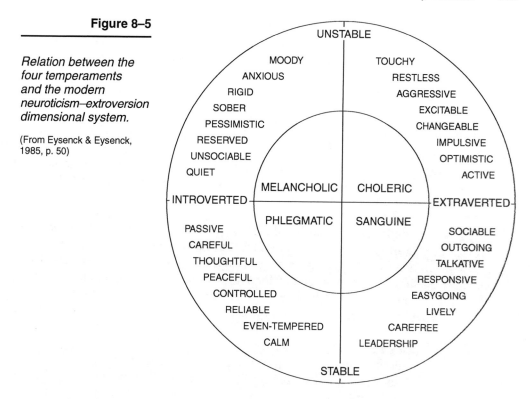

BIOLOGICAL BASES OF PERSONALITY

For Eysenck, it was not enough to establish a measurement system and a taxonomy of personality types. His quest to interrelate test scores, behaviour, and the underlying biological mechanisms with empirical data make his contribution to personality theory both unique and historically important.

Excitation and Inhibition.   In his first attempt to develop a biological explanation of personality, Eysenck adopted ideas from the Russian researcher who discovered classical conditioning, Ivan Pavlov, and an American neobehaviourist, Clark L. Hull. (For further reading concerning both Pavlov and Hull see Hergenhahn & Olson, 1997). In early theorizing, Eysenck (1957) used concepts that were *inferred* from behaviour rather than actually demonstrated in research. For example, Pavlov's explanation of classical conditioning relied heavily on his theoretical ideas about brain processes called excitation and inhibition. Noting that some dogs acquired conditioned responses more readily than others, Pavlov (1928) speculated that excitation dominated the nervous activity of some animals while inhibition dominated in others. Although Pavlov's studies were inconclusive, his ideas about excitatory versus inhibitory dominance captured Eysenck's attention. With respect to excitatory nervous activity, Eysenck borrowed from Pavlov's work and wrote in his typological postulate:

> Individuals in whom excitatory potential is generated slowly and in whom excitatory potentials so generated are relatively weak, are thereby predisposed to develop extraverted patterns of behavior . . . individuals in whom excitatory potential is generated quickly and in whom excitatory potentials so generated are strong, are thereby predisposed to develop introverted patterns of behavior. (1957, p. 114)

Eysenck's ideas about inhibition were greatly influenced by Hull's learning theory. Hull used the concept of *reactive inhibition* to explain phenomena like experimental extinction, in which a response decreases with experimental repetition. Basically, reactive inhibition is caused by fatigue—either muscular or neural—and acts to inhibit responding. Regarding the role of inhibition in personality, Eysenck (1957) continued,

> Similarly, individuals in whom reactive inhibition is developed quickly, in whom strong reactive inhibitions are generated, and in whom reactive inhibition is dissipated slowly, are thereby predisposed to develop extraverted patterns of behavior . . . conversely, individuals in whom reactive inhibition is developed slowly, in whom weak reactive inhibitions are generated, and in whom reactive inhibition is dissipated quickly, are thereby predisposed to develop introverted patterns of behavior. (p. 114)

Cortical and Emotional Arousal.   Later, Eysenck (1967) abandoned the excitation/inhibition approach in favour of **arousal theory**, which is based on well-documented brain processes. His use of arousal theory preserves the essential idea that the introvert's brain is characterized by higher levels of neural activity, and it improves on the earlier theory by providing an explanation for the neuroticism/stability (N) dimension of personality. The newer approach relies on two widely studied arousal systems in the brain. The first system, discovered by Moruzzi and Magoun (1949) is called the **ascending reticular activating system** (ARAS) and is responsible for patterns of excitation (and inhibition) of the cerebral cortex. The second system, referred to by Eysenck as the **visceral brain** (VB) is more often called the *limbic system*. It regulates emotional expression and controls autonomic responses (the symptoms of emotion) such as heartbeat, blood pressure, and sweating. Eysenck (1967) suggested that extroversion/introversion is controlled by the ARAS while emotional expression, including neuroticism, is *independently* mediated by the VB. As in the earlier theory summarized in the typological postulate, the introvert is characterized by higher levels of cortical excitation or arousal, mediated by the ARAS, than the extrovert. The neurotic is characterized by higher levels of autonomic activity (or reactivity), mediated by the VB, than the stable individual. Thus, the neurotic introvert, including Eysenck's *dysthymic,* has the highest overall arousal; both the ARAS and the VB are highly active. The individual that Eysenck called the "normal" extrovert experiences the lowest baseline arousal; both the ARAS and the VB are relatively inactive. The normal introvert and the neurotic extrovert are expected to fall between those extreme cases. Most recently, Eysenck (1990a) explored the relationships between psychoticism (P) and the activities of hormones such as testosterone and arousal-related enzymes such as monoamine oxidase (MAO). At this time, however, any links between hormones, enzymes, and psychoticism are only speculative.

Is Anatomy Destiny?

When posed for theorists like Freud, Jung, Horney, or Adler, this question addresses the issue of gender. For Cattell and Eysenck, the question of anatomy and destiny takes on special meaning. Both theorists provide strong evidence for the **heritability** of key traits or types. Heritability is defined as the "proportion of the total variance in the phenotype which is due to the genotype" (Eysenck & Eysenck, 1985, p. 88), in other words, those differences in expression or appearance of a trait that are attributed to genetic influences rather than to environmental events. Thus, to the extent that genetic and biological factors are critical determinants of personality, the answer to the question, although not necessarily concerned with gender, must be "Yes!"

Cattell: Heredity versus Environment.   No other personality theorist did more than Cattell to determine the relative contributions of heredity and environment to the development of each personality trait. To examine these contributions Cattell created a complicated statistical procedure called *Multiple Abstract Variance Analysis* (MAVA). In general, the method compares members of the same family raised together or raised apart, and unrelated persons raised either together or apart. Each person studied is given a test, or a series of tests, to assess a particular trait. More specifically, measurements are taken of identical twins raised together, identical twins raised apart, fraternal twins raised together, fraternal twins raised apart, siblings raised together, siblings raised apart, unrelated persons raised together, and unrelated persons raised apart (Cattell, 1982, p. 90). The number of genes in common is highest for identical twins, then fraternal twins and siblings, and is lowest for unrelated persons. The logic of such research is straightforward; if a trait is genetically determined, the degree to which it is possessed by two people should be correlated with the degree to which they share the same genes. For example, if a trait is completely genetically determined, then identical twins should possess that trait whether they are raised together or apart.

On the basis of the type of research just described, Cattell concluded that heredity plays a significant role in the development of at least some traits. He confirmed his earlier observation that intelligence (fluid intelligence) is about 65% genetically determined. Also the tendency to have a zestful, active disposition versus a reflective, circumspective one was found to be about 70% genetically determined. Cattell, Schuerger, and Klein (1982) studied the heritability of three source traits: ego strength (factor C), superego strength (factor G), and self-sentiment (factor Q_3). In this particular study, a 10-hour battery of tests was administered to 94 identical twins reared together, 124 fraternal twins reared together, 470 brothers reared together, and 2973 unrelated children reared apart. Using the MAVA procedure, the authors found that superego strength (factor G) is largely a function of environmental influences rather than heredity. However, ego strength (factor C) and self-sentiment (factor Q_3) were found to be strongly influenced by heredity. Cattell (1979, 1980, vol. 2, p. 58) reported that source traits are found to have a genetic component of about 30% or more. When the overall contribution of heredity to personality is considered, Cattell essentially confirmed his earlier conclusion that personality is about two-thirds determined by environmental influences and about one-third by heredity (Hundleby, Pawlik, & Cattell, 1965).

Eysenck: The Biological Argument.   Eysenck and Eysenck (1985) stated that, in order to demonstrate that P, E, and N have biological bases, four criteria must be met: (1) data must demonstrate heritability or a genetic contribution to P, E, and N; (2) observations must confirm traits similar to P, E, and N in nonhuman animals; (3) evidence of P, E, and N must be found in many different cultures; and (4) P, E, and N must be found to be stable over time.

After reviewing a large body of data from twin studies, Eysenck and Eysenck (1985) summarized findings:

> It is found that for practically all traits and dimensions of personality there is a considerable degree of genetic determination of individuals. . . . No serious worker in this field denies that genetic factors account for something like half the variance, and equally none would deny the importance of environmental variables. (p. 96)

The second criterion, the existence of personality in nonhuman animals, is an issue that must be approached carefully. We are often prone to anthropomorphize about our pets, attributing human moods and traits to their behaviour. At the same time, we cannot deny that members of the same species often differ remarkably in *temperament*. In fact, the breeding of domesticated animals has focused on both physical and *temperamental* traits.

Research in the area of nonhuman temperament has generally been conducted by recording the activities of different individual animals in social groups. Researchers can avoid anthropomorphizing but still record whether an animal affiliates with others, is aggressive, actively avoids others and so on. Using this method with rhesus monkeys, Chamove, Eysenck, and Harlow (1972) factor-analyzed their data and found that behaviours clustered in three, independent clusters that corresponded roughly to P, E, and N. Chimpanzees also exhibit behaviours that are best described by three independent dimensions like those proposed by Eysenck (Van Hooff, 1971).

Although conducting cross-cultural personality assessment has its own difficulties, many attempts to gather trait and type data across cultures have confirmed the widespread existence of P, E, and N. Again, summarizing a large data base, Eysenck and Eysenck (1985) wrote:

> Not wishing to paint the lily, we will refrain from commenting at too great length on the results, except to say that they are strongly in support of the view that *essentially the same dimensions of personality emerge from factor analytic studies of identical questionnaires in a large number of different countries* embracing not only European cultural groups but also many quite different types of nations. (p. 108)

And finally, many studies have demonstrated that Eysenck's superfactors, particularly E and N, are quite stable. They have been shown to be consistent over 12-year periods (Hindley & Giuganino, 1982), 15 to 20 year periods (Bronson, 1966, 1967), and even periods of more than 30 years (Conley, 1984; Leon, Gillenn, Gillenn & Ganze, 1979; Mussen, Eichorn, Hanzik, Bieher, & Meredith, 1980). Even those trait theorists who have developed alternatives to Eysenck's theory (whose work will be discussed below) have shown the long-term consistency of E and N (e.g., Costa & McCrae, 1980).

As we can see, the criteria that Eysenck identified as necessary in order to claim that a trait has a biological basis are satisfied. Most researchers working within the trait approach currently accept this conclusion to some degree, although the exact nature of the biological mechanisms underlying personality remain to be determined (Zuckerman, 1991, 1995).

Personality Development

CATTELL'S MULTIPLE INFLUENCE APPROACH

Like most personality theorists, Cattell believed personality development is a function of both motivation and learning. Motivation is responsible for many changes in perceptual and behavioural capabilities.

Learning.   Learning allows changes in the way ergs are satisfied; that is, learning is responsible for the development of sentiments and attitudes. Cattell believed that there are three types of learning: classical conditioning, instrumental conditioning, and structured learning. He defined **classical conditioning** as a situation in which "a new stimulus gets attached to an old response by occurring a moment before the old stimulus" (1965, p. 266). **Instrumental conditioning** (also called reward learning or operant conditioning) is learning to perform a response that will produce a reward.

Most important, however, is **structured learning.** According to Cattell, when an element of the personality changes, it changes the entire configuration of traits. Although the ergs are innate, ways of reducing ergic tensions are learned. For example, as we have seen, ergs manifest themselves in sentiments and attitudes. As these metaergs are learned, the entire structure of personality changes. The acquisition of a new trait, or the modification of an old one, is like throwing a pebble into a pond: The entire pond is influenced. One configuration of traits exists before learning; another exists after learning.

Importance of Early Experience.   Cattell believed that early experiences exert a strong influence on the development of certain personality traits. For example, he observed that adults displaying high *affectia* (see Table 8–2) typically come from a warm, loving home where the father was cheerful, the mother was calm, and the children were controlled through reasoning rather than punishment. The same is true for adults displaying a high level of ego strength (see Table 8–2). Proneness to dominance and guilt tends to characterize adults whose parents were authoritarian, used physical punishment, and were highly critical of their offspring. (For a further discussion of how various parental behaviours relate to the development of certain source traits see Cattell, 1973, pp. 158–178).

Cattell (1973) also studied the Adlerian contention that birth order significantly affects personality development. In general, he found that oldest children tend to be high in dominance, ego strength, and conservatism but low in self-sentiment strength. Only children tend also to be conservative but are high in self-sentiment strength. Children who are not the oldest tend to display surgency (see Table 8–2). Finally, Cattell found that ergic tension (trait Q 4) tends to increase as family size increases.

Syntality.   Cattell thought that because much of people's behaviour is determined by their group affiliations, it is important to know as much as possible about the groups to which people belong. The term *personality* summarizes a person's traits, whereas the term **syntality** summarizes a group's traits, and is akin to Allport's idea of common traits. For example, are there significant and consistent differences in the trait structure of English-speaking vs. French-speaking Canadians, or between Aboriginal and non-Aboriginal groups? Cattell studied groups such as families, various religions, schools, peer groups, and nations in the same way he studied people. For example, in one study (Cattell, Breul, & Hartman, 1952), 40 countries were evaluated on 72 variables. All measures were intercorrelated and factor-analyzed. It was found that the major differences between the countries could be explained using the following four factors:

Factor 1: Enlightened Affluence versus Narrow Poverty
Factor 2: Vigorous Order versus Unadapted Rigidity
Factor 3: Cultural Pressure and Complexity versus Direct Ergic Expression
Factor 4: Size

Thus the groups that influence people have traits, too, and these traits can be uncovered by factor analysis, just as the traits characterizing people can. Once group or national traits have been discovered, a wide variety of comparisons can be made.

EYSENCK AND HERITABLE TRAITS

Eysenck's theory does not focus on development of traits during infancy and childhood, but, as we have seen, on the genetic bases of P, E, and N. He did not, however, claim that types, traits, and the behaviours associated with them appear fully developed in human infants. A trait only provides a predisposition to behave in a certain way, and the behaviour in question does not appear without appropriate environmental stimulation. Eysenck and Eysenck (1985) wrote:

> Usually the name of a given trait also implies the situation in which it can be demonstrated and measured, thus a trait theory directly implies a taxonomy of situations. . . . In other words, trait and situation form the two sides of a coin that cannot be separated from each other, and classical trait theories do not neglect situations; they directly imply them. (pp. 38–39)

Eysenck's position, like that of Allport, exemplifies interactionism because it maintains that person variables (e.g., genetics and biological dispositions) and situation variables always interact to cause behaviour. We will say more about interactionism when we discuss Bandura and Mischel's theory in chapter 11.

Recent work by Jerome Kagan (1994) may help clarify the hereditarian position. Kagan's research demonstrates how a temperament-induced bias expresses itself both in infancy and in more fully developed adult behaviour. Kagan and his colleagues note that some infants are more reactive than others to aversive stimuli. Further, many of the extremely reactive infants grow, over the next few years, into what he calls *inhibited* children; and many of the extremely nonreactive children grow into what he calls *uninhibited* children (Kagan, 1994). Although Kagan does not refer directly to the similarities between inhibited children and introverts and between uninhibited children and extroverts, his research provides a glimpse of the early expression of these adult types. For example, inhibited children stay close to their mothers in novel situations, do not explore novel environments, and do not eagerly engage new people. That is, they behave in ways that Eysenck would call introverted. The uninhibited children, in contrast, leave their mothers' sides to explore new environments, play with new toys, and engage new people. They behave like Eysenck's classic extroverts.

For Eysenck, then, the development of personality is *directed* by genetically endowed traits but is tempered by environmental factors. Personality traits influence the kinds of situations that we find aversive and avoid as well as those that we enjoy and seek. Because they guide us toward some environments and turn us away from others, they influence the kinds of behaviours, experiences, and learning that we encounter and, therefore, indirectly shape the acquired, as opposed to the biological/genetic, aspects of our personalities.

Psychopathology

Cattell suggested two reasons for psychopathology. One is an abnormal imbalance of the normal personality traits; for example, those measured by the 16 PF. For example, an excessive amount of factor A (*affectia* versus *sizia*) could result in a manic-depressive disorder. The second reason for psychopathology is the possession of abnormal traits that are not found among normal individuals. Cattell and his colleagues isolated 12 abnormal traits that can be used to describe various types of neuroses and psychoses. Cattell (1975) devised the Clinical Analysis Questionnaire to assess those abnormal traits. The 12 abnormal traits Cattell discovered are listed in Table 8–3.

Cattell concluded that abnormal people are, first of all, like normal ones in that they possess all of the normal source traits. However, they may also possess pathological traits (Cattell, 1979, 1980, vol. 1, pp. 73–74). In Table 8–3, the first seven abnormal traits

Table 8–3

Cattell's 12 Abnormal Source Traits

(Adapted from Cattell, 1979, 1980)

FACTOR	LOW SCORE DESCRIPTION	HIGH SCORE DESCRIPTION
D1	Low hypochondriasis	High hypochondriasis
D2	Zestfulness	Suicidal disgust
D3	Low brooding discontent	High brooding discontent
D4	Low anxious depression	High anxious depression
D5	High energy euphoria	Low energy depression
D6	Low guilt and resentment	High guilt and resentment
D7	Low bored depression	High bored depression
Pa	Low paranoia	High paranoia
Pp	Low psychopathic deviation	High psychopathic deviaion
Sc	Low schizophrenia	High schizophrenia
As	Low psychasthenia	High psychasthenia
Ps	Low general psychosis	High general psychosis

(symbolized by the letter D) are depressive traits. The last five traits are considered relatively more powerful and more serious.

Cattell, then, saw some individuals with serious psychopathology as *quantitatively* different from normal individuals while others were seen as *qualitatively* different. That is, they possess qualities—abnormal traits—not found in people who are not suffering from psychological disorders. Eysenck, on the other hand, saw the differences between normal individuals and those with psychopathologies only as *quantitative.* In other words, their personalities are described in terms of the same types, P, E, and N, as normals, but they have abnormally high scores on one or more superfactors, particularly on P and/or N. Cattell's view would suggest that Montreal Massacre gunman Marc Lepine or convicted murderer Paul Bernardo do not merely have *more* psychologically unstable traits; they have instead a unique set of traits (e.g., psychotic thinking) not found in the average person. Perhaps that view is comforting, perhaps not.

Cattell believed that abnormal individuals possess pathological traits that are quantitatively and qualitatively different from normal individuals. This suggests that Marc Lepine, perpetrator of the Montreal massacre, or Paul Bernardo, convicted murderer, not only has more psychologically unstable traits than a normal person but also has a unique set of traits (e.g., psychotic thinking) not found in the average person.

It should be noted, however, that high scores on P or N do not necessarily guarantee psychopathology. As we saw above, traits require interaction with specific situations in order to attain full expression:

> There are many individuals whose psychoticism, neuroticism, and extraversion scores resemble those of the average manic-depressive or schizophrenic and yet who manage to lead relatively contented, symptom-free lives. Perhaps an individual's location within Eysenckian three-dimensional space can appropriately be regarded as a measure of his or her vulnerability to different kinds of mental illness. (Eysenck & Eysenck, 1985, p. 339)

Psychotherapy

Ideally for Cattell, psychotherapy should be preceded by a precise personality-factor assessment. Such a profile not only defines exactly what the problem is but also aids the clinician in determining the most effective treatment procedure. Furthermore, the P-technique should be used during treatment so that the changes occurring within the client during therapy can be assessed. As far as therapeutic treatment is concerned, Cattell was an eclectic. He thought that the type of treatment should be dictated by the type of disorder revealed by precise personality assessment. Severe psychoses may be best treated by drugs or electric shock; certain neuroses might be best treated by dream analysis and the reliving of traumatic experiences; and for relatively minor problems some form of behaviour therapy might be most effective (behaviour therapy is discussed in the next chapter).

Eysenck also suggested that accurate personality testing leads to correct diagnoses and results in appropriate and more effective treatment. Wolpe and Plaud (1997) praise Eysenck for identifying E and N as biological influences that affect both acquisition of maladaptive behaviours and responsiveness to behaviour therapies, such as systematic desensitization, used to treat them.

While Cattell was eclectic in his approach to therapy, Eysenck, a long-time critic of psychoanalysis and proponent of behaviour therapy, was far less accepting of therapies lacking empirical support. For Eysenck, therapy must be based on demonstrated psychological principles such as those derived from classical or operant conditioning. The ultimate test of a therapy lies not in its intent but in empirical evidence showing that patients receiving therapy actually improve more than no-treatment controls or patients receiving placebo treatments.

Contemporary Developments: The Big Five

During the last decade, a theory of personality called the "Big Five" or sometimes the Five-Factor Model has generated considerable interest among trait theorists. This approach has a number of active advocates (Costa & McCrae, 1985; Digman, 1989, 1996; Goldberg, 1990, 1993; McCrae & Costa, 1985, 1987, 1996) who challenge Cattell's and Eysenck's analyses and offer an alternative theory with five superfactors. Like Cattell and Eysenck, psychologists supporting the Big Five also use factor analysis as their primary analytical tool, and two of the five superfactors are virtually identical to two identified by Eysenck. And as we shall see, Cattell's research is often cited to support the contention that five factors are better than three or sixteen.

Specifically, the five superfactors include neuroticism and extroversion, defined in much the same way that Eysenck defined them. Also included are higher order factors called openness (to experience), agreeableness, and conscientiousness. (Students may want to use the acronym OCEAN to remember the five factors.) Definitions of these factors are found in Table 8–4.

Although research on the Big Five has become popular only in the last few years, the history of this approach can be traced back over 100 years to the work of Sir Francis Galton, and its history is grounded in what has become known as the **lexical hypothesis** (Goldberg, 1981, 1993). The basic premise of the lexical hypothesis is that all we need to know about personality is contained in natural language (i.e., folk psychology). That is, the terms we commonly (and sometimes uncommonly) use to describe ourselves and each other contain all the information necessary to discern the fundamental dimensions of human personality.

Galton (1884), without the statistical power of factor analysis, collected terms from the dictionary that were descriptive of personality and noted that many of the words shared common meanings. Years later, L. L. Thurstone (1934), who was instrumental in development of factor analysis, used an adjective checklist method in which he provided experimental participants with a list of 60 personality-descriptive adjectives. Participants were asked to think about some other person and to indicate whether each of the adjectives was descriptive of that person. Thurstone factor-analyzed the resulting data and concluded that the complexity of human personality could be described using as few as five major factors. He did not, however, suggest what those factors might be. Two years later, Allport and Odbert (1936), beginning with nearly 18 000 adjectives, developed a collection of approximately 4500 personality-descriptive terms, 35 of which were used by Cattell (1943) in a factor-analytic study. As we saw previously, Cattell preferred to extract as many factors as possible in his data sets, and in his treatment of the 35 personality terms, he found at least 12 factors. Although Cattell did not become an advocate of the Big Five and did not deviate from his 16 PF approach, he is often credited with an early version of the lexical hypothesis when he insisted that "all aspects of human personality which are or have been of importance, interest, or utility have already become recorded in the substance of language." (Cattell, 1943, p. 483). Different

---

Table 8–4

The Five-Factor Model of Personality

(Adapted from Costa & McCrae, 1986.)

Neuroticism
Calm—Worrying
Even-tempered—Temperamental
Self-satisfied—Self-pitying
Comfortable—Self-conscious
Unemotional—emotional
Hardy—Vulnerable

Extroversion
Reserved—Affectionate
Loner—Joiner
Quiet—Talkative
Passive—Active
Sober—Fun-loving
Unfeeling—Passionate

Openness to experience
Down-to-earth—Imaginative
Uncreative—Creative
Conventional—Original
Prefer routine—Prefer variety
Uncurious—Curious
Conservative—Liberal

Aggreeableness
Ruthless—Soft-hearted
Suspicious—Trusting
Stingy—Generous
Antagonistic—Acquiescent
Critical—Lenient
Irritable—Good-natured

Conscientiousness
Negligent—Conscientious
Lazy—Hardworking
Disorganized—Well-organized
Late—Punctual
Aimless—Ambitious
Quitting—Persevering

researchers (Digman & Takemoto-Chock, 1981; Norman, 1963. and most notably Tupes and Christal, 1961) reanalyzed Cattell's variables and concluded that only five of his factors could be replicated. Although some of the names have changed, those factors are the same as those that have been the basis of all subsequent work on the Big Five.

The researchers most often associated with the Big Five, Paul T. Costa and Robert R. McCrae, entered the trait debate with a three-factor theory derived from a personality questionnaire rather than from an adjective checklist. Their first set of superfactors consisted of neuroticism, extroversion, and openness, and the personality inventory that these authors developed is the NEO-PI (neuroticism, extroversion, openness-personality inventory). After attending two symposia held by Digman and Goldberg, (two researchers from the lexical school described above) Costa and McCrae were convinced that the two additional factors of agreeableness and conscientiousness should be added to their model. They further refined their personality questionnaire and arbitrarily developed six facets (lower order traits) for each of the five superfactors in the Big Five. These are shown in Table 8–4.

Does the Five-Factor Model apply to people of different cultures? To work around cultural and language differences, Sampo Paunonen of the University of Western Ontario developed a nonverbal personality inventory (using pictures instead of statements) to correspond to the Big Five, called the Five Factor Nonverbal Personality Questionnaire (FF-NPQ; Paunonen, Ashton, & Jackson, 2001; Paunonen, Jackson & Keinonen, 1990). When administered to university undergraduates from Canada, England, Norway, Israel, and the Netherlands, the results were useful and comparable across the different cultures, and reasonably corresponded to the Big Five factor structure (Paunonen, Zeidner, Engvik, Oosterveld & Maliphant, 2000).

HAVE THE BIG FIVE DISPLACED CATTELL AND EYSENCK?

Despite the current popularity of the Big Five approach to personality, the two most prolific trait theorists, Cattell and Eysenck, refused to adopt it. Eysenck (1991), perhaps, made the clearest argument against the position. Eysenck argued that agreeableness and conscientiousness are primary traits rather than superfactors. Eysenck concluded that advocates of the Big Five mix superfactors (e.g., neuroticism and extroversion) with primary traits (e.g., agreeableness and conscientiousness) in order to inflate the number of superfactors in their model from two to four. And what about openness? Eysenck suggested two possibilities. One (Eysenck & Eysenck, 1985) is that, like agreeableness and conscientiousness, openness is negatively related to P and is actually a primary trait rather than a superfactor. More recently, Eysenck (1991) indicated that several studies show openness to be correlated with intelligence and therefore a cognitive ability factor, not a temperament factor. Recall from our earlier discussion that Eysenck excluded ability factors from his formal analysis of personality. Draycott and Kline (1995) analyzed both Costa and McCrae's NEO-PI and the Eysenck Personality Questionnaire (Revised) (EPQ-R). They agree with Eysenck's earlier claim that the Big Five mixes lower order with higher order factors.

Paunonen tackled the question of whether specific lower-order traits or comprehensive Eysenckian supertraits would predict behaviour better (Paunonen, 1998). He found that both narrow traits and broad factors separately predicted most relevant behaviours.

A direct attack on the Big Five comes from Block (1995), who retraces the history of the Big Five and suggests that the emergence of five factors is more a matter of research planning than it is a matter of empirical discovery. He suggests that the advocates of the Big Five have invested their research interests in validating the five factors rather than testing the theory. Even Costa and McCrae indicate that, beyond explicit identification of openness, agreeableness, and conscientiousness, the Big Five add little to the current body of data about personality. They note that the theory contains "few surprises; the basic ideas are familiar from many personality theories" (McCrae & Costa, 1996, p. 75). Thus, while the Big Five model enjoys a degree of popularity, it has not replaced Eysenck's PEN or Cattell's 16 PF. Block (1995), for example, argues that the Big Five model is not at all what it claims to be:

> The Big Five are often called "the five-factor model of personality" and are referred to as providing an understanding of the "structure of personality." As the term "model" is used in conventional parlance among psychologists, it means a theoretically based, logically coherent, working representation or simulation that, in operation, attempts to generate psychological phenomena of interest. However, no identifiable hypotheses, theories, or models guided the emergence of or decision on this five-fold space. . . . Because the Big Five formulation was entirely atheoretical, usage of the term "model" may be premature. (p. 188)

Dissatisfaction with the Big Five has led Zuckerman (1991, 1995) to propose a biologically-based "Alternative Five," which includes sociability (related to extroversion), neuroticism-anxiety, impulsive sensation seeking, aggression-hostility, and activity.

Paunonen and Jackson (2000) returned to the lexical approach and tested whether a large set of adjectives would fall within the Five Factors (cf. Saucier & Goldberg, 1998). After eliminating variables that had little to do with personality (e.g., "tall"), they used stricter criteria in deciding whether an adjective fit within a factor. This reanalysis showed that almost a third of the adjectives failed to fit neatly into the five categories, and gelled instead into nine distinguishable (and currently unrepresented) personality dimensions: (a) religiosity; (b) deceptive and manipulative; (c) honest, moral, and ethical; (d) sexual, sensual, and erotic; (e) thrifty or miserly; (f) conservative, down-to-earth; (g) masculine-feminine; (h) egotistical, conceited, and snobbish; and (i) humorous, witty, and amusing. At least one of these factors seems to stand up to testing; Michael Ashton suggests that honesty may be the sixth factor (Ashton, Lee & Son, 2000).

Thus, although it may be intuitively appealing that the complexity of human personality requires more than three superfactors, it may be inappropriate to proclaim the overthrow of Eysenck's three-factor model by the Big Five. In fact, there is no consensus on how many factors are required to fully describe personality.

Evaluation

Cattell's and Eysenck's theories are unique among those presented so far in this text because of their substantial empirical support. Numerous studies have been discussed throughout this chapter and a few more are discussed below.

CATTELL: EMPIRICAL RESEARCH

The 16 PF. Cattell and Nesselroade (1967) used the 16 PF to determine the personality profiles of spouses in stable marriages and unstable marriages, defined as those in which at least one step had been taken toward dissolution. Contrary to the old saying that opposites attract, it was found that couples with similar traits were more likely to have stable marriages.

Cattell, Eber, and Tatsuoka (1970) used the 16 PF to study the personality profiles of men and women who had attempted suicide (see also Benitez, Ferrerro, & Marco, 1997). Those who had attempted suicide were more introverted, more anxious, and displayed lower superego strength than the general adult population. The same study found nearly opposite traits among airline pilots and flight attendants; they were more extroverted, less anxious, and displayed more superego strength than average.

Predictive Science and Determinism.   Like Eysenck, Cattell believed a theory of personality is of little value unless it can predict behaviour. Cattell was very much a **determinist;** that is, he believed behaviour is a function of a finite number of variables, and if those variables are completely known, human behaviour can be predicted with complete accuracy. Since all of the variables influencing behaviour can never be known, the prediction of behaviour will always be probabilistic; however, as more is known about the variables influencing human behaviour, predictions will become more accurate. According to Cattell, this is also true in the realm of personality research. The more we know about the various traits of a particular person, the better we will be able to predict his or her behaviour.

What, then, is personality to Cattell?

Personality is that which permits a prediction of what a person will do in a given situation. The goal of psychological research in personality is thus to establish laws about what different people will do in all kinds of social and general environmental situations . . . Personality is . . . concerned with *all* behavior of the individual, both overt and under the skin. (Cattell, 1950, pp. 2–3)

EYSENCK: EMPIRICAL RESEARCH

Experimental and correlational studies spanning over 40 years have provided an impressive database to support Eysenck's beliefs concerning E and to a lesser extent N and P (Wilson, 1997). These studies range from relatively straightforward confirmations concerning the behaviours of basic personality types to very complex attempts to reveal the brain functions assumed by the ARAS-VB arousal model. As the principal factor in several personality factor models, extroversion has been intensely studied.

Reaction Times.   Is there a biological basis for extroversion/introversion? To investigate this question, Robert Stelmack from the University of Ottawa looked for differences between introverts and extroverts in attention, motivation, learning, and both motor and sensory processes (1990, 1997; Doucet & Stelmack, 1994, 2000; Stelmack & Campbell, 1974; Stelmack & Geen, 1992; Stelmack & Pivik, 1996; Stelmack & Wilson, 1982). In one study, introverts and extroverts performed a simple task — quickly moving their hand from one button to another. Initial reaction time was the same, but extroverts moved their hands faster. However, no difference was found in cognitive processing speed.

Health Outcomes.   Another study investigated links between extroversion, stressful life events, and health; contrary to expectations, no relationship emerged between degree of extroversion and health outcome (Korotkov & Hannah, 1994).

Social Behaviour.   Both male and female extroverts are more likely to have sexual intercourse at younger ages than introverts; they are more likely to have multiple sexual partners; and they are more likely to engage in different types of sexual activities

(Eysenck, 1976; Giese & Schmidt, 1968). On the other hand, introverts tend to demonstrate superior academic achievement in both Western and nonwestern cultures (Furneaux, 1957; Kline, 1966; Lynn, 1959). Finally, Eysenck (1967, 1977) reports that individuals with high E, high N, and high P scores are more likely to engage in criminal activity.

Perceptual Phenomena.   Introverts, according to Eysenck, experience a high baseline arousal. They should, therefore, be more sensitive to high levels of environmental stimulation. Elliott (1971) and Ludvigh and Happ (1974) asked experimental participants to adjust auditory tones to levels that were just loud enough to be uncomfortable. In both experiments, extroverts adjusted tones to levels that were louder than those selected by introverts. Extroverts also have higher pain tolerance thresholds than do introverts (Bartol & Costello, 1976; Shiomi, 1978)

Conditioning.   Eyeblink conditioning is often used to demonstrate classical conditioning in humans; Eysenck (1965) and Jones, Eysenck, Martin, and Levey (1981) reported that, in general, introverts demonstrate more rapid eyeblink conditioning than extroverts. Eysenck and Levey (1972) examined the variables involved in classical conditioning experiments (see chapter 9) and determined that introverts develop a conditioned response faster under partial reinforcement schedules, with weak to moderately strong unconditioned stimuli, and at short intervals between conditioned and unconditioned stimuli, as might be predicted if they have higher cortical arousal. Conversely, extroverts acquire conditioned responses more rapidly under continuous reinforcement, with strong unconditioned stimuli, and when the interval is relatively long. If introverts demonstrate superior conditioning because of higher levels of cortical arousal, then drugs that increase cortical arousal should also enhance conditioning. This phenomenon has, in fact, been demonstrated by administering a stimulant (dexamphetamine sulfate) prior to classical conditioning (Franks & Trouton, 1958). Also as expected, administration of sedative drugs that reduce arousal inhibit classical conditioning (Franks & Laverty, 1955; Franks & Trouton, 1958; Willet, 1960). Similarly, administration of stimulants enhances operant conditioning while depressants interfere with it (Gupta, 1973).

Drug Effects.   An alternative method of testing the arousal model is called the *sedation threshold method*. In this approach, a sedative drug is given until a patient's behaviour reflects a predetermined sedation criterion. According to Eysenck's arousal theory, introverts have a higher baseline arousal level and should require more sedative drug to produce a given sedation effect. This prediction has been confirmed using barbiturates (Krishnamoorti & Shagass, 1963; Laverty, 1958; Shagass & Jones, 1958). Other studies have demonstrated that individuals with high levels of N and low E (introverts) require more sedative than other participants (Claridge, Donald, & Birchall, 1981; Claridge & Ross, 1973).

Electrophysiological Measures.   Numerous studies have attempted to detect differences between introverts and extroverts using electroencephalograms (EEGs) or a related technique called the event-related potential (ERP), which is an accumulated, averaged EEG elicited by a specific stimulus. Although results have been mixed, Eysenck (Eysenck & Eysenck, 1985; Eysenck, 1990a) reviewed the accumulated evidence and concluded that introverts usually show higher arousal, as measured in EEG recordings, especially when test conditions are moderately arousing (Gale, 1973, 1983). ERP evidence has been less supportive, although one experiment demonstrated higher ERPs for introverts (Stelmack, Achorn, & Michaud, 1977). Although some critics claim that electrophysiological evidence fails to confirm Eysenck's (1967) arousal hypothesis, the data from studies of conditioning, drug effects, and many other phenomena not discussed here reveal fundamental differences between extroverts and introverts that are not easily explained by theories that attribute personality differences primarily to socialization.

CRITICISMS

Too Subjective.   As scientifically rigorous as Cattell's and Eysenck's theories appear to be, a number of critics claim that they are still characterized by too much subjectivity. One source of subjectivity, say the critics, lies in determining what to study about people at the outset. What comes out of a factor analysis is totally dependent on what goes into it. Subjectivity is also involved in determining what will be accepted as evidence of a factor. That is, how many variables must be correlated and how high must the correlations be? Finally, how many factors need to be postulated to account for the data? As we have seen, there is some disagreement on the number of factors required to adequately describe human personality. The subjective nature of such decisions is reflected in the fact that, for example, others have not been able to replicate many of Cattell's factors or source traits (Digman & Takemoto-Chock, 1981).

Behaviour Not as Consistent as Factor Theories Suggest.   Although Cattell and Eysenck did not ignore the influence of specific environmental situations on behaviour, they assumed a considerable amount of cross-situational consistency. Critics claim that such consistency simply does not exist (see, for example, Mischel, 1968; Mischel & Peake, 1982).

Excessive Emphasis on Groups and Averages.   Although Cattell developed his P-technique partially to appease Allport, Allport was still dissatisfied with the way Cattell went about discovering traits to begin with. In a criticism that can be extended to Eysenck, Allport argued that Cattell's method yielded average traits that no person actually possessed:

> An entire population (the larger the better) is put into the grinder, and the mixing is so expert that what comes through is a link of factors in which every individual has lost his identity. His dispositions are mixed with everyone else's dispositions. The factors thus obtained represent only *average* tendencies. Whether a factor is really an *inorganic* disposition in any one individual is not demonstrated. All one can say for certain is that a factor is an empirically derived component of the *average* personality, and that the average personality is a complete abstraction. This objection gains point when one reflects that seldom do the factors derived in this way resemble the dispositions and traits identified by clinical methods when the *individual* is studied intensively. (Allport, 1937, p. 244)

Elsewhere Allport said that the traits produced by factor analysis "resemble sausage meat that has failed to pass the pure food and health inspection" (1958, p. 251). Allport's point is valid only when one looks at how traits or superfactors are identified. Most of this research did involve large groups of people and dealt with averages. Once the 16 personality traits or three superfactors were isolated, however, they were used to understand the behaviour of individuals and to predict individual behaviour. To say that Cattell and Eysenck were only interested in groups and in averages is incorrect.

Reification.   Reification occurs when it is assumed that a verbal label refers to something that exists physically. We saw in chapter 7 that Allport believed traits were real psychophysical structures that determined behaviour. Cattell and Eysenck, too, imply that the source traits and superfactors actually exist. If traits are considered convenient fictions postulated for scientific expediency, there is no problem. There is, however, little evidence that source traits and superfactors have material existence.

CONTRIBUTIONS

Both Cattell and Eysenck are notable for their pioneering scientific efforts in a field that was, in its early forms, riddled with unbridled speculation and unsubstantiated, near-mystical beliefs. Because the use of scientific methodology in the study of personality is often characterized as the most significant contribution made by Cattell and Eysenck, we will elaborate their scientific orientations next.

Cattell: Beyondism.   Throughout his career, Cattell combined scientific rigour with compassion for the human situation. These dual interests are exemplified in Cattell's books *A New Morality from Science: Beyondism* (1972) and *Beyondism: Religion from Science* (1987). Cattell (1987) defined **beyondism** as follows:

> What, briefly, is Beyondism? It is a system for discovering and clarifying ethical goals from a basis of scientific knowledge and investigation, by the objective research procedures of scientific method. This does not deny it emotional richness, but in fact calls for the deepest, most genuine emotional satisfaction and loyalty, unaided and unbetrayed by myths and illusions. It believes that the difficult and honest thinking that has given us power, light, warmth, speed of travel, and world-wide instant communication by the physical sciences, and health and longevity by the medical sciences, is capable of giving us definiteness of values, true social progress, and peace of mind, in our individual, national, and international behavior. (p. 1)

Beyondism places great value on evolutionary principles such as fitness and natural selection. As it is for the sociobiologists (see chapter 12), the relationship between biological and cultural evolution is extremely important for Cattell. The products of biological evolution (that is, people) create culture, and culture, in turn, influences biological evolution. The optimal situation occurs when biological and cultural evolution are compatible. For example, it is best when a moral system is conducive to biological survival and advancement. Traditional moral systems were based on "revealed" knowledge and were taken on faith. By contrast, the religion of beyondism will be based on scientific facts whose effectiveness can be objectively evaluated:

> With good fortune we shall before long see the revealed religions fading out of the more advanced countries. The great cathedrals will become spiritual landmarks of the past. . . . Out of the superstition-ridden night of the past two thousand years will gradually dawn the light of science-based evolutionary religion. It is to this new structuring of life that the present believers in Beyondism must apply themselves. (Cattell, 1987, p. 256)

Needless to say, Cattell's proposal to replace the traditional religious foundation of morality with scientific objectivity was another reason he was surrounded by controversy.

Eysenck: Farewell to Mythical Psychology.   As an advocate of the hypothetico-deductive method in scientific research, Eysenck attempted to develop a testable psychological theory in the natural science tradition. He challenged other psychologists to subject their own theories to the same scrutiny, and he rejected many theories—including many of those covered in this text—because of their scientific shortcomings:

> As an example, I would class among the inadmissable theories those of Freud, Adler, Jung, Binswanger, Horney, Sullivan, Fromm, Erikson, and Maslow. They fail essentially because for the most part they do not generate testable deductions; because where they do so the deductions have most frequently been falsified; and because they fail to include practically all the experimental and empirical studies which have been done over the last 50 years. Historically these theorists have had some influence, but their theorizing and their mode of working has not been in the tradition of natural science, and they have not been found responsive to adverse criticism or empirical disproof. (Eysenck, 1991, p. 774)

Why, then, are these theories popular? According to Eysenck, their popularity is largely explained by the common tendency of not letting the difficult, and often relatively uninteresting scientific truth, stand in the way of an unscientific good story.

> Most people of course, whatever they may say, do not in fact, want a scientific account of human nature and personality at all—indeed, this is the last thing they really wish for. Hence they much prefer the great story-teller S. Freud, or the great myth-creator, C. G. Jung, to those who, like Cattell or Guilford, expect them to learn matrix algebra, study physiological details of the nervous system, and actually carry out experiments, rather than rely on interesting anecdotes, sex-ridden case histories, and ingenious speculation. After all, after-dinner conversation can easily encompass the Oedipus complex, or penis envy; it would be much more difficult to talk about a non-Gramian matrix, or the reticular formation! (Eysenck, 1972, p. 24)

Applied Value.   Personality tests devised by Cattell and Eysenck have been used for clinical diagnoses, personnel selection, vocational counselling, and marital counselling. They have been used to predict accident proneness, the possibility of heart attacks in men, rates of recovery from cancer, and scholastic performance. Versions of Cattell's evaluative devices have been translated into more than a dozen languages, and in each language they are used extensively for both research and practical applications.

SUMMARY

1. Cattell and Eysenck began the study of personality by measuring a large group of individuals in as many ways as possible. Using a statistical technique called factor analysis, the measures were then intercorrelated; measures at least moderately correlated are thought to measure the same attribute (factor or trait). Cattell's theory emphasizes the source traits detected by factor analysis. Eysenck's theory emphasizes higher order traits called *superfactors* or *types*.

2. Cattell's most important distinction was between surface traits and source traits. Surface traits are actually measured and expressed in overt behaviour of some kind; source traits represent underlying causes of overt behaviour. Some source traits (genetically determined) are called constitutional traits. Other source traits (shaped by one's culture) are called environmental-mould traits.

3. Cattell also distinguished between ability, temperament, and dynamic traits. The most important ability trait is intelligence, described as fluid intelligence (general problem-solving ability and largely genetic) and crystallized intelligence (gained through experience). Temperament traits are constitutional and determine a person's emotional makeup and style of behaving. Dynamic traits determine a person's motivational makeup. Cattell distinguished two categories of dynamic traits: ergs (roughly equivalent to instincts, biological needs or primary drives) and metaergs (learned drives, divided into sentiments and attitudes). Cattell diagrammed the relationship among ergs, sentiments, and attitudes in the dynamic lattice. The fact that humans almost inevitably take indirect routes to satisfy ergic tensions is referred to as long-circuiting.

4. Eysenck also believed that intelligence is largely genetically determined; but the focus of his theory of personality is temperament, a concept that did not include intelligence or ability. Eysenck argued that traits are genetically influenced rather than learned and arranged hierarchically. Eysenck identified three superfactors that he believed are sufficient to describe human personality, all of which have biological bases. These include extroversion vs. introversion, whose differences stem from different levels of arousal of the cerebral cortex—at rest, extroverts have a lower level of cortical arousal than introverts. The second major factor is neuroticism vs. stability; high levels of neuroticism are attributed to excessive activity of the autonomic nervous system. The third major factor, psychoticism, is used primarily to explain severe psychotic disorders.

5. To explain how personality develops, Cattell postulated three types of learning: classical and instrumental conditioning and structured learning. The latter is most important because it involves a change in one's entire personality. Cattell has shown the relationship between early home environments and the development of various personality traits. He also found support for Adler's assertion that birth order and family size significantly affect personality development.

6. Using MAVA to assess the relative contribution of heredity and environment to trait development, Cattell found that some traits (e.g., intelligence) have a very strong genetic component, and some have practically none (e.g, superego strength). Cattell concluded that about one-third of personality is determined by genetics. Eysenck emphasized the genetic bases of traits and types and did not place great theoretical importance on developmental issues. He noted that situations in which traits and types manifest themselves always influence how they will be expressed.

7. Cattell believed that psychopathology can result from either an abnormal configuration of the normal source traits, or from the possession of one or more of the 12 abnormal traits. Eysenck attributed psychopathology only to abnormally high levels of the three superfactors that characterize all personality.

8. Cattell and Eysenck believed that trait analysis should precede psychotherapy; this provides an accurate diagnosis of the problem and will suggest the most effective method of treatment. Also trait evaluation should occur throughout therapy to determine how treatment is affecting the client's total personality. While Cattell was eclectic with respect to psychotherapy, Eysenck only advocated therapies (e.g., behaviour therapy) derived from empirically demonstrated psychological principles and shown to be effective.

9. Both theories are criticized for containing too many subjective elements, for assuming human behaviour is more consistent than it actually is, for concentrating too much on groups and group averages at the expense of the unique individual, and for implying that source traits have actual physical existence. Both theories have been praised for bringing scientific rigour to the study of personality and providing tools that can be used in a large number of applied areas (e.g., clinical diagnoses, vocational and marital counselling, and personnel selection).

EXPERIENTIAL EXERCISES

1. By referring to Table 8–2, administer Cattell's 16 PF questionnaire to yourself. Assume a 10 is the highest score you can attain on a factor and a 1 is the lowest. A score of 5 indicates you think you are about in the middle of the two extremes for any given factor. In other words, any score from 1 to 10 is possible for each of the 16 factors. Next create a personality profile for yourself in the form of a line graph showing the level for each factor. Cattell has found that, at least in the case of married couples, the more similar the profiles of two persons, the more positive is their relationship. Have someone you are close to respond to the 16 PF questionnaire, and summarize his or her performance in a personality profile. Compare yours with his or hers. What conclusions do you draw from the comparison?

2. Look at the traits assumed under each of the superfactors illustrated in Figure 8–4. To simplify, assume that either you have a trait or you don't. Using this all-or-nothing method, determine which of the traits under the P, E, and N types you possess. Do you have a majority of the traits under a particular type—enough to classify you as a "high P," "high E," or "high N"?

3. Give an example of how subsidiation and long-circuiting operate in your life. That is, show how a particular erg relates to one or more of your sentiments, which, in turn, relates to one or more of your attitudes.

4. Apply the theories of *either* Cattell or Eysenck to predict your own behaviour. Assume the more you know about yourself and the situation you are in, the more accurate will be your prediction of your behaviour in that situation. Take any situation that you will find yourself in shortly (for example a social event, a major test, going home for a visit with relatives) and list the types of information you would need to know about yourself and the situation to predict your behaviour accurately. For this exercise you will need to use some of the information that you learned about yourself in exercise 1 (if using Cattell's theories) or exercise 2 (if using Eysenck's). What conclusion do you reach concerning the prediction of your behaviour?

DISCUSSION QUESTIONS

1. Describe the technique of factor analysis as it is used to study personality.
2. Summarize Cattell's findings concerning the relative contributions of heredity and environment to personality development.
3. What are the four criteria that Eysenck claims must be satisfied in order to claim that personality factors are biological?
4. Summarize the Big Five theory of personality. Is it more like Eysenck's or Cattell's theory?
5. What are the major criticisms of Cattell's and Eysenck's theories?

KEY TERMS

Ability trait, p. 192
Arousal theory, p. 200
Ascending reticular activating system
    (ARAS), p. 200.
Attitude, p. 194
Beyondism, p. 213
Classical conditioning, p. 202
Cluster analysis, p. 186
Constitutional trait, p. 192
Correlation, p. 185
Correlation coefficient, p. 185
Correlation matrix, p. 185
Crystallized intelligence, p. 193
Culture Free Intelligence Test, p. 193
Determinism, p. 210
Dynamic lattice, p. 195
Dynamic trait, p. 193
Dysthymic, p. 197
Environmental-mould trait, p. 192
Erg, p. 193
Ergic tension, p. 194
Extroversion, p. 197
Factor, p. 186
Factor analysis, p. 185.
Fluid intelligence, p. 192
Heritability, p. 200
Hypothetico-deductive reasoning, p. 187
Hysteric, p. 197

Inductive reasoning, p. 187
Instrumental conditioning, p. 202
L-data, p. 187
Lexical hypothesis, p. 207
Long-circuiting, p. 195
Metaerg, p. 194
Negative correlation, p. 185
Neuroticism, p. 197
Personality sphere, p. 190
Positive correlation, p. 185
Psychoticism, p. 198
P-technique, p. 188
Q-data, p. 187
R-technique, p. 188
Self-sentiment, p. 194
Sentiment, p. 194
Source traits, p. 190
Structured learning, p. 203
Subsidiation, p. 194
Superfactor, p. 186
Surface traits, p. 190
Syntality, p. 203
T-data, p. 187
Temperament, p. 195
Temperament trait, p. 193
Trait, p. 186
Type, p. 186
Visceral brain (VB), p. 200

9 B. F. Skinner

Biographical Sketch

Burrhus Frederic Skinner was born on March 20, 1904, in Susquehanna, Pennsylvania. He was the first child of William Arthur and Grace Madge Skinner. A second son, Edward James, was born two-and-a-half years later but died suddenly of a cerebral aneurysm when Skinner was a freshman in college. Skinner considered his mother the dominant member of the family and was often reminded that she almost died bringing him into the world (Skinner, 1976, p. 23). The Presbyterian religion was a major theme in Skinner's early life. He attended bible classes and embraced a number of traditional religious beliefs. During adolescence, however, he abandoned his religious convictions and never returned to them. Skinner's father was a lawyer who wanted his son to follow in his footsteps, but that was not to be.

Skinner was raised according to strict standards but was physically punished only once:

> I was never physically punished by my father and only once by my mother. She washed my mouth out with soap and water because I had used a bad word. My father never missed an opportunity, however, to inform me of the punishments which were waiting if I turned out to have a criminal mind. He once took me through the county jail, and on a summer vacation I was taken to a lecture with colored slides describing life in Sing Sing. As a result I am afraid of the police and buy too many tickets to their annual dance. (Skinner, 1967, pp. 390–391)

B. F. Skinner

Perhaps this unusually small amount of physical punishment influenced Skinner's later theoretical emphasis on controlling behaviour through reward or lack of reward rather than through punishment.

Skinner's aptitude for creative apparatus building, for which he became widely known, was evident in his childhood:

I was always building things. I built roller-skate scooters, steerable wagons, sleds, and rafts to be poled about on shallow ponds. I made see-saws, merry-go-rounds, and slides. I made slingshots, bows and arrows, blow guns and water pistols from lengths of bamboo, and from a discarded water boiler a steam cannon with which I could shoot plugs of potato and carrot over the houses of our neighbors. . . . I worked for years on the design of a perpetual motion machine. (It did not work.) (Skinner, 1967, p. 388)

In high school, Skinner earned money by playing saxophone in a jazz band and with an orchestra. After Skinner graduated from high school, the Skinner family moved to Scranton, Pennsylvania and soon thereafter Skinner enrolled in Hamilton College, a small liberal arts school in Clinton, New York. Skinner believed he never fit into the life of the college student because he was terrible at sports and was "pushed around" by unnecessary requirements such as daily chapel. He wrote highly critical articles about the faculty and administration in the school paper and disrupted the campus with a number of tricks. For example, he caused the campus and the local railroad station to be jammed with people by falsely announcing a lecture by Charlie Chaplin. The college president told Skinner to quit his antics, or he would not graduate. Skinner did graduate in 1926 with a Phi Beta Kappa Key and a BA in English literature. It is interesting to note that Skinner never took a course in psychology as an undergraduate.

Skinner left college with a burning desire to be a writer. Part of this desire is explained by the fact that the famous American poet Robert Frost had favourably reviewed three of Skinner's short stories. Skinner's first attempt at writing was in the attic of his parents' home. This attempt failed. His next attempt was in Greenwich Village, in New York City. This attempt also failed. Skinner referred to the period following his graduation from college as his "dark year." He became so depressed during this time that he pondered seeing a psychiatrist. However, his father believed doing so would be a waste of time and money and the idea was apparently abandoned (Skinner, 1976, p. 278). After two years of trying, Skinner concluded he "had nothing important to say" and gave up the idea of becoming a writer. He spent the next summer in Europe.

While in Greenwich Village, Skinner read the works of Ivan Pavlov, Bertrand Russell, and J. B. Watson, which greatly influenced him. On returning from Europe in 1928, he enrolled in the graduate program in psychology at Harvard. According to Elms (1981), enrollment in graduate school finally resolved the identity crisis that Skinner experienced following graduation from college. At Harvard, Skinner pursued his studies with extreme intensity.

I would rise at six, study until breakfast, go to classes, laboratories, and libraries with no more than fifteen minutes unscheduled during the day, study until exactly nine o'clock at night and go to bed. I saw no movies or plays, seldom went to concerts, had scarcely any dates and read nothing but psychology and physiology. (1967, p. 398)

This high degree of self-discipline characterized Skinner's work habits throughout his life.

Skinner earned his MA in two years (1930), his Ph.D. in three years (1931), and then remained at Harvard for the next five years as a postdoctoral fellow. He began his teaching career at the University of Minnesota in 1936 and remained there until 1945. During this time, Skinner established himself as a nationally prominent experimental psychologist by publishing his now famous book *The Behavior of Organisms* (1938). This book, though instrumental in establishing Skinner's career as an experimental psychologist, was received very poorly. Initially 800 copies were printed, and in the four years that followed only 80 copies were sold (Wiener, 1996, p. ix).

Shortly after moving to Minnesota, Skinner married Yvonne ("Eve") Blue, an English major at the University of Chicago. The marriage, although at times stormy and unconventional (Wiener, 1996, p. 58), lasted until Skinner's death. Skinner and his wife had two daughters; Julie, born in 1938, and Deborah (Debbie), born in 1944.

In 1945, Skinner moved to Indiana University as chairman of the psychology department, where he remained until 1948, when he returned to Harvard. In 1974, Skinner became professor emeritus, and he remained affiliated with Harvard until his death in 1990.

Skinner was highly productive. In 1948, he published *Walden Two,* which describes a society that functions in accordance with his principles of learning. In 1953, he published *Science and Human Behavior,* perhaps the best overall presentation of his theory. *Verbal Behavior* was published in 1957, and in that same year he published (along with Charles B. Ferster) *Schedules of Reinforcement.* He wrote *Beyond Freedom and Dignity* in 1971, which garnered widespread controversy, *Walden Two* has sold over 3 million copies, and *Beyond Freedom and Dignity* was on the New York Times bestseller list for 20 weeks (Wiener, 1996).

Skinner was disturbed that his position had been misunderstood by so many (including many psychologists), so he wrote another book, *About Behaviorism* (1974), to clarify his position.

It is ironic that Skinner's views are being considered in a text on personality theory because he rejected the use of theory (1950) and any notions of the inner causation of behaviour. For Skinner, the term personality itself must be rejected because it suggests the inner causation of behaviour:

> It is often said that a science of behavior studies the human organism but neglects the person or self. What it neglects is a vestige of animism, a doctrine which in its crudest form held that the body was moved by one or more indwelling spirits. When the resulting behavior was disruptive, the spirit was probably a devil; when it was creative, it was a guiding genius or muse. Traces of the doctrine survive when we speak of *personality,* of an ego in ego psychology, of an *I* who says he knows what he is going to do and uses his body to do it, or of the role a person plays as a persona in a drama, wearing his body as a costume. (1974, p.167)

In describing how his own life unfolded, Skinner carefully avoided references to the nonobservable concepts employed by most personality theorists.

> I do not believe that my life shows a type of personality à la Freud, an archetypal pattern à la Jung, or a schedule of development à la Erikson. There have been a few abiding themes, but they can be traced to environmental sources rather than to traits of character. They became a part of my life as I lived it; they were not there at the beginning to determine its course. (1983, p. 401)

Behaviourism

It is impossible to fully understand Skinner's view of personality without first understanding the school of psychology to which he belonged: behaviourism. To understand behaviourism, we must briefly discuss three other schools of psychology. Psychology's first school was **voluntarism,** which developed in Germany toward the end of the nineteenth century under the leadership of *Wilhelm Wundt* (1832–1920). A primary goal of the voluntarist was to study the nature of consciousness through the use of introspection or self-analysis. The voluntarists believed the mind was capable of arranging the elements of thought in any number of creative configurations, thus the name *voluntarism.* When voluntarism was transported to the United States it became the school of **structuralism.** It was Wundt's student *Edward Titchener* (1867–1927) who founded the school of structuralism at Cornell University in 1892. The structuralists also searched for the elements of consciousness but were not interested in the mind's creative ability. The schools of voluntarism and structuralism were short-lived for several reasons, but the main one was the growing influence of Darwinism. Several American psychologists embraced the doctrine of evolution enthusiastically and created America's first school of psychology around it, which was **functionalism.** The school of functionalism developed under the leadership of *John Dewey* (1859–1952) and *William James* (1842–1910) in the 1890s. As the name implies, the functionalist was concerned primarily with discovering how various processes are related to survival. They studied both behaviour *and* cognitive processes but did so with the goal of discovering how they functioned to enhance adjustment to the environment.

John Broadus Watson

John B. Watson took the next step. According to Watson, if psychology wanted to be truly scientific, it would have to have a subject matter that could be reliably and objectively studied. This could not be consciousness because the study of consciousness had been notoriously unreliable and because it could be studied only indirectly via introspection. The subject matter on which Watson insisted was overt behaviour, and he thus founded the school of **behaviourism.** Watson insisted that the study of consciousness be abandoned completely. He also wanted to end explanations of human behaviour in terms of instincts. Likewise, he thought that setting humans artificially apart from the other animals made no sense. The behaviour of both, he said, is governed by the same principles.

Watson believed that, with the exception of a few basic emotions that are inherited, behaviour patterns are learned through experience. Therefore, if you can control a person's experiences, you can create any type of person you wish. Watson famously (or infamously) stated:

Give me a dozen healthy infants, well-formed, and my own specified world to bring them up in and I'll guarantee to take any one at random and train him to become any type of specialist I might select—doctor, lawyer, artist, merchant, chief, and yes, even beggarman and thief, regardless of his talents, penchants, tendencies, abilities, vocations, and race of his ancestors. (1926, p. 10)

Behaviourism became the rage in North American psychology, and although its popularity is diminishing, behaviourism is still an important part of North American psychology. This brings us back to B. F. Skinner, who became the world's leading behaviourist.

Like many behaviourists, Skinner bypassed the internal workings of the organism (for instance, cognitive and physiological processes) and concentrated on the relationship between environmental events and behaviour. For this reason, Skinner's approach has been characterized as the "empty organism" approach. Skinner believed that no information is lost by making a **functional analysis** between measurable experiences and measurable behaviour and leaving out the intervening activities. In fact, he said, all of the problems inherent in a study of consciousness can be avoided:

> The mentalistic problem can be avoided by going directly to the prior physical causes while bypassing intermediate feelings or states of mind. The quickest way to do this is to confine oneself to what an early behaviorist, Max Meyer, called the "psychology of the other one": consider only those facts which can be objectively observed in the behavior of one person in its relation to his prior environmental history. If all linkages are lawful, nothing is lost by neglecting a supposed non-physical link. (Skinner, 1974, p. 13)

As we see throughout this chapter, Skinner believed strongly that a behavioural technology based on behaviouristic principles can solve many of the world's major problems. He believed, however, that many nonscientific explanations of the causes of behaviour were inhibiting the use of such a technology. His book *Beyond Freedom and Dignity* (1971) described this problem in great detail. The following quotation from that book nicely summarizes Skinner's concerns:

> The environment is obviously important, but its role has remained obscure. It does not push or pull, it *selects,* and this function is difficult to discover and analyze. The role of natural selection in evolution was formulated only a little more than a hundred years ago, and the selective role of environment in shaping and maintaining the behaviour of the individual is only beginning to be recognized and studied. As the interaction between organism and environment has come to be understood, however, effects once assigned to states of mind, feelings, and traits are beginning to be traced to accessible conditions, and a technology of behaviour may therefore become available. It will not solve our problems, however, until it replaces traditional prescientific views, and these are strongly entrenched. (p. 25)

In the following section, we examine how, according to Skinner, the environment *selects* some behaviours and not others.

Respondent and Operant Behaviour

Although both John B. Watson and B. F. Skinner were behaviourists, each emphasized a different type of behaviour. Watson accepted the principles of learning developed by Ivan Pavlov as a model for his brand of behaviourism. Pavlov's work on learning contains the following ingredients:

> **Conditioned Stimulus** (CS)—A stimulus that does not elicit a predictable response from an organism at the beginning of training but does elicit a predictable response after training.
> **Unconditioned Stimulus** (US)—A stimulus that elicits an automatic, natural, and predictable response from an organism.
> **Unconditioned Response** (UR)—The natural and automatic response elicited by the unconditioned stimulus.

Pavlov found that if the conditioned stimulus was paired several times with the unconditioned stimulus, it gradually developed the capacity to elicit a response similar to the unconditioned response; such a response is called a **conditioned response** (CR). Pavlovian or **classical conditioning** can be diagrammed as follows:

$$CS \longrightarrow US \longrightarrow UR \qquad \text{Original pairing}$$

$$CS \longrightarrow CR \qquad \begin{array}{l}\text{Demonstration of a} \\ \text{Conditioned Response}\end{array}$$

To use an example, suppose a particular perfume, though pleasant, doesn't yield any noticeable physical changes. Now suppose that a man smells this perfume while he enjoys sexual contact with a woman. After enough pairings of the perfume (CS) with all the arousing stimuli from sexual contact (US) and the erection that naturally follows (UR), the man may get an erection (CR) from simply smelling the perfume during a casual stroll past the cosmetics counter in a department store.

Skinner referred to behaviour elicited by a known stimulus as **respondent behaviour,** and all conditioned and unconditioned responses are examples. He called Pavlovian or classical conditioning **respondent conditioning** or **type S conditioning,** to stress the importance of the stimulus. The important point to remember about respondent behaviour is that a direct link exists between its occurrence and the stimulus that preceded it. In other words, a direct stimulus-response association occurs. All reflexes, such as pupillary constriction when light intensity is increased or pupillary dilation when light intensity is decreased, are examples of respondent behaviour.

Unlike Pavlov and Watson, Skinner did not emphasize respondent behaviour in his theory. Rather, he emphasized behaviour that is *not* linked to any known stimulus. He emphasized behaviour that appears to be simply emitted by the organism rather than elicited by a known stimulus, which is labelled **operant behaviour.** Skinner believed that operant behaviour is indeed caused by stimulation, but the source of that stimulation is not known, so that behaviour *appears* to be emitted. Skinner also said that it is not important to know the origins of operant behaviour. The most important characteristic of operant behaviour is that it is under the control of its consequences. In other words, it is what happens *after* operant behaviour is emitted that determines its fate. The name *operant* now might make more sense; operant behaviour *operates* on the environment so as to change it in some way. The changes in the environment that it causes will determine the subsequent frequency with which the response is made. We have more to say about this concept in the next section, but for now suffice it to say that the conditioning of operant behaviour is called **type R conditioning** to emphasize the importance of the response. Skinner's work was primarily in the area of operant conditioning.

Operant Conditioning

Operant conditioning has been used in psychotherapy, education, and child rearing, and has been proposed as a means of redesigning cultures. A technique this powerful must be complex and not easily comprehensible, right? Wrong! Operant conditioning is summarized in the following statement: "If the occurrence of an operant is followed by presentation of a reinforcing stimulus the strength is increased" (Skinner, 1938, p. 21). Putting this in slightly different form, we can say, if a response is followed by a reward, the response will be strengthened. This enormously powerful rule could not be more simple: *If you want to strengthen a certain response or behaviour pattern, reward it!*

To modify behaviour, two elements are necessary—behaviour and a reinforcer. Having defined operant, or type R conditioning, we look in more detail at its characteristics.

It should be remembered as we go through these characteristics that, according to Skinner, personality is nothing more than consistent behaviour patterns that have been strengthened through operant conditioning. As we look more carefully at the principles of operant conditioning, we are at the same time examining Skinner's theory of personality.

ACQUISITION

To demonstrate operant conditioning, Skinner invented a small experimental chamber for use with small animals, such as rats or pigeons, that has come to be called a **Skinner box.** Typically, the chamber contains a lever, a light, a food cup, and a grid floor. The apparatus is arranged so that when the lever is pressed, a feeder mechanism is activated that delivers a pellet of food into the food cup. In this box, the lever-press response is the operant response of interest, and the food pellet is the reinforcer. Even before the reinforcer is introduced into the situation, the animal will probably press the lever now and then just as part of its random activity. The frequency with which an operant response occurs *before* the introduction of a reinforcer is called the **operant level** of that response. When the response is followed by a reinforcer, the frequency with which it is made increases, which is what Skinner meant when he said a response has been strengthened. Operant conditioning is measured by the change in **rate of responding.** Under the conditions we have described, the rate with which the lever-press response is made will increase (relative to its operant level) and operant conditioning is said to have been demonstrated. This process is also referred to as **acquisition** of a behaviour. Note that the origins of the initial lever-press responses are not known, nor do they need to be. The situation is arranged so that when a lever-press response is made, it is reinforced, and when it is reinforced, it is strengthened in that the frequency with which it is made increases.

So much for rats in Skinner boxes. Now, what about people? Remember, the behaviourist does not believe that one set of learning principles exists for humans and another set for nonhumans. It is assumed that the same principles apply to all living organisms. Such an assumption has not gone untested. Greenspoon (1955) hypothesized that the therapist's "mmm-hmm" is reinforcing in a situation in which a client is talking quietly. To verify this notion, Greenspoon tested many subjects, one at a time; each time the subject spoke a plural noun, he said "mmm-hmm." Subjects subsequently increased the frequency of speaking plural nouns, even though they were not aware that their verbal behaviour was being modified.

Verplanck (1955) had his experimental class at Harvard condition a wide range of simple motor responses using points as the reinforcer:

> After finding a fellow student who was willing to be a subject, the experimenter instructed him as follows: "Your job is to work for points. You get a point every time I tap the table with my pencil. As soon as you get a point, record it on your sheet of paper. Keep track of your own points." With these instructions, it seemed likely that a tap, a "point," would prove to be a reinforcing stimulus. The method worked very well. Indeed, the experimenters were now able to condition a wide variety of simple motor behaviours, such as slapping the ankle, tapping the chin, raising an arm, picking up a fountain pen, and so on. They were further able to differentiate out, or shape, more complex parts of behaviour, and then to manipulate them as responses. The data they obtained included the results of the manipulation of many of the variables whose effects were familiar in operant conditioning of rats and pigeons. Despite the fact that the experiments were carried out in a variety of situations, the experimenters were able to obtain graphical functions that could not be distinguished from functions obtained on the rat or the pigeon in a Skinner box. (pp. 598–599)

Verplanck and his students went on to condition the response of stating opinions (for example, I think that or I believe that):

> The results of these experiments were unequivocal. In the first experiment, on opinion-statements, every one of 23 subjects showed a higher rate of giving opinion-statements during the 10–minute period when the experimenter reinforced each of them by agreeing with it, or by repeating it back to him in paraphrase, than he showed in the first 10–minute period when the experimenter did not reinforce. (Verplanck, 1955, p. 600)

Verplanck, like Greenspoon, found that conditioning did not depend on the subject's awareness of what was happening. Most of Verplanck's subjects were totally unaware of the experimental conditions governing their behaviour.

The Greenspoon and Verplanck studies represent only a sample of the hundreds of studies which have confirmed that operant principles apply to human as well as to nonhuman behaviour. These two studies were chosen for this book because they show the ease with which operant principles are demonstrated.

SHAPING

What do we do if the response we want to strengthen is not in the organism's response repertoire? The answer is that it is shaped into existence. Assume the lever-press response is one a rat would initially not make on its own in a Skinner box. Using the principles of operant conditioning already described, the lever-press response can be developed through a series of several steps. Using an external hand switch to trigger the feeder mechanism, the rat would be reinforced only for behaviour that brings it closer and closer to making the response that is ultimately wanted which, in this case, is the lever-press. We see that the shaping process has two components, **differential reinforcement,** which means that some responses are reinforced and some are not, and **successive approximations,** which means the responses that are reinforced are those that are increasingly close to the response ultimately desired. Hergenhahn (1974) lists the following steps as one way of **shaping** the bar-press response:

1. Reinforce the rat for being on the side of the test chamber containing the bar.
2. Reinforce him for moving in the direction of the bar.
3. Reinforce him for rising up in front of the bar.
4. Reinforce him for touching the bar.
5. Reinforce him for touching the bar with both paws.
6. Reinforce him for exerting pressure on the bar.
7. Reinforce him only for the bar-press response. (p. 361)

According to operant theory, the best way to teach a complex skill is to divide it into its basic components and gradually shape it into existence one small step at a time. According to this viewpoint, the shaping process is extremely important to education and to child rearing. It is by the principle of shaping that we learn to write letters and numbers. However, shaping is not always planned. Skinner gave the following example of how a mother may unknowingly shape undesirable behaviour in her child:

> The mother may unwillingly promote the very behavior she does not want. For example, when she is busy she is likely not to respond to a call or request made in a quiet tone of voice. She may answer the child only when [he or she] raises [his or her] voice. The average intensity of the child's vocal behavior therefore moves up to

another level. . . . Eventually the mother gets used to this level and again reinforces only louder instances. This vicious circle brings about louder and louder behaviour. . . . The mother behaves, in fact, as if she has been given the assignment of teaching the child to be annoying. (1951, p. 29)

Extinction

If operant behaviour followed by a reinforcer is strengthened, it should follow that if the reinforcer is removed from the situation, the operant behaviour will be weakened. This is exactly what happens. If, for example, after the lever-press response was conditioned, the feeder mechanism was disconnected, thus creating a situation in which a lever-press response is no longer followed by a food pellet, eventually that response would return to its operant level. Likewise, a professor may choose to ignore a student's constantly raised hand in order to give other students an opportunity to answer some questions. After enough instances of unrewarded hand-raising behaviour, the eager student will be less likely to raise his or her hand when questions are asked. In other words, when a reinforcer no longer follows a response, the frequency with which the response is made returns to the level it was at before the reinforcer was introduced into the situation, and we say that **extinction** has occurred.

Extinction can be regarded as the counterpart of acquisition, and the two processes together, according to Skinner, explain much of what we call personality. Briefly stated, rewarded behaviour persists, and unrewarded behaviour is extinguished. For example, an infant emits the sounds contained in every language on earth. From these random babblings the child's language is shaped. Those sounds that resemble words of the parents' language are noticed or reinforced in some way, and those utterances that are irrelevant to the parents' language are ignored. The reinforced verbal responses are strengthened and are shaped further, whereas the nonreinforced verbal responses are extinguished. So it is with all the behaviour we refer to collectively as personality.

Extinction is important to the Skinnerian view of behaviour modification. This view is quite simple: *Reinforce desired behaviour and ignore undesirable behaviour.* Skinner viewed extinction as the proper method of dealing with undesirable behaviour, *not punishment.* He gave the following example:

> The most effective alternative process [to punishment] is probably *extinction.* This takes time but is much more rapid than allowing the response to be forgotten. The technique seems to be relatively free of objectionable by-products. We recommend it, for example, when we suggest that a parent "pay no attention" to objectionable behaviour on the part of his child. If the child's behaviour is strong only because it has been reinforced by "getting a rise out of" the parent, it will disappear when this consequence is no longer forthcoming. (1953, p. 192)

We will discuss the problems associated with punishment later in this chapter.

Discriminative Operants

A **discriminative operant** is an operant response made under one set of circumstances but not under others. The Skinner box typically contains a light, which is usually above the lever. The circuitry of the Skinner box can be arranged so a lever-press response is reinforced when the light is on but not reinforced when the light is off. Under these circumstances, the rate with which the lever is pressed is much higher when the light is on than it is when the light is off. We say that the light has become a **discriminative stimulus** (S^D) for the lever-press response. In other words, the light-on condition becomes the *occasion* for the lever-press response. With S^R symbolizing a reinforcing stimulus or simply a reinforcer, the situation can be diagrammed as follows:

Light on   Lever Press   Food
                    Response   Pellet

Everyday life is filled with discriminative operants. A few examples follow:

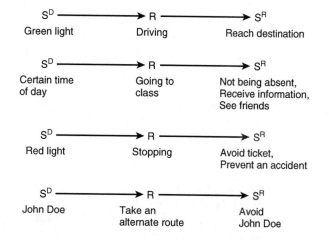

Green light   Driving   Reach destination

Certain time   Going to   Not being absent,
of day   class   Receive information,
                                           See friends

Red light   Stopping   Avoid ticket,
                                           Prevent an accident

John Doe   Take an   Avoid
                    alternate route   John Doe

According to the principles of operant conditioning, any response that is consistently reinforced in a particular situation will be repeated when that situation recurs. However, there will also be a tendency to respond to similar situations in a like manner. This tendency to emit an operant response in situations similar to the one in which it was originally reinforced is called **stimulus generalization**. Stimulus generalization explains why we emit learned responses in situations other than those in which the learning actually occurred. Thus, learning to avoid John Doe will also create a tendency to avoid individuals resembling him. The closer the resemblance, the greater will be the tendency to avoidance.

SECONDARY REINFORCEMENT

At this point, we must distinguish between a **primary reinforcer** and a **secondary reinforcer**. Primary reinforcers are factors related to survival such as food, water, oxygen, elimination, and sexual activity. These factors are not biologically neutral because if an organism (or in the case of sex, a species) goes long without any one of them, it will not survive. Food for a hungry animal is a natural, powerful, primary reinforcer, as is water for a thirsty animal. Secondary reinforcers are stimuli that are originally biologically neutral and thus not reinforcing but *acquire* their reinforcing properties through their association with a primary reinforcer. This principle can be stated as follows: *Any neutral stimulus that is consistently paired with a primary reinforcer takes on reinforcing properties of its own.*

It follows that every S^D that precedes a primary reinforcer, such as food, will become a secondary reinforcer. In our example in which a light was the occasion for a lever-press response to be reinforced by food, the light became a secondary reinforcer. Once a stimulus takes on reinforcing properties, it can be used to condition a new response or it can be used to maintain the response for which it was the occasion. For example, the light in the example can be used to teach the animal a response other than the lever-press response, for example, sticking its nose in a particular corner of the Skinner box. Likewise if the light followed the lever-press response during extinction, the animal would go on responding far beyond the point at which it would stop if the light did not follow the lever-press response.

According to Skinner, most human behaviour is governed by secondary reinforcers. For example, because mothers are typically associated with the satisfaction of the child's basic needs, they become secondary reinforcers. Eventually the sight of the mother is enough to pacify temporarily a hungry or thirsty child. In fact, attention alone is a powerful secondary reinforcer because it must precede the satisfaction of almost all, if not all, basic needs. Besides attention, which is a secondary reinforcer for children and adults alike, other common secondary reinforcers include the following:

kind words	awards
bodily contact	recognition
glances	gifts
money	privileges
medals	points

Secondary reinforcers that do not depend on a particular motivational state are called **generalized reinforcers.** A mother, for example, is a generalized reinforcer because her presence is associated with several primary reinforcers. Her reinforcing properties do not depend on the child being hungry or thirsty. Money is another generalized reinforcer because, like a mother, it usually is associated with several primary reinforcers.

CHAINING

For the Skinnerians, much complex behaviour is explained using the concept of **chaining,** which involves the notion of secondary reinforcement. We mentioned that any S^D that is the occasion for primary reinforcement becomes a secondary reinforcer. It is also true that all stimuli which consistently and immediately precede primary reinforcement will take on secondary reinforcing properties. In turn, stimuli associated with those stimuli will take on reinforcing properties, and so forth. In this way, stimuli far removed from the primary reinforcement can become secondary reinforcers, and as such can influence behaviour. These secondary reinforcers develop two functions: (1) They reinforce the response that preceded their appearance; and (2) they act as an S^D for the next response. The secondary reinforcers act as S^Ds that ultimately bring the organism into contact with the primary reinforcer. It is the primary reinforcer that

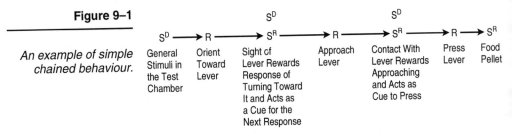

Figure 9–1

An example of simple chained behaviour.

$S^D \longrightarrow R \longrightarrow S^R \longrightarrow R \longrightarrow S^R \longrightarrow R \longrightarrow S^R$

| General Stimuli in the Test Chamber | Orient Toward Lever | Sight of Lever Rewards Response of Turning Toward It and Acts as a Cue for the Next Response | Approach Lever | Contact With Lever Rewards Approaching and Acts as Cue to Press | Press Lever | Food Pellet |

(From Hergenhahn & Olson, 1997, p. 91)

Figure 9–2

An example of chaining involving two people.

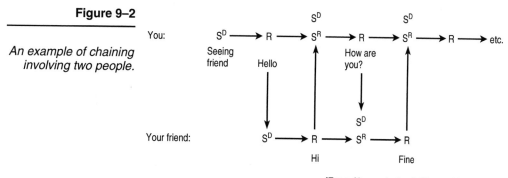

(From Hergenhahn & Olson, 1997, p. 92)

holds this entire chain of events together. The process of chaining is diagrammed in Figure 9–1.

Chained behaviour also results when two people confront each other. Typically, what one person says acts as an S^D for a response from the second person, and the second person's response not only rewards the first person's response but also acts as an S^D for another response, and so forth. An example of this process is diagrammed in Figure 9–2.

Skinner maintained that these principles also govern our behaviour when we simply roam about or even when we free associate:

> A response may produce or alter some of the variables which control another response. The result is a "chain." It may have little or no organization. When we go for a walk, roaming the countryside or wandering idly through a museum or store, one episode in our behaviour generates conditions responsible for another. We look to one side and are stimulated by an object which causes us to move in its direction. In the course of this movement, we receive aversive stimulation from which we beat a hasty retreat. This generates a condition of satiation or fatigue in which, once free of aversion stimulation, we sit down to rest. And so on. Chaining need not be the result of movement in space. We wander or roam verbally, for example, in a casual conversation or when we "speak our thoughts" in free association. (Skinner, 1953, p. 224)

Anyone who plays a musical instrument has experienced a form of chained behaviour. Within a musical piece, playing a note both reinforces the preceding response (S^R) and stimulates the next one (S^D). Everyday experiences with shopping, putting children to bed, even going on a date are little more than chainings of simple behavioural contingencies to construct a rather complex sequence of behaviours.

Verbal Behaviour

As indicated in chapter 1, the nativism-empiricism controversy is an ancient one. The nativist maintains that important attributes such as intelligence, creativity, or even personality are mainly genetically determined. The empiricist, conversely, insists that such attributes are the product of experience and not of genes. As one might expect, both viewpoints are represented in the explanation of language.

Skinner falls squarely in the empiricist camp. For him, language is simply verbal behaviour that is governed by the same principles as any other behaviour: Reinforced behaviour persists; nonreinforced behaviour is extinguished. Skinner (1957) did describe various categories of **verbal behaviour** that are distinguished by what is being done to be reinforced. The **mand** is a verbal command that specifies its own reinforcer. For example, the mand "pass the salt" is reinforced when the salt is passed. A **tact** is the accurate naming of something. For example, if a child says "doll" while holding a doll, he or she will be reinforced. **Echoic behaviour** is repeating something verbatim. For example, in the early stages of language training, a parent may point to her mouth and say "mouth"; if the child responds by saying "mouth," he or she will be reinforced.

We see then that Skinner's explanation of language is simply an extension of his general principles of learning. Skinner's most severe critic was Noam Chomsky (1959). Chomsky contended that language is simply too complex to be explained by learning. For example, it has been estimated that there are 10^{20} possible 20-word sentences in the English language, and it would take approximately 1000 times the estimated age of the earth just to listen to them all (G. A. Miller, 1965). Thus, said Chomsky, a process other than learning must be operating. Chomsky's answer is that the brain is structured in a way that causes it to generate language. In other words, our verbal skills are genetically determined. Chomsky's nativistic explanation of language was diametrically opposed to Skinner's empirical explanation. At present, the issue is far from settled.

Reinforcement Schedules

So far we have talked as if modifying behaviour necessitated reinforcing every desirable response that is made. That is, if we want to encourage children to read, they should be reinforced each time we observe them reading, or if we want a rat to continue to press a lever in a Skinner box, we should reinforce it with food each time it does so. If, indeed, each desirable response is followed by reinforcement, we say that the organism is on a 100% or **continuous reinforcement schedule.** A pay-phone works by this principle; one call for one quarter. However, if the phone does not work after you deposit your money, you likely won't deposit more money and you're less likely to return to this pay-phone in the future. Thus, this schedule is quite prone to extinction. Likewise, if a response that had been learned is now not followed by a reinforcement, we say that the organism is on a 0% reinforcement schedule that leads to extinction.

A response that is sometimes followed by a reinforcer and sometimes not followed by a reinforcer is said to be on a **partial reinforcement schedule.** Many believe the research by Ferster and Skinner (1957) on schedules of reinforcement represents a major contribution to experimental psychology. Although Ferster and Skinner studied many schedules, the following four have become most representative of their work:

1. **Fixed interval reinforcement schedule (FI).** On this schedule, the organism is reinforced for a response that is made following a certain time interval. For example, only the response made following a 30-second interval is reinforced. After an organism has been on this type of schedule for a while, its behaviour quickens toward the end of the time interval and then slows down drastically after reinforcement has been obtained. Individuals working for a fixed weekly or monthly salary are on this type of schedule. Students preparing for a term paper also will often wait until the deadline approaches before starting and then "work like mad" to finish. Such behaviour is typical of a FI schedule. If the mail is delivered at the same time daily, then this too would be a fixed interval schedule. Checking the mailbox after 1 p.m. (if that is the regular delivery time) should prove worthwhile, whereas checking before 1 p.m. should not. Note that

with this schedule, only one response is needed to obtain reinforcement if the response is made at just the right time.

2. Fixed ratio reinforcement schedule (FR).   On this schedule, the organism must make x number of responses before it is reinforced. For example, every fourth (FR4) response is reinforced. Such a schedule produces extremely high rates of responding and characterizes persons doing piecework or working for a commission. In both cases, the harder one works the more pay one receives because reinforcement is response-contingent instead of time-contingent.

3. Variable interval reinforcement schedule (VI).   On this schedule, the organism is reinforced at the end of variable time intervals. In other words, rather than reinforcing the organism after a fixed interval of, say, 10 seconds, it is reinforced *on the average* of every 10 seconds. For example, it may be reinforced for a response made after 7 seconds, then after 20 seconds, then after 2 seconds. Bosses who believe their workers should be periodically rewarded place them on such a schedule. At various times as they were working, the boss reinforces them with a kind word, although they have done nothing extra to deserve the kind word. Fishing is a prime example of this schedule. It is not certain how much time must pass before you get a nibble on your fishing line, but it's best to keep the line in the water just in case.

For interval schedules, it is not the *number* of responses made that is important; rather, it is the *passage of time* that determines when a response will be reinforced. For ratio schedules, however, the frequency of responding has a direct relationship to the number of reinforcers the organism will receive. For ratio schedules, the faster the organism responds, the more often it will be reinforced.

4. Variable ratio reinforcement schedule (VR).   This, like the FR schedule, is response-contingent but, on this schedule, the organism is reinforced on the basis of an average number of responses. That is, instead of being reinforced for *every* fourth response, it is reinforced on the *average* of every fourth response. Thus reinforcements could be close together or fairly far apart. On this schedule, however, the faster it responds, the more reinforcement it will obtain. This schedule produces the highest rate of responding. Gambling behaviour is under the control of a VR schedule, as is the behaviour of sales reps. For example, the faster one pulls the handle of a slot machine, the more often one will receive a payoff (and the faster one will go broke). With sales reps, the more contacts they make, the more likely they will be to make a sale, although exactly when a sale will be made cannot be predicted.

Partial reinforcement schedules have two important effects on behaviour: (1) They influence rate of responding. The VR schedule produces the highest rate of responding, followed by the FR schedule, then the VI schedule, and finally the FI schedule. (2) They increase resistance to extinction. All partial reinforcement schedules produce greater resistance to extinction than does a 100% or continuous schedule of reinforcement, and this fact is named the **partial reinforcement effect** (PRE). That is, a response followed by reinforcement only some of the time will persist much longer when reinforcement is discontinued than will a response followed by reinforcement each time it occurs. The PRE has implications for education and child rearing. For example, although a 100% schedule may be used in the early stages of training, a response should be switched to a partial reinforcement schedule as soon as possible. This will increase the perseverance of the response. In most cases, this will happen automatically because most behaviour that occurs outside a laboratory is on some type of partial reinforcement schedule.

Superstitious Behaviour

When a response leads to a reinforcer, we say that the reinforcer is *contingent* on the response. In our earlier example, a rat had to press the lever in a Skinner box *in order to* obtain a pellet of food. This is called **contingent reinforcement;** if the appropriate response is not made, the reinforcer will not become available.

Now let us imagine what would happen if a Skinner box were arranged so that the feeder mechanism would fire automatically, providing the animal with a pellet of food *regardless of what the animal was doing.* Let us imagine, for example, that the feeder mechanism is arranged so that it automatically provides a pellet of food on the average of every 15 seconds. According to the principles of operant conditioning, whatever the animal is doing when the feeder mechanism fires will be reinforced and thus tend to be repeated. As that response is being repeated, the feeder mechanism will again fire, further reinforcing the response. The end result will be that whatever the animal was "caught" doing when the feeder mechanism first fired will become a strong habit. Strange ritualistic behaviour develops under these circumstances. For example, one animal may learn to turn in a circle, another may learn to bob its head, and still another may learn to sniff air holes on the top of the Skinner box. Such behaviour is called **superstitious behaviour** because it appears *as if* the animal believes its ritualistic response is responsible for producing the reinforcer, when in fact it is not. Reinforcement that occurs regardless of what the animal is doing is called **noncontingent reinforcement.** Superstitious behaviour results from noncontingent reinforcement.

Numerous examples of superstitious behaviour on the human level exist. A baseball player, for example, who adjusts his hat a certain way just before hitting a home run will have a strong tendency to adjust his hat that way again the next time he comes up to bat. Many actors who are wearing a certain article of clothing before giving an outstanding performance may wear that same article of clothing whenever they perform. A native who beats on a drum in response to an eclipse of the sun may have a strong tendency to beat the drum the next time an eclipse occurs because his drum beating looked as if it brought the sun back.

Reinforcement Contingencies

POSITIVE REINFORCEMENT

As we have already seen, a **primary positive reinforcer** is something related to survival. If a response produces a primary positive reinforcer, the rate with which that response is made increases. We have seen too that any biologically neutral stimulus paired with a primary positive reinforcer takes on positive reinforcing characteristics of its own, thus becoming a **secondary positive reinforcer.** As with primary reinforcement, if a secondary positive reinforcer follows a response, the rate with which that response is made will increase.

NEGATIVE REINFORCEMENT

Positive reinforcement presents the organism with something it "wants" whereas **negative reinforcement** *removes* something the organism does not want. A **primary negative reinforcer** is a stimulus that is potentially harmful to the organism such as an extremely loud noise, a bright light, or an electric shock. Any response that removes or reduces one of these aversive stimuli will increase in frequency and is said to be negatively reinforced. For example, if a school has an ear-splitting morning bell, it reinforces the behaviour of coming to school late, which removes the aversive stimulus. This is labelled an **escape contingency** because the organism's response allows it to escape from an aversive situation. Any neutral stimulus consistently paired with a primary negative reinforcer becomes a **secondary negative reinforcer,** and an organism will work to escape from it just as it does from a primary negative reinforcer. Both primary and secondary negative reinforcement involve escaping from an aversive situation.

It is important to note that both positive and negative reinforcement result in an increase in response probability or in rate of responding. Both result in something desirable. In the case of positive reinforcement, a response produces something desirable. In the case of negative reinforcement, a response removes something undesirable.

AVOIDANCE

An **avoidance contingency** exists when engaging in certain behaviour prevents an aversive event from occurring. For example, opening an umbrella prevents getting wet, which is aversive. If a Skinner box is arranged so that a light precedes the onset of a shock, the animal will learn to respond to the light in such a way as to avoid the shock. With an avoidance contingency, the organism's behaviour prevents it from experiencing a negative reinforcer. As with our earlier example with John Doe:

$$S^D \longrightarrow R \longrightarrow S^R$$

Sight of   Take an   Avoid
John Doe   alternative   John Doe
         route

The sight of John Doe was a signal for an aversive encounter, and taking a route away from John Doe prevented or avoided that encounter. The reinforcement from negative reinforcement contingencies comes from *escaping* something aversive whereas the reinforcement from an avoidance contingency comes from *avoiding* an aversive experience.

PUNISHMENT

Punishment involves either removing a positive reinforcer or presenting a negative reinforcer. In other words, punishment either takes away something an organism wants or gives it something it does not want. A form of punishment that has become very popular among teachers and parents is called **time out from reinforcement.** With this technique, a child who has engaged in undesirable behaviour is denied access, for a period of time, to positive reinforcers that are normally available in the situation. Kazdin (1989) gives the following example: "A child may be isolated from others in class for 10 minutes. During that time, he or she will not have access to peer interaction, activities, privileges, and other reinforcers that are usually available" (p. 149).

Consistently, Skinner emphasized his belief that behaviour should be controlled using positive contingencies. He believed strongly that positive reinforcement and punishment are not opposite in their consequences. That is, although positive reinforcement strengthens behaviour, punishment does not necessarily weaken it:

Punishment is designed to remove awkward, dangerous, or otherwise unwanted behaviour from a repertoire on the assumption that a person who has been punished is less likely to behave in the same way. Unfortunately, the matter is not that simple. Reward and punishment do not differ merely in the direction of the changes they induce. A child who has been severely punished for sex play is not necessarily less inclined to continue; and a man who has been imprisoned for violent assault is not necessarily less inclined toward violence. Punished behaviour is likely to reappear after the punitive contingencies are withdrawn. (Skinner, 1971, pp. 61–62)

Even if punishment effectively eliminates undesirable behaviour, why use it if the same result can be accomplished with positive control? The use of punishment in controlling behaviour appears to have several shortcomings. For example, it causes the punished person to become fearful; it indicates what the person should *not* do, instead of what he or she *should* do; it justifies inflicting pain on others; it often causes aggression; and it tends to replace one undesirable response with another, as when a child who is spanked for a wrongdoing now cries instead.

Skinner stressed positively reinforcing desirable behaviour and ignoring undesirable behaviour (extinction). This should be viewed as an ideal, however, because instances occur when punishing a child is strongly reinforcing to a parent. A child acting up in a supermarket may stop doing so immediately if spanked by a parent, and this will vastly increase the likelihood of the child being spanked again next time he or she acts up. Even parents are capable of learning. As Skinner said, there are always two organisms whose behaviour is being modified in a learning situation, and sometimes it is difficult to know who is the experimenter and who is the subject. This point is made in the cartoon in Figure 9–3.

Although there is now considerable evidence that corporal punishment is ineffective in modifying a child's undesirable behaviour, and that more effective methods of positive control are available (for example, praise for desirable behaviour), the widespread use of corporal punishment persists. A recent survey indicates that 80% of parents in the United States spank their children. Perhaps more surprising is the fact that 60% of psychologists spank their children, although only 15% of those same psychologists believe in the effectiveness of corporal punishment (Murray, 1996a). Only five countries have outlawed the use of corporal punishment in child rearing (Austria, Cyprus, Finland, Norway, and Sweden) (Murray, 1996b). In Canada, there has been a movement to make physical punishment illegal on the grounds that spanking is assault, that it violates a child's constitutional rights, and that allowing any hitting of children makes it harder to demonstrate child abuse. However, in July 2000, Ontario Superior Justice David McCombs upheld section 43 of the Criminal Code, which allows parents to use "reasonable force" to discipline children, arguing that "parents and teachers require a protected sphere of authority within which to fulfill their respective roles." Yet the judge did not endorse spanking, stating that even mild forms of corporal

Figure 9–3

"Boy, have I got this guy conditioned. Every time I press the bar down he drops in a piece of food."

(From Skinner, 1959, p. 378)

Skinner believed in positively reinforcing desirable behaviour and ignoring undesirable behaviour. An Ontario judge recently upheld parents' right to spank their children, while emphasizing that he believes corporal punishment does more harm than good.

punishment do more harm than good. Parliament was also encouraged to better define the term "reasonable force." Clearly, the debate is far from over; it will likely surface in the Supreme Court of Canada in the coming years.

Our Biggest Problem

According to behaviourists, "Man's biggest problem is that his behavior is more easily influenced by small but immediate and definite reinforcers than it is by large, but distant and uncertain reinforcers" (Malott, Ritterby, & Wolf, 1973, pp. 4–2). This observation explains why many people remain smokers when they "know" they should not and overeaters when they "know" that in the long run it will be harmful. The prospect of a long, healthy life is no contest for a small amount of nicotine or the immediate taste of food in one's mouth.

Contingency Contracting.   So how do we solve this problem? One solution is to make the future immediate, and one way to do that is through **contingency contracting.** Let us say you want to quit smoking but cannot seem to do it on your own. Let us assume further that $100 is a substantial amount of money for you. One plan is to make an agreement with another person in which you turn over $100 to that person with the stipulation that every week you go without smoking you will get back $10. If you have even one cigarette during the week, you will lose $10. Many variations on such *contingency contracts* are possible. For example, the payoff could come daily instead of weekly, and the object of value could be such items as CDs or clothing instead of money. The point is that you have rearranged the reinforcement contingencies in your environment so that they now encourage desirable behaviour and discourage undesirable behaviour. In the case of smoking, rather than waiting for old age for the effects of nonsmoking to become manifest, you need wait only a day or a week. Now your behaviour is under the control of more immediate reinforcers instead of distant ones.

What happens when the contract expires? Perhaps other reinforcements will support the desired behaviour. Both smoking and nonsmoking produce reinforcers. The reinforcers for smoking include the effects of nicotine and perhaps a degree of social approval from other smokers. The reinforcers for not smoking include saving money, feeling better, not being the target of anticancer commercials, and social approval from other nonsmokers. Both smoking and nonsmoking produce reinforcement, and it is mainly a matter of switching from one source of reinforcement to another. Contingency contracting is one way of making the switch.

Since its early description as a behaviour modification technique (for example, Homme, Csanyi, Gonzales, & Rechs, 1969; Stuart & Lott, 1972), contingency contracting has been used to treat marital problems (Jacobson, 1978; Weiss, Birchler, & Vincent, 1974); study problems and other school-related behaviour problems (Blechman, Taylor, & Schrader, 1981; Kelley & Stokes, 1982; Speltz, Shimamura, & McReynolds, 1982); self-control problems, such as drug abuse (Boudin, 1972; Frederiksen, Jenkins, & Carr, 1976); weight control problems (Aragona, Cassady, & Drabman, 1975; Mann, 1972); alcoholism (P. M. Miller, 1972); and heavy smoking (Paxton, 1980, 1981).

Behaviour Disorders and Behaviour Therapy

BEHAVIOUR DISORDERS

For the Skinnerians, inappropriate behaviour is learned in the same way that appropriate behaviour is learned. That is, both desirable and undesirable behaviour are under the control of their consequences. In other words, so-called abnormal behaviour is not viewed by the Skinnerians as resulting from some underlying neurophysiological disease, nor from psychic conflicts such as those among the id, ego, and superego. As with normal behaviour, the Skinnerian analysis of abnormal behaviour stresses external, observable events, not inner causation. Skinner said, "A psychotic patient is psychotic because of his behaviour. You don't institutionalize a person because of his feelings" (quoted in Evans, 1976, p. 89). Like appropriate behaviour, inappropriate behaviour persists because it is maintained by reinforcement. Thus, according to the Skinnerians, if you want to eliminate undesirable behaviour you must prevent its reinforcement. Furthermore, you should specify the behaviour you want instead of the undesirable behaviour and reinforce it when it occurs. **Behaviour therapy** is a term used to describe any approach to psychotherapy that is based on a learning theory; however, several learning theories exist. For example, behaviour therapy may be based on Pavlovian learning theory, Bandura's observational learning theory (see chapter 11), or on Skinnerian learning theory. The Skinnerian version of behaviour therapy involves clearly specifying the undesirable behaviours that are to be extinguished, clearly specifying the desirable behaviours to be reinforced, and arranging reinforcement contingencies so they are responsive to the desirable behaviour but not to the undesirable behaviour. Because contingency contracting incorporates all of these procedures, it can be considered an example of Skinnerian behaviour therapy.

The Skinnerian version of behaviour therapy has been used successfully in treating a wide range of disorders such as alcoholism, drug addiction, mental retardation, autism, juvenile delinquency, phobias, speech disorders, obesity, sexual disorders, and various neuroses and psychoses. (For reviews of the applications of behaviour therapy see, for example, Craighead, Kazdin, & Mahoney, 1976; Kazdin & Hersen, 1980; Masters, Burish, Hollon, & Rimm, 1987.)

TOKEN ECONOMIES

An interesting example of the Skinnerian approach to therapy is **token economies.** In a token economy certain behaviours are deemed desirable, and other behaviours are deemed undesirable. When the participants in the economy act in desirable ways, they are given tokens (most often plastic discs like poker chips, but sometimes points or plastic cards). Because the tokens can subsequently be exchanged for items such as candy or cigarettes, they are secondary reinforcers. More specifically, the tokens are generalized reinforcers because they are paired with several primary reinforcers. Typically token economies are used in institutional settings such as schools or psychiatric hospitals. For a detailed description of the procedures, rules, and general considerations for such programs see Ayllon and Azrin, 1968; Schaefer and Martin, 1969; Thompson and Grabowski, 1972, 1977.

Token economies may sound contrived and unnatural, but perhaps it is the contingencies that exist within institutions without token economies that are unnatural. Masters, Burish, Hollon, and Rimm (1987) explain:

> Token economies are not really unnatural. Indeed, any national economy with a currency system is in every sense a token economy: any currency consists by definition of token or symbolic "reinforcers" that may be exchanged for items that constitute a more direct form of reinforcement. Whereas the individual in society works to earn tokens (money) with which he purchases his dwelling place, food, recreation, and so on, most institutions provide such comforts noncontingently and hence cease to encourage many adaptive behaviors that are appropriate and effective in the natural environment. (p. 222)

Ayllon and Azrin (1965, 1968) were among the first to use a token economy to treat maladaptive behaviour. Working with psychotic patients in a mental institution, Ayllon and Azrin first spent 18 months teaching attendants which behaviour to reinforce, how much to reinforce it, and when to reinforce it. By the time the behaviour modification program started, they had created a standardized list of behaviours to be changed as well as a list showing how many tokens were to be given when the patients engaged in various activities. Examples of behaviours that would earn tokens included washing dishes; helping to serve meals to other patients; cleaning tables; keeping oneself or one's room clean; proceeding to the dining room in an orderly fashion at mealtime; and washing sheets, pillowcases, and towels in the laundry. The tokens earned could be subsequently exchanged for such items as candy, cigarettes, coffee, privacy, a 30–minute grounds pass, a private audience with the ward psychologist or a social worker, the exclusive use of a radio, or the choice of a television program.

In general, Ayllon and Azrin found that the frequency of desirable behaviour increased significantly when it was reinforced by tokens. Furthermore, in another phase of the program, it was found that such behaviour decreased in frequency when the tokens were withdrawn and increased again when the tokens were reinstated.

Criticisms and Shortcomings of Token Economies.   Although token economies have tended to be successful, they have not gone uncriticized. One criticism directed at all forms of behaviour therapy is that it treats only symptoms and not the causes of those symptoms. Admittedly, say the critics, getting a psychotic patient to groom himself or herself is an improvement; however, the real problem, the psychosis itself, remains intact. Other critics complain that it may be unethical to deprive patients of goods and services to which they are legitimately entitled and then to provide those items selectively when the patients act in only appropriate ways.

A shortcoming of token economy programs is that the effects of the programs often do not generalize to other environments such as the home, the community, or the place of employment (see for example, Kazdin, 1977; Kazdin & Bootzin, 1972). A study by Becker, Madsen, Arnold, and Thomas (1967) even suggested that behaviours learned in a token economy program during one part of the day do not generalize to other parts of the day. These and other studies indicate that people in fact learn desirable behaviour when such behaviour leads to reinforcement but will stop engaging in that behaviour when the reinforcement is no longer forthcoming. Gagnon and Davison (1976) suggested that token economies actually do the participants a disservice because within the program certain behaviours are inevitably followed by reinforcement, whereas in the real world reinforcement is not nearly as predictable.

Finally, it seems that in some cases token economies simply do not work. For example, one token economy was designed to reduce the disruptive behaviour of nine adolescent boys in a psychiatric hospital school. It turns out that disruptive behaviour actually increased among the group when two of the boys realized the nature of the program. These two boys declared themselves "on strike" and labelled any boy willing to cooperate in the program "a fool" (Santogrossi, O'Leary, Romanczyk, & Kaufman, 1973).

Walden Two

The purposive manipulation of reinforcement contingencies so they encourage certain behaviours is called **contingency management.** We just saw how contingency management can be applied to the treatment of behaviour disorders. Skinner believed it can be used on a far larger scale. In fact, he defined *culture* as a set of reinforcement contingencies that encourages certain behaviours and discourages others. It follows that cultures, like experiments, can be designed to produce certain effects:

> A culture is very much like the experimental space used in the analysis of behavior. Both are sets of contingencies of reinforcement. A child is born into a culture as an organism is placed in an experimental space. Designing a culture is like designing an experiment; contingencies are arranged and effects noted. In an experiment we are interested in what happens, in designing a culture with whether it will work. (Skinner, 1971, p. 153)

When contingency management is used to design a culture, the effort is called **cultural engineering.** In 1948, Skinner published *Walden Two,* in which he described a utopian culture designed in accordance with the principles of operant conditioning.

Walden Two is a fictitious community of 1000 people. No private homes exist; rather, the inhabitants live in apartment complexes. No living quarters have cooking facilities; all meals are in community dining halls, which assures a healthy diet and frees people from the drudgery of preparing meals. Women of Walden Two are not burdened by cooking, cleaning, or mothering and are thus able to realize their full potential along with men. Marriage and child bearing are encouraged in the mid-teens. Marriages tend to last because couples are matched by interests, money is no problem, and child rearing is no burden. Children do not live with their parents rather, they live in nurseries and later dormitories, and move to their own apartments at about age 13. They are raised by experts because average parents do not have the knowledge or the facilities to raise children properly. The goal is "to have every adult member of Walden Two regard all the children as his own and to have every child think of every adult as his parent" (Skinner, 1948, p. 142).

Education is individualized, in that every child progresses at his or her own pace. No "formal" education exists, and teachers act only as guides. Education is provided in the actual workshops and laboratories of the community. Even at the college level, students are merely "taught to think" and are left to learn anything else on their own. No grades or diplomas are given.

No prisons, taverns, unemployment, narcotics, mental institutions, wars, or crime exist. Is such an "ideal" society possible? Frazier, the hero of the novel, who to many represents Skinner himself, said:

> The one fact that I would cry from every housetop is this: the Good Life is waiting for us. . . . It does not depend on a change in government or on the machinations of world politics. It does not wait upon an improvement in human nature. At this very moment we have the necessary techniques, both material and psychological, to create a full and satisfying life for everyone. (1948, p. 193)

Skinner believed that using the ideas contained in *Walden Two* could solve major societal problems:

> It is now widely recognized that great changes must be made in the American way of life. Not only can we not face the rest of the world while consuming and polluting as we do, we cannot for long face ourselves while acknowledging the violence and chaos in which we live. The choice is clear: Either we do nothing and allow a miserable and probably catastrophic future to overtake us, or we use our knowledge about human behavior to create a social environment in which we shall live productive and creative lives and do so without jeopardizing the chances that those who follow us will be able to do the same. Something like a *Walden Two* would not be a bad start. (1978, p. 66)

Several experimental communities have been designed according to the suggestions found in *Walden Two*. One of these communities, in Virginia, publishes a newsletter that describes its progress (Twin Oaks; Louisa, VA 23093). The history of this particular project is summarized in a book by K. Kinkade (1973). In an article entitled "Easing Toward Perfection at Twin Oaks," Cordes (1984) gives a progress report on the Twin Oaks experiment after 17 years of existence.

Beyond Freedom and Dignity

Skinner believed that cultural engineering need not be fictional but before such engineering will be possible, we need to develop a technology of behaviour:

> What we need is a technology of behaviour. We could solve our problems quickly enough if we could adjust the growth of the world's population as precisely as we adjust the course of a spaceship, or improve agriculture and industry with some of

the confidence with which we accelerate high-energy particles, or move toward a peaceful world with something like the steady progress with which physics has approached absolute zero (even though both remain presumably out of reach). But a behavioral technology comparable in power and precision to physical and biological technology is lacking, and those who do not find the very possibility ridiculous are more likely to be frightened by it than reassured. That is how far we are from "understanding human issues" in the sense in which physics and biology understand their fields, and how far we are from preventing the catastrophe toward which the world seems to be inexorably moving. (Skinner, 1971, p. 5)

What prevents the development of a technology of behaviour? According to Skinner, the main barrier is the traditional view of human nature that depicts people as autonomous—free to do as they choose—and therefore worthy of praise and dignity when they accomplish something. If those same accomplishments could be ascribed to outside influences, they would lose their meaning: "We stand in awe of the inexplicable, and it is therefore not surprising that we are likely to admire behavior more as we understand it less" (Skinner, 1971, p. 53). Skinner elaborated:

We recognize a person's dignity or worth when we give him credit for what he has done. The amount we give is inversely proportional to the conspicuousness of the causes of his behavior. If we do not know why a person acts as he does, we attribute his behavior to him. We try to gain additional credit for ourselves by concealing the reasons why we behave in given ways or by claiming to have acted for less powerful reasons. We avoid infringing on the credit due to others by controlling them inconspicuously. We admire people to the extent that we cannot explain what they do, and the word "admire" then means "marvel at." What we may call the literature of dignity is concerned with preserving due credit. It may oppose advances in technology, including a technology of behavior, because they destroy chances to be admired and a basic analysis because it offers an alternative explanation of behavior for which the individual himself has previously been given credit. The literature thus stands in the way of further human achievements. (1971, pp. 58–59)

The trouble with the notion of autonomous people, according to Skinner, is that it explains nothing about human behaviour; that is, in autonomous people the causes of behaviour are mystical. As our knowledge about human behaviour has increased, said Skinner, more of what once was attributed to autonomous people has been attributed to the environment. As we learn more, this trend will continue.

Evaluation

EMPIRICAL RESEARCH

Skinner's theory has no problem with empirical validation. Throughout this chapter, we have sampled research generated by Skinner's theory, and the studies we have mentioned indeed constitute only a sample. Because so many researchers follow Skinnerian principles, they have formed their own division of the American Psychological Association (Division 25, Experimental Analysis of Behavior). In addition, the Skinnerians have two journals in which to publish their research, *The Journal of Applied Behavior Analysis* and *Journal for the Experimental Analysis of Behavior.* With the possible exceptions of Cattell's and Eysenck's, no personality theory considered thus far is so intimately tied to experimental research as Skinner's.

Criticisms

Excessive Generalization from Nonhuman Animals to Humans.   Skinnerians believe that much, if not all, of what is learned by studying nonhuman animals applies to humans as well. For example, they believe the behaviour of all animals is controlled by its consequences. Therefore, if you can control consequences you can control behaviour; whether the behaviour in question is that of a rat, a pigeon, or a human. Many of the attributes thought to be uniquely human are essentially ignored in the Skinnerian analysis. For example, intentions, sense of self, thinking, reasoning, feeling, choosing, and reflecting have little or no place in Skinnerian theory. In fact, cognitive processes of any type are actively avoided by most Skinnerians. Skinner's relentless attack on cognitive psychology continued in the last article he wrote shortly before his death (Skinner, 1990). Given that cognitive psychology is currently very popular, while the influence of Skinner's brand of behaviourism is declining, we can conclude that Skinner lost his battle with cognitive psychology. Whether this continues to be the case, only time will tell.

Other critics agree with Skinner that some of the principles of learning that apply to nonhuman animals can be generalized to humans. They believe he goes too far, however, when he uses those principles in social, religious, economic, cultural, and philosophical speculations.

Radical Environmentalism.   The brand of determinism that Skinner embraced is called *radical environmentalism* because he assumed behaviour is caused by reinforcement contingencies found in the environment. We have seen throughout this chapter that all Skinnerian efforts to modify behaviour involved changing reinforcement contingencies. Critics say this view reduces humans to mindless automatons (or large white rats). Where in the Skinnerian analysis of behaviour, ask the critics, is the explanation for such phenomena and experiences as suicide, depression, love, wonder, hope, purpose, and awe?

Who Controls the Controllers?   This reaction to Skinner's writings is more of a concern than a criticism. Skinner believed strongly that operant principles can be, and should be, applied to cultural engineering. He believed an entire society could be arranged like a token economy. That is, desirable behaviour would be defined and would be reinforced with such items as tokens, money, goods, or services. Because behaviour is controlled by its consequences, members of this society would soon act as the dispensers of the reinforcers want them to act. Who, however, dispenses the reinforcers? Who decides what behaviour is desirable and what behaviour is undesirable? Skinner argued that the people in the society could determine the answers to these questions and could institute methods for countercontrolling the controllers. Many critics are not convinced, however, and continue to believe that the possibility of serious abuse exists within Skinner's notion of cultural engineering. Skinner was aware of this possibility, "I think a science of behavior is just as dangerous as the atom bomb. It has the potential of being horribly misused" (quoted in Evans, 1981, p. 54).

Contributions

Applied Value.   Throughout this chapter we have seen how Skinnerian principles have been applied to education, child rearing, therapy, personal improvement, and societal problems. Increasingly, Skinner's ideas have also been used in prison reform, in which positive control was explored as an alternative to negative control (see, for example, Boslough, 1972). A good theory explains, synthesizes large amounts of information, generates new information, and can be used as a guide in solving practical problems. Skinner's theory gets high marks in all of these categories. The criticisms that he generalizes too readily from the animal level to the human level and from the laboratory to the "real world" seem minor when compared to what has been accomplished using his theory as a guide.

Scientifically Rigorous Explanation of Human Behaviour. In an area such as personality theory, it is not uncommon to encounter terms, concepts, beliefs, and speculations that are difficult, if not impossible, to validate empirically. Skinner's theory (like Cattell's and Eysenck's) is an exception. All of the elements in Skinner's theory grew out of his laboratory research. The question concerning Skinner's theory is not whether or not it is correct. The question is not even whether it can be generalized to humans. The question is *to what extent* it can be employed to explain human behaviour.

How popular is Skinner among psychologists? In a 1966 survey, department heads of graduate psychology programs ranked Freud as the greatest psychologist of all time and ranked Skinner ninth. In 1981 a similar survey ranked Skinner first among living psychologists (Davis, Thomas, and Weaver, 1982). In a more recent survey taken just prior to Skinner's death (Korn, Davis, & Davis, 1991), historians of psychology and chairs of graduate departments of psychology ranked Skinner eighth on the all-time list but first among contemporary psychologists.

SUMMARY

1. Skinner's position falls into the behaviouristic camp because it stressed the study of overt behaviour and not internal mental or physiological events. He recognized two major categories of behaviour: respondent behaviour, which is elicited by a known stimulus, and operant behaviour, which appears to be emitted rather than elicited. Respondent behaviour is controlled by the events that precede it; operant behaviour is controlled by the events that follow it. Skinner focused on operant behaviour.

2. If an operant response is followed by reinforcement (either positive or negative) the rate at which it occurs will increase. If the desired response does not occur naturally, it can be shaped into existence using differential reinforcement and successive approximations. If the reinforcement for an operant response is discontinued, the rate eventually will return to its operant level, and extinction will have occurred. The situation can be arranged so that an operant response will be made under one set of circumstances but not under another set of circumstances. Such a response is called a discriminative operant. Any neutral stimulus consistently paired with a primary reinforcer becomes a secondary reinforcer, and thus all discriminative stimuli become secondary reinforcers. A stimulus that is paired with more than one primary reinforcer becomes a generalized reinforcer.

3. Much complex behaviour is explained using the concept of chaining. Chaining occurs when one response by an organism brings it into proximity with a reinforcer that both reinforces that response and triggers the next one. Chaining can also involve two people when the response of one triggers the response in the other. Verbal behaviour or language is thought to be governed by the same principles as is any other behaviour. Those utterances that are reinforced are repeated; those that are not reinforced are extinguished.

4. A response that is followed by a reinforcer on only some occasions is said to be on a partial reinforcement schedule. A response that is reinforced each time it occurs is said to be on

a continuous or 100% reinforcement schedule. A response that has been on a partial reinforcement schedule takes much longer to extinguish than one that has been on a continuous schedule.

5. When a response makes a reinforcer available, the reinforcer is contingent on the response. When a reinforcer appears independent of any response, we refer to it as noncontingent reinforcement. The ritualistic responses labelled superstitious behaviour result from noncontingent reinforcement.

6. A primary positive reinforcer is something that contributes to survival. A secondary positive reinforcer is anything that has been consistently paired with a primary positive reinforcer. A primary negative reinforcer is anything that is physically harmful to the organism. A secondary negative reinforcer is anything that has been consistently paired with a primary negative reinforcer. Positive reinforcement occurs when a response adds a primary or secondary positive reinforcer to the situation. Negative reinforcement occurs when a response removes a primary or secondary negative reinforcer from the situation. Punishment occurs when a response adds a primary or secondary negative reinforcer to the situation or removes a primary or secondary positive reinforcer. A popular type of punishment among educators and parents is called time out from reinforcement. Skinner opposed the use of punishment in the control of behaviour and stressed control through positive reinforcement.

7. A major problem for humans is that our behaviour is controlled by small, immediate reinforcers instead of by larger, more distant reinforcers. One way to remedy this problem is to use contingency contracting, which rearranges the reinforcement contingencies in the environment. Both appropriate and inappropriate behaviour is maintained by reinforcement. Skinner's version of behaviour therapy involves arranging reinforcement contingencies so they strengthen appropriate behaviour and weaken inappropriate behaviour. The Skinnerian belief that behaviour can be directed by controlling reinforcement contingencies has special relevance to child rearing because parents have considerable control over their child's environment. Skinner's utopian novel, *Walden Two*, describes a society designed in accordance with the principles of operant conditioning. Skinner believed cultural engineering could solve many of society's major problem but was impeded by the traditional view of autonomous people with freedom and dignity.

8. Skinner's theory grew out of empirical research and has generated a massive amount of subsequent empirical research since its inception. His theory has been criticized for generalizing findings too readily from the nonhuman to the human level, and for insisting that even complex human behaviour can be explained in terms of reinforcement contingencies. His notion of cultural engineering has also raised questions concerning decisions as to which behaviours will be deemed desirable and which undesirable, and who will control the controllers. Among the contributions of Skinner's theory are its widespread applied value and scientifically rigorous attempts to understand personality.

EXPERIENTIAL EXERCISES

1. Assume that Skinner was correct in his assumption that frequently occurring behaviour is maintained by reinforcement. First, note an activity that you engage in with considerable frequency, and then attempt to specify the reinforcers that maintain that activity.

2. According to the Skinnerians you need only two elements to modify behaviour: behaviour and reinforcement. With this point in mind, attempt to modify someone's behaviour. First, choose a behaviour that occurs with some moderate frequency and is easy to measure. Examples are uttering plural nouns, making opinionated statements, making various hand gestures, or laughing. When the person whose behaviour you are attempting to modify engages in the behaviour you have chosen, reinforce him or her with interest and attention. First observe and note the frequency with which the behaviour occurs initially and then note the frequency as the behaviour is reinforced. Make a tally mark on a sheet of paper each time the behaviour occurs within 3-minute intervals. After 15 minutes discontinue the reinforcement but continue to

count the occurrence of the behaviour. Did the frequency of the response increase as a function of reinforcement? If it did, what conclusions do you reach about human behaviour? If it did not, what conclusions do you reach?

3. Using the information in this chapter, work out a contingency contract with a friend to deal with some behaviour he or she considers undesirable. Describe the behaviour, what will reinforce abstaining from that behaviour, and the conditions under which the reinforcers will be dispensed. For example, if your friend wants to quit smoking, what reinforcement will be used and how often will nonsmoking behaviour be reinforced? Describe in detail your contingency contract program and its effectiveness.

4. Modify your own behaviour using Skinnerian principles. First, make a list of those items that you find reinforcing. The list should contain large reinforcers like going on vacation; medium-sized reinforcers like going to the movies, a play, or a concert; and small reinforcers like a snack, a cup of coffee, or watching a television program. Next, make a list of some of the behaviours you would like to change. Perhaps you would like to study longer, not smoke so much, not spend so much time socializing, or spend more time reading. Now arrange your life so you need to do something you do not enjoy to get something you do enjoy. For example, decide that you will not have the cup of coffee you desire until after you have studied for 45 minutes. In that way you create an incentive for yourself to do something that you otherwise would not enjoy doing. Describe and summarize your experience with the modification of your own behaviour.

DISCUSSION QUESTIONS

1. Describe the essential features of behaviourism.
2. Describe the nativism-empiricism debate as it applies to verbal behaviour. Summarize Skinner's explanations of verbal behaviour.
3. Describe "our biggest problem" and offer possibilities for its solution.
4. According to Skinner, what must be done before we can begin to solve our major problems? What did Skinner think is the major factor inhibiting us from making progress in this area?

KEY TERMS

Acquisition, p. 224
Avoidance contingency, p. 233
Behaviour therapy, p. 236
Behaviourism, p. 221
Chaining, p. 228
Classical conditioning, p. 223
Conditioned response (CR), p. 223
Conditioned stimulus (CS), p. 222
Contingency contracting, p. 235
Contingency management, p. 238
Contingent reinforcement, p. 232
Continuous reinforcement schedule, p. 230
Cultural engineering, p. 238
Differential reinforcement, p. 225
Discriminative operant, p. 226
Discriminative stimulus (S^D), p. 226

Echoic behaviour, p. 230
Escape contingency, p. 233
Extinction, p. 226
Fixed interval reinforcement schedule (FI), p. 230
Fixed ratio reinforcement schedule (FR), p. 231
Functional analysis, p. 222
Functionalism, p. 221
Generalized reinforcers, p. 228
Mand, p. 230
Negative reinforcement, p. 232
Noncontingent reinforcement, p. 232
Operant behaviour, p. 223
Operant conditioning, p. 223
Operant level, p. 224
Partial reinforcement effect (PRE), p. 231
Partial reinforcement schedule, p. 230

10 John Dollard Neal Miller

Biographical Sketches

JOHN DOLLARD

John Dollard was born in Menasha, Wisconsin, on August 29, 1900. When Dollard was approaching college age, his father, a railroad engineer, was killed in a train wreck. Dollard's mother, a former school teacher, then moved the family to Madison so that the children could more easily attend the University of Wisconsin. After a short time in the Army, Dollard enrolled in the University of Wisconsin, where he studied English and commerce. After obtaining his BA in 1922, Dollard remained at the university as a fundraiser for the Wisconsin Memorial Union. In his capacity as fundraiser Dollard met Max Mason, who became a second father to him. When Mason became president of the University of Chicago, Dollard went with him and acted as his assistant from 1926 to 1929. In 1930, Dollard earned an MA in sociology from the University of Chicago and in 1931 his Ph.D., also in sociology. During the year 1931 to 1932 Dollard travelled to Germany as a research fellow and, while there, was psychoanalyzed by Hans Sachs,

John Dollard

a colleague of Freud, at the Berlin Institute. Upon returning from Germany, Dollard took the position of assistant professor of anthropology at Yale University, and in 1933 he became an assistant professor of sociology in the newly formed Institute of Human Relations at Yale. In 1935, he became research associate at the institute, and in 1948 was appointed research associate and professor of psychology. Dollard was already at the Institute of Human Relations when Neil Miller became affiliated there in 1936, and the two soon formed a close working relationship. Dollard remained at Yale, where he became professor emeritus in 1969. He died on October 8, 1980, at 80 years of age.

Dollard was truly a generalist. Besides teaching anthropology, sociology, and psychology, he was also trained in psychoanalysis. He wrote *Caste and Class in a Southern Town* (1937), which is now considered a classic field study of the black person's social role in the South during the 1930s. Miller (1982) commented:

Today it is difficult to realize the courage that it took to make such a study and to write such a book. Southern whites, and some Northern white scholars as well, felt that it was despicable to describe such facts. The book was banned in South Africa and in Georgia. If conditions in this country are considerably better today, it is partly due to the long-term effects of the early insights provided by Dollard's classic study of *Class and Caste*. (p. 587)

NEAL MILLER

Neal Elgar Miller was born in Milwaukee, Wisconsin, on August 3, 1909. His family moved to Bellingham, Washington, so Miller's father, an educational psychologist, could teach at Western Washington State College (now Western Washington University). Miller received his BS degree from the University of Washington in 1931. While at the University of Washington, he studied with the famous learning theorist Edwin Guthrie. He received his MA degree from Stanford in 1932 and his Ph.D. degree from Yale in 1935. While at Yale he studied with another famous learning theorist, Clark L. Hull. As we shall see, Hull had a major influence on Miller's theory of personality. Miller undertook what Hull himself expressed an interest in doing but never did—he explored the relationship between Hull's theory and Freud's theory of personality.

Neal Miller

Shortly after obtaining his Ph.D., Miller went to Europe as a Social Science Research Council Travelling Fellow. While in Europe, he was psychoanalyzed by Heinz Hartmann, a colleague of Freud, at the Vienna Institute of Psychoanalysis. Miller could not afford the $20 an hour fee required to be analyzed by Freud himself (Moritz, 1974). From 1936 to 1941 he was an instructor, assistant professor, and associate professor at Yale's Institute of Human Relations. The Institute of Human Relations was founded in 1933 to explore the interdisciplinary relationships among psychology, psychiatry, sociology, anthropology, economics, and law. From 1942 to 1946 he directed psychological research for the Army Air Force. In 1946, he returned to Yale, and in 1952 he became the James Rowland Angell Professor of Psychology. In 1948, Miller married Marion Edwards and they subsequently had two children, York and Sara. Miller remained at Yale until 1966, and then moved to Rockefeller University to become professor of psychology and head of the laboratory of physiological psychology. Miller is currently professor emeritus at Rockefeller University, and a research affiliate at Yale.

Through the years Miller has been a courageous researcher, who has been willing to apply the rigorous methods of science to the more subjective aspects of human experience, such as conflict, language, and unconscious mechanisms. This boldness continued with Miller's exploration of the conditions under which people can learn to control their own internal environment. His pioneer research in this area of **biofeedback** is but one area in which Miller has stimulated research and to which he has made significant contributions. Until the 1960s, it was believed that operant conditioning was possible for responses involving the skeletal or striped muscles but not for responses involving smooth muscles and glands. Examples of the latter include heart rate, salivation, blood pressure, and skin temperature. Miller and his colleagues found that when a mechanical device, such as an auditory signal or flashing light, was used to display the status of the internal biological event of concern, individuals were often able to control them. The medical implications of biofeedback were immediately apparent. Heart patients could learn to control their cardiac abnormalities, epileptics could learn to suppress abnormal brain activity, and those suffering from migraine headaches could learn to control the dilation of blood vessels surrounding the brain. Furthermore, it was found that after using biofeedback for a period of time patients became aware of their internal states and modified them as necessary. For example, patients could raise or lower their blood pressure, without the aid of biofeedback (for more details concerning the use of biofeedback and its current status, see Hergenhahn and Olson, 1997). More recently Miller has been concerned with the relatively new topic of *behavioural medicine* that, to a large extent, is an outgrowth of his research on biofeedback (see for example, Miller, 1983, 1984).

Among Miller's many honours are included the presidency of the American Psychological Association, a position he held from 1960 to 1961; the Warren Medal from the Society of Experimental Psychologists in 1957; and the U.S. President's Medal of Science in 1965.

On August 16, 1991, the American Psychological Association presented Miller with an award for Outstanding Lifetime Contribution to Psychology (*American Psychologist,* 1992, p. 847). In his acceptance of this award, Miller (1992) emphasized the importance of basic scientific methodology and animal models to the understanding of such topics as social learning, psychopathology, and health. Miller argued that most significant advances in understanding human behaviour, and, therefore, in the solution of social problems, have come from scientific research. For this reason, the teaching of science and scientific methodology should be a substantial part of even introductory psychology courses. According to Miller, the greater the number of future leaders and citizens of our country who understand science, the better off we all are.

The combined efforts of Dollard and Miller created a framework within which complex topics such as personality and psychotherapy could be understood more clearly than they had ever been before. As we shall see, they took two pre-existing systems—Freud's and Hull's—and synthesized them, thus creating a more comprehensive and more useful theoretical structure than either Freud's theory or Hull's theory alone had been.

Goal of Dollard and Miller.   Dollard and Miller dedicated their 1950 book, *Personality and Psychotherapy,* to "Freud, Pavlov and their students." The first paragraph of this book reads:

> This book is an attempt to aid in the creation of a psychological base for a general science of human behavior. Three great traditions, heretofore followed separately, are brought together. One of these is psychoanalysis, initiated by the genius of Freud and carried on by his many able students in the art of psychotherapy. Another stems from the work of Pavlov, Thorndike, Hull, and a host of other experimentalists. They have applied the exactness of natural-science method to the study of the principles of learning. Finally, modern social science is crucial because it describes the social conditions under which human beings learn. The ultimate goal is to combine the

vitality of psychoanalysis, the rigor of the natural-science laboratory, and the facts of culture. We believe that a psychology of this kind should occupy a fundamental position in the social sciences and humanities—making it unnecessary for each of them to invent its own special assumptions about human nature and personality. (p. 3)

Why the emphasis on learning principles? Miller and Dollard believed most human behaviour is learned. In their earlier book, *Social Learning and Imitation* (1941), which was dedicated to Clark Hull, they explained:

Human behavior is learned; precisely that behavior which is widely felt to characterize man as a rational being, or as a member of a particular nation or social class, is acquired rather than innate. To understand thoroughly any item of human behavior—either in the social group or in the individual life—one must know the psychological principles involved in its learning and the social conditions under which this learning took place. It is not enough to know either principles or conditions of learning; in order to predict behavior both must be known. The field of psychology describes learning principles, while the various social science disciplines describe the conditions. (p. 1)

It is not just simple overt behaviour that Dollard and Miller believed is learned, but also the complex processes such as language and the processes described by Freud such as repression, displacement, and conflict. Because of their willingness to postulate and investigate mental events and processes, the work of Dollard and Miller can be seen as representing the transition from the radical behaviourism of Watson and Skinner to contemporary cognitive psychology.

Hull's Theory of Learning

In chapter 9, we said that Skinner defined a reinforcer as anything that modified either the probability of a response or the rate of responding. Hull (1943) was more specific about the nature of **reinforcement.** He said that for a stimulus to be a reinforcer it must reduce a drive. Therefore Hull had a **drive reduction** theory of learning. A stimulus capable of reducing a drive is a **reinforcer**, and the actual drive reduction is the reinforcement.

The cornerstone of Hull's theory is the concept of **habit,** which is an association between a stimulus and a response. If a stimulus (S) leads to a response (R), which, in turn, produces a reinforcer, the association between that stimulus (S) and that response (R) becomes stronger. We say that the habit of performing that response in the presence of that stimulus becomes stronger. Because habits describe relationships between stimuli and responses, Hull's theory is referred to as an S-R theory of learning.

In addition to the concepts of drive and habit, Dollard and Miller borrowed other concepts from Hull's theory of learning. Among them are the concepts of response hierarchies, stimulus generalization (which Hull borrowed from Pavlov), primary and secondary drives, primary and secondary reinforcers, anticipatory goal responses, and cue-producing responses.

A few of the Freudian concepts that Dollard and Miller attempted to explain or equate with learning principles are the pleasure principle, the relationship between frustration and aggression, the importance of early childhood experience to the formation of adult personality, conflict, repression, and the importance of the unconscious mind in the formation and maintenance of neurotic behaviour. Dollard and Miller also attempted to explain many of the effective procedures in psychotherapy in terms of Hullian learning principles.

For the remainder of this chapter, we review certain aspects of Freudian theory and place them within the context of **Hull's theory of learning.**

Like Skinner, the Hullians, including Dollard and Miller, made no apologies for using lower animals, such as rats, to study human behaviour. In fact, Dollard and Miller believed that two of the best sources of information about the normal human personality are the rat and neurotic humans who seek professional help. They thought that studying rats is useful because their histories (both genetic and environmental) can be controlled; they are less complex than humans; and the simple behavioural "units" found in rats are also the ingredients of human behaviour. Being a lifelong supporter of animal research, Miller has often defended such research against radical animal rights advocates (e.g., Coile & Miller, 1984; Miller, 1985, 1991).

Dollard and Miller thought that studying neurotics is useful because they seek help and therefore can be observed under controlled conditions; their behaviour can be systematically studied during a fairly long period of time; they are more willing than normal people to speak openly about sensitive and highly personal aspects of their lives; and the same variables govern both neurotic and normal behaviour, but the variables appear in exaggerated form in neurotics, making them easier to observe. Incidentally, Freud also believed that much could be learned about normal people by studying abnormal people: "Pathology has always done us the service of making discernible by isolation and exaggeration conditions which would remain concealed in a normal state" (Freud, 1933/1964, p. 150). Dollard and Miller did caution, however, that any generalizations from rats or neurotics applied to normal humans should be checked empirically to test their validity. Dollard and Miller believed that a combination of psychotherapy and laboratory experimentation offers the best means of studying personality.

Drive, Cue, Response, and Reinforcement

Dollard and Miller's theory of personality relies heavily on four concepts that they borrowed from Hull's theory of learning: drive, cue, response, and reinforcement.

DRIVE

A **drive** is any strong stimulus that impels an organism to action and the elimination or reduction of which is reinforcing. Drives may be *internal,* such as hunger or thirst, or they may be *external,* such as a loud noise or intense heat or cold. A drive may be *primary,* in that it is directly related to survival—for example, hunger, thirst, pain, sex, and elimination—or it may be *secondary,* or learned, such as fear, anxiety, or the need to be successful or attractive. Secondary drives are usually culturally determined, whereas primary drives are not. It is important to note that primary drives are the building blocks of personality, and all **acquired drives** ultimately depend on them. This concept is similar to Freud's position that many of the everyday behaviours we observe in people are indirect manifestations of basic instincts such as sex or aggression.

Drive is the motivational concept in Miller and Dollard's theory; it is the energizer of personality. The stronger the stimulus, the stronger the drive and the greater the motivation:

> A drive is a strong stimulus that impels action. Any stimulus can become a drive if it is made strong enough. The stronger the stimulus, the more drive function it possesses. The faint murmur of distant music has but little primary drive function; the infernal blare of the neighbour's radio has considerably more. (Miller & Dollard, 1941, p. 18)

CUE

A **cue** is a stimulus that indicates the appropriate direction an activity should take. Drives energize behaviour; cues guide behaviour:

> The drive impels a person to respond. Cues determine when he will respond, where he will respond, and which response he will make. Simple examples of stimuli which function primarily as cues are the five o'clock whistle determining when the tired worker will stop, the restaurant sign determining where the hungry man will go, and the traffic light determining whether the driver will step on the brake or on the accelerator. (Dollard & Miller, 1950, p. 32)

Any stimulus can be thought of as having certain drive properties, depending on its strength, and certain cue properties, depending on its distinctiveness. Seeing a delicious dessert can motivate you to eat, or seeing your home athletes win Olympic medals may stimulate you to take up the sport.

RESPONSE

Responses are elicited by the drive and cues present and are aimed at reducing or eliminating the drive. In other words, the hungry (drive) person seeing a restaurant (cue) must get into the restaurant (response) before the hunger drive can be reduced. In Dollard and Miller's theory (and in Hull's) a **response** can be *overt*—it can be directly instrumental in reducing a drive—or it can be *internal*, entailing the thinking, planning, and reasoning that will *ultimately* reduce a drive. Dollard and Miller refer to internal responses as cue-producing responses. We have more to say about such responses later in the chapter.

Some responses are more effective than others in reducing a drive and are the ones expected to occur when next the drive occurs. New responses must be learned to new situations, and old responses must be discouraged if they are no longer maximally effective. The rearrangement of response probabilities as new conditions emerge or as old conditions change is called **learning.** We say more about the circumstances under which response probabilities change in the next section.

REINFORCEMENT

As we said earlier, reinforcement, according to Dollard and Miller, is equated with drive reduction: "Reward is impossible in the absence of drive" (Miller & Dollard, 1941, p. 29). Any stimulus that causes drive reduction is said to be a reinforcer. A reinforcer can be primary, in which case it satisfies a need related to survival, or it can be secondary. A secondary reinforcer, as in Skinner's theory, is a previously neutral stimulus that has been consistently paired with a primary reinforcer. A mother, for example, becomes a powerful secondary reinforcer because of her association with the reduction of primary drives.

If a cue leads to a response and the response leads to reinforcement, the association between the cue and the response will be strengthened. If this process is repeated, eventually the organism develops a strong habit.

As we have seen, Dollard and Miller's goal was to explain personality in terms of learning theory. They summarized what learning theorists call **reinforcement theory** in a simple statement: "In order to learn one must want something, notice something, do something, and get something" (Miller & Dollard, 1941).

Response Hierarchies

Every cue elicits several responses simultaneously that vary in terms of their probability of occurrence. This group of responses elicited by a cue is what Hull called the **habit family hierarchy,** which can be diagrammed as follows:

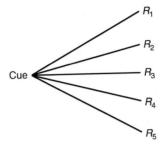

In the preceding diagram, R_1 is the most likely response to be made when the cue is encountered, R_2 is next likely, and so forth. If R_1 is prevented, R_2 will occur, and if R_1 and R_2 are blocked, R_3 will occur, and so on.

When a newborn child experiences an irritation, a set of responses is triggered, and because no learning is involved, it is called the **innate hierarchy of responses.** This hierarchy is a genetically determined set of responses that is triggered by certain drive conditions. The hungry infant may first become restless, then cry, and then kick and scream. Note that the innate hierarchy of responses exists for only a short period of time. As certain responses in the hierarchy are reinforced, they change their position in the hierarchy. The response most likely to occur at any given time is called the **dominant response** in the hierarchy and is the one that has been most successful in bringing about drive reduction.

Learning is constantly rearranging responses in the various habit family hierarchies. Prior to a learning experience, the arrangement of responses elicited by a cue is called the **initial hierarchy of responses.** After learning has occurred, the revised arrangement of responses is called the **resultant hierarchy of responses.** Note that what is called the initial hierarchy of responses refers to either an innate hierarchy of responses or to a hierarchy that resulted from prior learning. In either case, it is the hierarchy that exists before a *new* learning experience that will rearrange the hierarchy, thus creating a resultant hierarchy of responses. The term *initial* refers to clusters of response probabilities that exist *before* a learning experience, whether those probabilities are determined by genetics or by prior learning experience.

It is also important to note that if the dominant response in a hierarchy always reduces the existing drive, no learning will occur. If, for example, the innate response of blinking always removes stray particles from one's eye, no need will exist to learn to rub the eye or roll it or wash it. According to Dollard and Miller, all learning, which we can now equate with the rearrangement of response hierarchies, depends on failure. This concept is labelled the **learning dilemma,** and has important implications for both education and child rearing:

> In the absence of a dilemma, no new learning of either the trial-and-error or the thoughtful problem-solving type occurs. . . . The absence of a dilemma is one of the reasons why it is often difficult to teach successful people new things. Old, heavily rewarded habits must be interrupted before new learning can occur. When the accustomed rewards are withdrawn by unusual circumstances such as revolution,

new responses may occur and, if rewarded, may be learned; Russian Counts *can* learn to drive taxicabs and Countesses to become cooks. (Dollard & Miller, 1950, pp. 45–46)

THE GRADIENT OF REINFORCEMENT

Responses that are reinforced immediately after they are made are strengthened more than they would be if reinforcement was delayed. In other words, "Delayed reinforcements are less effective than immediate ones" (Dollard & Miller, 1950, p. 54). But there is another sense in which reinforcement can be delayed in a learning situation. Dollard and Miller observe that most learning involves a sequence of responses only the last of which is reinforced. In such a sequence, the last response made will be strengthened the most, then the second to the last, etc. Dollard and Miller (1950) give the following example:

> When a hungry boy takes off his hat in the hall, dashes through the dining room into the kitchen, opens the icebox, and takes a bit to eat—the connections more remote from the reward are strengthened less than those closer to the reward. In this series, the connection between the sight of the hall closet and the response of hanging up the hat will be strengthened less than the connection between the sight of the icebox door and the response of opening it. (p. 54)

This **gradient of reinforcement** explains why activity quickens as a positive goal is approached: "A hungry man on his way to dinner has a tendency to quicken his pace in rounding the last corner on the way home" (p. 55). This also explains why you are more likely to protest if someone cuts in line when you're second from the movie ticket booth rather than twenty-second. Your proximity to the goal yields a steeper reinforcement gradient. The gradient of reinforcement also explains why when two or more routes to a positive goal are available, the shorter route tends to be preferred.

Fear as an Acquired Drive

We have looked in detail at the complexities of Dollard and Miller's concepts of response and reinforcement. In this section, we focus on their concept of drive, and in the next section we discuss some additional properties of cues.

We mentioned earlier that two types of drives exist—primary and secondary. Primary drives are biologically determined, and secondary drives are learned or culturally determined. One of the most important secondary drives is fear, because it is so important to both adaptive and maladaptive human behaviour (for our present purposes we will use the terms fear and anxiety as synonyms). Freud observed that anxiety serves as a warning of impending danger. Events that accompanied a painful experience, when re-encountered, would cause fear or anxiety, thus warning the person to be careful. For example, a child burned by a hot stove would experience fear when next seeing a stove even though there was no pain in merely seeing the stove.

In 1948 Miller performed his now-famous experiment exploring the acquisition of fear (1948a). His apparatus consisted of an experimental chamber with black and white compartments. When a rat was allowed to roam freely, it showed no aversion to either the white or the black compartment. Next, Miller shocked the rat in the white compartment, and it was allowed to escape the shock by running through an open door into the black compartment. The rat quickly learned to escape the shock by leaving the white compartment. Later when the animal was placed in the white compartment without being shocked, it urinated, defecated, crouched, and ran into the black compartment. The animal had learned to fear the white compartment because it had been associated with shock.

Miller next arranged the experiment so the animal could escape the white compartment only by first turning a small wheel. The animal learned to do this, even though no additional shocks were given. Miller replaced the wheel with a lever and found the animal quickly extinguished the wheel-turning response, which was now ineffective, and learned the lever-pressing response, again with no further shocks. The animal had developed a **conditioned fear reaction** to the white chamber.

The most important point about Miller's experiment is that it demonstrates that fear itself becomes a drive that can be reduced, resulting in reinforcement. It was the reduction of fear, not pain, that caused the animal to learn the wheel-turning and the lever-pressing responses. Such behaviour is highly resistant to extinction, because as long as fear is present, its reduction will be reinforcing. Note that, under these circumstances, the animal does not stay in the situation long enough to learn that it will not receive additional shocks and thereby extinguish its fear reaction. It continues to behave *as if* it will be shocked again if it lingers in the situation.

It is Dollard and Miller's contention that phobias and other irrational fears are produced by similar experiences on the human level. Such behaviour appears irrational to the observer because the history of its development is not known as it is with the rat. For example, a person who is afraid of crowds may have become lost in a large group of people as a young child, too young to remember the experience. Similarly, a traumatic event (like a spanking) could have occurred while a child was riding in an elevator, causing a fear of elevators. Or it may be that because of harsh physical punishment for sexual behaviour in early childhood, a person has an aversion to sexual activities and sexual thoughts. For this person, even approximating such activities or thoughts elicits fear, which is reduced by escape or avoidance. Like the rat in Miller's experiment, this person never dwells long enough in the anxiety-provoking situation to learn that he or she will no longer be punished for such thoughts or activities. As with the rat, extinction of the fear reaction is extremely difficult. As we see later in this chapter, the main job of psychotherapy, as Dollard and Miller view it, is to provide a situation in which the client is encouraged to experience threatening thoughts without punishment and, in that way, to finally extinguish them. This goal is similar to what Freud attempted to do when he used free association and dream analysis to discover repressed thoughts.

Stimulus Generalization

As we mentioned in chapter 9, if an association exists between S_1 and R_1, not only will S_1 elicit R_1, but so will various stimuli similar to S_1. The greater the similarity of a stimulus to S_1, the greater will be the tendency for it to elicit R_1. This is called **stimulus generalization**. In Miller's experiment on fear, we would expect not only the white compartment but also various shades of grey compartments to elicit fear. The lighter the shade of the compartment, however, the greater will be the fear response because it was the white compartment that was originally associated with pain.

All learned responses generalize to other stimuli. If a child learns to fear snakes, he or she probably will also, at least at first, fear rope. If an adolescent fears his or her father, he or she will also tend to fear men who resemble the father. A woman who is raped may shortly thereafter hate all men. With further experience, however, most normal humans learn to discriminate. **Discrimination** is the opposite of generalization.

Thus the child learns that some snakes are to be feared but ropes are safe. The adolescent learns that the father perhaps should be feared under some circumstances but that men of similar appearance pose no threat, and the rape victim realizes that her attacker is not typical of all men. Therefore, generalization causes the initial tendency for learned responses to be elicited by a wide range of stimuli, but further experience allows the person to discriminate and thus respond selectively to stimuli. This is true, at least, of normal people. As we see later in this chapter, neurotics often lose their ability to discriminate and therefore tend to overgeneralize their anxieties.

Dollard and Miller distinguished two types of generalization: primary and secondary. **Primary generalization** is based on the physical similarity among stimuli. The closer two stimuli are in their physical attributes, the greater the probability is that they will elicit the same response. Primary generalization is innate and governed by a person's sensory apparatus. **Secondary generalization** is based on verbal labels. Thus one responds to all individuals labelled "friendly" in a similar way. Likewise the word "dangerous" equates many dangerous situations that tend to elicit similar types of responses. Secondary generalization is what Dollard and Miller called learned equivalence, which is mediated by language. It is important to realize that secondary generalization is not based on physical attributes; in fact, it can counteract primary generalization by labelling one event "good" and another event "bad," although the two events are physically similar.

Conflict

One of Freud's concepts that Miller studied intensively was that of **conflict.** Lewin (1935) had studied the concept earlier, and Miller borrowed from both Freud and Lewin. It was Miller, however, who experimentally analyzed in depth the concept of conflict. Freud had talked about the continuous conflict between libidinal desires and the demands of the ego and superego. To Freud, a person can be both attracted to an object and repelled by it at the same time. This was later called an approach-avoidance conflict and is one of four types of conflict studied by Miller. Each of the four is now described.

APPROACH-APPROACH CONFLICT

Here the conflict is between two positive goals that are equally attractive at the same time. Such a conflict can be diagrammed as follows:

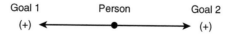

An **approach-approach conflict** exists when two equally attractive people ask you for a date on the same night or when you are both hungry and sleepy. Typically, this type of conflict is easily solved by attaining first one goal and then the other; for example, you could first eat and then go to bed. It may also be seen when you have to choose a single scoop of ice cream from two equally attractive flavours—fortunately, you won't come away disliking your choice. Dollard and Miller (1950) say, "Donkeys do not starve between two equally desirable stacks of hay, unless there are thorns, eliciting avoidance, concealed in the haystacks" (p. 366). If there were thorns, the hungry donkeys would have an approach-avoidance conflict, which, as we shall see, is more difficult to resolve.

AVOIDANCE-AVOIDANCE CONFLICT

Here the person must choose between two negative goals. For example, the child must eat her spinach or be spanked, the student must do his homework or get low grades, or a person must either go to a job she dislikes or lose the income. A person having such a conflict is "damned if he does and damned if he doesn't"; he or she can also be said to be "caught between the devil and the deep blue sea." Such a conflict can be diagrammed as follows:

Two types of behaviour typically characterize an organism having an **avoidance-avoidance conflict**: (1) vacillation or indecision and (2) escape. Escape can be either actually leaving the conflict situation or it can be mental escape such as daydreaming or mental preoccupation with other thoughts.

APPROACH-AVOIDANCE CONFLICT

Here the person is both attracted to and repelled by the *same goal.* A job may be attractive because of the money it generates but be unattractive because it is boring, or because it keeps the person from engaging in more enjoyable activities. A young woman may be attracted to an executive position because of the challenge, income, and responsibility involved but may have reservations because such a position might undermine her family life. Such a conflict can be diagrammed as follows:

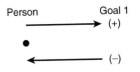

Dollard and Miller (1950) listed the most significant features of the **approach-avoidance conflict**:

1. The tendency to approach a goal is stronger the nearer the subject is to it. This will be called the *gradient of approach.*
2. The tendency to avoid a feared stimulus is stronger the nearer the subject is to it. This will be called the *gradient of avoidance.*
3. The strength of avoidance increases more rapidly with nearness than does that of approach. In other words, the gradient of avoidance is *steeper* than that of approach.
4. The strength of tendencies to approach or avoid varies with the strength of the drive upon which they are based. In other words, an increase in drive raises the *height* of the entire gradient. (pp. 352–353)

It is on the approach-avoidance conflict that Miller did his most extensive research (for example, 1944, 1959, and 1964). Figure 10–1 summarizes many of the characteristics of the approach-avoidance conflict.

Figure 10–1

Diagram of an approach-avoidance conflict.

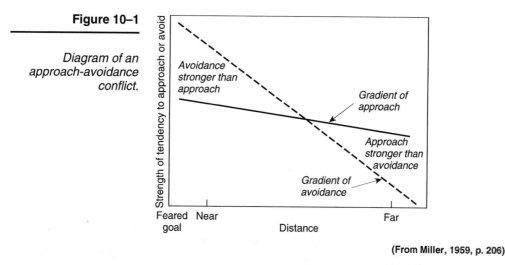

(From Miller, 1959, p. 206)

Among the many deductions that can be made from Figure 10–1 is that as long as the approach gradient is higher than the avoidance gradient, the person will approach the goal. As soon as the avoidance gradient becomes higher, the person will avoid the goal. Therefore, because the approach gradient becomes higher the farther one is from the goal, a strong approach tendency will occur. As one approaches the goal, however, the avoidance tendency increases and eventually is stronger than the approach tendency. At that point, the person will retreat from the goal. Thus we would expect vacillation at the point at which two gradients cross. We all know couples who have doubts about their relationship and who are constantly separating and reconciling. While apart, the favourable aspects of their relationship are dominant, and therefore they are driven back together. Once reunited, however, they confront the troubling aspects of their relationship and are once again driven apart. Approach-avoidance conflicts can be resolved either by increasing the strength of the approach tendency or by reducing the strength of the avoidance tendency. In the therapeutic situation, it is usually the latter that is attempted.

We have more to say about the approach-avoidance conflict in subsequent sections of this chapter.

DOUBLE APPROACH-AVOIDANCE CONFLICT

Here the person has ambivalent feelings about two goal objects. Such a conflict can be diagrammed as follows:

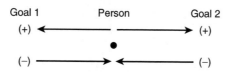

One example of a **double approach-avoidance conflict** comes from a girl's position relative to her parents in Freudian theory. She is attracted to her mother because the mother satisfies her biological needs but is repelled by the mother because she is thought responsible for denying the girl a penis. She is attracted to her father because he possesses the valued organ and yet is envious of him because he does. According to Freud, girls have ambivalent feelings about both parents.

Dollard and Miller agree with Freud that most neurotic behaviour involves conflict. For example, when neurotics begin to engage in activities or thoughts that will lead to the reduction of a strong drive such as sex, they are overwhelmed with anxiety. The closer they come to approaching a goal that will satisfy their need for sex, the stronger their anxiety will become, until eventually they retreat from the goal. Because their original need was not satisfied, however, they again approach sex-related goals, only to be eventually driven from them by anxiety, and on it goes. Only psychotherapy, or its equivalent, will rescue them from this vicious circle.

Displacement

Dollard and Miller also thoroughly explored the Freudian concept of **displacement.** One of the most important aspects of Freud's theory was his contention that frustrated drives do not simply go away but rather surface in disguised form. In other words, if a need cannot be satisfied directly, it is displaced and satisfied indirectly. As we saw in chapter 2, Freud's term for the displacement of the sex drive to more socially acceptable activities such as hard work, and creativity in general, is sublimation.

Miller's first step was to verify experimentally the phenomenon of displacement. To do this, Miller (1948b) placed two rats in an apparatus and shocked them until they started fighting, at which point the shock was turned off. In other words, the aggressive act of fighting was reinforced by escape from shock. Training continued in this manner until the animals began fighting immediately after the shock was turned on. At this point, a doll was placed in the apparatus, and the animals were shocked. Again they fought with each other and ignored the doll. This is shown in Figure 10–2.

When only one animal was placed in the apparatus and shocked, however, it attacked the doll. This is shown in Figure 10–3. When the object of aggression was not available to the animal, it aggressed toward a substitute object—that is, the doll. Thus **displaced aggression** was demonstrated.

To show that displacement occurs is important, but it leaves unanswered questions as to what determines which objects are involved in displacement and why. For example, if an employee cannot aggress toward his or her boss after being refused a raise, toward what object or objects will he or she aggress? Miller (1959, pp. 218–219) reached the following conclusions about displacement:

Figure 10–2

This figure shows two rats that have been trained to fight each other to terminate an electric shock.

(From Miller, 1948b, p. 157)

Figure 10–3

This figure shows the displacement of an aggressive response.

(From Miller, 1948b, p. 157)

1. When it is impossible for an organism to respond to a desired stimulus, it will respond to a stimulus that is most similar to the desired stimulus. For example, if a woman is prevented from marrying the man she loved by his death, she will tend to marry someday a man similar to him.

2. If a response to an original stimulus is prevented by conflict, displacement will occur to an intermediate stimulus. For example, if a girl leaves her boyfriend after a quarrel, her next boyfriend will tend to be similar to her original boyfriend in many ways and yet also different from him.

3. If there are strong avoidance tendencies to an original stimulus, displacement will tend to occur toward a dissimilar stimulus. For example, if a girl's original romance was extremely distressing, her next boyfriend will tend to be very different from the first.

If displacement occurs because of conflict, the strength of the conflicting responses will determine where displacement occurs. Figure 10–4 shows the nature of displacement when a weak conflicting response and a strong conflicting response occur.

Figure 10–4

This figure shows that with a weak avoidance tendency, fear is not experienced until objects very near or very similar to the goal are encountered. When there is a strong avoidance tendency, however, fear is caused by objects more distant from and more dissimilar to the goal.

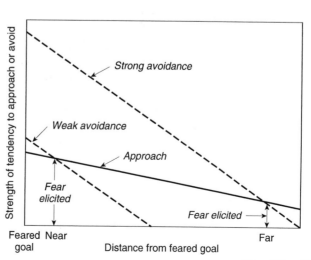

(From Miller, 1959, p. 208)

We can see in Figure 10–4, for example, that if a desire to aggress toward a goal and a weak fear of punishment exist, a tendency to displace to an object similar to the original goal will occur. If a desire exists to aggress toward a goal and there is a strong fear of punishment, however, the aggression will probably be directed toward objects dissimilar to the original goal. In other words, increasing a person's fear will decrease the tendency to displace the response to similar objects, and decreasing a person's fear increases the tendency to displace the response to similar objects. For example, if an employee has no fear of her boss and her boss frustrates her, she will aggress directly toward the boss. If an employee has a mild fear of her boss and the boss frustrates her, she will not aggress toward the boss but will aggress toward someone similar to the boss—for instance, the vice president or manager. If an employee has a strong fear of her boss and the boss frustrates her, she will aggress toward objects dissimilar to the boss, such as other cars on the way home from work, her husband and children, or perhaps her pet.

We see, then, that if an object of choice is not available and no conflict exists, displacement is simply a matter of stimulus generalization. That is, an object most like the one not available will be chosen. If a conflict exists, however, displacement will be governed by the net of the approach and avoidance tendencies.

Frustration-Aggression Hypothesis

Aggressive behaviour pervades the news: from Marc Lepine's shooting of 14 women in Montreal, to a school shooting in Taber, Alberta, to violent confrontations between protesters and policemen in Vancouver and Quebec City. Each of these incidents can be traced to a trigger of frustration.

In 1939, Dollard and Miller (along with Doob, Mowrer, and Sears) published their first book together, *Frustration and Aggression*. They analyzed the contention, derived from Freudian theory, that frustration leads to aggression, better known as the **frustration-aggression hypothesis.** They made the following assumptions:

> This study takes as its point of departure the assumption that *aggression is always a consequence of frustration.* More specifically, the proposition is that the occurrence of aggressive behavior always pre-supposes the existence of frustration and, contrariwise, that the existence of frustration always leads to some form of aggression. (1939, p. 1)

Frustration was defined as "that condition which exists when a goal-response suffers interference," and *aggression* was defined as "an act whose goal-response is injury to an organism (or organism-surrogate)" (1939, p. 11). It was assumed that the disruption of goal-directed behaviour causes frustration, and frustration causes aggression toward the person or object acting as a barrier between the person and his or her goal.

Dollard and colleagues(1939, pp. 28–32) concluded that three main factors determine how much aggression will result from frustration:

1. Drive level associated with the frustrated response.   The more intensely the person wants to attain a goal, the more frustrated he or she will be when the goal-directed activity is blocked, and thus the more aggressive that person will become.

2. Completeness of the frustration.   Goal responses that are only partially blocked will lead to less frustration and therefore less aggression than produced by goal responses that are completely blocked.

Dollard and Miller believed that frustration leads to aggression. In April, 1999, a 14-year-old boy entered a high school, where he shot and killed one student and badly wounded another. His act can be traced to the frustration of having to study at home because, as a victim of bullying, he was afraid of going to school.

3. Cumulative effect of minor frustrations.   Minor frustrations or interferences will eventually add up to produce considerable frustration and therefore considerable aggression. If on the way to a restaurant to eat, for example, one is interrupted first by a friend who wants to chat, then by unusually heavy traffic, and then finds the restaurant closed, one is likely to become more frustrated than one would have been if one had gone directly to the restaurant and found it closed.

In all of these points, the message is always the same—the strength of aggression is a function of the magnitude of frustration.

In the last section we learned that as the threat of punishment for a direct act of aggression increases, the tendency for the act of aggression to be displaced to less threatening people or objects also increases. According to Dollard et al., "It follows that the *greater the degree of inhibition specific to a more direct act of aggression, the more probable will be the occurrence of less direct acts of aggression*" (1939, p. 40).

Through the years, the relationship between frustration and aggression has been found to be less direct than originally thought. Subsequent research has confirmed that frustrated people act more aggressively than people who are not frustrated. However, Miller and Dollard (1941) concluded that aggression is only one possible result of frustration. Other possible reactions include withdrawal or apathy, depression, regression, sublimation, creative problem solving, and fixation (stereotyped behaviour).

Furthermore, it has been found that acting aggressively does not reduce the aggressive tendency, as Freud and Dollard et al. (1939) believed. A number of studies have shown that acting aggressively actually *increases* the aggressive tendency (e.g., Geen & Quanty, 1977; Geen, Stonner, & Shope, 1975). In order to account for the evidence that is inconsistent with its original formulation, Leonard Berkowitz (1989) has proposed that the frustration-aggression hypothesis be reformulated. Berkowitz finds that if the aversiveness or unpleasantness of an event is emphasized, instead of its capacity to frustrate, many of the current findings are more comprehensible.

Most researchers still believe, however, that aggression is one of the most common and important reactions to frustration and that the relationship between the two has many implications for penal reform, child rearing, and behaviour modification in general.

Importance of Language

Response is one of the four essential ingredients in Dollard and Miller's theory. A major distinction between their theory and Skinner's was that they considered two types of responding to be important—instrumental, or overt, and internal, or thinking. Although Skinner did not avoid the topic of language, to him, language was simply verbal behaviour and was governed by the same laws as any other behaviour. Dollard and Miller speculated on the nature of internal thought processes and their relationship to language. Furthermore, they analyzed Freudian notions of repression and neurosis in terms of internal response mechanisms. Dollard and Miller thought that people's ability to use language accounts for their higher mental processes, which are part of both neurotic and normal functioning.

Many years ago, Pavlov referred to physical stimuli that precede biologically significant events as the **first signal system.** Such stimuli allow an organism to anticipate biologically significant events and thus deal with them effectively when they occur. For example, we avoid hot stoves, and we salivate when we are hungry and see food. Pavlov called the first signal system "the first signals of reality." In addition to learning anticipatory responses to physical stimuli, however, humans also learn to respond to symbols of reality. For example, we become fearful when we hear words like "fire," "danger," or "enemy." Likewise, we feel good when we hear the name of a loved one or hear such words as "love," "peace," or "friend." Pavlov called the words that symbolize reality "signals of signals" or the **second signal system.**

Dollard and Miller followed Pavlov in believing that language becomes a symbolic representation of reality. As this set of symbols develops, one can think through experiences without actually having them. Thinking, then, is a kind of talking to oneself about several behavioural possibilities. Dollard and Miller called images, perceptions, and words **cue-producing responses** because they generally determine the next responses in a sequence. Counting, for example, is a series of cue-producing responses because the response "one" triggers the response "two," and so forth. Thoughts constitute responses but they also act as cues in eliciting further responses.

Two of the most useful functions of cue-producing responses are **reasoning** and **planning.** Reasoning replaces overt-behaviour trial and error with cognitive trial and error. The latter is far more efficient because *mentally* a problem can be approached from various viewpoints and no set sequence needs to be followed. Figure 10–5 shows the advantage of reasoning in problem solving.

Figure 10–5

In this example of reasoning, the driver in the black car is blocked from making a left turn by the traffic jam in the left lane. In the distance, he sees the cars in the lighter traffic coming from the opposite direction making the right turn easily on to the road he wants to take. He thinks, "If I were only going the other way." This stimulates him to think of how he could be going the other way. He pulls out into the right lane, passes the cars ahead, turns around, comes back the other way, and makes a right turn onto the highway. (The small circle at the centre intersection indicates a traffic light.)

1/4 mile

(From Dollard and Miller, 1950, p. 112.)

When cue-producing responses are part of solving an immediate problem, the process is called reasoning. When the cue-producing responses are directed at the solution of a future problem, the process is called planning.

Unconscious Mind

Like Freud, Dollard and Miller considered unconscious processes to be extremely important in determining behaviour. They described two major categories of unconscious material: (1) experiences that were never verbally labelled and (2) experiences that have been repressed.

EXPERIENCES THAT WERE NEVER VERBALIZED

Learning that occurs before language is developed is not labelled or recorded in a way that allows it to be recalled, and therefore, such learning becomes part of the unconscious:

According to our hypothesis, drives, cues, and responses that have never been labeled will necessarily be unconscious. One large category of this kind will be experiences that occurred before the child learned to talk effectively. Since the effective use of speech develops gradually and may not be established for certain categories until long after the child has learned to say "Mamma," the period during which major parts of social learning are unconscious extends over a considerable number of years and has no set boundaries. (Dollard & Miller, 1950, p. 198)

At the time in life thought by Freud to be critical to adult personality development, experiences are unlabelled and thus cannot be recalled. These early experiences have a profound effect on one's later conscious life, and yet they themselves remain unconscious:

The young child does not notice or label the experiences which it is having at this time. It cannot give a description of character traits acquired during the first year of life nor yet of its hardships, fears, or deep satisfactions. What was not verbalized at the time cannot well be reported later. An important piece of history is lost and cannot be elicited by questionnaire or interview. Nevertheless, the behavioural record survives. The responses learned occur and may indeed recur in analogous situations throughout life. They are elicited by unlabeled cues and are mutely interwoven into the fabric of conscious life. (Dollard & Miller, 1950, p. 136)

REPRESSED EXPERIENCES

Some thoughts are uncomfortable because they cause anxiety. A few examples are: thinking about an automobile accident in which a loved one was killed or injured; thinking about sex after learning how evil some believe such thoughts are; thinking about how you would like to steal something from a store; thinking about how you would like to caress your teacher or minister. Anxiety is a negative drive, just as pain, hunger, and thirst are, and therefore anything that reduces anxiety is reinforcing. In other words, *anything that terminates an anxiety-provoking thought will be learned as a habit.*

If suddenly during a conversation, you find yourself pondering sexual activity with your best friend's boyfriend, you may find such a thought anxiety-provoking because of your early moral training. If so, you may respond by consciously "putting the thought out of your mind." Such a conscious and deliberate effort to stop an anxiety-provoking thought is called **suppression.** Suppression is learned just like any other response; that is, because it is followed by drive reduction (in this case, anxiety is reduced) it gains in strength. Suppression is a common way of stopping thoughts that cause anxiety.

Eventually the suppression of anxiety-provoking thoughts becomes *anticipatory* in that such thoughts are terminated automatically before they can cause anxiety. When a potentially painful thought is aborted before it enters consciousness, the process is called **repression.** Repression is the learned response of *not thinking* thoughts that are unpleasant. In repression, early thoughts act as signals that, if a line of thought is continued, it will result in the experience of anxiety. Therefore the line of thought is terminated before it can become painful. For this reason, repression is said to be anticipatory, and because it prevents the experience of anxiety, it is said to be a conditioned avoidance response. Suppression allows *escape* from anxiety-provoking thoughts whereas repression allows *avoidance* of them. In other words, repression is triggered when unacceptable material starts to emerge from the unconscious, and suppression is triggered when such material is already conscious. Both processes are learned responses that are maintained by the elimination, reduction, or prevention of anxiety.

It may appear that a process such as repression is beneficial because it allows a person to avoid many painful thoughts, and this is certainly true. Repression also has a negative side. A thought that is repressed cannot be treated rationally because it does not enter consciousness. As we saw in the preceding section, it is conscious mechanisms that are part of the problem-solving processes of reasoning and planning. If a category of experience is repressed, it cannot be considered logically, and the activities related to it will be irrational. Furthermore, any attempt to bring repressed material into consciousness is typically met with great resistance, which is the case during psychoanalysis.

As you may have deduced by now, Dollard and Miller thought (as did Freud) that the mechanism of repression was causally related to most neurotic behaviour. The goal of psychotherapy is to free certain thoughts from repression so they may be treated logically and realistically.

Neurosis and Symptom Formation

NEUROSIS

As we have seen, Dollard and Miller followed Freud in assuming that conflict is at the heart of neurotic behaviour, and that this conflict is unconscious and usually learned in childhood:

> An intense emotional conflict is the necessary basis for neurotic behavior. The conflict must further be unconscious. As a usual thing, such conflicts are created only in childhood. How can it be that neurotic conflicts are engendered when there is no deliberate plan to do so? Society must force children to grow up, but it does not idealize neurosis and makes no formal provision in its system of training for the production of neurotic children. Indeed we deplore the neurotic and recognize him as a burden to himself and others. How then does it happen? Our answer is that *neurotic conflicts are taught by parents and learned by children* [italics added]. (Dollard & Miller, 1950, p. 127)

Although the term **neurosis** is hard to define precisely, it is clear the neurotic is miserable, unwise about certain aspects of his or her own existence, and often develops physical symptoms that are manifestations of the repressed conflict. For example, a person might stutter in social situations, perhaps as a result of being embarrassed on numerous occasions in the past. Likewise, a person may be fearful of relationships after a string of bad experiences in the past.

If children are severely punished for sexual activities, they will learn to repress sexual behaviours and thoughts as adults. They will therefore need to live with a sex drive that strongly impels them to engage in sexual activities but with a strong fear of punishment if they do so. As we saw in the last section, thoughts of sexual activity will be repressed under these circumstances and, as a result, this strong approach-avoidance conflict will remain unconscious, so that language cannot be used to describe and analyze it:

> Without language and adequate labeling, the higher mental processes cannot function. When these processes are knocked out by repression, the person cannot guide himself by mental means to a resolution of his conflict. Since the neurotic cannot help himself, he must have the help of others if he is to be helped at all—though millions today live out their lives in strong neurotic pain and never get help. The neurotic, therefore, is, or appears to be, stupid because he is unable to use his mind in dealing with certain

of his problems. He feels that someone should help him, but he does not know how to ask for help since he does not know what his problem is. He may feel aggrieved that he is suffering, but he cannot explain his case. (Dollard & Miller, 1950, p. 15)

The neurotic, therefore, is caught in an unbearable conflict between frustrated drives, on the one hand, and the fear connected with the approach responses that would bring about their satisfaction, on the other.

SYMPTOM FORMATION

Neurotics often develop symptoms such as phobias, inhibitions, avoidances, compulsions, and physical disorders such as paralysis or nervous tics. Although it is common for neurotics to think their symptoms constitute their problem, they do not. Neurotic symptoms are manifestations of repressed conflicts. As an example, Dollard and Miller (1950) cited the case of Mrs. A., who was an orphan, born of unknown parents in a southern city. She was raised by foster parents, who gave her very repressive sex training. Although she had strong sexual appetites, sex became a dirty, loathsome activity about which it was painful for her to talk or think. Eventually she developed several phobias and a preoccupation with her heartbeat. In analysis, it was learned that her preoccupation with her heartbeat was used as a means of preventing sex-related thoughts. Dollard and Miller summarized the case of Mrs. A. as follows:

> When on the streets alone, her fear of sex temptation was increased. Someone might speak to her, wink at her, make an approach to her. Such an approach would increase her sex desire and make her more vulnerable to seduction. Increased sex desire, however, touched off both anxiety and guilt, and this intensified her conflict when she was on the street. . . . When sexy thoughts came to mind or other sex stimuli tended to occur, these stimuli elicited anxiety. . . . Since [heartbeat] counting is a highly preoccupying kind of response, no other thoughts could enter her mind during this time. While counting, the sexy thoughts which excited fear dropped out. Mrs. A. "felt better" immediately when she started counting, and the counting habit was reinforced by the drop in anxiety. (1950, p. 21)

Neurotic symptoms are learned because they reduce fear or anxiety:

> The symptoms do not solve the basic conflict in which the neurotic person is plunged, but they mitigate it. They are responses which tend to reduce the conflict, and in part they succeed. When a successful symptom occurs it is reinforced because it reduces neurotic misery. *The symptom is thus learned as a habit* [italics added]. One very common function of symptoms is to keep the neurotic person away from those stimuli which would activate and intensify his neurotic conflict. Thus, the combat pilot with a harrowing military disaster behind him may walk away from the sight of any airplane. As he walks towards the plane his anxiety goes up; as he walks away it goes down. Walking away is thus reinforced. It is this phobic walking away which constitutes his symptom. If the whole situation is not understood, such behaviour seems bizarre to the casual witness. (Dollard & Miller, 1950, pp. 15–16)

Psychotherapy

The major assumption that Dollard and Miller made about neurosis is that it is learned, and because it is learned, it can be unlearned. Psychotherapy provides a situation in which neurosis can be unlearned:

If neurotic behavior is learned, it should be unlearned by some combination of the same principles by which it was taught. We believe this to be the case. Psychotherapy establishes a set of conditions by which neurotic habits may be unlearned and nonneurotic habits learned. Therefore, we view the therapist as a kind of teacher and the patient as a learner. In the same way and by the same principles that bad tennis habits can be corrected by a good coach, so bad mental and emotional habits can be corrected by a good psychotherapist. There is this difference, however. Whereas only a few people want to play tennis, all the world wants a clear, free, efficient mind. (Dollard & Miller, 1950, pp. 7–8)

As we have seen, the only way for a learned response to be extinguished is for it to occur and not be followed by reinforcement. For unrealistic fears to be extinguished, they must occur and then not be followed by the type of events that produced the fears in the first place. As previously mentioned, however, the person has learned to repress such fears, thus preventing their expression and therefore their subsequent extinction. Psychotherapy can be regarded as a situation in which the expression of repressed thoughts is encouraged. If the patient can be made to express these painful thoughts, the therapist is extremely careful to be encouraging, positive, and not punitive. Dollard and Miller (1950) explained:

> In addition to permitting free speech, the therapist commands the patient to say everything that comes to mind. By the free-association technique the therapist sets the patient free from the restraint of logic. The therapist avoids arousing additional anxiety by not cross-questioning. By encouraging the patient to talk and consistently failing to punish him, the therapist creates a social situation that is the exact opposite of the one originally responsible for attaching strong fears to talking and thinking. The patient talks about frightening topics. Since he is not punished, his fears are extinguished. This extinction generalizes and weakens the motivation to repress other related topics that were originally too frightening for the patient to discuss or even to contemplate. Where the patient cannot say things for himself, the therapist helps by attaching a verbal label to the emotions that are being felt and expressed mutely in the transference situation. (p. 230)

To persuade the patient to express a repressed thought is no easy matter, however, and typically a procedure similar to successive approximations is used. Let us imagine that a patient, for whatever reason, has learned to fear his mother to the point at which he cannot talk about her or anything directly related to her. The therapist using Dollard and Miller's theory would not confront the patient directly with a conversation about his mother. Rather, the therapist would begin the discussion with events only indirectly related to the patient's mother. How indirect this needs to be depends on how strong the patient's avoidance is. As the therapist and patient discuss events only remotely related to the mother *in a nonthreatening environment,* a small amount of the avoidance of the mother is extinguished, or what Freud called catharsis occurs. With the avoidance response somewhat reduced, the therapist can steer the conversation a bit closer to the mother but still stay a safe distance away. The avoidance response is further reduced, and the therapist can move still closer to the ultimate target, the mother. Gradually, usually over several sessions, the therapist moves closer and closer to a discussion of the mother and then, when the avoidance response is sufficiently reduced, to a discussion of the mother herself. Now with the avoidance reduced, the patient can talk about his mother phobia openly and rationally.

Psychotherapy, as viewed by Dollard and Miller (and also by Freud) is a process of gradual extinction that depends on generalization, because the events discussed must be related in some way to the object, person, or event of ultimate concern. It can also be said that avoidance is displaced onto objects similar to the one that is avoided the most, so that not only will the patient avoid his mother, but he will also avoid people who look like her (primary generalization) or all mothers (secondary generalization); he may even be mildly apprehensive of women in general. Thus conflict, extinction, generalization, and displacement are part of the therapeutic process.

Psychotherapy usually does not end when repressions have been released. Because repressed thoughts have persisted for so much of the patient's life, and because it is impossible to deal effectively with repressed material, there will be significant gaps in the person's life even after successful therapy. For example, a person who is suddenly able to ponder her sex drive at the age of 35 will need some guidance as to how best to adjust to the relative absence of inhibition.

Four Critical Training Situations of Childhood

As we have seen throughout this chapter, Dollard and Miller agreed with Freud that most neuroses originate in early childhood. This is an especially vulnerable time because children have no verbal labels for their feelings and experiences and are not aware of time; for example, they do not know that "in a little while" their hunger, thirst, or pain will be reduced. Their lives vacillate from extreme discomfort to bliss and back again. In fact, Dollard and Miller (1950) referred to early childhood as a period of "transitory psychosis" (p. 130). Also, infants, because of their helplessness, are completely at the mercy of their parents for the satisfaction of their needs, and how the parents go about satisfying their infants' needs will make the difference between a normal healthy adult and a neurotic. Dollard and Miller (1950, pp. 132–156) described four critical training situations they believed have a profound influence on adult personality:

1. Feeding situation (occurs primarily during the Freudian oral stage). The conditions under which the hunger drive is satisfied will be learned and generalized into personality attributes. If, for example, children are fed when active, they may become active people; if they are fed while quiet and passive, they may become passive or apathetic individuals. If their hunger drives are satisfied in an unpredictable manner, they may grow up believing the world is an unpredictable place. If children are left alone for long periods when they are hungry, they may develop a fear of being alone. If the mother is harsh and punitive during the feeding situation, the child may grow up disliking other people and avoid them at all costs. If, however, the mother is kind, warm, and positive during the feeding situation, the child may grow up with a positive attitude toward other people and seek them out as friends.

2. Cleanliness training (occurs primarily during the Freudian anal stage). Dollard and Miller, like Freud, believed the events surrounding toilet training are extremely important to personality development. If the parents respond negatively to children's inability to control their bladder or bowels, the children may not be able to distinguish between parental disapproval of what they have done and disapproval of themselves:

> The child may not be able to discriminate between parental loathing for its excreta and loathing for the whole child himself. If the child learns to adopt these reactions, feelings of unworthiness, insignificance, and hopeless sinfulness will be created—feelings which sometimes so mysteriously reappear in the psychotic manifestations of guilt. (Dollard & Miller, 1950, pp. 139–140)

Although it is necessary to toilet train a child, how it is done may have a profound influence on the child's emerging personality.

3. Early sex training (occurs primarily during the Freudian phallic stage).   The first sex training a child normally receives in our culture is related to the child's early efforts to masturbate. Often, such behaviour elicits physical punishment or such terms as *nasty* and *dirty*. So it may be with most sexually oriented activities in which the child engages. There are probably more taboos in our culture related to sexual matters than there are for any other type of activity, and these taboos are all part of our child rearing practices. No wonder sexual conflict is such a common theme in the analyst's office. The sex drive is innate, but the fear of sexual thoughts and activities is learned in childhood.

4. Anger-anxiety conflicts (this training is not specific to any Freudian stage of development).   Frustration is inevitable in childhood (and at any other age), and as we learned earlier, the most common reaction to frustration is aggression. However, aggressive behaviour on the part of children in our culture is often met with parental disapproval or punishment. Children are placed in still another approach-avoidance conflict; that is, they want to be aggressive but inhibit this impulse because of fear of punishment. This may result in being too passive to compete successfully in modern society:

> After this learning has occurred, the first cues produced by angry emotions may set off anxiety responses which "outcompete" the angry emotional responses themselves. The person can thus be made helpless to use his anger even in those situations where culture does permit it. He is viewed as abnormally meek or long-suffering. Robbing a person of his anger completely may be a dangerous thing since some capacity for anger seems to be needed in the affirmative personality. (Dollard & Miller, 1950, p. 149)

Dollard and Miller described the types of childhood experiences they believed lead to adult neuroses and their message was, *change these childhood conditions and neuroses can be eliminated*:

> As a learning theorist sees it, the existence of neuroses is an automatic criticism of our culture of child rearing. Misery-producing, neurotic habits which the therapist must painfully unteach have been as painfully taught in the confused situation of childhood. A system of child training built on the laws of learning might have the same powerful effect on the neurotic misery of our time as Pasteur's work had on infectious diseases. (1950, p. 8)

Evaluation

EMPIRICAL RESEARCH

Dollard and Miller's theory is firmly grounded in empirical research. Almost without exception, when a concept is used in their theory, several experiments are cited that empirically verify that concept. Dollard and Miller's theory is, to a large extent, an extension of Hullian learning theory, which itself is one of the most scientifically rigorous theories in psychology's history. Throughout this chapter, we have reviewed experiments that Dollard, Miller, and their colleagues ran to verify or test their theoretical concepts. For example, research was cited showing how fear is acquired; how fear and other tendencies generalize; how various conflicts affect behaviour; how fear and other tendencies are displaced; how frustration and aggression are related; how physical symptoms partially reduce neurotic conflict; and how learning principles operate in the therapeutic process. Recent work by Campbell and Campbell (2000), Collins and Onwuegbuzie (2001), and Merckelbach, Muris, and Rossin (2000) support these findings. Dollard and Miller have carefully outlined the role of language in normal and abnormal personality development, and these views have been shared by many other theorists. The interactionist perspective, for example, states that we derive self-understanding, even elements of self-concept, from our own and others' verbal comments and appraisals. Alain Morin of Acadia University (1995, 1999; Morin & Everett, 1990) considered the role of what we say to ourselves, or inner-speech, with respect to self-awareness, wherein we become the object of our own attention. Research shows that self-awareness and inner speech are at least modestly related. Highly self-aware individuals use self-talk more frequently—so the more you focus on yourself, the more you talk to yourself about yourself, your personal characteristics, and behaviours. Indeed, early research showed that the more people talk to themselves about their self-image, the more that image began to take form with some coherence and sophistication.

CRITICISMS

Unsuccessful Synthesis of Hullian Learning Theory and Psychoanalysis.
Prominent members of both camps have complained that Dollard and Miller's attempt to synthesize Hullian learning theory and psychoanalysis did not work. Learning theorists such as Bandura (whose theory we review in the next chapter) and Skinner complained that no need exists to use nebulous, subjective psychoanalytic terminology to explain personality. Bandura and Skinner (and others) claimed that learning principles alone can do the job. As we saw in the last chapter, Skinner went so far as to say that personality can be understood without reference to mental events of any type.

Skinner believed that even Dollard and Miller's use of such "hypothetical fictions" as cues, drives, conflicts, and cue-producing responses was not only unnecessary but may, in fact, interfere with a true understanding of personality. In the next chapter, we see that Bandura's analysis *does* allow, even emphasizes, mental events, but those events are not the unconscious variety stressed by the psychoanalysts.

Many psychoanalysts were equally unimpressed by the efforts of Dollard and Miller. Their argument was that the dynamics of the human mind are far more complicated than Dollard and Miller's analysis suggests. To them phenomena such as displacement, repression, conflict, and neuroses are too complex to be understood in terms of a few principles of learning. Furthermore, they say, it is foolish to suggest that the processes occurring during psychotherapy (especially psychoanalysis) can be demonstrated by a rat running a maze.

Overgeneralization from Nonhuman Animals to Humans.
Like Skinner, Dollard and Miller have been criticized for assuming that the principles observed in nonhuman animals also apply to humans. What good, ask the critics, are all of the carefully controlled laboratory experiments on nonhuman animals if a tenuous assumption concerning the generalizability of the findings must be made? Insofar as humans are different from rats and pigeons, the findings from such research is irrelevant. In fairness to Dollard and Miller, however, it must be noted they stressed that any such generalizations should be carefully investigated; they did do a considerable amount of research on humans as well as nonhuman animals.

Overly Simplistic Approach.   Some critics say that a theory such as Dollard and Miller's that stresses environmental stimuli, a few mental events, and overt responses misses the richness and complexity of human personality. Love, despair, the importance of the future, the meaning of life, and the experience of the self, are just a few of the human experiences that are not addressed by such a theory. In addition, to suggest that dysfunctional mental or emotional habits can be corrected by a therapist in much the same way that a good coach corrects bad tennis habits is just too simplistic, say the critics.

CONTRIBUTIONS

Synthesis of Hullian Learning Theory and Psychoanalysis.   As so often happens, what some find to be a weakness in a theory, others view as a strength. For many, Dollard and Miller's synthesis of Hullian learning theory and psychoanalysis was a milestone in the history of psychology. The synthesis achieved two goals: It broadened the application of an otherwise limited theory of learning to a wide array of human phenomena; and it made several psychoanalytic concepts more testable than they had been. Until Dollard and Miller's efforts, the gulf between the research laboratory and the clinical consulting room was enormous. Their work provided a bridge across that gulf, and ideas have been flowing back and forth ever since. In fact, Dollard and Miller were the first theorists to explore the role of learning in personality development specifically, a role now accepted by most theorists as substantial.

Scientifically Respectable Approach to the Study of Personality.   In an area of psychology in which the early theories were difficult to test empirically, a scientifically rigorous theory is welcomed. Most of the terms and concepts in Dollard and Miller's theory are defined precisely enough to allow them to be empirically verified. In terms of testability, Dollard and Miller's theory ranks high, along with the theories of Cattell, Eysenck, and Skinner.

Clear Description of Therapeutic Process.   By describing traditional psychotherapeutic procedures in terms of learning principles, Dollard and Miller were able to account for successful therapy and to make sound recommendations for the improvement of the therapeutic process. It is now widely accepted that at least some forms of anxiety are learned, and once learned, thoughts and events that elicit such anxiety are avoided. It is, according to Dollard and Miller, this avoidance that causes anxiety-provoking thoughts to persist. Effective therapy creates a situation in which such thoughts can be expressed without experiencing the unpleasant consequences originally associated with them. As this change occurs, extinction gradually takes place, and the thoughts that were once too anxiety provoking to entertain can now be dealt with rationally. All of these elements of the therapeutic process were discussed by Freud but restating them using the terminology of learning theory makes them clearer and more testable. What has become known as behaviour therapy was given a tremendous boost by the work of Dollard and Miller.

Dollard and Miller provided information that is certainly helpful in treating neuroses, and that information may also someday be responsible for a reduction in their prevalence. If this turns out to be true, one can forgive them for favouring animal research and for having a deterministic model of human nature. Every theory must be judged by its ultimate effectiveness, not by its origins or assumptions.

SUMMARY

1. Dollard and Miller's goal was to combine Hullian learning theory with Freud's theory of personality. Hull's theory of learning equated reinforcement with drive reduction and defined a habit as a strong association between a stimulus (cue) and a response. Central to Dollard and Miller's theory were the concepts of drive, cue, response, and reinforcement. Drive impels an organism to action, cue directs its behaviour, response is what the organism does either overtly or internally, and reinforcement occurs when the motivational drive is either reduced or terminated. In other words, in order to learn, the organism must want something, notice something, do something, and get something.

2. Every cue elicits several responses arranged in accordance with their probability of occurrence. This set of responses is called the habit family hierarchy. Before new learning occurs, there is an initial hierarchy of responses; after learning, there is a resultant hierarchy of responses. The most likely response to any situation is called the dominant response. The learning dilemma refers to the fact that previously learned responses or innate responses must fail to solve a problem before learning can take place. Thus all learning depends on failure. The gradient of reinforcement refers to the fact that when a series of responses ultimately results in reinforcement, the last response in the series is strengthened the most, then the second to the last, etc.

3. Dollard and Miller demonstrated that events associated with pain will themselves become feared, and an organism will learn responses that allow it to escape from those fear-producing cues. Stimulus generalization occurs when a learned response is elicited by stimuli similar to the cue in the actual learning. The more similar a cue is to the original one, the greater the probability that it will elicit the same response. Primary generalization is determined by the physical properties of stimuli. Secondary generalization is caused by using the same verbal label to describe events. Discrimination is the opposite of generalization.

4. Dollard and Miller studied four types of conflict: approach-approach conflicts, in which the organism is attracted to two goals at the same time; avoidance-avoidance conflicts, in which the organism is repelled by two goals at the same time; approach-avoidance conflicts, in which the organism is attracted and repelled by the same goal; and double approach-avoidance conflicts, in which the organism is both attracted and repelled by two goals at the same time. Dollard and Miller did most of their research on approach-avoidance conflict and found that at great distances from the goal the approach tendency is strongest, but as one approaches the goal, the avoidance tendency becomes stronger. This causes vacillation at the point that the two tendencies have about equal strength.

5. If the goal of choice is not available, the organism will choose a substitute goal, which is called displacement. If one cannot aggress toward the object, event, or person that caused frustration, one will aggress toward a substitute object; this is called displaced aggression. If one is fearful of aggressing toward an object, event, or person causing frustration, displacement will be toward dissimilar objects, events, or people. If little fear exists, displacement will be to more similar things.

6. The frustration-aggression hypothesis originally stated that aggression followed from frustration and that frustration always resulted in aggression. This was later modified to state that aggression was one possible result of frustration. Recent research indicates that aggression does not necessarily result in a reduction of the aggressive tendency.

7. Language is important to Dollard and Miller's theory. Thinking is essentially talking to oneself, and allows cognitive trial and error to replace behavioural trial and error. Dollard and Miller called images, perceptions, and words cue-producing responses because they determine the next response in a series. Thinking consists of a series of cue-producing responses. Two important types of thinking are reasoning—directed at solving a current problem—and planning—directed at solving a future problem.

8. The unconscious mind consists of experiences that were never verbalized and experiences that have been repressed. Repression, a response of not thinking, is reinforced because it prevents an anxiety-provoking thought from becoming conscious. Suppression is the act of driving an anxiety-provoking thought out of consciousness. Repressed thoughts are practically immune to extinction because they are not experienced consciously long enough for the person to realize that they are no longer followed by negative consequences.

9. Most neurotic conflicts are learned in childhood and are not verbally labelled. Neurotics are miserable and unwise about matters related to their repressions. Neurotic symptoms stemming from repressed conflict, such as phobias, compulsions, or physical disorders, temporarily relieve neurotics' distress by blocking anxiety-provoking situations. Both repression and neurotic symptoms are learned because they temporarily reduce or prevent anxiety.

10. In psychotherapy, patients are encouraged to label their conflicts verbally and to confront them gradually. The therapist is encouraging and nonthreatening, so that if and when repressed material emerges, it can be extinguished. Therapy usually approaches the source of anxiety indirectly and by stages so that anxiety is extinguished. Psychotherapy treats conflict and repression using the processes of generalization, displacement, and extinction.

11. Dollard and Miller believed the difference between a mentally healthy adult and a neurotic adult generally lies in how parents handled feeding, cleanliness training, sex training, and anger-anxiety training.

12. Dollard and Miller's theory is firmly grounded in empirical research but has been criticized for failing to synthesize Hullian learning theory and psychoanalysis successfully; generalizing too freely from nonhuman animals to humans; and being too simplistic in its account of personality and of the therapeutic process. Their theory has been praised for combining Hullian learning theory and psychoanalytic theory, thereby making both more useful; clarifying the processes that are actually involved in effective psychotherapy; and being scientifically rigorous.

EXPERIENTIAL EXERCISES

1. Give at least one example of an approach-approach, avoidance-avoidance, and approach-avoidance conflict that you have experienced and state how you resolved each conflict. In the case of the approach-avoidance conflict, did your experiences conform to Miller's description? That is, did you experience a great deal of vacillation and indecision as the goal was approached?

2. Give an example of displaced aggression in your life. That is, describe a situation in which you could not aggress directly toward a source of frustration and therefore aggressed, in some way, toward a person or an object other than the one that actually frustrated you. Explain, in terms of Dollard and Miller's theory, why you chose that object or person.

3. Privately ponder an idea or topic that you cannot openly discuss without experiencing considerable anxiety. Review how Dollard and Miller suggest such anxiety-provoking thoughts should be approached and resolved. Do you believe that by following their procedure of systematic extinction your anxiety-provoking thought will become increasingly more tolerable? Why or why not?

4. Ask someone who would know (e.g., your mother) how the four critical training situations of feeding, cleanliness, sex, and anger-anxiety were handled in your life. Do notable relationships exist among these early training experiences and your current personality characteristics? If they do, describe them. If they do not exist, try to explain why.

DISCUSSION QUESTIONS

1. Dollard and Miller's theory is often called a blending of Hullian learning theory and Freudian psychoanalytic theory. Explain why their theory is identified this way. Give several examples of such a blend.

2. Give the formal definitions and then examples of each of the following types of conflict: approach-approach, avoidance-avoidance, approach-avoidance, and double approach-avoidance.

3. What is the frustration-aggression hypothesis? How was it first stated by Dollard and Miller and how was it later revised?

4. Of what, according to Dollard and Miller, does the unconscious mind consist? Give examples.

5. Describe what Dollard and Miller meant when they referred to repression as the conditioned avoidance response of not thinking.

KEY TERMS

Acquired drive, p. 250
Approach-approach conflict, p. 255
Approach-avoidance conflict, p. 256
Avoidance-avoidance conflict, p. 256
Biofeedback, p. 248
Conditioned fear reaction, p. 254
Conflict, p. 255
Cue, p. 251
Cue-producing responses, p. 262
Discrimination, p. 254
Displaced aggression, p. 258
Displacement, p. 258
Dominant response, p. 252
Double approach-avoidance conflict, p. 257
Drive p. 250
Drive reduction, p. 249
First signal system, p. 262
Frustration-aggression hypothesis, p. 260
Gradient of reinforcement, p. 253
Habit, p. 249

Habit family hierarchy, p. 252
Hull's theory of learning, p. 250
Initial hierarchy of responses, p. 252
Innate hierarchy of responses, p. 252
Learning, p. 251
Learning dilemma, p. 252
Neurosis, p. 265
Planning, p. 262
Primary generalization, p. 255
Reasoning, p. 262
Reinforcement, p. 249
Reinforcement theory, p. 251
Reinforcer, p. 249
Repression, p. 264
Response, p. 251
Resultant hierarchy of responses, p. 252
Second signal system, p. 262
Secondary generalization, p. 255
Stimulus generalization, p. 254
Suppression, p. 264

11 Albert Bandura
Walter Mischel

Chapter Outline

Although Bandura and Mischel have not collaborated on major books, as did Dollard and Miller, their viewpoints are so similar that we consider them together. The position of Bandura and Mischel is referred to as **social cognitive theory.** Bandura (1986) explains the reasons for the name: "The social portion of the terminology acknowledges the social origins of much human thought and action; the cognitive portion recognizes the influential causal contribution of thought processes to human motivation, affect, and action" (p. xii).

Biographical Sketches

ALBERT BANDURA

Albert Bandura was born on December 4, 1925, in Mundare, a small town in Alberta. His parents were wheat farmers of Polish heritage. The high school he attended had only 20 students and two teachers. Following graduation from high school, Bandura spent the summer working on the Alaskan highway. Many of the men with whom he worked had fled to Alaska to escape "creditors, alimony, and probation officers." Working with such characters instilled in Bandura "a keen appreciation for the psychopathology of everyday life" (*American Psychologist*, 1981). Bandura entered the University of British Columbia in 1946 and obtained his BA in 1949, with a major in psychology. He then went to the University of Iowa where he obtained his MA in 1951 and his Ph.D. in 1952. It was at the University of Iowa that Bandura met his future wife, Virginia (Ginny)

Albert Bandura

Varns, who was teaching in the school of nursing there. Bandura and his wife eventually had two daughters, Mary and Carol. After a year's clinical internship at the Wichita, Kansas, Guidance Center, he moved to Stanford University, where he has been ever since.

After arriving at Stanford, Bandura began working on the familial causes of aggression with his first graduate student, Richard Walters (1918–1967). It was during this work that Bandura became aware of the importance of modelling and observational learning for personality development. A section on observational learning appears later in this chapter. Bandura's first book (coauthored with Richard Walters) was *Adolescent Aggression* (1959). His second book (also written with Richard Walters) was *Social Learning and Personality Development* (1963). Subsequent books were *Principles of Behavior Modification* (1969), *Aggression: A Social-Learning Analysis* (1973), *Social Learning Theory* (1977), *Social Foundations of Thought and Action: A Social Cognitive Theory* (1986), *Self-Efficacy in Changing Societies* (1995) of which he was editor; and *Self-Efficacy: The Exercise of Control* (1997). In addition to his books, Bandura has written many influential articles.

WALTER MISCHEL

Walter Mischel

Walter Mischel, the second son of upper-middle-class parents, was born on February 22, 1930 in Vienna, Austria, within walking distance of Freud's house. In 1938, when Mischel was eight years old, the Nazis invaded Austria, and his family moved to the United States. After living in various parts of the country, the family settled in Brooklyn, New York in 1940. There, Mischel attended primary and secondary school and earned a college scholarship, but because his father became ill he was forced to work. He worked as a stock boy, elevator operator, and assistant in a garment factory before he was finally able to attend New York University, where he pursued his interests in painting, sculpture, and psychology.

In university, Mischel was disenchanted by behaviouristic psychology but was attracted to psychoanalysis. At the same time, he strengthened his humanistic inclinations by reading existential philosophy and poetry. After graduation, Mischel entered the MA program in clinical psychology at City College of New York. While working on his degree Mischel became a social worker, working primarily with juvenile delinquents in the lower east side slums of New York. It was this work that caused Mischel to doubt the usefulness of psychoanalytic theory.

Between 1953 and 1956 Mischel worked on his Ph.D. at Ohio State University, where he came under the influence of George Kelly and Julian Rotter. Rotter's work emphasized the importance of expectancies in human behaviour, and Kelly stressed the importance of the formulation of mental concepts (personal constructs) in dealing with the world. Both Rotter and Kelly emphasized cognitive events in dealing with the current situations and de-emphasized the importance of traits and early developmental experience. The influence of both men is seen in Mischel's work. George Kelly's theory is covered in chapter 13.

From 1956 to 1958, Mischel lived in a village in Trinidad, studying religious cults that practised spirit possession. It was at this time that Mischel observed that some people have the ability to reject small, immediate rewards in favour of larger, but delayed, rewards. Mischel also observed that people with this ability to delay gratification had higher needs for achievement and showed more social responsibility (1958, 1961a, 1961b). As we will see later in this chapter, delayed gratification became one of Mischel's lifelong interests.

Mischel next taught for two years at the University of Colorado before joining the Department of Social Relations at Harvard. While at Harvard his interests in personality theory and assessment were furthered by discussions with Gordon Allport. It was also at Harvard that Mischel met his future wife, Harriet Nerlove, who was a graduate student in cognitive psychology. The Mischels eventually had three daughters and have collaborated on several studies. In 1962, Mischel moved to Stanford, where he became a colleague of Bandura. In 1983, after more than 20 years at Stanford, Mischel returned to New York City, where he joined the faculty at Columbia University. There, Mischel continues to pursue his long-standing interests in delayed gratification, self-control, and the cognitive processes used by individuals in their interactions with the world.

Consistency of Human Behaviour

Through the years, most personality theorists have assumed that a person's behaviour is fairly consistent over time and across similar situations. That is, it was assumed that how people act at one time in their lives will be more or less how they act at other times, and that they will tend to respond to similar situations in similar ways. For example, if a person was outgoing in one social situation, it was assumed he or she would be outgoing in other situations and would continue to respond in that characteristic way throughout most of his or her life. It was also assumed that scores on various personality tests and questionnaires would correlate significantly with actual behaviour. That is, if a person scored high on a scale intended to measure introversion, he or she would tend to be introverted in social situations. The question was not whether behaviour was consistent; rather, theorists attempted to account for the consistency they assumed existed. Psychoanalytic theory attempted to account for it by postulating repressed experiences, complexes, fixations, or internalized values. Within psychoanalytic theory, however, the conclusion of consistency can sometimes only be reached by a trained psychoanalyst because it is assumed that sometimes extreme aggression really means passivity, love really means hate, and repulsion really means attraction, to give but a few examples. Trait theory postulated enduring traits to explain why, for example, a neat person tended to be neat in a wide variety of situations. Learning theory emphasized the role of reinforcement. That is, behaviour that was reinforced tended to persist and to transfer to situations similar to the one in which the reinforcement had occurred.

Traditionally, personality theory has attempted to account for individual differences among people, but it was always assumed that although people differ from one another, the behaviour of any given individual tended to be consistent across similar situations and over time. In the early 1960s, Mischel was given the task of predicting the success of Peace Corps volunteers. In this effort, he found that standardized personality tests designed to measure traits were weak predictors of behaviour (Mischel, 1965). He found that people are better predictors of their own behaviour than the best available personality tests. It was this work that led to Mischel's highly influential book *Personality and Assessment* (1968). In this book, Mischel reviewed many studies designed to measure consistency of behaviour across situations or to measure the relationship between performance on personality questionnaires and actual behaviour. He found the typical correlation to be about 0.30. Mischel called this weak correlation the **personality coefficient,** and he argued that the weakness of the coefficient was not due to problems in measuring such characteristics as traits or behaviour but, rather, to the fact that human behaviour is simply not very consistent.

Thus, according to Mischel, although traits and various other inner states have been used to describe behaviour for a long time, they are of limited use in actually predicting behaviour. The use of traits to describe and explain behaviour, says Mischel, often indicates what the theorist thinks *should be* the case rather than what actually is the case. Mischel (1990) uses the term **consistency paradox** to describe the fact that both laypeople and professional psychologists persist in believing that people's behaviour is consistent when evidence indicates that it is not (e.g., Carlson & Mulaik, 1993; Hayden & Mischel, 1976). Chapman and Chapman (1969) coined the term *illusory correlation* to describe the belief or perception that variables are correlated when, in fact, they are not. According to Mischel, the belief that traits and behaviour are highly correlated is an example. Mischel ended *Personality and Assessment* (1968) with the plea to abandon the trait approach to understanding personality, "This conceptualization of man, besides being philosophically unappetizing, is contradicted by massive experimental data" (p. 301).

Since 1968, Mischel and many others have performed research that confirms the inconsistency of human behaviour. For example, in a much cited study, Mischel and Peake (1982) examined the consistency of college students on two "traits"—conscientiousness and friendliness. While common sense, and many psychologists, would predict that students would behave consistently across situations according to the degree to which they possess the traits in question, the prediction was not confirmed. There was essentially no intersituational consistency ($r = .13$).

In the years since 1968, Mischel has moderated his attack on trait theory (1979, 1984, 1990). He no longer denies the value of *describing* people in terms of such traits as intelligence, friendliness, and aggressiveness. He does say, however, that it is practically impossible to predict how these, and other, traits will manifest themselves in a person's behaviour in any given situation. Thus, Mischel no longer wishes to purge psychology of the concept of trait. Rather, he seeks to clarify how the traits that an individual may possess actually contribute to that person's behaviour. For example, he wants to be able to make conditional statements such as "person A, in situation x, tends to do y" (Wright & Mischel, 1987). In other words, Mischel remains opposed to making generalized predictions about people based on the traits that they supposedly possess. Whatever consistency a person may demonstrate can only be discovered by observing how he or she responds to specific situations. Cantor and Mischel (1979) say, "Consistency of personality may be demonstrable only when theorists abandon their search for distinctive nomothetic traits and instead look for more idiographic patterns of person-environment interactions" (p. 43).

Although Mischel's observation that human behaviour is not as consistent as was traditionally believed caused quite a stir among personality theorists, he believes their concern was misguided. Mischel believes that the degree of consistency previously thought to exist may actually be maladaptive.

> Personologists have long searched for behavioral consistencies from situation to situation as if such consistency were the essence of personality. Perhaps that form of consistency will prove to be more characteristic of rigid, maladaptive, incompetent social functioning than of the integrated individual. (1984, p. 360)

Mischel's major criticism of traditional personality theories is that they emphasize **person variables** and de-emphasize **situation variables.** Person variables are those aspects of a person, like traits, habits, and repressed experiences, that are assumed to cause the person to act consistently in a variety of similar situations. Situation variables consist of the person's environmental circumstances at a given time.

Although Mischel believes situation variables have been de-emphasized by most personality theories, he believes they have been overemphasized by certain behaviouristic theories—for instance, Skinner's. According to Mischel, Skinner's attempt to explain behaviour entirely in terms of environmental conditions overlooks the significant contributions made by the person to his or her own behaviour. What is needed, says Mischel, is a theory that considers the contributions of both the person *and* the situation.

RECIPROCAL DETERMINISM

The position taken by the social cognitive theorist is called **reciprocal determinism**, which means that person variables, situation variables, and behaviour continuously interact with one another. Situation variables provide the setting in which a person behaves, person variables determine how a situation is analyzed and which behaviours are chosen, and behaviour both provides information concerning the person's analysis of the situation and modifies the environment. Bandura (1986, p. 24) diagrams reciprocal determinism as follows, where P is the person, E is the environment, and B is the person's behaviour:

One implication of reciprocal determinism is that people's beliefs about themselves and the world will influence both how they behave and the environments in which they place themselves. In turn, feedback from behaviour and environmental experience will confirm or disconfirm people's beliefs. For example, a gregarious person believing that people are generally friendly will tend to respond warmly to strangers. Such positive responses tend to create an environment that encourages positive human interactions. Thus the person's gregarious tendency is confirmed and strengthened. In contrast, a shy, withdrawn person will dread interpersonal interactions and therefore avoid or minimize them. Such reactions create social environments that are negative and encourage the person to remain shy and withdrawn. However, beliefs are not the only aspect of a person that influences his or her environment. Person variables also include a person's gender, social position, size, and physical attractiveness. Bandura (1978) says, "People activate different environmental reactions, apart from their behavior, by their physical characteristics (e.g., size, physiognomy, race, sex, attractiveness) and socially conferred attributes, roles, and status" (p. 346).

Social cognitive theory, then, does not exclude person variables. In fact, they are considered extremely important. The person variables postulated, however, are not the traditional types such as traits, habits, and repressed experiences. Rather, they are beliefs, values, and information-processing strategies. Furthermore, they are important only insofar as they manifest themselves in the present.

Cognitive Social Person Variables

Social cognitive theory views the interaction between the person and the environment as highly complex and individualistic. Each individual brings to each situation the remnants of previous experience, which are used to deal with the present situation.

The outcome of the negotiations with the present situations, in turn, influence how similar situations are dealt with in the future. How a given individual will interact with a situation is determined by what Mischel calls **cognitive social person variables** (1993, p. 403). It is these variables that determine which of the myriad stimuli confronted by a person are perceived, selected, interpreted, and used. Unlike the traditional person variables, the person variables in social cognitive theory are active cognitive processes that operate in the present. These variables provide dynamic, reciprocal relationships among the person, the person's behaviour, and the environment.

Mischel (1993, pp. 403–411) describes five cognitive social learning person variables.

1. Encoding strategies: How we see things.   People not only select different aspects of the environment to attend to, but they also assign different meanings to the stimuli selected, for instance race, gender, weight, even eye-glasses. Mischel (1993) says:

> People differ greatly in how they encode (represent, symbolize) and group information from stimulus inputs. The same "hot weather" that upsets one person may be a joy for another who views it as a chance to go to the beach. The same stranger in the elevator who is perceived as "dangerous" by one person may be seen as "attractive" by another. (p. 404)

To understand a person it is necessary to know the categories with which he or she embraces the world. Here we see the influence of George Kelly (see chapter 13) on Mischel. Kelly suggested that any given event can be construed (interpreted) in any number of ways and that people are free to choose the constructs (concepts, categories, symbols, or words) with which they interpret their experiences. This means that in the same physical situation, people will encode it, construe it, and respond to it differently. Furthermore, because person variables are dynamic, we should not assume that even for a given person the same situation will be construed the same way twice. It is a person's **encoding strategies** that provide some consistency in behaviour, but the fact that those strategies can be changed by the individual at any time at least partially accounts for the fact that cross-situational behaviour is not very consistent. Encoding strategies determine what aspects of the world are attended to and how they are interpreted.

2. Expectancies: What we think will happen.   The person variable of encoding strategies determines how one categorizes experience. At some point, however, people must actually act on the environment. The most important variable for actual performance is a person's expectations. For example, in a given situation, the person hypothesizes, If I act in this way, it will have the following result. This is called a **behaviour-outcome expectancy.** In the absence of any information about a specific situation, one tends to create **expectancies** based on past experience with similar situations. If specific information is available, however, one's expectations change accordingly. In preparation for a job interview, for example, if one hears that the job interviewer is especially impressed by assertiveness, one might expect that acting assertively would increase the probability of getting the job, and then would act on this newly formed expectancy. Likewise, society hopes to deter crime by announcing the punishment associated with various crimes, so that people need not commit a particular act to learn the likely penalty.

Mischel refers to a second type of hypothesis we formulate in dealing with our experience as a **stimulus-outcome expectancy.** We learn that if event 1 occurs, event 2 is likely to follow. For example, if we hear a siren, we expect a speeding emergency vehicle will soon be seen; or, noting that it is six o'clock, we expect that dinner will soon be available. Similarly, seeing red and blue flashing lights in the rear-view mirror often yields a fearful reaction if we know we have broken the traffic laws.

A third type of hypothesis we use in dealing with the world is called a **self-efficacy expectancy.** It is one thing to know what behaviour would be effective in a given situation and another to be able to perform that behaviour. One's ability to perform the behaviours required in a particular situation is called self-efficacy. Because what one can actually do often differs from what one thinks one can do, social cognitive theory places great stress on **perceived self-efficacy,** which is what a person *thinks* he or she is capable of doing in various situations—for example, whether a person thinks she can complete a marathon run of 26 miles. We return to a discussion of self-efficacy later in the chapter.

In general, the person variable of expectancies answers the questions, What should I expect if I act in a certain way? If I see one thing, what should I expect to see next? and Am I capable of doing what I think needs to be done?

3. Subjective values: What is worth having or doing?   Even if a person has a strong behaviour outcome expectancy and a strong self-efficacy expectancy, he or she may decide not to translate those expectancies into behaviour because what would be gained simply is not seen as worth the effort. For example, a student may know exactly what needs to be done to write an outstanding term paper, and may believe he or she has the ability to do what is necessary but may decide that getting an A on a term paper is not worth the time and effort. Another student in the same situation may value an A more, and thus engage in the behaviours necessary to obtain it. Likewise, a given student may, at one time, under certain conditions, decide an A is worth pursuing and at another time, under different circumstances, decide that it is not. One's values will to a large extent determine whether or not the other person variables will be translated into performance. A person's **subjective values** determine what is worth having or doing.

4. Self-regulatory systems and plans: How do we attain our goals?   According to social cognitive theory, human behaviour is largely self-regulated. Performance standards are established, and when actual performance meets or exceeds those standards, one feels good; when it does not, one feels bad. Behaviour, then, is influenced more by **intrinsic** (internal) **reinforcement** and punishment than it is by **extrinsic** (external) **reinforcement** and punishment.

Humans also set future goals and then plan the events in their lives so that they are compatible with those goals. Typically, a major future goal is approached by first reaching a sequence of lesser short-term goals. For example, the goal of obtaining a university degree is met by doing well in high school, graduating from high school, applying for university admission, surviving the first term, and so on. Thus social cognitive theory views much human behaviour as teleological, that is, purposive. **Self-regulatory systems and plans** make it possible to attain those goals deemed important. We say more about self-regulated behaviour later in this chapter.

5. Competencies: What we are capable of doing.   Through observational learning, which is discussed shortly, the person acquires information about the physical and social worlds and his or her relationship to them. The person develops skills, concepts, and problem-solving strategies that are actively used in dealing with the environment. Mischel stresses the fact that these **competencies** are not static memories that are mechanically activated by environmental stimuli. Rather, they are active processes that can be used by the person to generate a wide variety of creative constructions or responses to any given situation. Competencies, then, are seen as tools available to the individual in doing commerce with the environment. Like any tools, what can be done with them is limited only by the imagination of those using them. Competencies refer to what a person knows and what he or she is capable of doing—for instance, whether he has the attention span and stamina to read 100 textbook pages per night.

It is not only one's competencies that are learned from observational learning but also one's encoding strategies, expectancies, values, and self-regulatory systems and plans. We turn next to the important topic of observational learning.

Observational Learning

At the heart of social cognitive theory is the notion of **observational learning.** The most important fact about observational learning is that it requires no reinforcement. According to Bandura and Mischel, humans learn what they attend to, and therefore, for them, learning is a perceptual process. Thus social cognitive theory contrasts sharply with the theories of Skinner and Dollard and Miller, which rely heavily on the concept of direct reinforcement. To illustrate, take a group of five people, and ask one to guess your favourite number (between 1 and 10), awarding a dollar upon a successful guess. Supposing it takes the first person (by trial and error) four attempts to arrive at your favourite number, and you reward her with a dollar; then you move on to the next person. Without hesitation, he will guess the number in one trial. In fact, this will be the same for all people subsequent to the first. Although no person but the first ever received a reward for learning the favourite number, everyone learned it. Learning without reinforcement is not only possible, it is quite common.

Although, according to social cognitive theory, reinforcement does not influence learning, it is key to *performance* and to perceptual processes. In other words, reinforcement influences what is attended to, and thus learned; more importantly, it determines which aspect of what has been learned is translated into behaviour.

The distinction between learning and performance is illustrated in a famous study performed by Bandura (1965). In this experiment, a five-minute film was shown of a **model** aggressing toward a large Bobo doll. In social cognitive theory, a model is anything that conveys information—for instance, a person, a book, a film, a demonstration, or instructions. In this experiment, the model was an adult human.

> The film began with a scene in which a model walked up to an adult-sized plastic Bobo doll and ordered him to clear the way. After glaring for a moment at the noncompliant antagonist the model exhibited four novel aggressive responses each accompanied by a distinctive verbalization.
>
> First, the model laid the Bobo doll on its side, sat on it, and punched it in the nose while remarking, "Pow, right on the nose, boom, boom." The model then raised the doll and pommelled it on the head with a mallet. Each response was followed by the verbalization, "Sockeroo . . . stay down." Following the mallet aggression, the model kicked the doll about the room, and these responses were interspersed with the comment, "Fly away." Finally, the model threw rubber balls at the Bobo doll, each strike punctuated with "Bang." This sequence of physically and verbally aggressive behaviour was repeated twice. (Bandura, 1965, pp. 590–591)

Following presentation of the film, one group of children were shown a second film in which a second adult was shown praising the model for his aggressive behaviour and rewarding him with pop and candy. A second group of children saw a film in which a second adult punished the model for his aggressive behaviour. In this group, the model was called a coward and a bully, spanked with a rolled-up newspaper, and threatened with a beating if he was caught being aggressive again. A third group of children, the control group, saw only the first five-minute film. The children were then exposed to a doll similar to that in the film, and their aggressiveness toward it was measured. Results indicated that the group who saw the model being reinforced for aggressiveness was most aggressive; the group who saw the model punished for aggressiveness was least aggressive; and the control group was between the other two groups in aggressiveness.

This portion of Bandura's study demonstrated that children performed on the basis of what they had seen happen to someone else. That is, rather than performing on the basis of direct reinforcement and punishment, they were responding to **vicarious reinforcement** and **vicarious punishment.** To put this in terms of the person variables described earlier, it was as if the children had formulated behaviour-outcome expectancies on the basis of what they had seen in the film. The children who saw the model's aggressiveness reinforced appeared to develop the hypothesis that if they acted aggressively, they, too, could expect reinforcement. Those children who saw the model punished for aggressiveness expected similar behaviour on their part would yield similar results.

The first phase of Bandura's study seemed to indicate that reinforcement was still important for learning, but that it could be vicariously experienced and need not be contingent on one's own behaviour. This finding alone was in contradiction to the theories of Skinner and Dollard and Miller which state that for reinforcement to be effective, it must be contingent on one's own behaviour. In their view, seeing someone else's behaviour being reinforced or punished should have no effect on one's own behaviour.

The results of the second phase of Bandura's study were even more surprising. In this phase, all the children were offered attractive incentives (stickers and juice) to act as the model had acted in the film. Remember that in the first film the model was shown aggressing toward the doll, but the consequences of the model's aggression varied according to what group the children were in. When offered the incentive to replicate the model's behaviour, *the children in all three groups did so.* This means that all the children had learned what they had observed—that is, the model being aggressive—but they had translated what had been learned into the type of behaviour they expected would be either reinforced or at least not punished. Bandura's experiment shows that indeed what is observed is learned, and that how what is learned is translated into performance depends on the learner's behaviour-outcome expectancies. The behaviour-outcome expectancies in this case came vicariously from observing the consequences of a model's behaviour. Bandura indicates that the research just discussed made the Bobo doll famous in psychology, "When I'm introduced at invited lectures at other universities the students place a Bobo doll by the lectern. From time to time I have been asked to autograph one. The Bobo doll has achieved stardom in psychological circles" (quoted in Evans, 1989, p. 23).

Sometimes signals can be mixed, as in an ice hockey brawl, when viewers on the one hand see penalties and even fines meted out for fighting, but on the other hand realize that hockey "goons" can achieve fame and fortune. Consider one of the most famous cases of violence in professional ice hockey, what was to be later called the "the chop heard 'round the world." In February 2000, Boston Bruin defenceman Marty ("the Enforcer") McSorley hit Vancouver Canuck forward Donald Brashear in the head with his stick. Brashear would receive a concussion, and McSorley would receive a season suspension and $100 000 fine. A Vancouver judge, wanting to send a message that criminal law applies on the ice as well as off, found McSorley guilty of assault with a weapon but handed down no jail time. What would viewers learn from their observations? Would the sport and criminal penalties meted out to McSorley be sufficient to curb others' violence in both professional and amateur hockey arenas?

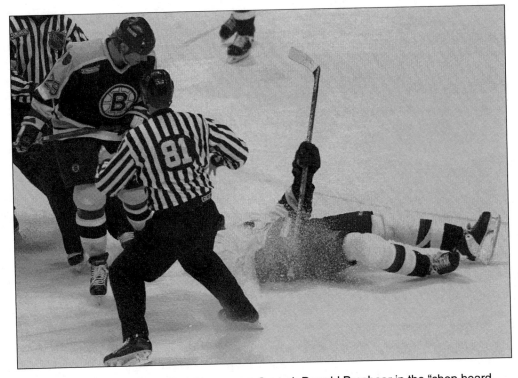

Boston Bruin Marty McSorley hits Vancouver Canuck Donald Brashear in the "chop heard round the world." Bandura believed that children respond to vicarious reinforcement and punishment. Were McSorley's suspension, fine, and criminal conviction enough vicarious punishment to curb others' violence on ice?

Research has shown that emotional responses can also be learned vicariously (for example, Bandura & Rosenthal, 1966; Berger, 1962; Craig & Weinstein, 1965). Berger (1962) found that when a model was shown reacting with pain, presumably in response to extreme electric shock, following the sound of a tone, the observer, too, would develop an emotional response to the tone. Physiological measures indicated that after observing a model experience what appeared to be a tone-shock relationship, the observer responded emotionally when the tone sounded even when the model was no longer present. Thus a conditioned emotional response was developed on the basis of what appeared to be happening to another person.

Bandura (1986) notes that the ability to learn by observing the consequences of other people's behaviour not only enhances survival but also makes life less tedious:

> If human behavior depended solely on personally experienced consequences, most people would not survive the hazards of early development. Of those who managed to outlive their mistakes, each would have to rediscover, through tiresome trial and error, what works and what fails in everyday transactions with their environment. Fortunately, people are spared many hazards and much tedium by their capacity to benefit from the experiences of others. (p. 283)

Elsewhere, Bandura says, "One would not teach military recruits how to lob grenades through trial and error. This mode of learning would create a situation of, 'Look, sergeant, no arms.' It would give new meaning to the wartime movie, 'A Farewell to Arms'" (quoted in Evans, 1989, p. 8). Similarly, direct reinforcement is not used to teach doctors to perform heart surgery, to teach air traffic controllers to guide planes, or to teach children that electricity is fatal.

We do, of course, learn by observing the consequences of our own behaviour but, according to Bandura, whatever can be learned by direct experience can also be learned by vicarious experience. Bandura (1986) says, "Virtually all learning phenomena resulting from direct experience, can occur vicariously by observing other people's behavior and its consequences for them" (p. 19).

NEWS AND ENTERTAINMENT MEDIA AS MODELS

Because, according to social cognitive theory, we learn from what we observe, it follows that newspapers, television, and films can act as influential models. To use a recent example, let's return to the 1999 Columbine shootings in Littleton, Colorado, and the tragedy that occurred days later in Taber, Alberta. The armed student in Taber reportedly wore a blue trench coat, like those worn by the Colorado killers, so police and news media immediately referred to this as a "copy-cat crime." Similarly, full television coverage of APEC protests in Vancouver may have led to more intense conflict at later trade protests in Seattle, Quebec City, and Windsor.

Bandura (1986) makes the following observations about fictional television:

> Analyses of televised programs reveal that violent conduct is portrayed, for the most part, as permissible, successful, and relatively clean. . . . Witnesses to the violence in the dramatic presentations are more likely to approve of such behavior or to join in the assaults rather than to seek alternative solutions. Violence not only is shown to pay off but is readily used by superheroes, who dispose of their adversaries in a quick, perfunctory way as though slaying human beings was of no great concern. (p. 292)

Since Bandura's early work on modelled aggression, numerous studies have examined the relationship between television violence and aggression and other forms of antisocial behaviour. Typically these studies confirm a positive relationship between the two (e.g., Geen & Thomas, 1986; Huesmann & Malamuth, 1986; Turner, Hesse, & Peterson-Lewis, 1986). Recent research has indicated that despite considerable current societal concern, 58% of television programs still contain violence and that in 78% of violent incidents, the perpetrator is depicted as at least unremorseful, if not actually glamourized. Concerned citizens have urged Canadian broadcasters to adopt the program ratings used in the United States, where a code in the corner of the screen alerts parents and viewers to objectionable content. However, evidence indicates that the use of warning labels has not prevented children from watching violent programs (Seppa, 1997). It has also been found that violent rock videos can create, in some men, violent attitudes toward women (Peterson & Pfost, 1989).

Clearly, not everyone exposed to violence becomes violent nor does everyone exposed to sexually explicit literature or movies become sexually deviant. For some, however, such modelling provides learning experiences that promote antisocial behaviour. Nor are the news and entertainment media the only places in society where violence is modelled. For example, parents who spank their children are modelling aggression. Bandura (1973) observes that children whose parents employ considerable corporal punishment often become highly aggressive. Such children also tend to be less obedient (Power & Chapleski, 1986). Bandura supports neither the extensive use of corporal punishment nor "unconditional love."

> Some child-rearing authorities have popularized the view that healthy personality development is built on "unconditional love." If this principle were, in fact, unfailingly

applied, parents would respond affectionately regardless of how their children behaved—whether or not they mistreated others, stole whatever they wanted, disregarded the wishes and rights of others, or demanded instant gratification. Unconditional love, were it possible, would make children directionless and quite unlovable. Most readers are undoubtedly acquainted with families where parents who attempted to approximate this condition succeeded in producing "self-actualized" tyrants. (Bandura, 1977, p. 102)

In any case, news and entertainment media are among society's influential models and "humane living requires reducing social influences that promote cruelty and destructiveness [and] . . . society has the right to regulate obscene materials that can cause harm" (Bandura, 1986, p. 296). However, Bandura recognizes that controlling such material is complex. First, there is disagreement over what is harmful. Second, the suppression of material considered harmful may conflict with the basic right of free expression.

Although social cognitive theory maintains what is observed is learned, certain processes influence what is attended to, what is retained, how what is learned is translated into behaviour, and why it is translated into behaviour. Bandura (1986) describes four such processes.

ATTENTIONAL PROCESSES

These processes include aspects of the environment that influence attention, such as the complexity, distinctiveness, and prevalence of the stimulation. For example, screeching brakes attract almost everyone's attention. Certain characteristics of models determine the extent to which they are observed. For instance, it has been found that models are attended to more if they are seen as similar to oneself, are respected, are considered powerful, or are attractive. Related to the concept of power, it has been found that adults who control resources, that is, have the ability to dispense rewards, are more powerful models for children than adults who do not control resources (Bandura, Ross, & Ross, 1963; Grusec & Mischel, 1966).

Attentional processes also include observer characteristics such as sensory capacities. Blind and deaf people, for example, do not respond to the same stimuli as people with normal sight and hearing.

Also, the consequences of past behaviour can create a perceptual set in the observer. For example, if attending to certain stimuli in the past resulted in positive consequences, a tendency will exist to attend to similar stimuli in similar situations.

RETENTIONAL PROCESSES

What is learned by observation is of no value unless it is retained. We saw earlier that how information is encoded and construed varies from person to person but, in general, Bandura (1986) says that experiences are stored either imaginally or verbally. That is, our **retentional processes** lead to either an actual cognitive picture of what was experienced or the words that describe the experience. The memories make **delayed modelling** possible: that is, information gained by observational learning may not be translated into behaviour until much later.

MOTOR REPRODUCTION PROCESSES

To translate learning into performance, one needs to have the necessary motor apparatus. Granted that apparatus, one can be temporarily prevented from performing by injury, fatigue, or illness. Moreover, complex skills cannot simply be observed and immediately translated into performance. First, many observations may be required to attend to and remember all the relevant information. Second, many rehearsals may be necessary to match performance with what has been learned and retained. All these steps make up **motor reproduction processes**. According to Bandura (1986), it is the observer's conceptualization of modelled behaviour that provides the frame of reference necessary for skill improvement:

> The conceptual representation provides the internal model for response production and the standard for response correction. Behavioural production primarily involves a conception-matching process in which the incoming sensory feedback from enactments is compared to the conception. The behavior is then modified on the basis of the comparative information to achieve progressively closer correspondence between conception and action. (p. 64)

MOTIVATIONAL PROCESSES

No matter how much one has learned, and no matter what one's capabilities are, learning will not be translated into performance unless there is an incentive to do so. Observational learning may create potentially effective behaviour-outcome expectations, but unless the person believes that behaviour will yield something valued, no behaviour will occur. According to social cognitive theory, **reinforcement,** either direct or vicarious, provides the *information* necessary for the development of effective behaviour-outcome expectancies. Even with direct reinforcement, however, it is assumed that learning is observational and not an automatic, unconscious strengthening of response tendencies, as Skinner and Dollard and Miller had assumed. According to social cognitive theory, a person learns from *observing* the consequences either of his or her own behaviour (direct reinforcement) or of other people's behaviour (vicarious reinforcement). In either case, information is provided about what behaviours lead to what consequences.

In addition to information concerning what behaviours lead to what consequences, reinforcement provides an *incentive* for action, leading to **motivational processes.** Within social cognitive theory, reinforcement is equated with something of value to the person under existing circumstances. People, then, are motivated to act in ways that provide things they value and that allow them to avoid things considered aversive. Bandura's views on observational learning and the translation of that learning into behaviour can be summarized as follows: A person must observe something; remember what was observed; be able to perform the behaviours necessary to reproduce what was observed; and want to reproduce those behaviours.

Self-Regulated Behaviour

Social cognitive theory maintains that most human behaviour is **self-regulated.** Through cumulative direct and vicarious experience, people develop **performance standards** that they use to evaluate their own behaviour. Almost constantly, the person compares what he or she does in a situation with some performance standard. If performance meets or exceeds the standard, the person experiences intrinsic reinforcement. If a performance falls short of a standard, the person experiences intrinsic punishment.

Modelling has been found to influence the formulation of one's performance standards. Bandura and Kupers (1964), for example, found that children exposed to models who set high performance standards reinforced themselves only for superior performance, whereas children exposed to models accepting minimal performance standards reinforced themselves for minimal performance. It would be expected, then, that relevant people in a child's life—for instance, parents, siblings, and peers—would have a profound influence on the development of a child's performance standards.

Goals and *plans* extend self-directed behaviour over long periods of time. Once a future goal has been established, a person organizes his or her experiences so they increase the probability of goal attainment. Bandura (1991) says, "People form beliefs about what they can do, they anticipate the likely consequences of prospective actions, they set goals for themselves, and they otherwise plan courses of action that are likely to produce desired outcomes" (p. 248). Experiences that keep the person on track toward the goal result in self-reinforcement; those that are incompatible with the goal cause self-punishment. As mentioned earlier, major goals are seldom attained all at once. Rather, a series of subgoals are established, that approximate the major goal. Personal frustration and depression can occur if goals are either too distant or too difficult. Goals must be related to one's capabilities and must be attainable through the achievement of reasonable subgoals that are of moderate difficulty relative to a person's competencies. Performance standards, too, must be realistic. If they are too lenient, they will be too easily met, and little, if any, self-reinforcement will result from performing in accordance with them. If they are too stringent, one will experience frustration or worse. Consider two-time Olympic gold medalist in women's speed-skating, Catriona LeMay Doan. Deemed "the fastest woman on ice" when she set a world record in the 500-metre sprint at the 1998 Nagano Olympics, she broke her own record at the 2002 games in Salt Lake City. For LeMay Doan to set her sights on the world record was reasonable; the same goal would be unrealistic for the average speed-skater.

Bandura (1986) says, "In its more extreme forms, harsh standards for self-evaluation give rise to depressive reactions, chronic discouragement, feelings of worthlessness, and lack of purposefulness" (p. 358). Bandura (1991) finds that people prone to depression generally judge themselves more harshly than people not prone to depression, "Compared to nondepressed persons, those who are prone to depression react less self-rewardingly for similar successes but more self-critically for similar failures" (pp. 274–275).

Ideally performance standards are modified as a function of one's accomplishments and failures. Bandura (1986) notes:

> One's previous behavior is continuously used as a reference against which ongoing performance is judged. In this referential process, self-comparison supplies the measure of adequacy. Past attainments affect self-appraisal mainly through their effects on standard setting. . . . After a given level of performance has been attained, it is no longer challenging, and people seek new self-satisfactions by means of progressive improvement. Hence, people tend to raise their performance standards after success and to lower them to more realistic levels after repeated failure. (pp. 347–348)

SELF-EFFICACY

Bandura (1989) observes, "Among the mechanisms of personal agency, none is more central or pervasive than people's beliefs about their capabilities to exercise control over events that affect their lives" (p. 1175). **Self-efficacy** refers to what a person is *actually* capable of doing. More important, however, is what a person *thinks* he or she is capable of doing, or perceived self-efficacy. Perceived self-efficacy is influenced by several factors—for example, personal accomplishments and failures, seeing models perceived as similar to oneself succeed or fail at various tasks, and verbal persuasion. Through verbal persuasion, persons can often be encouraged to try to achieve goals they would otherwise avoid; an example is when a coach "fires up" his team before a game. The effects of verbal persuasion are short-lived, however, if the resulting perceived self-efficacy is not manifested in real performance. It has also been found that people tend to judge their self-efficacy in a potentially threatening situation in terms of their emotional arousal. Because high arousal typically inhibits performance, strong emotion is usually correlated with feelings of perceived self-inefficacy. Conversely, being relaxed in such a situation facilitates perceived self-efficacy.

Research performed by Bandura and others (for a summary of this research see Bandura, 1986, 1989, 1995) has demonstrated that, compared to individuals with low perceived self-efficacy, individuals with high perceived self-efficacy have the following characteristics:

> they set more challenging goals and performance standards
> they persist longer in the pursuit of goals
> they are more venturesome in their behaviour
> they recover more quickly from setbacks and frustrations
> they experience less fear, anxiety, stress, and depression

As with goals and performance standards, the situation is best when one's perceived self-efficacy is in line with one's true capabilities. Thinking one can do more than one can actually do results in frustration. Thinking that one can do less than one can actually do inhibits personal growth. Both distortions of one's self-efficacy result in dysfunctional (erroneous) self-expectancies which, if severe enough, can cause a person to seek psychotherapy.

Bandura's concept of perceived self-efficacy has become one of the most popular research topics in the realm of personality theory. Researchers have found perceived self-efficacy to be related to many aspects of people's lives, from academic and athletic performance to depression to immune system functioning. Canadian researchers have participated enthusiastically in the study of self-efficacy and its relation to other variables, including frequency of physical exercise, high-risk sexual behaviours, and the ability to cope with chronic pain. Table 11-1 lists just some of the areas in which researchers have found a relationship.

Later in this chapter we will also see that the concept of perceived self-efficacy is central to Bandura's approach to, and understanding of, psychotherapy.

MORAL CONDUCT

Standards of right and wrong are also highly personal and are also derived from one's direct and vicarious experience. As with performance standards, moral principles are usually modelled by a child's parents and are eventually internalized (Blatny & Cermak, 1995). Once internalized, these moral principles determine which behaviours and thoughts are self-sanctioned and which result in self-contempt. Thus moral behaviour comes to be self-regulated and is maintained independently of, and in many cases despite, environmental consequences. Bandura (1977) says, "The anticipation of self-reproach for conduct that violates one's standards provides a source of motivation to keep behavior in line with standards in the face of opposing inducements. There is no more devastating punishment than self-contempt" (p. 154).

Certain cognitive mechanisms, however, allow a person to act contrary to his or her moral principles without experiencing self-contempt. These **self-exonerating mechanisms** (Bandura, 1986, pp. 375–385) are summarized on page 291:

Table 11–1

Variables Found to be Associated with Perceived Self-Efficacy

VARIABLE	RESEARCH
the effectiveness of smoking cessation programs	Mitchell & Stuart, 1984 Weinberg, Hughes, Critelli, England, & Jackson, 1984, Baer, Holt, & Lichtenstein, 1986 Garcia, Schmitz, & Doerfler, 1990, Wojcik, 1988
the effectiveness of alcohol treatment programs	Annis, 1990
AIDS prevention	Bandura, 1990a, O'Leary, 1992
academic performance	Multon, Brown, & Lent, 1991, Tuckman, 1990
depression	Bandura, 1989 Bandura, Adams, Hardy, & Howells, 1980 Davis-Berman, 1990
job burnout	Meier, 1983
maternal competence	Teti & Gelfand, 1991
occupational choice	Bonett, 1994 Bores-Rangel, Church, Szendre, & Reeves, 1990 Betz & Hackett, 1981
athletic performance	Gould, Hodge, Peterson, & Giannini, 1989
managerial decision making	Bandura & Jourden, 1991 Bandura & Wood, 1989, Wood & Bandura, 1989 Wood, Bandura, & Bailey, 1990
gender differences	Lent, Brown, & Larkin, 1986 Nevill & Schlecker, 1988, Poole & Evans, 1989
developmental experiences	Skinner, Chapman, & Baltes, 1988 Holden, Moncher, Schinke, & Barker, 1990
physiological reactions	Bandura, Reese, & Adams, 1982 Bandura, Taylor, Williams, Mefford, & Barchas, 1985
coping ability	Ozer & Bandura, 1990
job satisfaction and performance	Saks, 1995
adherence to mammography schedules	Black, Stein, & Loveland-Cherry, 2001
beginning exercise program	Dawson & Brawley, 2000
frequency of physical exercise	Rodgers & Sullivan, 2001
university students' stress levels	Dwyer & Cummings, 2001
medical students' patient communications	Kaufman, Laidlaw, Langille, Sargeant, & MacLeod, 2001
coping, perceived control, and cognitive performance for sufferers of acute and chronic illnesses	Endler, Speer, Johnson, & Flett, 2001
high-risk sexual behaviours	Nadeau, Truchon, & Biron, 2000
frequency of emergency visits for asthmatics	Nouwen, Freeston, Labbe, & Boulet, 1999 Senecal, Nouwen, & White, 2000
chronic pain	LeFort, 2000
immune system functioning	Bandura, Cioffi, Taylor, Brouillard, 1988 Bandura, O'Leary, Taylor, Gauthier, & Gossard, 1987 Wiedenfeld, O'Leary, Bandura, Brown, Levine, & Raska, 1990

1. **Moral justification.** One's otherwise reprehensible behaviour becomes a means to a higher purpose and therefore is justifiable. "I committed the crime so I could provide food for my family." Bandura (1986) says, "Over the years, much destructive and reprehensible conduct has been perpetrated by decent people in the name of religious principles, righteous ideologies, and nationalistic imperatives" (p. 377).

2. **Euphemistic labelling.** By calling an otherwise reprehensible act something other than what it really is, one can engage in an act without self-contempt. For example, nonaggressive individuals are far more likely to aggress toward another person when doing so is called a game.

Through the power of words, even killing a human being loses much of its repugnance. Soldiers "waste" people rather than kill them, CIA operatives "terminate (them) with extreme prejudice." When mercenaries speak of "fulfilling a contract," murder is transformed by admirable words into the honourable discharge of duty (Bandura, 1986, p. 378). Attempting to destroy a race or culture is merely "ethnic cleansing."

3. **Advantageous comparison.** Comparing one's self-deplored acts with even more heinous acts makes one's own wrongdoing look trifling by comparison. "Sure I did that, but look at what he did."

Promoters of the war in Vietnam, for example, minimized the slaying of countless people as a way of checking massive communist enslavement. Given the trifling comparison, supporters of American military action remained unperturbed by the fact that the intended beneficiaries were being killed at an alarming rate. American protesters, on the other hand, characterized their own violence against educational and political institutions as trifling, or even laudable, by comparing it with the carnage perpetrated by their country's military forces in foreign lands. (Bandura, 1986, p. 379)

4. **Displacement of responsibility.** Some people can readily depart from their moral principles if they believe a recognized authority sanctions their behaviour and takes responsibility for it. "I did it because I was ordered to do so."

Nazi prison commandants and their staffs felt little personal responsibility for their unprecedented inhumanities. They were simply carrying out orders. Impersonal obedience to horrific orders was similarly evident in military atrocities, such as the My Lai massacre. (Bandura, 1986, p. 379)

Bandura (1990b) observes that terrorists who have taken hostages often "warn officials of targeted nations that if they take retaliatory action they will be held accountable for the lives of the hostages" (p. 175).

5. **Diffusion of responsibility.** A decision to act in an otherwise reprehensible manner that is made by a group is easier to live with than an individual decision. Where everyone is responsible, no single individual feels responsible. "I couldn't be the only one saying no." The attack on Reena Virk (see chapter 6) was carried out by at least eight teenagers. This fact diffused the responsibility so that no one individual feels especially responsible for the attack, since "everyone else is doing it."

6. **Disregard or distortion of consequences.** Here people ignore or distort the harm caused by their conduct and therefore do not experience self-contempt. The farther people remove themselves from the ill effects of their immoral behaviour the less pressure there is to censure it. The 1992 Gulf War was characterized by many as "Nintendo warfare," since pilots viewed targets such as troop barracks or munitions plants as coloured squares on a screen. So long as they do not associate those coloured squares with real people, pilots have no qualms about firing deadly missiles.

7. **Dehumanization.** If some individuals are looked upon as subhuman, they can be treated inhumanely without experiencing self-contempt.

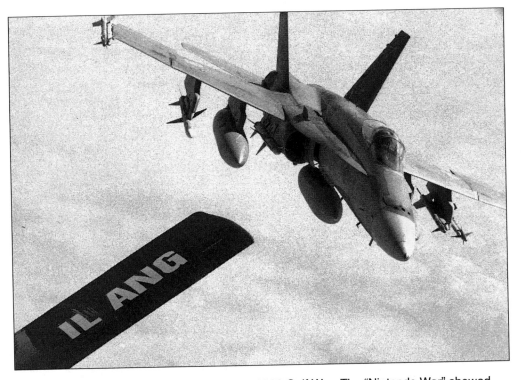

Canadian pilots flying combat missions in the 1992 Gulf War. The "Nintendo War" showed their targets as coloured squares; they did not see the people and buildings they were shooting, allowing them to salve their consciences by disregarding the consequences of their actions.

> Once dehumanized, [individuals] are no longer viewed as persons with feelings, hopes, and concerns but as subhuman objects demeaningly stereotyped as "gooks," "fags," or "niggers." Subhumans are presumably insensitive to maltreatment and influenceable only through more primitive methods. If dispossessing disfavored people of their humanness does not blunt self-reproof, it can be fully eliminated by attributing bestial qualities to them. They become "degenerates," "pigs," and other bestial creatures. Over the years slaves, women, manual laborers, and religious and racial minorities have been treated as chattel or as subhuman objects. (Bandura, 1986, p. 382)

8. Attribution of blame.   One can always choose something that a victim said or did and claim that it caused one to act in a reprehensible way.

> Rapists and males who acknowledge a proclivity to rape subscribe to myths about rape embodying the various mechanisms by which moral self-censure can be disengaged. . . . These beliefs hold rape victims responsible for their own victimization because they have supposedly invited rape by sexually provocative appearance and behavior and by resisting a sexual assault weakly. (Bandura, 1986, pp. 384–385)

The self-exonerating mechanisms provide another reason why human behaviour tends to be inconsistent. Even if a person's moral principles were known with certainty, employing one or more of these mechanisms would make the person's moral behaviour unpredictable to the outside observer. Such behaviour would, however, undoubtedly seem consistent and logical to the person himself or herself.

Delay of Gratification

In a series of experiments that began soon after he received his Ph.D. from Ohio State University in 1956, Mischel and his colleagues have extensively explored the variables related to the ability to delay gratification. In one early study, Mischel and Metzner (1962) found that the ability to delay gratification increased with age, intelligence, and with shorter intervals of delay. Later, Mischel and his colleagues began their influential research on four- and five-year-old children attending the Bing nursery school at Stanford University (Mischel & Ebbesen, 1970; Mischel, Ebbesen, & Zeiss, 1972). In these studies, children were given a choice between a small reward given immediately (e.g., one marshmallow or pretzel) or a larger reward given after a delay (e.g., two marshmallows or pretzels). There were four experimental conditions: (1) both the immediate and delayed rewards were visible; (2) neither the immediate nor the delayed rewards were visible; (3) only the immediate reward was visible; and (4) only the delayed reward was visible. The researchers predicted that being able to see the rewards would enhance the ability to delay. The opposite was true: children waited the longest when no rewards were visible. It turned out that when rewards were visible it caused the children to think about them, and thinking about them reduced their ability to delay gratification. It was also found that children who could delay the longest employed a number of self-distraction strategies in order to make the aversive delay period more pleasant. These children talked to themselves, sang, invented games to be played with their hands and feet, and even tried to fall asleep (one child was successful). Mischel and Moore (1973) found that instructing children to think of pictures of rewards instead of actual rewards increased their ability to delay gratification. Other studies showed that instructing children to think of otherwise desirable rewards in undesirable ways (e.g., to think of pretzels as little brown logs or of marshmallows as round white clouds or as balls of cotton) increased their ability to delay (Mischel & Baker, 1975; Mischel & Moore, 1980; Moore, Mischel, & Zeiss, 1976). From the experiments just described, Mischel (1993) concludes, "What is in the children's heads—not what is physically in front of them—determines their ability to delay [and] if you can make the waiting easier for yourself, you are more likely to wait successfully" (pp. 457, 458). Numerous studies have confirmed the contention that imposed or self-created distractions facilitate the ability to delay gratification (Mischel, Shoda, & Rodriguez, 1989).

In the more than 40 years of research on **delay of gratification,** one of the most dramatic findings is the relationship between the ability to delay gratification as a preschool child and a number of positive adolescent personality characteristics. Mischel and his colleagues followed up their research on the Stanford preschool children 10 years after the original research (Mischel, Shoda, & Peake, 1988; Mischel, Shoda, & Rodriguez, 1989; Shoda, Mischel, & Peake, 1990). Of special interest were the children who were able to delay even when rewards were visible and who were not given strategies to facilitate delay. It was assumed that such children were capable of generating their own self-distracting strategies, and that this capability would continue to exist later in life. These assumptions were clearly supported. Preschool children who could delay gratification with rewards visible and without imposed distractions were rated positively by their parents on a variety of social and academic skills when they were high school students. Table 11–2 summarizes the attributes these parents saw in these adolescents. They also had higher verbal and quantitative scholastic aptitude test (SAT) scores. In contrast, preschool delay behaviour when rewards were not visible or when distraction strategies were provided did not reliably predict either positive parental ratings or SAT scores. Mischel (1993, p. 460) notes evidence that people with the ability to self-distract can also deal more effectively with pain, stress, and severe life crises.

Table 11–2	Less likely to be sidetracked by minor setbacks.
	More likely to exhibit self-control in frustrating situations.
	Copes well with important problems.
Characteristics of	Capable of doing well academically when motivated.
Adolescents Who, as	Less likely to yield to temptations.
Preschoolers Had	When faced with a choice, is less likely to settle for an immediate but less
Delayed Gratification	desirable choice.
	More able to pursue goals when motivated.
	Intelligent.
	When motivated, is capable of exhibiting self-control in tempting
	situations.
	Skilled in maintaining friendships and getting along with peers.
	Not distractible when trying to concentrate.
	Capable of exhibiting self-control when frustrated.
	Can effectively pursue goals.
	Can divert attention from the frustration of having to postpone a desired
	gratification while continuing to pursue it.

From Mischel, 1993, p. 459

What determines the extent to which one possesses such an important personality attribute? As with other factors influencing self-regulated behaviour, it has been found that the willingness to delay gratification can be learned by observing models (Bandura & Mischel, 1965; Mischel & Liebert, 1966; Stumphauzer, 1972). The fact that the ability to delay gratification can be taught to young children, and that the ability is clearly advantageous later in life, suggests that such teaching be incorporated into early education and child-rearing practices. In any case, it is vital that we understand the kind of **self-control** necessary to delay gratification because, according to Mischel (1993), without it humans are as impulsive as nonhuman animals, and the goal-oriented behaviour necessary for civilized living is impossible.

Dysfunctional Expectancies and Psychotherapy

According to social cognitive theory, psychological problems result from **dysfunctional expectancies** (that is, erroneous, nonfunctional, or faulty expectancies), and any type of therapy that corrects them—that is, brings them in line with reality—will be, by definition, effective.

If, for example, one believes that developing a close relationship with a member of the opposite sex will bring pain and frustration, one will avoid such relationships. Such expectancies are usually based on real experiences, but they are overgeneralized and prevent the person from having the types of experiences that would disconfirm them. The defensive behaviour based on a dysfunctional expectancy is therefore often difficult to remedy.

Some dogs do bite, some airplanes do crash, some intimate relationships do result in pain and frustration, some members of minorities do commit crimes, and some men and some women are insensitive. To generalize on the basis of a few cases to all possible experiences, however, does not accurately represent reality. Bandura (1986) observes, "What such individuals need in order to relinquish their erroneous beliefs are powerful disconfirming experiences, which verbal assurances alone do not provide" (p. 190). Providing such experiences is a key ingredient of the kind of therapy promoted by social cognitive theory.

Another type of dysfunctional expectancy concerns perceived self-efficacy. As we have seen, if people believe they are incapable of doing something, they will not try to do it. A person who believes she cannot touch dogs, cats, snakes, children, or members of the opposite sex will not do so. Likewise, a person who believes he is incapable of handling success will avoid success. Thus, according to social cognitive theory, a major goal of psychotherapy is to change the client's perceived self-efficacy. The assumption is that behaviour will then become more adaptive. Bandura summarizes: "Treatments that are most effective are built on an empowerment model. If you really want to help people, you provide them with . . . competencies, build [in them] a strong self-belief, and create opportunities for them to exercise these competencies" (quoted in Evans, 1989, p. 16).

To test the effects of perceived self-efficacy on behaviour Bandura, Adams, and Beyer (1977) recruited seven men and 26 women who suffered a chronic snake phobia. Before treatment, each person was given a Behavioural Avoidance Test that consisted of 29 performance tasks requiring increasingly close interactions with a red-tailed boa constrictor. Self-efficacy expectancies were also measured before treatment. Subjects were asked to indicate which interactions they would or would not be able to perform, and their certainty about these beliefs.

After pretesting, subjects were randomly assigned to one of three treatment groups. In the **participant modelling** condition, subjects first watched a live model handle a boa constrictor in a series of interactions ranging from mildly threatening to extremely threatening and were then asked to perform these same interactions. The time required for these interactions ranged from 40 minutes to 7 hours, with the average time being 1½ hours. Some subjects were so fearful that a baby boa had to be used initially. In the *modelling condition*, subjects observed a model engage in a series of interactions with the snake but did not actually come into contact with the snake themselves. In the *control condition,* subjects neither watched nor participated in interactions.

After the various treatments, subjects were again given the Behaviour Avoidance Test, the final step of which was to let the boa constrictor crawl on the subject's lap while his or her hands were held passively to the side. Both the participant modelling and the modelling conditions significantly reduced avoidance behaviour, but the participant modelling condition was more effective.

Efficacy expectations were measured again after conclusion of treatment. Again, modelling alone significantly changed expectations, but participant modelling was more effective. Most important, however, was the finding that self-efficacy expectations were accurate predictors of behaviour. Those subjects who indicated they now believed they could handle a snake *actually did so.* Maximal efficacy expectations, however, did not always result from maximal interactions with the snake; that is, some of the individuals in the participant modelling group who were able to perform the most threatening interactions with the snake during treatment did not believe that they would be able to interact that way with a snake on subsequent occasions, and they were correct. Successful performance has a powerful influence on the formation of efficacy expectations, but is not the only factor.

Further measures indicated that the reduction of avoidance generalized to other snakes, that the results of the experiment persisted over time, and that the results generalized positively into other aspects of the subjects' lives. For instance, some subjects were later able to deal effectively with other animal and social threats. Similar results were obtained from an experiment on people with spider phobias (Bandura, Reese, & Adams, 1982).

In another study, Bandura, Blanchard, and Ritter (1969) tested the effectiveness of various techniques in dealing with a snake phobia. In this experiment, adults and adolescents were divided into four groups: **symbolic modelling**, in which subjects were shown a film showing models interacting with a snake; *live modelling with participation,* in which subjects interacted with a snake along with the model; **systematic desensitization**, in which subjects were asked to imagine interactions with a snake. Subjects started by imagining low-anxiety scenes, continued to imagine each scene until it no longer caused anxiety, and then moved on to imagine a higher-anxiety scene, continuing until they could imagine all the scenes without anxiety. The *control group* received no treatment. Results are shown in Figure 11–1.

Again live modelling with participation was most effective, followed by symbolic modelling and then desensitization. Follow-up research again indicated that the effects of the experiment endured and generalized positively to other sources of anxiety.

Many other experiments have shown the effectiveness of modelling in dealing with a wide variety of dysfunctional expectancies. In all of this research, the emphasis is on the person's current perceptions and expectancies. There is no mention of traits, reinforcement histories, or internal conflicts. In fact, Bandura (1986) believes those therapists looking for such things tell us more about themselves than they tell us about the source of their client's problems:

> Advocates of differing theoretical orientations repeatedly discover their chosen motivators at work but rarely find evidence for the motivators emphasized by the proponents of competing viewpoints. . . . Hence, one can predict better the types of insights and unconscious motivators that persons are apt to discover in themselves in the course of psychodynamic analysis from knowledge of the therapists' conceptual belief system than from the clients' actual psychological status. (p. 5)

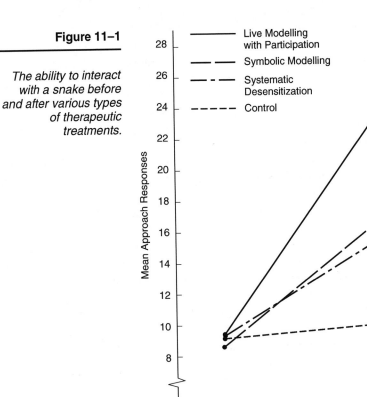

Figure 11–1

The ability to interact with a snake before and after various types of therapeutic treatments.

(From Bandura, Blanchard, & Ritter, 1969, p. 183. Copyright 1999 by the American Psychological Association. Reprinted by permission.)

Social Cognitive Theory View of Human Nature

FREEDOM VERSUS DETERMINISM

Social cognitive theory portrays human nature as complex and rational but is that the same as saying humans possess a free will? Bandura rejects the notion that humans are autonomous, that is, free to act independently of the environmental and personal influences impinging on them. He also rejects the notion that humans respond mechanistically to those influences. Rather, as we have seen, Bandura accepts reciprocal determinism, in which people can influence both their behaviour and their environment. "[T]hrough their capacity to manipulate symbols and to engage in reflective thought, people can generate novel ideas and innovative actions that transcend their past experiences" (Bandura, 1989, p. 1182). However, says Bandura, "self-generated influences operate deterministically on behaviour the same way as external sources of influence do" (1989, p. 1182). Thus, according to Bandura, humans are rational but they do not possess an autonomous free will.

William James (1884/1956) distinguished between hard and soft determinism. Hard determinism is the belief that the causes of human behaviour function in an automatic, mechanistic manner, thus rendering the idea of personal responsibility meaningless. Hergenhahn (1997) describes soft determinism.

> With soft determinism, . . . cognitive processes such as intentions, motives, beliefs, and values intervene between experience and behavior. The soft determinist sees human behavior as resulting from thoughtful deliberation of the options available in a given situation. Because rational processes manifest themselves prior to actions, the person bears responsibility for those actions. Although soft determinism is still determinism, it is a version that allows uniquely human cognitive processes into the configuration of the causes of human behavior. Soft determinism, then, offers a compromise between hard determinism and free will—a compromise that allows for human responsibility. (p. 13)

Bandura is a soft determinist. This conception allows human behaviour to be viewed as teleological, or goal-oriented: "By representing foreseeable outcomes symbolically, people can convert future consequences into current motivators and regulators of foresightful behaviour" (Bandura, 1986, p. 19). It also allows people to be viewed as at least partially responsible for their own behaviour, "[People can] serve as a causal contributor to their own life course by selecting, influencing, and constructing their own circumstances" (Bandura, 1986, p. 38). Elsewhere, Bandura (1989) says, "the capacity to exercise control over one's own thought processes, motivation, and action is a distinctively human characteristic. Because judgment and actions are partly self-determined, people can effect change in themselves and their situations through their own efforts" (p. 1175).

Freedom as Options.   Within the context of social cognitive theory, **freedom** is defined as "the number of options available to people and their right to exercise them. The more behavioural alternatives and prerogatives people have, the greater is their freedom of action" (Bandura, 1986, p. 42). Bandura (1989) elaborates:

> Given the same environmental conditions, persons who have developed skills for accomplishing many options and are adept at regulating their own motivation and behavior are more successful in their pursuits than those who have limited means of personal agency. It is because self-influence operates deterministically on action that some measure of self-directedness and freedom is possible. (p. 1182)

Anything that reduces a person's options, then, limits his or her freedom. According to Bandura (1986, pp. 42–43) the factors that can limit personal freedom include the following:

deficiencies in knowledge and skills

perceptions of self-inefficacy

internal standards that are too stringent

social sanctions that limit a person's opportunities because of his or her skin colour, sexual orientation, gender, religion, ethnic background, or social class

Chance Encounters and Life Paths.   Bandura (1982) observes that chance encounters—unintended meetings with unfamiliar people—can significantly impact people's lives and provide another reason for the unpredictability of human behaviour.

> Some chance encounters touch people only lightly, others leave more lasting effects, and still others branch people into new trajectories of life. Psychology cannot foretell the occurrence of fortuitous encounters, however sophisticated its knowledge of human behavior becomes. This factor introduces a measure of unpredictability about the direction of the flow of human lives. Patterns of change can therefore vary widely in different individuals. They may display basic continuities throughout their life spans, continuities in some aspects of life but discontinuities in others, or a vast discontinuity at any point along the way affecting virtually all domains of functioning. (p. 749)

Reciprocal determinism is not violated by noting the importance of fortuitous experience. Such experience indicates an additional way in which the environment can influence people and their subsequent behaviour.

MIND-BODY RELATIONSHIP

Although social cognitive theory gives cognitive events a prominent role as causative agents, it does not accept psychophysiological dualism. Bandura (1989) states, "Thoughts are higher brain processes rather than psychic entities that exist separately from brain activities. Ideational and neural terminology are simply different ways of representing the same cerebral processes" (p. 1181). However, at least at the present time, psychological laws cannot be derived from neurophysiological laws:

> One must distinguish between biological laws governing the mechanics of cerebral systems and psychological laws of how cerebral systems can be orchestrated to serve different purposes. Psychological knowledge of how best to structure influences to create belief systems and personal competencies is not derivable from knowledge of the neurophysical mechanisms that subserve such changes. Thus, understanding the brain circuits involved in learning does not tell one much about how best to present and organize instructional contents, how to code them for memory representation, and how to motivate learners to attend to, cognitively process, and rehearse what they are learning. Nor does understanding of how the brain works furnish rules on how to create social conditions that cultivate the skills needed to become a successful parent, teacher, or executive. The optimal conditions must be specified by psychological principles. (Bandura, 1989, p. 1182)

Thus while it is true psychological laws cannot violate the laws of the neurophysiological systems that subserve them, attempting to reduce psychology to biology serves no useful purpose:

Were one to embark on the road to reductionism, psychology would be reduced to biology, biology to chemistry, and chemistry to physics, with the final stop in atomic particles. Neither atomic particles, chemistry, nor biology will provide the psychological laws of human behavior. (Bandura, 1989, p. 1182)

Evaluation

EMPIRICAL RESEARCH

Like the theories of Cattell, Eysenck, Skinner, and Dollard and Miller, the theory of Bandura and Mischel is well grounded in empirical research. Throughout this chapter we have sampled numerous experimental studies that Bandura and Mischel and their colleagues have run to test their concepts. Social cognitive theory continues to generate an enormous amount of research. Also, Mischel's book, *Personality and Assessment* (1968), triggered a debate among personality theorists concerning the consistency of human behaviour that has lasted to the present time. This debate has stimulated research programs designed to answer the question, Is human behaviour consistent? If so, to what extent, and in what areas? (For an extensive review of this research, see Zuckerman, 1991). It now appears that whether behaviour consistency is found or not depends on what is meant by consistency and how the research is performed. For example, if *average* behaviour is measured, it pools those behaviours that are consistent with those that are not. The result tends to support the notion that behaviour is inconsistent. Bowers (1973) and Bem and Allen (1974) argue that research on consistency should be correlational rather than experimental because the correlational method preserves individual differences. Bem and Allen tested the hypothesis that "individuals who identify themselves as consistent on a particular trait dimension will in fact be more consistent cross-situationally than those who identify themselves as highly variable" (p. 512). The hypothesis was supported, indicating that some people are consistent on some traits and others are not; further, people themselves know whether or not they are consistent.

After reviewing the literature and the arguments, Pervin (1984) commented:

> Perhaps the conclusion that makes most sense is that most people are consistent in their behavior some of the time and variable in their behavior the rest of the time. . . . In other words, each person can be expected to be consistent in ways that are salient or meaningful for him or her. The areas of consistency differ with different individuals. Thus, for example, for some individuals it may be important to be always honest while for others it may be important to be always dominant. Each individual may have many or few such areas in which there exists cross-situational consistency. Sampling of a large group of individuals on any one characteristic might suggest little cross-situational consistency since it is unlikely that more than a small proportion of the total sample will be consistent in that particular area. The consistency of a subgroup in the population can be masked by the situational specificity of the larger group: this is true for every personality characteristic that is assessed. The conclusion might then be that behavior is situationally specific rather than that behavior is stable in some ways for some individuals and in other ways for other individuals. What appears to be needed is a more differentiated picture of consistency and of the relationship between person and situational determinants. (p. 17)

The information just summarized refutes the position of neither the social cognitive theorist nor the trait theorist (Beaty, Cleveland, & Murphy, 2001). Just as showing consistency of behaviour is no longer a valid argument against social cognitive theory, finding inconsistency in behaviour is not necessarily an argument against trait theory. We saw in chapter 7 that Allport believed the possession of personality traits did not cause a person's behaviour to be fixed and stable. Rather, Allport viewed traits as representing ranges of possible behaviour. He believed differing situations determined which behaviour, in the possible range of behaviours, occurred. Thus Allport's theory was in fact similar to the interactionism of social cognitive theory. The major differences are in Allport's use of the term *trait* and his belief that a person's behaviour must occur within a specified range of possibilities. Also, we saw in chapters 8 and 9 that Cattell and Eysenck believed traits interact with situational variables to produce behaviour in any given situation. Thus none of these theorists believed behaviour was entirely consistent or that it could be predicted on the basis of personality traits alone.

Recent research shows considerable support for the interactionist position. Peter Crocker and Kim Isaak (1997) from the University of Saskatchewan evaluated the consistency of swimmers' coping strategies across three competitions. Analysis of person or situation data alone showed little consistency. Each swimmer appeared to use unique coping patterns for each competition, so that person variables (each swimmer) interacted with situation variables (each competition). Likewise, Robert Gifford and Timothy Gallagher (1985) at the University of Victoria considered whether peer-group sociability was a function of traits, social context, and/or physical setting. Adolescents were asked to discuss various topics in a group setting. Whether they chose to participate in the discussion was a function of dispositions brought to a setting by an individual, the social context of that setting, and the physical arrangement of the setting. In short, the interactionist position appears to be well founded in the empirical arena.

CRITICISMS

Behaviour Is More Consistent Than Social Cognitive Theory Claims.   A great deal of criticism was triggered by Mischel's early book (1968), which seemed to emphasize situation variables almost to the exclusion of person variables and in which he suggested that little consistency exists in human behaviour. Since that time, however, Mischel has accepted an **interactionist** position, in which both the person and the environment are considered important. Also, Mischel claims that his earlier statements about the consistency of behaviour were misunderstood. He notes that he never said *no* consistency existed; if that were the case, he said, memory would have no value (1977, p. 333). Rather, he argued that the amount of consistency predicted by trait and psychoanalytic theories did not exist.

Mental Events Cannot Cause Behaviour.   Radical behaviourists, such as Skinner, take issue with any theory that contains mentalistic concepts. They believe that mental events are irrelevant to understanding human behaviour. Terms like *perceived self-efficacy* and *functional* and *dysfunctional expectancies,* say the radical behaviourists, confuse the study of human behaviour rather than clarify it. Also, say the Skinnerians, *observational learning* is probably just a special case of operant conditioning in which acts of imitation sometimes lead to reinforcement and are thus repeated. Therefore, observational learning is under the control of reinforcement, not independent of it as the social cognitive theorists claim (see for example, Gewirtz, 1971).

Unfair to Psychoanalytic Theory.   The social cognitive theorists have been harshly critical of both traditional psychoanalytic theory and Dollard and Miller's attempt to synthesize psychoanalytic theory and Hullian learning theory. Social cognitive theorists claim that no need exists to employ the nebulous language of psychoanalytic theory because the clearly defined terms from social cognitive theory work as well, if not better. Psychoanalytic theorists believe this position is naive and misses the complex interplay between the conscious and unconscious mind. It is because social cognitive theory does not understand the workings of the human mind, say these critics, that it can only deal with relatively simple psychological problems such as phobias, and with nothing more complex.

Important Aspects of Personality Neglected.   The psychoanalysts criticize social cognitive theory because it does not recognize the importance of unconscious motivation. Another important area neglected by social cognitive theory is development. Other theorists have found that maturational factors are important in determining the emotions people experience and how they process information. Little is said in social cognitive theory about the biological, hormonal, or maturational influences on personality development. Other topics neglected or minimized by social cognitive theory include motivation and conflict. Motivation appears to be covered by the social cognitive theorists mainly in relationship to goal formulation and in the formulation of plans to reach goals. Also the concept of conflict, so important to so many personality theorists (e.g., Freud, and Dollard and Miller), does not appear in the index of Bandura's most comprehensive book (1986).

Social Cognitive Theory Is Not Unified.   Social cognitive theory has been criticized for being neither systematic nor unified. Several important topics have been studied extensively (e.g., the variables governing observational learning, perceived self-efficacy, and the self-regulation of behaviour) but how these topics are related to each other is not clear. The same is true for Mischel's cognitive social learning person variables; they are simply listed and described but little discussion occurs on how they relate to each other, let alone to social cognitive theory in general.

CONTRIBUTIONS

Emphasis on Human Empirical Research.   One reason that social cognitive theory is currently so popular among personality psychologists is that its terms are defined precisely enough to be verified empirically. Bandura and Mischel, and their colleagues, have always been associated with active research programs. Furthermore, Bandura and Mischel have avoided the touchy problem of generalizing research on nonhumans to humans by performing all of their research on humans. Likewise, they have avoided the problem of generalizing from simple behaviour to complex behaviour by doing research on complex behaviour originally. By concentrating on human subjects and on complex behaviour, social cognitive theory avoids many of the criticisms of Skinner's and Dollard and Miller's theories.

Applied Value.   Social cognitive theory has been extremely heuristic. It has provided information about topics of vital importance in today's world: aggression, moral behaviour, delay of gratification, the influence of models (e.g., parents, television, and films) on behaviour, dysfunctional expectancies and how to correct them, self-regulation of behaviour, and the importance of perceived self-efficacy.

For many, the social cognitive theory view of humans as thinking, planning, reasoning, expecting, and reflecting organisms is more realistic than the mechanistic, simplistic view of humans derived from animal research. Social cognitive theory recognizes the importance of language, symbols, and cognitive information-processing mechanisms; the research it generates is usually directed at something relevant; it views humans optimistically; and it emphasizes the importance of the present or the future, rather than the past.

SUMMARY

1. As spokespersons for social cognitive theory, Albert Bandura and Walter Mischel (a) stress cognitive factors in learning and performing, and (b) emphasize that behaviour in any given situation is a function of the characteristics of both the person and the situation. Early in his career, Mischel took both trait and psychoanalytic theories to task; human behaviour was not nearly as consistent as it should be if it was determined by factors thought to exist within the person, such as traits or repressed experiences.

2. Although in 1968 Mischel was basically a situationalist (i.e., believing the probability of reward or punishment was the strongest determinant of behaviour in any given situation), he later became an interactionist, recognizing the importance of both person and situation variables. Bandura labelled the latter position *reciprocal determinism,* or the interplay among the person, the person's behaviour, and the environment. Mischel replaced the traditional person variables such as traits and internal conflicts with cognitive social person variables: encoding strategies, expectancies, subjective values, self-regulatory systems and plans, and competencies.

3. According to social cognitive theory, we learn by either observing the consequences of our own behaviour or observing the consequences of other people's behaviour. Although learning is an almost continuous process, we only translate what we have learned into performance when there is an incentive to do so. Because they believe humans learn through observation, the content of television programs and films are of special interest to social cognitive theorists.

4. According to Bandura, observational learning is influenced by four variables: attentional processes, which determine what we can and do attend to; retentional processes, which determine how experience is encoded in memory; motor reproduction processes, which determine what behaviours can be performed; and motivational processes, which determine the circumstances under which learning is translated into performance.

5. Most human behaviour is, according to social cognitive theory, self-regulated. If one's behaviour meets or exceeds one's own standards, one experiences self-reinforcement; if they do not, one experiences self-punishment. Humans also formulate future goals and then plan to attain them. Usually, future goals are approached via smaller, immediate subgoals. A great deal of self-regulated behaviour is influenced by one's perceived self-efficacy, or one's own view of what one is capable of doing. Those people with high perceived self-efficacy try more, do more, persist longer, and are less anxious than those with low perceived self-efficacy. Moral conduct is governed by internalized moral principles which, if violated, cause a person to experience self-contempt. Self-contempt can be escaped, however, by using one of the self-exonerating mechanisms.

6. The ability to delay gratification develops early in life for some individuals and has a positive influence on later personality characteristics. Like the other variables involved in self-regulated behaviour, the ability to delay gratification is influenced by modelling.

7. Psychological and behavioural problems result from dysfunctional expectancies. Such erroneous expectancies can result from the overgeneralization of negative personal experiences or from modelling. Within social cognitive theory, psychotherapy is seen as a means of changing self-efficacy expectations. Although all forms of modelling have been found effective in treating many types of phobias, live modelling with participation is usually the most effective. Modelling changes a person's perceived self-efficacy, which, in turn, changes behaviour.

8. Social cognitive theory views humans as thoughtful problem solvers dealing with the present while planning for the future. Bandura rejects both the notion that humans are autonomous and the notion that they respond mechanically to external or internal events (hard determinism). Reciprocal determinism portrays humans as capable of reflective, imaginative thought, which, in part, determines a person's behaviour (soft determinism). In this view, the level of personal freedom is determined by the number of options available to a person. Social cognitive theory also recognizes fortuitous experience as a major determinant of human behaviour. Although psychological laws cannot violate the neurophysiological laws that subserve them, social cognitive theory contends that psychological laws must be studied independently of neurophysiological laws.

9. Social cognitive theory is firmly grounded in empirical research but has been criticized for claiming human behaviour is more inconsistent than it actually is; suggesting that mental events can cause behaviour; being too critical of psychoanalytic theory and thus missing the importance of unconscious motivation; neglecting important aspects of personality such as development, motivation, and conflict; and not being a systematic, unified theory. Social cognitive theory has been praised for emphasizing empirical research using human subjects; performing research on complex, socially relevant topics; and for recognizing the many cognitive processes that differentiate humans from non-human animals.

EXPERIENTIAL EXERCISES

1. According to social cognitive theory, most human behaviour is self-regulated. For example, it is claimed that much of our behaviour is guided by internalized performance and moral standards. If performance meets or exceeds these standards we feel good about ourselves, and if it does not we feel bad. Give an example of how such standards guide your behaviour. Do you agree with the social cognitive contention that intrinsic reinforcement has more of an impact on behaviour than extrinsic reinforcement? Explain. Also, attempt to account for the origins of your moral and performance standards.

2. A key concept within social cognitive theory is perceived self-efficacy. Discuss how your *perceptions* of your abilities influence your behaviour. That is, how do they influence what you try, how long you persist, and what you avoid doing? Discuss how you think your perceived self-efficacy originated and the circumstances under which you think it can be changed. Do you agree with the contention of the social cognitive theorists that changing dysfunctional expectancies is largely a matter of changing perceived self-efficacy? Explain.

3. An important concept within social cognitive theory is that of modelling. Describe a person who has acted as an influential model in your life. What important values did you learn from this person? Discuss the topic of observational learning as it applies to this modelling experience.

4. Evaluate your behaviour in terms of consistency. List two of your personality characteristics that have remained stable during the past few years and two that have changed. Also evaluate your consistency across similar situations. For example, do you tend to act the same way at all social events? If not, why not? What conclusion do you reach concerning the consistency of your behaviour?

5. Give an example of each of Mischel's five cognitive social learning person variables as they apply to you. Those variables are encoding strategies; expectancies; subjective values; self-regulatory systems and plans; and competencies.

6. Describe someone you know who has a strong ability to delay gratification (perhaps yourself) and someone you know who has a weaker ability. What are some of the other characteristics that differentiate the two people?

7. Has a chance encounter played a significant role in your life? Explain.

DISCUSSION QUESTIONS

1. What is reciprocal determinism? Give an example.

2. Why, according to social cognitive theory, should we be concerned about the contents of television programs and films?

3. What influences a person's perceived self-efficacy? What are some differences between people with high perceived self-efficacy and people with low perceived self-efficacy?

4. Discuss the major variables to which Mischel and his colleagues found the ability to delay gratification to be related. Provide evidence that the ability to delay gratification early in life is related to positive personality characteristics later in life.

5. Summarize the criticisms that have been made of social cognitive theory. Do you agree or disagree with them?

KEY TERMS

Attentional processes, p. 286
Behaviour-outcome expectancy, p. 280
Cognitive social person variables, p. 280
Competencies, p. 281
Consistency paradox, p. 278
Delay of gratification, p. 293
Delayed modelling, p. 286
Dysfunctional expectancies, p. 294
Encoding strategies, p. 280
Expectancies, p. 280
Extrinsic reinforcement, p. 281
Freedom, p. 297
Interactionist, p. 300
Intrinsic reinforcement, p. 281
Model, p. 282
Motivational processes, p. 287
Motor reproduction processes, p. 287
Observational learning, p. 282
Participant modelling, p. 295
Perceived self-efficacy, p. 281

Performance standards, p. 287
Person variables, p. 278
Personality coefficient, p. 277
Reciprocal determinism, p. 279
Reinforcement, p. 287
Retentional processes, p. 286
Self-control, p. 294
Self-efficacy, p. 288
Self-efficacy expectancy, p. 281
Self-exonerating mechanisms, p. 289
Self-regulated behaviour, p. 287
Self-regulatory systems and plans, p. 281
Situation variables, p. 278
Social cognitive theory, p. 297
Stimulus-outcome expectancy, p. 280
Subjective values, p. 281
Symbolic modelling, p. 295
Systematic desensitization, p. 296
Vicarious punishment, p. 283
Vicarious reinforcement, p. 283

12

Edward O. Wilson
David P. Barash

In 1975, Edward O. Wilson published *Sociobiology: The New Synthesis*, which marked the formal beginning of the discipline of **sociobiology.** In his book, Wilson defines sociobiology as "the systematic study of the biological basis of all social behavior" (1975, p. 4). The major contention of the sociobiologists is that certain social behaviours have been selected by evolution because they contribute to the biological fitness of those who engage in them. In other words, just as various bodily structures and physiological processes are the products of the natural selection that has occurred in our evolutionary past, so too are patterns of social behaviour.

Although this chapter discusses the work of several authors, it features the works of Edward O. Wilson and David P. Barash.

Biographical Sketches

Edward O. Wilson

EDWARD O. WILSON

Wilson was born in Birmingham, Alabama on June 10, 1929. He was an only child. Wilson had many colourful relatives. On his father's side, the men were mainly ship owners and river pilots, although his grandfather was a railroad engineer. During the Civil War, his paternal great-grandfather (William "Black Bill" Wilson) used his ship to smuggle guns past a federal blockade until he was captured by Admiral Farragut and sent to prison in Tampa (Wilson, 1994, pp. 65–66). On his mother's side, his relatives were mainly farmers from northern Alabama.

Wilson's mother and father divorced when he was seven, and he was raised by his father and stepmother. His father was a federal employee whose job required him to move frequently. Between the first and twelfth grades Wilson attended 16 schools. The numerous school changes, along with the fact that Wilson skipped third grade because of exceptional performance, steered him in the direction of his later career choice. Because he was a perpetual newcomer, without siblings, and younger than his classmates, he took to the woods and fields, where he found surrogate companionship in the organisms he discovered and studied there (Wilson, 1985, p. 465).

Wilson fell in love with the outdoors and the organisms found there; he could easily have become a zoologist if it were not for a childhood accident. At the age of seven he lost the sight in his right eye by accidentally jerking a fish fin into it. As a result of his monocular vision, he found it difficult to locate birds and mammals in the field. The vision in his left eye, however, became, and remains, exceptionally acute. "I am the last to spot a hawk sitting in a tree, but I can examine the hairs and contours of an insect's body without the aid of a magnifying glass" (Wilson, 1985, p. 466).

Wilson was also slightly hearing impaired. So, not only was he unable to see various species of birds, he was also unable to hear their songs. Thus it was Wilson's love of nature combined with his monocular vision and his hearing difficulty that led him in the direction of entomology (the study of insects).

Wilson majored in biology at the University of Alabama, where he obtained his BS in 1949 and his MS in 1950. He received his Ph.D. in biology from Harvard in 1955. Wilson joined the Harvard faculty in 1956, was promoted to full professor in 1964, and became Frank B. Baird, Jr., Professor of Science in 1976. He was given the National Medal of Science by President Carter in 1977. In *The Insect Societies* (1971), Wilson attempted to explain the behaviour of social insects using principles from physiology, population biology, and evolutionary theory. Wilson's evolutionary analysis was applied specifically to ants in *The Ants* (1990), co-authored with Bert Hölldobler. This book was awarded a Pulitzer Prize in 1991, the first book with a primarily scientific content to do so (Wilson, 1994, p. 306). This was Wilson's second Pulitzer Prize. Wilson extended his evolutionary analysis to all organisms in *Sociobiology: The New Synthesis* (1975). Only the last chapter of Wilson's 1975 book pertained to humans, whereas in *On Human Nature* (1978) Wilson focused exclusively on human social behaviour. Wilson was awarded his first Pulitzer Prize for *On Human Nature* in 1979. He is currently the curator in entomology at the Museum of Comparative Zoology at Harvard. As of July 1987, Wilson had authored or coauthored 10 books and about 310 technical articles focusing mainly on social insects and evolutionary theory. Barash (1982) says affectionately of Wilson, "Long before jogging became a national fad, E. O. Wilson was an enthusiastic runner—both with his legs and with new concepts in evolutionary biology" (p. 5).

The many colourful details of Wilson's life are reported in his delightful autobiography (Wilson, 1994).

DAVID P. BARASH

David P. Barash

Barash was born in New York City on January 9, 1946. He obtained his BA in biology in 1966 from the State University of New York (SUNY) Binghamton (then known as Harpur College), and his MA in 1968 and his Ph.D. in 1970 from the University of Wisconsin. Barash taught for three years at SUNY, Oneonta, before moving to the University of Washington in 1973, where he has been ever since. Barash is currently professor of psychology at the University of Washington.

Barash's books *The Whisperings Within: Evolution and the Origin of Human Nature* (1979), and *Sociobiology and Behavior* (2nd ed., 1982) have done much to extend and popularize sociobiology. In the foreword of the latter book, E. O. Wilson said, "*Sociobiology and Behavior* is the best introductory textbook available on the subject, and it is not likely to be surpassed in the near future" (p. xi). One of Barash's major concerns is with specifying the problems that result when cultural evolution proceeds at a much faster rate than biological evolution. This concern is addressed in his book *The Hare and the Tortoise: Culture, Biology, and Human Nature* (1986). The "hare" is fast-moving cultural evolution, and the "tortoise" is slow-moving biological evolution. Barash believes that much of what is wrong with humanity today stems from the incompatibility between human culture and human biology. "This incongruity (literally: an inability to fit), between our biology, which has evolved by the laborious process of natural selection, and our culture, which has appeared with explosive speed through cultural evolution, is the root of nearly every human difficulty" (p. 60). Barash is especially concerned with the problems that result when prenuclear thought processes and brain mechanisms are used to deal with a world in which nuclear weapons are a reality. With his psychiatrist wife, Judith Eve Lipton, Barash wrote *Stop Nuclear War! A Handbook* (1982) and *The Caveman and the Bomb: Human Nature, Evolution, and Nuclear War* (1985). More recently he has published *The Arms Race and Nuclear War* (1987).

Darwin's Theory of Evolution

Because to a large extent, sociobiology is an effort to apply Darwinian evolutionary theory to the explanation of human social behaviour, we spend a moment here reviewing Darwinian theory.

Darwin (1859) observed that all species of living organisms are capable of producing more offspring than environmental resources can support. When this happens a **struggle for survival** occurs. Because individual differences exist among members of a species in terms of the traits necessary for survival, only those members possessing traits allowing **adaptation** (successful adjustment) to the environment survive and reproduce. If the traits that allow adaptation to an environment are at least partially heritable, the offspring of parents who previously survived in that environment will also tend to possess traits conducive to survival. This tendency will continue to be true as long as the environment does not radically change. The term **survival of the fittest** refers to the fact that only those members of a species who are best adapted to their environment survive and reproduce. **Fitness,** then, is measured by an organism's ability to survive and reproduce, and nothing else. Crawford (1987) cautioned us not to confuse fitness with social standing: "It is essential to distinguish biological fitness from social standing. Michelangelo, Isaac Newton, and Leonardo da Vinci had zero reproductive fitness since they apparently did not leave offspring. However, their social standing is beyond question" (p. 16). Also fitness is often equated with such factors as physical size, strength, or aggressiveness. As we have just seen, however, an organism's fitness is determined only by its ability to survive and reproduce in a given environment, and this ability often involves complex behaviour patterns that are anything but aggressive. As we shall see, the tendencies to like and eat ripe fruit, to love children, and to cooperate with fellow humans can all be fitness enhancing, but none involves aggression. Within Darwinian theory, any anatomic structure, physiological process, or pattern of behaviour is said to be adaptive if it contributes to an organism's ability to survive and reproduce. The term **natural selection** refers to the fact that only organisms possessing adaptive traits in a given environment are "selected" to survive and reproduce. Naturally selected characteristics, then, are those that increase the chances of survival in the struggle for existence.

INCLUSIVE FITNESS

When Darwin published his theory of evolution he knew nothing about genes. All he knew was that organisms possessing adaptive characteristics tended to leave more organisms like themselves in future generations than organisms possessing fewer adaptive characteristics. For Darwin, fitness was assessed by counting the number of offspring produced by an organism. If Darwin had known about genes he might have defined fitness in terms of the number of genes (or more accurately, replicas of genes) that an organism leaves in subsequent generations. The difference between defining fitness in terms of offspring or in terms of gene replicas is highly significant. It is true the most direct way to perpetuate our genes is to produce offspring, but it is not the only way because our offspring are not the only persons carrying our genes. Our brothers and sisters, nieces and nephews, and aunts and uncles also carry our genes. Thus, in addition to producing offspring, another way of perpetuating our genes is to help our relatives survive and reproduce.

It is this expanded theory of evolution that is accepted by sociobiology. Instead of concentrating exclusively on a person's ability to survive and create offspring (fitness), sociobiology concentrates on the many other ways that a person can increase the probability of copies of his or her genes being represented in subsequent generations. This expanded notion of gene reproduction is called **inclusive fitness**. Although suggested by others earlier, including Darwin himself (1859, pp. 250–257), it was most fully developed in two highly influential papers by W. D. Hamilton (1964). Silverman (1987) describes inclusive fitness as "undoubtedly the most heuristic, sociobiological principle of the past two decades" (p. 214).

Basic Assumptions of Sociobiology

PERPETUATION OF THE GENES

According to the sociobiologists, whether we know it or not, our primary goal in life is to perpetuate copies of our genes into the next generation, which was also true of our ancestors. It is because of the natural selection of genes that we now possess the types of brains, minds, bodies, and behavioural tendencies we do. As Barash (1979) put it, "Genes need not know what they are doing in order to function effectively, and—here is the painful part—neither need we. We can spend a whole lifetime serving their purposes without ever knowing it" (p. 25).

This assumption, then, underlies all of sociobiology: *We live to pass copies of our genes into the next generation.* Everything we do serves this goal or, if not, is deleterious to us. Those experiences that are neither biologically helpful nor harmful are irrelevant. One may argue, however, that life seems to involve more than doing those things necessary to perpetuate copies of one's genes. Perhaps it just *seems* that way. Wallace (1979) comments:

> So what does all this make us? Genetic caretakers? Temporary housings for chromosomes? Slaves to tiny, coiled molecules that operate us by remote control? Ponderous robots, full of rationalizations, explanations, superstitions, and excuses but blindly following the Reproductive Imperative? What about the fact that we are learning classical guitar? That we have an interest in tap dancing and may start lessons soon? That we are very tidy and responsible and hold darned good jobs? That we have read Camus and don't pronounce the "s"? That we have good, really good, friends? That we are fine people and our parents are proud of us? How about all that? Chromosomes make us do all that? "No," comes the answer from the mountain, "but they don't care if you do"—*as long as* it doesn't interfere with your reproduction. Being such a splendid person may even help you find a mate more easily and leave *more* genes. (p. 183)

NATURAL SELECTION SHAPES SOCIAL BEHAVIOUR

A second basic assumption of sociobiology is that evolution selects certain patterns of social behaviour just as it selects certain anatomic structures or physiological mechanisms. Lumsden and Wilson (1981) say, "The central tenet of sociobiology is that social behaviours are shaped by natural selection" (p. 99). The assumption is that complex social behaviours such as courting, associating with friends, and caring for children can be as much related to fitness as are certain anatomical or physiological characteristics. That is, people who are *socially* effective are more adaptive than those who are not. If this assumption is correct, it means that much of our current social behaviour is engaged in because similar behaviour was adaptive for our ancestors.

This sociobiological view of human social behaviour may be disturbing to some, but the fact that it is disturbing does not mean it is necessarily incorrect and should be rejected. Any objective seeker of truth cannot disregard facts simply because they are not to his or her liking. Barash (1979) comments:

> We human beings like to think we are different. We introspect, we are confident that we know what we are doing, and why. But we may have to open our minds and admit the possibility that our need to maximize our fitness may be whispering somewhere deep within us and that, know it or not, most of the time we are heeding these whisperings. (p. 31)

On the other hand, the disturbing quality of sociobiology does not mean it is necessarily correct either. Objective inquirers will weigh the actual evidence offered to support or refute sociobiology (or any other theory), and arrange their beliefs accordingly.

Nature of Human Nature

A theory of human nature attempts to describe what it means to be human. Theories of human nature are extremely important within the realm of personality theory because every theory of personality accepts a theory of human nature either explicitly or implicitly. Here we discuss only two theories of human nature: the empirical and the sociobiological.

EMPIRICAL THEORY

The **empirical theory of human nature** maintains that what characterizes a person at any given time is a function of what that person has experienced in his or her lifetime. Although John Locke (1631–1704) was not the first to offer an empirical view of human nature, his was among the most clearly articulated. According to Locke, except for a few innate faculties such as the ability to reflect upon experience, the mind is essentially a *tabula rasa* (a blank tablet) at birth, and experience writes on that tablet. For Locke, what you become as a person depends on what you experience. According to this view, there is no human nature: environment is all-important in determining human behaviour. Other than this capacity to become whatever you experience, we come equipped with *no* inherited predispositions. In chapter 9 we noted that J. B. Watson believed if he could control the environments of healthy infants he could make them into any type of adult he chose. Other learning theorists, for example, Dollard and Miller, and Skinner, claimed behaviour is controlled by the reinforcement contingencies found in the environment. Reinforcement theorists also accept an empirical theory of human nature because they believe that if one changes the environment (reinforcement contingencies) one changes the person.

SOCIOBIOLOGICAL THEORY

The sociobiologists strongly disagree with the empirical theory of human nature. Their entire theory is built on the assumption that the human mind is not a blank tablet at birth. Instead, they view the mind as programmed by evolution to influence its possessor to act in certain ways and not in others. For example, children of all cultures develop language and motor skills. All cultures have customs for caring for children, some sort of religion, and a taboo against incest. Sociobiologists are interested in **cultural universals** because they assume if a category of social behaviour appears in every culture, chances are good it is genetically influenced. Such a category of behaviour could not have been transmitted from one culture to another because, in many cases, no way could have existed for cultures to communicate with each other. Exactly how a particular category of experience is responded to may vary from culture to culture, but the category itself is responded to in some way and is therefore a cultural universal. Barash (1979) explains:

> Human beings are, after all, still human beings, and as such, there is a certain range within which their behaviour will fall. They may develop distinctive customs of dress and adornment, perhaps parrot feathers in one place, strange patterns of head shaving in another, the ritual carving of deep scars on cheeks and foreheads in yet another, but some pattern of dress and adornment is always found. Similarly, marriage in one place might be sanctified by a ceremonial sharing of food, or maybe by the union of menstrual blood with semen, or by the payment of tokens from one partner to the other or by signing a document and uttering officially approved words, but some ritualized sanctioning of male-female association seems almost always to take place. . . . While it is true that culture makes people, people also make cultures, and there is much to gain by looking at what remains the same about people underneath their customs and habits. (pp. 4–5)

Biogrammar.   According to Barash (1979, p. 10), just as a grammar structures our verbal behaviour, a **biogrammar** structures our social behaviour. The rules of grammar allow ideas to be expressed in many ways without the essential meaning of those ideas being lost. Biogrammar allows innate social behavioural tendencies to be expressed in many ways without the essential function of that behaviour being lost. People may learn different languages in different cultures but *the capacity for humans to learn some language* is universal.

The sociobiologists believe social science has provided little information as to why people act as they do, and the reason for this failure is social science's widespread acceptance of the empirical theory of human nature. For the sociobiologists, the empirical view of human nature has not been informative, heuristic, or flattering:

> If we maintain that there is no "us" located inside, beneath or beyond our customs, we are in danger of missing ourselves altogether. For anyone concerned about human dignity I would happily recommend a sociobiological recognition of human nature grounded in evolution over the extreme social science view that people are merely empty shells waiting for culture to fill them up, ghostly actors waiting for their lines. (Barash, 1979, p. 13)

So, for the sociobiologists, a human nature indeed exists. During our long evolutionary past, those of our ancestors who possessed genes that caused them to engage in adaptive behaviour survived and reproduced. The genes that caused adaptive behaviour were perpetuated; those that did not were not. Thus, according to the **sociobiological theory of human nature** each human being is well endowed at birth with the genetically determined behavioural tendencies that allowed his or her ancestors to perpetuate their genes.

PROXIMATE VERSUS ULTIMATE CAUSATION

What one seeks and accepts as a cause of behaviour varies with one's conception of human nature. Those who accept the empirical theory of human nature tend to seek the causes of an organism's behaviour in its immediate environment, its current motivational state, its memories of past experiences, or in some combination of the three. These environmental, physiological, and experiential factors constitute the **proximate causation** of behaviour. Social scientists tend to explain human behaviour in terms of proximate causation. For example, in answer to the question, What causes learning? the learning theorist might say that learning occurs when, in a given environmental situation, an organism does something that produces a result it wants, or that learning occurs when two stimuli are consistently experienced together.

In contrast, the sociobiologists attempt to explain why a characteristic was selected and maintained by evolutionary pressures. That is, the sociobiologists seek to discover the adaptive significance of various behaviours, sensory capabilities, and physiological mechanisms. Why, they ask, does the human body maintain its temperature within certain limits? Why do humans, and other animals, have the ability to learn from experience? Why are some experiences learned more easily than others? Why, for example, are some phobias so easy to learn and so difficult to forget? Why do some species of animals learn with ease what other species learn with great difficulty or not at all? Why can we see some colours, hear some sounds, taste some tastes, smell some odours, and not others? Why do we tend to love children, especially our own? By seeking the evolutionary significance of abilities and behaviours, sociobiologists are seeking their **ultimate causation**.

The sociobiologists believe, however, that a complete explanation of behaviour must involve both proximate and ultimate explanations. It is important to know under what circumstances a behaviour occurs in an organism's lifetime (proximate causation), but it is equally important to know why that behaviour potential exists in that organism's behavioural repertoire to begin with (ultimate causation).

WHY ARE SOME BEHAVIOURS "SWEETER" THAN OTHERS?

In *The Whisperings Within* (1979) Barash addresses the question, Why is sugar sweet?

> The reason is clear enough: we are primates, and some of our ancestors spent a great deal of time in trees, where they ate a great deal of fruit. Ripe fruit is more nutritious than unripe, and one thing about ripe fruit is that it contains sugars. It doesn't take much imagination to reconstruct the evolutionary sequence that selected for a strong preference among our distant ancestors for the taste that characterized ripe fruit. Genes that influenced their carriers to eat ripe fruit and reject the unripe ultimately made more copies of themselves than did those that were less discriminating. (Barash, 1979, p. 39)

Now we address the more crucial question: Why are some *behaviours* "sweeter" than others? Why, under certain circumstances, does acting one way feel better, more natural, or more satisfying than acting in other ways? For example, why do we cooperate with others, why do males tend to be more aggressive than females, why do men find younger women more attractive, and why are women left with most of the work of looking after children? The answer to this more crucial question forms the heart of sociobiology. Sociobiologists answer that our evolutionary past has genetically programmed us to respond to certain situations with any one of a certain range of possible responses. Those behaviours compatible with our biogrammar will be sweet, those incompatible will not be. Barash puts the matter as follows: "The process of evolution, operating on human beings, has produced a creature for whom certain behaviors just don't go at all, whereas others go very well indeed" (1979, p. 11). According to the sociobiologists, then, those behaviours we find sweet are those that increased the fitness of our ancestors. Sweetness and fitness go hand in hand. For example, it is sweet for us to love our children and for them to love us, but why is it sweet? Barash (1979) answers:

> Here we are back in the realm of evolutionary events, where human inclinations are so often revealed as the handmaidens of fitness. We love our children "because" it is adaptive for us to do so. Love of parent for child is an evolutionary stratagem insuring that parents will invest in the child in a manner that maximizes each parent's fitness. The child, of course, is equally motivated to love its parents "because" such an attachment to appropriate adults enhances its own chances of ultimate evolutionary success. In other words, parental and filial love, solicitude and care are ultimately selfish. (p. 94)

All of the usual reasons given by parents for loving their children, such as because they are so cute, or helpless, or because it feels good to love them, constitute proximate causes of parental love. The ultimate cause, however, is the fact that surviving offspring perpetuate the genes of the parents.

According to the sociobiologists, then, any behaviour that increases a person's inclusive fitness will be preferred over other behaviours. If this sounds selfish it is because it *is* selfish. It is assumed that everything living organisms do—humans included—is selfish.

What Is Inherited?

It is extremely important to note that the sociobiologists do not say that genes are the only cause of human social behaviour, or even that they are the primary cause. Rather, they say we inherit behavioural *tendencies,* and that these tendencies are always modified by culture. Social behaviour, then, is always the result of the interaction between biological and cultural influences. For the title of his book, *The Whisperings Within* (1979), Barash chose the term **whisperings** (rather than *shoutings, yellings, cravings,* or *urges*) to describe our inherited predispositions. A whisper is a slight biological push to act in some general way as opposed to others. It is even possible for culture to inhibit many of these behavioural tendencies altogether. The sociobiologists do not draw a direct cause-and-effect relationship between genes and behaviour. What the genes provide, according to the sociobiologists, is not a strict **biological determinism** but a **behavioural potentiality**.

Our biogrammar, then, provides only a general game plan for social behaviour. A genetic tendency exists to adorn one's body but how it is adorned is culturally determined. A genetic tendency exists to learn a language but which language one learns is culturally determined. A genetic tendency exists to attend to a child's needs but how children are reared is culturally determined. Of course, people *can* behave competitively, men *can* judge older women as attractive, and men *can* be passive and nurturing to children.

The sociobiologists fully appreciate the contributions of both biology and culture in determining human social behaviour. Barash (1979) urges all who attempt to explain such behaviour to avoid "nothing butism," which is

> the notion that just because we are animals we are nothing but animals. And, again, the opposite is equally misleading: beware the notion that we are "nothing but" the products of social learning. For too long social science and biological science have pursued "nothing but" approaches. Sociobiology may just help redress that imbalance. (p. 45)

Relationship between Biology and Culture

INNATE TENDENCY TO CREATE CULTURE

According to the sociobiologists, one of our whisperings predisposes us to create and participate in a culture of some sort. Barash (1979) says, "Culture is, in fact, one of our most important biological adaptations, and it therefore need not be opposed to biology. In behaving culturally, we are also behaving biologically. Our culture is natural to us, just as quills are natural to a porcupine" (p. 221).

LIMITATIONS OF CULTURE AS A MODIFIER OF HUMAN BEHAVIOUR

Culture is a powerful modifier of human behaviour, but it is not all-powerful. The range of behaviours that can occur within a category of social behaviour is often vast, but a range still exists. In other words, our biological heritage places a limit on the extent to which our behaviour is modifiable by culture. Wilson (1978) warns what might happen if we try to live in accordance with social systems that are too incompatible with our biological nature:

> It is inconceivable that human beings could be socialized into the radically different repertoires of other groups such as fishes, birds, antelopes, or rodents. Human beings might self-consciously *imitate* such arrangements, but it would be a fiction played out on a stage, would run counter to deep emotional responses and have no chance of persisting through as much as a single generation. To adopt with serious intent, even

in broad outline, the social system of a nonprimate species would be insanity in the literal sense. Personalities would quickly dissolve, relationships disintegrate, and reproduction cease. (pp. 21–22)

Leash Principle.   In fact, our biogrammar normally functions to keep culture compatible with our biological makeup. This is because we are genetically predisposed to seek experiences and establish institutions that enhance our genetic fitness. Wilson (1980) describes his **leash principle**: "The genes hold culture on a leash. In some categories of behaviour—eating, voiding, and the basic facial expressions, the predisposition toward sexual behavior—the leash is short and tight. In others—the form of dress, religious ritual, artistic expression—it is very long and flexible" (p. 64). For example, all societies care for children, but this care is provided in many ways: babies may be held close to the mother's body most of the day, strapped to a board, or put in a playpen; young children may be expected to play at their mother's feet, help with household tasks, run and climb, or sit straight at school desks; a child approaching puberty may be considered still a child in one society and a marriageable worker in another. But all these customs have the common elements of nurturing children and teaching them the ways of their culture. We have more to say about the leash principle when we discuss mind-body relationships shortly.

Hypertrophy.   One way for biology and culture to be incompatible is for biology to be *over*represented in culture. The tendency for a relatively weak biological tendency to be amplified out of proportion in culture is what Wilson calls **hypertrophy**. Wilson (1978) defines hypertrophy as "the cultural inflation of innate human properties" (p. 172). Wilson (1978) believes that civilization itself exemplifies hypertrophy: "In my opinion the key to the emergence of civilization is *hypertrophy,* the extreme growth of preexisting structures . . . the basic social responses of the hunter-gatherers have metamorphosed from relatively modest environmental adaptation into unexpectedly elaborate, even monstrous forms in more advanced societies" (p. 92). For example, the relative vulnerability of women and their connection to childbearing may tend to keep them closer to home than men. But from that slight evolutionary difference, the society of Victorian England crafted a complex and highly constraining set of rules about where a lady was allowed to be, in what company, and what dress, and what she was allowed to say.

What Wilson calls hypertrophy Barash (1986) calls **cultural hyperextension**, about which Barash says, "Rather than setting itself in opposition to innate human inclinations, culture often seeks to mimic and extend these inclinations, in the process outdoing nature itself and going too far" (p. 58). According to Barash (1986), the male physical and behavioural traits that led to male domination over females were selected because, at the time, male aggressiveness, competitiveness, and defence of the family enhanced male fitness. Under current circumstances, however, these traits are essentially obsolete. Barash (1986) elaborates:

We are stuck, saddled with an outdated biological system, rendered anachronistic by our rapidly evolving culture, and unacceptable by our expanding social consciousness. We possess physical characteristics and behaviours such as male dominance and aggressiveness that are offensive, inappropriate, and often downright dangerous. . . . It seems especially likely that society, seizing on a degree of evolutionary reality, has hyperextended it, making awkward, unjust, and offensive cultural mountains out of what may, in essence, be biological molehills. Men and women are indeed different, but in most cases they are less different than human social traditions have demanded them to be. Give cultural evolution a hand in such cases, and it takes the whole arm, ultimately, perhaps, to the detriment of all concerned. (pp. 105–106)

Human biology, then, can be underrepresented in culture, and it can be over-represented; in either case, problems can result.

MIND-BODY RELATIONSHIP

As we noted in chapter 1, determining how the mind and body are related has been a persistent problem throughout the history of psychology. As you may recall, the problem is determining how something purely mental (for example, consciousness, ideas, awareness, or rationality) can result from something purely physical (for example, the brain). Unlike most who study human behaviour the sociobiologists tackle the mind-body problem enthusiastically. Barash (1979) says:

> The mind-body problem is an ancient one: a tremendous gap seems to exist between our unique, personal thoughts and emotions on the one hand and the cells, chemicals and electrical circuits that make up our brains on the other. Yet the human mind—its conscious as well as its unconscious aspects, its thoughts as well as its emotions—springs somehow from the concrete, impersonal human brain, and that brain is the product of evolution. . . . Our bodies . . . are the vehicles created by our genes in the service of themselves. And our minds are among the devices that serve to control those bodies. Both the cellular structure of the brain and the psychic structure of consciousness are the results of millions of generations of evolution, during which genes that were more successful at reproducing themselves prospered at the expense of those that were less adept. Our genes have programmed us and every other living thing to do what is best for them. Our minds are likely to serve that ultimate end no less than are our hands or our kidneys. (pp. 199–200)

Epigenetic Rules.   In *Genes, Mind, and Culture: The Coevolutionary Process* (1981) Lumsden and Wilson describe how they believe the genes influence the mind. It is postulated that environmental experience is filtered through and mediated by innate **epigenetic rules** before one cognitively experiences and acts on environmental information. Lumsden and Wilson (1981) discuss two types of epigenetic rules: *primary epigenetic rules*, which determine what types of sensory experiences and perceptions we can have; and *secondary epigenetic rules,* which determine how those sensations and perceptions are evaluated and responded to emotionally. Both levels of information processing are the product of evolution and therefore have adaptive significance. The first level, for example, determines what can be a biological stimulus for a human being. Primary epigenetic rules determine what can be seen, heard, smelled, tasted, and felt. Secondary epigenetic rules determine which of those sensations or perceptions are attended to, retained, learned, and responded to with an appropriate emotional response. Secondary epigenetic rules also determine what courses of action, if any, will be taken in response to various sensations or perceptions.

According to Lumsden and Wilson (1981), it is the epigenetic rules (mainly the secondary ones) that hold culture on a leash. Because they are innate in all humans, the epigenetic rules will always make some decisions, evaluations, emotional responses, learning experiences, and memories more likely than others. Wilson (1980) says, "Long-term defections from the innate censors and motivators of the brain can only produce an ultimate dissatisfaction of the spirit and eventually social instability and massive losses in genetic fitness" (p. 69).

Elsewhere, Lumsden and Wilson (1983) say, "The human genes prescribe the epigenetic rules, which channel behavior toward the characteristic human forms of thought" (p. 83). This means that "the genes and culture are inseverably linked. Changes in one inevitably force changes in the other, resulting in what we have termed gene-culture coevolution" (Lumsden & Wilson, 1983, p. 117). In other words, "Culture is created and shaped by biological processes while the biological processes are simultaneously altered in response to culture change" (Lumsden & Wilson, 1983, p. 118). This brings us back to the leash principle, "Gene-culture coevolution expanded the human mind but did not, could not, and perhaps *should* not fully emancipate it. . . . People are neither genetically determined nor culturally determined. They are something in between, a much more interesting circumstance" (Lumsden & Wilson, 1983, pp. 83–84).

Prepared Learning.   Among other things, the secondary epigenetic rules predispose humans to learn some experiences more easily than others. The fact we are biologically disposed to learn with ease those experiences that enhance fitness is referred to as **prepared learning.** Thus we readily learn the rules and regulations that characterize our culture, we learn a language, we learn incest avoidance, we learn those qualities necessary to attract a mate, and we learn to distrust strangers. The development of phobias also exemplifies prepared learning:

> The preparedness of human learning is most clearly manifested in the case of phobias, which are fears defined by a combination of several traits. They are first of all extreme in response. . . . They typically emerge full-blown after only a single negative reinforcement [and] they are exceptionally difficult to extinguish. . . . It is a remarkable fact that the phenomena that evoke these reactions consistently (closed spaces, heights, thunderstorms, running water, snakes, and spiders) include some of the greatest dangers present in mankind's ancient environment, while guns, knives, automobiles, electric sockets, and other far more dangerous perils of technologically advanced societies are rarely effective. It is reasonable to conclude that phobias are the extreme cases of irrational fear reactions that gave an extra margin needed to ensure survival during the genetic evolutions of human epigenetic rules. Better to crawl away from a cliff, nauseated with fear, than to casually walk its edge. (Lumsden & Wilson, 1981, pp. 84–85)

Altruism

Countless examples exist to illustrate the seemingly selfless nature of people helping family and friends, but also of helping complete strangers in times of need. Power line engineers from the Prairies and the United States came out to Montreal to speed the reconnection of downed power lines in the aftermath of the Ice Storm in January 1998. Hundreds of firefighters lost their lives trying to rescue victims in the New York Trade Tower attacks in September, 2001. If human behaviour is ultimately selfish, why do we spend so much time doing things that benefit our fellow humans? Is the unselfish, or altruistic, nature of these actions illusory? According to the sociobiologists the answer is yes, it is illusory. Barash (1979) says, "Real, honest-to-God altruism simply doesn't occur in nature" (p. 135). This statement does not mean that people do not help each other; clearly they do. According to the sociobiologists, however, they do so for reasons that are ultimately selfish. The sociobiologists discuss two types of **altruism:** one that involves blood relatives (kin) and one that does not.

KIN ALTRUISM

Darwin's theory emphasized an organism's ability to adapt to its environment and to successfully reproduce. The sociobiologists have emphasized, however, the fact that because our relatives possess copies of many of our genes, we have reason to be concerned for their survival and reproduction. The greater the degree of genetic relatedness, the deeper will be our concern and the greater will be our willingness to help them. As Wilson (1994) says, "You may be willing to risk your life for a brother, for example, but the most you are likely to give a third cousin is a piece of advice" (p. 318). The offering of help to genetic relatives is called **kin altruism.** This is not true altruism because, in looking out for our relatives, we are actually looking out for ourselves (or more accurately, for our genes).

As we saw earlier, when fitness is viewed as perpetuating our genes into future generations by producing offspring or by helping relatives survive and reproduce, it is called *inclusive fitness.* When a person's genes are perpetuated (or selected) because that person confers advantages on his or her relatives, the process is called **kin selection.** Thus kin selection is accomplished through kin altruism. **Nepotism** is another term for kin altruism. Both terms refer to the tendency to show favouritism toward one's relatives. Whether it is guard bees allowing closer family relations into the hive ahead of distant relations or an uncle offering you a job in the company, we take care of family in many ways. Because this tendency is culturally universal the sociobiologists suggest that it has a biological basis.

RECIPROCAL ALTRUISM

Of course, the firefighters in New York and the power line engineers in Montreal were not related to the people they were helping. But in everyday life, we help strangers in many ways—we tell them the time, we give them directions, we help look for a lost child or contact lens, we might even given them money. Altruism among nonrelatives is called **reciprocal altruism** (Trivers, 1971), and it is based on the evolutionary fact that humans who cooperate with one another have a better chance of surviving than those who do not. In primitive times, humans who cooperated in the hunting of large animals or in defending their village had a better chance of surviving than those who did not. Reciprocal altruism is based on the assumption that if I help you, you, at some time in the future, will help me. With reciprocal altruism you "do unto others as you would have others do unto you," and you are willing to "scratch my back" if you are convinced that someday I will scratch yours. The person returning the help may be the same one who received it (*direct reciprocity*) or it may be returned by someone else in the social group (*indirect reciprocity*). Indirect reciprocity is more likely to occur within a social system in which helping others is encouraged by rules and regulations, and accepting help without offering it to others (cheating) is actively discouraged or punished.

Cheating.   With reciprocal altruism there is always the possibility that **cheating** will occur. That is, someone will take and not give, or someone will take more than he or she gives. Barash (1979) elaborates:

> A system of this sort is vulnerable, as any good con man knows. Why not take the altruism from another, then refuse to pay it back? If this happens, genes for altruism are at a disadvantage, since they incur a cost but no benefit. And cheaters gain doubly, since they profit once from the others' altruism and again by never incurring the cost of repayment. Perhaps crime does pay.
>
> Of course, the evolutionary process can be as calculating as the cheater, maybe more so. If selfish individuals are cheating in a reciprocal system, selection would favour those altruists who could discriminate true reciprocators from those who had cheated the last time around. It could become a never-ending spiral: greater care by

would-be reciprocators selects for greater slyness on the part of the cheaters, which in turn selects for greater discrimination by the altruists, and so on. Where does it all lead? Just look around. (pp. 158–159)

Thus, according to the sociobiologists, we agree to help our close relatives because in doing so we promote our own fitness, and we agree to help nonrelatives because we expect that they, or other members of the community, will help us in return. In neither case is true altruism (giving help and expecting nothing in return) involved. True altruism, however, seems to occur on some occasions. What about the famous Japanese kamikaze pilots who flew to their deaths by diving into American ships during World War II? Because these pilots sacrificed their lives for their country, should one consider their actions truly altruistic? Before deciding, Barash (1979, p. 168) asks that the following facts be considered: The kamikazes were promised eternal life if they died for their country, they were given national recognition and special privileges (including sexual privileges), and their families gained status. Also, when the moment for self-sacrifice came, if they refused to fly they were shot. If they did take off they had no parachute and only enough gasoline to make it to their target. Barash (1979) concludes, "Perhaps there is a question here whether the bargain these men were making was a fully altruistic one" (p. 168).

Male and Female Criteria for Mate Selection

As should be clear by now, the sociobiologists believe the master motive for every living organism (including humans) is to perpetuate copies of its genes into the next generation. A major variable determining whether one's genes will be perpetuated is mate selection. The question here is, do men and women choose mates in the same way and for the same reasons? The answer, according to the sociobiologists, is that they do not. Although the major goal of both males and females is to produce healthy offspring successfully, they use different strategies in attempting to reach that goal because of the biological differences between them. What happens when a man and a woman copulate? Wallace (1979) facetiously describes the experience from the man's viewpoint: "A male can make up the energy expended in a sexual episode by eating a grape. His cost is low, and—who knows?—perhaps it will result in a child for him" (p. 74). If pregnancy does result from copulation, however, the consequences for the woman are enormous. Barash (1979) explains:

Eggs are fertilized by sperm, not vice versa. And women become pregnant, not men. It is the woman who must produce a placenta and nourish her unborn child; who must undergo the metabolic and hormonal stresses of pregnancy; who must carry around an embryo that grows in bulk and weight, making her more and more ungainly as her pregnancy advances; and who, when the child is born, must nurse it.

Because women become pregnant, they simply cannot produce as many children as can men. We may regret this fact, glory in it or simply accept it, but it remains, nevertheless, an indelible part of our biology. (p. 47)

What does all this have to do with male and female criteria for mate selection? A lot! Women have a much greater stake in any one reproductive act than men do:

In virtually all species males are selected to be aggressive—sexual advertisers—while females are selected to be choosier—comparison shoppers. Again, these behaviours follow directly from the biology of what it is to be male or female. For males, reproduction is easy, a small amount of time, a small amount of semen, and the potential evolutionary return is very great if offspring are produced. On the other hand, a female who makes a "bad" choice may be in real evolutionary trouble. If fertilization occurs, a baby is begun, and the ensuing process is not only inexorable but immensely demanding. . . . Small wonder that females in virtually every species are more discriminating than males in the choice of sexual partners. . . . For males, a very different strategy applies. The maximum advantage goes to individuals with fewer inhibitions. A genetically influenced tendency to "play fast and loose"—"love 'em and leave 'em"—may well reflect more biological reality than most of us care to admit. (Barash, 1979, p. 48)

DOUBLE STANDARD

The sexual activities of men and women are often evaluated differently. For example, male promiscuity is almost universally accepted and is often encouraged whereas female promiscuity is simply not tolerated. Barash (1979) reviews the possible biological reasons for this **double standard**:

> Compare these two situations: (1) you are a male animal, paired with a single female, and your "wife" goes around copulating with other males; (2) you are a female animal, paired with a single male, and your "husband" goes around copulating with other females. In which case is your fitness likely to be lower? In the first situation, if you (as male) remain faithful to your "swinging" spouse, she will eventually conceive offspring via other males, and you will have lost out in the evolutionary sweepstakes. However, in the second case, if you (as female) remain faithful to your mate, you can still breed successfully despite his philandering, provided he includes you among his girlfriends. This is the basic biology of the double standard: males are expected to be sexually less discriminating, more aggressive and more available than females. They are also expected to be more intolerant of infidelity by their wives than wives will be of infidelity by their husbands. (p. 53)

We expect men to "come on" to women, and in most cases the man will be rejected. This reflects the fact that through the eons men have had little to lose by copulating whereas women have had much to lose if copulation was not with the right man under the right circumstances. Wallace (1979) describes a fictitious experiment that clearly reflects the double standard:

> I once facetiously suggested that my students in an "adult" class perform an experiment in which members of a pair (man and wife) would enter a crowded bar and see which sex could persuade a stranger to copulate with them first. We decided that the success of most women could be measured with a stopwatch but that the men might well require a calendar. (p. 71)

Female Criteria for Mate Selection.   In what follows, the term *good* means fitness-enhancing for the female (Barash, 1982, p. 252). Females tend to seek males with good genes (for example, genes that will produce an offspring with survival and reproductive potential); with good resources (for example, food, territory, shelter, and protection); and with good behaviour, or a willingness to invest some of those resources in them and their offspring. A male's resources, then, tend to be important to females. According to Buss (1987), "In humans, resources can take many forms . . . [for example] income, occupational and social status, possessions, networks of alliance, and family background. Personality characteristics such as hard-working, ambitious, energetic, industrious, and persevering also appear to be correlated with achievement potential" (p. 340). Females will tend to reject sexual overtures until all or most of the preceding criteria are met.

Because females can produce only a relatively small number of offspring in their lifetimes, and because they choose only males with special characteristics as mates, females tend to be a limited resource and therefore a source of male competition. Under these circumstances, attractive females can choose males with the greatest resources. **Hypergamy** or the widespread tendency for females to benefit themselves through marriage (marrying up) appears to have its roots in biology. After reviewing the data on the subject, Buss (1987) concludes, "Physically attractive females tend to marry high-status males who have access to resources" (p. 347).

Male Criteria for Mate Selection.　For many males the most important attribute in a mate is **reproductive value**, which Buss (1987) defines as "the extent to which persons of a given age and sex (and other features) will contribute, on the average, to the ancestry of future generations" (p. 340). According to Buss (1987), it is important to differentiate between reproductive value and **fertility**: "Fertility reflects immediate probability of reproduction, while reproductive value reflects long-term probability of reproduction" (p. 341).

According to Buss (1987), males seeking a temporary sex partner will tend to seek females with the highest fertility (early twenties in North America). Males seeking a long-term relationship will tend to seek females with the highest reproductive value (mid-teens in North America). The question is, What cues do males use in assessing a female's reproductive capability? Buss suggested that the two strongest cues are *age* and *health*. How, in our evolutionary past, was age determined?

> In our evolutionary past prior to the development of counting systems . . . age was not a characteristic that could be evaluated directly. Instead, cues that correlated with age and health could be used by males to identify reproductively capable females. Physical appearance probably provides the strongest set of cues, and these include features such as clear, smooth, and unblemished skin, lustrous hair, white teeth, clear eyes, and full lips. . . . Behavioral cues such as sprightly gait and high activity level also provide cues to youth.
>
> According to this evolutionary argument, males should come to value and view as attractive those physical and behavioral cues in potential mates that correlate with female reproductive capability. (Buss, 1987, p. 341)

By contrast, age should be less of a factor in female mate selection because age does not provide a reliable cue concerning a male's ability to fertilize eggs. Much data need to be collected and analyzed before the predictions based on evolutionary theory concerning mate selection can be accepted or rejected. Some data, however, already appear to substantiate the predictions suggested earlier. Buss (1987) reviewed seven studies of mate selection criteria conducted over more than 40 years. These studies and their major findings are summarized in Table 12–1. The data support the contention that qualities directly or indirectly related to resources are more important for females than for males, and physical attractiveness is more important for males than for females. However, Buss also found that both men and women valued such personal characteristics as kindness, understanding, and intelligence more highly than either resources or physical attractiveness (Buss, 1994, cited in Rathus, Nevid, and Fichner-Rathus, 1998).

About the results of these studies, Buss (1987) said, "This sex difference does not appear to be a transient generational phenomenon, and the magnitude of this sex difference does not appear to have changed over the past 40 years. . . . The findings are so consistent across studies that they qualify as among the most robust and

Table 12–1

Summary of Seven Studies on Sex Differences in Mate Selection Criteria

AUTHORS	YEAR	SAMPLE SIZE	METHOD	FEMALES VALUE MORE	MALES VALUE MORE
Hill	1945	600	Ratings	Ambition & industrious; good financial prospect	Good looking
Langhorne & Secord	1955	5000	Nominations	Getting ahead; ambitious; enjoys work; high-status profession; good provider; wealth	Physical attractiveness
McGinnis	1958	120	Ratings	Ambition & industrious; favourable social status; good financial prospect	Good looks
Hudson & Henze	1969	566	Ratings	Ambition & industrious; favourable social status; good financial prospect	Good looks
Buss	1985	162	Rankings	Good earning capacity	Physical attractiveness
Buss & Barnes*	1986	186	Ratings	Good earning capacity; ambitious & career-oriented	Good looking; Physically attractive
Buss & Barnes	1986	100	Rankings	Good earning capacity	Physically attractive

*This sample was composed of married couples between the ages of 20 and 42. (From Buss, 1987, p. 345.)

consistently replicated psychological findings that have been documented across several generations" (p. 344).

BIOLOGY OF MATING ARRANGEMENTS

As we have seen, the most effective reproductive strategy for males is to mate with as many females as possible. As far as marital arrangements are concerned this means that **polygyny**, the reproductive system in which one male mates with more than one female, is probably the most natural one for males. Such an arrangement is also conducive to the female's fitness because it allows each female involved to reproduce. **Polyandry**, the reproductive system in which one female mates with more than one male is very rare:

> About three-fourths of all human societies permit the taking of multiple wives, and most of them encourage the practice by law and custom. In contrast, marriage to multiple husbands is sanctioned in less than one percent of societies. The remaining monogamous societies usually fit that category in a legal sense only, with concubinage and other extramarital stratagems being added to allow *de facto polygyny*. (Wilson, 1978, p. 130)

About **monogamy**, a mating system consisting of one male and one female, Barash (1979) says:

> Monogamy is rare in mammals, almost unheard of in primates, and, despite our Judeo-Christian fondness for the "nuclear family," it appears to be a relatively recent invention of certain human cultures. Our biology may permit this social form, but it certainly doesn't demand it—and may not even like it. (pp. 65–66)

Jealousy.   According to the sociobiologists, the emotion of jealousy suggests some important male-female differences in criteria for mate selection and mate retention. In general, a male experiences jealousy when he feels his mate's activities may result in the perpetuation of someone else's genes—that is, when her activities raise doubts about his parenthood. A female, conversely, tends to experience jealousy when she feels that another female is threatening the resources that her mate is providing to her and her offspring. According to Wallace (1979), "We must realize that, on an evolutionary basis, jealousy is important. Women must see to it that they and their offspring are the sole recipients of a male's services. The male must see to it that he does not raise someone else's chromosomes" (p. 63).

Teismann and Mosher (1978) studied the patterns of jealousy reported by undergraduate dating couples and essentially confirmed the sociobiological analysis. Primarily, but not exclusively, for males, the emotion of jealousy can become intense enough to lead to homicide. On June 20, 2000 in Pickering, Ontario, 34-year-old Ralph Hadley shot and killed his estranged wife, Gillian, before he turned the gun on himself. And in 1998, a coroner's inquest was called in to examine the murder of Arlene May of Collingwood, Ontario, by her boyfriend Randy Isles. Concerning such cases Margo Wilson (1989) says:

> Police files, psychiatric reports, and case law reveal a remarkable consistency of motives underlying spousal homicides: In any sample of well-described cases, a large majority were evidently precipitated by the husband's accusing the wife of sexual infidelity and/or her unilateral decision to terminate the relationship. Several studies of spouse-killers demonstrate the overwhelming predominance of male sexual jealousy and proprietariness as motives in spousal homicide. (p. 54)

Biology of Parenting

Barash (1979) points out that parenting has been, and is, largely the job of females:

> There is no human society, historically or in recent times, in which women have not borne the primary responsibility for child care. Parenting is a largely sex-linked occupation. In all societies, men do men things and women are left holding the babies. But why does this occur? Since one-half of the genes making up every individual have been contributed by each parent, then each parent should have the same interest in each child. Right? Wrong. (p. 108)

According to the sociobiologists, a major reason for this inequality in involvement in parenting is the fact that each child reflects a large proportion of the mother's total reproductive potential and a large investment of her time and energy. As we have seen, for the male the investment is only a tiny amount of sperm. For these reasons, females tend to be far more committed to a child's survival than are their mates. A second reason why females tend to be more devoted parents than males concerns certainty of parenthood. When a child is born, only the female knows with certainty that her genes have been passed on. Therefore, the female knows that everything that she invests in her offspring is ultimately to her own evolutionary benefit. Males have no such guarantee and, therefore, it is always possible that investing in an offspring might turn out to be a wasted effort in terms of the male's fitness.

Yet behaviours shaped by evolution can adapt to changed circumstances. While women still carry more than half the responsibility for child rearing, the expectation that men are breadwinners and women are home with the children is fast disappearing.

Environment is a factor. In small towns, where there are fewer employment opportunities and lower costs of living, women are somewhat more likely to stay home with young children; in expensive urban areas like Toronto or Vancouver, where two incomes are needed to meet the high costs of housing and transportation, families are more likely to delegate some of the labour of child-rearing to a sitter or daycare centre.

INVOLVEMENT OF MEN IN PARENTING

First of all, relative to most other living organisms, human infants remain dependent on adults for a long period of time. During this period of dependency a mother's chances of successfully rearing a child are greatly increased if she has someone to help her obtain food, and to protect her and her offspring from harm, that is, a mate who engages in good behaviour. The mother, therefore, has pragmatic reasons for attempting to entice the father into sharing child-rearing responsibilities. What does she use to entice him? The answer appears to be sex. Human females are unique among primates in that they are not sexually receptive only during ovulation or estrus. Human females remain sexually receptive throughout their entire menstrual cycle. Wilson (1978) explains why this may be the case:

> Why has sexual responsiveness become nearly continuous? The most plausible explanation is that the trait facilitates bonding; the physiological adaptation conferred a Darwinian advantage by more tightly joining the members of primitive human clans. Unusually frequent sexual activity between males and females served as the principal device for cementing the pair bond. . . . Love and sex do indeed go together. (pp. 146–147)

Barash (1979) also suggests that the evolution of the female orgasm may have occurred because it helps to keep the father of a child close:

> What about the female orgasm, another uniquely human trait?. . . . Nonreproductive sex could represent an evolutionary strategy for keeping the male nearby, but not simply as an appeal to pleasure. . . . Female sexual receptivity throughout the reproductive cycle may actually be a loving form of deceit. . . . If women enjoy making love and are motivated to do so (enter: the female orgasm), men might not want to stay away too long. They will remain nearby and look after their genetic investment. (pp. 88–89)

Although it appears that shared sexual activity can create a bond between a male and a female, it does little to create a bond between a father and his offspring. If a male agrees to share in the responsibilities of parenting, he must be convinced to do so by the mother or encouraged by considerable social pressure. "My guess is that male parenting in human beings, as in virtually all mammals, is not nearly as innate as modern sexual egalitarians might wish it to be" (Barash, 1979, p. 88).

STEPPARENTING

It comes as no surprise to sociobiologists that there are more problems involving children in homes with stepparents than in homes with natural parents. Martin Daly (1989) summarizes his extensive research on the abuse of stepchildren as follows:

> Do stepparents resent, exploit, and mistreat their fictive children while nurturing their own? Although step-relationships clearly can and often do work reasonably well, the short answer is yes: Step-relationships are vastly more conflictual and unsatisfying than genetic parent-child relationships, and vastly more dangerous to the children. (pp. 38–39)

Daly (1989) indicates how dangerous the situation can become, "An American child living with one or more substitute parents in 1976 was approximately 100 times as likely to be fatally abused as a same-aged child living with genetic parents only" (p. 39).

The tendency to abuse stepchildren has been found to be independent of socioeconomic status, family size, and the ages and personality characteristics of the abusers (Daly, 1989, p. 39). The phenomenon is also culturally universal. Concerning the universality of stepchild abuse, Daly (1989) says, "This phenomenon is not peculiar to industrialized societies. . . . The cross-cultural ubiquity of 'cruel stepparent' stories . . . apparently reflects an endemic problem in human social life" (p. 39).

ADOPTION

Do the preceding observations imply that the sociobiologists believe only natural parents can be good parents? On the contrary, they believe humans are capable of developing as much love for an adopted child as they do toward their own children. People will, in fact, go to considerable lengths to adopt children. For example, some Canadians travelled to Bucharest, Romania to adopt one or more of the several thousand orphans left to institutional care following the breakdown of that country's government and social structure in 1989. Barash suggests that humans may even have a natural inclination to adopt children. This natural inclination may have developed because for much of evolutionary history, humans lived in small groups of about 50 people who were all probably closely genetically related. Under such circumstances, if a child was orphaned he or she could be adopted by one or more adults in the band who would likely be the child's uncle, aunt, or cousin. Adoption, then, becomes a way of increasing the adopter's inclusive fitness.

It seems, however, that such an evolutionary history makes adoption acceptable or tolerable, but not optimal. Barash (1979) explains:

> Adoption is rarely as smooth and trouble free as many would think, or wish. If we take a hard, unromanticized look at adoption in Western culture two significant facts stand out. First, despite a great deal of social approval, adoption is overwhelmingly a second choice of parents. Given the option, most people prefer to produce their own children. Although extended-family members—grandparents, aunts and uncles, cousins—may sincerely attempt not to treat the adopted child differently, it is notable that such effort is required at all. A second fact about adoption is that our society subjects would-be adoptive parents to intensive scrutiny, while extending virtually none to would-be biological parents. It is remarkable that we require a license to drive an automobile but none to carry out the much more difficult task of having and raising a child. (pp. 106–107)

The reason that would-be adoptive parents are scrutinized so thoroughly is because it is assumed biological parents will naturally care for their offspring but adoptive parents must prove they are capable and willing to do so. Barash (1979) says, "In fact, there is probably real wisdom involved in this assumption; in scrutinizing the motives and suitability of would-be adopters, child welfare agencies may be good sociobiologists without being aware of it" (p. 107).

INTENTIONAL CHILDLESSNESS

According to Barash (1979), intentional childlessness is a sociobiological puzzle. He says, "Women may have been less than wildly enthusiastic about spending a large percentage of their adult lives either pregnant or nursing, yet as long as they ultimately became pregnant, such feelings had no real evolutionary consequences" (p. 107). Now, however, because of the existence of various contraceptive devices, females have the opportunity to act on whatever ambivalence they may feel toward child bearing. This opportunity may create an approach-avoidance conflict toward having children, however. On the one hand, to choose not to have children would help alleviate the world overpopulation problem and would spare one the physical, psychological, and financial expense of having and rearing them. Conversely, such a choice runs contrary to the tendency to have children that has developed during millions of years of evolution. Barash believes it will be interesting to study the long-term consequences (both costs and benefits) of deciding not to become a parent. He also believes the long-term genetic consequences of intentional childlessness must also be considered, "Because, by definition, selection will favor those people who wish to have children, and any genetically influenced tendency for lesser reproduction will eventually disappear, leaving us with a population of even more eager breeders" (Barash, 1979, p. 108).

Aggression, Territoriality, and Warfare

ARE HUMANS INNATELY AGGRESSIVE?

Although the sociobiologists believe humans are innately aggressive, an important difference exists between what they mean by that contention and what Freud meant by it. In explaining his version of innate human aggressiveness, Freud followed a drive-discharge model. The **drive-discharge model of aggression** assumes that humans, like other animals, have a need to be aggressive that must be periodically satisfied. Freud believed the human aggressive need could be, and should be, displaced so that its satisfaction would not be harmful and could even be beneficial to society. Competitive sports is but one example of displacement. According to Freud, humans have a need to be aggressive just as they have a need for food or water. Being deprived of any of these things too long builds up a drive that must eventually be discharged. The sociobiologists believe the analysis of aggression by Freud is incorrect.

The sociobiological explanation of aggression emphasizes the interaction between genetic potential and learning. This explanation assumes that humans have the inherited potential to be aggressive, but it is through learning (culture) that we learn what form of aggression is tolerated and under what circumstances it should occur. According to the sociobiologists, we engage in aggressive behaviour when it is advantageous for us to do so.

According to the sociobiologist, then, aggressive behaviour will occur when it maximizes fitness—that is, when the benefits of such behaviour exceed the costs. In fact, the terms *strategy* and **cost–benefit analysis** are popular ones in sociobiology, suggesting that humans, consciously or unconsciously, weigh various alternatives before deciding on a course of action.

TERRITORIALITY AND WARFARE

The sociobiologists define a **territory** as any defended area (Barash, 1982, p. 394). Thus a territory can be an area of land, a house, a country, or even a person. According to Wilson (1978), "Each culture develops its own particular rules to safeguard personal property and space" (p. 112). Wars occur when some humans do not respect the rules and regulations by which the territories of other humans can be penetrated. Wilson (1978) elaborates: "War can be defined as the violent rupture of the intricate and powerful fabric of the territorial taboos observed by social groups" (p. 113). A major reason for territoriality is the feeling of kinship that one has toward either his or her relatives or toward those with whom he or she shares beliefs. Wilson (1978) says, "The force behind most warlike policies is ethnocentrism, the irrationally exaggerated allegiance of individuals to their kin and fellow tribesman" (pp. 113–114).

Organized aggression directed toward those perceived as threatening one's territory evolved into warfare, and warfare as a means of defending and expanding one's territory was effective indeed:

> Primitive men cleaved their universe into friends and enemies and responded with quick, deep emotion to even the mildest threats emanating from outside the arbitrary boundary. With the rise of chiefdoms and states, this tendency became institutionalized, war was adopted as an instrument of policy of some of the new societies, and those that employed it best became—tragically—the most successful. The evolution of warfare was an autocatalytic reaction that could not be halted by any people, because to attempt to reverse the process unilaterally was to fall victim. A new mode of natural selection was operating at the level of entire societies. (Wilson, 1978, p. 119)

Sociobiologists believe the primitive tendencies just described are still whispering within us and, therefore, we are in trouble. We are dealing with a complex modern world with behavioural tendencies that developed hundreds of thousands of years ago. Is there hope? Wilson (1978) says yes, but improvement will not come easily:

> The learning rules of violent aggression are largely obsolete. We are no longer hunter-gatherers who settle disputes with spears, arrows, and stone axes. But to acknowledge the obsolescence of the rules is not to banish them. We can only work our way around them. To let them rest latent and unsummoned, we must consciously undertake those difficult and rarely traveled pathways in psychological development that lead to mastery over and reduction of the profound human tendency to learn violence. (p. 123)

Time and time again, the sociobiologists go out of their way to avoid committing the **naturalistic fallacy,** which is believing that just because something is natural it is necessarily good. Barash (1979) says, "No claim is made that what is natural is therefore good. 'Smallpox is natural,' Ogden Nash pointed out. 'Vaccine ain't.' And there isn't very little good that anyone can see in smallpox" (p.15). The innate tendency toward warfare is another example. Barash (1979) asks, "Can we recognize that, because of modern technology, the rules of the game have been changed? Can we use our understanding and our reason to overrule our dangerously outmoded whisperings from within?" And his answer is, "We had better do so" (p. 198).

Rape, Incest, and Suicide

RAPE

As we have seen, social scientists tend to study the proximate causes of behaviour and sociobiologists tend to study the ultimate causes. When studying rape, then, the social scientists seek the physiological and cultural variables leading to such behaviour whereas the sociobiologists seek an explanation based on evolutionary principles.

Thornhill and Thornhill (1983, 1987b) attempted to explain the phenomenon of rape in evolutionary terms by assuming that rape is engaged in by men who cannot successfully compete for the resources and status necessary to attract and successfully reproduce with a desirable mate. In other words, rapists are losers in the competition for available women. Thornhill and Thornhill (1987b) said, "When female mate choice is based importantly on resources and male striving for resources produces losers and winners, forced copulation may be a viable alternative for losers" (p. 277).

Thornhill and Thornhill discussed the two most common explanations of rape offered by social scientists. The first is that rape represents a behavioural pathology that somehow grew out of modern industrial societies. This hypothesis is rejected because the evidence indicates that rape occurs in many different cultures. The second hypothesis, derived from feminist ideology, is that men use rape to dominate women. Thornhill and Thornhill (1987b) gave the reasons why they reject the second hypothesis: "The feminist hypothesis seems to predict that men will rape powerful, older women. . . . This is false. Rape is directed primarily at young poor women. . . . The feminist view would also predict that rapists will derive equally from all walks of life and adult age categories. This appears to be false in all human societies for which there are data. Rapists primarily are young, poor men" (pp. 283–284).

Thus the sociobiological explanation of rape is based on the assumption that rape is an effort to reproduce on the part of men who cannot successfully compete for mates. If this assumption is correct, the typical targets of rape will tend to have certain characteristics. Earlier in this chapter we distinguished between the reproductive value of a female and her current fertility. Female reproductive value peaks sometime in the mid-teens and fertility in the early twenties in the United States. According to Thornhill and Thornhill (1987b), "Rapists in particular are expected to unconsciously evaluate fertility of potential victims to a greater degree than reproductive value because fertility is most closely related to the probability that a copulation will lead to conception and successful gestation and live birth" (pp. 284–285).

Do the data support the sociobiological explanation of rape? Thornhill and Thornhill (1987b) reported the following:

> We compared the ages of rape victims with ages of females in the general population of the U.S. Statistically, young women are greatly overrepresented and older women are greatly underrepresented in the data on victims of rape. The peak in rape victims in relation to age corresponded with ages of high reproductive capacity. We also examined all major data sets on ages of rape victims in the U.S. The same pattern is revealed by all data sets: Young females of high reproductive capacity are raped most often. . . . It is interesting that ages of rape victims seem to follow fertility distributions to a greater extent than reproductive value distributions.
>
> Clearly our prediction about female age in relation to rape victimization was supported, and there is suggestion that fertility of females is more important than reproductive value in rape victimization. (p. 285)

Thornhill and Thornhill tested several other predictions concerning the characteristics of rapists and rape victims, and in each case the data supported an evolutionary explanation. Thornhill and Thornhill (1987b) concluded, "The general conclusion that emerges is that evolutionary theory is very relevant to any attempt to understand rape and any of its ramifications. . . . In fact, it appears that significant understanding of rape will derive primarily from the evolutionary approach" (p. 287).

INCEST

If people who are closely genetically related mate (for example, parents and offspring, siblings, and half-siblings), the probability of genetic defect in any resulting offspring is significantly higher than for offspring of unrelated mates. Therefore, it makes good evolutionary sense to avoid such mating arrangements. In fact, an inherited tendency should exist to avoid incestuous sexual relationships, and indeed an inherited mechanism does appear to discourage incest. If such an innate inhibitory mechanism against incest exists, however, why do so many cultures, including our own, spend so much time and energy discouraging incestuous sexual relationships? In his effort to explain why both cultural prohibitions and an innate inhibitory mechanism are involved in incest avoidance, van den Berghe (1987) first reviewed the statements on incest made by Freud (1913/1958) and by Westermarck (1891).

Freud (1913/1958) took the position that cultural incest taboos were necessary to counteract the strong sexual attractions that occur between members of a nuclear family. In other words, Freud believed a natural tendency toward incest existed that needed to be inhibited by cultural rules and regulations. Westermarck (1891) took the opposite viewpoint. According to Westermarck, close association among young children (apparently between the ages of 2 and 6) inhibits the development of sexual attraction between them. This avoidance of sex by those who experienced each other as young children is called the **Westermarck effect** and it results in a natural avoidance of at least brother-sister incestuous relationships. As Lumsden and Wilson (1985) say, "To put the matter simply, little children who use the same potty do not, in later life, fall in love" (p. 355).

Israeli anthropologist Joseph Shepher (1971) studied the eventual marriages of people who grew up together in a kibbutz in which they had been treated as if they were all members of one large family. Of the 2769 marriages studied, only six were between members of the same kibbutz who had been together since birth, despite the fact that such marriages were actively encouraged by the authorities. Wolf and Huang (1980) reported similar findings. *Shim-pua* marriages in China involve adopting a young girl and raising her together with the family's biological children, with the understanding she will marry one of the family's sons. Although such marriages were sanctioned by society, they failed at an incredible rate. Often the married couples had to be forced to occupy the same room. Also, adultery and divorce for these couples were much higher than the average, and birth rate was much lower.

The fact that the Westermarck effect occurs whether those involved are related or not, and the fact that it comes from *experience*, seems to suggest it is learned rather than an inherited disposition. Trigg (1982), however, suggests this is not the case:

> The absence of genetic ties in such a case might seem to be an argument against a sociobiological explanation but it can in fact easily be taken to confirm it. Natural selection will have found it simpler to favour those who behave towards others as if they are genetically related when they *normally* would be. The alternative would involve a discrimination perhaps amounting to conscious understanding of when people were genetically related and when they were not. It may even demand some knowledge of the significance of this. Such an enterprise would be ridiculously complicated. Simple instinctual reactions in what would usually be the appropriate situations would further genetic fitness just as well, even if such reactions sometimes occurred when they were unnecessary. (p. 122)

Some believe the Westermarck effect will occur only if the interacting children are between two and six (for example, Shepher, 1983). If true, the Westermarck effect would explain incest avoidance only among those who experienced each other as young children (for example, brother-sister incest). Others, however, believe that anyone, of any age, who interacts with a young child will develop a sexual aversion to that child as a child and later as an adult. For example, Thornhill and Thornhill (1987a) responded to the contention that the Westermarck effect results only when young children interact:

We disagree and suggest that a more parsimonious hypothesis is that cosocialization of an individual of any age with a child who is experiencing the sensitive stage (2 to 6 years of age), should lead to sexual aversion between them. This eliminates the need for hypothesizing complex mechanisms of mother/son and father/daughter incest avoidance. . . . When cosocialization does *not* occur during the sensitive stage it appears that the mechanism for avoiding close inbreeding is not learned, and incest might occur. (p. 377)

We now return to the question, with such a powerful natural mechanism preventing incestuous relationships, why are there so many cultural prescriptions against them, and why do they still occur so often? Recent cases in North America indicate that incest, while not rampant, still exists. In August 2001, Renald Côté of Sherbrooke, Quebec, was charged with raping his daughter in over a 17-year period. And in February 2002, Samuel Patrick of Glades County, Florida, was charged with incest. He and his wife Debbie, who police say is also his sister, had nine children together; it was also alleged that Patrick was the father of his daughters' children. Van den Berghe (1987) examined several societies and found some of them encouraged sexually permissive relationships among family members and some did not. In those that did allow such relationships, the Westermarck effect occurred; when such relationships were discouraged, the Westermarck effect did not occur. Thus, according to van den Berghe (1987), both Freud and Westermarck were correct.

SUICIDE

Living organisms generally act in ways that are conducive to their survival. They will seek food, water, and safety, and will actively escape or avoid experiences that threaten their continued existence. Natural selection easily explains such tendencies: Organisms that display them are far more likely to survive and reproduce than those that do not. Thus, over many generations, any predispositions toward self-preservation are passed on whereas predispositions not conducive to self-preservation are not. It is assumed that humans also have evolved in this way. But if humans have such a propensity for self-preservation, why do so many of us engage in self-destructive behaviour—suicide being the most dramatic example?

As we have often seen, the concept of inclusive fitness is central to sociobiology. De Catanzaro emphasized this concept in his analysis of suicide. He asks, Do circumstances exist under which a person's genes would have a better chance of being perpetuated if that person ceased to exist? De Catanzaro (1987) answers in the affirmative: "It could be predicted that once an individual is postreproductive or otherwise excluded from reproduction, and has no further role to play in nurturance of its progeny, self-preservation is of little or no value for the individual's inclusive fitness" (p. 316). De Catanzaro (1987) elaborates:

> Any genetic predispositions favoring a self-preserving orientation of behavior, when expressed prior to or during reproductive (including nurturant) phases of the life cycle, would confer a strong selective advantage for the individual. However, expression of such predispositions after all reproductive opportunities had passed would have no positive reproductive consequences. In fact, to the extent that postreproductive or nonreproductive individuals consumed resources that otherwise would be available to potential reproducing kin, their self-preservation could actually have adverse effects upon their inclusive fitnesses . . . . Wherever the continued existence of one individual impedes the reproduction of close kin . . . more than it enhances the reproduction of the individual himself, self-destructiveness is at least theoretically possible. (p. 317)

So much for the predictions concerning suicide based on sociobiological theory; what do the facts show? De Catanzaro (1987) reports that suicide typically occurs among people whose capacity to promote inclusive fitness is seriously impaired. That is, suicide is related to diminished reproductive potential, absence of or unfavourable relations to one's kin or one's social group, or the lack of coping skills. One of the best predictors of true suicidal intent is the feeling of hopelessness or desperation. According to de Catanzaro, such a feeling usually means that a person finds himself or herself incapable of engaging in reproductive and productive behaviour that would promote his or her inclusive fitness:

> Suicide is very common in the terminally ill and those with permanently debilitating handicaps . . . Suicide is also very common in the chronically unemployed and others with severe economic difficulties . . . such difficulties may engender problems in attracting a mate and supporting offspring, rendering the individual incapable of reproducing, and may preclude other activity that indirectly advances the individual's inclusive fitness. (de Catanzaro, 1987, p. 319)

Among the other variables that de Catanzaro (1987) found to be related to suicide were social isolation (a socially isolated person would be relatively incapable of engaging in productive or reproductive behaviour); age (suicide is rare in children under 14, but is a major cause of death in adolescence and early adulthood); sex (men are much more likely to commit suicide than women); marital status (people in a stable marriage are less likely to commit suicide than those who are single, divorced, widowed, or have an unstable marriage); and culture (learning may provide the means by which one commits suicide but the ultimate cause of such an act must be understood in evolutionary terms).

Evidence for a genetic component to suicide came in January 2000 from scientists at the Royal Ottawa Hospital, who discovered a genetic abnormality that might lead to suicide. The genetic photographs of depressive patients with mild to moderate suicidal thoughts were carefully reviewed to identify the gene. The authors of the study argue that this genetic marker might just make it harder for some people to resist the deadly urge. Although this does not explain every suicide, it does offer evidence for a biological condition that contributes to suicidal impulses, a condition that could one day be treated.

OTHER FORMS OF SELF-DESTRUCTIVE BEHAVIOUR

Many people smoke, drink alcohol, take drugs, or overeat, activities not conducive to self-preservation. In their attempt to explain behaviour that appears to be contrary to self-preservation, the sociobiologists tend to (1) show that the self-abusive behaviour is actually conducive to the person's inclusive fitness (for example, suicide); or (2) stress the fact that the environment in which we evolved is, in many ways, different from the one in which we now live. Barash (1979) gives the following examples:

> Most of us over-indulge in foods that are high in saturated fats and cholesterol, despite the fact that these materials are clearly harmful and may in fact be life threatening when consumed in sufficient quantities. Fats cause our arteries to clog up and lead to heart disease, the foremost killer in the United States today. This dietary imprudence is aggravated by our tendency to avoid exercise. We drive when we could walk, use the elevator when we could take the stairs and so on. . . . Dangerous Western eating and exercise habits may well be the effects of our cultural developments outstripping our biological evolution. Human beings evolved as part-time carnivores, probably on the African savannah. There is every reason to suspect that we are programmed to relish

animal fat, a very concentrated food source and, not surprisingly one that is prized by all meat-eating animals. Most wild game is actually quite lean, and a fatty meal would therefore be a rare and sought-after treat. Because we undoubtedly got more than enough exercise during our long African evolution, any opportunity to avoid exercise and to leave ourselves with enough physical activity to keep our bodies in good order would be seized upon.

But nowadays we fatten our livestock in feedlots; slather butter and oils on everything; and compound the problem by adding unnecessary calories through sugar, candies and other worthless confections. For a savannah-bred protohuman, this diet would be heaven. For us, it may well be lethal. Having provided us with an opportunity to satisfy (in excess) our primitive needs, modern culture then adds to the villainy by designing all sorts of "labor-saving devices" that enable us to avoid the exercise that might otherwise be our bodily salvation. (pp. 228–229)

Religion

Artifacts have been found indicating that Neanderthals engaged in religious practices 60 000 years ago, and since that time humans have produced about 100 000 religions (Wilson, 1978, p. 176). Religion is culturally universal, uniquely human, and, according to the sociobiologists, part of human nature (that is, part of our biogrammar). Wilson (1978) says, "The predisposition to religious belief is the most complex and powerful force in the human mind and in all probability an ineradicable part of human nature" (p. 176).

According to Wilson, religion plays a vital role in allowing humans to live in groups such as tribes or nations. Wilson (1978) says, "Religion is above all the process by which individuals are persuaded to subordinate their immediate self-interest to the interests of the group" (p. 183). Religion does this in several ways but one way is to generate a feeling of kinship among persons who share common beliefs. By holding similar beliefs people, at least symbolically, become related; feeling related, they are more likely to engage in reciprocal altruism. Furthermore, religions almost always sanctify the principles by which believers should conduct themselves. Wilson (1978) says, "To sanctify a procedure or a statement is to certify it as beyond question and imply punishment for anyone who dares to contradict it" (p. 191). Rules concerning reciprocal altruism, for example, Do unto others as you would have them do unto you, are a vital part of religion, as are the procedures used to deal with cheaters. Thus society depends on reciprocal altruism, and religion encourages its practice and creates fear or guilt in those who are inclined to cheat.

Another important function of religion is to simplify life, and religion does this in several ways. In addition to providing believers with a feeling of kinship, religion also encourages the human tendency to divide humans into two categories, such as believers and nonbelievers, members of the in-group and members of the out-group, friends and enemies. We seem to be willing to accept any doctrine that simplifies life, and the dichotomization of people is one way to do just that. Related to the strong human tendency to dichotomize is **xenophobia,** the fear of strangers. From our distant past comes the tendency to distrust anyone who is not like us—for example, someone not from the same clan, village, or tribe, someone who lives life according to different (and therefore inferior) rules. Such a person is at least a potential enemy and should be treated as such. Since the terrorist attacks on the World Trade Center in September 2001, distrust of strangers has increased among Canadians, as seen in tighter immigration policies and "racial profiling" in security checks at airports and along border crossings.

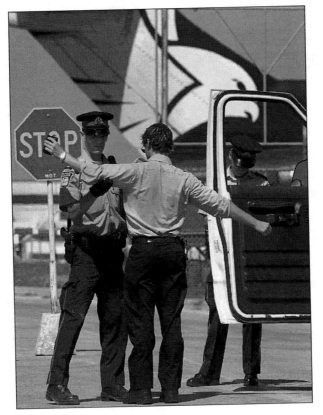

A traveller goes through a security check. According to Wilson, distrust of strangers comes from our distant past. In the wake of the World Trade Center bombings in 2001, Canada has increased scrutiny of anyone entering the country, especially those whose skin and dress indicate they are "not like us."

NEED FOR RULES AND REGULATIONS

Social living requires rules and regulations and historically it has been religion, in one form or another, that has furnished and enforced them. Although it appears necessary that these rules and regulations encourage reciprocal altruism, give a sense of kinship to members of the community, and discourage any practice that is not conducive to survival and reproduction, they can provide these functions in a wide variety of ways. In other words, rules and regulations are necessary for societal living, but any number of systems of rules and regulations are possible.

The willingness to accept a system of rules and regulations, and to live according to them, may have a biological basis. Perhaps we are born to be team players as long as the game does not stray too far from our biological makeup. Thus Wilson (1975) says, "The enduring paradox of religion is that so much of its substance is demonstrably false, yet it remains a driving force in all societies. Men would rather believe than know. . . . Human beings are absurdly easy to indoctrinate—they *seek* it" (pp. 561–562). In other words, humans readily embrace any beliefs that simplify their lives and allow cooperative living, and it appears that the ultimate validity of those beliefs is irrelevant as long as they have pragmatic value. Furthermore, because good "team players" are more likely to survive and reproduce, parents eagerly pass on the rules of societal living to their offspring, and the offspring are eager to learn them. Lumsden and Wilson (1981) say, "Adults are strongly prone to provide complex instructions, and the young are predisposed to follow them" (p. 5). Smith (1987) compared the typical goals toward which parents socialize their children with the goal suggested by the sociobiologist:

> In Western culture, these goals [according to parents] often involve producing polite, active, law-abiding adults who will have the skills to secure fulfilling, lucrative employment and a similarly socialized spouse. An evolutionary perspective views these end-points of socialization as intermediate steps in achieving the real goal of parenting: the maximization of inclusive fitness through the maximal production of grandchildren. (p. 235)

BIOLOGY OF ETHICS

Every human society has some ethical code of behaviour for its members to follow and although ethical codes vary significantly from society to society, there are common elements among them. All encourage reciprocal altruism and specify punishment for cheaters, all promote patriotism, and all encourage behaviours that are conducive to the survival and reproductive success of its members. Religion typically functions to strengthen and maintain the ethical code by which a society functions, therefore, it is not surprising to find that all of the major religions make strong statements about reciprocal altruism. In his book *The Expanding Circle: Ethics and Sociobiology,* Singer (1981) summarizes several of these statements:

> In Judaism the rule is to love your neighbor as yourself; a rule which Jesus elevated to the status of one of the two great commandments. About the same time, Rabbi Hillel said: "What is hateful to you do not do to your neighbor; that is the whole Torah, the rest is commentary thereof." Jesus also put it another way: "As you would that men should do to you, do ye also to them likewise." When Confucius was asked for a single word which could serve as a rule of practice for all one's life, he replied: "Is not reciprocity such a word? What you do not want done to yourself, do not do to others." In Indian thought we find the Mahabharata saying: "Let no man do to another that which would be repugnant to himself; this is the sum of righteousness." (p. 136)

In his book *The Genesis Factor,* Wallace (1979) said all life must obey the **reproductive imperative**: *"Reproduce, and leave as many offspring as possible"* (p. 17). In time, according to Wallace, those activities conducive to the reproductive imperative determine the norm of a society and become formally encoded by tradition, laws, religions, and ethics. Those activities not conducive to the reproductive imperative are viewed as crimes or sins and are discouraged. According to Wallace, activities contrary to the reproductive imperative include oral and anal sex, masturbation, necrophilia (a sexual attraction to dead bodies), pederasty (sexual relations between a man and a boy), sex with young children in general, adultery, rape, fornication, and incest. All of the activities listed either cannot produce offspring and are therefore wasted activities or they may produce offspring that have a low probability of being cared for and therefore may not survive. Although, as we have seen, some sociobiologists consider both adultery (for men) and rape to be biologically adaptive, Wallace considers adultery (sexual activity with someone other than one's spouse), fornication (copulation involving unmarried partners), and rape to violate the reproductive imperative because they may produce offspring that may not be cared for adequately.

Homosexuality.   You may have noticed that homosexuality did not appear on the list of sexual activities that violate the reproductive imperative. The relatively widespread practice of homosexuality seems to run contrary to a genetic account of sexual preferences. That is, if homosexuality is at least partially genetically determined, how can it be perpetuated, since homosexuals tend not to leave offspring? Wilson (1978) answers this question by once again employing the concept of *inclusive fitness*. Wilson suggests that homosexuals perpetuate their genes by helping their relatives rear and protect their children. Because it is assumed that those closely related to homosexuals carry homosexual genes, homosexuals who assist their relatives in child bearing and child rearing actually enhance their own inclusive fitness. Thus, according to Wilson, homosexuality is not abnormal or unnatural and it is perpetuated genetically via kin selection.

IMPORTANCE OF MYTH

In addition to encouraging and enforcing codes of conduct, and giving people a sense of group identity, religion also provides simple answers to complex questions. Typically, religion provides the answers to the most perplexing questions such as Where did we come from? Why are we here? and What is our ultimate fate? in the form of myths. For example, the universe is divided into heaven and hell; human existence is viewed as a struggle between good and evil; various gods or spirits control natural events, for example, volcanoes, earthquakes, and storms; and a God, gods, spirits, or demons are available to enforce whatever societal taboos exist. Lastly, religion, again through myth, explains why its adherents have a special place in the world.

Religion, then, facilitates societal living in several ways. On the negative side, however, is the fact that religions are seldom tolerant of each other. Wilson (1978) says, "The one form of altruism that religions seldom display is tolerance of other religions" (pp. 182–183). This is as true for ancient religions as it is for more modern religions. Each religion is made up of rules, regulations, myths, and ceremonies and rituals. Each religion sanctifies a particular way of societal life, provides answers to the great mysteries of life, and makes its adherents believe they are special in some way, for example, that they are God's favourite people. All of this would be fine if only one religion generated one way of life but when more than one religion exists trouble often occurs. After all, only one set of sanctified rules and regulations can be the correct set, and only one group of people can be God's favourite. Many wars have been fought attempting to straighten out such matters, and no doubt there will be more.

Sociobiology and Freudian Theory

In their article "Freudian Psychoanalysis and Sociobiology: A Synthesis," Leak and Christopher (1982) outlined several points of agreement between Freud's theory and sociobiology.

ID, EGO, AND SUPEREGO

Id.   Like the gene, the id is inherited from our evolutionary past, is ultimately selfish, is totally unconscious, and has as its goal the survival and reproductive success of the person.

Ego.   Because neither the genes nor the id come into contact with social and physical reality, they require a mediating structure to satisfy their selfish needs. In sociobiology, this mediating mechanism is that cortical region of the brain responsible for consciousness;

for Freud it was the ego. In both cases, the mechanisms are responsible for allowing the person to deal effectively with physical reality in meeting his or her survival and reproductive needs. Thus for both Freud and the sociobiologists much human behaviour and most cognitive processes are rooted in biology.

Furthermore, both Freud and the sociobiologists view humans as flexible problem solvers whose primary goal is to maximize fitness under varied and changing circumstances. Leak and Christopher (1982) say:

> The concept of the ego as a reality-oriented system that maximizes instinctual gratification while minimizing punishment accords perfectly with the cost-benefit-analyzing, fitness-maximizing view of behavior derived from natural selection theory. (p. 317)

Leak and Christopher (1982) continue:

> Since the advent of sociobiology, *strategy* has become a ubiquitous term in the literature of animal behavior. The implication that organisms exercise choices among an array of options is quite deliberate. In this . . . sociobiology and psychoanalytic theory seem . . . congruent. Freud argued that although individuals work toward similar goals, their methods of obtaining them differ according to historical and situational factors. This is a position sociobiologists find easy to defend. (p. 321)

Superego.   As we have seen, it is often adaptive to conform to norms and standards of a group even when doing so seems in opposition to one's selfish biological interests. It is also advantageous to help fellow humans if they are likely to help you in return. In Freudian theory, the superego accounts for altruistic behaviour. The values of the culture are instilled into children, usually via their parents, by rewarding "appropriate" behaviour (resulting in the ego ideal) and punishing "inappropriate" behaviour (resulting in the conscience). Once instilled, these values will promote positive feelings when doing what is culturally appropriate and negative feelings (for example, guilt) when doing what is inappropriate. Getting along with others, conforming to societal norms, and helping others in times of need are among the behaviours usually considered appropriate, and according to Freud, these actions are learned. The sociobiologists reject the heavy emphasis on learning in the Freudian analysis of altruism and other forms of social behaviour. According to them, if learning is involved at all, it is *prepared learning.* That is, the person is biologically prepared to learn such behaviour and, therefore, learns it with ease.

Both Freud and the sociobiologists believe it is the experience of various emotions that cause a person to conform to the norms and standards of a group. Leak and Christopher (1982) summarize the importance of emotions for altruistic behaviour:

> It is possible to view emotions such as guilt, gratitude, sympathy, and pride as proximate mechanisms which motivate appropriately adaptive behavior. For example, guilt may in fact be a selfishly motivated emotion that causes a cheater to make reparations, hence increasing the cheater's chances of being allowed to remain in the altruism network and reap its benefits. Similarly, moral indignation is a way of galvanizing the person into taking appropriate action against a cheater. . . . The reliance on norms and customs may be a way of simplifying the problem of identifying cheaters, and the tendency to conform may increase one's chances of being perceived as a genuine altruist, one worth trusting. (p. 317)

Leak and Christopher (1982, p. 317) speculate that perhaps the id reflects tendencies developed before humans lived in social groups, and the superego reflects tendencies that developed to enhance living in social groups.

AGGRESSION

As we have seen, Freud viewed aggression as a tension that must be periodically relieved. The sociobiologists disagree with the Freudian position on aggression, arguing instead for an interactionist position that stresses the importance of both genes and the environment. The sociobiological position is that humans inherit the capacity to act aggressively but will do so only when it maximizes fitness. For example, humans are likely to fight among themselves in environments where valuable resources are scarce. Should circumstances change and resources become more plentiful, aggression among humans decreases. Unfortunately, many occasions have occurred in human history when aggression has been effective in protecting or expanding one's resources. So, although Freud and the sociobiologists disagree on the exact nature of human aggression, they do agree that a great deal of aggression characterizes the human animal.

UNCONSCIOUS

The notion of the unconscious mind is central to Freudian theory and it also plays a prominent role in sociobiological theory. According to the sociobiologists, remaining unconscious of one's true motives makes good evolutionary sense. As we have seen, the sociobiologists assume that all human motives are ultimately selfish. Yet, for practical reasons we must cooperate with fellow humans. This whole process might be facilitated if one's selfish motives remained unconscious and only more altruistic motives were entertained consciously. This type of self-deception is fitness enhancing because the person believes he or she is motivated by social rather than individual motives.

IRRATIONALITY AND RATIONALITY

Finally, Freud believed that although it is extremely difficult, unconscious motives can be made conscious and thereby dealt with rationally. Although Freud believed most human behaviour was unconsciously motivated, he also believed it did not need to be. In fact, he hoped his theory would provide the information necessary for human behaviour to become more rational. Assuming that what Barash calls whisperings are unconscious and realizing they have a different origin than the unconscious motives in Freud's theory, Freud and the sociobiologists seem to be making the same point. To know which whisperings to allow full expression, which to encourage, and which to discourage, we must first know what those whisperings are. It may not be possible to eliminate a whispering without somehow changing our genetic makeup but, once known, like unconscious motives made conscious, they can be dealt with rationally.

Sociobiology and Jungian Theory

Similarity exists between Jung's concept of archetypes and what the sociobiologists call whisperings (or the biogrammar). Both Jung and the sociobiologists stress general inherited predispositions to respond to certain categories of experience. According to the sociobiologists, these predispositions were selected by evolution because of their survival value. Jung does not give a mechanism for the perpetuation of these predispositions but he does say they represent the collective memory of universal human emotional experiences. The important similarity between Jung and the sociobiologists is that both say our behaviour is strongly influenced by what has happened to our ancestors throughout evolutionary history. Also, both agree that neither specific ideas nor specific behaviour patterns are inherited. Rather, a general tendency to respond to certain categories of experience is inherited from our distant past.

Evaluation

EMPIRICAL RESEARCH

If what is meant by empirical research is controlled experimental research, not much exists to substantiate sociobiology. It should be realized, however, that sociobiologists study behaviour in the natural environment. Therefore, much of the research offered to support sociobiology is based on naturalistic observations. Such research *is* empirical but it is not experimental. A major problem with naturalistic observation is that it is difficult to determine, with any degree of certainty, the causes of the behaviour that is observed. Because the causes of complex, naturally occurring behaviour are hard to specify, they are, to a large extent, a matter of speculation. For example, the explanation of the social behaviour observed by the sociobiologists based on evolutionary theory is only one possible explanation. As we shall see, some critics of sociobiology maintain that everything it explains in evolutionary terms can be better explained in terms of learning.

Evolutionary theorists believe that females should value specific attributes in their mates to increase the probability of reproductive success, including fondness for children, ambition, and earning potential. This idea has been recently evaluated in the context of artificial insemination. Would the same mate selection criteria be imposed on an unseen sperm donor? Joanna Scheib (1994) from McMaster University asked female undergraduates to state their preference for either a long-term mate or a sperm donor. The sperm donor group rated health, physical attributes, and abilities as more important than the long-term mate group; highly heritable factors, such as eye colour, hair colour, height, and health were especially important to the donor group. This seems to support the evolutionary principle, since the sperm donor need neither care for the children nor support them financially.

Sociobiology explains behaviour as based on interactions between behavioural tendencies and culture. How heritable are factors that affect behaviour, such as personality traits and intelligence? Much of the work exploring the relation among genetics, intelligence, and personality has been conducted by Phillip Vernon from the University of Western Ontario and Kerry Jang from the University of British Columbia. One twin study (Harris, Vernon, & Jang, 1998) showed that intelligence correlated positively with personality dimensions of achievement, autonomy, dominance, endurance, sentience, and understanding, and correlated negatively with harm avoidance and order. Furthermore, heritability estimates (indexing the contribution of genetic factors) were high for both the IQ scores and the personality dimensions, suggesting moderate to substantial genetic influence on both.

The same researchers (Jang, Livesley, & Vernon, 1996) analyzed personality data for several hundred identical and fraternal twins. They found that identical twins had more similar personalities than fraternal twins, suggesting at least a moderate genetic influence on personality development. Moreover, the correlations were significantly higher for twins aged 30 to 65 years than for those aged 18 to 25 years. That the genetic contribution to personality increases with age suggests that our personality profile may grow more rigid over time, or that characteristics may be more malleable earlier in life.

CRITICISMS

Sociobiology Is Not Falsifiable.   In chapter 1, we saw that, according to Karl Popper, for a theory to be considered scientific it must be falsifiable. That is, it must make risky predictions. If no conceivable observation would refute or falsify the theory, then the theory is not scientific. According to Harvard paleontologist Stephen Jay Gould (1978), sociobiology is like Christian fundamentalism because for both no possible negative cases, exceptions, or refutations exist. In other words, neither can be falsified. According to Gould, whenever sociobiologists want to demonstrate that a current form of social behaviour has been naturally selected because it has adaptive value they make up a "just-so story." A just-so story is an explanation of behaviour that sounds plausible and, in fact, may be true but is not supported by any solid evidence.

Sociobiology Is Based on Adaptationism.   Similarly, Gould and Lewontin (1979) criticized sociobiology for accepting an adaptationist program. The adaptationists believe if a structure or a behavioural tendency exists now, it must have been conducive to the survival of our ancestors. Gould and Lewontin (1979) found three faults with this view (1) factors other than adaptation cause evolutionary change (genetic drift and genetic mutations are two examples); (2) a trait is not necessarily adaptive in our present environment because it was adaptive in the environments of our distant relatives; and (3) a characteristic may have evolved for specific reasons in the past but may be used in totally different ways in the modern world. The way the brain functions, for example, is a result of its evolution, but the computing powers of the brain are now used to solve the problems of modern living, which are often unlike any experienced in our evolutionary past.

Gould and Lewontin (1979) also say that accepting an adaptationist program results in believing that this must be the best of all possible worlds. This is because human social behaviour is the product of millions of years of evolution and should, therefore, be maximally adaptive. Lewontin, Rose, and Kamin (1984) also make this point:

> The claim that genetically determined social organization is a product of natural selection has the further consequence of suggesting that society is in some sense optimal or adaptive. While genetic fixity in itself is logically quite sufficient to support the status quo, the claim that present social arrangements are also optimal adds to their palatability. It is rather a handy feature of life that what must be is also the best. (p. 237)

As we have seen, however, this concept is *not* what the sociobiologists believe. Rather they believe that many of the tendencies we inherit are obsolete, troublesome, or even dangerous, and that such tendencies should be actively inhibited. Surely the sociobiologists see that the world is anything but perfect.

Sociobiology Legitimizes the Status Quo.   The above criticism is closely related to the criticism that sociobiology legitimizes the status quo. Lewontin, Rose, and Kamin (1984) say:

> The general appeal of sociobiology is in its legitimation of the *status quo*. . . . If men dominate women, it is because they must. If employers exploit their workers, it is because evolution has built into us the genes for entrepreneurial activity. If we kill each other in war, it is the force of our genes for territoriality, xenophobia, tribalism, and aggression. Such a theory can become a powerful weapon in the hands of ideologues who protect an embattled social organization by "a genetic defense of the

free market." It also serves at the personal level to explain individual acts of oppression and to protect the oppressors against the demands of the oppressed. It is "why we do what we do" and "why we sometimes behave like cavemen." (pp. 236–237)

As we have seen throughout this chapter, however, the sociobiologists do not believe that just because something is natural, it is necessarily good. Believing that would be committing the naturalistic fallacy. They do say, however, that natural behaviours are learned and maintained more easily than unnatural behaviours. In other words, if a culture decides that unnatural behaviour is more desirable than natural behaviour, that culture will need to expend vast resources developing and maintaining the unnatural behaviour. According to the sociobiologists, this can be done and, in many cases, should be done.

Sociobiology Accepts a Rigid, Biological Determinism. Some have criticized sociobiology for accepting the position that humans are "hard wired" by genetics to respond to specific situations in specific ways.

Because the sociobiologists spend so much time emphasizing that human behaviour is *always* the result of the *interaction* between biological predispositions *and* culture, it is hard to understand how they can be accused of promoting a strict biological determinism. As we have seen, Barash pleads with students of human behaviour not to follow "nothing butism"—that is, believing that human behaviour is nothing but genetically determined, or that it is nothing but culturally determined.

> Fortunately, there is some good news. Human beings, intelligent primates that we are, can exercise choice. We can overcome our primitive limitations and short-sightedness. We can learn all sorts of difficult things, once we become convinced that they are important, or unavoidable. We can even learn to do things that go against our nature. A primate that can be toilet trained could possibly even be planet trained someday. (Barash, 1986, p. 254)

Sociobiology Is Racist. Through the theory of kin altruism, which holds that people are more likely to help someone closely related to them and to fear those most unlike themselves, sociobiologists have been accused of justifying xenophobia and racism. Barash (1979) says:

> People of different races *are* different. Although we are all one species and quite capable of exchanging genes, the fact remains that members of any race seem likely to share more genes with each other than with individuals of a different race. Physical resemblance almost certainly has some correlation with genetic resemblance, and, accordingly, we can expect the principles of kin-selected altruism to operate on this fact. More to the point, we can expect the other side of the coin—antagonism toward those who are different. (p. 153)

Again, the sociobiologists are not saying that what is natural is good; rather, they argue that society must commit resources to encourage what is best.

Sociobiology Is Sexist. Sociobiology does specify several biologically based male-female differences—for example, those involved in parental investment, mate selection strategies, and aggressiveness. Because of these observations, sociobiology has been criticized for being sexist. To *describe* male and female traits, say the sociobiologists, is not the same as the differential *valuing* of those traits (for example, claiming that one sex is somehow better than the other). Disciplines such as anatomy and physiology describe male-female differences without being accused of sexism; so it should be with sociobiology.

In response to the question, Is sociobiology sexist? Barash (1979) says:

Evolution simply *is*—or better yet, evolution *does*. It says nothing whatever about what ought to be. . . . If females appear to be scheming and yet basically passive, males are nasty and aggressive, sometimes ridiculous and, given modern weaponry, very, very dangerous. There is probably a risk that the sociobiological understanding of male-female differences will be used to justify sexist attitudes to defend the view that it is only "natural" for men to be aggressive and for women to be more passive, and all the rest. But, as we've said before, what is natural is not necessarily what is good. Furthermore, the inclinations predicted by sociobiology are just that: inclinations! They are not certainties. . . . To my thinking, sexism occurs when society differentially values one sex above another, providing extra opportunities for one (usually the males) and denying equal opportunities for the other (usually the females). As such, it has nothing to do with sociobiology. On the other hand, sexism is also sometimes applied to the simple identification of male-female differences, and on this count sociobiology is, I suppose sexist. No one would think it awful to state that a man has a penis and a woman, a vagina. Or that a man produces sperm and a woman, eggs. But when we begin exploring the behavioral implications of these facts somebody is sure to cry "Foul." If male-female differences are sexist, we should put the blame where it really belongs, on the greatest sexist of all: "Mother" Nature! (p. 90)

CONTRIBUTIONS

Scientific Framework to Study Human Social Behaviour.   The social sciences have long suffered from what biologist Joel Cohen calls **physics envy** (Barash, 1979, p. 3). That is, social scientists are impressed by how much reliable information physics can generate using only a few scientifically rigorous theoretical principles. The social scientists have no such structure. As a result, Barash (1979) says:

The "essence" of human beings has escaped their analysis, and indeed the social sciences have never been able to agree on even the most basic principles governing their work. They have much to envy in physics.

The real strength of physics, and to a lesser extent the other natural sciences, lies in their intellectual coherence. In most cases, good science derives from a small number of relatively simple but enormously powerful ground rules. Indeed, it is re-markable how simplicity and explanatory power often go together. By contrast, the social sciences have erected an incredibly intricate but rickety Tower of Babel. Theories have proliferated with almost the abundance of their expounders, and there has been over the years a succession of Spencerians, Durkheimians, Weberians, Marxists, Freudians, Adlerians, Jungians, Piagetians, Skinnerians—and countless others. (p. 3)

Lopreato (1989) agrees with Barash that the scientific status of the social sciences leaves much to be desired, "What we have is an endless series of debates carried out in a language that shows how quarrelsome, deaf, and disoriented we are" (p. 124). With the advent of sociobiology, however, Lopreato believes this chaos may finally come to an end, "Sociobiology represents the first serious indication that a science of human behavior is finally possible" (p. 124).

Sociobiology Is Heuristic.   Many believe that sociobiology will provide several new, important, and interesting avenues of research in psychology. For example, Symons (1987) says:

The potential contribution of Darwinism to psychology does not lie merely in assigning ultimate causes to psychological mechanisms. Rather . . . Darwinism can aid our understanding of the mind: It guides research, prevents certain kinds of errors, inspires new questions, and calls attention to aspects of the mind that are normally too mundane or uniform to be noticed. . . . Even such a modest contribution to the formidable task of understanding the most complex thing in the known universe, the human brain/mind, surely will be welcomed. (pp. 143–144)

Crawford, Smith, and Krebs (1987) describe what they view as sociobiology's heuristic potential:

As a synthesis of ideas from behavioral ecology, population genetics, ethology, comparative psychology and behavior genetics, sociobiology offers the opportunity of integrating ideas from biology into the social sciences and even into the humanities. Some believe that its eventual impact may be as great as that of psychoanalysis and behaviorism. (p. xi)

SUMMARY

1. Sociobiology is based on Darwin's theory of evolution, which includes the concepts of struggle for survival, survival of the fittest, and natural selection. For Darwin, an organism's fitness was determined by its ability to survive and produce offspring. Sociobiology emphasizes inclusive fitness—that is, perpetuating copies of our genes either by producing offspring, or by assisting close relatives so they can survive and reproduce.

2. The two basic assumptions of sociobiology are: (1) The primary motive for every living organism, including humans, is to perpetuate copies of its genes into the next generation; and (2) adaptive social behaviour is shaped by natural selection just as anatomical features and physiological mechanisms are.

3. Most social scientists accept the empirical theory of human nature, which assumes that a person's nature is determined by his or her cumulative experiences; for them learning is all-important in determining human social behaviour. Sociobiologists believe that humans are born with a biogrammar (whisperings, innate predispositions) that has been selected by evolution. Cultural universals are seen as evidence that the human mind is not a blank tablet at birth. Many social scientists seek the causes of human behaviour in proximate causes: a person's internal and external environment and life's experiences. The sociobiologists, conversely, consider the ultimate causes of behaviour to lie in the evolutionary process.

4. We inherit general tendencies or predispositions to act in some ways instead of others. Because these tendencies are modified by culture, human social behaviour results from an interaction between innate tendencies and cultural influences. Culture must always maintain a reasonable relationship to human biology. If it strays too far from human biology, social behaviour will disintegrate and eventually reproduction will cease. Human biology, then, holds culture on a leash, sometimes a long leash. Both Wilson and Barash believe that much in culture represents the extension or amplification of slight biological tendencies (called hypertrophy or cultural hyperextension).

5. Sociobiologists believe both the human mind and body are the products of evolution. Mental processes, both conscious and unconscious, exist as they do because they enhanced the survival and reproduction of our ancestors. The genes influence cognitive processes through epigenetic rules. Primary epigenetic rules determine what types of sensations and perceptions we can have. Secondary epigenetic rules determine which sensations or perceptions are selected for further processing, and how they are evaluated intellectually and emotionally and then acted on. Evaluation via the secondary epigenetic rules is always done relative to survival and reproduction.

6. We are willing to help our close relatives because in doing so we are increasing our inclusive fitness. Through the preferential treatment

of relatives we perpetuate our genes through kin selection. We agree to help nonrelatives because it is understood that if and when we need help, we, too, will receive it. The help you receive may come from the person you helped (direct reciprocity) or from someone else in the community (indirect reciprocity). With reciprocal altruism cheating is possible—that is, taking but not giving. In every human society, rules and regulations reward reciprocal altruism and punish cheaters. Sociobiologists conclude that true altruism (giving and expecting nothing in return) does not exist.

7. For males, a sexual act may result in offspring and, therefore, would enhance their fitness. The more females a male can inseminate, the greater is his fitness. For the female, childbearing involves an enormous investment of time, energy, and resources. To maximize her investment, a female tends to seek a mate who carries genes that are likely to create healthy offspring, has resources that would enhance the survival of her and her offspring, and would be willing to share those resources. The optimal female strategy is to discriminate among males. The optimal male strategy is to be promiscuous. The difference between these strategies is believed to be the basis for the double standard.

8. Because males have such a small investment in reproduction and because they can never be absolutely certain an offspring carries their genes, they tend not to get involved in parenting. According to the sociobiologists, females tend to become jealous when another female threatens to reduce the resources being provided to her by her mate. Males tend to become jealous when their mates associate with other males, thereby bringing into question the authenticity of their parenthood. The fact that males become involved in parenting at all may be explained by the mate's sexual availability. Frequent sex creates a bond between partners. For males, the most natural mating arrangement appears to be polygyny (having more than one mate). Polyandry (females having more than one mate) is extremely rare, and monogamy (having one mate) may be biologically unnatural for males.

9. Humans are more interested in their own genes than in those of others. Thus, stepparents tend to have more problems with children than natural parents and adoption is an overwhelming

second choice among parents. The sociobiologists suspect that intentional childlessness could cause some psychological or emotional damage because such a decision runs contrary to millions of years of evolution.

10. The sociobiologists do not accept the drive-discharge model of aggression offered by Freud. Rather, humans are capable of acting aggressively but do so only when a cost-benefit analysis justifies aggression Often organisms will act aggressively in defence of their territories. Members of a tribe or nation may engage in war if they believe their territory is threatened. However, to claim such a tendency is good because it is natural is to commit the naturalistic fallacy.

11. Sociobiologists believe that rapists tend to be men who are losers in the competition with other males for females. Rape is a desperate attempt to perpetuate one's genes when one is not chosen by a female. This theory of rape predicts that rapists will tend to be poor young men, and rape victims will tend to be fertile young women. Research has supported both predictions.

12. Offspring resulting from an incestuous relationship are at increased risk for genetic defects. Therefore, it makes good evolutionary sense to avoid such relationships, and taboos against incest are culturally universal. Freud believed incest taboos were necessary to inhibit strong sexual attractions among family members. Westermarck believed at least brother-sister incest was naturally inhibited if brother and sister interacted closely as young children. In societies in which close, intimate contact is encouraged between children and between children and adults, the Westermarck effect operates to inhibit incestuous relationships. In societies in which close, intimate contact among family members is discouraged (such as the one in which Freud grew up), strong taboos appear to be needed to inhibit incestuous relationships.

13. De Catanzaro speculated that people who commit suicide are those whose continued existence would not contribute to their inclusive fitness and may even operate against it. Groups with a high risk of suicide include the terminally ill; the chronically unemployed; the socially isolated; and those who are single, divorced, widowed, or in an unstable marriage. Other forms of self-destructive behaviour such as overeating, smoking, drinking alcohol, or taking drugs are

thought to result from the incompatibility between the conditions under which humans evolved and those under which we now live.

14. Religion plays several important roles in human society: It gives its adherents a sense of kinship; it sanctifies the rules and regulations governing social life, including those related to reciprocal altruism; it simplifies life by dichotomizing the people in the world into friends and enemies, and by providing myths that offer simple answers to complex questions; and it encourages people to subordinate their selfish interests to those of the community. In general, religion functions to encourage behaviour conducive to survival and to discourage behaviour that is not. For this reason, many religions contain sanctions against nonreproductive sexual behaviour.

15. Freud and the sociobiologists agree that humans are basically selfish; the unconscious mind is important; humans are flexible problem solvers; emotional experience guides behaviour; and self-deception plays a significant role in behaviour. Freud and the sociobiologists disagree on the origin of the superego and in their explanations of human aggression. Both Jung and the sociobiologists believe that much current human behaviour can be understood in terms of our evolutionary past, and that myth plays a prominent role in human existence.

16. Sociobiology has been criticized for accepting or supporting an array of radical, political viewpoints; not being falsifiable; accepting an adaptationist program; accepting a rigid, biological determinism; legitimizing the status quo; supporting racism; and being sexist. The contributions of sociobiology include providing the social sciences a scientific theory from which to study human behaviour and providing many new avenues of research.

EXPERIENTIAL EXERCISES

1. List those aspects of your life that are of special importance, for example, relationships, education, health, employment, or finances. Which of these areas of concern could have a biological basis? That is, which of them could reflect whisperings within you? Explain.

2. Ponder a few members of the opposite sex you find especially attractive. Determine what characteristics those persons have in common. Are the characteristics you find attractive in accordance with the predictions made by sociobiology? Explain.

3. Describe an experience you have had with the double standard. Do you agree with sociobiology's explanation of the origin of the double standard?

4. Has it been your experience that females are more committed to parenting than males? Do you think our culture values mothers more than fathers as parents? Are your observations in accordance with sociobiology or not? Explain.

5. List the 10 people you care the most about. For example, for whom would you be most willing to make a sacrifice? According to sociobiology, your list should be dominated by persons with whom you are either genetically related or with whom you are bonded through sexual intimacy. How does your list compare to the one predicted by sociobiology?

6. Do you agree with the sociobiologists that all human behaviour is ultimately selfish? Explain.

7. Based on your own life experiences, describe the conditions under which females and males experience jealousy. Are the reasons the same? Different? Are the reasons in accordance with those suggested by sociobiology? Explain.

8. Is your experience with religion compatible with the sociobiological explanation of religion? Explain why or why not.

9. Summarize aspects of sociobiology with which you agree or disagree. Do you agree that sociobiology offers a valuable framework within which to study human behaviour?

DISCUSSION QUESTIONS

1. Briefly discuss the following terms: *struggle for survival, adaptation, survival of the fittest, fitness, inclusive fitness, natural selection.*
2. According to Barash, why are some behaviours and experiences "sweeter" than others?
3. According to the sociobiologists, what do females tend to look for in a mate? What do males tend to look for in a mate?
4. What is the naturalistic fallacy?
5. Describe each of the following criticisms of sociobiology, and indicate whether you accept or reject it and why: Sociobiology is not falsifiable, sociobiology is based on adaptationism, sociobiology accepts a rigid biological determinism, sociobiology legitimizes the status quo, sociobiology is racist, and sociobiology is sexist.

KEY TERMS

Adaptation, p. 307
Altruism, p. 316
Behavioural potentiality, p. 313
Biogrammar, p. 310
Biological determinism, p. 313
Cheating, p. 317
Cost-benefit analysis, p. 325
Cultural hyperextension, p. 314
Cultural universals, p. 310
Double standard, p. 319
Drive-discharge model of aggression, p. 325
Empirical theory of human nature, p. 310
Epigenetic rules, p. 315
Fertility, p. 320
Fitness, p. 307
Hypergamy, p. 320
Hypertrophy, p. 314
Inclusive fitness, p. 308
Kin altruism, p. 317
Kin selection, p. 317
Leash principle, p. 314

Monogamy, p. 321
Natural selection, p. 308
Naturalistic fallacy, p. 326
Nepotism, p. 317
Physics envy, p. 340
Polyandry, p. 321
Polygyny, p. 321
Prepared learning, p. 316
Proximate causation, p. 311
Reciprocal altruism, p. 317
Reproductive imperative, p. 333
Reproductive value, p. 320
Sociobiological theory of human nature, p. 311
Sociobiology, p. 308
Struggle for survival, p. 307
Survival of the fittest, p. 307
Territory, p. 325
Ultimate causation, p. 311
Westermarck effect, p. 328
Whisperings, p. 313
Xenophobia, p. 331

13 George Kelly

Chapter Outline

Biographical Sketch

George Alexander Kelly was born on a farm near Perth, Kansas, on April 28, 1905. He was an only child. Kelly's father had been a Presbyterian minister but because of poor health he gave up the ministry and turned to farming. In 1909, Kelly's father converted a lumber wagon into a covered wagon and used it to move his family to Colorado, where they staked a claim to a plot of land offered free to settlers. They returned to their farm in Kansas, however, when they were unable to find water on their claim. Kelly never lost the pioneer spirit derived from his early experiences. He remained a practical person throughout his life; his overriding concern with an idea or a device was whether it worked; if it did not, he had no time for it. Furthermore, Kelly was strongly influenced by his parents' deep religious convictions and remained an active member of the church.

Kelly's early education consisted of attending a one-room schoolhouse and being tutored by his parents. When he was 13, he was sent to Wichita, where he eventually attended four high schools. After the age of 13, Kelly seldom lived at home again. On graduation from high school, he enrolled in the Friends University in Wichita, a Quaker school. After three years he moved to Park College in Parkville, Missouri, where he earned his BA degree in physics and mathematics in 1926. Kelly remembered his first psychology class as totally unimpressive. For the first few weeks he waited in vain for something interesting to be said. One day the instructor began to discuss stimulus-response psychology and placed "SR" on the blackboard. Finally, Kelly thought, they were getting to the crux of the matter. Kelly (1969) recalled his disappointment:

George Kelly

Although I listened intently for several sessions, after that the most I could make of it was that the "S" was what you had to have in order to account for the "R" and the "R" was put there so the "S" would have something to account for. I never did find out what that arrow stood for—not to this day—and I have pretty well given up trying to figure it out. (p. 47)

Kelly had originally planned on a career as an engineer but decided such a career would not allow him to deal with social problems, with which he was becoming increasingly concerned. As a result, he enrolled in the MA program at the University of Kansas, with a major in educational sociology and a minor in labour relations. For his master's thesis, he studied how workers in Kansas City spent their leisure time. He was awarded an MA degree in 1928. It was during his graduate training at the University of Kansas that Kelly decided it was time for him to become acquainted with the writings of Freud. He was about as impressed by Freud's theory as he was by SR psychology. "I don't remember which one of Freud's books I was trying to read, but I do remember the mounting feeling of incredulity that anyone could write such nonsense, much less publish it" (Kelly, 1969, p. 47).

The next year was a busy one for Kelly. He taught part-time in a labour college in Minneapolis, speech classes for the American Bankers Association, and an Americanization class to immigrants wishing to become citizens. Finally, in the winter of 1928, he joined the faculty at a junior college in Sheldon, Iowa, where he met his future wife, Gladys Thompson. Among his other duties, he coached dramatics and that, as we shall see, may have influenced Kelly's later theorizing.

In 1929, Kelly was awarded an exchange scholarship, which enabled him to spend a year at the University of Edinburgh, in Scotland, where he worked closely with Sir Godfrey Thomson, who was largely responsible for Kelly developing an interest in psychology. In 1930, Kelly earned a degree in education from the University of Edinburgh. His thesis, under the supervision of Thomson, was on predicting teaching success.

On returning to the United States in 1930, Kelly enrolled in a psychology program at the State University of Iowa, where he earned his Ph.D. in 1931. His dissertation was on the common factors in speech and reading disabilities. Two days after graduation, he married Gladys Thompson, and they eventually had two children. By the time Kelly obtained his Ph.D. in psychology at the age of 26, he had already studied physics, mathematics, sociology, education, labour relations, economics, speech pathology, cultural anthropology, and biometrics.

Kelly's academic career began at Fort Hays Kansas State College, in the midst of the Great Depression. He soon learned that his interest in physiological psychology, which he had pursued at the State University of Iowa, would do him little good under his present circumstances. He noted that the people with whom he had contact simply did not know what to do with their lives—they were confused. Kelly, therefore, switched his interests to clinical psychology, for which there was a great need. It turns out that Kelly had a great advantage at this point, in that *he was not formally trained in any particular clinical technique*. This, along with his practical nature, gave him great latitude in trying a variety of approaches in treating emotional problems. What worked was salvaged; what did not work was discarded.

During his 13-year (1931 to 1943) stay at Fort Hays, Kelly developed travelling clinics, which served the state's public school system, making Kelly an early school psychologist (Guydish, Jackson, Markley, & Zelhart, 1985). This service allowed Kelly and his students to encounter a wide range of psychological problems and to experiment with ways of treating them. Initially, Kelly returned to the Freudian notions that, as a student, he found to be untenable, and he found them to be effective; "Through my

Freudian interpretations, judiciously offered at those moments when clients seemed ready for them, a good many unfortunate persons seemed to be profoundly helped" (Kelly, 1963, p. 51). However, Kelly was haunted by the feeling that Freudian therapy worked only because his clients believed it should. It was at this time that Kelly made two observations that were to have a profound influence on his later theory. First, he found that even if he made up a radical explanation for a client's problem, the client would accept it and usually improve. In other words, Kelly noted that anything that caused clients to look at themselves or their problems differently caused improvement in the situation. Logic, or "correctness," seemed to have little to do with it. Kelly described his experiment with psychotherapy as follows:

> I began fabricating "insights." I deliberately offered "preposterous interpretations" to my clients. Some of them were about as un-Freudian as I could make them—first proposed somewhat cautiously, of course, and then, as I began to see what was happening, more boldly. My only criteria were that the explanation account for the crucial facts as the client saw them, and that it carry implications for approaching the future in a different way. (1969, p. 52)

Second, Kelly noted that a teacher's complaint about a student often said more about the teacher than it did about the student. It was the way the teacher was *seeing things* that determined the nature of the problem rather than some objective event that everyone could experience. It was observations like these that stimulated Kelly to develop perhaps one of the boldest theories of personality since Freud's.

At the beginning of World War II, Kelly was in charge of a local civilian pilot-training program. Eventually he joined the navy as a psychologist in the Bureau of Medicine and Surgery and was stationed in Washington, D.C. While in the service, he did much to improve the quality and effectiveness of clinical psychology in the armed forces. Kelly remained active in a number of government programs related to clinical psychology until his death.

In 1945, when the war ended, Kelly was appointed associate professor at the University of Maryland, where he remained for one year. In 1946, he became professor of psychology and director of clinical psychology at Ohio State University. Although the department was extremely small, Kelly, along with Julian B. Rotter, also destined to become a prominent psychologist, developed a clinical psychology program that many considered to be the best in the country. It was during his 19 years at Ohio State that Kelly refined and tested his theory of personality. As we mentioned in chapter 11, Walter Mischel was a student of Rotter's and Kelly's and their influence is clearly evident in social cognitive theory.

During 1960 to 1961, Kelly and his wife received a grant from the Human Ecology Fund that allowed them to travel around the world lecturing on the relationship between Kelly's theory and various international problems. Their journey carried them to Madrid, London, Oslo, Louvain, Copenhagen, Prague, Warsaw, Moscow, the Caribbean area, and South America. It was quite an adventure for someone who claimed never to have gotten all the Kansas mud off his shoes. In 1965, Kelly left Ohio State to accept an appointment to an endowed chair at Brandeis University. Kelly died on March 6, 1967, at the age of 62.

Kelly was remembered by his students and colleagues as a warm, accepting person. His outgoing nature was apparent during the summer of 1965 when his colleagues at Ohio State gathered to congratulate him for having been awarded an endowed chair at Brandeis University. At the end of the presentations, Kelly rose to invite the entire gathering to his house for dinner. Nearly a hundred accepted the offer, yet Kelly managed "good food for all and a characteristic abundance of warm fellowship" (Thompson, 1968, p. 22). Compared to the other theorists covered in this book, Kelly wrote relatively little. The major presentation of his theory is found in his two-volume work *The Psychology of Personal Constructs* (1955). In the preface to volume 1 of this work, Kelly gave his readers fair warning about what they were about to read:

> It is only fair to warn the reader about what may be in store for him. In the first place, he is likely to find missing most of the familiar landmarks of psychology books. For example, the *learning*, so honorably embedded in most psychological texts, scarcely appears at all. That is wholly intentional; we are for throwing it overboard altogether. There is no *ego*, no *emotion*, no *motivation*, no *reinforcement*, no *drive*, no *unconscious*, no *need*. There are some words with brand-new psychological definitions, words like *foci of convenience, preemption, propositionality, fixed-role therapy, creativity cycle, transitive diagnosis*, and *the credulous approach. Anxiety* is defined in a special systematic way. *Role, guilt*, and *hostility* carry definitions altogether unexpected by many; and to make heresy complete, there is no extensive bibliography. Unfortunately, all this will make for periods of strange, and perhaps uncomfortable, reading. Yet, inevitably, a different approach calls for a different lexicon; and, under its influence, many old terms are unhitched from their familiar meanings.
>
> To whom are we speaking? In general, we think the reader who takes us seriously will be an adventuresome soul who is not one bit afraid of thinking unorthodox thoughts about people, who dares peer out at the world through the eyes of strangers, who has not invested beyond his means in either ideas or vocabulary, and who is looking for an ad interim, rather than an ultimate, set of psychological insights. (pp. x–xi)

Categorization of Kelly's Theory

Without formal clinical training, Kelly was not indoctrinated in any particular school of thought. Confronted by people with problems, he had to improvise his own techniques. He had no mentor to guide him; he came from no department with a particular philosophical leaning; and he was not surrounded by clinical colleagues who steered him in a certain direction. Thus, if Kelly's theory resembles anyone else's, it is coincidental. As we shall see, Kelly believed that a person's present personality need not be tied to his or her past. He believed the same to be true of personality theories; that is, to be valid, a theory need not grow out of those theories already in existence. Kelly's theory of personality is probably as independent of other theoretical positions as a theory can be.

Kelly's theory, however, can be classified in certain ways. First, Kelly was a **phenomenologist** (see, for example, Walker, 1990). Phenomenologists believe that intact conscious experience should be psychology's focus of attention. It should not matter where such experiences originate; the important thing to study, the phenomenologists believe, is a person's individual conscious experiences, without breaking them down into component parts or attempting to determine their origin. Unlike some phenomenologists, however, he was only interested in such experience in relationship to objective reality. That is, he was interested in how thought processes are used while interacting with the environment.

Kelly's theory can also be labelled cognitive (see, for example, Cantor & Zirkel, 1990). It is not a behavioural theory because the emphasis is not on behaviour and its causal relationships to the environment; it is not a psychoanalytic theory because it does not stress unconscious mechanisms or early experience in the determination of adult personality; and it is not a trait theory because it does not attempt to categorize people in terms of their traits. It is a **cognitive theory** because it stresses how people *view* and *think about* reality.

Kelly's theory can also be considered an **existential theory** because it emphasizes the present and the future rather than the past, and because it assumes that humans are free to choose their own destinies. In general, existentialism assumes that humans are free and future oriented, that their subjective feelings and personal experience are extremely important, and that they are concerned with the meaning of life. The existentialists also believe that because humans are free, they are responsible for their own destinies. Generally, existentialists examine the problems of human existence. The statement that man "is what he wills to be," by the famous existential philosopher Jean-Paul Sartre (1956, p. 291), fairly well summarizes both Kelly's and the existentialist's position.

Last, Kelly's theory can be considered a **humanistic theory** (see, for example, Epting & Leitner, 1992) because it stresses the human capacity for improvement. Kelly urged each person to continue to explore new possibilities for living, possibilities that may turn out to be more effective than those already tried. Both Kelly and the humanists believed humans sought, and were capable of, better personal, sociological, and international conditions.

It should be emphasized that all of these labels were provided by others. Kelly believed that his theory was "too fluid to be pinned down by verbal labels" (1966, p. 15).

Basic Postulate—People as Scientists

Kelly took the scientist as the model for describing all humans. He noted that scientists constantly seek clarity and understanding in their lives by developing theories that will allow them to predict future events; in other words, *the scientist's main goal is to reduce uncertainty*. Kelly believed that, like scientists, all humans attempt to clarify their lives by reducing uncertainty. For example, you might routinely expect a bus driver to greet you when you step on, and say good-bye when you exit. If one day the driver does neither, you may be troubled, and would at least ask yourself (and possibly the driver) why. Therefore the distinction between the scientist and the nonscientist is not a valid one:

> It is as though the psychologist were saying to himself, "I, being a *psychologist*, and therefore a *scientist*, am performing this experiment in order to improve the prediction and control of certain human phenomena; but my subject, being merely a human organism, is obviously propelled by inexorable drives welling up within him, or else he is in gluttonous pursuit of sustenance and shelter." (Kelly, 1955, p. 5)

According to Kelly, all humans are like scientists in that they are interested in the future and use the present only to test a theory's ability to anticipate events. "Anticipation is not merely carried on for its own sake; it is carried on so that future reality may be better represented. It is the future which tantalizes man, not the past. Always he reaches out to the future through the window of the present" (Kelly, 1955, p. 49).

The major tool a person uses in anticipating events is the **personal construct**. Personal constructs are used by individuals to **construe** or interpret, explain, give meaning to, or predict experiences. A **construct** is an idea that a person uses when attempting to interpret his or her own personal experiences. A construct is like a mini-scientific theory, in that it makes predictions about reality. If the predictions generated by a construct are confirmed by experience, it is useful; if the predictions are not confirmed, the construct must be revised or abandoned. "Man looks at his world through transparent patterns or templets which he creates and then attempts to fit over the realities of which the world is composed. . . . Let us give the name *constructs* to these patterns that are tentatively tried on for size. They are ways of construing the world" (Kelly, 1955, pp. 8–9).

We have more to say about constructs in the next section, but it is important to note they are usually verbal labels that a person applies to environmental events and then tests with subsequent experience with those events. For example, on meeting a person for the first time, one might construe that person with the construct of "friendly." If the person's subsequent behaviour is in accordance with the construct of friendly, then the construct will be useful in anticipating that person's behaviour. If the new acquaintance acts in an unfriendly manner, he or she will need to be construed either with different constructs or by using the other pole (see the Dichotomy Corollary in the next section) of the friendly–unfriendly construct. The point is that constructs are used to anticipate the future, so they must fit reality. Arriving at a **construct system** that corresponds fairly closely to reality is largely a matter of trial and error. According to Kelly, a person's **personality** refers to the collection of constructs that constitute his or her construct system at any given time.

Kelly emphasized the fact that each person *creates his or her own constructs* for dealing with the world. He believed that, although all people have the goal of reducing future uncertainty, they are free to construe reality any way they wish. He called this belief **constructive alternativism**, which he described as follows: "We take the stand that there are always some alternative constructions available to choose among in dealing with the world. No one needs to paint himself into a corner; no one needs to be completely hemmed in by circumstances; no one needs to be the victim of his biography" (1955, p. 15).

Although it is true that no one *needs* to "paint himself into a corner," it does not mean people do not do so. Here we have an interesting distinction between freedom and determinism. Kelly believed individuals are free to create their own construct systems, but he also believed they are controlled by them after they are created.

Kelly noted that some of the construct systems created by people were more effective than others. Some individuals arrive at inflexible convictions about the world and become slaves to them. The lives of such individuals are dominated by rules and regulations, and they live within a narrow range of highly predictable events. Others have a broader perspective. They live their lives in accordance with flexible principles rather than rigid rules. Such individuals live a richer life because of their openness to experience:

> Ultimately a man sets the measure of his own freedom and his own bondage by the level at which he chooses to establish his convictions. The man who orders his life in terms of many special and inflexible convictions about temporary matters makes himself the victim of circumstances. Each little prior conviction that is not open to review is a hostage he gives to fortune; it determines whether the events of tomorrow will bring happiness or misery. The man whose prior convictions encompass a broad perspective, and are cast in terms of principles rather than rules, has a much better chance of discovering alternatives which will lead eventually to his emancipation. (Kelly, 1955, pp. 21–22)

The 11 Corollaries

Kelly embellished his basic postulate by adding 11 corollaries.

1. Construction Corollary.   "A person anticipates events by construing their replications" (Kelly, 1955, p. 50).

Events in one's life occur with some regularity; for example, a friendly person will tend to remain friendly; day follows night; it tends to be cold in winter; and the physical objects in one's environment will tend to remain in place—for instance, the refrigerator probably will still be in the kitchen tomorrow. Although no two events are exactly the same ("No man ever steps into the same river twice"), nonetheless, themes running through events bind them together. It is on the basis of these themes that constructs are formed and that predictions about the future are made. In other words, if the events in our lives did not occur with some regularity, it would be impossible to form constructs that represent them.

2. Individuality Corollary.   "Persons differ from each other in their construction of events" (Kelly, 1955, p. 55).

This corollary cannot be stressed too much; it is the essence of Kelly's theory. According to Kelly, not only is beauty in the eye of the beholder, so is everything else. Reality is what we perceive it to be. This, of course, is a restatement of Kelly's notion of constructive alternativism, which says that we are free to construe events as we wish. This freedom is thought to apply not only to our interpretation of external reality but to ourselves as well.

> On occasion I may say of myself . . . "I am an introvert." "I," the subject, "am an introvert," the predicate. The language form of the statement clearly places the onus of being an introvert on the subject—me. What I actually am, the words say, is an introvert.
>
> The proper interpretation of my statement is that *I construe* myself to be an introvert, or, if I am merely being coy or devious, I am inveigling my *listener into construing me* in terms of introversion. The point that gets lost in the shuffle of words is the psychological fact that I have identified myself in terms of a personal construct—"introversion." (Kelly, 1958, p. 38)

3. Organization Corollary.   "Each person characteristically evolves, for his convenience in anticipating events, a construction system embracing ordinal relationships between constructs" (Kelly, 1955, p. 56).

Not only do individuals differ in the constructs they use to construe events but they also differ in how they organize their constructs. According to Kelly, personal constructs are arranged in a hierarchy, some being more comprehensive than others. For example, the construct extrovert–introvert subsumes such constructs as likes people–dislikes people and likes parties–dislikes parties. A construct that subsumes other constructs within it is called a **superordinate construct**, and the constructs that are subsumed under it are called **subordinate constructs**.

Neimeyer (1985) discusses a patient who viewed herself as "businesslike" as opposed to "emotional." When asked why she chose to be viewed as businesslike, she said that she regarded it as a "mature approach to life" as opposed to an "unstable" one. When asked her definition of maturity she said that it meant "being in control" as opposed to "being controlled by others." When asked why it was important to be in control, she answered that her very "survival" depended on it and the opposite of survival was viewed as "just death." Figure 13–1 summarizes the constructs the patient used to describe herself and shows that some of those constructs were superordinate and some were subordinate.

Kelly believed that without this hierarchical arrangement of constructs, one would experience contradictions and would make inaccurate predictions of events. Because this is undesirable, a person organizes constructs in a way that reduces contradictions and increases predictive efficiency.

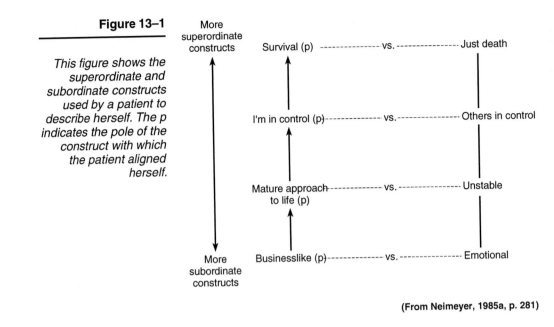

Figure 13–1

This figure shows the superordinate and subordinate constructs used by a patient to describe herself. The p indicates the pole of the construct with which the patient aligned herself.

More superordinate constructs

Survival (p) -------------- vs. -------------- Just death

I'm in control (p) -------------- vs. -------------- Others in control

Mature approach to life (p) -------------- vs. -------------- Unstable

Businesslike (p) -------------- vs. -------------- Emotional

More subordinate constructs

(From Neimeyer, 1985a, p. 281)

4. Dichotomy Corollary. "A person's construction system is composed of a finite number of dichotomous constructs" (Kelly, 1955, p. 59).

According to Kelly, all constructs are bipolar or dichotomous. He believed that for a construct to be significant, it must indicate at least two elements that are similar to each other and a third element that is different from those two. One might say, for example, that males and females are similar in that they are both humans. This, in turn, implies that some organisms are not humans, for example, apes. Also, after observing a person who provides help to his aging parents and another who donates substantially to charity, one may conclude that both individuals are "good" or "generous." This implies that people who do not engage in such activities are perhaps "bad" or "stingy" or "insensitive." It is important to note, however, that for Kelly not only is the choice of the constructs used to construe reality a personal matter but so is the choice of the poles of a construct. The dichotomous poles of a construct are not determined by logic or convention; they are whatever a person views them to be. For example, for one person, one pole of a construct may be beautiful and the contrasting pole may be insensitive. For another person, beautiful might be contrasted with ugly. For still another person, beautiful might be contrasted with unsexy. Because a person uses these personally defined constructs to construe his or her world, if one is ever going to know another person, one must know his or her construct system. For Kelly, then, a construct is a personal way of construing certain experiences as being alike and yet different from other experiences.

It has been observed that under stress people sometimes abruptly switch from construing events with one pole of an important construct to construing them using the opposite pole. For example, people previously construed as friendly may now be construed as unfriendly. Winter (1993) argues that the conversion of law-abiding police officers to law breakers can be explained by such an abrupt change in the way events are construed. The Kellians refer to such pole shifts as **slot movements.** Because therapy can be stressful, it is not uncommon for slot movements to occur during the therapeutic process (Landfield & Epting, 1987).

5. Choice Corollary. "A person chooses for himself that alternative in a dichotomized construct through which he anticipates the greater possibility for extension and definition of his system" (Kelly, 1955, p. 64).

Here the person can either be safe or take a risk. If one applies previously effective constructs to new but similar experiences, one is merely seeking further validation of one's construct system. Kelly referred to this relatively safe path as **definition** because such experiences further define or validate a construct system. Conversely, one can use the occasion to try new constructs which, if validated, would further expand one's construct system, thereby making it better able to assimilate experiences that previously were foreign to it. Kelly referred to this as **extension**. The danger in extension, as opposed to definition, is the possibility of failure. When choosing a construct, one is torn between security and adventure. One can make safe predictions or one can attempt to expand one's construct system, thereby making an ever-increasing number of experiences understandable. In Kelly's words, "One may anticipate events by trying to become more and more certain about fewer and fewer things [definition] or by trying to become vaguely aware of more and more things on the misty horizon [extension]" (1955, p. 67). According to Kelly, too much emphasis on definition may result in too much certainty and in a very restricted view of life. Conversely, emphasis on extension may result in too much uncertainty and confusion. A *middle ground is best.*

6. Range Corollary. "A construct is convenient for the anticipation of a finite range of events only" (Kelly, 1955, p. 68).

A construct such as hot versus cold cannot be applied to a situation that requires a good versus bad judgment. Each construct has a **range of convenience** that includes all of the events to which the construct is relevant:

> Suppose, for example, A and B are men, C is a woman, and O is the time of day. We abstract an aspect of A, B, and C which we may call *sex*. Sex, then is our z. Sex is not applicable to O, the time of day; at least most of us would not so abstract it. The time of day, O, does not fall within the range of convenience of sex, z. Now, with respect to sex, z, the two men, A and B, are alike and in contrast to the woman, C. (Kelly, 1955, p. 60)

The events within the range of convenience for which a construct is maximally pertinent define the construct's **focus of convenience**. For example, if one sees a wild animal rapidly approaching, the construct of dangerous–safe may be a useful one to employ in construing the situation. Certainly the event of being charged by a wild animal would fall within the range of convenience of the dangerous–safe construct. Furthermore, the notion of very dangerous would seem especially appropriate within that construct. In this situation, the construct of dangerous–safe would be employed, and the notion of very dangerous would be the focus of convenience within that construct's range of convenience. Constructs such as nice weather–bad weather or politically liberal–politically conservative would seem irrelevant to the situation. In other words, the range of convenience of the latter constructs would not include the situation at hand.

7. Experience Corollary. "A person's construction system varies as he successively construes the replications of events" (Kelly, 1955, p. 72).

Experience alone was unimportant to Kelly; what was important was the construing of experience:

> Experience is made up of the successive construing of events. It is not constituted merely by the succession of events themselves. A person can be a witness to a tremendous parade of episodes and yet, if he fails to keep making something out of them, or if he waits until they have all occurred before he attempts to reconstrue them,

he gains little in the way of experience from having been around when they happened. It is not what happens around him that makes a man experienced; it is the successive construing and reconstruing of what happens, as it happens, that enriches the experience of life. . . . The person who merely stands agog at each emerging event may experience a series of interesting surprises, but if he makes no attempt to discover the recurrent themes, his experience does not amount to much. It is when man begins to see the orderliness in a sequence of events that he begins to experience them. (Kelly, 1955, pp. 73–74)

Thus, for Kelly, experience alone is not the best teacher but the active construing of experience is. With his characteristic wit, Kelly (1963) recalled a school administrator who "had one year of experience—repeated thirteen times" (p. 171).

8. Modulation Corollary. "The variation in a person's construction system is limited by the permeability of the constructs within whose range of convenience the variants lie" (Kelly, 1955, p. 77).

Some constructs are more **permeable**—that is, open to experience—than are others. "A construct is permeable if it will admit to its range of convenience new elements which are not yet construed within its framework" (Kelly, 1955, p. 79).

For example, a person's construct nice people–awful people might be defined in terms of certain individuals, nice people consisting of a circle of close friends and awful people consisting of everyone else. Such a person is not open to experience because one pole of the construct nice people–awful people is not permeable. Thus, even if the individual encountered a person with several admirable characteristics, that person could not be assimilated into the individual's construct system because of its lack of permeability.

A person who has several permeable constructs will be in a better position to extend his or her construct system than a person who has an abundance of impermeable constructs will. The former person can be characterized as open-minded and the latter as close-minded.

9. Fragmentation Corollary. "A person may successively employ a variety of construction subsystems which are inferentially incompatible with each other" (Kelly, 1955, p. 83).

Kelly said that a person's construct system is in a state of continual flux. Different constructs are constantly being tested, and new elements are constantly entering into one's more permeable constructs. Likewise, one is constantly reorganizing one's construct system so the most reliable predictions are made. This experimentation with one's construct system creates the possibility for inconsistent behaviour. One may not respond in a consistent way to the same event each time that it is encountered. For example, the interaction with one's boss on the job and in a local bar may be totally different. One may act differently because the situation has changed, one's constructs have changed, or the organization of one's constructs has changed. Kelly believed a certain number of inconsistencies are inevitable because construct systems "are in flux," but he believed even with minor inconsistencies the overall outcome is still consistent. "We can say that while a person's bets on the turn of minor events may not appear to add up, his wagers on the outcome of life do tend to add up" (Kelly, 1955, p. 88).

10. Commonality Corollary. "To the extent that one person employs a construction of experience which is similar to that employed by another, his psychological processes are similar to the other person" (Kelly, 1955, p. 90).

With this corollary Kelly emphasized the point that it is not common *experiences* that make people similar but the fact that they construe their experiences in a similar way. Two people can have the same physical experiences but construe them differently. Likewise, it is conceivable that two similar construct systems can result from distinctly different sets of physical experiences.

11. Sociality Corollary.   "To the extent that one person construes the construction processes of another, he may play a role in a social process involving the other person" (Kelly, 1955, p. 95).

The concept of **role** was important to Kelly's theory but he did not use the concept in the traditional way. Kelly defined role as "an ongoing pattern of behavior that follows from a person's understanding of how the others who are associated with him in the task think" (1955, pp. 97–98).

In other words, playing a role is acting in accordance with the expectations of others. To play a role one must understand another person's construct system. For example, if a man wants to play the role of husband to his wife, he must first understand her expectations for the construct husband and then act accordingly. Kelly called our understanding of another person's outlook and expectations a **role construct**; how we act in light of this understanding is called a role. "A *role* is a psychological process based upon the role player's construction of aspects of the construction systems of those with whom he attempts to join in a social enterprise" (Kelly, 1955, p. 97).

This corollary was Kelly's major statement on social behaviour. He said that if we want to engage in constructive interactions with other people, we must first determine how other people see things and then take their perceptions into consideration when dealing with them. For example, consider the way Native and Non-Native Canadians view taxation, fishing rights, and cultural assimilation. Or consider how a separatist and a federalist view issues like signs on businesses, immigration, and cultural destiny. Kelly's theory suggests that what creates divided positions on these key issues is the application of different sets of constructs. The deepest social interaction occurs when this role playing is reciprocal.

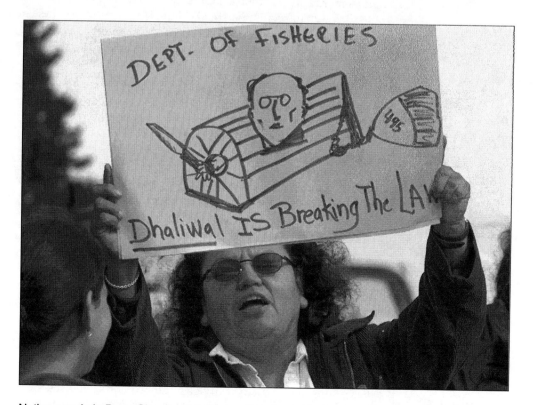

Native people in Burnt Church, New Brunswick, demand what they see as their treaty rights to harvest fish. Kelly's theory explains why Aboriginal groups clashed with Non-Native fishermen over fishing rights: the two groups used different constructs to understand the issues.

CPC Cycle

According to Kelly, the **CPC cycle** characterizes the actions of a person confronted with a novel situation. The initials CPC symbolize the three phases of the cycle: *circumspection, pre-emption,* and *control*. In the **circumspection phase**, the person ponders several **propositional constructs** that could possibly be used to interpret the situation. The thinking during this phase is hypothetical and tentative, and might be labelled cognitive trial and error.

In the **pre-emption phase**, the person chooses from all the constructs pondered in the preceding phase the one construct that seems especially relevant to the situation. In other words, a person cannot go on pondering the situation forever; he or she must choose a strategy for dealing with the experience.

In the **control phase,** the person decides which pole of the dichotomous construct chosen during the preemption phase is most relevant to the situation. Thus the CPC cycle involves pondering several possible constructs with which to construe a situation, deciding on one of those constructs, and then deciding which pole of that construct seems best for construing the situation. Once the final choice is made, subsequent experience will validate or invalidate the person's predictions.

We can again use the example of an attack by a wild animal to demonstrate the CPC cycle. On seeing the animal approaching, the person enters the circumspection phase of the CPC cycle by pondering several constructs that seem to be pertinent to the situation—for example, stand still–run, fight–not fight, or hide–not hide. In the pre-emption phase, the person chooses from among these the construct stand still–run. In the control phase, he or she will choose that pole of the chosen construct that seems most useful under the circumstances and will then act on it. Let us say the person chooses to run. Because the whole idea was to predict personal safety, if the person's course of action gets him or her out of trouble, the construct stand still–run would be validated and would thus tend to dominate the person's thinking if again attacked by a wild animal.

Kelly's Interpretation of Traditional Psychological Concepts

As Kelly himself pointed out, he ignored many traditional concepts, redefined others, and invented several new ones. In this section, we review some of the traditional psychological concepts that Kelly redefined in accordance with his personal construct theory.

MOTIVATION

Kelly disagreed with most of the traditional views of motivation. He thought they looked on humans as naturally inert and therefore in need of being set in motion by something. In other words, traditional theories of motivation claimed that humans needed a drive, a need, a goal, or a stimulus to set them in motion. Kelly thought this was nonsense. He believed that humans are born motivated, and nothing more needs to be said. Every person, according to Kelly, is motivated "for no other reason than that he is alive" (1958, p. 49):

> Motivational theories can be divided into two types, push theories, and pull theories. Under push theories we find such terms as drive, motive, or even stimulus. Pull theories use such constructs as purpose, value, or need. In terms of a well-known

metaphor, these are the pitchfork theories on the one hand and the carrot theories on the other. But our theory is neither of these. Since we prefer to look to the nature of the animal himself, ours is probably best called a jackass theory. (Kelly, 1958, p. 50)

Examples of what Kelly called **push theories of motivation** include those of Freud, Skinner, and Dollard and Miller. Examples of what Kelly called **pull theories of motivation** include those of Jung and Adler. Other jackass theories include those of Rogers, Maslow, and May, to which we turn in the next three chapters. Concerning motivation, social cognitive theory is also more like a **jackass theory of motivation** (because motivation is viewed as inherent) than it is a push or pull theory.

ANXIETY

Kelly defined **anxiety** as "the recognition that the events with which one is confronted lie outside the range of convenience of one's construct system" (1955, p. 495). As we have seen, the ability to predict the future accurately is everyone's goal. The extent to which our predictions are invalid is the extent to which we experience anxiety. Young children on road trips can't help asking "are we there yet" because they cannot use the maps and road signs to anticipate how long it will take to reach their destination. Likewise, some parents don't want to wait nine months to find out the sex of the fetus, nor its genetic health; they use medical technology to avoid uncertainty.

Because the primary function of a construct system is to accurately anticipate events, anxiety is evidence of a failed construct system and, therefore, one requiring modification. According to Kelly (1955) the necessary modifications to one's construct system may be large or small:

> From the standpoint of the psychology of personal constructs, anxiety . . . represents the awareness that one's construction system does not apply to the events at hand. It is, therefore, a preconsideration for making revisions. . . . Our definition of anxiety . . . covers the little confusions and puzzles of everyday living. The sum of a column of numbers does not check. Anxiety! We add it up again, it still does not check. More anxiety! We add it up another way. Good adjustment. Ah, there was our error! (pp. 498–499)

In the extreme, life can become so unpredictable that the only certain thing one can imagine is death. For some this may stimulate suicide. "For the man of constricted outlook whose world begins to crumble, death may appear to provide the only immediate certainty which he can lay his hands on" (Kelly, 1955, p. 64). Anxiety is caused by the uncertainty that results when one's construct system does not permit the accurate construing of life's experiences. In some extreme cases, the certainty of death may be preferred to the uncertainty of the future.

It should be pointed out that some construct systems may require modification even if anxiety is not experienced. Kelly (1963) gave an example:

> A friend of mine, while driving her car, customarily closes her eyes when she gets in a tight spot. This is an anticipatory act; she suspects something may happen that she would prefer not to see. So far, it hasn't happened though it's hard to understand why. (p. 26)

HOSTILITY

Kelly defined **hostility** as the "continued effort to extort validational evidence in favor of a type of social prediction which has already proven itself a failure" (1955, p. 510).

Hostility is related to anxiety. Anxiety is experienced when one's predictions are incorrect. When it is clear that one's construct system has failed to construe the situation properly (that is, when anxiety is inevitable), one may refuse to accept this fact and attempt to demand validation from the environment. Such demands characterize hostility. Bannister and Fransella (1971) said:

> There are times when, if his construct system is to be preserved, a person simply cannot afford to be wrong. If he acknowledges that some of his expectations are ill-founded, this might involve the modification or abandonment of the constructions on which those expectations were based. If, in turn, these constructions are central to the whole of his system, he might well be faced with chaos, having no alternative way of viewing his situation. In such a position the person is likely to become *hostile,* to extort evidence, to bully people into behaving in ways which confirm his predictions, to cook the books, to refuse to recognize the ultimate significance of what is happening. (p. 35)

Leitner and Pfenninger (1994) give the example of a man who became violent with his wife when she asked him for a divorce, an idea he could not tolerate.

AGGRESSION

Kelly (1955) defined **aggression** as "the active elaboration of one's perceptual field" (p. 508). Thus, according to Kelly, the aggressive individual opts to extend his construct system rather than define it (see the choice corollary). He or she seeks adventure rather than security, to expand his or her construct system so that it includes an increasing range of events. Aggression, then, in Kelly's theory, is the opposite of hostility. Bannister and Fransella (1971) put it as follows:

> It is interesting to note that Kelly is here attempting to define aggression (and similarly attempts to define hostility) in terms of what is going on *within the individual* rather than in terms of other people's reaction to him. Thus, a person is being aggressive when he actively experiments to check the validity of his construing; when he extends the range of his constructions (and thereby his activities) in new directions; when he is exploring. Obviously from the point of view of the people around and about such a person, this can be a very uncomfortable process and they may well see it as an attack upon them and handle it as such. But in terms of the aggressive person's construction system it is essentially an extending and elaborating process and thereby the opposite of hostility. (pp. 37–38)

To Kelly, hostility is the unwillingness to give up an ineffective construct system, and aggression is an attempt to expand one's construct system to an ever-increasing range of events.

GUILT

Kelly defined **guilt** as the "perception of one's apparent dislodgement from his core role structure" (1955, p. 502). The term **core role structure** refers to the roles we play while interacting with the relevant individuals and groups in our lives. According to Kelly, "Guilt arises when the individual becomes aware that he is alienated from the roles by which he maintains his most important relationships to other persons" (1963, p. 228). Thus if a man construes his relationship with his wife as loving, reliable, and caring, he will feel guilty if he acts in an unloving, unreliable, and uncaring way toward her.

In Kelly's view, the experience of guilt has nothing to do with good versus evil or right versus wrong. It has to do with the consistency or inconsistency with which one interacts with significant people or groups in one's life. It is inconsistency in these relationships that causes guilt. Even as Kelly defined it, however, guilt can be devastating:

> If you find yourself doing, in important respects, those things you would not have expected to do if you are the kind of person you always thought you were, then you suffer from guilt. . . . To live in a world where you cannot understand and predict others can be terrifying—how much more terrifying is it to find that one cannot understand and predict oneself. (Bannister & Fransella, 1971, p. 36)

THREAT

Kelly defined **threat** as the "awareness of imminent comprehensive change in one's core structures" (1955, p. 489).

Just as we have a core role structure that governs our significant interpersonal relationships, we have other constructs, on which we rely heavily, for predicting external events. These **core structures** are used to make sense out of life. They become the heart of what others may call our belief system. When these basic core constructs suddenly seem no longer validated by experience, we feel threatened. To challenge our core constructs is to challenge our very existence, and that could be dangerous.

For Kelly, we feel guilty when the constructs we use to predict our significant interpersonal relationships are not validated, and we feel threatened when previously validated constructs for dealing with external events lose their validity. For example, a person who spent most of his life avoiding alcohol would feel guilty if he accepted a drink at a party; if a person looked out her window in the middle of summer and saw snow, she would feel threatened. Threat can also be caused by the anticipation of one's death (Moore & Neimeyer, 1991; Neimeyer, Moore, & Bagley, 1988).

It should be clear that because people have different core structures, they will find different situations threatening. Furthermore, threat is not only caused by negative events. Kelly (1955) gave an example: "A prisoner of twenty years, while eager, is nevertheless threatened on the last day by the imminence of his release" (p. 490). Likewise, many students find that as they approach the end of the final examination period, they feel directionless and uncertain about what to do next, because all their time and attention for the preceding few weeks has been focused on preparing for examinations instead of preparing for what to do after examinations are over.

FEAR

Fear, according to Kelly, is similar to threat but less severe. Fear results when a peripheral element of one's construct system is invalidated rather than one's core constructs. "Fear is like threat, except that, in this case, it is a new incidental construct, rather than a comprehensive construct, that seems about to take over" (Kelly, 1955, p. 494). A person may experience fear if a previously friendly dog growls at him. The change this experience necessitates in one's construct system is a minor one; for instance, a friendly dog now becomes a friendly dog that sometimes growls.

UNCONSCIOUS

Kelly believed constructs could be described in terms of their cognitive awareness. Constructs with low cognitive awareness are considered more or less as **unconscious**. According to Kelly, there are three types of constructs with low cognitive awareness: preverbal, submerged, and suspended.

Preverbal Constructs.   Kelly defined a **preverbal construct** as "one which continues to be used even though it has no consistent word symbol" (1955, p. 459). Preverbal constructs typically are formed early in life, before language is available. Although words are not available to infants, they still describe and anticipate events in terms of nebulous, nonverbal constructs such as feelings of warmth and security. Because verbally labelling a construct makes it easier to use, preverbal constructs are less definite than those that are verbally labelled. For example, several psychological phenomena, including identity crisis, multiple personalities, panic attacks, even eating disorders, have seen an increase in their incidence following media attention. This is not to say the condition did not exist before it was labelled, but the condition becomes more real and understandable once it is named.

Submergence.   As stated earlier, every construct has two poles. Sometimes a person will act as if only one of the two poles exists, however: for example, believing that all people are good or everything is living. Emphasizing one pole of a construct and ignoring the other pole is what Kelly called **submergence.** "There is the *likeness* and the *contrast* end. Sometimes one of these two ends is less available than the other. When this is markedly true we may refer to the less available end as the *submerged* end" (Kelly, 1955, p. 467). A person may choose not to entertain one pole of a construct because doing so challenges his or her construct system. Kelly's notion of submergence is somewhat similar to Freud's notion of repression. For example, it is socially unacceptable to deeply dislike (even hate) your own children, so that even when parents' frustration and despair might begin to mount, they may actively push aside that way of thinking. Consider the case of Andrea Yates, a Houston mother convicted for the drowning deaths of her five children in June 2001. People who heard this story could not believe that a loving mother would harm her own children; in short, the explanation lay outside the realm of possibilities.

Suspension.   Another way by which an element of experience can have low cognitive awareness is through **suspension.** An experience is suspended when it cannot be used constructively in one's construct system. For example, suppose that you have an entertaining and rather illuminating way of explaining lightning and thunder to a child. But with no child present, this viewpoint or explanation remains dormant until it is needed. It is as if an experience is kept in a holding pattern until a construct system that can assimilate it is created:

> Our theory does not place the emphasis upon remembering what is pleasant or forgetting what is unpleasant; rather, it emphasizes that one remembers what is structured and forgets what is unstructured. In contrast with some notions of repression, suspension implies that the idea or element of experience is forgotten simply because the person can, at the moment, tolerate no structure within which the idea would have meaning. Once he can entertain such a structure the idea may become available within it. (Kelly, 1955, p. 473)

Experiences that cannot be construed by one's construct system have no meaning. Therefore, such experiences must be suspended until a construct system develops that can assimilate them. What can be understood by a person is always determined by his or her construct system. In chapter 4, we noted that Adler believed experiences incompatible with a person's world view, final goal, and lifestyle cannot be pondered consciously and therefore cannot be understood. Although they employed different terminology, Adler and Kelly agreed that only those experiences capable of assimilation into one's personality structure can be experienced consciously. In their own ways, Adler and Kelly viewed the unconscious as the "not understood." Here we have another of the several points of agreement between Adler and Kelly.

LEARNING

Learning, for Kelly, was the constant alteration of one's construct system with the goal of increasing its predictive efficiency. Any change in one's construct system exemplifies learning. When Kelly considered the value of classical conditioning, so popular at the time, Pavlov fared no better than Freud had:

> Salivation . . . takes place in a manner that suggests the anticipation of food, or perhaps hunger—I am not sure which. Perhaps what is anticipated is an activity we call eating. Whatever it indicates, Pavlov seems to have demonstrated it and there is no reason we should not be grateful even though we are not quite sure what it was he demonstrated. (1980, p. 29)

REINFORCEMENT

Kelly replaced what others call reinforcement or reward with the concept of **validation.** According to Kelly, people do not seek reinforcement or the avoidance of pain. People seek validation of their construct systems. If a person predicts that something unpleasant will occur and it does, his or her construct system will have been validated even though the experience was a negative one. Again, according to Kelly, the primary goal in one's life is to reduce uncertainty by accurately predicting future events. "Confirmation and disconfirmation of one's predictions [have] greater psychological significance than rewards, punishments, or . . . drive reduction" (Kelly, 1970, p. 11).

Psychotherapy

According to Kelly, neurotic people are like bad scientists; they keep making the same predictions in the absence of validating experiences. "From the standpoint of the psychology of personal constructs, we may define a disorder as any personal construction which is used repeatedly in spite of consistent invalidation" (Kelly, 1955, p. 831). In other words, a neurotic's construct system does not adequately predict future events, and therefore anxiety is inescapable. What the neurotic person needs is a more effective construct system, and psychotherapy is a procedure designed to help that person develop one. For Kelly, psychotherapy provides a person with an opportunity to examine and reformulate his or her construct system. In other words, psychotherapy trains people to be better scientists.

ROLE CONSTRUCT REPERTORY TEST

Because psychotherapy must deal with a client's constructs, the therapist must first discover what those constructs are. Kelly devised the **Role Construct Repertory Test** to identify the constructs a client uses to construe the relevant people in his or her life. This test has come to be called the *Rep test*. A typical form used in administering the Rep test is shown in Figure 13–2.

(From Kelly, 1955, p. 270)

Figure 13–2 *A typical form used for Kelly's Role Construct Repertory (Rep) Test.*

The first step in administering the Rep test is to ask the client to fill in the grid portion of the form, numbered 1 to 22, with the names of 22 persons relevant to his or her life. The client taking the test usually is asked to place the names of the following people in the blanks above the numbers on the test sheet (see Figure 13–2):

1. The name of the client taking the test.
2. Mother's first name (or the person who acted as your mother).
3. Father's name (or the person who acted as your father).
4. Brother nearest to you in age, or if no brother, a boy near your age most like a brother.
5. Sister nearest to you in age, or if no sister, a girl near your age most like a sister.
6. Your wife or husband, or if not married, your closest friend of the opposite sex.
7. Closest friend of the opposite sex after the person listed in item 6.
8. Closest friend of your own sex.
9. A person who was once a close friend but no longer is.
10. A religious leader, for example, a minister, priest, or rabbi with whom you would be willing to discuss your feelings about religion.
11. Your medical doctor.
12. The neighbour you know best.
13. A person you now know who dislikes you.
14. A person for whom you feel sorry and whom you would like to help.
15. The person with whom you feel most uncomfortable.

16. A recent acquaintance you would like to know better.
17. Your most influential teacher when you were in your teens.
18. The teacher with whom you disagreed the most.
19. An employer or supervisor for whom you worked while you were experiencing stress.
20. The most successful person you know personally.
21. The happiest person you know personally.
22. The most ethical person you know personally.

When the names have been furnished, the client is asked to compare them in groups of three. The three names that are to be compared are indicated by circles on the test sheet. For example, the first comparison is of the individuals whose names appear in blanks 20, 21, and 22. The second comparison is of the individuals whose names appear in blanks 17, 18, and 19, and so on. For each triad the client is asked to choose a word or phrase that describes how two of the three individuals are alike and a word or phrase that describes how the third person is different from the other two. The way in which the two people are the same is listed under construct, and the way in which the third person is different is listed under contrast. An X is placed in the circles of the two people who are alike, and the circle of the person thought to be different is left blank. A partially completed Rep test is shown in Figure 13–3.

It can be seen in Figure 13–3 that the client construed individuals 20 and 22 as highly motivated but individual 21 as lazy; individuals 18 and 19 were thought to be mean whereas individual 17 was thought to be understanding, and so forth.

By analyzing the client's performance on the Rep test, the psychotherapist can answer a number of questions about a client's construct system. For example, which constructs are used? What aspects of people do they emphasize, for example, physical characteristics and social characteristics? Which people are seen as most like or different from the client? Does the client have many constructs available or only a few? What poles does a client use to define the ranges of the constructs?

The Rep test was only one tool that Kelly used to learn about his clients' construct systems. Another tool was simply to ask the clients about themselves. Kelly adopted what he called a **credulous attitude** toward his clients. In other words, he believed that the information they furnished about themselves should be trusted. *"If you don't know what's wrong with a client, ask him; he may tell you"* (Kelly, 1955, p. 201). What a client reports may not be true in an objective sense, but what a client believes to be true *is* true in at least a subjective sense. Because these personal beliefs or perceptions determine the client's behaviour, they must be understood by the therapist:

> A person may misrepresent a real phenomenon, such as his income or his ills, and yet his misrepresentation will itself be entirely real. This applies even to the badly deluded patient: What he perceives may not exist, but his perception does. (Kelly, 1955, p. 8)

	CONSTRUCT	CONTRAST
1	Highly motivated	Lazy
2	Mean	Understanding
3	Needs me	Independent of me
4	Fun loving	Serious
5	Easy going	Tense
6	Intelligent	Unintelligent

Figure 13–3 *An example of a partly completed Rep test, showing six of the 22 comparisons.*

Like Allport's theory (see chapter 7), Kelly's theory is idiographic and values the narrative accounts people provide of their lives (Harvey, 1989; Neimeyer, 1994). In fact, Allport's classic idiographic study, *Letters From Jenny* (1965), has been reinterpreted from a personal construct perspective (Feixas & Villegas, 1991). Although Kelly did not dwell on a client's past, he did acknowledge the usefulness of case histories (a kind of narrative). According to Kelly (1955) the events contained within a case history provide

> the validational evidence against which [the client] won and lost his wagers, against which he tested his personal constructs. They are the checkpoints he had to use in charting the course of his life. To understand what they actually were is to get some notion of the ranges of convenience of the client's constructs, what the system was designed to deal with, one way or another. Moreover, many of these events will have to be given some stabilizing interpretation in the new construct system produced under therapeutic intervention. (Kelly, p. 688)

In keeping with his credulous attitude, Kelly often had his clients write a **self-characterization**:

> I want you to write a character sketch of Harry Brown (i.e., client's name), just as if he were the principal character in a play. Write it as it might be written by a friend who knew him very *intimately* and *very sympathetically*, perhaps better than anyone ever really could know him. Be sure to write it in the third person. For example, start out by saying, "Harry Brown is . . . " (Kelly, 1955, p. 323).

Again, as with the Rep test, the purpose of this sketch was to help the therapist see how clients construed themselves and their interactions with the world and with other people.

FIXED-ROLE THERAPY

Kelly believed that one way to help clients explore different ways of construing is to have them pretend they are different people. In **fixed-role therapy,** the therapist presents the client with a personality sketch and asks the client to act it out, just as an actor would play a part in a play. To enhance the development of new constructs, the personality of the person the client is asked to play is markedly different from the client's own personality. Kelly asked the client to try on a new personality as one would try on a new set of clothes. Under these circumstances, the therapist becomes a supporting actor. Kelly said the therapist must "play in strong support of an actor—the client—who is continually fumbling his lines and contaminating his role" (1955, p. 399).

The client plays his role for about two weeks, during which time he lives as if he were the person in the role he is playing. The therapist, during this time, responds to the client as if he were the person in the part and offers encouragement and validating experiences for the new constructs with which the client is experimenting. The therapist must give the client enough courage to overcome the threat involved in giving up his core constructs and developing new ones:

> What I am saying is that it is not so much what man is that counts as it is what he ventures to make of himself. To make the leap he must do more than disclose himself; he must risk a certain amount of confusion. Then, as soon as he does catch a glimpse of a different kind of life, he needs to find some way of overcoming the paralyzing moment of threat, for this is the instant when he wonders what he really is—whether he is what he just was or is what he is about to be. (Kelly, 1964, p. 147)

> By providing validating data in the form of responses to a wide variety of constructions on the part of the client, some of them quite loose, fanciful, or naughty, the clinician gives the client an opportunity to validate constructs, an opportunity which is not normally available to him. (Kelly, 1955, p. 165)

We see, then, that Kelly maintained his cognitive viewpoint even in psychotherapy. Emotional problems are *perceptual* problems. To resolve a perceptual problem, one must be made to *look at* experiences differently. Psychotherapy is a process by which a client is encouraged to look at experiences differently, while the therapist attempts to minimize the anxiety or threat in doing so.

Kelly suggested that neurotics have lost their ability to make-believe, and the therapist tries to help them regain it. Healthy people make-believe all the time. In fact, in Kelly's opinion, brilliant novelists and brilliant scientists do much the same thing; that is, they make-believe:

> Both [the novelist and the scientist] employ . . . human tactics. The fact that the scientist is ashamed to admit his phantasy probably accomplishes little more than to make it appear that he fits a popular notion of the way scientists think. And the fact that a novelist does not continue his project to the point of collecting data in support of his portrayals and generalizations suggests only that he hopes that the experiences of man will, in the end, prove him right without anyone's resorting to formal proof.
>
> But the brilliant scientist and the brilliant writer are pretty likely to end up saying the same thing—given, of course, a lot of time to converge upon each other. The poor scientist and the poor writer, moreover, fail in much the same way—neither of them is able to transcend the obvious. Both fail in their make-believe. (Kelly, 1964, p. 140)

Construct Systems and Paradigms

In many ways, Kelly's view of personality is similar to Kuhn's view of science. Kelly maintained that the way in which an individual construes reality is only one of many possible ways, but for that particular individual his or her construct system *is* reality, and it is sometimes difficult for him or her to imagine other constructions. For Kuhn, as we saw in chapter 1, a paradigm is a way of looking at a subject matter, and scientists doing research while following a paradigm are said to be doing normal science. Such scientists, according to Kuhn, are often blinded to other, perhaps more effective, ways of looking at a body of information.

Perhaps the most important similarity between Kelly and Kuhn is that they both emphasized *perceptual mechanisms.* For Kelly, a construct system is a set of personal constructs that result in a person construing the world in a certain way. Likewise, Kuhn's paradigm is a perceptual habit shared by several scientists that causes them to *view* their subject matter in a similar way.

Both Kelly and Kuhn insisted there are many equally valid interpretations of reality. Whereas Kelly took this view of an individual's adjustment to the world and Kuhn took this view of science, we take the same view of personality theory. One of the main functions of this book is to offer the various personality theories, not as *truths* but as *ways of viewing* personality. In other words, we believe that, like reality in general, personality can be construed in several equally valid ways. We hope that your construct for personality is permeable enough to allow various viewpoints to enter it.

We end our coverage of Kelly's theory with the following quotation, which seems to summarize Kelly's philosophy of the individual, Kuhn's philosophy of science, and this book's approach to personality theory: "Whatever nature may be, or howsoever the quest for truth will turn out in the end, the events we face today are subject to as great a variety of constructions as our wits will enable us to contrive" (Kelly, 1970, p. 1).

Evaluation

CURRENT STATUS

A relatively small but highly productive group of Kellians currently exists (Jankowicz, 1987). There is a clearinghouse for research generated by Kelly's theory at the University of Nebraska, Lincoln, headed by Al Landfield, which issues a newsletter and publishes bibliographies of recent research on personal construct theory. Similar clearinghouses are scattered throughout the world. Worldwide membership in these clearinghouses has risen from 112 in 1970 to over 500.

Although interest in Kelly's theory is increasing in North America, the theory is most popular in England, where prominent clinical psychologist Donald Bannister, a former student of Kelly's, effectively promoted it for many years. The London-based Centre for Personal Construct Psychology, under the direction of Fay Fransella, is also influential in disseminating Kelly's ideas in England. So popular is Kelly's theory there that exposure to it is required in most clinical programs approved by the British Psychological Society (Jankowicz, 1987, p. 483).

A major reason why Kelly's theory did not become more popular in North America was that it was extremely critical of the other approaches to psychology that were so popular at the time—for example, behaviourism and psychoanalysis. Because Kelly actively avoided forming links between his theory and those of others, they, in turn, avoiding forming links to his. As psychology in the United States has become increasingly cognitive in nature, however, Kelly's theory has become more popular. In fact, for many, Kelly is viewed as having been ahead of his time.

EMPIRICAL RESEARCH

Almost every aspect of Kelly's theory has received some research attention but most of that attention has involved the Rep test. In an early research project, James Bieri (1955), one of Kelly's students, used the Rep test to distinguish between a **cognitively complex person** and a **cognitively simple person** (Procter, 2001). A cognitively complex person has many highly differentiated constructs available. As a result, such a person can cast other people into many categories and can perceive much variety among them. Conversely, a cognitively simple person has a limited, poorly differentiated construct system. As a result, such a person casts all of humanity into a few categories such as good–bad. Bieri was able to substantiate Kelly's assumption that the more constructs one has available, the better one will be at predicting future events. Bieri found that cognitively complex people are far better at predicting the behaviour of others than cognitively simple ones. Other variables related to cognitive complexity include: age (Signell, 1966; Vacc & Greenleaf, 1975); adaptive flexibility (Stein, 1994); vocational choice (Bodden, 1970; Harren, Kass, Tinsley, & Moreland, 1979; Neimeyer, 1988, 1992a, 1992b; Schoenbach & Schooler, 1995); decisions of Supreme Court justices (Gruenfeld, 1995); the ability to cope with stress (Dixon & Baumeister, 1991; Linville, 1985; Niedenthal, Setterlund, & Wherry, 1992; Smith & Cohen, 1993); and gender differences (Engelhard, 1990; Mau, 1997; Pratt, Pancer, Hunsberger, & Manchester, 1990).

The Rep test has been found useful in industrial-organizational psychology. Bannister and Fransella (1971) pointed out that the Rep test can be adapted to evaluate how individuals construe most anything. One non-clinical application has been market research to determine how consumers perceive (construe) various products, which may be expected to determine their purchasing decisions. One study, for example, explored the constructs used by a panel of home testers to describe a range of cosmetics and perfumes (Stewart & Stewart, 1982). Personal construct theory is being used by industrial-organizational psychologists, management development specialists, and occupational counsellors. Jankowicz (1987) concludes: "In all these fields of psychology, finding out what the other person thinks, as a guide to discovering why he or she acts, is a central undertaking" (p. 481).

The Rep test has also been found useful in studying the decision-making processes of managers and school psychologists (Jankowicz, 1987; Salmon & Lehrer, 1989); marital satisfaction (G. J. Neimeyer, 1984; Neimeyer & Hall, 1988; Neimeyer & Hudson, 1984, 1985); friendship formation (Duck, 1979); values and beliefs (Horley, 1991); gender roles (Baldwin, Critelli, Stevens, & Russell, 1986); and recidivism rates of psychiatric patients (Smith, Stefan, Kovaleski, & Johnson, 1991). For further examples of how the Rep test has been used as a research tool, see Bannister and Mair (1968); Landfield and Leitner (1980); and Mancuso and Adams-Webber (1982).

Given the complexity of the REP test, it was inevitable that computers would be used to administer and score it. For examples of such efforts, see Bringmann, 1992; Ford and Adams-Webber, 1991; Lane, Miller, & Woehr, 1998; and Sewell, Adams-Webber, Mitterer, and Cromwell, 1992.

According to Kelly's fundamental postulate, personality is fuelled by differences in how we predict and control events. Herbert Lefcourt (1973, 1991) from the University of Waterloo and Paul Wong (1992) from Trent University spoke of the benefits of feeling in control over important aspects of one's life. James Nickels at the University of Manitoba distinguished between prediction and control. Prediction exists when one can anticipate a given outcome: for example, that if a button on a remote control is pushed, television volume will increase. Control exists when one's choice makes a difference in the outcome: a person who operates the remote has control over volume. Note that the two concepts are defined independently: it is not necessary to anticipate an outcome in order to control it. However, critics of this model suggest that control and prediction are hopelessly intertwined (Peterson, Maier, & Seligman, 1993; Seligman, 1975) so that when outcomes are controlled, we must necessarily be able to predict them. Nickels and colleague Ken Cramer from the University of Windsor have conducted several studies to evaluate whether prediction and control have separate effects (Cramer, Nickels, & Gural, 1997; Langlois, Cramer, & Mohagen, 2002; Nickels et al., 1992).

In one study (Nickels et al., 1992), participants had to listen to several minutes of aversive noise, including loud random blasts of ambulance sirens, horns, and whistles. However, noise duration could be changed by inserting one of two identically marked plugs into a countdown timer. One plug increased the time (an undesired outcome), the other decreased the time (a desired outcome), but participants were not told which plug yielded which outcome. Participants with actual control selected one of the plugs, inserting it into the timer; participants with no actual control had the plug selected by a coin flip. Participants with prediction learned (before completing the dependent measures) whether their noise duration increased or decreased; participants without prediction did not. Results supported the hypothesis that regardless of knowing the outcome (prediction), participants who chose the plug (actual control) felt more influence, control, and responsibility, and less helplessness over noise duration than participants whose plug was randomly chosen. In other words, feeling in control over important events in our lives has more to do with making a difference in those outcomes (cf. Bandura's self-efficacy, chapter 11) than being able to anticipate what those outcomes will be.

But was it actual control over the outcome that made people feel better, or merely being given the choice of plugs? To separate these effects, Langlois et al. (2002) gave three groups of participants the opportunity to reduce the amount of time they would spend proofreading technical medical papers by selecting one of two identically marked envelopes. Participants with actual control knew the envelopes contained different proofreading time periods (either two minutes or twenty minutes). Participants with no actual control knew the envelopes contained identical proofreading time periods—both short or both long, but they were not told which. Participants with choice (actual control) selected the envelope; participants without choice had the envelope randomly selected by the outcome of a spinner. Participants with prediction were told their time period before they completed the dependent measures; participants without prediction were not. Even without being able to predict their time period, those with both choice *and* actual control reported stronger feelings of control, influence, and responsibility than participants without actual control, regardless of choice. That is, merely having a choice among options does not render feelings of influence and responsibility. One's choice must *make a difference* in the outcome, even if one cannot predict that outcome.

CRITICISMS

Limited Empirical Research.   Although Kelly's theory has generated a considerable amount of empirical research, most of it has involved the Rep test. Little research has been designed to test the theory of personal constructs on which the Rep test is based; it therefore remains more or less as Kelly originally proposed it in 1955.

Important Aspects of Personality Neglected or Denied.   In his effort to create a new way of viewing personality, Kelly may have gone too far in his rejection of other theoretical approaches. In his rather flippant rejection of learning, motivation, and the developmental aspects of personality, Kelly may have discarded information vital to a comprehensive understanding of personality. Others think that his treatment of the unconscious mind and of human emotions was superficial, at best. For example, Jerome Bruner (1956) referred to Kelly's theory as "a genuine new departure and spirited contribution to the psychology of personality" (p. 356). However, he went on to say that the theory's greatest failure was its inability to deal with the human passions (for example, love). In this, according to Bruner, Freud did a much better job.

Several theorists have attempted to revise or expand Kelly's theory so that it will more adequately address the emotions (for example, Fisher, 1990; Katz, 1984; McCoy, 1977; Miall, 1989).

Difficulty in Predicting Behaviour.   For Kelly, construing was a private, creative process. Furthermore, construct systems are constantly being tested and revised. These features of Kelly's theory make it practically impossible to predict what a person will do in a particular situation. In fact, Kelly insisted that unpredictability is an important characteristic of a healthy person. For many, this violates the scientific definition of understanding. That is, if something is truly understood its behaviour can be predicted and controlled. Kelly focused his attention on the unique person almost as much as Allport did. For many, this violates the tenets of science, since individual focus does not seek the general laws that govern human behaviour.

Many Unanswered Questions.   Kelly left unanswered such basic questions as, Why do some people have more constructs available to them than others? Why do some people opt for the definition of their construct systems and others opt for extension? What is the origin of a personal construct? What causes people to construe the same situation differently? Is the model of humans as scientists really an accurate one? That is, do people really spend that much time trying to accurately predict future events?

CONTRIBUTIONS

Emphasis on Cognition.   Just as Kelly has been criticized for emphasizing the cognitive aspects of humans, others have praised him for doing just that. Both the psychoanalysts and the behaviourists (for different reasons) played down the type of rational thought that Kelly made the cornerstone of his theory. As other personality theorists were attempting to explain human behaviour in terms of repressed memories, stimuli and responses, reinforcement, habits, ego-defence mechanisms, or the built-in tendency toward self-actualization, Kelly was attempting to explain it in terms of cognitive hypotheses testing. It is a tribute to Kelly that the newer theories (e.g., information-processing psychology) are more like his own than those he opposed. His theory is compatible with the popular interactionist position because it stresses both person variables (constructs and construct systems) and situation variables (those events people construe). As we have seen, Kelly rejected pure phenomenology because it was concerned only with subjective reality, and he rejected behaviourism because it was concerned only with objective reality. Kelly's concern was with the relationship between subjective and objective reality.

Applied Value.   Kelly's ideas have been applied to a number of different areas. His ideas are now widely used in industrial-organizational settings. There are also applications or research in the areas of friendship formation, developmental psychology, person perception, education, political science, and environmental psychology (Adams-Webber, 1979; Mancuso & Adams-Webber, 1982).

Construct theory has been applied clinically in the areas of suicide (R. A. Neimeyer, 1984; Parker, 1981); obsessive-compulsive disorder (Rigdon & Epting, 1983); drug abuse (Dawes, 1985; Rivers & Landfield, 1985); childhood disorders (Agnew, 1985); physical illness (Robinson & Wood, 1984; Viney, 1983, 1984); couples in conflict (Neimeyer & Hudson, 1984); and other relationship disorders (Leitner, 1984; Neimeyer & Neimeyer, 1985).

Starting with practically no formal training in clinical psychology, Kelly developed a unique theory of personality and therapeutic procedures that were both innovative and effective. Kelly's belief that truth is mainly a way of looking at things freed him from the dogma of the past and gave him latitude to experiment with his theorizing. We agree with Pervin's eloquent evaluation of Kelly's theory:

> George Kelly, then, was a person who refused to accept things as black or white, right or wrong. He was a person who liked to test new experiences; a person who dismissed truth in any absolute sense and, therefore, felt free to reconstrue or reinterpret phenomena; a man who challenged the concept of "objective" reality and felt free to play in the world of "make-believe"; a person who perceived events as occurring to individuals and, therefore, was interested in the interpretations of these events by individuals; a person who viewed his own theory as only a tentative formulation and who, consequently, was free to challenge views that others accepted as fact; a man who experienced the frustration and challenge, the threat and joy, of exploring the unknown. (Pervin, 1989, p. 235)

The criticisms of Kelly's theory should not disturb those who find it enlightening. No personality theory—indeed, no theory of any type—is without valid criticism. As Kelly would have said, every theory, like any construct, has a range of convenience and a focus of convenience, and that includes his own theory as well.

As we have seen, many aspects of Kelly's theory are found in social cognitive theory, which is popular today. Kelly's theory also has much in common with the popular existential-humanistic theories, to which we turn in the next three chapters.

SUMMARY

1. Born in the Midwest and raised by educated, religious parents, Kelly gained from his early pioneering experiences a lifelong practical, flexible outlook. Kelly's theory is phenomenological because it studied intact, conscious experiences; cognitive because it studied mental events; existential because it emphasized the present and future and people's freedom to choose their own destinies; and humanistic because it emphasized people's creative powers and was optimistic about people's ability to solve their problems.

2. Kelly's major premise was that all humans act like scientists: they attempt to reduce uncertainty by developing theories (construct systems) that allow them to anticipate future events accurately. People construe—interpret, explain or predict—the events in their lives by using constructs: categories of thought that describe how events are similar to one another and yet different from other events. All individuals are free to create whatever constructs they choose in their attempts to give meaning to their experiences, but are more or less bound to them once they have been selected.

3. Kelly elaborated his theory through 11 corollaries. The construction corollary states that constructs are formed on the basis of the common themes in our experiences. The individuality corollary states that all individuals construe their experiences in their own unique way. The organization corollary states that some constructs are subsumed under other constructs. The dichotomy corollary states that each construct must describe how certain events are similar and also how those events are contrasted with other events. Under stress, people sometimes display slot movement. That is, they switch abruptly from construing with one pole of a construct to construing with its other pole.

The choice corollary states that those constructs are chosen that have the best chance of either defining (validating) or extending (generalizing) one's construct system.

4. The range corollary states that each construct has a range of convenience consisting of the events to which the construct is relevant and a focus of convenience to which the construct is maximally relevant. The experience corollary states that it is not physical experience that is important but the active construing of physical experiences. It is construing that allows one's construct system to be tested and revised. The modulation corollary states that some constructs are more permeable—that is, more open to experience—than other constructs. The fragmentation corollary states that while trying new constructs people may at times be inconsistent, but in the larger picture, people tend to be consistent. The commonality corollary states that in order for two individuals to be considered similar they must construe their experiences in a similar manner. The sociality corollary states that in order to play a role, one must first determine what another person's expectations are and then act in accordance with those expectations.

5. When individuals are confronted with a novel situation, they apply the CPC cycle: they ponder a number of possibly relevant constructs (circumspection phase); choose the most relevant construct (pre-emption phase); and then choose one pole of the dichotomous construct and act on it (control phase).

6. Kelly redefined several traditional psychological concepts in terms of his theory. He thought the concept of motivation was unnecessary because humans are born motivated. He defined anxiety as a response to experiencing something outside one's construct system. In Kelly's view, anxiety indicates that a construct system has

failed and must be modified. He defined hostility as an attempt to force the validation of one's construct system when it is clear that it is generating inaccurate predictions. He defined aggression as the attempt to expand one's construct system. Guilt, according to Kelly, is experienced when one's core role structure is threatened; in other words, when one acts contrary to one's typical role in relation to a significant person or group. Threat was defined a reaction to the invalidation of one's core structures. Fear was defined as the feeling one has when constructs other than core constructs are invalidated. The unconscious, to Kelly, was made up of preverbal constructs; submergence, in which one pole of a construct is emphasized; and suspension, in which certain experiences are ignored until they can be assimilated into one's construct system. Learning was defined as any change in one's construct system.

7. Kelly envisioned neurotic people as bad scientists because they continue to make inaccurate predictions in the absence of validating experiences. Psychotherapy, to Kelly, was a process in which a client could try out different, potentially more effective, construct systems. To discover clients' constructs, Kelly devised the Role Construct Repertory (Rep) Test. Kelly believed that clients could provide a great deal of valid information about themselves. He often had his clients describe themselves in the third person. To allow clients to test alternative construct systems, Kelly used fixed-role therapy, in which clients act as if they were different people and the therapist a supporting actor.

8. Currently Kelly's theory has a relatively small but highly productive group of supporters scattered throughout the world. The empirical research generated by Kelly's theory has concentrated on the Rep test but almost all aspects of Kelly's theory have generated some research. Kelly's ideas are widely applied in industrial-organizational psychology, management development, and occupational counselling.

9. Kelly's theory has been criticized for generating a limited amount of empirical research; neglecting or denying important aspects of personality; having difficulty in predicting behaviour; and leaving too many important questions unanswered. Kelly's theory has been praised for refocusing the study of personality on the rational, intellectual aspects of human behaviour and for having considerable applied value. Because many aspects of Kelly's theory are found in both social cognitive theory and in existential-humanistic theory, it promises to remain influential.

EXPERIENTIAL EXERCISES

1. Choose an issue in your life about which you feel strongly—perhaps abortion, the existence of God, women's rights, or gay rights, Write down the issue and how you feel about it. Next, try taking a stand that is diametrically opposed to your own. Try to think about the issue as would those with views contrary to your thinking. Can you "see" their viewpoint? Is one viewpoint concerning this issue clearly correct and others clearly incorrect? With regard to this exercise, comment on Kelly's contention that "truth" is largely a viewpoint.

2. Describe in a few words the roles you have assumed while interacting with the relevant people or groups in your life. For example, what role describes your relationship with your parents, your loved one, and your closest friends? Kelly claimed one experiences guilt when one acts contrary to the role one assumes while interacting with the significant others in one's life. Explain why you agree or disagree with Kelly.

3. Take the Role Construct Repertory Test found earlier in this chapter yourself. Carefully note the number and the variety of the constructs that you use in construing other people. Also note what you listed as the two poles of your constructs. What does the Rep test tell you about your construct system? Next, administer the Rep test to someone you are very close to and compare responses. Summarize your observations.

4. To experience what fixed-role therapy is like, write a self-characterization of yourself in the third person. Next, write a description of a person very unlike yourself. For the next few days, keep this fictitious description in mind. As you have various experiences, note not only how you interpret and respond to them but try

to imagine how the fictitious person might construe and respond. Remember Kelly's clients were instructed to *actually* construe and respond as if they were the fictitious person. Do you think it would be easy to try on a new personality as one would try on a new set of clothes? Explain.

5. To what extent do you feel arguments, or even wars, result because people construe events with different construct systems? What can be done to reduce such confrontation? What can be done to improve the interpersonal relationships in your own life?

6. Kelly suggested that if you do not like the way something looks, you should look at it differently. Try his advice. Isolate a source of frustration, anger, or discouragement in your life. Attempt to view that negative aspect of your life positively. For example, if lack of money is a source of frustration in your life, try to see the positive aspects of having limited funds. Describe the outcome of your experience with constructive alternativism.

DISCUSSION QUESTIONS

1. Explain how Kelly used the model of the scientist to explain the psychological processes of all humans.

2. Discuss each of the following terms from Kelly's point of view: motivation, anxiety, hostility, aggression, guilt, threat, fear, learning, and reinforcement.

3. What, in Kelly's theory, corresponds to the concept of the unconscious in other theories?

4. Answer the following question as if you were Kelly: If playing different parts is so useful in calling different construct systems to the attention of a client, why is it that there seem to be so many emotionally disturbed actors and actresses? Are they not experimenting with different construct systems all the time?

KEY TERMS

Aggression, p. 358
Anxiety, p. 357
Choice corollary, p. 353
Circumspection phase, p. 356
Cognitive theory, p. 348
Cognitively complex person, p. 366
Cognitively simple person, p. 366
Commonality corollary, p. 354
Construct, p. 349
Construct system, p. 350
Construction corollary, p. 350
Constructive alternativism, p. 350
Construe, p. 349
Control phase, p. 356
Core role structure, p. 358
Core structures, p. 359
CPC cycle, p. 356
Credulous attitude, p. 363
Definition of a construct system, p. 353

Dichotomy corollary, p. 352
Existential theory, p. 349
Experience corollary, p. 353
Extension of a construct system, p. 353
Fear, p. 359
Fixed-role therapy, p. 364
Focus of convenience, p. 353
Fragmentation corollary, p. 354
Guilt, p. 358
Hostility, p. 357
Humanistic theory, p. 349
Individuality corollary, p. 351
Jackass theory of motivation, p. 357
Learning, p. 361
Modulation corollary, p. 354
Organization corollary, p. 351
Permeable construct, p. 354
Personal construct, p. 349
Personality, p. 350

14 Carl Rogers

Biographical Sketch

Carl Ranson Rogers was born to Walter and Julia Cushing Rogers on January 8, 1902, in Oak Park (a Chicago suburb), and he was the fourth of six children. Because his father was a successful civil engineer and contractor, there were no economic problems in Rogers's early life. Rogers described himself as "the middle child in a large, close knit family, where hard work and a highly conservative (almost fundamentalist) Protestant Christianity were about equally revered" (1959, p. 186). Rogers (1961) commented on the religious and ethical atmosphere that characterized his childhood home, "I have a hard time convincing my children that even carbonated beverages had a faintly sinful aroma, and I remember my slight feeling of wickedness when I had my first bottle of 'pop'" (p. 5). Rogers's parents discouraged the development of friendships outside their home because, it was argued, nonfamily members engaged in questionable activities. Rogers commented:

> I think the attitudes toward persons outside our large family can be summed up schematically in this way: Other persons behave in dubious ways which we do not approve in our family. Many of them play cards, go to movies, smoke, drink, and engage in other activities—some unmentionable. So the best thing to do is to be tolerant of them, since they may not know better, and to keep away from any close communication with them and live your life within the family. (1973, p. 3)

Carl Rogers

As a result of this attitude toward "outsiders," Rogers spent a great deal of time by himself, reading everything he could get his hands on, including encyclopedias and a dictionary. In Oak Park, the Rogers family lived in an upper-middle-class neighbourhood, where young Carl attended the Holmes elementary school. His classmates included Ernest Hemingway (who was two years older than Carl) and the children of Frank Lloyd Wright, the famous American architect.

When he was 12 years old, Rogers and his family moved to a farm about 30 miles from Chicago. Moving to a farm, however, did not require that the Rogers family give up their middle-class lifestyle: "It is widely known that Carl Rogers grew up on a farm, but not so widely known that the farm house had a slate roof, tile floors, eight bedrooms and five baths, and a clay tennis court behind the house" (Kirschenbaum, 1979, p. 10). On this farm, Rogers first developed an interest in science. Because his father insisted the farm be run scientifically, Rogers read about many agricultural experiments. From his reading, he developed an interest in a species of moth that he captured, raised, and bred. This interest in science is something that never left Rogers, although he worked in one of the more subjective areas of psychology all of his professional life.

Rogers's tendency toward solitude lasted throughout high school, during which time he only had two dates. He was an excellent student and obtained almost straight As. His main interests were English and science.

In 1919, Rogers enrolled at the University of Wisconsin, where both parents, two brothers, and a sister had attended, and chose to study agriculture. Rogers was very active in church work through his early university years. In 1922, he was one of 10 university students selected to attend the World Student Christian Federation Conference in Peking, China. This six-month trip had a profound effect on Rogers. Having experienced, firsthand, people of different cultures with different religions, Rogers (1961) reflected on an insight that he had aboard ship on his return from China: "It struck me one night in my cabin that perhaps Jesus was a man like other men—not divine! As this idea formed and took root, it became obvious to me that I could never in any emotional sense return home. This proved to be true" (p. 351). Rogers wrote to his parents declaring his independence from their conservative religious viewpoint. Rogers found his declaration of independence intellectually refreshing, but it seems he had to pay an emotional price for his newfound freedom. Shortly after he returned from the Orient, he was increasingly troubled by abdominal pains that were diagnosed as a duodenal ulcer. Rogers was hospitalized for several weeks and received intensive treatment for six months. Rogers was not the only child in the family to develop ulcers; "Something of the gently suppressive family atmosphere is perhaps indicated by the fact that three of six children developed ulcers at some period during their lives. I had the dubious distinction of acquiring mine at the earliest age" (1967, p. 353). On returning to the University of Wisconsin, he changed his major from agriculture to history. Rogers received his BA degree in 1924.

After graduation, Rogers married (despite strong parental disapproval) his childhood sweetheart, Helen Elliott, and they later had two children (David, born in 1926 and Natalie, born in 1928). When David was born, Rogers was inclined to raise him according to the principles of Watsonian behaviourism. He notes, however, that Helen "had enough common sense to make a good mother in spite of all this damaging psychological 'knowledge' " (1967, p. 356). Rogers said observing his children grow up taught him "far more about individuals, their development, and their relationships than I could ever have learned professionally" (1961, p. 12). Following his graduation from the University of Wisconsin, Rogers enrolled in the liberal Union Theological Seminary in New York. Although by now Rogers was interested in helping people with problems, he was increasingly doubtful that the best vehicle for help was to be found in religious doctrine. After two years at the seminary, Rogers transferred to Columbia University to study clinical and educational psychology. He received his MA in 1928 and his Ph.D. in 1931. His dissertation was on the measurement of personality adjustment in children.

On receiving his Ph.D., Rogers accepted a position as psychologist in the Child Study Department of the Society for the Prevention of Cruelty to Children in Rochester, New York, where he had worked as an intern. It was here that Rogers had a number of experiences that greatly influenced his later theory of personality and his approach to psychotherapy. First, he learned that the psychoanalytic approach to therapy, which dominated the department, was often ineffective. Second, because of the vastly different approaches to therapy he had studied at Columbia and in the Child Study Department, he learned that so-called authorities could not agree on what constituted the best treatment for a troubled person. Third, he learned that looking for an "insight" into a problem is often met with frustration. Rogers described one situation in which he believed a mother's rejection of her son was the cause of his delinquent behaviour. He tried his best to share this "insight" with the mother but failed:

> Finally I gave up. I told her that it seemed we had both tried, but we had failed. . . . She agreed. So we concluded the interview, shook hands, and she walked to the door of the office. Then she turned and asked, "Do you ever take adults for counseling here?" When I replied in the affirmative, she said, "Well then, I would like some help." She came to the chair she had left, and began to pour out her despair about her marriage, her troubled relationship with her husband, her sense of failure and confusion, all very different from the sterile "case history" she had given before. Real therapy began then. . . .
>   This incident was one of a number which helped me to experience that fact—only fully realized later—that it is the *client* who knows what hurts, what directions to go, what problems are crucial, what experiences have been deeply buried. It began to occur to me that unless I had a need to demonstrate my own cleverness and learning, I would do better to rely upon the client for the direction of movement in the process. (Rogers, 1961, pp. 11–12)

It was also about this time that Rogers was influenced by Alfred Adler:

> I had the privilege of meeting, listening to, and observing Dr. Alfred Adler. This was the winter of 1927–28, when I was an intern. . . . Accustomed as I was to the rather rigid Freudian approach of the Institute [where he was interning]—seventy-five-page case histories, and exhaustive batteries of tests before even thinking of "treating" a child— I was shocked by Dr. Adler's very direct and deceptively simple manner of relating to the child and the parent. It took me some time to realize how much I learned from him. (quoted in Ansbacher, 1990, p. 47)

From Adler, Rogers learned that lengthy case histories are cold, mechanical, and unnecessary. He also learned that a therapist need not spend time probing the past of a patient. Rather, a therapist could learn more by determining how the patient relates to the here and now.

Rogers wrote his first book, *The Clinical Treatment of the Problem Child* (1939), while at the Child Study Department. In 1940, Rogers moved from a clinical setting to an academic setting by accepting a faculty position in clinical psychology at Ohio State University. It was here that Rogers began to formulate and test his own approach to psychotherapy. In 1942, Rogers published his now-famous book, *Counseling and Psychotherapy: Newer Concepts in Practice*, which described the first major alternative to psychoanalysis (for a discussion of how revolutionary Rogers's ideas were, see Hergenhahn, 1997). The publisher was reluctant to publish, believing the book would not sell 2000 copies, the number necessary to break even. By 1961 it had sold more than 70 000 copies, and it is still going strong.

In 1944, as part of the war effort, Rogers left Ohio State and moved back to New York as Director of Counseling Services for the United Service Organization (USO). After a year, he moved to the University of Chicago as professor of psychology and director of counselling. It was during his stay at the University of Chicago that Rogers published what many consider to be his major work: *Client-Centered Therapy: Its Current Practice, Implications, and Theory* (1951).

In 1957, Rogers left the University of Chicago to return to the University of Wisconsin, where he held the dual position of professor of psychology and professor of psychiatry. At Wisconsin, Rogers found the atmosphere to be overly competitive and nonsupportive. He was primarily concerned with what he perceived as the inhumane treatment of graduate students (Kirschenbaum, 1979, pp. 291–292). Failing in his attempt to improve the situation, he resigned his positions at the University of Wisconsin to become a member of the Western Behavioral Sciences Institute (WBSI) in La Jolla, California. In 1968, Rogers, and several of the more humanistically oriented members of WBSI, left the organization to form the Center for the Studies of the Person, also in La Jolla.

Many of Rogers's moves were coupled with a shift in his interests, techniques, or philosophy. His last move stressed his interest in the individual as he or she experiences the world. Rogers explained, "We are deeply interested in persons but are rather 'turned-off' by the older methods of studying them as 'objects' for research" (1972a, p. 67). In his later years, Rogers worked with encounter groups and taught sensitivity training. He was mainly interested in discovering the conditions under which a person can fully develop his or her potentialities. Also toward the end of his life, Rogers became interested in promoting world peace. He organized the Vienna Peace Project, which in 1985 brought leaders of 13 countries together, and conducted peace workshops in Moscow in 1986. Rogers continued to work on these and other projects until his death on February 4, 1987, from cardiac arrest following surgery for a broken hip. He was 85 years old.

Actualizing Tendency

Rogers postulated one master motive, which he called **self-actualization,** "The organism has one basic tendency and striving—to actualize, maintain, and enhance the experiencing organism" (Rogers, 1951, p. 487). Rogers further postulated that

> there is one central source of energy in the human organism; that is a function of the whole organism rather than some portion of it; and that it is perhaps best conceptualized as a tendency toward fulfillment, toward actualization, toward the maintenance and enhancement of the organism. (Rogers, 1963, p. 6)

According to Rogers, all humans, as well as all other living organisms, have an innate need to survive, grow, and enhance themselves. All biological drives are subsumed under the **actualizing tendency** because they must be satisfied if the organism is to continue its positive development. This "forward thrust of life" continues despite many obstacles. For example, children first learning to walk stumble frequently, but, despite the pain, press on with their attempts to walk. There are numerous examples of humans who, while living under dire circumstances, not only survive but continue to enhance their lives.

One might ask, Toward what is the actualizing tendency moving? Rogers's answer to this question specified a view of human nature that is essentially the opposite of the view suggested by Freud. Freud viewed humans as having the same needs, drives, and motives as any other animal. Therefore, humans' tendencies toward uninhibited sex and aggression must be controlled by society. Rogers believed that humans are basically good and therefore need no controlling. In fact, he believed it is the attempt to control humans that makes them *act* bad. Rogers's view of human nature clearly placed him in the humanistic camp:

> I have little sympathy with the rather prevalent concept that man is basically irrational, and that his impulses, if not controlled, will lead to the destruction of others and self. Man's behavior is exquisitely rational, moving with subtle and ordered complexity toward the goals his organism is endeavoring to achieve. (Rogers, 1961, pp. 194–195)

> I am inclined to believe that fully to be a human being is to enter into the complex process of being one of the most widely sensitive, responsive, creative, and adaptive creatures on this planet.
>   So when a Freudian such as Karl Menninger tells me (as he has, in a discussion of this issue) that he perceives man as "innately evil" or more precisely, "innately destructive," I can only shake my head in wonderment. (quoted in Kirschenbaum, 1979, p. 250)

In 1962, Rogers joined Gordon Allport, George Kelly, Abraham Maslow, Rollo May and others to establish the American Association of Humanistic Psychology (DeCarvalho, 1990a). All the members of this group acknowledged the influence of Adler. We will have more to say about humanistic psychology when we discuss Maslow in the next chapter.

Rogers was aware that people sometimes act negatively. But, he claimed, such actions are not in accordance with human nature. Such actions result from fear and defensiveness:

> I do not have a Pollyanna view of human nature. I am quite aware that out of defensiveness and inner fear individuals can and do behave in ways which are incredibly cruel, horribly destructive, immature, regressive, anti-social, and hurtful. Yet one of the most refreshing and invigorating parts of my experience is to work with such individuals and to discover the strongly positive directional tendencies which exist in them, as in all of us, at the deepest levels. (Rogers, 1961, p. 27)

The actualizing tendency, which is the driving force in everyone's life, causes the person to become more differentiated (complex), more independent, and more socially responsible. We say more about the actualizing tendency when we describe the fully functioning person later in this chapter.

ORGANISMIC VALUING PROCESS

All of the organism's experiences can be evaluated using the actualizing tendency as a frame of reference. Rogers called this method of evaluation of one's experiences the **organismic valuing process.** Those experiences that are in accordance with the actualizing tendency are satisfying and therefore are approached and maintained. Those experiences that are contrary to the actualizing tendency are unsatisfying and therefore are avoided or terminated. The organismic valuing process, therefore, creates a feedback system that allows the organism to coordinate its experiences with its tendency toward self-actualization. This means that people can trust their *feelings*. Rogers believed that even infants, if given the opportunity, will choose what is best for them:

> The simplest example is the infant who at one moment values food, and when satiated, is disgusted with it; at one moment values stimulation, and soon after, values only rest; who finds satisfying the diet which in the long run most enhances his development. (Rogers, 1959, p. 210)

In his own life, Rogers learned the value of acting on his own feelings:

> One of the basic things which I was a long time in realizing, and which I am still learning, is that when an activity *feels* as though it is valuable or worth doing, it *is* worth doing. Put another way, I have learned that my total organismic sensing of a situation is more trustworthy than my intellect.
>
> All of my professional life I have been going in directions which others thought were foolish, and about which I have had many doubts myself. But I have never regretted moving in directions which "felt right," even though I have often felt lonely or foolish at the time. . . . *Experience is, for me, the highest authority.* . . . Neither the Bible nor the prophets—neither Freud nor research—neither the revelations of God nor man—can take precedence over my own experience. (1961, pp. 22–24)

Valuing feelings (emotions) over the intellect and believing in the inherent goodness of humans places Rogers in the philosophical tradition of romanticism (Hergenhahn, 1997). There is a close correspondence between romanticism and humanistic psychology.

Phenomenological Field

The following quotation identifies Rogers as a phenomenologist and shows a kinship between his position and Kelly's:

> The only reality I can possibly know is the world as *I* perceive and experience it at this moment. The only reality you can possibly know is the world as you perceive and experience it at the moment. And the only certainty is that those perceived realities are different. There are as many "real worlds" as there are people! (Rogers, 1980, p. 102)

According to Rogers, all people live in a subjective world, which can be known, in any complete sense, only to themselves. It is this **phenomenological reality,** rather than the physical world, that determines people's behaviour. In other words, how people interpret things is, for them, the only reality. This private reality will correspond in varying degrees to objective reality, depending on the individual. It is this subjective, phenomenological reality that the therapist, according to Rogers, must attempt to understand. Again, a great deal of similarity exists on this point between Rogers's theory and Kelly's. Both stressed the individual's singular, subjective interpretation of experience. The major difference between Rogers and Kelly is in the actualizing tendency. Kelly's major point was that people continue to try new constructs in order to find the set that best anticipates the future. There was, for Kelly, no innately determined condition toward which all humans were evolving. Rather, each individual, in a sense, invents his or her personality. The view of the social cognitive theorist (see chapter 11) is similar to Kelly's.

Rogers differentiated between **experience** and **awareness.** Experience is all that is going on within the organism's environment at any given moment that is potentially available to awareness. When these potential experiences become *symbolized,* they enter awareness and become part of the person's **phenomenological field.** The symbols that act as vehicles for experiences to enter awareness are usually words but they need not be. Rogers believed that symbols also could be visual and auditory images. The distinction between experience and awareness was important to Rogers because, as we shall see, certain conditions cause people to deny or distort certain experiences, thereby preventing them from entering their awareness. For example, a person stubbornly debating an issue may be unprepared to actively listen to opposing arguments. Arguments counter to the debater's position are ignored, likely unremembered, and perhaps not even heard.

Emergence of the Self

At first, infants do not distinguish between events in their phenomenological field; the events all blend together in a single configuration. Gradually, however, through experiences with verbal labels such as "me" and "I," a portion of their phenomenological field becomes differentiated as the **self.** At this point, a person can reflect on himself or herself as a distinct object.

The development of the self is a major manifestation of the actualizing tendency, which, as stated earlier, inclines the organism toward greater differentiation and complexity. The actualizing tendency that, prior to the development of the self, characterized the organism as a whole, now characterizes the self as well. In other words, those experiences viewed as enhancing one's self-concept are positively valued; those viewed as detrimental to the self-concept are negatively valued.

Need for Positive Regard

With the emergence of the self comes the **need for positive regard**, which Rogers believed was universal although not necessarily innate (whether it was learned or innate was unimportant to Rogers). Positive regard means receiving warmth, love, sympathy, care, respect, and acceptance from the relevant people in one's life. In other words, it is the feeling of being prized by those people who are most important to us.

As a typical part of the socialization process, children learn there are things they can and cannot do. For instance, they can and should use manners. However, parents' list of behavioural don'ts tends to be much longer: Don't play ball in the house, don't swear, don't break or steal others' property.

Most often parents will make positive regard contingent on desirable behaviour on the part of their children. That is, if the children do certain things, they will receive positive regard; if they do other things, they will not. This creates what Rogers called **conditions of worth**, which specify the circumstances under which children will receive positive regard. These conditions will depend, of course, upon the prejudices and customs of a particular culture. Through repeated experiences with these conditions of worth, children internalize them, making them part of their self-structure. Once internalized, they become a conscience, or superego, guiding the children's behaviour even when the parents are not present.

Parents can find unspoken ways to give children the message "I love you as you are. I love you no matter what you do." Rogers believed that children need such unconditional positive regard to grow up as congruent people with their own organismic valuing process intact.

From the need for positive regard comes the **need for self-regard.** That is, children develop the need to view themselves positively. In other words, children first want others to feel good about them and then they want to feel good about themselves. This explains why children are routinely encouraged to take part in individual or team sports. The conditions that make relevant people in their lives regard them positively are introjected into their self-structure and thereafter they must act in accordance with those conditions in order to regard themselves positively. The children are now said to have acquired conditions of worth. Unfortunately, when conditions of worth have been established, the only way children can view themselves positively is by acting in accordance with someone else's values, which they have internalized. Now children's behaviour is no longer guided by their organismic valuing process but by the conditions in their environment that are related to positive regard.

Whenever there are conditions of worth in children's lives, they may be forced to deny their own evaluations of their experiences in favour of someone else's evaluation, and this causes an alienation between people's experiences and their self. This alienation creates a condition of incongruence, which we discuss in the next section.

The only way not to interfere with children's actualizing tendencies is to give them **unconditional positive regard**, which allows them to experience positive regard no matter what they do:

> If an individual should *experience only unconditional positive regard*, then no *conditions of worth* would develop, *self-regard* would be unconditional, the needs for *positive regard* and *self-regard* would never be at variance with *organismic evaluation*, and the individual would continue to be *psychologically adjusted*, and would be fully functioning. (Rogers, 1959, p. 224)

This does not mean that Rogers believed children should be allowed to do whatever they please. He believed a rational, democratic approach to dealing with behaviour problems is best. Because, according to Rogers, conditions of worth are at the heart of all human adjustment problems, they should be avoided at all costs. Rogers suggested the following strategy for dealing with a misbehaving child:

> If the infant always felt prized, if his own feelings were always accepted even though some behaviours were inhibited, then no conditions of worth would develop. This could at least theoretically be achieved if the parental attitude was genuinely of this sort: "I can understand how satisfying it feels to you to hit your baby brother (or to defecate when and where you please or to destroy things) and I love you and am quite willing for you to have those feelings. But I am quite willing for me to have my feelings, too, and I feel very distressed when your brother is hurt, . . . and so I do not let you hit him. Both your feelings and my feelings are important, and each of us can freely have his own." (1959, p. 225)

In other words, Rogers believed the following message should be conveyed to the child: We love you deeply as you are but what you are doing is upsetting and therefore we would be happier if you would stop. The child should always be loved, but some of his or her behaviours may not be.

Incongruent Person

Incongruency exists when people no longer use their organismic valuing process as a means of determining whether their experiences are in accordance with their actualizing tendency. If people do not use their own valuing process for evaluating their experiences, then they must be using someone's **introjected values** in doing so. That is, conditions of worth have replaced their organismic valuing process as the frame of reference for evaluating their experiences. This results in an alienation between the self and experience because, under these circumstances, what may truly be satisfying to the person may be denied awareness because it is not in accordance with the person's introjected conditions of worth.

Rogers looked on incongruence as the cause of all human adjustment problems. It follows then, that eliminating incongruence will solve those problems:

> This, as we see it, is the basic estrangement of man. He has not been true to himself, to his own natural organismic valuing of experience, but for the sake of preserving the positive regard of others has now come to falsify some of the values he experiences and to perceive them only in terms based upon their value to others. Yet this has not been an obvious choice, but a natural—and tragic—development in infancy. The path of development toward psychological maturity . . . is the undoing of this estrangement in man's functioning . . . the achievement of a self which is congruent with experience, and the restoration of a unified organismic valuing process as the regulator of behavior. (Rogers, 1959, pp. 226–227)

When an incongruency exists between self and experience the person is, by definition, maladjusted and is vulnerable to anxiety and **threat** and therefore is defensive.

Anxiety results when people *subceive* an experience as being incompatible with their self-structure and its introjected conditions of worth. In other words, anxiety is experienced when an event is encountered that *threatens* the existing self-structure. Note that Rogers said that the event is *subceived* rather than *perceived*. **Subception** is the detection of an experience before it enters full awareness. This way a potentially threatening event can be denied or distorted before it causes anxiety. According to Rogers, the process of **defence** consists of editing experiences, using the mechanisms of **denial** and **distortion,** to keep them in accordance with the self-structure. It is important to note that an experience, according to Rogers, is not denied **symbolization** because it is "sinful" or "naughty" or contrary to cultural mores, as Freud believed, but because it is contrary to the self-structure. For example, if a person's introjected conditions of worth include being a poor student, then receiving a good grade on a test would be threatening, and the experience would tend to be distorted or denied. The person may say, for example, that he or she was just lucky or that the teacher made a mistake. Or suppose your children colour with permanent marker on your walls and neatly transport water from the toilet onto your bed. You subceive a black fury against your children. But your conditions of worth include being a loving parent, so you deny your feelings of rage and convince yourself you're just acting as a responsible parent in disciplining them.

According to Rogers, almost all individuals experience incongruency and therefore defend against symbolization of certain experiences into awareness. It is only when the incongruency is severe that adjustment problems occur.

Psychotherapy

Like Kelly's, Rogers's notion of personality came from his therapeutic practice. Psychotherapy was paramount to Rogers; his personality theory developed only as he tried to become more effective as a therapist, and as he tried to comprehend the principles that operated during the therapeutic process.

> The gradually formed and tested hypothesis [was] that the individual has within himself vast resources for self-understanding, for altering his self-concept, his attitudes, and his self-directed behavior—and that these resources can be tapped if only a definable climate of facilitative psychological attitudes can be provided. (1974, p. 116)

Through the years, Rogers's description of the therapeutic process changed (Holdstock & Rogers, 1977). First, he referred to his approach to therapy as **nondirective therapy,** a term that emphasized clients' ability to solve their own problems if they were given the proper atmosphere for doing so. Next, Rogers labelled his technique **client-centred therapy.** Now therapy was regarded as a joint venture deeply involving both client and therapist. Instead of simply providing an atmosphere in which clients could gradually comprehend the nature of their problems, as was the case in the earlier stage, the therapist's job was to attempt *actively* to understand the client's phenomenological field or **internal frame of reference.** The next stage was called the **experiential stage.** During this stage in the evolution of Rogers's thinking, the therapist became as free as the client. Now the deep personal feelings of both therapist and client were equally important, and the therapeutic process was regarded as a struggle to put these feelings into words.

The last stage in Rogers's thinking was labelled the **person-centred stage.** During this stage, Rogers's theory was extended to many areas beyond the therapeutic process. A sample of the areas to which his theory has been applied includes education, marriage and the family, encounter groups, problems of minority groups, and international relations. But to Rogers, that wasn't the main point:

The shift in emphasis to person-centered points out more than the widespread applicability of the theory. It attempts to emphasize that it is as *person; as I am*, as *being*, and not just in terms of some role identity as client, student, teacher, or therapist that the individual is the unit of all interactions. The name change conveys the full complexity of each person; it indicates that each individual is more than the sum of the parts that make the person. (Holdstock & Rogers, 1977, p. 129)

In 1980, Rogers described his person-centred approach as follows:

I am no longer talking simply about psychotherapy, but about a point of view, a philosophy, an approach to life, a way of being, which fits any situation in which *growth*—of a person, a group, or a community—is part of the goal. (p. ix)

With the many changes in Rogers's thinking through the years, however, certain basic components of his theory have remained unchanged. These are the importance of the actualizing tendency, the importance of the organismic valuing process as a frame of reference in living one's life, and the importance of unconditional positive regard in allowing a person to live a rich, full life.

Rogers (1959, p. 213) summarized the necessary conditions for effective therapy as follows:

1. The client and the therapist must be in psychological contact; that is, both must make a difference in the phenomenological field of the other.
2. The client must be in a state of incongruence and therefore vulnerable or anxious.
3. The therapist must be in a state of congruency in relation to the client.
4. The therapist must give the client unconditional positive regard.
5. The therapist must seek an empathic understanding of the client's internal frame of reference.
6. The client must perceive the fact that the therapist is giving him or her unconditional positive regard and is attempting to understand empathetically his or her internal frame of reference.

If the above conditions have been met, then, according to Rogers (1959, p. 216), the following changes in the client will be observed:

1. Clients express their feelings with increased freedom.
2. Clients become more accurate in their description of their experiences and of the events around them.
3. Clients begin to detect the incongruity between their concept of self and certain experiences.
4. Clients feel threatened as incongruity is experienced, but the unconditional positive regard of the therapist allows them to go on experiencing incongruent experiences without the necessity of distorting or denying them.
5. Clients eventually are able to symbolize accurately, and thus be aware of, feelings which in the past had been denied or distorted.
6. Clients' concepts of self become reorganized and thus are able to include those experiences which had previously been denied awareness.
7. As therapy continues, clients' concepts of self become increasingly congruent with their experience; that is, they now include many experiences which were previously threatening. As clients feel less threatened by experience, they become less defensive.

8. Clients become increasingly able to experience, without feeling threatened, the therapist's unconditional positive regard.
9. Clients feel an increasing amount of unconditional positive self-regard.
10. Therapy is successful if, in the end, clients' experiences are evaluated in terms of their organismic valuing process and not in terms of conditions of worth.

Therapy, then, is designed to eliminate incongruity between experience and the self. When the person is living in accordance with his or her organismic valuing process, rather than conditions of worth, the defences of denial and distortion are no longer necessary and the individual is referred to as a **fully functioning person.**

Fully Functioning Person

In many ways, the fully functioning person is like a young infant because he or she lives in accordance with his or her own organismic valuing process rather than conditions of worth. Rogers equated "being true to oneself" with the good life. Happiness is not the tranquillity that comes when all of one's biological needs are satisfied or when one attains a sought-after goal, such as a house, a large amount of money, or a college degree. Happiness comes from the active participation in the actualizing tendency that is a continuous process. It is important to note that Rogers stressed the actualizing tendency, and not the *state* of self-actualization.

We have seen that to use one's organismic valuing process as a guide for living one's life, it is necessary to exist in an unconditional environment. Rogers believed unconditional positive regard was an essential ingredient of psychotherapy but one need not undergo psychotherapy in order to experience unconditional positive regard. A few people experience it in their home, in their marriage, or with close friends.

In 1980, Rogers extended the conditions that he believed must be present in any human relationship if growth is to occur:

> There are three conditions that must be present in order for a climate to be growth promoting. These conditions apply whether we are speaking of the relationship between therapist and client, parent and child, leader and group, teacher and student, or administrator and staff. The conditions apply, in fact, in any situation in which the development of the person is a goal. . . . The first element could be called genuineness, realness, or congruence. . . . The second attitude of importance in creating a climate for change is acceptance, or caring, or prizing—what I have called "unconditional positive regard ." . . . The third facilitative aspect of the relationship is empathic understanding . . . . This kind of sensitive, active listening is exceedingly rare in our lives. We think we listen, but very rarely do we listen with real understanding, true empathy. Yet listening, of this very special kind, is one of the most potent forces for change that I know. (pp. 115–116)

For Rogers, it was important not to confuse empathy with passive listening or with sympathy. Empathy, he said, "means temporarily living in the other's life, moving about in it delicately without making judgments" (1980, p. 142). In an article published after his death, he explained further:

> To be really empathetic is one of the most active experiences I know. You have to really understand what it feels like to this person in this situation. . . . To really let oneself go into the inner world of this other person is one of the most active, difficult, and demanding things I know. (Rogers, 1987, p. 45)

If people are fortunate enough to have a generous portion of the three types of experiences just described, they will be free to act in accordance with their feelings—that is, in accordance with their organismic valuing process. Such people will be fully functioning and, according to Rogers (1959, pp. 234–235), they will have at least the following characteristics:

1. They will be open to experience—that is, they will exhibit no defensiveness. Therefore, their experiences will be accurately symbolized and thus available to awareness.
2. Their self-structures will be congruent with their experiences and will be capable of changing so as to assimilate new experiences.
3. They will perceive themselves as the locus of evaluation of their experiences. In other words, they will use their organismic valuing process, rather than conditions of worth, to evaluate their experiences.
4. They will experience unconditional self-regard.
5. They will meet each situation with behaviour that is a unique and creative adaptation to the newness of that moment. In other words, they meet each new experience with honest spontaneity instead of with a preconception of what those experiences should mean. In 1961, Rogers referred to this characteristic of a fully functioning person as "existential living," which he described as follows: "What I will be in the next moment, and what I will do, grows out of that moment, and cannot be predicted in advance either by me or by others" (p. 188).
6. They will live in harmony with others because of the rewarding nature of reciprocal unconditional positive regard.

In 1961, Rogers added two characteristics to his description of fully functioning persons. One was the experience of subjective freedom:

He is *free*—to become himself or to hide behind a facade; to move forward or to retrogress; to behave in ways which are destructive of self and others, or in ways which are enhancing; quite literally free to live or die, in both the physiological and psychological meaning of those terms. (p. 192)

The other was creativity:

With his sensitive openness to his world, his trust of his own ability to form new relationships with his environment, he would be the type of person from whom creative products and creative living emerge. He would not necessarily be "adjusted" to his culture, and he would almost certainly not be a conformist. (p. 193)

Q-Sort Technique

One of the more interesting aspects of Rogers's theory is that he stressed, on the one hand, the importance of the completely subjective phenomenological field of the individual and, on the other hand, the importance of scientific methodology:

Therapy is the experience in which I can let myself go subjectively. Research is the experience in which I can stand off and try to view this rich subjective experience with objectivity, applying all the elegant methods of science to determine whether I have been deceiving myself. The conviction grows in me that we shall discover laws of personality and behaviour which are as significant for human progress or human understanding as the law of gravity or the laws of thermodynamics. (Rogers, 1961, p. 14)

As a therapist with an inclination toward science, Rogers could not accept on faith the changes that were *supposed* to occur during therapy, or the changes that *appeared* to take place. Like any good scientist, Rogers had to find a way to *quantify* the extent to which a client changed as a function of therapy. The technique that Rogers found most useful was the **Q-sort technique**, developed by William Stephenson, his colleague the University of Chicago (Stephenson, 1953).

The Q-sort technique can be administered in a number of different ways, but all of them use the same basic concepts and assumptions. First, it is assumed that the client can describe himself or herself accurately, and this is called the **real self**. Second, it is assumed that a person can describe those attributes that he or she would like to possess but currently does not; this is called the **ideal self**. Typically, when therapy begins there is a discrepancy between a person's real self (what he or she is) and the ideal self (what he or she would like to be).

The procedures used in administering the Q-sort are as follows:

1.   The client is given 100 cards, each containing a statement such as the following:
     I have a warm, emotional relationship with others.
     I put on a false front.
     I am intelligent.
     I have a feeling of hopelessness.
     I despise myself.
     I have a positive attitude toward myself.
     I often feel humiliated.
     I can usually make up my mind and stick to it.
     I express my emotions freely.
     I am fearful of sex.

2.   The client is asked to choose those statements that best describe the way he or she is. This creates the **self-sort**. To facilitate the statistical analysis of the results of the various Q-sorts, the client is asked to select cards in a manner that approximates a normal distribution. This is done by asking the client to place the cards in nine piles. The piles are arranged to reflect those statements that are most like the client, on one extreme, to the statements least like the client, on the other. Statements placed in the middle pile are those for which the client cannot decide whether the trait listed is like him or her or not; that is, they are neutral.

3.   Next, the client is asked to sort the cards again but this time in such a way that they describe the person he or she would most like to be. This creates the **ideal-sort**.

Repeating the Q-sort during and after therapy can give an indication of any change in the discrepancy between the client's real self and ideal self.

In addition to being the first therapist actually to measure the effectiveness (or ineffectiveness) of therapy, Rogers was also the first to record and film therapy sessions. He did this, with the client's permission, so that the therapist would not need to rely on his or her memory (perhaps selective) of what happened to evaluate the session. In addition, recording and filming allows the careful analysis of aspects of behaviour such as speech mannerisms and physical gestures as possible indicators of the extent to which the client was experiencing stress or anxiety.

Again, it is somewhat paradoxical that the theorist who insisted the only way to know a person is to attempt to understand his or her private, unique, subjective world was also the therapist who did the most to stimulate the scientific evaluation of the therapeutic process.

The Rogers-Skinner Debate

On September 4, 1955, members of the American Psychological Association held their breath as two of the world's most influential psychologists climbed on stage at the association's annual meeting in Chicago to engage in debate. What psychologist could ask for more? In one corner was Carl Rogers, representing the phenomenological, subjective approach to understanding humans, who claimed the master motive behind human action is the actualizing tendency. Rogers also represented the belief in the innate goodness of the individual whose freedom comes from within. In the other corner was B. F. Skinner, representing the behaviouristic, objective approach to understanding humans. Skinner also represented the belief that what a person becomes is explained in terms of environmental reinforcement contingencies, not of a built-in actualizing tendency. The stage was set for an intense philosophical confrontation. What actually happened was less than a battle; in fact, there was about as much agreement between the two men as there was disagreement.

Both Rogers and Skinner agreed that humans have always attempted to understand, predict, and control human behaviour; that the behavioural sciences have made vast progress in developing the ability to predict and control human behaviour; and both stated their commitment to the further development of the behavioural sciences.

The most important difference between Rogers and Skinner was over the idea of cultural engineering. Skinner believed behavioural principles should be used in designing a culture that more efficiently satisfied human needs. To Rogers that notion raised the following important questions: "Who will be controlled? Who will exercise control? What type of control will be exercised? Most important of all, toward what end or what purpose, or in the pursuit of what value, will control be exercised?" (1956b, p. 1060).

Rogers proposed a model of humans that emphasizes their actualizing tendency and creative powers. Rather than controlling human behaviour from the outside, Rogers suggested that principles developed in the behavioural sciences be applied to the creation of conditions that would release and facilitate humans' inner strengths.

Another major difference between Rogers and Skinner was over the issue of whether human behaviour is free or determined. Skinner maintained that human behaviour is determined by reinforcement contingencies. Rogers, however, maintained that the existence of choice cannot be denied. He agreed that science must assume determinism, but believed this did not conflict with the existence of responsible choice on the individual level:

Behavior, when it is examined scientifically, is surely best understood as determined by prior causation. This is one great fact of science. But responsible personal choice, which is the most essential element in being a person, which is the core experience in psychotherapy, which exists prior to any scientific endeavor, is an equally prominent fact in our lives. To deny the experience of responsible choice is, to me, as restricted a view as to deny the possibility of a behavioural science. That these two important elements of our experience appear to be in contradiction has perhaps the same significance as the contradiction between the wave theory and the corpuscular theory of light, both of which can be shown to be true, even though incompatible. We cannot profitably deny our subjective life, any more than we can deny the objective description of that life. (Rogers, 1956b, p. 1064)

My experience in therapy and in groups makes it impossible for me to deny the reality and significance of human choice. To me it is not an illusion that man is to some degree the architect of himself . . . for me the humanistic approach is the only possible one. It is for each person, however, to follow the pathway—behavioristic or humanistic—that he finds most congenial. (Rogers, 1974, p. 118)

Skinner maintained that his major argument with Rogers was over method, because they both wanted to see approximately the same type of person in the future:

The whole thing is a question of method. That's the crux of my argument with Carl Rogers; I'd like people to be approximately as Rogers wants them to be. I want independent people, and by that I mean people who don't have to be told when to act or who don't do things just because they've been told they're the right things to do. . . . We agree on our goals; we each want people to be free of the control exercised by others—free of the education they have had, so that they profit by it but are not bound by it, and so on. (quoted in Evans, 1968, pp. 67–68)

As already mentioned, Rogers agreed with Skinner that the behavioural sciences are, and should be, advancing but he contended that to have such knowledge is not necessarily to know how to use it. Depending on how this information is used, Rogers said, we may experience great positive growth or destruction:

So I conclude that knowledge in the science of psychology will in the near future be used and exploited as fully as knowledge in the physical sciences is used today. The challenge for educators is unreal only if we are looking a year or two ahead. From the long view I know of no problem holding greater potentiality of growth and of destruction than the question of how to live with the increasing power the behavioral sciences will place in our hands and the hands of our children. (Rogers, 1956c, p. 322)

Freedom to Learn

We have already seen that Rogers was very disturbed by the cold, mechanical way that graduate students were trained when he was a faculty member at the University of Wisconsin (see, for example, Rogers, 1968). However, Rogers was also highly critical of the American educational system in general and suspected that the worst would happen unless our educational system was changed radically.

What Rogers was calling for was nothing short of a revolution: "We should recognize that the transformation to a truly humanistic, person-centered education constitutes a full-scale revolution. It is not a way of tinkering with conventional education. Rather, it entails turning the politics of education upside down" (1980, pp. 307–308).

Rogers believed education in the United States was based on faulty assumptions about the learner. For example, it is widely believed that students must have information given to them and digested for them while they remain passive in the process. Instead of basing education on these and other faulty assumptions, Rogers believed education would be improved if it took into consideration the following facts about the learning process (Rogers, 1969, pp. 157–163):

1. Humans have a natural potential for learning.
2. Learning is best when the student sees relevance in what is being learned.
3. Some learning may require a change in the learner's self-structure, and such learning may be resisted.
4. Learning that necessitates a change in the learner's self-structure occurs more easily in a situation in which external threats are at a minimum.
5. When threats to the learner's self-concept are small, experience can be perceived in great detail, and learning will be optimal.
6. Much learning takes place by doing.
7. Learning proceeds best when the student participates responsibly in the learning process.
8. Self-initiated learning which involves the whole person, that is, both intellectually and emotionally, is the most long-lasting learning.
9. Independence and creativity are facilitated when self-criticism and self-evaluation are of primary importance, and evaluation by others is of secondary importance.
10. The most useful type of learning is the learning to learn that results in a continuing openness to experiences and a tolerance of change.

In general, Rogers (1968, 1969, 1983) believed that it was wrong to assume that students cannot be trusted to pursue their own educational goals, that creative people develop from passive learners, and that evaluation is the same as education. Rogers (1968) observed with dismay that "examinations have become the beginning and end of education" (p. 691)

Rogers thought the term *teacher* was unfortunate because it suggests a person who dispenses information to students. Instead, Rogers suggested the term *facilitator,* to emphasize the fact that the person is there to create an atmosphere conducive to learning. A **facilitator of education** acts on the principles of learning we have listed, and thereby treats each student as a unique person with feelings of his or her own rather than as an object to be taught something.

Think about what a student-governed university class would be like. Would such a class be possible if the academic culture stressed competition for grades, jobs, and scholarships? Is a democratic classroom, with student votes on lecture content, testing format, and performance evaluation, feasible? Would these changes effectively cripple the learning environment? Would this idea have a better chance of taking off at a smaller school? Would this idea be better suited if the grades were assigned at the start of the year (as a pledge of commitment) so that students would worry less about performance evaluation and focus on skill development and growth?

We see that Rogers's approach to education was not unlike his approach to psychotherapy. In both cases, he insisted it must be recognized that each person is unique, each person has feelings, and each person has an actualizing tendency that functions best when experiencing unconditional positive regard and freedom.

Modern Marriage

Statistics indicate that the institution of marriage in our culture is in trouble and, according to Rogers, this is because marriages are too often based on outdated, simplistic, fallacious, or selfish assumptions. For example, couples frequently believe that simply being in love or being committed to each other is enough to sustain a marriage. Rogers (1972b) gathered statements that he believed signalled these dangerous assumptions:

"I love you"; "We love each other." . . . "I commit myself wholly to you and your welfare" . . . "I am more concerned for you than I am for myself." . . . "We will work hard on our marriage." . . . "We hold the institution of marriage sacred, and it will be sacred for us" . . . "We pledge ourselves to each other until death do us part." . . . "We are destined for each other." (pp. 199–200)

According to Rogers, all of the preceding statements miss the important point that for marriage to work it must be egalitarian, enriching, and satisfying for *both* partners. Marriage should be a dynamic process within which both partners continually grow. The only pledge that made any sense to Rogers is, "We each commit ourselves to working together on the changing process of our present relationship, because that relationship is currently enriching our love and our life and we wish it to grow" (1972b, p. 201). A good marriage is one that is *mutually beneficial* to the partners involved.

Rogers observed themes running through the apparently successful marriages of couples who had learned the person-centred philosophy from discussion groups, encounter groups, or individual therapy. Rogers summarized those themes:

Difficulties already present in the partnership are brought into the open. . . . Communication becomes more open, more real, with more mutual listening. . . . The partners come to recognize the value of separateness. . . . The woman's growing independence is recognized as valuable in the relationship. . . . There is increasing recognition of the importance of feelings, as well as reason, of emotions as well as intellect. . . . There is a thrust toward the experiencing of greater mutual trust, personal growth, and shared interests. . . . Roles, and role expectations, tend to drop away and are replaced by the person choosing her own way of behaving. . . . There is a more realistic appraisal of the needs each can meet in the other. . . . So-called satellite relationships may be formed by either partner, and this often causes pain as well as enriching growth. (1977, pp. 45–52)

Rogers (1977) elaborated on the point concerning **satellite relationships**:

Satellite relationship means a close secondary relationship outside the marriage which may or may not involve sexual intercourse, but which is valued for itself. . . . When two persons in a partnership learn to look upon each other as separate persons, with separate as well as mutual interests and needs, they are likely to discover that outside relationships are one of those needs. (pp. 52–53)

The notion of satellite relationships brings jealousy to mind. For Rogers, however, jealousy suggested possessiveness:

To the extent that jealousy is made up of a sense of possessiveness, any alteration in that feeling makes a profound difference in the politics of the marriage relationship. To the degree that each partner becomes truly a free agent, then the relationship only has permanence if the partners are committed to each other, are in good communication with each other, accept themselves as separate persons, and live together as persons, not roles. This is a new and mature kind of relationship toward which many couples are striving. (1977, p. 55)

Rogers (1977) described a married couple that apparently had overcome possessiveness and its related feeling of jealousy:

Fred and Trish endeavored to make their marriage a relationship in which primary value is placed on each of them as persons. They have tried to share in decision-making, the desires of each having equal weight. Each seems to have avoided, to an unusual degree, any need to possess or control the other. They have developed a partnership in which their lives are both separate *and* together. They have each developed relationships outside of marriage, and these intimate interactions have often been sexual in nature. They have communicated openly about these relationships and appear to have accepted them as a natural and rewarding part of their individual lives and of their marriage. They like their life-style. Theirs is a marriage both person-centered and far from conventional. (p. 205)

Permitting an intimate satellite relationship within a marriage is apparently easier to accept intellectually than it is emotionally because many of the couples that have tried one or more of them have ended in divorce. For it to work, according to Rogers, the idea must be acceptable to both marital partners on both an intellectual and an emotional level.

Person of Tomorrow

On June 7, 1969 Rogers was at Sonoma State College to deliver the commencement address. He began by saying:

As an undergraduate student I majored in medieval history. I have enormous respect for the scholars of the Middle Ages and their contributions to learning. But I want to speak to you as Carl Rogers, in 1969, not as a medieval symbol. So I hope I will not offend you if I remove these medieval trappings—this nonfunctional cap, this handsome but useless hood, and this robe, designed to keep one warm even in the rigors of a European winter. (quoted in Kirschenbaum, 1979, p. 395)

After removing the garments, the 67-year-old Rogers began discussing "the person of tomorrow." Rogers believed that a "new person" is emerging who has many of the characteristics of a fully functioning person. Such a person is humanistically oriented rather than technologically oriented. It was because of the emergence of such a person that Rogers was optimistic about the future:

In all candor I must say that I believe that the humanistic view will in the long run take precedence. I believe that we are, as a people, beginning to refuse to allow technology to dominate our lives. Our culture, increasingly based on the conquest of nature and the control of man, is in decline. Emerging through the ruins is the new person, highly aware, self-directing, an explorer of inner, perhaps more than outer, space, scornful of the conformity of institutions and the dogma of authority. He does not believe in being behaviorally shaped, or in shaping the behavior of others. He is most assuredly humanistic rather than technological. In my judgment he has a high probability of survival. (1974, p. 119)

Rogers (1980, pp. 350–352) enumerated 12 characteristics of the person of tomorrow:

1. An openness to both inner and outer experience.
2. A rejection of hypocrisy, deceit, and double talk. In other words, a desire for authenticity.
3. A skepticism toward the kind of science and technology that has as its goal the conquest of nature or the control of people.
4. A desire for wholeness. For example, equal recognition and expression of the intellect and the emotions.

5. A wish for shared purpose in life or intimacy.

6. A tendency to embrace change and risk-taking with enthusiasm.

7. A gentle, subtle, nonmoralistic, nonjudgmental caring.

8. A feeling of closeness to, and a caring for, nature.

9. Antipathy for any highly structured, inflexible, bureaucratic institution. They believe that institutions should exist for the people, not the other way around.

10. A tendency to follow the authority of their own organismic valuing process.

11. An indifference toward material comforts and rewards.

12. A desire to seek a meaning in life that is greater than the individual. Rogers referred to this characteristic as "a yearning for the spiritual."

Rogers believed the emergence of the humanistic person of the future will not go unopposed. He summarized what he considered to be the sources of opposition to such a person in the form of slogans:

1. "The State above all." . . . 2. "Tradition above all." . . . 3. "The intellect above all." . . . 4. "Human beings should be shaped." . . . 5. "The status quo forever." . . . 6. "Our truth is the truth." (1980, pp. 353–355)

Rogers was confident that person-centred individuals will prevail, however, and the result will be a more humane world.

Evaluation

EMPIRICAL RESEARCH

Among Rogers's accomplishments is the fact that he, more than any other therapist, exposed the psychotherapeutic process to scientific examination. Using techniques such as the Q-sort, Rogers and his colleagues were able to examine a client's tendency toward congruency as a function of therapy. Research has supported the Q-sort as a measure of therapeutic success (Deal, 1996; Du Caju, Fraile, Gonzales de Chavez, & Gutierrez (2000). Butler and Haigh (1954) found that the average correlation between real self and ideal self for 25 clients before therapy was .01, indicating essentially no relationship. Following therapy, the average correlation between real self and ideal self rose to +.34, indicating significant movement toward the clients' ideal selves. A control group not undergoing therapy did the Q-sort at the same time. The initial average correlation for the control group was +.58 and the second Q-sort yielded an average correlation of +.59 between real and ideal self. Thus, people not involved in therapy showed less of a discrepancy between their real and ideal selves than the clients involved in therapy and this small discrepancy persisted over time.

Rogers was also responsible for creating encounter groups (sometimes called sensitivity groups or T-groups), and there have been several studies designed to determine their effectiveness. For example, Dunnette (1969) observed that people were found to be more empathetic following an encounter group experience, and Diamond and Shapiro (1973) observed that encounter group participants subsequently felt more in control of their own lives.

The Q-sort has also been widely used as a research tool outside the therapeutic situation. Turner and Vanderlippe (1958) studied the relationships among the discrepancy between the real self and the ideal self, general effectiveness, and degree of satisfaction for 175 college students. Students whose real and ideal selves were close were more active, sociable, and emotionally stable and had higher scholastic averages than those with a wider discrepancy. Rosenberg (1962) found that small discrepancies between the real and the ideal selves related to a variety of measures of successful living. Mahoney and Harnett (1973) found that a measure of self-actualization correlated with degree of congruence. That is, as the discrepancy between the real and ideal selves became smaller, the tendency to display the characteristics of a self-actualizing person became greater. Recent work by Cramer (2001) and Lawson (2000) offer further support.

A great deal of research has aimed to validate Rogers's claim that empathy, unconditional positive regard, and genuineness are the necessary ingredients for personal growth. Aspy and Roebuck (1974) tested the Rogerian hypothesis in the realm of education. They recorded more than 3500 hours of student-teacher interactions involving 550 primary and secondary school teachers in the United States and abroad. They found that the most important variable in producing favourable educational outcomes was teacher empathy, or the effort to understand the meaning of the school experience from the student's viewpoint. Taken together, empathy, unconditional positive regard, and genuineness correlated strongly with academic achievement, positive self-concepts in the students, decreased discipline problems, decreased truancy, and higher student morale, creativity, and problem-solving ability.

In the realm of psychotherapy, Truax and Mitchell (1971) found that the extent to which genuineness, unconditional positive regard, and empathy characterized the therapeutic process, it was successful. Likewise, in a review of 22 studies, Gurman (1977) found that clients who perceived their therapist as displaying empathy, unconditional positive regard, and genuineness tended to perceive their therapy as effective. Because empathy is an important characteristic of effective therapy and other forms of helping relationships, it is important to know if it is something that can be learned or if it is something one is born with. Research strongly suggests that it can be learned (Aspy, 1972; Aspy & Roebuck, 1974; Goldstein & Michaels, 1985).

While numerous studies have supported Rogers's contention that empathy, unconditional positive regard, and genuineness are *necessary* for effective therapy to occur, other studies suggest that these ingredients are not *sufficient* for effective therapy (Sexton & Whiston, 1994; Truax & Carkhuff, 1967). It appears that the personality characteristics of clients play a role in how much they benefit from these attributes.

Many studies have also been performed to investigate the Rogerian hypothesis that incongruent individuals must defend themselves by denying or distorting certain experiences. For example, using male undergraduates as subjects, Chodorkoff (1954) confirmed the hypothesis that congruent people will display less perceptual defence than incongruent individuals. Incongruent subjects took significantly longer to identify emotional words (for example, whore, bitch, or penis) than they did to identify neutral words (for example, tree, house, or book). For congruent subjects, there was no difference in time of recognition. Congruent people have also been found to be better socially adjusted than incongruent people (Chodorkoff, 1954; Sackett, 1995). Cartwright (1956) and Suinn, Osborne, and Winfree (1962) also supported the Rogerian contention that congruent individuals tend to be open to experience whereas incongruent individuals tend to be less open to experience.

Rogers emphasized the discrepancy between real and ideal selves in personality development and psychological adjustment. Perfectionists in particular are feverishly driven to seek congruence between real and ideal selves; unfortunately, the standards set for the ideal self are unrealistically high. Gordon Flett from York University and Paul Hewitt from the University of British Columbia suggest three dimensions of perfection (Hewitt & Flett, 1991). Self-oriented perfectionism refers to high self-imposed standards, increased motivation, and compulsive strivings for self-enhancement. Other-oriented perfectionism represents the tendency to expect perfection of significant others. Socially prescribed perfectionism denotes responding to other people's (perhaps parents' or peers') unrealistic expectations. Although many humanist thinkers believed perfection was inherent in the self-actualized person, these researchers suggest instead that perfectionism correlates with guilt, neuroticism, and anxiety and depression. To test this, undergraduates completed the Multidimensional Perfectionism Scale, a depression inventory, and a short index of self-actualization. The researchers found that self-actualization was negatively related to both socially prescribed and self-oriented perfectionism, but not to other-oriented perfectionism. Depression was associated with high socially prescribed perfectionism and low self-actualization. In other words, setting high personal standards with little success is likely to lead to sadness.

Moreover, self-oriented perfectionism was found to increase a person's vulnerability to stress, perhaps because it leads to more punitive responses to the self when goals are not attained (Hewitt, Flett, & Ediger, 1996). We are, it has been said, our worst judge. Researchers at Concordia University also found that all three dimensions of perfectionism contributed, among women, to the kind of excessive dieting associated with eating disorders.

CRITICISMS

Overly Simplistic and Optimistic Approach.   Many believe Rogers's assumption that humans are basically good and born with a tendency toward self-actualization is nothing more than wishful thinking. Carl Rogers has been sarcastically compared to Mr. Rogers, the kind, sensitive neighbour on children's television (Palmer & Carr, 1991). Real people, say some critics, experience hate as much as love and are often motivated by intense sexual desires. Moreover, except for subception, Rogers denies the importance of unconscious motivation. For those who experience bizarre dreams, intense conflict, deep depression, anger, or psychosomatic illness, the Rogerian view of humans does not ring true. Also considered simplistic is Rogers's heavy reliance on self-reports, which others have found to be notoriously unreliable. Many have criticized Rogers for a simplicity that is opposite to the simplicity of which Kelly was accused. Rogers emphasized the emotional aspect of personality by saying that what truly feels good is the best guide for action. For Rogers, emotions were more important than the intellect; for Kelly, the opposite was true.

Failure to Credit Those Who Have Influenced His Theory.   Many elements are similar in Rogers's and Adler's theories. Both emphasized the whole individual, conscious experience, and an innate drive toward harmonious relationships with fellow humans. A strong relationship also exists between Rogers's theory and Horney's. The crux of Horney's theory was that psychological problems begin when the healthy real self is displaced by the unhealthy idealized self and its associated tyranny of the should. For Horney, the way to make unhealthy people healthy is to bring them back in touch with their real selves so that the real self, instead of the externally imposed idealized self, would be used as a guide for living. Except for differences in terminology, Rogers and Horney were saying much the same thing. There is also considerable similarity between Rogers's theory and that of Allport. For example, both describe the characteristics of psychologically healthy individuals, emphasize the innate goodness of humans, and emphasize conscious rather than unconscious motivation. Although Rogers did acknowledge the influence of Adler on his early thinking, he said little about the influence of Horney or Allport.

Important Aspects of Personality Ignored or Denied.   Rogers essentially dismissed the darker side of human nature (for example, aggressive, hostile, and selfish, motives). He also said very little about the development of personality. Except for the fact that for some the organismic valuing process is displaced by conditions of worth, Rogers said little about the developmental experiences that are conducive to healthy growth.

CONTRIBUTIONS

Alternative, Positive View of Humans.   Rogers helped illuminate a facet of human nature that was previously obscure. He contributed to the development of a "third force" in psychology that successfully challenged psychology's other two dominant forces, behaviourism and psychoanalysis. This third force has been named humanistic psychology because of its emphasis on the goodness of human nature and its concern with the conditions that allow humans to reach their full potential. These concerns run through every aspect of Rogers's writings.

New Form of Therapy.   No one since Freud has had more influence on psychotherapy than Rogers. His humanistic approach to counselling and therapy has become extremely popular because it is effective, it is optimistic about human nature, and it does not require the long, tedious training that psychoanalysis does. Rogers created not only a new form of therapy but also methods for evaluating the effectiveness of therapy. By recording therapeutic sessions, making recordings and transcripts available to other professionals, and developing objective measures of personality change as a function of the therapeutic experience, Rogers, for the first time, made research on psychotherapy scientifically legitimate.

Applied Value.   Again, no one since Freud has had more of an impact on both psychology and on other disciplines. Rogers's person-centred psychology has been applied in such diverse areas as religion, nursing, dentistry, medicine, law enforcement, social work, race and cultural relations, industry, politics, and organizational development (for the various applications of person-centred psychology see, for example, Levant & Schlien, 1984). In an interesting paper, Rogers and Ryback (1984) showed how person-centred psychology might be used to reduce or avoid international conflict and conflict within nations among warring factions (see also, McGaw, Rice, & Rogers, 1973). Toward these ends Rogers, in the last years of his life, led workshops in such countries as Brazil, England, Germany, Hungary, Ireland, Japan, South Africa, the former Soviet Union, and Switzerland (Gendlin, 1988; Heppner, Rogers, & Lee, 1984). Lastly, Rogers (1969, 1983) showed how his person-centred principles might be used to improve education at all levels.

In his 1973 address to the American Psychological Association upon receipt of that organization's first Distinguished Professional Contribution Award, Rogers assessed the impact of his own work:

> It turned the field of counseling upside down. It opened psychotherapy to public scrutiny and research investigation. It has made possible the empirical study of highly subjective phenomena. It has helped to bring some change in the methods of education at every level. It has been one of the factors bringing change in concepts of industrial (even military) leadership, of social work practice, of nursing practice, and of religious work. It has been responsible for one of the major trends in the encounter group movement. It has, in small ways at least, affected the philosophy of science. It is beginning to have some influence in interracial and intercultural relationships. It has even influenced students of theology and philosophy. (1974, p. 115)

So who was Carl Rogers? Rogers himself offered an answer:

So, who am I? I am a psychologist whose primary interest, for many years, has been in psychotherapy. . . . I rejoice at the privilege of being a midwife to a new personality—as I stand by with awe at the emergence of a self, a person, as I see a birth process in which I have had an important and facilitating part. (1961, pp. 4–5)

In his comments on the occasion of Rogers's death, Gendlin (1988) succinctly described the type of person Rogers was. "He cared about each person—but not about institutions. He did not care about appearances, roles, class, credentials, or positions, and he doubted every authority including his own" (p. 127).

SUMMARY

1. Rogers was born into a financially successful, religious family. He spent his adolescent years on a farm, where he first became interested in science. A trip to the Far East while in college was highly influential, introducing Rogers to several different cultures, with their own religions and philosophies.

2. The main premise of Rogers's theory is that all people are born with an actualizing tendency, which causes them to seek those experiences that will maintain and enhance their lives. This tendency drives individuals toward greater complexity, independence, creativity, and social responsibility. Ideally, individuals evaluate their experiences using the organismic valuing process, which indicates if experiences are in tune with the actualizing tendency. Healthy people use their organismic valuing processes as guides in living their lives.

3. All people live in their own subjective reality, called their phenomenological field. People act in accordance with their phenomenological field rather than objective reality. Experience is defined as all of those events occurring around people of which they could be aware. However, only a small portion of those events is symbolized, thus entering awareness. Gradually, a portion of the phenomenological field becomes differentiated as the self. The self-concept emerges as a result of repeated experiences involving such terms as *I*, *me*, and *mine*.

4. With the emergence of the self comes the need for positive regard—warmth, love, sympathy, and respect from the relevant people in one's life. This need expands into the need for self-regard: children also need to respond positively to themselves. Typically, adults give children positive regard only after certain behaviours but not after other behaviours. This creates conditions of worth that specify how children must behave or feel. These conditions of worth are introjected into children's self-concept and thereby control their self-regard. Now, even in the absence of adults, children must act in accordance with these conditions of worth in order to feel good about themselves. The only way to escape imposing conditions of worth on children is to give them unconditional positive regard.

5. Conditions of worth create incongruent people because they force them to live in accordance with introjected values rather than their own organismic valuing process. Incongruent people are vulnerable because they must constantly guard against experiences or feelings that violate conditions of worth, threatening their self-structure and therefore causing anxiety. When an experience is perceived or subceived as threatening, it is either distorted or denied symbolization.

6. The goal of client-centred psychotherapy is to make the incongruent person congruent again. The Rogerian approach emphasized unconditional positive regard, which presumably will reduce threat, eliminate conditions of worth, and align the person with his or her own organismic valuing process, thereby becoming a fully functioning person, who is open to experience, not defensive, creative, capable of living harmoniously with others, and subjectively free. Genuineness and empathy are also needed in any human relationship in which positive growth is sought.

7. Rogers had two major interests in his professional life: to encourage the phenomenological person-centred approach in psychology, and to study the outcomes of therapy scientifically. To do this, he created the Q-sort technique, in which the client sorts 100 cards containing trait descriptions into nine piles depending on how well the card describes him or her. The client

sorts the cards first to describes how he or she is at the moment (self-sort) and then to describe the type of person he or she would like to become (ideal sort). These two sorts allow the therapist to make many comparisons; for example, real self-concept before therapy versus real self-concept after therapy, or real self-concept after therapy versus ideal self-concept after therapy. Research has indicated that Rogerian therapy can effectively improve a client's self-concept.

8. In 1955, Rogers debated with B. F. Skinner, the world's leading behaviourist. Both men agreed that the behavioural sciences had been growing exponentially, and that such growth was beneficial. Skinner maintained that behavioural principles should be used as a guide in creating an environment that would encourage desirable behaviour and satisfy human needs. His approach emphasized control of behaviour from the outside. Rogers maintained that control from the outside should be avoided; behavioural principles should be used to create an environment that gives humans maximal freedom so their actualizing tendencies can function without interference.

9. Rogers believed our educational system is in poor shape. It treats the student as an object to be taught and the teacher as an authority figure who dispenses information in a highly structured environment. Rogers believed that it would be more constructive if we assumed that each human wants to learn and will learn if placed in a nonthreatening learning environment characterized by unconditional positive regard. Learning will occur much faster and will be retained better if the material to be learned has personal relevance to the learner.

10. Rogers thought that many marriages fail because they are based on outdated, superficial, or selfish assumptions. He thought that for a marriage to work it must be viewed as a dynamic, mutually satisfying relationship by both partners. Both partners must remain free, autonomous individuals; one or both may choose to develop a close relationship with someone other than one's marital partner.

11. Rogers envisioned a *person of tomorrow* who would display many of the characteristics of a fully functioning person. Such a person rejects hypocrisy, respects nature and other people, and resists any attempts to control his or her thoughts or behaviour externally. The emergence of such a person, according to Rogers, will be resisted by those who want to maintain the status quo, maintain tradition, or emphasize the intellect over emotions, or who believe they possess the one truth.

12. A considerable amount of empirical research has been generated by Rogers's theory and most of it has been supportive. Rogers's theory has been criticized for portraying an overly simplistic and optimistic view of humans; not giving proper credit to other theories on which his is based; and ignoring important aspects of personality. His theory has been praised for promoting a positive view of humans; creating a new form of therapy as well as methods that can be used to test its effectiveness; and creating a heuristic theory of personality.

EXPERIENTIAL EXERCISES

1. Rogers thought any relationship characterized by unconditional positive regard, empathy, and genuineness is conducive to positive growth. On the other hand, relationships characterized by conditions of worth stifle positive growth. First, describe a relationship within which you *receive* unconditional positive regard, empathy, and genuineness and another one in which conditions of worth are placed on you. Do you agree with Rogers that the former is more conducive to your positive growth than the latter? Next, describe what you feel you *give* in an important relationship. Ask the person involved in this relationship if he or she agrees with your assessment. What is his or her response?

2. Explain why you agree or disagree with Rogers's assertion that humans are basically good and if left alone to live in accordance with their organismic valuing process, would live in peace and harmony with their fellow humans. How do you think Rogers would explain criminal activities? How would Rogers recommend dealing with criminals to reduce their likelihood of reoffending?

3. Make a list of at least 15 statements that you believe accurately describe you as you really are. Some possibilities include:

   I am basically lazy.
   I am overly sensitive.

I am very moody.
I am optimistic.
I am intelligent.
I am able to express my feelings openly.
I feel others control me too much.
I am reliable.
I am pessimistic.
I make new friends easily.
I often feel phony.
I am confused about my future.
I understand myself quite well.
I frequently feel guilty.
I am too critical of myself.

Next, make a list of at least 15 statements that describe the type of person you would ideally like to become. Carefully examine the two lists. If the two lists have many characteristics in common, Rogers would say you are a congruent person. If the lists are quite different,

he would say you are an incongruent person. Which are you? In either case, does Rogers's description of the congruent or the incongruent person (whichever applies to you) accurately describe you? Explain.

4. Review the characteristics of a fully functioning person. How many of those characteristics do you display? Relate your response to your answer to the previous question.
5. Did your own educational experiences support or refute Rogers's denunciation of educational practices in North America? Explain why or why not.
6. Explain why you do or do not agree with Rogers's thoughts on marriage. Include in your answer a reaction to his thoughts on satellite relationships.
7. Do you share Rogers's hope that a person of tomorrow will emerge and eventually populate the world? Explain.

DISCUSSION QUESTIONS

1. Define the actualizing tendency and discuss its importance to Rogers's theory. Include in your answer a discussion of the organismic valuing process.
2. Describe the need for positive regard, the need for self-regard, and conditions of worth, and explain how the three are interrelated.

3. Describe the fully functioning person.
4. Summarize the Rogers-Skinner debate.
5. Summarize the characteristics that Rogers thought the "person of tomorrow" will possess. Who, according to Rogers, will oppose the emergence of such a person?

KEY TERMS

Actualizing tendency, p. 377
Anxiety, p. 382
Awareness, p. 380
Client-centred therapy, p. 383
Conditions of worth, p. 380
Defence, p. 383
Denial, p. 383
Distortion, p. 383
Experience, p. 380
Experiential stage, p. 383
Facilitator of education, p. 390
Fully functioning person, p. 385
Ideal self, p. 387
Ideal-sort, p. 387
Incongruency, p. 382
Internal frame of reference, p. 383
Introjected values, p. 382

Need for positive regard, p. 380
Need for self-regard, p. 381
Nondirective therapy, p. 383
Organismic valuing process, p. 378
Person-centred stage, p. 383
Phenomenological field, p. 380
Phenomenological reality, p. 379
Q-sort technique, p. 387
Real self, p. 387
Satellite relationships, p. 391
Self, p. 380
Self-actualization, p. 377
Self-sort, p. 387
Subception, p. 382
Symbolization, p. 383
Threat, p. 382
Unconditional positive regard, p. 381

15 Abraham Maslow

Biographical Sketch

Abraham Harold Maslow was born on April 1, 1908, in Brooklyn, New York. He was the first of seven children. His parents were poor, uneducated Jewish immigrants from Russia. Being the only Jewish boy in his neighbourhood, he was alone and unhappy much of the time. Like Rogers, Maslow took refuge in books. Maslow described his childhood as follows: "With my childhood, it's a wonder I'm not psychotic. I was a little Jewish boy in the non-Jewish neighborhood. It was a little like being the first Negro enrolled in the all-white school. I was isolated and unhappy. I grew up in libraries and among books, without friends" (quoted in Hall, 1968, p. 37).

Unfortunately, not all of Maslow's problems were outside of his home. Maslow recalled his father as loving whiskey, women, and fighting (Wilson, 1972, p. 131) and belittling him as ugly and stupid. Once, at a large family gathering, his father, Samuel, asked, "Isn't Abe the ugliest kid you've ever seen?" Hoffman (1988) describes the impact of such remarks on young Maslow: "Such thoughtless remarks affected the boy's self-image so much that for a time he sought out empty cars when riding the subway, 'to spare others the sight' of him, as though he were horribly disfigured" (p. 6).

If anything, Maslow's mother, Rose, was worse than his father:

[Maslow] grew to maturity with an unrelieved hatred for her and never achieved the slightest reconciliation. He even refused to attend her funeral. He characterized Rose Maslow as a cruel, ignorant, and hostile figure, one so unloving as to nearly induce madness in her children. In all of Maslow's references to his mother—some uttered publicly while she was still alive—there is not one that expresses any warmth or affection. (Hoffman, 1988, p. 7)

Abraham Maslow

One reason for Maslow's bitterness toward his mother was the miserly way in which she ran her household:

[Maslow] recalled bitterly that she kept a bolted lock on the refrigerator, although her husband was making a good living. Only when she was in the mood to serve food would she remove the lock and permit her children to take something to eat. Whenever the young Maslow had a friend over to the house, she was especially careful to keep the refrigerator bolted. (Hoffman, 1988, p. 7)

And then there was the episode with the cats.

As a youngster, [Maslow] was walking alone one day, when he discovered two abandoned baby kittens on the street. He decided to take them home and care for them. Quietly he carried them into the house and down into the basement. That evening, Rose came home and heard the kittens' meows. She descended to the basement and found her son feeding the kittens from a dish of milk. Doubly enraged that he had brought stray cats into her house and then used her dishes to feed them, she seized the kittens. Before his horrified eyes, Rose smashed each one's head against the basement wall until it was dead. (Hoffman, 1988, p. 8)

It is ironic that one so closely associated with humanistic psychology found the motivation for his life's work in his hatred of his mother. In 1969, shortly before his death, Maslow entered the following comments in his personal journal:

What I had reacted against and totally hated and rejected was not only [my mother's] physical appearance, but also her values and world view, her stinginess, her total selfishness, her lack of love for anyone else in the world, even her own husband and children . . . her assumption that anyone was wrong who disagreed with her, her lack of concern for her grandchildren, her lack of friends, her sloppiness and dirtiness, her lack of family feeling for her own parents and siblings. . . . I've always wondered where my Utopianism, ethical stress, humanism, stress on kindness, love, friendship, and all the rest came from. I knew certainly of the direct consequences of having no mother-love. But the whole thrust of my life-philosophy and all my research and theorizing also has its roots in a hatred for and revulsion against everything she stood for. (Lowry, 1979, p. 958)

Maslow eventually made peace with his father and often spoke of him kindly. Not so, however, with his mother.

In 1925, Maslow enrolled at the City College of New York (CCNY) at the age of 17. In 1926, while still a student at CCNY, Maslow, in an effort to please his father, enrolled in an evening program at the Brooklyn Law School. After only two weeks, however, he decided his interests were elsewhere and he abandoned law school. In 1927, Maslow transferred to Cornell University in Ithaca, New York. At Cornell, Maslow took an introductory psychology course from the illustrious Edward B. Titchener, who lectured wearing full academic robes. Maslow found Titchener's "scientific introspection" cold and boring, and lost interest in psychology temporarily. After only one semester at Cornell, Maslow returned to New York City and re-enrolled at CCNY. In 1928, Maslow transferred to the University of Wisconsin, where he received his BA in 1930, his MA in 1931, and his Ph.D. in 1934.

Shortly after moving to Wisconsin in 1928, Maslow married Bertha Goodman (his first cousin and childhood sweetheart), and they eventually had two children. Maslow claimed that his life really did not start until he married. He was 20 years old at the time, and Bertha was 19. They remained happily married until Maslow's death.

As strange as it now seems, Maslow decided to study psychology when, while a student at CCNY, he discovered the behaviourism of J. B. Watson. He described his excitement over his discovery:

> I had discovered J. B. Watson and I was sold on behaviorism. It was an explosion of excitement for me. . . . Bertha came to pick me up and I was dancing down Fifth Avenue with exuberance; I embarrassed her, but I was so excited about Watson's program. It was beautiful. I was confident that here was a real road to travel, solving one puzzle after another and changing the world. (Hall, 1968, p. 37)

This infatuation with behaviourism ended when Maslow and his wife had their first child:

> Our first baby changed me as a psychologist. It made the behaviorism I had been so enthusiastic about look so foolish I could not stomach it anymore. That was the thunderclap that settled things. . . . I was stunned by the mystery and by the sense of not really being in control. I felt small and weak and feeble before all this. I'd say anyone who had a baby couldn't be a behaviorist. (Hall, 1968, p. 55)

While at the University of Wisconsin, Maslow became the first doctoral student of Harry Harlow, the famous experimental psychologist, who was just in the process of developing a primate laboratory to study the behaviour of monkeys. Maslow's dissertation was on the establishment of dominance in a colony of monkeys. He noted that dominance appeared to result from a type of inner confidence or dominance-feeling rather than through physical strength or aggression. Maslow also observed that sexual behaviour within a primate colony was determined by a member's dominance or subservience, and he wondered if the same was true for humans. He would soon explore that possibility.

After receiving his Ph.D. in 1934, Maslow continued to teach at the University of Wisconsin for a short time and even enrolled in medical school there. He found that medical school, like law school, reflected a dispassionate and negative view of people and he soon dropped out. In 1935, he moved to Columbia University as a Carnegie fellow, where he worked for 18 months with the eminent learning theorist Edward L. Thorndike. Thorndike administered one of his intelligence tests to Maslow and it revealed an IQ of 195, the second highest ever recorded by the test. When Maslow expressed his interest in pursuing the relationship between dominance and sexuality, Thorndike expressed his dismay but gave his permission saying:

> I dislike your work [on dominance and sexuality], I wish you wouldn't do it, but if I don't have faith in my intelligence tests, who will? And I'll assume that if I give you [permission], it'll be the best for you and me—and for the world. (quoted in Hoffman, 1988, p. 74)

With this freedom Maslow began his research on human sexuality in late 1935. He began by interviewing both males and females to determine their feelings of dominance or subservience and their sexual preferences. He soon abandoned males, however, because they were evasive and "tended to lie, exaggerate, or distort their sexual experiences" (Hoffman, 1988, p. 77). Between 1937 and 1942 Maslow published several articles on female sexuality. In general he found that when compared to subservient females, dominant females tended to be unconventional, less religious, less tolerant of female stereotypes, extroverted, more sexually adventuresome, and less anxious, jealous, and neurotic. Maslow also found that the high-dominance female was attracted to the high-dominance male, who was described as "highly masculine, self-confident, fairly aggressive, sure of what he wants and able to get it, generally superior in most things" (quoted in Lowry, 1973, p. 126). In the realm of sex, high-dominance women expressed preference for:

> Straightforward, unsentimental, rather violent, animal, pagan, passionate, even sometimes brutal lovemaking. It must come quickly, rather than after a long period of wooing. She wishes to be suddenly swept off her feet, not courted. She wishes her favors to be taken, rather than asked for. In other words she must be dominated, must be forced into subordinate status. (quoted in Lowry, 1973, p. 127)

Low-dominance women, conversely, were attracted to men who were kind, friendly, gentle, faithful, and showed a love for children. It is interesting to note that Maslow's work on human sexuality appeared several years before Kinsey's famous research appeared in the mid-1940s.

In 1937, Maslow moved to Brooklyn College where he remained until 1951. At Brooklyn College, Maslow taught a full load, continued his research on human sexuality, and advised students. Maslow became so popular as a teacher that the college newspaper referred to him as the Frank Sinatra of Brooklyn College. In 1947, an illness, later diagnosed as a heart attack, forced Maslow to take a medical leave. The Maslows, with their two daughters, moved to Pleasanton, California, where Maslow temporarily managed a branch of the Maslow Cooperage Corporation, and read biographies of illustrious historical figures. In 1949, he returned to Brooklyn College.

We have seen that Maslow's early work was concerned with the healthy, exceptional, dominant specimen. It was but a minor step from these early interests to a concern for the most outstanding human beings. This step in the evolution of Maslow's concerns was stimulated by the tragedy of World War II. Maslow explained:

> I gave up everything I was fascinated with in a selfish way around 1941. I felt I must try to save the world and to prevent these horrible wars and this awful hatred and prejudice.
>
> It happened very suddenly, you know. One day just after Pearl Harbor I was driving home and my car was stopped by a poor, pathetic parade. Boy Scouts and fat people and old uniforms and a flag and someone playing a flute off-key. . . . As I watched, tears began to run down my face. I felt we didn't understand—not Hitler, nor the Germans, nor Stalin, nor the communists. We didn't understand any of them. I felt that if we could understand, then we could make progress. I had a vision of a peace table, with people sitting around it, talking about human nature and hatred and war and peace and brotherhood.
>
> I was too old to go into the army. It was at that moment that I realized that the rest of my life must be devoted to discovering a psychology for the peace table.
>
> That moment changed my whole life and determined what I have done since. . . . I wanted to prove that human beings are capable of something grander than war and prejudice and hatred. I wanted to make science consider all the problems that nonscientists have been handling—religion, poetry, values, philosophy, art.
>
> I went about it by trying to understand great people, the best specimens of mankind I could find. (quoted in Hall, 1968, pp. 54–55)

Maslow was in New York in the late 1930s and early 1940s, when the best minds in Europe were arriving in the United States to escape Nazi Germany. Among those individuals Maslow sought out and learned from were Alfred Adler, Max Wertheimer, Karen Horney, and Erich Fromm.

American anthropologist Ruth Benedict also had a strong influence on Maslow at this time. In fact, it was Maslow's deep admiration for Benedict and for Max Wertheimer, a founder of the school of Gestalt psychology that finally stimulated his interest in self-actualizing people. Maslow described how his efforts to understand these two individuals evolved into what became his life's work.

> My investigations on self-actualization were not planned to be research and did not start out as research. They started out as the effort of a young intellectual to try to understand two of his teachers whom he loved, adored, and admired, and who were very, very wonderful people. It was a kind of high-IQ devotion. I could not be content simply to adore, but sought to understand why these two people were so different from the run-of-the-mill people in the world. These two people were Ruth Benedict . . . and Max Wertheimer. They were my teachers after I came with a Ph.D. from the West to New York City, and they were most remarkable human beings. My training in psychology equipped me not at all for understanding them. It was as if they were not quite people but something more than people. My own investigation began as a prescientific or nonscientific activity. I made descriptions and notes on Max Wertheimer, and I made notes on Ruth Benedict. When I tried to understand them, think about them, and write about them in my journal and my notes, I realized in one wonderful moment that their two patterns could be generalized. I was talking about a kind of person, not about two noncomparable individuals. There was wonderful excitement in that. I tried to see whether this pattern could be found elsewhere, and I did find it elsewhere, in one person after another.
>
> By ordinary standards of laboratory research, i.e., of rigorous and controlled research, this simply was not research at all. (1971, pp. 40–41)

The deep admiration Maslow had for Wertheimer and Benedict was only an extension of the admiration he generally had for highly esteemed individuals. He referred to his college professors and illustrious historical figures as his angels because they were always there when he needed help. Maslow idealized his angels and was shocked whenever he learned they were merely human. For example, Maslow once found himself in a washroom with his philosophy professor at the next urinal. "It stunned me so that it took hours, even weeks, for me to assimilate the fact that a professor was a human being and constructed with the plumbing that everyone else had" (quoted in Wilson, 1972, p. 138). Throughout his professional career Maslow's angels were always there when he needed them.

> I have worked out a lot of tricks for fending off professional attacks. . . . I have a secret. I talk over the heads of the people in front of me to my own private audience. I talk to people I love and respect. To Socrates and Aristotle and Spinoza and Thomas Jefferson and Abraham Lincoln. And when I write, I write for them. This cuts out a lot of crap. (quoted in Hall, 1968, p. 56)

In 1951, Maslow moved to the then new Brandeis University in Waltham, Massachusetts as chairman of the psychology department. During his early years at Brandeis, administrative duties and personal problems kept Maslow from pursuing his theoretical goals. At this time, he underwent psychoanalysis because of his persistent hostility toward his mother and of the remnants of his childhood experience with anti-Semitism (Hoffman, 1988, p. 203). Before long, however, Maslow was able to resume his study of psychologically healthy humans, and he soon emerged as the leader of third force psychology (to be discussed shortly). His highly influential book *Motivation and Personality* was published in 1954. Following several highly productive years, however, Maslow's academic life became increasingly turbulent.

In the mid-1960s, there was widespread social unrest in the United States, and a growing counterculture was seeking leadership. Although Maslow appeared to be a likely candidate, Hoffman (1988, pp. 287–312) discusses the reasons why Maslow was a poor choice. Those in the counterculture movement wanted to emphasize feelings, intuition, and spontaneity at the expense of objective inquiry into human nature. Maslow's position was always that the higher aspects of human nature can be, and should be, studied objectively. He refused to totally condemn the American presence in Indochina. He resigned from the American Civil Liberties Union because he believed it was becoming too soft on criminals. He criticized as simplistic the pacifism and other political views of his younger daughter, Ellen, and the former Brandeis psychology major, Abbie Hoffman. He openly disagreed with Timothy Leary's advice to "tune in, turn on [with drugs], and drop out." More generally, he further alienated himself from the academic community by criticizing universities in the United States for not contributing to the solution of world problems, and by criticizing faculty members for clinging to medieval guild privileges such as tenure. Furthermore, he concluded that colleges and universities were among the country's most poorly managed organizations. In the midst of all this dissension, Maslow was stunned to learn on July 8, 1966, that he was elected president of the American Psychological Association (Hoffman, 1988, p. 294).

During these turbulent times Maslow viewed his students as self-indulgent and intellectually undisciplined. In one case, Maslow's students wanted to take over a class and teach themselves. Maslow initially resisted but finally conceded. Hoffman (1988) describes what followed:

> Matters improved after he let the malcontents form their own class. He now believed that they had craved fellowship so intensely that they had simply been unable to participate in serious intellectual dialogue. They were merely confused adolescents, not deliberately hurtful. He realized, too, that his own theory of human nature cogently explained their behaviour: the need for belongingness is more pressing than the need for self-actualization. But he considered it a pity, and a waste of his intellect, that these young adults were still struggling to satisfy basic needs that should have been met when they were children. As he told Bertha . . . and a few trusted friends, "I'm too old for this sort of work anymore." (p. 314)

The student takeover of the library and administration building at Columbia University, along with failing health, finally convinced Maslow it was time to quit teaching.

Escape from the academic world came when, in late 1968, Maslow was offered a fellowship by the Saga Administrative Corporation. And what a fellowship it was:

> Laughlin [the president and chairman of the Saga Corporation] cheerfully informed Maslow, the fellowship was ready. He was prepared to offer Maslow a two-to-four-year commitment with the following conditions: a handsome salary, a new car, and a personally decorated private office with full secretarial services at Saga's attractive campuslike headquarters on Stanford University's suburban outskirts. What would Maslow have to do in return? Nothing. Laughlin explained that he had heard of Maslow's discontent with full-time teaching and simply wished to give him unlimited free time for writing and scholarly work. Maslow would not be expected to perform any duties at the company; the fellowship would be created out of Laughlin's personal funds, and there would be no connection with the Saga Administrative Corporation at all. (Hoffman, 1988, p. 316)

Maslow accepted the offer and enjoyed his freedom immensely. Unfortunately this ideal situation did not last long. On June 8, 1970, Maslow suffered a fatal heart attack while slowly jogging. He was 62 years old.

Although a number of personality theorists fall into the humanistic camp (for instance Allport and Rogers), it was Maslow who emerged as spokesperson for humanistic psychology. It was Maslow who took the development of humanistic psychology on as a cause, and he did so with a religious fervour.

Third Force Psychology

As noted earlier, Maslow believed his training in psychology did not equip him to understand the positive qualities of remarkable people. By viewing humans as victims of animal instincts and of the conflicts caused by culture, the psychoanalytic camp told only part of the story. Likewise, the behaviourists, who viewed humans as creatures whose behaviour is moulded by the environment, shed only limited light on the mysteries of human existence. In fact, Maslow believed all of psychology had concentrated on the dark, negative, sick, and animalistic aspects of humans. He hoped that **humanistic psychology** would provide information that could be used in formulating a comprehensive theory of human motivation, a theory that would include both the positive and the negative aspects of human nature. For Maslow it was clear that if we wanted to discover the best in humans we had to study exceptional humans.

It was to the study of exceptional people that Maslow dedicated most of his professional life. Maslow believed the typical **reductive-analytic approach to science**, which reduces human beings to a collection of habits or conflicts, overlooks the essence of human nature. For example, love can be described as the combination of behavioural changes (increased smiling), cognitive changes (recurrent mental images), and physiological changes (increased heart rate) in response to specific stimuli. Yet to a person in love, this description misses the point. The **holistic-analytic approach to science,** which studies the person as a thinking, feeling totality, is more likely to yield valid results. If, said Maslow, the standard scientific techniques cannot be applied to the study of the whole person, throw them out and develop techniques that can be used: It is the understanding of humans that is important, and if traditional scientific procedures do not aid in gaining that understanding, so much the worse for them. Maslow even suggested that some scientists are preoccupied with the reductive-analytic approach because it serves as a defence against knowing their own nature. In other words, some scientists in the name of scientific rigour cut themselves off from the poetic, romantic, tender, and spiritual aspects of themselves and other people. Maslow said that such scientists **desacralize** people by making them less marvellous, beautiful, and awesome than they really are.

Maslow's goal was to round out psychology by making it focus on a subject that it had ignored through the years, that is, the healthy, fully functioning human being. This effort was to become psychology's **third force,** with psychoanalysis and behaviourism constituting the other two forces. Maslow (1968) said, "Freud supplied to us the sick half of psychology and we must now fill it out with the healthy half" (p. 5). Maslow was impressed with behaviourism's scientific objectivity but not with its relevance to the real world: "Behaviorism's fatal flaw is that it's good for the lab and in the lab, but you put it on and take it off like a lab coat. It's useless at home with your kids and wife and friends" (quoted in Lowry, 1973, p. 5).

In 1962, Maslow, along with several other humanistically oriented psychologists (including Gordon Allport, George Kelly, Carl Rogers, and Rollo May) established the American Association of Humanistic Psychology, which operated in accordance with the following principles:

1. The primary study of psychology should be the experiencing person.
2. Choice, creativity, and self-realization, rather than mechanistic reductionism, are the concern of the humanistic psychologist.
3. Only personally and socially significant problems should be studied—significance, not objectivity, is the watchword.
4. The major concern of psychology should be the dignity and enhancement of people.

A humanistic science of psychology would consider these principles, and the result would be *less* external prediction and control of human behaviour, but greater self-knowledge:

> If humanistic science may be said to have any goals beyond sheer fascination with the human mystery and enjoyment of it, these would be to release the person from external controls and to make him *less* predictable to the observer (to make him freer, more creative, more inner determined) even though perhaps more predictable to himself. (Maslow, 1966, p. 40)

Maslow was not antiscience. What he opposed was science that excluded important aspects of human nature. Maslow always viewed himself as an objective scientist:

> It may sound peculiar in view of [my humanistic psychology work], but I still feel the same love and admiration for objective research. I have not repudiated it nor will I attack it as such. All that happened is that I was forced to realize its limitation, its failure to generate a true and useful image of man. (quoted in Hoffman, 1988, p. 40)

Hierarchy of Needs

The cornerstone of Maslow's position is his theory of motivation, which he first proposed in two articles published in 1943 when he was at Brooklyn College (1943a, 1943b). Maslow centred his theory of motivation on the **hierarchy of human needs**. He contended that humans have a number of needs that are **instinctoid,** that is, innate. Maslow chose the term *instinctoid* instead of *instinctive* to demonstrate the difference between our biological heritage and that of nonhuman animals:

> This inner core, even though it is biologically based and "instinctoid," is weak in certain senses rather than strong. It is easily overcome, suppressed or repressed. It may even be killed off permanently. Humans no longer have instincts in the animal sense, powerful, unmistakable inner voices which tell them unequivocally what to do, when, where, how and with whom. All that we have left are instinct-remnants. And furthermore, these are weak, subtle and delicate, very easily drowned out by learning, by cultural expectations, by fear, by disapproval, etc. (Maslow, 1968, p. 191)

Maslow also assumed our needs are arranged in a hierarchy in terms of their potency. Although all needs are instinctoid, some are more powerful than others. The lower the need is in the hierarchy, the more powerful it is. The higher the need is in the hierarchy, the weaker and the more distinctly human it is. The lower, or basic, needs in the hierarchy are similar to those possessed by nonhuman animals, but only humans possess the higher needs.

PHYSIOLOGICAL NEEDS

These are the needs directly related to survival that we share with other animals. Included here are the needs for food, water, sex, elimination, and sleep. If one of the **physiological needs** is not met, it will completely dominate the individual's life:

> For our chronically and extremely hungry person, Utopia can be defined simply as a place where there is plenty of food. He or she tends to think that, if only guaranteed food for the rest of life, he or she will be perfectly happy and will never want anything more. Life itself tends to be defined in terms of eating. Anything else will be defined as unimportant. Freedom, love, community feeling, respect, philosophy, may all be waved aside as fripperies that are useless, since they fail to fill the stomach. Such a person may fairly be said to live by bread alone. (Maslow, 1954/1987, p. 17)

Consider the airplane crash in the Andes Mountains in 1972, where the remaining passengers survived over 90 days without food by cannibalizing the dead. Clearly, the satisfaction of basic physiological needs can drive people to behaviour they have never before dreamed of; hunger became the salient motive over those three months. Or consider the struggle of millions of Canadians during the Great Depression in the 1930s, the flood in Southern Manitoba in 1997, or the ice storm in Montreal in 1998. Loftier goals such as the meaning of life become secondary to finding warm shelter, food, and water.

According to Maslow's famous hierarchy of needs, if one of the physiological needs—for food, water, sex, elimination, and sleep—is not met, it will dominate the individual's life. During the Great Depression, the struggle for food and shelter was paramount for many Canadians.

Obviously, such needs are extremely important and must be satisfied. But, according to Maslow, psychology has overemphasized the importance of such needs in determining the behaviour of humans in a modern society. For most humans, these needs are easily satisfied. The real question, to Maslow, was what happens *after* the physiological needs are satisfied. "It is quite true that humans live by bread alone—when there is no bread. But what happens to their desires when there *is* plenty of bread and when their bellies are chronically filled?" (Maslow, 1954/1987, p. 17). Maslow's answer was that the individual is then dominated by the next level or cluster of needs. It is important to note that Maslow did not believe one set of needs had to be completely satisfied before the individual was released to deal with the next level. Rather, he believed one set of needs had to be consistently and substantially satisfied. In other words, a person can be periodically hungry or thirsty and still be able to deal with higher needs but the person's life cannot be *dominated* by hunger or thirst.

SAFETY NEEDS

When the physiological needs are satisfactorily met, the **safety needs** emerge as dominant motives. Included here are the needs for structure, order, security, and predictability. For example, a person might keep a large bank account in preparation for unexpected expenses or emergencies. The person operating at this level is very Kellian, in that the primary goal is to reduce uncertainty in his or her life. These needs are most clearly seen operating in children, who typically show great fear when confronted with novel (unpredictable) events. The satisfaction of the safety needs assures individuals they are living in an environment free from danger, fear, and chaos.

BELONGINGNESS AND LOVE NEEDS

With the physiological and safety needs essentially satisfied, the person now is driven by the need for affiliation. Included here are the needs for friends and companions, a supportive family, identification with a group, and an intimate relationship. If these needs are not met, the person will feel alone and empty. Maslow believed the failure to satisfy needs at this level is a major problem in North America, and explains why so many people seek psychotherapy and join support groups.

ESTEEM NEEDS

If one has been fortunate enough to satisfy one's physiological, safety, and **belongingness and love needs,** the need for esteem will begin to dominate one's life. This group of needs requires both recognition from other people, which results in feelings of prestige, acceptance, and status, and self-esteem, which results in feelings of adequacy, competence, and confidence. Both types of feelings usually result from engaging in activities considered to be socially useful. Lack of satisfaction of the **esteem needs** results in discouragement and feelings of inferiority.

SELF-ACTUALIZATION

If all the lower needs have been adequately satisfied, the person is in a position to become one of the rare people who experiences **self-actualization:**

> So far as motivational status is concerned, healthy people have sufficiently gratified their basic needs for safety, belongingness, love, respect, and self-esteem so that they

are motivated primarily by trends to self-actualization [defined as ongoing actualization of potentials, capacities and talents, as fulfillment of mission (or call, fate, destiny, or vocation), as a fuller knowledge of, and acceptance of, the person's own intrinsic nature, as an unceasing trend toward unity, integration or synergy within the person]. (Maslow, 1968, p. 25)

Musicians must make music, artists must paint, poets must write if they are to be ultimately at peace with themselves. What humans *can* be, they *must* be. They must be true to their own nature. This need we may call self-actualization. (Maslow, 1954/1987, p. 22)

We have more to say about the characteristics of self-actualized people later in this chapter. Maslow's hierarchy of needs is diagrammed in Figure 15–1.

EXCEPTIONS IN THE HIERARCHY OF NEEDS

Maslow believed that most people progress through the hierarchy of needs in the order shown in Figure 15–1. Exceptions occur, however. For example, some people have gone so long with their physiological needs only partly satisfied that they lose all desire to ever progress beyond them. For the rest of their lives, these people may be satisfied if only they can get enough food to eat. Something similar may happen with the need for love. If a person is starved for love in early childhood, the desire for and the ability to give affection may be lost forever. Both of these cases are reminiscent of a Freudian fixation. In the first case, the person is "fixated" on the physiological level of the hierarchy, and in the second case, on the belongingness and love level. Maslow (1954/1987, p. 26) also suggested that the creativity of some innately talented people does not seem to require the satisfaction of the pre-self-actualization needs. Rather, their creativity seems to occur despite unsatisfied needs. This can be seen in the case of starving artists like Michelangelo, who went days without food in an effort to complete the Vatican ceiling. Martyrdom in general thrives on sacrificing basic needs for higher ones.

DEGREES OF SATISFACTION

We saw earlier that one set of needs does not require complete satisfaction before the next higher set is reached. It is also true that no matter what set of needs in the hierarchy a person is concentrating on, he or she is also addressing other sets of needs at the same time. Maslow (1954/1987) explained:

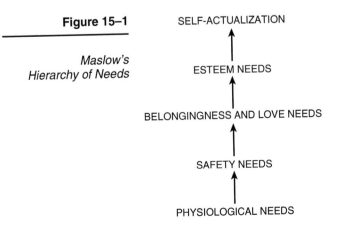

Figure 15–1

Maslow's Hierarchy of Needs

SELF-ACTUALIZATION

ESTEEM NEEDS

BELONGINGNESS AND LOVE NEEDS

SAFETY NEEDS

PHYSIOLOGICAL NEEDS

So far, our theoretical discussion may have given the impression that these five sets of needs—physiological, safety, belongingness, esteem, and self-actualization—are somehow in such terms as the following: If one need is satisfied, then another emerges. This statement might give the false impression that a need must be satisfied 100 percent before the next need emerges. In actual fact, most members of our society who are normal are partially satisfied in all their basic needs and partially unsatisfied in all their basic needs at the same time. A more realistic description of the hierarchy would be in terms of decreasing percentages of satisfaction as we go up the hierarchy of prepotency. For instance, to assign arbitrary figures for the sake of illustration, it is as if the average citizen is satisfied perhaps 85 percent in physiological needs, 70 percent in safety needs, 50 percent in love needs, 40 percent in self-esteem needs, and 10 percent in self-actualization needs.

As for the concept of emergence of a new need after satisfaction of the prepotent need, this emergence is not a sudden, saltatory phenomenon, but rather a gradual emergence by slow degrees from nothingness. For instance, if prepotent need A is satisfied only 10 percent, then need B may not be visible at all. However, as this need A becomes satisfied 25 percent need B may emerge 5 percent, as need A becomes satisfied 75 percent need B may emerge 50 percent, and so on. (pp. 27–28)

It should also be noted that no matter how far one has progressed up the hierarchy, if lower needs are frustrated for a considerable length of time, one will regress to the level of the hierarchy corresponding to those needs and will remain there until those needs are satisfied. Thus, no matter what one has accomplished in life, if the need for food is suddenly unsatisfied, that need will again dominate one's life. Maslow said, "For the man who is extremely and dangerously hungry, no other interests exist but food" (quoted in Lowry, 1973, p. 156). Elsewhere he said, "Respect is a dispensable luxury when compared with food or safety" (1954/1987, p. 57).

DESIRE TO KNOW AND UNDERSTAND

Maslow believed the desire to know and understand was related to the satisfaction of the basic needs. In other words, knowing and understanding were thought to be tools used in solving problems and overcoming obstacles, thereby allowing the satisfaction of the basic needs:

If we remember that the cognitive capacities (perceptual, intellectual, learning) are a set of adjustive tools, which have among other functions that of satisfaction of our basic needs, then it is clear that any danger to them, any deprivation or blocking of their free use, must also be indirectly threatening to the basic needs themselves. Such a statement is a partial solution of the general problems of curiosity, the search for knowledge, truth, and wisdom, and the ever-persistent urge to solve the cosmic mysteries. Secrecy, censorship, dishonesty, and blocking of communication threaten *all* the basic needs. (Maslow, 1954/1987, p. 23)

Thus the needs to know and understand exist at all motivational levels but will be directed at the satisfaction of different needs depending on a person's position in the hierarchy. To progress upward in the hierarchy, the needs to know and understand must be unencumbered.

THE AESTHETIC NEEDS

The **aesthetic needs** are for order, symmetry, closure, structure, and for completion of actions, which are seen in some adults and almost universally in children. Maslow believed that evidence exists for such needs in every culture as far back as the cavepeople.

Although the physiological, safety, love and belongingness, and esteem needs and the need for self-actualization form a hierarchy, and the needs to know and understand are functionally related to their satisfaction, it is not clear how the aesthetic needs relate to other needs. Two things are clear, however. First, Maslow believed the aesthetic needs are instinctoid, and second, they are given their fullest expression in self-actualizing individuals.

Being Motivation

What happens to an individual when all of the basic needs have been met to a satisfactory degree, and he or she enters the realm of self-actualization? Maslow's answer was that, in a sense, the person becomes qualitatively different from those who are still attempting to meet their basic needs. The self-actualizing person's life is governed by **being values** (B-values), which Maslow also labelled **metamotives.** "Self-actualizing people are not primarily motivated (i.e., by basic needs); they are primarily metamotivated (i.e., by metaneeds = B-values)" (Maslow, 1971, p. 311). Because **being motivation** affects personal inner growth, it is also called **growth motivation.** Examples of B-values are beauty, truth, and justice.

The lives of nonactualizing people are governed by **deficiency motivation (D-motivation or D-motives)**; in other words, they are influenced by the absence of such things as food, love, or esteem. The perception of a nonactualizing person is influenced by his or her deficiencies and is therefore called **need-directed perception** (also called **D-perception** or **D-cognition**). "Need-directed perception is a highly focused searchlight darting here and there, seeking the objects which will satisfy needs, ignoring everything irrelevant to the need" (Jourard, 1974, p. 68).

Being cognition (B-cognition or **B-perception)**, on the other hand, is qualitatively different from need-directed perception. "Being-cognition . . . refers to a more passive mode of perceiving. It involves letting oneself be reached, touched, or affected by what is there so that the perception is richer" (Jourard, 1974, p. 68).

As an example of the difference between D-motivation and B-motivation, Maslow used the concept of love. He differentiated between D-love and B-love. **D-love** is motivated by the lack of fulfillment of the need for love and belongingness. A person in such a need-state craves love as a hungry person craves food. Such love is selfish because, when obtained, it satisfies a personal deficiency. In contrast to D-love, Maslow (1968, pp. 42–43) listed some of the characteristics of **B-love:**

1. B-love is nonpossessive.
2. B-love is insatiable, it can be enjoyed without end. It usually grows stronger rather than disappearing. D-love, however, can be satiated.
3. The B-love experience is often described as having the same effect as an aesthetic or mystic experience.
4. B-love has a profound and widespread therapeutic effect.
5. B-love is a richer, higher, and more valuable experience than D-love.
6. There is a minimum of anxiety and hostility in B-love.
7. B-lovers are more independent of each other, less jealous, less needful, more interested, and more autonomous than D-lovers. Also, they are more eager to help the other toward self-actualization and are genuinely proud of the other's triumphs.
8. B-love makes the truest, most penetrating perception of the other possible.

9. B-love, in a sense, creates the partner. It offers self-acceptance and a feeling of love-worthiness, both of which permit the partner to grow. Perhaps full human development cannot occur without the experience of B-love.

The list of 15 B-values that Maslow believed dominated the lives of self-actualizing people is shown in Table 15–1.

Although B-values are metaneeds, they are still needs and must be satisfied if a person is to experience full psychological health. Failure to satisfy a metaneed (B-value) causes what Maslow called a **metapathology.** A description of the metapathologies caused by the failure to satisfy the various B-values is shown in Table 15–1.

Moments of intense B-cognition cause feelings of ecstasy or rapture. Maslow called these mystic or oceanic feelings **peak experiences,** and we have more to say about them in the next section as we consider the characteristics of self-actualizing people.

Characteristics of Self-Actualizing People

As noted earlier, Maslow's interest in self-actualizing people began with his great admiration for Ruth Benedict and Max Wertheimer. After discovering that these two people had much in common, he began to search for others with the same qualities. He searched for people who seemed to be operating at full capacity, that is, doing the best they were capable of doing. Such people were found among his students, his personal acquaintances, and historical figures. But they were not found very often. Of the 3000 college students Maslow screened for his study, he found only one useful subject and a few others that showed promise as future subjects (Maslow, 1954/1987, p. 126). The general population fared only slightly better. Maslow estimated that only 1% of the entire human population becomes self-actualized. The group he finally isolated for more detailed study consisted of 23 people: nine highly probable actualizers, nine fairly sure actualizers, and five partial actualizers. Among the public or historical figures listed as highly probable actualizers were Albert Einstein, Eleanor Roosevelt, Jane Addams, William James, Albert Schweitzer, Aldous Huxley, and Benedict Spinoza (Maslow, 1954/1987, p. 128).

Maslow realized full well that his research on self-actualizers was not scientific and could be criticized on several levels, but he was so startled by what he found that he felt obliged to share his observations with others:

> [This] study . . . is unusual in various ways. It was not planned as ordinary research; it was not a social venture but a private one, motivated by my own curiosity and pointed toward the solution of various personal, moral, ethical, and scientific problems. I sought only to convince and to teach myself rather than to prove or demonstrate to others.
>
> Quite unexpectedly, however, these studies have proved to be so enlightening to me, and so laden with exciting implications, that it seems fair that some sort of report should be made to others in spite of its methodological shortcomings. (Maslow, 1954/1987, p. 125)

Maslow compared his method of gathering data on his self-actualizing individuals to the gradual development of a global impression of a friend or acquaintance. In other words, the impression came from a large number of informal observations, under a wide variety of circumstances, rather than from controlled observations under laboratory conditions. This, along with the fact that his conclusions were based on such a small sample, has stimulated much criticism of Maslow's work.

Table 15–1

B-Values, Conditions That Exist if a B-Value Is Not Satisfied, and The Effect of Not Satisfying a B-Value on One's Life (Specific Metapathologies)

B-VALUES AND SPECIFIC METAPATHOLOGIES

B-Values	Pathogenic Deprivation	Specific Metapathologies
1. Truth	Dishonesty	Disbelief; mistrust; cynicism; skepticism; suspicion
2. Goodness	Evil	Utter selfishness; hatred; repulsion; disgust; reliance only on self and for self; nihilism; cynicism
3. Beauty	Ugliness	Vulgarity; specific unhappiness, restlessness, loss of taste, tension, fatigue; philisitinism; bleakness
4. Unity; wholeness	Chaos, atomism, loss of connectedness	Disintegration; "the world is falling apart"; arbitrariness
4A. Dichotomy-Transcendence	Black-and-white dichoto-mies; loss of gradations, of degree; forced polar-ization; forced choices	Black-and-white thinking, either/or thinking; seeing everything as a duel or war, or a conflict; low synergy; simplistic view of life
5. Aliveness; process	Deadness; mechanization of life	Deadness; robotizing; feeling oneself to be totally determined; loss of emotion; boredom (?); loss of zest in life; experiential emptiness
6. Uniqueness	Sameness; uniformity; in-terchangeability	Loss of feeling of self and of individuality; feeling oneself to be interchangeable, anonymous, not really needed
7. Perfection	Imperfection; sloppiness; poor workmanship, shoddiness	Discouragement (?); hopelessness; nothing to work for
7A. Necessity	Accident; occasionalism; inconsistency	Chaos, unpredictability; loss of safety; vigilance
8. Completion; finality	Incompleteness	Feelings of incompleteness with perseveration; hopelessness; cessation of striving and coping; no use trying
9. Justice	Injustice	Insecurity; anger; cynicism; mistrust; lawlessness; jungle worldview; total selfishness
9A. Order	Lawlessness; chaos; break-down of authority	Insecurity; wariness; loss of safety, of predictability; necessity for vigilance, alertness, tension, being on guard
10. Simplicity	Confusing complexity; disconnectedness; disintegration	Overcomplexity; confusion, bewilderment, conflict, loss of orientation
11. Richness; totality; comprehensiveness	Poverty; coarctation	Depression; uneasiness; loss of interest in world
12. Effortlessness	Effortfulness	Fatigue, strain, striving, clumsiness, awkwardness, gracelessness, stiffness
13. Playfulness	Humorlessness	Grimness; depression; paranoid humorlessness; loss of zest in life; cheerlessness; loss of ability to enjoy
14. Self-sufficiency	Contingency; accident; occasionalism	Dependence on the perceiver; it becomes his responsibility
15. Meaningfulness	Meaninglessness	Meaninglessness; despair; senselessness of life

(From Maslow, 1971, pp. 308–309)

From his informal research, Maslow concluded that self-actualizing people exhibit the following characteristics:

1. They perceive reality accurately and fully.   Their perceptions are not coloured by specific needs or defences. In other words, their perception of the world is characterized by B-cognition rather than by D-cognition. They also have "an unusual ability to detect the spurious, the fake, and the dishonest in personality, and in general to judge people correctly and efficiently" (1954/1987, p. 128).

2. They demonstrate a greater acceptance of themselves, others, and of nature in general.   Self-actualizers accept themselves as they are. They lack defensiveness, phoniness, and are not burdened by undue guilt, anxiety, or shame. "Self-actualizing people tend to be good animals, hearty in their appetites and enjoying themselves without regret or shame or apology. They seem to have a uniformly good appetite for food; they seem to sleep well; they seem to enjoy their sexual lives without unnecessary inhibition and so on for all the relatively physiological impulses" (Maslow, 1954/1987, p. 131). Similarly, they accept others and have no need to instruct, inform, or convert them. Not only can they tolerate weakness in others, but they are not threatened by their strengths. Nature is also accepted as it is.

3. They exhibit spontaneity, simplicity, and naturalness.   Self-actualizers tend to be true to their feelings; what they really feel they tend to say or experience. They do not hide behind a mask and do not act in accordance with social roles. They are true to themselves.

4. They tend to be concerned with problems rather than with themselves.   Self-actualizers are typically committed to some task, cause, or mission toward which they can direct most of their energies. This is contrasted with the preoccupation with oneself often found in nonactualizers.

5. They have a quality of detachment and a need for privacy.   Because self-actualizing individuals depend on their own values and feelings to guide their lives, they do not need constant contact with other people:

> It is often possible for them to remain above the battle, to remain unruffled, undisturbed by that which produces turmoil in others. They find it easy to be aloof, reserved, and also calm and serene; thus it becomes possible for them to take personal misfortunes without reacting violently as the ordinary person does. They seem to be able to retain their dignity even in undignified surroundings and situations. Perhaps this comes in part from their tendency to stick by their own interpretation of a situation rather than to rely upon what other people feel or think about the matter. This reserve may shade over into austerity and remoteness. (Maslow, 1954/1987, p. 134)

6. They are autonomous.   Because self-actualizers are B-motivated rather than D-motivated, they are more dependent on their inner world than on the outer world:

> Deficiency-motivated people must have other people available, since most of their main need gratifications (love, safety, respect, prestige, belongingness) can come only from other human beings. But growth-motivated [B-motivated] people may actually be *hampered* by others. The determinants of satisfaction and of the good life are for them now inner-individual and *not* social. They have become strong enough to be independent of the good opinion of other people, or even of their affection. The honors, the status, the rewards, the popularity, the prestige, and the love they can bestow must have become less important than self-development and inner growth. (Maslow, 1954/1987, p. 136)

7. They exhibit a continued freshness of appreciation.   Self-actualizers continue to experience the events of their lives with awe, wonder, and pleasure. Every baby or sunset is as beautiful and exciting as the first they had seen. Marriage is as exciting after 40 years as it was in the beginning. Sex, too, can have special meaning to self-actualizers: "For several of my subjects the sexual pleasures and particularly the orgasm provided not pleasure alone, but some kind of basic strengthening and revivifying that some people derive from music or nature" (1954/1987, p. 137). Generally such individuals derive great inspiration and ecstasy from the basic experiences of everyday life.

8. They have periodic mystic or peak experiences.   Maslow believed that all humans had the potential for peak experiences, but only self-actualizers could have them full-blown, because such people were not threatened by them and therefore would not inhibit or defend against them in any way. Generally, peak experiences are the embracing of B-values:

> Feelings of limitless horizons opening up to the vision, the feeling of being simultaneously more powerful and also more helpless than one ever was before, the feeling of great ecstasy and wonder and awe, the loss of placing in time and space with, finally, the conviction that something extremely important and valuable had happened, so that the subject is to some extent transformed and strengthened even in his daily life by such experiences. (Maslow, 1954/1987, p. 137)

One of Maslow's own peak experiences involved his "angels." He imagined that he was part of the greatest commencement exercise of all time:

> I was in a faculty procession here at Brandeis. I saw the line stretching off into a dim future. At its head was Socrates. And in the line were the ones I love most. Thomas Jefferson was there. And Spinoza. And Alfred North Whitehead. I was in that same line. Behind me that infinite line melted into the dimness. (quoted in Hall, 1968, p. 35)

Maslow concluded that some self-actualizers peak more often than others. The *nonpeakers* (low frequency of peak experiences) tend to be practical, effective people. *Peakers* (relatively high frequency of peak experiences) tend to be more poetic, aesthetically oriented, transcendent, and mystical.

We will have more to say about peak experiences when we consider the empirical research supporting Maslow's theory later in this chapter.

9. They tend to identify with all of humankind.   The concerns that self-actualizers have for other people extend not only to their friends and family but to all people in all cultures throughout the world. This feeling of fellowship extends also to individuals who are aggressive, inconsiderate, or otherwise foolish. Self-actualizers have a genuine desire to help humanity.

10. They develop deep friendships with only a few individuals.   Self-actualizers tend to seek out other self-actualizers as their close friends. Such friendships are few in number but are deep and rich.

11. They tend to accept democratic values.   Self-actualizers do not respond to individuals on the basis of race, status, or religion. "They can be and are friendly with anyone of suitable character regardless of class, education, political belief, race, or color. As a matter of fact it often seems as if they are not even aware of these differences, which are for the average person so obvious and so important" (Maslow, 1954/1987, p. 139)

12. They have a strong ethical sense.   Although their notions of right and wrong are often unconventional, self-actualizers, nonetheless, almost always know the ethical implications of their actions. The ethical issues with which self-actualizers become involved are substantial. They avoid trivial issues such as the morality of "card playing, dancing, wearing short dresses, exposing the head (in some churches) or not exposing the head (in others), drinking wine, or eating some meats and not others, or eating them on some days but not on others" (1954/1987, p. 147).

13. They have a well-developed, unhostile sense of humour. Self-actualizers tend not to find humour in things that injure or degrade other humans. Rather, they are more likely to laugh at themselves or at human beings in general.

14. They are creative. Maslow found this trait in all of the self-actualizers:

> This is a universal characteristic of all the people studied or observed. . . . There is no exception. . . . This creativeness appears in some of our subjects not in the usual forms of writing books, composing music or producing artistic objects, but rather may be much more humble. It is as if this special type of creativeness, being an expression of healthy personality, is projected out upon the world or touches whatever activity the person is engaged in. In this sense there can be creative shoemakers or carpenters or clerks. (Maslow, 1954/1987, pp. 142–143)

This creativity comes from the fact that self-actualizers are more open to experience and more spontaneous in their feelings. It is directly related to B-motivation.

15. They resist enculturation. Self-actualizers tend to be nonconformists because they are inner-directed people. If a cultural norm is contrary to their personal values, they simply will not adhere to it.

NEGATIVE CHARACTERISTICS OF SELF-ACTUALIZING PEOPLE

Most people would describe these 15 characteristics as positive, but Maslow wanted to make it clear that self-actualizing people are far from perfect:

> Our subjects show many of the lesser human failings. They too are equipped with silly, wasteful, or thoughtless habits. They can be boring, stubborn, irritating. They are by no means free from a rather superficial vanity, pride, partiality to their own productions, family, friends, and children. Temper outbursts are not rare.
>
> Our subjects are occasionally capable of an extraordinary and unexpected ruthlessness. It must be remembered that they are very strong people. This makes it possible for them to display a surgical coldness when this is called for, beyond the power of the average man. The man who found that a long-trusted acquaintance was dishonest cut himself off from this friendship sharply and abruptly and without any observable pangs whatsoever. Another woman who was married to someone she did not love, when she decided on divorce, did it with a decisiveness that looked almost like ruthlessness. Some of them recover so quickly from the death of people close to them as to seem heartless. (Maslow, 1954/1987, p. 146)

Maslow concluded that as healthy, creative, democratic, and spontaneous as his self-actualizers were, *"there are no perfect human beings!"* (Maslow, 1954/1987, p. 146)

Why Self-Actualization Is Not Universal

Why, if the tendency toward self-actualization is innate, is not every mature adult self-actualized? Maslow suggested four basic explanations for the rarity of self-actualized people:

1. Because self-actualization is at the top of the hierarchy, it is the weakest of all the needs and therefore easily impeded. "This inner nature is not strong and overpowering and unmistakable like the instincts of animals. It is weak and delicate and subtle and easily overcome by habit, cultural pressure, and wrong attitudes toward it" (Maslow, 1968, p. 4).

2. Most people fear the kind of knowledge about themselves that self-actualization requires. Such knowledge requires giving up the known and entering a state of uncertainty:

> More than any other kind of knowledge we fear knowledge of ourselves, knowledge that might transform our self-esteem and our self-image. . . . While human beings love knowledge and seek it—they are curious—they also fear it. The closer to the personal it is, the more they fear it. (Maslow, 1966, p. 16)

Related to the fear of self-knowledge is the **Jonah complex**, which Maslow (1971) defined as "fear of one's own greatness . . . evasion of one's destiny . . . running away from one's best talents" (p. 34). The complex is named after the Biblical Jonah, who tried, in vain, to escape his fate. Thus according to Maslow, not only do we fear our weaknesses but we fear our strengths as well:

> We fear our highest possibilities (as well as our lowest ones). We are generally afraid to become that which we can glimpse in our most perfect moments, under the most perfect conditions, under conditions of greatest courage. We enjoy and even thrill to the godlike possibilities we see in ourselves in such peak moments. And yet we simultaneously shiver with weakness, awe, and fear before these very same possibilities. (1971, p. 34)

The Jonah complex explains why peak experiences are brief and transitory: "*We are just not strong enough to endure more!*" (1971, pp. 36–37)

Not only does the Jonah complex explain the aversion to our own potential greatness, it also explains why we often resent greatness in others:

> Not only are we ambivalent about our own highest possibilities, we are also in a perpetual and I think universal—perhaps even *necessary*—conflict and ambivalence over these same highest possibilities in other people, and in human nature in general. Certainly we love and admire good men, saints, honest, virtuous, clean men. But could anybody who has looked into the depths of human nature fail to be aware of our mixed and often hostile feelings toward saintly men? Or toward very beautiful women or men? Or toward great creators? Or toward intellectual geniuses? (1971, p. 35)

3. The cultural environment can stifle one's tendency toward actualization by imposing certain norms on segments of the population. For example, the way our culture defines *manly* tends to prevent the male child from developing such traits as sympathy, kindness, and tenderness, all of which characterize the self-actualized individual.

4. As indicated in item 2, in order to become self-actualized one must choose growth over safety. Maslow observed that children from warm, secure, friendly homes are more likely to choose experiences that lead to personal growth than children from insecure homes. Thus childhood conditions influence the probability of a person becoming self-actualized. Maslow characterized what he believed was the optimal set of circumstances for a child as *freedom within limits*. He believed too much permissiveness is as harmful as too much control; what is needed is a proper mixture of the two.

CONDITIONS NECESSARY FOR SELF-ACTUALIZATION

In addition to satisfying the physiological needs, the safety needs, and the love and belongingness needs, an environment must have several other characteristics before self-actualization can occur. These characteristics, according to Maslow, include freedom of speech, freedom to do what one wants to do as long as it harms no one else, freedom of inquiry, freedom to defend oneself, order, justice, fairness, and honesty. Later Maslow added "challenge" (proper stimulation) as a characteristic of an environment conducive to self-actualization.

We can now see why only about 1% of the population becomes self-actualized. Most of the rest of us live out our days somewhere between the love and belongingness and self-esteem needs.

Eupsychia

Because Maslow believed all human needs, including the need for self-actualization, were instinctoid, it must be the environment (society, culture) that determines the highest level of attainment in the hierarchy of needs one will reach. Maslow rejected the Freudian notion that humans and society had to be engaged in constant conflict. Rather, he believed society could be designed to maximize the probability of self-actualization. Because Maslow believed people's needs are good, their satisfaction should be encouraged rather than discouraged.

Maslow speculated on the type of utopia that would develop if 1000 healthy families moved to a deserted island where they could determine their own destiny. He called this potential utopia **Eupsychia** (pronounced yew-sigh-key-a), which can be broken down as follows: Eu = good, psych = mind, and ia = country. In Eupsychia, there would be complete **synergy**, a concept he borrowed from Ruth Benedict: syn = together, and ergy = working. Thus, in Maslow's utopia, there would be complete cooperation, or working together. What other features would characterize Eupsychia?

> What kind of education would they choose? Economic system? Sexuality? Religion?
> I am very uncertain of some things—economics in particular. But of other things I am *very* sure. One of them is that this would almost surely be a (philosophically) anarchistic group, a Taoistic [nature-oriented] but loving culture, in which people (young people too) would have much more free choice than we are used to, and in which basic needs and metaneeds would be respected much more than they are in our society. People would not bother each other so much as we do, would be much less prone to press opinions or religions or philosophies or tastes in clothes or food or art on their neighbors. In a word, the inhabitants of Eupsychia would tend to be more Taoistic, nonintrusive, and basic need-gratifying (whenever possible), would frustrate only under certain conditions that I have not attempted to describe, would be more honest with each other than we are, and would permit people to make free choices wherever possible. They would be far less controlling, violent, contemptuous, or overbearing than we are. Under such conditions, the deepest layers of human nature could show themselves with greater ease. (Maslow, 1954/1987, pp. 121–122)

In 1962, Maslow went to Non-linear Systems, Inc. as a visiting fellow. His experiences at this voltmeter factory resulted in his book ***Eupsychian Management*** (1965). The basic message in the book was that if industrial management were more aware of human needs and what is required to satisfy those needs, both the worker and the industry would be far healthier. "Eupsychian . . . conditions of work are often good not only for personal fulfillment, but also for the health and prosperity of the organization, as well as for the quantity and quality of the products or services turned out by the organization" (Maslow, 1971, p. 227). Eupsychian management, then, is an attempt to create a working situation conducive to satisfying human needs as Maslow described them.

Ashrams—Places for Personal Growth

For hundreds of years, India has had **ashrams,** or retreats, where people could escape the anxieties associated with everyday life. The pace of living in the ashram is radically slowed down, so that individuals can meditate and reflect on the meaning of their lives. Each ashram is led by a **guru** (spiritual teacher) who acts as a guide for those seeking inner peace. People stay in the ashram for a day, a week, months, or, in some cases, years. Others, however, visit the ashram for a few hours, and then return to their regular, routine lives.

In 1963, Michael Murphy and Richard Price developed the first North American equivalent to the Indian ashram in Big Sur, California. The philosophy of the ashram was directly in accordance with Maslow's views that psychology should concentrate more on *healthy* people than on unhealthy ones. Ashrams were places where nonneurotic individuals could go and search themselves and reflect on their own values and thus become even more effective in their daily lives. Whereas psychotherapy is available to the emotionally disturbed, ashrams are places where the already healthy person can become healthier. It is not surprising, then, that Maslow was among the first to conduct seminars at this newly founded ashram, which was named the Esalen Institute, after the Esalen Indians, who once inhabited the Big Sur region. The Western version of the Indian ashram has come to be called a **growth centre.**

Although the Esalen Institute and its participants embraced Maslow's humanistic psychology enthusiastically, they provided Maslow with one of the most unpleasant experiences of his life. While on sabbatical leave from Brandeis in 1966, Maslow agreed to conduct a workshop at Esalen. The approximately 25 people in the workshop included Fritz Perls, the renowned and irascible psychotherapist. When Maslow began the workshop in the academic style of questions and answers, the group was confused and irritated. They sought (as Maslow's students at Brandeis did later) a more personal sharing of experiences. Perls exclaimed, "This is just like school. . . . Here is the teacher, and there is the pupil, giving the right answer" (Hoffman, 1988, p. 290). Perls became increasingly bored and "began crawling toward an attractive woman across the room chanting 'you are my mother; I want my mother; you are my mother'" (Maslow, 1954/1987, p. xi). The situation became increasingly tense but neither Maslow nor the Esalen leaders did anything about it. The next day the climax came when, during Maslow's presentation, Perls "dropped to the floor and began to make whining, infantlike sounds before the astonished gathering as he slowly wrapped himself around Maslow's knees. . . . The meeting broke up in confusion" (Hoffman, 1988, p. 291).

Maslow finally had enough and the next day he gave the leaders of Esalen and its participants a scolding. He said they valued spontaneous feelings over rationality and objective research. They wanted to be childlike, he said, not to engage in the difficult work necessary for understanding human nature. "If you don't just want to be a selfish person contemplating your navel . . . you put your shoulder to the wheel. . . . If you don't use your brain, you're not fulfilling your potential" (quoted in Hoffman, 1988, pp. 292–293).

After the Esalen fiasco, Maslow and his wife Bertha gladly returned home. They spent the remainder of his sabbatical travelling through the southern and eastern United States. They were unaware that soon an experience similar to that at Esalen would be repeated at Brandeis.

Transpersonal Psychology

Toward the end of his life, Maslow began to realize that even humanistic psychology could not adequately explain certain aspects of humans. For example, various mystical, ecstatic, or spiritual states were viewed by Maslow as experiences beyond self-actualization. They were experiences that transcended the customary limits of personal identity and experience. Maslow believed the study of such phenomena should constitute a **fourth force** in psychology, which he called **transpersonal psychology.** In the preface of his book *Toward a Psychology of Being* (1968) he summarized his views on transpersonal psychology:

> I consider Humanistic, Third Force Psychology to be transitional, a preparation for a still "higher" Fourth Psychology, transpersonal, transhuman, centered in the cosmos rather than in human needs and interest, going beyond humanness, identity, self-actualization, and the like. . . . These new developments may very well offer a tangible, usable, effective satisfaction of the "frustrated idealism" of many quietly desperate people, especially young people. These psychologies give promise of developing into the life-philosophy, the religion-surrogate, the value-system, the life-program that these people have been missing. Without the transcendent and the transpersonal, we get sick, violent, and nihilistic, or else hopeless and apathetic. We need something "bigger than we are" to be awed by and to commit ourselves to in a new, naturalistic, empirical, nonchurchly sense. (pp. iii–iv)

Maslow lived to see the founding of the *Journal of Transpersonal Psychology* in 1969. This journal was organized by Anthony Sutich, the same person who founded the *Journal of Humanistic Psychology*. Following is Sutich's statement of the purpose of the *Journal of Transpersonal Psychology*, a statement that was enthusiastically endorsed by Maslow:

> The emerging Transpersonal Psychology ("Fourth Force") is concerned specifically with the empirical, scientific study of, and responsible implementation of the findings relevant to, becoming, individual and species-wide meta-needs, ultimate values, unitive consciousness, peak experiences, B-values, ecstasy, mystical experience, awe, being, self-actualization, essence, bliss, wonder, ultimate meaning, transcendence of the self, spirit, oneness, cosmic awareness, individual and species-wide synergy, maximal interpersonal encounter, sacralization of everyday life, transcendental phenomena, cosmic self humor and playfulness, maximal sensory awareness, responsiveness and expression, and related concepts, experiences, and activities. (Sutich, 1976, pp. 13–14)

Maslow's "The Farther Reaches of Human Nature" was the lead article in the first issue of the new journal. By 1985, there were 1200 members in the Association for Transpersonal Psychology, and the International Transpersonal Association has sponsored conferences on transpersonal psychology throughout the world.

With the emergence of transpersonal psychology in North America came an appreciation for non-Western psychologies, philosophies, and religions. It was realized that such views have for centuries offered ways, such as intense meditation, of inducing and understanding the "higher" states of consciousness.

Evaluation

EMPIRICAL RESEARCH

A major criticism of Maslow's theory has concerned the subjective way he and his colleagues described and studied self-actualizing people. One response to this criticism has been the development of the Personal Orientation Inventory (POI) by Everett Shostrom (Shostrom, 1963, 1964, 1974; Shostrom, Knapp, & Knapp, 1976). In the POI, respondents choose one each from 150 pairs of statements; for example, "my ethical standards are dictated by society" and "my ethical standards are self-determined"; "I find some people to be uninteresting," and "I never find people to be uninteresting." The test yields two overall scores. One is for *inner-directed support*, or the degree to which a person is his or her own source of support. The other is *time competence*, or the degree to which a person lives in the present. Ten subscales measure self-actualizing values, existentiality, feeling reactivity, spontaneity, self-regard, self-acceptance, nature of humans, synergy, acceptance of aggression, and capacity for intimate contact.

The POI has proved to be a reliable measure of self-actualization, as Maslow defined the term (Draguns, Krylova, Martin, Oryol, & Rukavishnikov, 2000; Ilardi & May, 1968; Klavetter & Mogar, 1967; Shostrom, 1966). The POI has also proved to be a valuable research tool. For example, Dosamantes-Alperson and Merrill (1980) administered the POI to people before and after they participated in several group therapy sessions. Results indicated that those receiving therapy became more inner-directed, spontaneous, and self-accepting—that is, they became more self-actualizing. POI scores have also been found to be positively correlated with academic achievement (LeMay & Damm, 1968; Stewart, 1968), teaching effectiveness (Dandes, 1966), and the effectiveness of psychotherapists (Foulds, 1969). Additional research involving measures of self-actualization has found that those having relatively high scores tend to be more creative (Buckmaster & Davis, 1985; Kiel, 1999; Satopathy, 2001; Runco, Ebersole & Mraz, 1991; Schulz, 2000; Yonge, 1975); more assertive (Ramanaiah, Heerboth & Jinkerson, 1985); more capable of sexual enjoyment (McCann & Biaggio, 1989); less influenced by social pressure (Bordages, 1989); and less likely to become bored (McLeod & Vodanovich, 1991).

Graham and Balloun (1973) found support for Maslow's concept of the hierarchy of needs. Thirty-seven participants were asked to describe the most important things in their lives. Judges rated these responses on a scale ranging from "very high" to "little or no" desire expressed for physiological, safety, love and belongingness, and self-actualization needs. Results supported Maslow's hypothesis that individuals at different levels of the hierarchy show greater satisfaction of the needs below their level than of the needs above it. Lester, Hvezda, Sullivan, and Plourde (1983), using their Need Satisfaction Inventory, found a significant, positive relationship between the satisfaction of the basic needs and psychological health. In the area of industrial-organizational psychology, Marrow, Bowers, and Seashore (1967) found that providing conditions that gratify higher needs improves both employee production and morale (see also Alderfer, 1972; Buttle, 1989; Johnston, 1995; Massarik, 1992). Using their own Maslowian Assessment Survey (MAS), Williams and Page (1989) found—as Maslow would have predicted—that esteem needs were the most salient, among college students, with love and belongingness needs a close second. There was little concern either for physiological and safety and security needs or for the self-actualizing needs. Finally, researchers have found Maslow's concept of the hierarchy of needs to be valid across cultures (Davis-Sharts, 1986).

With its stress on fulfilling potentials and self-improvement, the humanist perspective helped fuel the era of self-help literature, the scope of which is readily appreciated by a quick browsing of any popular bookstore. James Forest and colleagues from the University of Manitoba studied the usefulness of such books in helping individuals solve personal and social problems (Forest, 1987, 1988, 1991; Saper & Forest, 1992; Scholz & Forest, 1997). In one study, students completed a self-actualization scale to assess feelings of inner-directedness and mental wellness. Some students then read a best-selling self-help book emphasizing psychological issues; a control group did not. All students repeated the self-actualization measure two weeks later. As expected, self-actualization scores were significantly higher for students who read the self-help psychology book.

Maslow's notion of peak experiences has been studied extensively. For example, Panzarella (1980) found that artistically and musically oriented people claim that peak experiences have deepened their appreciation of music or art and that such mystical moments provide them with a sense of renewal and an urge to be creative. Ravizza (1977) had 20 athletes in 12 different sports describe their "greatest moments" as athletes. Their descriptions had much in common with Maslow's description of peak experiences. During their greatest moments the athletes felt no fear; were totally immersed in their activity; had a God-like feeling of control; felt a sense of self-validation; felt a unity with the experience and with the universe; viewed themselves as passive and their activity as effortless; and described their activity in terms of awe, ecstasy, and wonder. Mathes, Zevon, Roter, and Joerger (1982) developed the Peak Scale to measure the tendency to have peak experiences. Several studies using the Peak Scale yielded results consistent with Maslow's theorizing (Gordon, 1985; Keutzer, 1978; Yeagle, Privette, and Dunham, 1989). For example, those scoring high on the scale tended to have experiences of a mystical nature as well as feelings of intense happiness. High scorers also reported living in terms of B-values (for example, truth, beauty, and justice) instead of D-values. Contrary to what Maslow suggested, several researchers have found that peak experiences can be negative as well as positive (e.g., Acevedo & Hollander, 2000; Blanchard, 1969; Hoffman, 1998; Wilson & Spencer, 1990).

In his mention of the Jonah Complex, Maslow implied that we sometimes shy away from success because of excessive self-awareness. The intense scrutiny of fame induces chronic self-awareness, which highlights the celebrity's shortcomings. An attempt to escape such thoughts may explain self-destructive behaviours such as drugs and alcohol. Case studies have explored whether self-consciousness increases with fame. Mark Schaller (1997) of the University of British Columbia studied the songs of Kurt Cobain, lead singer and songwriter for the popular band *Nirvana*. Cobain, who committed suicide in 1994, suffered from depression and alcohol abuse. The percentage of first-person singular pronouns in Cobain's songs—a measure of self-consciousness—rose dramatically after Cobain signed a contract with a major record label. Similarly, Alain Morin and Lisa Craig (2000) studied self-awareness in Nobel Prize winner Ernest Hemingway, a heavy drinker who also committed suicide. They found that the number of first-person narratives in Hemingway's short stories doubled after he achieved fame with the publication of *A Farewell to Arms* in 1929 (Morin & Craig, 2000).

CRITICISMS

Too Many Exceptions.   Too many people seem to be highly productive and creative even though their basic needs do not seem to have been satisfied. Although Maslow noted such exceptions to his theory, he did little to account for them. Also, there are people who appear to have satisfied all their deficiency needs but do not become self-actualized. Maslow was struggling with this problem shortly before his death (see his interview with Frick, 1989) but he never solved it.

Unscientific Approach.   Maslow has been accused of using uncontrolled and unreliable research techniques, basing his conclusions about self-actualizing people on a small sample of people, accepting as valid the conscious self-reports of his subjects, using his own intuitive criteria as to what constitutes a self-actualizing person, and using ambiguous terms in his theory such as *metaneed, metapathology, love, beauty,* and *peak experience.* To be fair, we must realize that Maslow was aware the higher aspects of humans had not previously been investigated objectively. However, he desperately wanted psychology to expand its domain so these aspects could be studied scientifically. Several psychologists have followed the leads of Allport, Rogers, Maslow and others and have attempted to develop a scientifically rigorous humanistic psychology (e.g., Giorgi, 1992; Polkinghorne, 1992; Rychlak, 1988, 1991, 1997).

Overly Optimistic View of Human Nature.   Like Rogers, Maslow has been criticized for assuming humans have an innate tendency toward self-actualization. Critics say that many humans are too violent, insensitive, and inhumane to justify such an assumption. To these critics, theories such as those of Freud, Jung, and the sociobiologists present a more realistic picture of humans, and the theories of Rogers and Maslow represent wishful thinking rather than fact.

Several Unanswered Questions.   For example, who can become self-actualized? Most, if not all, of Maslow's subjects were highly intelligent and financially successful. What about less intelligent and financially successful people? Can they also become self-actualized? Also, can people intentionally become self-actualized or is it something that must occur naturally? That is, if one knows the criteria for self-actualization, can one adopt those characteristics and thus be self-actualized? Finally, as we have seen, Maslow was vague about how much satisfaction must be achieved at a given level of the hierarchy before the next higher needs become prominent in a person's life.

Concepts Biased Toward Western Culture.   Maslow's description of optimal psychological health emphasized personal achievement, autonomy, and self-esteem. This emphasis on the individual is contrary to the concept of "fulfillment" in a number of non-Western cultures. For example, in Japan and China, people are taught to value autonomy less than cooperation and not to demonstrate superiority over other people (Markus & Kitayama, 1991). Kitayama and Markus (1992) found that Japanese college students associated positive emotions with interpersonal relationships whereas American college students associated them with personal accomplishments. Furthermore, the conception of enlightenment offered by Buddhism emphasizes mental discipline as a means of overcoming the suffering, craving, and disappointment that would otherwise dominate one's life (Das, 1989). This conception of optimal psychological health is distinctly different than Maslow's. Similarly, Daniels (1988) criticizes Maslow's conception of psychological health for neglecting the hard work and pain involved in growth and development.

It has also been suggested that Maslow's description of optimal psychological health reflects male values (e.g., personal accomplishment) rather than female values (e.g., interpersonal relationships) (Josephs, Markus, & Tafarodi, 1992).

CONTRIBUTIONS

Vastly Increased Psychology's Domain.   Maslow took a position essentially opposite Freud's. In discussing Freud, we pondered a view of humans as animals in conflict with a society that imposes restrictions on their animal impulses. When we considered Maslow, we pondered a view of humans as basically good, nonaggressive seekers of truth, beauty, and perfection. For Freud, given complete freedom, humans would become sexually promiscuous and aggressive. For Maslow, given complete freedom, humans would create Eupsychia, a loving, harmonious, and nonaggressive society. The views of human nature held by Freud and Maslow are about as different as two views of human nature can be.

There is no doubt Maslow's contention that psychologists had traditionally focused on the darker side of human nature was valid. Of course, there have been exceptions: for example, Adler, Allport, Bandura, Mischel, Kelly, and Rogers. In general, however, psychology has been preoccupied with either the importance of the physiological drives in determining behaviour or the conditions under which neuroses and psychoses develop. Maslow did about as much as one person could have done to extend the domain of psychology to the study of healthy humans. His efforts, along with those of other theorists such as Rogers, have indeed created a viable third force in psychology.

Applied Value.   In addition to its impact on psychology, Maslow's theory has been highly influential in the areas of education, business, religion, and child rearing.

We conclude this chapter with the last entry that Maslow made in his diary a month before he died. The entry, dated May 7, 1970, attempts to explain why he was willing to take so many unpopular positions and what he was attempting to accomplish in his life:

> Somebody asked me the question . . . How did a timid youngster get transformed into a (seemingly) "courageous" leader and spokesman? How come I was willing to talk up, to take unpopular positions, while most others didn't? My immediate tendency was to say: "Intelligence—just realistic seeing of the facts," but I held that answer back because—alone—it's wrong. "Good will, compassion *and* intelligence," I finally answered. I think I added that I'd simply *learned* a lot from my self-actualizing subjects and from their way of life and from their metamotivations, which have now become *mine.* So I respond emotionally to the injustice, the meanness, the lies, the untruths, the hatred and violence, the simplistic answers. . . . So I feel cheap and guilty and unmanly when I *don't* talk up. So then, in a sense, *I have to.*
>
> What the kids *and* the intellectuals—and everybody else too—need is an ethos, a scientific value system and way of life and humanistic politics, *with* the theory, the facts, etc., all set forth soberly. . . . So *again* I must say to myself: to work! (Lowry, 1979, Vol. 2, p. 1309)

SUMMARY

1. Maslow survived the many bad experiences of his early years by taking refuge in books. Maslow's early research on dominance in monkeys led to research on dominance in humans and finally to an interest in "the good specimen." His interest in actualizing humans was stimulated by his efforts to understand two individuals he admired very much, Ruth Benedict and Max Wertheimer. He was distressed that his training in psychology had not equipped him to understand truly healthy, well-adjusted individuals. He concluded that psychology had been preoccupied with the study of lower animals, children, or maladjusted adults. Borrowing the reductive-analytic approach from the natural sciences, psychology attempted to understand humans as a collection of habits or conflicts. This technique does not tell the whole story; it denies or distorts many positive human qualities. Instead, Maslow suggested a holistic-analytic, or humanistic, approach that studies the total person.

2. Human nature, according to Maslow, consists of a number of instinctoidal (innate but weak) needs that are arranged in a hierarchy according to their potency. As one group of needs is satisfied, the next group in the hierarchy comes to dominate a person's life until they too are satisfied, at which time the next group becomes dominant, and so on. The needs, starting from the most basic, are physiological needs, safety needs, belongingness and love needs, esteem needs, and the need for self-actualization.

3. Self-actualizing people are no longer motivated by deficiencies (D-motivation); they are motivated by *being values* (B-motivation). B-values, also called metamotives, include such things as truth, goodness, beauty, justice, and perfection. D-motivated people search for specific need-related events in their environment; this is called D-perception (or D-cognition). B-motivated people perceive their environments most fully because they are not looking for anything in particular; this is called B-perception (or B-cognition). Failure to give expression to a B-value results in a metapathology.

4. Maslow attempted to correct the limited scope of psychology by studying the characteristics of the healthiest individuals he could find, among his friends, famous living people, and historical figures. He found that self-actualizing people tended to have in common the following characteristics: They perceive reality accurately; show great acceptance of themselves, others, and nature; are spontaneous; are problem-oriented rather than self-oriented; tend to be detached and private; are autonomous; exhibit continued freshness of appreciation; have peak experiences; identify with all of humanity; have only a few deep friendships; accept democratic values; have a strong ethical sense; have a well-developed sense of humour that is not hostile; are creative; and tend to be nonconformists. They also show some negative qualities such as vanity, pride, partiality, silliness, temper outbursts, and a coldness toward death.

5. Although Maslow thought the tendency toward self-actualization is innate, it is not universally experienced because the need is so weak that it is easily impeded; it takes considerable courage to be self-actualized (the fear of one's own potential greatness is called the Jonah complex); cultural norms are often incompatible with the self-actualizing process; and few childhoods instill enough security so that the child is willing to grow.

6. Maslow described a utopian society (Eupsychia) that he speculated a group of healthy people might design. He thought there would be complete synergy, or working together, in Eupsychia because all human needs would be recognized, respected, and gratified. When an industry attempts to consider human needs, as Maslow defined them, the process is known as Eupsychian management.

7. Maslow's humanistic psychology was enthusiastically embraced by an ashram in California called the Esalen Institute. There are now several hundred of these centres for personal growth in the Western world. Later in his life, Maslow became interested in transpersonal or fourth force psychology, which examines the human relationship to the cosmos and the various emotional experiences that an awareness of such a relationship creates.

8. The Personal Orientation Inventory has been used successfully to determine the extent to which individuals are self-actualized. Other research has supported Maslow's notion of the hierarchy of needs and of peak experiences. Maslow's theory has been criticized for having too many exceptions to its predictions, being unscientific, being overly optimistic about human nature, leaving many important questions unanswered, and being biased toward Western (and also perhaps male) values. His theory has been praised for vastly increasing psychology's domain and for having substantial applied value.

EXPERIENTIAL EXERCISES

1. At what level of Maslow's hierarchy of needs do you think you are currently operating? Justify your answer.

2. Evaluate your personality in terms of the 15 characteristics of the self-actualizing person. Indicate which characteristics you possess to some degree and which you do not. What conclusions do you draw?

3. Review Maslow's distinction between D-love and B-love and then evaluate a loving relation-

ship that you have had, or are having, in light of that distinction.

4. As part of his research on peak experiences, Maslow (1968) gave 190 college students the following instructions:

> I would like you to think of the most wonderful experience or experiences of your life; happiest moments, ecstatic moments, moments of rapture, perhaps from being in love, or from listening to music or suddenly "being hit" by a book or a painting, or from some great creative moment. First list these. And then try to tell me how you feel in such acute moments, how you feel differently from the way you feel at other times, how you are at the moment a different person in some ways. (p. 71)

Respond to Maslow's instructions.

5. Respond to Maslow's utopian society (Eupsychia). Which aspects of this society do you agree with and which ones do you disagree with? Do you believe that such a society is even theoretically possible? Explain.

DISCUSSION QUESTIONS

1. What is third force psychology? Why did Maslow feel that his third force was needed? Include in your answer the difference between the reductive-analytic approach to science and the holistic-analytic approach. Also discuss the term *desacralization*.

2. Discuss the hierarchy of needs. Which needs are included and how are they related to one another?

3. Differentiate between deficiency motivation (D-motivation) and being motivation (B-motivation).

4. If the tendency toward self-actualization is innate, why isn't self-actualization universal?

5. Compare Maslow's view of human nature with Freud's.

KEY TERMS

Aesthetic needs, p. 411
Ashram, p. 420
B-cognition, p. 412
Being cognition, p. 412
Being motivation, p. 412
Being values (B-values), p. 412
Belongingness and love needs, p. 409
B-love, p. 412
B-perception, p. 412
D-cognition, p. 412
D-love, p. 412
Deficiency motivation (D-motivation), p. 412
D-motive, p. 412
Desacralization, p. 406
D-perception, p. 412
Esteem needs, p. 409
Eupsychia, p. 419
Eupsychian management, p. 419
Fourth force psychology, p. 421

Growth centre, p. 420
Growth motivation, p. 412
Guru, p. 420
Hierarchy of human needs, p. 407
Holistic-analytic approach to science, p. 406
Humanistic psychology, p. 406
Instinctoid, p. 407
Jonah complex, p. 418
Metamotives, p. 412
Metapathology, p. 413
Need-directed perception, p. 412
Peak experiences, p. 413
Physiological needs, p. 408
Reductive-analytic approach to science, p. 406
Safety needs, p. 409
Self-actualization, p. 409
Synergy, p. 419
Third force psychology, p. 406
Transpersonal psychology, p. 421

16 Rollo Reese May

The theories of Adler, Allport, Kelly, Rogers, and Maslow have a clear existential orientation, in that they are concerned with the meaning of human life. However, it is May's theory that is most compatible with existential philosophy. In fact, May was as responsible as anyone for incorporating European existential philosophy into American psychology. Although humanistic and existential psychology have much in common, there are important differences between the two. For example, humanistic psychologists assume humans are inherently good whereas existential psychologists view human nature as neutral. That is, for the existentialists, whether a person becomes good or evil is essentially a matter of personal choice. (For other differences between humanistic and existential psychology see, for example, DeCarvalho, 1990b; Hergenhahn, 1997).

Biographical Sketch

Rollo Reese May was born to Earl Tittle and Matie Boughton May in Ada, Ohio, on April 21, 1909, and grew up in Marine City, Michigan. He was the first son, and the second child, in a family of six children. Neither of his parents were well educated and there was little intellectual stimulation in his home. When his older sister became schizophrenic, May's father blamed it on too much education. May was not close to either parent but he especially disliked his mother whom he described as a "bitch-kitty on wheels." May believed his mother's erratic behaviour and his older sister's schizophrenia contributed to his own two failed marriages later in his life (Rabinowitz, Good, & Cozad, 1989). May's first marriage, to Florence DeFrees, lasted from 1938 to 1968

Rollo Reese May

and produced three children: Robert Rollo, who is Director of Counseling at Amherst College, and twins Carolyn Jane, a social worker-therapist and artist, and Allegra Anne, a documentary film writer and single mother of two adopted multiracial children (Bugental, 1996, p. 418). After about 10 years, it became clear to May that his marriage to Florence was unsuccessful but he persisted in it for an additional 20 years for the sake of the children (Rabinowitz et al., 1989, pp. 438–439). His second marriage, to Ingrid Scholl from 1971 to 1978, was also unsuccessful and ended in divorce. His third marriage to Georgia Miller Johnson, a Jungian analyst, was successful and lasted from 1988 until May's death in 1994.

May first attended college at Michigan State University, where he majored in English, but was asked to leave when he became editor of a radical student magazine. He transferred to Oberlin College in Ohio, where he obtained his BA in 1930.

Following graduation, May pursued his interest in art by roaming through Europe with a group of artists. He remained in Europe from 1930 to 1933, and during that time, in addition to studying art, he taught at an American college in Greece and took summer school seminars from Alfred Adler in Vienna. During his second year in Europe, May began questioning the meaning in his life and finally had a "nervous breakdown."

Finally, in the spring of that second year I had what is called euphemistically a nervous breakdown. *Which meant simply that the rules, principles, values by which I used to work and live simply did not suffice anymore.* I got so completely fatigued that I had to go to bed for two weeks to get enough energy to continue my teaching. I had learned enough psychology at college to know that these symptoms meant that something was wrong with my whole way of life. I had to find some new goals and purposes for my living and to relinquish my moralistic, somewhat rigid way of existence. (May, 1985, p. 8)

In 1932, while still in Europe, May had an important insight while sketching a field of poppies.

I realized that I had not listened to my inner voice, which had tried to talk to me about beauty. I had been too hard-working, too "principled" to spend time merely looking at flowers! It seems it had taken a collapse of my whole former way of life for this voice to make itself heard. (May, 1985, p. 13)

In addition to learning to listen to his inner voice, May learned from this experience that psychological health often required challenging one's old values and replacing them with new ones. Incidentally, the impressive sketch of the poppies that May was making as he had these insights is reproduced on page 13 of May's book *My Quest for Beauty* (1985).

In 1934, May returned to the United States and enrolled in the Union Theological Seminary—not, May said, to become a preacher but to study the basic questions related to human existence. It was at this time that May met Paul Tillich, the eminent Protestant theologian and existential philosopher, who was a recent refugee from Germany and a faculty member at the seminary. Tillich became May's lifelong friend, and in 1973 May wrote *Paulus: Reminiscences of a Friendship* as a tribute to Tillich, who died in 1965. It was through Tillich that May was exposed to existential thought, although he had already concluded, after his exposure to Adler's thinking, that he could never accept a mechanistic, deterministic view of humans. May, then, was ready for the existential view of humans, and he embraced that view enthusiastically. After a year at Union

Seminary, May learned that his parents had divorced and his father had left the home. May returned to Michigan to provide for his mother and a sister and brother still living at home. During this time (1934–1936) he was employed by Michigan State College as a student advisor and counsellor. In 1936, May returned to Union Seminary and he received his BD *cum laude* from Union Theological Seminary in 1938, and served as a minister for two years in Montclair, New Jersey.

May's first book, written during his senior year at Union Seminary, was *The Art of Counseling* (1939), and his second was *The Springs of Creative Living: A Study of Human Nature and God* (1940). Both books were religiously oriented, but neither endorsed blind obedience to religious dogma. May considered religions that required blind acceptance of dogma to be unsound and unhealthy. He defined healthy religion as follows: "Call it confidence in the universe, trust in God, belief in one's fellow-men, or what not, the essence of religion is the belief that something matters—the *presupposition that life has meaning.*" (1940, pp. 19–20). So the religious person is one who has found meaning in life, and an *atheist* is one who cannot, or has not, found it.

In the 1940s, May studied psychoanalysis at the William Alanson White Institute of Psychiatry, Psychoanalysis, and Psychology in New York, where he was influenced by such illustrious individuals as Harry Stack Sullivan and Erich Fromm. May remained affiliated with the institute in a variety of capacities for many years. He became a practising psychoanalyst in 1946, and shortly thereafter enrolled in the Clinical Psychology Program at Teacher's College, Columbia University. It was about this time that he contracted tuberculosis and lived for 18 months in a sanatorium in upstate New York. His close brush with death had a profound influence on his thinking and brought him still closer to existential philosophy.

During his illness, May read both Kierkegaard's and Freud's analyses of anxiety. Søren Kierkegaard (1813–1855) was a Danish theologian and philosopher who rejected the attempts of other philosophers to view humans as totally rational and logical. He viewed humans as largely emotional and free to choose their own destinies. Although May agreed with Freud on many points, he agreed most with Kierkegaard's conclusion that anxiety results from a threat to one's existence. This definition of anxiety has become a focal point in May's theory and is elaborated later in this chapter. May's analysis of anxiety was submitted to Columbia University as his Ph.D. dissertation and was published as *The Meaning of Anxiety* (1950). In 1949, May was granted the first Ph.D. in clinical psychology ever awarded by Columbia University. The degree was granted *summa cum laude*.

In 1975, May moved to Tiburon, California, where he resumed his private practice and served in various capacities at the Saybrook Institute, a graduate school and research centre in San Francisco, and at the California School of Professional Psychology. He also continued to elaborate his version of existential psychology. In poor health the last two years of his life, May died of multiple causes in his home on October 22, 1994 (Bugental, 1996, p. 418).

In 1987, the Saybrook Institute established a Rollo May Center consisting of a library and a program designed to encourage research and publication in the spirit of May. The Saybrook Institute also granted an honorary doctorate to May accompanied by the following citation:

> [To Rollo May] a man of mythic vision and dedication, who has explored the borderlands of our art and science of psychology. . . . You have devoted your long, productive, and courageous life to the study of the human soul. . . . [through examining] love, will, courage, anxiety, innocence, beauty, and existence. . . . You are [William] James's worthy successor in the breadth of your vision, the articulateness of your descriptions, and the productiveness of your conceptions. (Bugental, 1996, p. 419)

Existentialism

Although elements of existential philosophy are embodied in several of the theories we have reviewed, May's theory has the most in common with existential philosophy. Therefore, to review the major concepts of **existentialism** is also to review much of May's theory of personality. The concepts and terms that follow have come from various sources including the writings of such existential thinkers as Kierkegaard, Nietzsche, Heidegger, Binswanger, Boss, Jaspers, Sartre, Camus, Frankl, and Tillich.

DASEIN

Dasein literally means to be there (German, *da* = there; *sein* = to be). The term indicates that the focus of interest for the existentialist is a particular person experiencing and interpreting the world at a particular time in a particular place. It is the study of a person as a being-in-the-world. The world and the person exist simultaneously and cannot be separated. To say that a human being exists at a certain time and in a certain place is not the same as saying a physical object exists there. Guignon (1984) discusses the complex nature of *Dasein:*

> To be human, as [Heidegger's] term Dasein suggests, is to be "there," caught up [in the world], taking a stand on one's life, active and engaged in ordinary situations, with some overview of what is at stake in living. What characterizes human life in its most natural ways of being is not a relationship between mind and body but a concrete "existing" in a world. Our most natural experience of ourselves is described as "Being-in-the-world," where "world" refers not to the universe studied by physics, but rather to a life-world in the sense in which we speak of "the academic world" or the "world of the theater." To be "in" such a world is not like a pencil's being "in" a drawer; it is more like being engaged or involved in something. (p. 231)

For humans then, existence is a complex, dynamic process. By choosing, valuing, accepting, and rejecting, humans are constantly **becoming** something different than they were. That personality is a dynamic, ever-changing process is echoed in previous theorists' views, including Adler's creative self, and even Allport's original definition of personality.

THREE MODES OF EXISTENCE

Many existential writers divide human existence into three categories: the *Umwelt,* the physical aspects of the internal and external environments; the *Mitwelt,* the realm of interpersonal relationships; and the *Eigenwelt,* a person's consciousness. Each person is thought to live in all three worlds simultaneously, and only the three worlds taken together give a full account of human existence.

ALIENATION

Alienation refers to a person's estrangement from some aspect of his or her nature. Alienation results in feelings of loneliness, emptiness, and despair. Because there are three modes of existence, one can become alienated from nature (*Umwelt*), from other people (*Mitwelt*), or from oneself (*Eigenwelt*). The devastating effects of this alienation and despair were made graphically clear to Canadians in November 2000 with news broadcasts from Labrador's Innu communities of Sheshatshiu and Davis Inlet. Young addicts, some as young as six years old, were found sniffing solvents from plastic garbage bags in an effort to forget poverty, family alcoholism, and death.

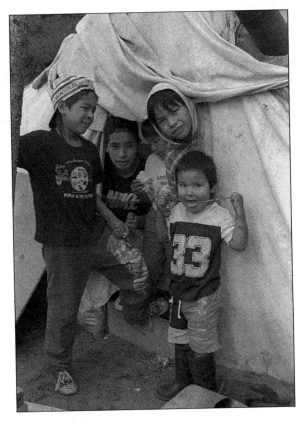

Innu children who face the difficulties of poverty and family alcoholism may turn to gas sniffing in just one manifestation of alienation.

Freedom

The most important human attribute, and the attribute that makes humans unique, is freedom of choice. **Freedom** exists only as a potentiality, however, and can be underdeveloped in some people, or even denied. One increases freedom by expanding consciousness. It is through freedom of choice that the person can transcend immediate circumstances, so no human needs to be a victim of environment, genetics, early experiences, or anything else. In the words of Sartre, "Man is nothing else but what he makes of himself. Such is the first principle of existentialism" (1957, p. 15).

Responsibility

Because we have the freedom to become whatever type of person we choose, we must assume full responsibility for what we become. No other person(s), circumstances, or fate can be praised or blamed for the nature of our existence; we alone are responsible. Freedom and responsibility are inseparable. In short, it becomes *our* job, and *our* marriage, and *our* health.

Ontology

In philosophy, **ontology** is the study of existence, or what it means to be. An ontological analysis of such concepts as time, knowledge, or love attempts to determine what all instances of each concept have in common. For example, such an analysis seeks to determine the essential ingredients of the experience of love. The existentialists are concerned with two ontological questions: (1) What is the essence of human nature, or what does it mean to be human? and (2) What does it mean to be a particular human, or what makes a person the way he or she is? In other words, the existentialist is interested in discovering the essence of people in general and of individuals in particular.

PHENOMENOLOGY

The existentialists use the person's consciousness as their subject matter. Awareness of all types is analyzed—for instance, awareness of the external world, awareness of bodily events, and awareness of awareness. It is generally assumed by the existentialists that humans are the only animals that are aware and know they are aware. Furthermore, consciousness is studied as an intact, meaningful phenomenon, and is not divided or compartmentalized for further study. Phenomenon means that which is given, and **phenomenology** is the study of that which is given in human consciousness. In other words, the person's view of reality is sacrosanct, and cannot be questioned or tampered with; it cannot be broken down and still maintain its meaning.

AUTHENTICITY

If a person exercises his or her free will to expand consciousness further, to establish values that minimize anxiety and provide positive relationships with fellow humans, and to create the challenges necessary for further personal growth, then he or she is living an authentic life. If, however, a person lives in accordance with someone else's values and does not exercise his or her free will to enhance personal growth and effective living, the person is said to be living an inauthentic life. **Authenticity** necessarily involves risk, and therefore living an authentic life takes courage—thus the title of Paul Tillich's book *The Courage to Be* (1952).

Many famous examples exist to illustrate the struggle between authentic and inauthentic living. Ellen Degeneres revealed her sexual orientation during an episode of her situation comedy *Ellen,* saying she could no longer maintain the act of being straight. Canada's surviving Dionne Quintuplets, who had spent their childhoods on display as cute scientific curiosities, broke their long silence to speak out about sexual and physical abuse at the hands of their parents and about the artificial life they had been forced to lead.

DEATH

Most existentialists emphasize the importance of the fact that humans are aware they must someday die. Death represents nothingness or nonbeing and is the polar opposite of the rich, full, creative life. It therefore represents the opposite of what most existentialists are urging people to become. No one can escape this dichotomy: We seek a full life but at the same time we are aware we must die. The knowledge of our mortality causes anxiety but this anxiety need not be negative; it can be (and should be) used to motivate people to get as much out of life as they can in the time available to them. May (1983) said, "To grasp what it means to exist, one needs to grasp the fact that he might not exist" (p. 105). Furthermore, death is not viewed as an all-or-nothing phenomenon. People die symbolically, by degrees, each time one of their established values is threatened. As Cole Porter wrote, "every time we say good-bye, I die a little." Such a threat is perceived as an attack on one's existence and therefore it too causes anxiety. Living an authentic life necessarily involves dealing with both literal and symbolic death and, therefore, authenticity and anxiety are inseparable. Symbolically, we die whenever we have the opportunity to grow, to develop in positive and creative ways, but yet we choose not to because of the anxiety that necessarily comes with it.

THROWNNESS

Thrownness (also called *facticity* and *ground of existence*) refers to the facts that characterize a person's existence over which he or she has no control. The facts that one is born and ultimately must die are two examples. Other examples include natural events such as earthquakes, volcanoes, and hurricanes; genetic factors, such as the colour of one's skin, one's gender, and the possession of exceptional talents (for example, artistic, musical, or mathematical abilities); familial and societal factors into which one is born (for example, being rich or poor, American or Russian, or being born during peacetime or wartime). It is these natural, familial, historical, and cultural conditions that, to a large extent, constitute the *da* of *Dasein*. It is thrownness that determines the conditions under which we exercise our personal freedom. That is, some facts characterizing our existence are impossible for us to control; how we interpret, value, and act on those facts, however, is a matter of personal choice.

What other existentialists call thrownness, facticity, or ground of existence, May called **destiny,** which he defined as the "pattern of limits and talents that constitutes the 'givens' in life" (1981, p. 89). According to May, these personal limitations in our existence give meaning to our personal freedom. It is true that the givens in one's life are determined by circumstances beyond one's control, but the meaning assigned to those givens is freely chosen. Thus, determinism and freedom are closely related.

> Freedom and determinism give birth to each other. Every advance in freedom gives birth to new determinism, and every advance in determinism gives birth to a new freedom. Freedom is a circle within a larger circle of determinism, which is, in turn, surrounded by a larger circle of freedom. And so on, ad infinitum. (May, 1981, p. 84)

All of the foregoing terms and concepts are found in May's theory of personality. Next, we turn to some of May's specific applications of existential philosophy to psychology.

The Human Dilemma

May (1967) stated that the **human dilemma** is the fact that humans are capable of viewing themselves as both subject and object at the same time. May described the **object-subject dichotomy** in various ways, which have not always been consistent (see Reeves, 1977, pp. 198–201). In general, however, May said that humans are capable of seeing themselves as an object to which things happen. For example, as people, we are influenced by the physical environment, the presence or absence of other people, genetics (we are tall, short, male, female, light-skinned, dark-skinned, and so on), and by social or cultural variables. In other words, we are influenced by our destiny.

These objective events are those variables that deterministically oriented theories stress as the causes of behaviour. That is, because we are stimulated in certain ways, we respond in certain ways. As subjects, however, we are aware of the fact that these things are happening to us. We perceive, ponder, and act on this information. We determine which experiences are valuable and which are not, and then act according to these personal formulations.

May said that **self-relatedness** is what distinguishes humans from the rest of nature. It is "man's capacity to stand outside himself, to know he is the subject as well as the object of experience, to see himself as the entity who is acting in the world of objects" (1967, p. 75). As humans, we view the world, and we can view ourselves viewing. It is this self-relatedness, or consciousness of self, that allows humans to escape determinism and personally influence what they do. "Consciousness of self gives us the power to stand outside the rigid chain of stimulus and response, to pause, and by this pause to throw some weight on either side, to cast some decision about what the response will be" (May, 1953, p. 161).

In short, a turtle does not realize that it is a turtle, nor does it contemplate the meaning of life, the meaning of being a turtle, and whether it is being the best turtle it can possibly be. The torment of awareness, at the heart of the human dilemma, was captured in a line by actor John Cusack in *Being John Malkovich*, "consciousness — I think, I feel, I suffer."

Here we have the concept of *Dasein* in May's theory. "Being there" is to be understood as a being who is there. The "there" is whatever deterministic forces are present in a given situation, whereas the being (the person) brings to bear on these forces his or her own freedom, values, interpretations, and so forth. For May, then, both ends of the dichotomy need to be taken into consideration to reach a full understanding of a person—that is, both one's physical circumstances (the objective part) and how one subjectively structures and values those circumstances (the subjective part).

May believed it is a mistake to stress one pole of the object-subject dichotomy at the expense of the other pole. "Curiously enough, both these alternatives—being purely free and purely determined—amount to the same kind of playing God in the respect that we arrogantly refuse to accept the dilemma which is our fate and our great potentiality as humans" (May, 1967, p. 9).

May thought that Skinner and Rogers both emphasized one side of the dilemma at the expense of the other. Skinner avoided subjective experience, but May asked, "Is it not a fact that people *do* react to an inner experience of their environment, *do* see their environment in terms of their past experiences, and *do* interpret it in terms of their own symbols, hopes and fears?" (May, 1967, p. 15).

May criticized Rogers for both his emphasis on subjectivity and for omitting from his analysis the negative components of human existence such as the emotions of anger, aggression, hostility, and rage. In an open letter to Rogers, May (1982) said we must "actively confront the issues of evil and good in ourselves, our society, and our world" (p. 19). Elsewhere, May said "We need, therefore, to put the question, Does not Rogers' emphasis on rationality, and his belief that the individual will simply choose what is *rational* for him, leave out a large section of the spectrum of human experience, namely, all the *irrational* feelings?" (1967, p. 18).

As we see when we discuss the daimonic later in this chapter, May believed the potential for evil is part of human nature and must be taken into consideration in fully understanding humans.

INTENTIONALITY

In *Love and Will* (1969), May spoke of **intentionality** as the means by which the dichotomy between subject and object is partially overcome. Although mental acts are purely subjective, they always intend, or relate to, events outside of themselves. Love, for example, is a subjective experience but one must love someone or something. Likewise, perception is a subjective experience but one must perceive something. So it is with all mental and emotional experiences; they must intend, or relate to, objects or events outside of themselves. In the object-subject dichotomy, the object pole is given, but it is the individual who determines which aspects of objective reality are valued positively or negatively, attended to or ignored, or approached or avoided. Intentionality, then, is the human capacity to perceive selectively and to assign meaning to objects and events in the world; it describes the relationship between the thinking person and the outside world. Thus the same environmental event will be responded to differently depending on what meaning the person assigns to it. For example, the same house in the mountains will have different meaning depending on whether it is perceived as a possible temporary vacation home, a possible permanent residence, the home of friends, the home of enemies, or as an object to be sketched (May, 1969, pp. 224–225).

For May, then, intentionality elaborates an important aspect of *Dasein*. As beings-in-the-world, our interactions with the physical world are highly personal and dynamic. Each person responds to the world in terms of a personal structure of meaning (for example, beliefs, values, and expectations). We see here considerable similarity between May's version of existential theory and Kelly's constructive alternativism (see chapter 13).

Will and wish are closely related to intentionality. May defined **will** as "the capacity to organize oneself so that movement in a certain direction or toward a certain goal may take place" (1969, p. 218). He defined **wish** as "the imaginative playing with the possibility of some act or state occurring" (1969, p. 218). Thus, given an individual structure of meaning, a person will use his or her imagination to ponder several possible future courses of action. It is this wishing that provides vitality, imagination, and innovation to the personality. From the many possible courses of action, the person chooses those that are possible and most meaningful, and organizes his or her life so that the chosen goals can be attained (will).

Intentionality, wish, and will are three of the most important concepts in May's theory because they relate to several other human attributes. Reeves (1977) says, "It is, then, asserts May, in intentionality and will, in the broad reach of human orientation toward meaning, decision, and act, in the weighing, deciding, and acting on possibilities sensed, that the individual person experiences his identity, exercises his freedom, and senses his being" (p. 158). For example, you may *wish* to be a lawyer, but it is by your own *will* that you pursue the right schooling, excel in classes, and succeed during articling and thereafter.

Anxiety and Guilt

Most existential thinkers assume that the experience of **anxiety** is part of the human condition, and May was no exception. As mentioned earlier, May studied the theories of anxiety proposed by Kierkegaard (for example, *The Concept of Anxiety,* 1844/1944) and Freud while he was in the sanatorium. He rejected Freud's interpretation of anxiety as resulting from a conflict between one's biological needs and the demands of society. For May, Freud's analysis of anxiety was too biological and compartmentalized. That is, for Freud, anxiety was viewed as resulting from the conflicts among the id, ego, and superego.

Instead of accepting Freud's complex and ultimately biological explanation of anxiety, May accepted Kierkegaard's existential definition. For Kierkegaard, human freedom and anxiety go hand in hand. When freedom is threatened, as it always is, anxiety results:

> The distinctive quality of human anxiety arises from the fact that man is the valuing animal, the being who interprets his life and world in terms of symbols and meanings, and identifies these with his existence as a self. . . . It is the threat to these values that

causes anxiety. Indeed, I define anxiety as *the apprehension cued off by a threat to some value which the individual holds essential to his existence as a self.* The threat may be to physical life itself, i.e., death; or to psychological life, i.e., loss of freedom. Or it may be to some value the person identifies with his existence as a self: patriotism, the love of a special person, prestige among one's peers, devotion to scientific truth or to religious belief. (May, 1967, p. 72)

May pointed out it is a uniquely human characteristic that we sometimes prefer death to the abandonment of a cherished value:

Death is the most obvious threat cueing off anxiety, for unless one holds beliefs in immortality, which is not common for our culture, death stands for the ultimate blotting out of one's existence as a self. But immediately we note a very curious fact: some people *prefer to die rather than to surrender some other value.* The taking away of psychological and spiritual freedom was not infrequently a greater threat than death itself to persons under the dictatorships of Europe. "Give me liberty or give me death" is not necessarily histrionic or evidence of a neurotic attitude. Indeed, there is a reason for believing . . . that it may represent the most mature form of *distinctively* human behavior. (May, 1967, p. 73)

NORMAL ANXIETY

To grow as a person, one must constantly challenge one's structure of meaning, which is the core of one's existence, and this necessarily causes anxiety. Thus to be human is to have the urge to expand one's awareness, but to do so causes anxiety. Such anxiety is not only inescapable; it is normal and healthy. "All growth consists of the anxiety-created surrender of past values as one transforms them into broader ones. Growth, and with it normal anxiety, consists of the giving up of immediate security for the sake of more extensive goals" (May, 1967, pp. 80–81). The authentic person recognizes the hazards of exploring uncharted territory and does so nonetheless. The anxiety associated with moving forward into the unknown is an unfortunate concomitant of exercising one's freedom.

One will experience **normal anxiety** from ordinary change and growth; for example, when starting new classes or a new job, in the purchase of a new home, the advent of a new relationship, or the breakup of a struggling one. Normal anxiety is viewed as part of the growth process, and no attempt should ever be made to eliminate it from a person's experience. May strongly disagreed with those psychotherapists who have as their goal the elimination of anxiety.

NEUROTIC ANXIETY

A certain amount of anxiety is normal, but nonetheless it is still anxiety, and some people attempt to escape from it. People who decide to conform to values arrived at by others, for example, give up their own personal freedom and the possibility for personal growth by seeking "security" in conformity. Such attempts to escape normal anxiety, which is healthy, result in **neurotic anxiety,** which is unhealthy. It is neurotic anxiety that must be addressed by a psychotherapist. May (1967) distinguished between normal and neurotic anxiety:

Normal anxiety is anxiety which is proportionate to the threat, does not involve repression, and can be confronted constructively on the conscious level. . . . *Neurotic* anxiety, on the other hand, is a reaction which is disproportionate to the threat, involves repression and other forms of intrapsychic conflict, and is managed by various kinds of blocking-off of activity and awareness. The anxiety connected with the "loneliness at the top" and the "loneliness of the long distance runner" which the movies tell us about can be seen as *normal* anxiety. The anxiety that comes from conforming, to escape this loneliness, is the *neurotic* transformation of the original, normal anxiety.

Actually, neurotic anxiety develops when a person has been unable to meet normal anxiety at the time of the actual crisis in his growth and the threat to his values. Neurotic anxiety is the end result of previously unmet normal anxiety. (p. 80)

To summarize, normal anxiety is experienced when one attempts to expand one's consciousness or when new values displace old ones because of changing circumstances. Normal anxiety is an integral part of healthy growth: "All growth consists of the anxiety-creating surrender of past values" (May, 1967, p. 80). Neurotic anxiety is experienced when consciousness is restricted, old values are clung to at all costs, or when one attempts to escape normal anxiety by accepting dogma. "Dogma, whether of the religious or scientific variety, is a temporary security bought at the price of surrendering one's opportunity for fresh learning and new growth. Dogma leads to neurotic anxiety" (May, 1967, p. 80). Neurotic anxiety leads to psychological stagnation and to intense feelings of guilt.

NORMAL AND NEUROTIC GUILT

Anyone who does not live up to his or her potentiality as a human feels guilty; therefore, all humans experience a certain amount of **guilt.** May referred to guilt as ontological because it, like anxiety, is part of the human condition. Guilt, according to May, does not result from violating a generally accepted moral code; rather, it results from not approaching or striving toward one's full potential as a human. "Ontological guilt does not consist of I-am-guilty-because-I-violated-parental-prohibitions, but arises from the fact that I can see myself as the one who can choose or fail to choose. Every developed human being would have this ontological guilt" (May, Angel, & Ellenberger, 1958, p. 55).

Normal guilt is part of a healthy existence and can be used constructively. Guilt, however, if not recognized and dealt with, can, like anxiety, become neurotic and debilitating. There is a close relationship between the experience of anxiety and guilt. The more one takes risks to expand consciousness the more one experiences normal anxiety, but this very risk taking reduces normal guilt. On the other hand, avoiding such risk taking—choosing to turn down an opportunity to grow—results in neurotic anxiety, which, in turn, results in **neurotic guilt.** Furthermore, because there are three modes of existence, there are three major sources of anxiety and guilt. Various levels of anxiety and guilt result from how we embrace the *Umwelt,* the *Mitwelt,* and the *Eigenwelt.*

Importance of Values

Values summarize in symbolic form those classes of experience we deem especially important. Valuing some experiences more than others cannot be avoided because the valuing process is part of human nature. A person's value system determines how much meaning an experience will have, how much emotionality it elicits, and what is worth aspiring to in the future. To a large extent, how much anxiety a person experiences will be determined by the adequacy of his or her value system. "A person can meet anxiety to the extent that his values are stronger than the threat" (May, 1967, p. 51).

According to May, a developmental pattern in the formation of values exists. A baby values most the love, care, and nourishment provided by the mother. Any threat to these causes the infant to experience anxiety. The maturing child typically values approval, success, and status among peers. Mature values, however, are not viewed as outgrowths of previously held values. Rather, they reflect basic human nature by emphasizing freedom, the future, and the betterment of the human condition:

> The criteria for mature values follows from the distinctive characteristics of the human being . . . mature values are those which transcend the immediate situation in time and encompass past and future. Mature values transcend also the immediate in-group, and extend outward toward the good of the community, ideally and ultimately embracing humanity as a whole. . . . The more mature a man's values are, the less it matters to him whether his values are literally satisfied or not. The satisfaction and security lie in the *holding* of values. To the genuine scientist or religious person or artist, security and confidence arise from his awareness of his devotion to the *search* for truth and beauty rather than the finding of it. (May, 1967, p. 82)

For May, the **Oedipal conflict** is not an attraction toward one parent and a feeling of hostility toward the other, as Freud had proposed. Rather, it is a struggle between dependence and independence. That is, as young children our needs for food, shelter, and safety are satisfied by our parents. We have a tendency to continue to depend on them, or others, for need satisfaction even when it is no longer necessary to do so. To approximate our potential as humans, we must give up the dependence that we valued in our early years. This is not easy to do, and yet it is a prerequisite for positive growth.

When conditions remain stable for a long time, it is possible for people to develop values that are effective in dealing with the world and also in manifesting themselves as human beings. It is even possible for many people to hold more or less the same values. This was the case for the pioneers in the United States, when individualism and pragmatism were widely accepted. In our modern world, however, conditions have changed so rapidly we have not had time to evolve values that are adequate for coping with modern life. "In a period of transition, when old values are empty and traditional mores no longer viable, the individual experiences a particular difficulty in finding himself in his world" (May, 1967, p. 25).

When we do not have adequate values, we feel alienated from the world and we lose our sense of identity, worth, and significance. May believed it was the breakdown of traditional values that caused a widespread identity crisis in North America in the 1950s. However, he observed that this identity crisis developed into an even more serious problem:

> Persons of all sorts these days, especially younger people, diagnose their trouble when they come to a counselor or therapist as an "identity crisis"—and the fact that the phrase has become trite should not lead us to overlook the fact that it may also be importantly true. . . . My thesis is that the problem of identity in the 1950's has now become, more specifically, the crisis of the loss of the sense of significance. . . . The feeling tends to be, "Even if I did know who I am, I couldn't make any difference as an individual anyway." (1967, p. 26)

According to May, people today are confronted with "mass" everything—for example, mass communication and mass education. The emphasis is on sameness not individuality. Yet we were brought up believing in the power and worth of the individual. Thus the values we learned as children do not fit the modern world, and therefore we feel insignificant, alone, and anxious. Without functional values, one has nothing to be committed to and one feels helpless. Without a strong value system, it is difficult, if not impossible, for a person to choose a course of action or a way of life. According to May, then, the major problem of our time is that "the younger generation . . . do not have viable values available in the culture on the basis of which they can relate to their world" (1967, p. 42).

Without an adequate system of values, people tend to be outer directed. That is, people with inadequate values depend on things outside of themselves to indicate their significance—for instance, social mores, peer evaluation, church dogma, teachers' opinions, and grades. Those people with strong values know they are significant independent of these external events and are therefore able to experience these things in a much different perspective. Peer approval may be valued, for example, but it is not depended on for a sense of worth.

For May, as well as many other existential thinkers, values and **commitment** go hand in hand. Mature values allow a person not only to deal effectively with present events but to consider the feelings and values of others and therefore to form deep, meaningful interpersonal relationships. Also, mature values allow one to become future oriented. Such values give a person hope and therefore a reason to make a commitment to a course of action. A person without an adequate value system has no good reason to be committed to anything (as noted by Allport in his theory of functional autonomy.) For this reason, the existentialists include commitment as an ontological human characteristic; that is, commitment characterizes every normal, healthy, mature human being.

A person's values determine how he or she acts, and because values are consciously and freely chosen, one is fully responsible for one's actions:

> *It is in the act of valuing that consciousness and behavior become united.* One can take over rote values . . . from the church, or the therapist, school, American Legion, or any other group in the culture. But the act of valuing, in contrast, involves a commitment on the part of the individual which goes beyond the "rote" or automatic situation. This, in turn, implies some conscious choice and responsibility. (May, 1967, p. 220)

The Nature of Love

In his book *Love and Will* (1969), May describes four types of love and states that authentic love is a blending of the four. The four types of love are sex, eros, philia, and agapé.

SEX

Sex is one of our biological drives, and it can be satisfied by engaging in sexual intercourse, just as eating a meal can satisfy the hunger drive. Both sexual intercourse and eating can be almost automatic activities triggered by a need and the availability of an object that will satisfy that need. "Sex can be defined fairly adequately in physiological terms as consisting of the building up of bodily tensions and their release" (May, 1969, p. 73).

EROS

Eros is the desire for union with another person. With sex the goal is termination, gratification, and relaxation. In contrast, we seek to continue the experience of eros. Eros causes us to seek a tender, creative relationship within the context of sexual experience. In addition, eros is responsible for humans seeking such a relationship with the world and with people in general. Eros is the human drive to seek wholeness or interrelatedness among all of our experiences. Seeking such feelings in a sexual relationship is but one manifestation of eros.

Although it may appear eros must always be experienced positively, that is not the case because eros exemplifies the daimonic forces within us. May (1969) defined the **daimonic** as

> any natural function which has the power to take over the whole person. Sex and eros, anger and rage, and the craving for power are examples. The daimonic can be either creative or destructive and is normally both. . . . The daimonic is the urge in every being to affirm itself, assert itself, perpetuate and increase itself. The daimonic becomes evil when it usurps the total personality without regard to the integration of that self, or to the unique forms and desires of others and their need for integration. It then appears as excessive aggression, hostility, cruelty—the things about ourselves which horrify us most, and which we repress whenever we can, or more likely, project on others. But these are the reverse side of the same assertion which empowers our creativity. All life is a flux between these two aspects of the daimonic. (p. 123)

The term *daimonic* comes from the Greek word meaning both divine and diabolic. Thus we have forces within us that in moderation lead to personal growth and creativity, but when allowed to dominate become negative and destructive. So it is with eros. One must be assertive to have a loving union with another person but when assertiveness dominates, one is in danger of exploiting one's partner.

The existence of daimonic forces within humans provides the continuing potential for cruel, irrational, and inhumane behaviour. An extreme example of harmful daimonic forces in eros may be seen in the notorious Jeffrey Dahmer, convicted in 1992 of the mutilation, murder, and in some cases cannibalism of 15 young men in Milwaukee. Interviews showed that Dahmer's horrendous crimes were performed as acts of love: to ensure his lovers would never leave him, he felt he had to destroy them, preserve them, and in some cases incorporate them. It is both unnecessary and impossible for humans to rid themselves of daimonic forces. What is important is to keep daimonic urges under control and to use them productively rather than to harm. May viewed the tension between the positive and negative forces within each human as the greatest source of the creativity shown in art, drama, literature, and even science.

There is another danger associated with eros. Merging with another person can be viewed as a form of death: the death of the person who existed before the merger took place. By entering into a loving relationship one is exposed to the possibilities of grief, sorrow, and disappointment as well as to the many delights such a relationship can bring. It is a major gamble.

> For death is always in the shadow of the delight of love. In faint adumbration, there is present the dread, haunting question, Will this new relationship destroy us? When we love, we give up the center of ourselves. We are thrown from our previous state of existence into a void; and though we hope to attain a new world, a new existence, we can never be sure. . . . This experience of annihilation is an inward one and, as the myth rightly puts it, is essentially what *eros* does to us. To love completely carries with it the threat of annihilation of everything. This intensity of consciousness has something in common with the ecstasy of the mystic in his union with God: just as he can never be *sure* God is there, so love carries us to that intensity of consciousness in which we no longer have any guarantee of security. (May, 1969, p. 101)

PHILIA

The third type of love is **philia**, which is ordinarily defined as friendship or brotherly love. According to May, eros cannot last for long without philia because the tension of continuous attraction and passion would be too great. May (1969) explained philia further:

Philia is the relaxation in the presence of the beloved which accepts the other's being as being; it is simply liking to be with the other, liking to rest with the other, liking the rhythm of the walk, the voice, the whole being of the other. This gives a width to eros, it gives it time to grow; time to sink its roots down deeper. Philia does not require that we do anything for the beloved except accept him, and enjoy him. It is friendship in the simplest, most direct terms. (p. 317)

For May, then, for a deep, loving relationship to exist, the partners must, in addition to seeking a creative union, truly like each other as individuals. Many people believe that their partner in a significant intimate relationship should also be their best friend. To be able to say honestly, "I like you" to one partner is an important part of authentic love.

AGAPÉ

The fourth type of love is **agapé**, which May (1969) defined as follows:

Esteem for the other, the concern for the other's welfare beyond any gain that one can get out of it; disinterested love, typically, the love of God for man. It is an analogy— though not an identity—with the biological aspect of nature which makes the mother cat defend to her death her kittens, and the human being love his own baby with a built-in mechanism without regard for what that baby can do for him. (p. 310)

Agapé is an unselfish giving of one's self to another; a giving of one's self without any concern of what one will get in return. May's concept of agapé is similar to what Rogers called unconditional positive regard. In both cases, the love offered to another has no conditions placed on it.

May believed that in modern times many have had an unfortunate tendency to equate love with sex. For May, however, authentic love must involve a blending of sex, the biological component of love; eros, the seeking of a creative union with another human, the sharing and combining of two selves; philia, friendship, a simple liking of one's partner even when sex and eros are not involved; and agapé, the unselfish concern for one's partner, the aspect of love that is unconditional.

Psychotherapy

For May, the goal of psychotherapy is *not* to eliminate anxiety or guilt but rather to convert neurotic anxiety or guilt to normal anxiety or guilt, which, as we have seen, are part of being human and are necessary for personal growth:

Our chief concern in therapy is with the potentiality of the human being. The goal of therapy is to help the patient actualize his potentialities. . . . The goal of therapy is not the absence of anxiety, but rather the changing of neurotic anxiety into normal anxiety, and the development of the capacity to live with and use normal anxiety. The patient after therapy may well bear more anxiety than he had before, but it will be conscious anxiety and he will be able to use it constructively. Nor is the goal the absence of guilt feeling, but rather the transformation of neurotic guilt into normal guilt, together with the development of the capacity to use this normal guilt creatively. (May, 1967, p. 109)

May used the term **unconscious** to describe cognitive experiences that are denied awareness because a person is not living an authentic life. May's treatment of the unconscious is similar to Kelly's. Kelly said that certain experiences are suspended because they do not fit into a person's construct system. For May, certain experiences are denied because they would cause too much anxiety if experienced. For both Kelly and May, repression in the Freudian sense is not involved because the person is at least partly aware of these experiences but they are denied full conscious expression. For May, then, the unconscious is not a reservoir of unacceptable impulses, thoughts, and wishes. Rather, it consists of *"those potentialities for knowing and experiencing which the individual cannot or will not actualize"* (1983, pp. 17–18).

According to May, effective therapy cannot occur if the therapist views the client as an object and attempts to explain his or her problem in terms of various causes—for example, past experiences. Rather, the therapist must try to determine what the client is attempting to express via his or her "problem":

> From the ontological approach . . . we see *that sickness is precisely the method that the individual uses to preserve his being.* We cannot assume in the usual oversimplified way that the patient automatically wants to get well; we must assume, rather, that he cannot permit himself to give up his neurosis, to get well, until other conditions in his existence and his relation to his world are changed. (May, 1967, p. 95)

In a manner reminiscent of Adler and Kelly, the existential therapist encourages clients to view the events into which they have been thrown, that is, their destiny, differently. In this sense, the goal of therapy is to help clients find meaning in circumstances they otherwise find meaningless or hopeless. In his classic book *Man's Search for Meaning* (1946/1984), Viktor Frankl (1905–1997) argued that meaning can be found in even the most dire circumstances.

> We must never forget that we may also find meaning in life even when confronted with a hopeless situation, when facing a fate that cannot be changed. For what then matters is to bear witness to the uniquely human potential at its best, which is to transform a personal tragedy into a triumph, to turn one's predicament into a human achievement. When we are no longer able to change a situation—just think of an incurable disease such as inoperable cancer—we are challenged to change ourselves. . . . In some way, suffering ceases to be suffering at the moment it finds a meaning. (p. 135)

May used the term **encounter** to describe the therapeutic process. By encounter May meant two selves coming together and sharing aspects of their existence:

> Encounter is what really happens; it is something much more than a relationship. In this encounter I have to be able, to some extent, to experience what the patient is experiencing. My job as a therapist is to be open to his world. He brings his world with him and therein we live for fifty minutes. . . . In addition, the therapeutic encounter requires that we ourselves be human beings in the broadest sense of the word. This brings us to a point where we can no longer talk about it merely psychologically, in any kind of detached way, but must "throw" ourselves into the therapeutic encounter. In this it helps to realize that we also have gone through similar experiences, and though perhaps not involved in them now, we know what they mean. (1967, p. 108)

We see, then, that both Rogers and May viewed empathetic understanding as a key ingredient in effective therapy.

May's approach to psychotherapy includes all the terms and concepts of his theory of personality. Humans, he believes, have the potential to be free and to live authentic lives but many factors can inhibit this freedom and authenticity. People who have adequate values can see their normal anxiety and guilt constructively and creatively. People without adequate values must block out various categories of experience, and healthy anxiety and guilt become neurotic. Such people cannot reach their full potential as human beings. The job of the therapist is to help the client approximate his or her full potential. The therapist's job, according to May, is to help the client to live an authentic life. What May meant by authenticity is much the same as what Rogers called congruency and what Maslow called self-actualization.

The Importance of Myth

In the same spirit as Jung's contention that archetypes guide human existence through symbolization and myths or Adler's guiding fictions, May believed "myth is a way of making sense in a senseless world. Myths are narrative patterns that give significance to our existence" (1991, p. 15). According to May, many of the problems in our society such as cults, drug addiction, suicide, and depression can be traced to the lack of myths that provide individuals with a sense of inner security. Many Native people in Canada would argue that many of the problems in daily living and the lack of spiritual wellness we suffer arise from losing touch with the mythic aspect of nature (*Umwelt*). About people seeking psychological help, May (1991) said, "As a practicing psychoanalyst I find that contemporary therapy is almost entirely concerned, when all is surveyed, with the problems of the individual's search for myths" (p. 9).

In close agreement with Jung, May (1991) believed "myths are archetypal patterns in human consciousness [and therefore] where there is consciousness, there will be myth" (p. 37). Also like Jung, May believed myths reflect the core of human nature: "Individual myths will generally be a variation on some central theme of the classical myths" (p. 33). The universal themes of which individual myths are usually some variation include birth; death; love and marriage; the Oedipal complex, which May viewed as the struggle for independence; and the conflict between good and evil, which May explained as the manifestation of the daimonic. "In the moments when eternity breaks into time, there we find myth. Myth partakes of both dimensions: it is of the earth in our day-to-day experiences, and is a reaching beyond our mundane existence" (May, 1991, p. 297). May also demonstrated his agreement with Adler by noting that we forget most of our early experiences but a few are remembered. These "first memories," whether they are accurate or not, become the main ingredients of our "guiding fictions" or the myths according to which we live our lives. Thus "memory and myth are inseparable" (May, 1991, p. 70).

To illustrate how myths give expression to the universal truths of human nature, May (1991) analyzed the myths portrayed in such classics as the Bible, Homer's *Odyssey*, Sophocles's *Oedipus Rex* and *Oedipus in Colonus*, Sartre's *The Flies*, Dante's *Divine Comedy*, Ibsen's *Peer Gynt*, Grimm's *Briar Rose* (later renamed *Sleeping Beauty*), Melville's *Moby Dick*, Goethe's *Faust*, Fitzgerald's *The Great Gatsby*, Poe's *The Raven*, and Shakespeare's *Hamlet, King Lear,* and *Macbeth.* In all of these, and other works, May showed how important aspects of human nature are given expression, allowing the reader to experience catharsis. May noted that one of the most common themes in classical literature is the portrayal of the conflict between the positive and negative aspects of human nature. For May, this eternal conflict between good and evil (for example, between God and Satan) is the greatest source of creativity. As we have seen, May had little patience with those who portray humans as only good or only bad. For May, we are both, and therein lies the primary drama of human existence.

According to May, myths serve four primary functions in our lives: They give us a sense of personal identity; they give us a sense of community; they support our moral values; and they allow us to deal with the mysteries of creation. Above all the "hunger for myth is a hunger for community. . . . To be a member of one's community is to share in its myths" (1991, p. 45). However, different communities (societies, cultures) are bound together by different myths and therein lies the potential for friction among people. Xenophobia may be explained by the fact that an outsider may not share one's myths and is therefore to be feared: "The outsider, the foreigner, the stranger is the one who does not share our myths, the one who steers by different stars, worships different gods" (1991, p. 45). Thus, like other aspects of human nature, the same characteristic that can bind people together has the potential to drive them apart.

Are some myths better than others? May's answer was yes. Some myths are undesirable because they do not encourage a sense of kinship among humans. According to May, many of the current problems in the United States stem from the myth of the rugged individualist attempting to live in isolation from other people. This myth has resulted in the Age of Narcissism and thus loneliness and violence. According to May, true happiness can result only from positive interpersonal relationships and, therefore, only myths that bind people are conducive to psychological health. Survival itself depends on caring for our fellow humans—all of them. May (1991) offered the type of myth that he believed we now need to embrace:

> We awake after a sleep of many centuries to find ourselves in a new and irrefutable sense in the myth of humankind. We find ourselves in a new world community; we cannot destroy the parts without destroying the whole. In this bright loveliness we know now that we are truly sisters and brothers, at last in the same family. (p. 302)

This thinking echoes Adler (chapter 4), who used social interest to index mental health. May also had common ground with Allport (chapter 7), who argued that friction among humans could be substantially reduced by adopting a one-world perspective, that is, by each individual identifying with all humankind.

Evaluation

EMPIRICAL RESEARCH

Most existential theorists are unconcerned with the empirical validation of their concepts. They believe the place to validate their concepts is in the arena of everyday life, or in the therapeutic situation, and not with systematic laboratory or field investigations. Van Kaam (1966), an existential psychologist, summarized this viewpoint: "Experiences such as responsibility, dread, anxiety, despair, freedom, love, wonder or decision cannot be measured or experimented with. . . . They are simply there and can only be explicated in their givenness" (p. 187).

Some, however, have made efforts to validate existential concepts empirically. Gendlin and Tomlinson (1967) created the *Experiencing Scale*, designed to measure the extent to which a person is in touch with his or her true feelings. Because a major goal of psychotherapy is to encourage people to recognize, accept, and live in accordance with their feelings, the scale can be used to measure the effectiveness of therapy (Gendlin, Beebe, Cassens, Klein, & Oberlander, 1968; see also Angus, Korman, & Levitt, 2000; Martin & Sells, 2001; Muran, Samstag, Segal, Ventur, & Winston, 2001). Crumbaugh (1968) devised the Purpose-in-Life Test to measure the extent to which a person's life is meaningful. It was found that individuals scoring low on the test tend to have negative worldviews and lack purpose. Also, the test was found to negatively correlate with a scale of depression. That is, people who scored high on the Purpose-in-Life Test were less likely to be depressed (see also Griffin & Roberts, 2000; McFarlane & Rhodes, 2000). Thorne and Pishkin (1973) developed the Existential Study, which consists of seven scales: self-status, self-actualization, existential morale, existential vacuum, humanistic identification, existence and destiny, and suicidal tendency. Thus the scales are designed to quantify several terms and concepts from existential theory.

Both humanistic and existential theorists believe that researchers have ignored many important elements of the human condition, including authenticity, despair, and loneliness. Researchers distinguish between social loneliness (an inadequate social network) and emotional loneliness (an absence of an intimate attachment relationship). Loneliness is common: approximately 80% of first-year university students (undergoing a major life transition and often away from home for the first time) report moderate to severe levels of loneliness (Cutrona, 1982). Daniel Perlman from the University of British Columbia has been instrumental in outlining the theory and relevant variables in loneliness (Perlman, 1987, 1988; Borys & Perlman, 1986; Dufton & Perlman, 1986; Gerson & Perlman, 1979; Peplau & Perlman, 1982). Loneliness was once considered an inappropriate topic for empirical research, but, perhaps because of the attention paid to it by existentialists, researchers from many theoretical perspectives and backgrounds have entered the arena of investigation.

Ken Rotenberg and colleagues at Lakehead University in Thunder Bay, Ontario have made considerable advances in understanding the relation of loneliness to stigmatization, dietary restraint, interpersonal trust, and self-disclosure, and even to the prediction of university drop-out rates (Rotenberg, 1994, 1998, 1999; Rotenberg & Flood, 1999; Rotenberg & MacKie, 1999; Rotenberg & Morrison, 1993). In one study, respondents attributed more psychological difficulty and interpersonal problems to hypothetical individuals described as having lonely characteristics. Interestingly, respondents who were lonely themselves judged non-lonely individuals more harshly than did other respondents (Rotenberg & Kmill, 1992).

Despite some attempts to quantify existential concepts, most existentialists believe that attempting to study and understand humans by using the traditional methods of science misses those qualities that are truly important. May (1967) captured this view with a fable:

> A psychologist—any psychologist, or all of us—arrives at the heavenly gates at the end of his long and productive life. He is brought up before St. Peter for the customary accounting. . . . An angel assistant in a white jacket drops a manila folder on the table which St. Peter opens and looks at, frowning. Despite the awesome visage of the judge, the psychologist clutches his briefcase and steps up with commendable courage.
>
> But St. Peter's frown deepens. He drums with his fingers on the table and grunts a few nondirective "uhm-uhm"s as he fixes the candidate with his Mosaic eyes.
>
> The silence is discomfiting. Finally the psychologist opens his briefcase and cries, "Here! The reprints of my hundred and thirty-two papers."
>
> St. Peter slowly shakes his head.
>
> Burrowing deeper into the briefcase the psychologist offers, "Let me submit the medals I received for my scientific achievement."
>
> St. Peter's frown is unabated as he silently continues to stare into the psychologist's face.
>
> At last St. Peter speaks. "I'm aware, my good man, how industrious you were. It's not sloth you're accused of. Nor is it unscientific behavior." . . .

Now St. Peter slaps his hand resoundingly down on the table, and his tone is like Moses breaking the news of the ten commandments: "You are charged with *nimis simplicandum* [oversimplification]!

"You have spent your life making molehills out of mountains—that's what you're guilty of. When man was tragic you made him trivial. . . . When he suffered passively, you described him as simpering; and when he drummed up enough courage to act, you called it stimulus and response. . . . You made man over into the image of your childhood Erector Set or Sunday School maxims—both equally horrendous.

"In short, we sent you to earth for seventy-two years to a Dantean circus, and you spent your days and nights at sideshows!" (pp. 3–4)

CRITICISMS

Philosophy Not Psychology.   Historically, concepts such as values, responsibility, and commitment have been studied by philosophers and theologians, not by psychologists. Many critics of existential psychology would like this historical trend to continue.

Unscientific Approach.   As we have seen, most existential psychologists reject traditional scientific methodology as a valid way of studying humans. Such methodology, say the existentialists, treats humans as passive objects not as authors of their own existence. Furthermore, the existentialists reject the assumption of determinism made by traditional science. Human behaviour, the existentialists say, is freely chosen, not determined. Critics say that the rejection of scientific methodology and the assumption of determinism represent a throwback to psychology's prescientific past—a throwback to the time when psychology, philosophy, and religion were indistinguishable. Existential psychology, then, say the critics, is jeopardizing the scientific respectability that psychology has gained since its prescientific era.

Nebulous Terminology.   It is difficult to define precisely terms such as freedom, responsibility, commitment, guilt, intentionality, love, and courage. Often the meanings of these and other terms change from one existential theorist to another, and sometimes for the same theorist at different times. This lack of precision makes understanding difficult and quantification practically impossible.

CONTRIBUTIONS

Call for Human Science.   Like Maslow, May did not reject the idea of objectively studying humans; he simply felt that traditional scientific methodology is not appropriate for doing so and that an approach is needed that studies humans as whole, unique, complex beings. Many welcome May's idea of developing a science more appropriate to the study of humans—one *not* based on the assumptions and techniques of the natural sciences.

Important, New Way of Conceptualizing Personality.   For many, the existential description of humans rings true: We do seek meaning in our lives and seem lost without it; some humans do seem to grow constantly by exercising their choices whereas others seem to escape from their freedom; most humans are aware of and disturbed by our finitude; and humans do differ in the experiences they seek and in their interpretations of those experiences. Many believe the existential view of humans has breathed new life into psychology. Hall and Lindzey (1978) exemplify such a belief:

Whatever the future of existential psychology may be—and at the present time it appears to have sufficient vigor and vitality to last a long time—it has already served at least one very important function. That function is to rescue psychology from being drowned in a sea of theories that have lost contact with the everyday world and with the "givens" of experience. . . . Existentialism is helping to revitalize a science that many feel has become theoretically moribund. It has done this by insisting on using a strictly phenomenological methodology. It has tried to see what is actually there and to describe human existence in concrete terms. . . . Whatever the future of existential psychology may be . . . it is clear that now it offers a profoundly new way of studying and comprehending human beings. For this reason, it merits the closest attention by serious students of psychology. (pp. 343–344)

SUMMARY

1. Under the influence of Freud, Kierkegaard, and Tillich, and with a special interest in the nature and causes of anxiety, May developed a theory of personality based on existential philosophy. From existential philosophy, May accepted the following concepts: (1) the term *Dasein*, which is the study of a particular person in the world at a particular time and existing under a particular set of circumstances; (2) a description of three modes of human existence; the *Umwelt*, or our interactions with the physical world; the *Mitwelt*, or our interactions with other humans; and the *Eigenwelt*, or one's interactions with oneself; (3) alienation, or separation from one or more of the modes of existence; (4) the belief that each person is free to choose the meaning of his or her own existence; (5) responsibility, which goes hand in hand with freedom; (6) ontology, which attempts to determine the essential features of human nature in general or of a particular human; (7) the importance of phenomenology, or the study of intact, meaningful conscious experience *without* dividing it or reducing it for study or analysis; (8) authenticity, or the effort to live one's life in accordance with freely chosen values rather than having values imposed on one from the outside; (9) the importance of death in the ontology of humans (for example, death is the ultimate state of nonbeing, and to ponder the inevitability of one's death is a source of great anxiety); and (10) thrownness (which May called destiny), referring to the circumstances of our lives over which we have no control.

2. May described the human dilemma as our ability to view ourselves as both an object in the world to which things happen and a subject who acts on things by interpreting them, valuing them, projecting them into the future, and thus transforming them. To develop a complete understanding of humans, both aspects must be studied.

3. *Intentionality* refers to the fact that mental events are directed toward objects outside of themselves. It is through intentionality that we interact with the objective world and, therefore, it is the means by which the object-subject dichotomy is bridged. After a structure of meaning has been developed and intentions formulated, we must act on those intentions. *Will* is a commitment to action. *Wish* is the imaginative playing with possible courses of action before actually committing ourselves to one.

4. According to May, to be human is to experience anxiety and guilt. Normal anxiety results when we ponder death or when our values are threatened. Likewise, when we become aware we are not living up to our full potential, we experience guilt. Some people, instead of using normal anxiety and guilt for personal growth, refuse to acknowledge them or attempt to escape them by conforming to external values. When normal anxiety and guilt are not dealt with consciously and constructively, they become neurotic. Neurotic anxiety and guilt cause a person to deny important areas of personal experience and therefore stifle personal growth. It is neurotic anxiety and guilt that typically cause a person to seek psychotherapy.

5. Our values summarize those experiences we deem most valuable. Mature values seek a harmony among people and are future oriented. Because each person can freely choose his or her values, each person is responsible for the actions derived from them. The amount of anxiety that one experiences is directly related to one's values. If one's value structure is adequate, one will experience normal anxiety. Value structures must be dynamic, however, because an unwillingness to change values stifles personal growth and results in excessive guilt.

6. May described four types of love. Sex is attraction based solely on biology. Eros seeks a union and a sharing of one's self with one's lover. Philia, the friendship that holds two people together even when sex and eros are not involved, means liking as well as loving the other person. Agapé means caring for the other person even when one gets nothing in return. Authentic love, according to May, involves a blending of all four types. Entering a loving relationship is risky because there is no guarantee that the personal sacrifices required will benefit those involved.

7. Effective psychotherapy attempts to understand what the client is trying to do or say through an emotional problem. In other words, the therapist must try to see experiences as the client does. The therapist attempts to help the client convert neurotic anxiety or guilt into normal anxiety or guilt and begin to live an authentic life. Another goal of existential therapy is to help clients find meaning in circumstances that appear to them as meaningless or hopeless.

9. For May, the unconscious consists of potential experiences that must be denied because of defences used to avoid normal anxiety, or because of a very restrictive value structure. When those barriers are overcome, the person becomes open to experience, becomes aware of previously denied possibilities, and in general, becomes freer as a human being.

10. May contended that it is through myth that the basic components of human nature are given expression. Myths that give people a sense of community are conducive to mental health. Myths that encourage individualism isolate people and result in feelings of loneliness and despair.

11. A few attempts have been made to verify existential concepts, such as loneliness, empirically but most existential psychologists believe concepts should be verified in the arena of everyday life or in the therapeutic situation. May's theory has been criticized for representing philosophy (or perhaps religion) instead of psychology, for being unscientific, and for containing nebulous terminology. May's theory has been praised for calling for the development of a human science and for offering a new way of conceptualizing personality.

EXPERIENTIAL EXERCISES

1. May defined an atheist as a person with little or no meaning in his or her life. According to May's definition, are you an atheist? Explain.

2. List your important values and describe how you organize your life around them.

3. According to the existentialists' definition of authenticity, would you consider yourself an authentic or an inauthentic person? Explain.

4. Analyze a loving relationship that you have, or have had, in terms of May's four-part definition of love. Indicate if you agree or disagree with May's description of love.

5. Using the existentialists' definitions of anxiety and guilt, describe the circumstances under which you have experienced these two emotions. Have you ever experienced what the existentialists call neurotic anxiety or neurotic guilt? Explain.

6. Give an example of how intentionality, wish, and will have combined and manifested themselves in your life.

7. According to the existentialists, some people accept the challenge of their individual freedom with courage and live authentic lives. Others, however, escape from their freedom and live inauthentic lives. From the people you know or have known, describe one person you think is (or was) authentic and one who is (or was) inauthentic.

8. According to May, myths serve four primary functions in our lives. List each function and indicate to what extent it operates in your life, if at all.

DISCUSSION QUESTIONS

1. Briefly describe the following terms from existential philosophy: Dasein, Umwelt, Mitwelt, Eigenwelt, alienation, ontology, phenomenology, responsibility, and thrownness.
2. What, according to May and other existentialists, is an authentic life?
3. What, according to May, is the human dilemma? Give an example.
4. What did May mean by authentic love? Include in your answer the roles played by sex, eros, philia, and agapé. Why did May refer to entering an authentic, loving relationship as risky?
5. Describe the model of humans that May thought current scientific psychology is using, and then describe the model proposed by May.

KEY TERMS

Agapé, p. 442
Alienation, p. 431
Anxiety, p. 436
Authenticity, p. 433
Becoming, p. 431
Commitment, p. 440
Daimonic, p. 441
Dasein, p. 431
Destiny, p. 434
Eigenwelt, p. 431
Encounter, p. 443
Eros, p. 440
Existentialism, p. 431
Freedom, p. 432
Guilt, p. 438
Human dilemma, p. 434
Intentionality, p. 435

Mitwelt, p. 431
Neurotic anxiety, p. 437
Neurotic guilt, p. 438
Normal anxiety, p. 437
Normal guilt, p. 438
Object-subject dichotomy, p. 434
Oedipal conflict, p. 439
Ontology, p. 432
Phenomenology, p. 433
Philia, p. 441
Self-relatedness, p. 434
Thrownness, p. 434
Umwelt, p. 431
Unconscious, p. 442
Values, p. 438
Will, p. 436
Wish, p. 436

17 A Final Word

After our review of the major theories of personality in the preceding chapters, the following four conclusions seem warranted:

1. Personality theories often reflect the biographies of their authors.
2. Much about personality remains unknown.
3. The best available explanation of personality comes from a composite of all the major theories (rather than from any single theory or paradigm).
4. Each person must judge for himself or herself what information from each theory is useful or not useful.

Personality Theories Often Reflect the Biographies of Their Authors

Students sometimes wonder why so many different personality theories exist. One reason is that personality is so complex that different theories can focus on different aspects of it. Given the fact that personality can be defined and studied in several different ways, the question remains, What causes a *particular* theorist to choose one approach to defining and studying personality over others? The answer seems to be that, at least in part, personality theories are biographical. That is, they often reflect the significant experiences of the particular theorist. George Atwood and Silvan Tomkins (1976) make this point: "Every theorist of personality views the human condition from the unique perspective of his own individuality. As a consequence, personality theories are strongly influenced by personal and subjective factors" (p. 166). Atwood and Tomkins (1976) argue that theories of personality cannot be fully understood without recognizing the biographical contributions to each theory.

> A truly unifying theory of personality ought to be able to account not only for the phenomena to which all theories address themselves, but also for the other theories themselves. This is because each of these constructions embodies a vision of the human situation which is rooted in the theorist's own development as a person. . . . If the science of human personality is ever to achieve a greater degree of consensus and generality, it should begin to turn back on itself and question its own psychological

foundations. There should be sustained study not only of the phenomena which have always been the province of personality theory, but also of the biasing subjective factors which contribute to the continuing confusion and diversity in the field. (p. 167)

Stolorow and Atwood (1979) apply the analysis suggested in the above quotation to a number of the theories we have covered in this text. Salvatore Maddi (1996) also recognizes the importance of a theorist's personal intuition for determining how he or she views personality. Maddi defines intuition as "an inarticulate, private, and emotional, as well as vivid, immediate, and compelling, sense of the meaning of what is happening" (1996, p. 9).

Does the fact that personality theories reflect the personalities and experiences of their authors invalidate the theories? Not at all. A theory can be valid or invalid, useful or useless, regardless of what motivated its origin. For example, much in Freud's theory reflects his personal experiences and concerns, yet most would agree that his is among the most influential theories ever constructed. We should realize, however, that because any particular theory is partly biographical, it will tend to apply more to certain types of people than to others, and it will ring true to some people more than to others—presumably to those with a personality most like that of the theorist. Perhaps this is why, at the end of a course such as this one, different students have different favourite theories. Thus tastes in personality theories might also be biographical. For example, Vyse (1990) found that psychology majors prefer psychological theories perceived as facilitating their self-understanding.

The following observation made by Robinson (1985) pertains to psychoanalytic theory but it could as easily apply to almost any personality theory:

The psychoanalytic account is a story, a narrative, but not a scientific one. It is rather a historical narrative—something of a saga—which is "good" or less than good depending upon the contact it makes with the reader's own experiences and thoughts. We ask of such accounts only whether they make sense, recognizing they are but one of an indefinite number of possible accounts all of which may make as much (or as little) sense. (p. 123)

Much about Personality Remains Unknown

The theories covered in this text, individually and collectively, do not adequately account for personality. Although each theory illuminates part of what we call personality, much remains in darkness. Existing theories need to be extended and new theories need to be developed before we will be able to approximate a thorough understanding of personality.

To test what you have learned about personality and what remains unknown, just attempt one day to account for your own actions and the actions of others by using what you have learned in this text. Perhaps you will have a better understanding of many events now. No doubt, you will encounter examples of repression (evidenced by such examples as slips of the tongue, dreams, and humour) and other ego-defence mechanisms such as projection, identification, and reaction formation. You may find that the emotion-producing symbols found in art, music, and religion reflect our evolutionary experiences as a species. You may see parents instilling either basic anxiety or basic trust in their children. You may conclude that the consistent patterns of behaviour observed in people reflect underlying traits, and you may see examples of how reinforcement contingencies influence behaviour. You may see people showing favouritism toward their relatives, and you may observe that many apparent acts of altruism are actually selfish. You may see that much of life is a matter of interpretation or attitudinal. You may see different people struggling to satisfy different levels of needs, and perhaps you will see a person who appears to be self-actualizing. You may observe that some people have been more successful than others in developing their own values with which to deal with the world. You may note that you, and others, find meaning in life by embracing personal or collective myths.

At the end of the day, many behaviours that were previously a mystery will have been at least partly explained, but many mysteries will remain. Their solution will require the work and imagination of future personality theorists.

Composite of All Major Theories Best Explains Personality

The position we have taken throughout this text is that all the major personality theories add to our understanding of personality, and therefore it is not necessary to search for *the* correct theory or even the *most* correct theory. As mentioned in chapter 1, just as a carpenter would not attempt to build a house with only one tool, a person cannot hope to understand personality with only one theory. It is nonsensical to say that a screwdriver is any more correct or useful than a hammer. It is simply that different tools have different functions; the same is true for personality theories. In other words, which personality theory is "best" depends on which aspect of personality one is attempting to explain. This position is *eclecticism:* taking the best from several different viewpoints. The eclectic is not bound to any single theory but chooses useful information from any theory or theories.

Is it not possible that society forces people to repress sexual and aggressive urges, and that such repressed urges manifest themselves indirectly in a person's life, as Freud and Dollard and Miller maintain? Is it not possible that we are born with predispositions to respond emotionally to the major categories of existence such as birth, death, and members of the opposite sex, and to symbols of perfection, as Jung suggested? Is it not possible that most of us choose a lifestyle with which to strive for perfection or superiority, and for the betterment of society, as Adler suggested? Does not evidence exist that some neurotics attempt to adjust to life by moving toward people, others by moving away from people, and still others by moving against people, as Horney suggested? Does not evidence exist that life consists of various stages each characterized by different needs and potential accomplishments, and that one of the most significant events in one's life is the development of an identity, as Erikson suggested? Does it not make sense to say that each person is unique, and that some adult motives are no longer tied to their earlier origins, as Allport proposed? Is it not possible, as Cattell suggests, that the many variables affecting human behaviour, including constitutional, learning, and situational variables, can be stated in a single equation that can be used in predicting behaviour? Is it not reasonable to assume that personality can be described in terms of a few important dimensions that have a substantial biological basis, as Eysenck insisted? Is there not evidence that reinforcement contingencies exert a powerful influence on behaviour, as Skinner maintained? Is it not possible to think of the various ego-defence mechanisms and neurotic symptoms as learned because they temporarily reduce anxiety, as Dollard and Miller suggest? Is it not also possible, as Bandura and Mischel maintain, that we learn some things simply by observing them, and that modelling experiences are extremely important to personality development? Is it not possible, as the sociobiologists claim, that various dating, mating, and child-rearing practices, the tendency to protect what belongs to us, and differential male-female parenting can be explained, at least in part, by urges within us that have been shaped by natural selection? Is it not possible that the reduction of uncertainty is a major motive in human behaviour, as Kelly suggested? Does not the possibility exist that much of our behaviour is in accordance with our subjective reality rather than with physical reality, as both Kelly and Rogers maintained? Is it not possible to confirm Rogers's contention that because of our need for positive regard and for self-regard many of us internalize conditions of worth that become our frame of reference for living rather than our own organismic valuing process? Is there not evidence for Maslow's contention that the motives of people with their basic needs satisfied are qualitatively different from the motives of people still struggling to satisfy their basic needs? Lastly, is it not possible to find people attempting to live the type of authentic life that May describes and to find others turning their back on such a life by blindly conforming to values established by others?

Perhaps what the realm of personality theory needs is a grand synthesizer, a person who could coordinate the various terms and concepts from all the various theories. This person would look carefully at all the theories that discuss developmental stages—for example, Freud, Erikson, and Allport—and attempt to derive a more comprehensive picture of personality development. If our contention is true that all of the various theories add something different to our knowledge of personality, it would make sense for a person like Newton to come along and somehow put it all together. Because such a synthesis does not seem possible in the foreseeable future, however, one can only make the best use of the existing paradigms or perhaps create new ones.

You Are the Final Judge

As we have seen, each theory of personality has generated at least some empirical research that supports it. It is also true that at least some empirical research refutes each theory of personality. Because the results of the empirical research are equivocal, they cannot be used as a basis for accepting or rejecting a theory. This situation may change as more studies are performed, and they collectively suggest acceptance or rejection of a theory or of parts of a theory. As it is now, however, relatively little unambiguous empirical research is available to help decide what is valid or invalid in the realm of personality theory. How, then, does one know what information to accept or reject? It seems that under existing circumstances, Buddha gave the best answer to this question:

> Believe nothing on the faith of traditions, even though they have been held in honour for many generations, and in divers places. Do not believe a thing because many speak of it. Do not believe on the faith of the sages of the past. Do not believe what you have imagined, persuading yourself that a god inspires you. Believe nothing on the sole authority of your masters or priests. After examination, believe what you yourself have tested and found to be reasonable, and conform your conduct thereto. (Hawton, 1948, p. 200)

SUMMARY

1. Four conclusions seem justified after our review of the major personality theories: (1) Most, if not all, of the theories of personality reflect the biographies of their authors. (2) Although the major theories of personality illuminate many aspects of personality, much about personality remains unknown. (3) The best available explanation of personality comes from using the best of all the theories rather than attempting to use one or a few of them. (4) Until more unambiguous empirical research is available, the best one can do is to evaluate the various theories personally, and to accept concepts that make sense and reject those that do not. This guideline means that which theories are found valid and useful will vary from person to person.

EXPERIENTIAL EXERCISES

1. Suppose you are the grand synthesizer mentioned in this chapter; describe how you might go about your task of synthesizing the various personality theories.

2. Review the theory of personality that you formulated as part of the experiential exercises for chapter 1. Reformulate your original theory using what you have since learned about personality. Summarize the major differences between your first and second formulations.

Glossary

Ability trait. Trait that determines how effectively a person works toward a desired goal. Intelligence is such a trait.

Accusation. Form of neurotic aggression that involves blaming other people for one's shortcomings and seeking revenge against those people.

Acquired drive. Drive that is learned, not innate. Fear is an example of an acquired drive.

Acquisition. That part of operant conditioning in which an operant response is followed by a reinforcer, thereby increasing the rate with which the response occurs.

Actualizing tendency. Innate tendency in all humans to maintain and enhance themselves.

Adaptation. Any anatomical structure, physiological process, or behaviour pattern that enhances an organism's chances of surviving and reproducing; the process of successfully adjusting to the environment.

Aesthetic needs. Innate need for such qualities as symmetry, closure, and order, observed most clearly in children and in self-actualizing adults.

Affiliation. Ritualization characterizing Erikson's sixth stage of development. This involves sharing one's identity with fellow humans in a caring, productive way, for example, by entering into an intimate relationship with someone who has also gained an identity.

Agapé. Unselfish giving of one's self in a loving relationship. One loves but expects nothing in return.

Aggression (Kelly). Effort to expand one's construct system so it is capable of assimilating a greater range of experiences.

Alienation. Separation from nature, other people, or oneself that results in feelings of loneliness, emptiness, or despair.

Altruism. Making a sacrifice to help someone else without expecting anything in return. (See also Kin altruism and Reciprocal altruism.)

Altruistic surrender. An ego-defence mechanism postulated by Anna Freud by which a person internalizes the values of another person and lives his or her life in accordance with those values.

Anal stage (Freud). Second psychosexual stage, which occurs during about the second year of life, during which time the anal area is the primary erogenous zone.

Anal-expulsive character (Freud). Character type that results from a fixation at the early anal stage. Such a person may have trouble with bowel control and may be overly generous.

Anal-retentive character (Freud). Character type that results from a fixation at the late anal stage. Such a person may suffer from constipation and may be stingy.

Anima. Female component of the male psyche.

Animus. Male component of the female psyche.

Anticathexis. Expenditure of energy to prevent a cathexis that would cause anxiety.

Anxiety. The general feeling of impending danger. (See also Moral anxiety, Neurotic anxiety, and Reality anxiety.

Anxiety (Kelly). Feeling caused by realizing that an experience lies outside one's construct system.

Anxiety (May). The experience we have when our existence as an individual is threatened; an unavoidable component of a normal, healthy life. (See also Normal anxiety and Neurotic anxiety.)

Anxiety (Rogers). Feeling that arises when a person perceives or subceives an experience as being incompatible with his or her self-structure and its introjected conditions of worth.

Approach-approach conflict. Situation that exists when a person must choose between two equally attractive goals.

Approach-avoidance conflict. Situation that exists when a person is both attracted to and repelled by the same goal.

Arbitrary rightness. Exemplified when issues arise that have no clear solution one way or the other, and a person arbitrarily chooses one solution, thereby ending debate.

Archetype. Inherited predisposition to respond emotionally to certain aspects of the world. All the archetypes taken together make up the collective unconscious.

Arousal theory. A general class of theories that assume behaviour is partly a function of the general state of arousal (excitation) or de-arousal (inhibition) of the cortex and/or other brain structures.

Ascending reticular activating system (ARAS). A network of neurons in the reticular formation of the brain stem that is responsible for cortical arousal and de-arousal.

Ashram. Retreat in India where ordinary citizens can go for various periods of time and search themselves and the meaning of their lives.

Attentional processes. Processes that determine what is attended to and therefore what is learned through observation.

Attitude (Allport). Attitudes, like habits, are more specific than traits. One can, for example, have a favourable attitude toward boxing but this may be only a single manifestation of the more general trait of aggressiveness.

Attitude (Cattell & Eysenck). A learned tendency to respond in a particular way in a particular situation to a particular object or event. Attitudes derive from sentiments, which in turn derive from ergs. An attitude is one type of metaerg.

Attitude (Jung). General orientation of the psyche when relating to the world. The two basic attitudes are introversion and extroversion.

Authenticity (Erikson). Ritualization characterizing the third stage of development. This involves playful role playing to discover possible ways of living one's adult life.

Authenticity (May). The quality of living one's life in accordance with values that are freely chosen.

Authoritism. Ritualism that can occur during Erikson's seventh stage of development. This involves using power for selfish gains instead of helping others.

Avoidance contingency. Situation in which the organism can avoid an aversive stimulus by engaging in appropriate activity.

Avoidance-avoidance conflict. Situation that exists when a person must choose between two equally aversive goals.

Avoiding type person. Person exhibiting the mistaken lifestyle of avoiding the attempt to solve life's problems thereby escaping possible defeat. Such a person lacks adequate social interest.

Awareness. Characterizes the events in one's experience that have been symbolized and therefore have entered consciousness.

B-cognition. See Being cognition.

B-love. Deep, nonpossessive, insatiable, emotional relationship that is not aimed at satisfying any particular need. Such love contrasts with D-love.

B-perception. See Being cognition.

Basic anxiety (Horney). Psychological state that exists when basic hostility is repressed. It is the general feeling that everything and everyone in the world is potentially dangerous.

Basic evil. Anything that parents do that undermines a child's security.

Basic hostility. Feeling generated in a child if needs for safety and satisfaction are not consistently and lovingly satisfied by the parents.

Basic mistrust. Lack of trust of the world and the people in it that arises if the crisis dominating Erikson's first stage of development is resolved negatively.

Basic trust. General feeling of trust of the world and the people in it which arises if the crisis dominating Erikson's first stage of development is resolved positively.

Becoming. May's contention that through their active involvement with their life's circumstances, authentic people are constantly changing.

Behaviour therapy. Approach to treating behaviour disorders that is based on any one of several learning theories.

Behaviour-outcome expectancy. Belief that acting a certain way in a certain situation will have a certain consequence.

Behavioural potentiality. Ability to respond with any one of a range of behaviours to a category of environmental experience.

Behaviourism. School of psychology, founded by J. B. Watson, whose members believe that the only scientifically valid subject matter for psychology is measurable behaviour.

Being cognition (also called *B-perception* or *B-cognition*). Thinking or perceiving that is governed by B-values rather than by D-motives. Such cognition is richer and fuller than D-cognition.

Being motivation (also called *growth motivation*). Motivation governed by the pursuit of B-values instead of by the satisfaction of basic deficiencies. (See also Being values.)

Being values (B-values) (also called *metamotives*). Those higher aspects of life pursued by self-actualizing individuals. Included are such values as truth, goodness, beauty, justice, and perfection.

Belongingness and love needs. Third cluster of needs in Maslow's hierarchy of needs. Included are the needs for affiliation with others and for the feeling of being loved.

Beyondism. Cattell's proposal that scientific facts, rather than religious illusions or philosophical speculation, be used to create moral systems.

Biofeedback. The use of some mechanical device, such as an auditory signal or flashing light, to provide individuals with information about the functioning of one or more of their internal biological processes.

Biogrammar. Genetic program believed by sociobiologists to be responsible for culturally universal human behaviour. Our biogrammar structures our social behaviour just as grammar structures our verbal behaviour.

Biological determinism. In the strong sense, the inherited predisposition to respond in a specific way to specific categories of environmental experience. In the weak sense, the predisposition to respond in any one of several ways to categories of environmental experience. Weaker biological determinism assumes that behavioural potentiality is inherited. It is the weaker form of biological determinism that is accepted by sociobiology.

Blind spots. Denying or ignoring certain aspects of experience because they are not in accordance with one's idealized self-image.

Bodily "me." In Allport's theory, attribute that emerges during the first stage in the development of the proprium. At this stage, infants learn that their bodies exist because of their sensory experience.

Cardinal dispositions. "Ruling passion" that influences almost everything a person does. Only a few individuals possess a cardinal disposition.

Castration anxiety. Boy's fear that he is going to lose his sex organs because they are regarded as the source of conflict between the boy and his father.

Catharsis. Emotional relief that results when a person is able to ponder pathogenic ideas consciously.

Cathexis. Investment of psychic energy in the image of an object that will satisfy a need.

Causality. Belief that a person's personality can be explained in terms of past experiences.

Central dispositions. Those qualities about a person that you would mention in a letter of recommendation. The five to ten characteristics that summarize a particular person's personality.

Chaining. Situation in which one response brings the organism into contact with stimuli that (1) reinforce that response and (2) stimulate the next response. Chaining can also involve other people; for example, one person's response can both reinforce another person's response and determine the next course of action.

Character. Description of a person that includes a value judgment. A person's character can be "good" or "bad" whereas a personality cannot be.

Cheating. Accepting help from someone without the intention of reciprocating. The cheater either takes and does not give, or takes more than he or she gives.

Choice corollary. Statement that people will choose a construct that will either further define or extend their construct system. (See also Definition of a construct system and Extension of a construct system.)

Circumspection phase. That phase of Kelly's CPC cycle in which a person ponders several constructs which might be useful in construing a novel situation.

Classical conditioning. Type of conditioning studied by Ivan Pavlov and used by J. B. Watson as a model for his version of behaviourism.

Classical conditioning (Cattell). Type of learning in which a stimulus that did not originally elicit a response is made to do so. Cattell believed many emotional responses to persons, objects, or events are learned through classical conditioning.

Client-centred therapy. Description of Rogers's second approach to therapy in which the therapist makes an active effort to understand the client's subjective reality.

Cluster analysis. Systematic search of a correlation matrix in order to discover factors.

Cognitive social person variables. Those variables thought by Mischel to determine how a person selects, perceives, interprets, and uses the stimuli confronting him or her. (See also Encoding strategies; Expectancies; Subjective values; Self regulatory systems and plans; and Competencies.)

Cognitive theory. Any theory that focuses on the study of mental events.

Cognitively complex person. Person with many well-differentiated constructs in his or her construct system.

Cognitively simple person. Person with only a few poorly differentiated constructs in his or her construct system.

Collective unconscious (Jung). Collection of inherited predispositions that humans have to respond to certain events. These predispositions come from the universal experiences humans have had throughout their evolutionary past.

Common traits. Traits used to describe a group of individuals.

Commonality corollary. The statement that people can be considered similar not because of similar physical experiences but because they construe their experiences in a similar fashion.

Compartmentalization. Dividing one's life into various components with different rules applying to the different components.

Compensation. Making up for a weakness, such as organ inferiority, by emphasizing functions that substitute for the weakness.

Competencies. Cognitive social person variables that describe what a person knows and is capable of doing.

Complex. Set of interrelated ideas that are highly valued and that exist in the personal unconscious.

Compliant type person. Person who uses moving toward people as the major means of reducing basic anxiety.

Condensation. Form of dream distortion in which one dream element represents several ideas at the same time.

Conditioned fear reaction. Learning to fear something that was not previously feared.

Conditioned response (CR). Response similar to an unconditioned response that is elicited by a previously neutral stimulus (CS).

Conditioned stimulus (CS). Stimulus that, before classical conditioning principles are applied, is biologically neutral; that is, it does not elicit a natural reaction from an organism.

Conditions of worth. Conditions under which an incongruent person will experience positive regard.

Conflict. Situation in which two or more incompatible response tendencies exist simultaneously.

Conscience (Freud). That part of the superego that results from the internalized experiences for which a child had been punished. This component of the personality is responsible for the experience of guilt. (See also Ego ideal.)

Consistency paradox. According to Mischel, the persistent belief that human behaviour is more consistent than is indicated by experimental evidence.

Constitutional trait. Genetically determined trait.

Construct. See Personal construct.

Construct system. Collection of constructs used by a person at any given time to construe the events in his or her life.

Construction corollary. Statement that constructs are formed on the basis of the recurring themes in one's experience.

Constructive alternativism. Term that reflects Kelly's belief that there are numerous ways of construing one's experience and therefore one is free to choose from a number of construct systems.

Construe. One's active effort to interpret, explain, and give meaning to experiences.

Contingency contracting. Agreement between two people that when one acts in an appropriate way, the other one gives him or her something of value.

Contingency management. Purposive manipulation of reinforcement contingencies so they encourage desirable behaviours.

Contingent reinforcement. Situation in which a certain response must be made before a reinforcer is obtained; that is, no response, no reinforcer.

Continuous reinforcement schedule (also called a 100% schedule of reinforcement). Schedule of reinforcement that reinforces a desired response each time it occurs.

Control phase. That phase of Kelly's CPC cycle in which people choose a pole of the construct chosen in the preemptive phase of the cycle and act in accordance with that pole.

Core role structure. Roles we play while interacting with the important people and groups in our lives.

Core structures. Those constructs on which we rely most heavily when construing experience—that is, those that have been most consistently validated.

Correlation. Condition that exists when the values of two variables vary together in some systematic way.

Correlation coefficient. Mathematical expression indicating the extent to which two variables are correlated. Correlation coefficients can vary from +1.00, indicating a perfect positive correlation, to -1.00, indicating a perfect negative correlation.

Correlation matrix. Display of the many correlation coefficients that result when many sources of information are intercorrelated.

Cost-benefit analysis. Analysis of the risks and benefits involved in a certain behaviour. Such an analysis increases the probability that an organism will engage in fitness-enhancing behaviour.

Countertransference. Phenomenon that sometimes occurs during therapy in which the therapist becomes emotionally involved with a patient.

CPC cycle. In Kelly's theory, series of activities engaged in by a person confronted with a novel situation. (See also Circumspection phase, Control phase, and Preemption phase.)

Creative illness. According to Ellenberger, a period of intense preoccupation with a search for a particular truth. This search is usually accompanied by depression, psychosomatic ailments, neuroses, and perhaps psychotic episodes.

Creative self. Free element of the personality that allows the person to choose between alternative fictional goals and lifestyles. It is the differential exercise of this creative power that is mainly responsible for individual differences.

Credulous attitude. Assumption that the information provided by clients about themselves can be trusted as accurate and valid.

Crisis. In Erikson's theory, conflict that becomes dominant during a particular stage of development that can be resolved positively thus strengthening the ego, or resolved negatively thus weakening the ego. Each crisis, therefore, is a turning point in one's development.

Crystallized intelligence. Type of intelligence that comes from formal education or from general experience and is the type of intelligence that most intelligence tests attempt to measure.

Cue. Stimulus that indicates the appropriate direction an activity should take.

Cue-producing responses. Images, perceptions, and words, the main functions of which are to determine subsequent behaviour. Thinking is an example of a cue-producing response.

Cultural engineering. Use of contingency management in designing a culture.

Cultural extension. (see hypertrophy)

Cultural universals. Categories of human social behaviour that are found in all human cultures.

Culture. For Erikson, a version of human existence.

Culture Free Intelligence Test. Test designed to measure fluid intelligence rather than crystallized intelligence.

D-cognition. See Need-directed perception.

D-love. Love motivated by the need for love and belongingness. Such love is selfish because it satisfies a personal deficiency. Such love contrasts with B-love.

D-motive. See Deficiency motivation.

D-perception. See Need-directed perception.

Daimonic. Potential for evil or harm that is part of human nature. The daimonic occurs when any natural function that in moderation is positive, dominates the individual—for example, when assertiveness becomes aggression or hostility or when eros causes one to dominate one's lover and thereby destroy his or her individuality.

Dasein. Study of the individual as a being in the world. The emphasis is on an individual's existence at a certain time under certain circumstances.

Defence. Effort to change a threatening experience through distortion or denial.

Deficiency motivation (D-motivation). Motivation governed by the basic needs. Characterizes the lives of individuals who are not self-actualizing.

Definition of a construct system. Choice of a construct in construing a situation that has already been successful in construing similar situations. Such a choice has the effect of further validating one's construct system.

Delay of gratification. Postponement of a small, immediate reinforcer in order to obtain a larger, more distant reinforcer.

Delayed modelling. Refers to the fact that there is often a long delay between when something is learned observationally and when that learning is translated into behaviour.

Denial (Rogers). Refusal to allow threatening experiences to enter awareness.

Denial of reality (Freud). Refusing to accept a potentially anxiety-provoking aspect of reality despite abundant information testifying to its existence.

Depreciation. Neurotic safeguarding strategy whereby one's accomplishments are overvalued and the accomplishments of others are undervalued. Depreciation can take the form of *idealization*—judging people by impossibly high standards,—or of *solicitude*,—acting as if other people could not get along without one.

Desacralization. Any process that distorts human nature and depicts it as less marvellous and dignified than it is.

Destiny. According to May, the givens in one's life that are creatively interpreted, and are thus provided meaning. For example, it is a given that all humans will die, but whether this fact is a source of vitality or despair is a personal choice. (See also Thrownness.)

Detached type person. Person who uses moving away from people as the major means of reducing basic anxiety.

Determinism. Belief that all behaviour is caused and is therefore not free. Some theorists (e.g., Cattell) believe that if all variables affecting behaviour were known, behaviour could be predicted with complete accuracy.

Dichotomy corollary. The statement that each construct has two poles, one of which describes what characteristics the events to which the construct is relevant have in common, the other of which describes events without those characteristics. For example, if one pole of a construct describes beautiful things, the other pole may describe things without beauty, or ugly things.

Differential reinforcement. Situation in which some responses are reinforced and others are not.

Discrimination. Opposite of generalization. That is, stimuli similar to the stimulus in the learning process do *not* elicit a learned response.

Discriminative operant. Operant response that is made under one set of circumstances but not under others.

Discriminative stimulus (S^D). Cue indicating that if a certain response is made it will be followed by reinforcement.

Displaced aggression. Aggressing toward a substitute person or object when the actual object of aggression is either not available or is feared.

Displacement. Act of substituting one goal for another when the primary goal is not available or is feared.

Displacement (Freud). Substituting a cathexis that is not anxiety-provoking for one that is. Also a form of dream distortion in which an acceptable image is substituted for an unacceptable one—for example, when one dreams of mountains instead of breasts.

Distancing. Safeguarding strategy used by neurotics that involves creating barriers between themselves and their problems in life.

Distortion. Modification of a threatening experience so it is no longer threatening.

Dominant response. That response in a habit family hierarchy which has the greatest probability of occurrence.

Double approach-avoidance conflict. Situation that exists when a person has both positive and negative feelings about two goals.

Double standard. Fact that male and female sexual behaviour is evaluated differently. For example, male promiscuity is generally tolerated and female promiscuity is not.

Dream analysis (Adler). Studying dreams to learn about the lifestyles of the dreamer, in the belief that the primary purpose of dreams is to create emotions that can be used by dreamers to support their mistaken lifestyles.

Dream work. Various mechanisms that distort a dream's latent content.

Drive (Dollard & Miller). Any strong stimulus that impels an organism to action and whose elimination or reduction is reinforcing.

Drive reduction. Lessening of a drive; constitutes reinforcement in Hull's theory of learning.

Drive-discharge model of aggression. Freudian view that the need to act aggressively increases if it is not periodically satisfied. According to this view, the need to act aggressively must be satisfied just as the hunger and thirst drives must.

Dynamic lattice. Diagram showing the relationships among ergs, sentiments, and attitudes.

Dynamic trait. Motivational trait that sets a person in motion toward a goal. Cattell postulated the existence of two types of dynamic traits: ergs and metaergs.

Dysfunctional expectancies. Expectancies that do not result in effective interactions with the environment.

Dysthymic. In Eysenck's theory, a diagnosis given to severely disordered introverted neurotics whose symptoms include anxiety, sensitivity, fatigue, and exhaustion.

Echoic behaviour. Accurate repeating of what someone else had said.

Ego (Freud). Executive of the personality whose job it is to satisfy the needs of both the id and the superego by engaging in appropriate environmental activities. The ego is governed by the reality principle.

Ego (Jung). For Jung, the ego is everything of which we are conscious and entails performing the functions related to everyday life.

Ego ideal (Freud). That portion of the superego that results from the internalized experiences for which a child has been rewarded.

Ego integrity (Erikson). The satisfaction with life and the lack of fear of death that characterize the person who has positively resolved the crisis that dominates the eighth and final stage of development.

Ego psychology. Theoretical system that stresses the importance of the ego as an autonomous part of the personality instead of viewing the ego as merely the servant of the id.

Ego-defence mechanisms. Unconscious processes that falsify or distort reality to reduce or prevent anxiety.

Eigenwelt. The intrapersonal world. An individual's self-awareness.

Elitism. Ritualism that can occur during Erikson's sixth stage of development. This involves the superficial relationships with groups of like-minded individuals that people without identities seek.

Elusiveness. Opposite to arbitrary rightness. The elusive person is highly indecisive. Without commitments to anything this person is seldom wrong.

Emotional security and self-acceptance. Two of the characteristics of a healthy, mature adult.

Empirical theory of human nature. Contention that the human mind is blank at birth and becomes furnished by experience.

Empiricism. Contention that an attribute is determined by experience rather than by genetics. Within epistemology, it is the belief that all knowledge is derived from sensory experience.

Encoding strategies. Cognitive social person variables that determines which aspects of the environment are selected for attention and how those aspects are interpreted by the individual.

Encounter. The meeting of two selves; seeing things as the other sees them and vice versa; an honest sharing of one's self with another person. For May, an encounter is a necessary component of successful psychotherapy.

Environmental-mould trait.   Trait that is determined by experience rather than by heredity.

Environmentalism.   Belief that the determinants of behaviour are found in the environment rather than in the person.

Epigenetic principle.   According to Erikson, the innate biological principle that determines the sequence in which the eight stages of psychosocial development occurs.

Epigenetic rules.   Innate rules that mediate between experience and the processes of the mind. Primary epigenetic rules determine which aspects of the physical environment can be sensed or perceived. Secondary epigenetic rules determine how information provided by the primary epigenetic rules is evaluated, responded to emotionally, learned and remembered, and how decisions are made with regard to that information.

Epiphenomenalism.   Contention that mental events are the by-products of bodily events. Mental events, therefore, can be ignored in the analysis of human behaviour.

Epistemology.   Study of the nature of human knowledge.

Erg.   Constitutional dynamic source trait that provides the energy for all behaviour. Much the same as what other theorists call a primary drive. Hunger and thirst are examples of ergs.

Ergic tension.   Tension that varies as the intensity of an erg varies.

Erogenous zone.   Area of the body that is a source of pleasure.

Eros (Freud).   All the life instincts taken collectively.

Eros (May).   Desire to form a union with or to feel at one with one's partner in love.

Escape contingency.   Situation in which an organism must respond in a certain way to escape from an aversive stimulus. All negative reinforcement involves an escape contingency.

Esteem needs.   Fourth cluster of needs in Maslow's hierarchy of needs. Included are the needs for status, prestige, competence, and confidence.

Eupsychia.   Maslow's name for the utopia that he believed a community of healthy adults could create.

Eupsychian management.   Industrial or societal management that attempts to consider the basic human needs as Maslow viewed them.

Existential theory.   Any theory that focuses on the nature of, or the problems related to, human existence.

Existentialism.   Philosophy that studies the essence of human nature. The emphasis is on freedom, individuality, and phenomenological experience.

Expectancies.   Cognitive social person variables that determine how individuals anticipate events in their lives. (See also Behaviour-outcome expectancy, Self-efficacy expectancy, and Stimulus-outcome expectancy).

Experience (Rogers).   All the events of which a person *could* be aware at any given moment.

Experience corollary.   The statement that mere passive experience is unimportant. It is the active construing of experience that ultimately results in a more effective construct system.

Experiential stage.   Third stage in the evolution of Rogers's approach to therapy in which the feelings of the therapist become as important as the feelings of the client.

Extension of a construct system.   Choice of a new construct in construing a situation. Such a choice can extend one's construct system to assimilate a greater range of experience.

Externalization.   Belief that the causes of one's major experiences are external to oneself.

Extinction.   Weakening of an operant response by removing the reinforcer that had been following the response during acquisition. When a response returns to its operant level, it has been extinguished.

Extrinsic reinforcement.   Reinforcement that results from sources outside of the person.

Extrinsic religion.   Superficial religion that is participated in for selfish, pragmatic reasons. Allport considered such religion to be unhealthy.

Extroversion.   Tendency to be externally oriented, confident, outgoing, and gregarious.

Extroversion (Eysenck).   The superfactor or type that includes the traits of sociability, activity, assertiveness, and sensation-seeking, to name a few.

Facilitator of education.   Rogers's preferred term (rather than teacher) for an educator who provides the freedom necessary for learning to take place.

Factor.   Ability or characteristic that is thought to be responsible for consistent behaviour. In Cattell's system, a factor is also called a trait.

Factor analysis.   Complex statistical technique based on the concept of correlation, which Cattell and Eysenck used to discover and investigate personality traits.

Fear (Kelly).   Feeling one has when a relatively unimportant construct is about to be invalidated thus requiring a minor change in one's construct system.

Feeling.   Function of thought that determines whether an object or event is valued positively or negatively.

Feelings of inferiority.   Feelings of being inferior, whether or not these feelings are justified by real circumstances. Such feelings, according to Adler, can lead either to positive accomplishments or to an inferiority complex.

Fertility.   For a female, the current ability to become pregnant. For a male, the current ability to impregnate a female.

Fictional finalism (Adler).   (Also called a guiding self-ideal and guiding fiction.) Fictional future goal to which a person aspires.

First signal system.   According to Pavlov, physical stimuli that precede biologically significant events, allowing their anticipation and thus appropriate responses to them.

Fitness.   Ability to survive and reproduce. (See also Inclusive fitness.)

Fixation (Freud).   Arrested development at one of the psychosexual stages because of the undergratification or overgratification of a need. Fixation determines the point to which an adult regresses under stress.

Fixed interval reinforcement schedule (FI). Reinforcement schedule that reinforces a response that is made only after a specified interval of time has passed.

Fixed ratio reinforcement schedule (FR). Reinforcement schedule that reinforces every nth response. For example, every fifth response the organism makes is reinforced (FR5).

Fixed-role therapy. Clinical technique used by Kelly that asks clients to act as if they were other people. The idea is to have the clients try different ways of construing their experiences in a nonthreatening situation as the therapist provides validating information about their new construct systems.

Fluid intelligence. General problem-solving ability that is largely innate.

Focus of convenience. Events within the range of convenience of a construct to which that construct is maximally significant.

Formalism. Ritualism that can occur during Erikson's fourth stage. This involves a preoccupation with how things work, or with one's work, and a disregard for the reason why things function as they do or why various types of jobs exist.

Formality. Ritualization corresponding to Erikson's fourth stage of development. This involves learning how various things work in one's culture.

Fourth force psychology. See Transpersonal psychology.

Fragmentation corollary. Statement that as a construct system is being tested, revised, or extended, certain inconsistencies in behaviour may result.

Free association. Called by Freud the fundamental rule of psychoanalysis, it entails instructing the patient to say whatever comes to his or her mind no matter how irrelevant, threatening, or nonsensical it may seem.

Freedom (May). According to May, not the absence of negative conditions, but the potential to set future-oriented goals and then to act in accordance with them.

Freedom (social cognitive theory). The number of options available to people and their right to exercise them.

Freudian slip. Verbal "accident" that is thought to reveal the speaker's true feelings.

Frustration-aggression hypothesis. Originally the contention that frustration always leads to aggression and aggression results only from frustration. Later modified to state that aggression is only one of several possible reactions to frustration.

Fully functioning person (Rogers). Person whose locus of evaluation is his or her own organismic valuing process rather than internalized conditions of worth.

Functional analysis. Skinner's approach to research, which attempted to relate measurable environmental events to measurable behaviour and bypass cognitive and physiological processes altogether.

Functional autonomy. An acquired system of motivation in which a motive that once existed as a means to an end becomes an end in itself. Allport's most famous and controversial concept.

Functionalism. America's first school of psychology. The major goal of the functionalist was to relate various behaviour and psychological processes to survival.

Functions of thought (Jung). The ways in which a person perceives the world and deals with information and experience. The four functions of thought are sensing, thinking, feeling, and intuiting.

Fundamental fact of life. In Adler's theory, people's aspirations to become superior or perfect. Adler's final position was that healthy persons aspire toward social rather than individual perfection.

Generalized reinforcers. Class of secondary reinforcers that have been paired with more than one primary reinforcer.

Generationalism. Ritualization that characterizes Erikson's seventh stage of development. This involves the many ways in which healthy individuals help younger people to have experiences conducive to healthy personality growth.

Generativity. Impulse to help members of the next generation that arises when the crisis dominating Erikson's seventh stage of development is resolved positively.

Genital stage. In Freud's theory, final psychosexual stage and the one that follows puberty. It is a time when the full adult personality emerges and when the experiences that occurred during the pregenital stages manifest themselves.

Getting-leaning type person. Person exhibiting the mistaken lifestyle that expects everything to be given to him or her by others. Such a person lacks adequate social interest.

Gradient of reinforcement. The observation that if a series of responses leads to reinforcement, the last response in the series will be strengthened the most, then the second to the last, etc.

Growth centre. Western equivalent of the Indian ashram. A place where healthy individuals can expand their potentialities.

Growth motivation. See Being motivation.

Guilt (Kelly). Feeling one has when one acts contrary to a role one has assumed while interacting with a significant person or group in one's life.

Guilt (May). Feeling we have when we realize we are not living up to our full potential. (See also Normal guilt and Neurotic guilt.)

Guru. Spiritual leader of an ashram.

Habit (Allport). Specific mode of responding—for example, putting on clean clothing in the morning—that develops because a more general trait exists, for example, the trait of cleanliness.

Habit (Dollard & Miller). Association between a stimulus and a response.

Habit family hierarchy. Group of responses elicited by a single stimulus that are arranged in accordance with their probability of occurrence.

Hedonism. Contention that the major motive in life is to seek pleasure and avoid pain.

Heritability. The proportion of variability in the phenotype (expression of a trait) that is accounted for by the genotype (the genes themselves).

Heuristic function of a theory. A theory's ability to generate new information.

Hierarchy of human needs. Maslow's arrangement of the needs from lowest to highest in terms of their potency.

Holistic-analytic approach to science. Strategy of studying an object of interest as a totality rather than attempting to reduce it to its component parts.

Hostile type person. Person who uses moving against people as the major means of reducing basic anxiety.

Hostility (Kelly). Attempt to force the validation of a prediction that has already proved to be erroneous.

Hull's theory of learning. Theory of learning that equates reinforcement with drive reduction. In other words, for learning to take place, the organism must engage in an activity that leads to the elimination or reduction of a need.

Human dilemma. Capacity of humans to see themselves both as objects to which things happen and as subjects who act on their experiences and thereby give them meaning.

Human nature. Those qualities that characterize all humans. One task of the personality theorist is to specify the nature of human nature.

Humanistic psychology (also called third force psychology). Approach to psychology that emphasizes the experiencing person, creativity, the study of socially and personally significant problems, and the dignity and enhancement of people.

Humanistic theory. Any theory that assumes that humans are basically good and rational and their behaviour is purposive.

Hypergamy. Tendency for females to benefit themselves through their selection of a mate.

Hypertrophy (also called cultural hyperextension). Cultural exaggeration of innate human predispositions.

Hypothetico-deductive reasoning (or hypothetico-deductive research). A method (exemplified in Eysenck's research) that begins with a hypothesis that guides data collection.

Hysteria. General term describing disorders such as paralysis of the arms or legs, loss of sensation, disturbances of sight and speech, nausea, and general confusion. Because hysteria has no known organic cause, its root is assumed to be psychological. Until Charcot, hysteria was generally assumed to be exclusively a female disease. *Hystera* is the Greek word for uterus.

Hysteric. In Eysenck's theory, a diagnosis given to severely disordered neurotic extroverts whose symptoms may include hysterical conversion(s) such as non-neurological paralysis or blindness.

Id. In Freud's theory, the component of the personality that is completely unconscious and contains all the instincts. It is the animalistic portion of the personality that is governed by the pleasure principle.

Ideal self (Rogers). Client's description of how he or she would like to be.

Ideal-sort (Rogers). Statements chosen by a client as best describing the person he or she would most like to be. Part of the Q-sort technique.

Idealized self (Horney). Fictitious view of oneself, with its list of "shoulds" that displaces the real self in the neurotic personality.

Identification. A term used in two ways by Freud: (1) the matching of an idinal image with its physical counterpart, and (2) the incorporation of another person's values or characteristics either to enhance one's self-esteem or to minimize that person as a threat.

Identity (also called ego identity). Sense of knowing who you are and where you are going in life that develops when Erikson's fifth stage of development is resolved positively. Probably Erikson's most famous concept.

Identity crisis. Crisis that dominates Erikson's fifth stage of development, which results either in the person gaining an identity (positive resolution) or in role confusion (negative resolution).

Ideology. Ritualization characterizing the fifth stage of development. This involves embracing a philosophy of life that makes one's past, present, and future meaningful.

Idiographic method. Research method that studies a single case in great detail and depth.

Idiographic research. Intense study of a single person.

Idolism. Ritualism that can occur during Erikson's first stage of development where instead of learning a warm, positive feeling toward others, the child tends to worship them.

Impersonation. Ritualism that can occur during Erikson's third stage of development. This involves confusing playing a role with one's true personality.

Inclusive fitness. Person's success in perpetuating copies of his or her genes into subsequent generations either by producing offspring himself or herself, by helping relatives survive and reproduce, or both.

Incongruency. In Rogers's theory, the condition of a person who no longer uses the organismic valuing process as a means of evaluating experiences.

Individual psychology. Adler's term to describe his theory. The term individual was used to stress his belief that each person is an integrated whole striving to attain future goals and attempting to find meaning in life while working harmoniously with others.

Individual traits. Either the unique patterns of traits possessed by an individual or the unique way that a particular trait manifests itself in the personality of a particular person—for example, a particular person's way of displaying aggressiveness. Later in the development of his theory, Allport changed the term *individual trait* to personal disposition.

Individuality corollary. Statement that each person is unique in his or her manner of construing experience.

Individuation (Jung). Process whereby a person comes to recognize the various components of his or her psyche and gives them expression within the context of his or her life. A process that is prerequisite to approximating self-realization.

Inductive reasoning (or inductive research). A method (exemplified in Cattell's research) that begins with collection of data that then leads to hypotheses.

Industry. Sense of enjoyment from work and from sustained attention which arises if the crisis dominating Erikson's fourth stage of development is resolved positively.

Inferiority. Loss of confidence in one's ability to become a contributing member of one's society which arises if the crisis dominating Erikson's fourth stage of development is resolved negatively.

Inferiority complex (Adler). Psychological condition that exists when a person is overwhelmed by feelings of inferiority to the point at which nothing can be accomplished.

Inflation of the persona (Jung). Condition that exists when one's persona is too highly valued.

Initial hierarchy of responses. Hierarchy of responses elicited by a cue before new learning occurs.

Innate hierarchy of responses. Habit family hierarchy that is genetically determined.

Instinct. The cognitive reflection of a biological deficiency; for Freud, the stuff from which personality is shaped.

Instinctoid. Term Maslow used to describe needs that are innate but weak and easily modified by environmental conditions.

Instrumental conditioning. Learning to make a response that will either make a reward available or remove an aversive stimulus.

Integralism. Ritualization characterizing Erikson's eighth stage of development. This involves the wisdom to place one's own life in a larger perspective, that is, to see one's finite life as contributing to immortal culture.

Intellectualization (also called isolation of affect). The minimization of the negative emotions associated with an event by a detached, logical analysis of the event.

Intentionality (May). The fact that mental events are directed toward objects outside of themselves. For example, perception always involves the perception of something. It is through intentionality that a relationship between objective and subjective reality is formed.

Interactionism. Contention that the mind influences the body and the body influences the mind. That is, the mind and the body are causally related.

Interactionist. Any theorist who contends it is the interaction of person variables and situation variables that determines behaviour at any given moment.

Internal frame of reference. Subjective reality, or phenomenological field, according to which a person lives his or her life.

Intrinsic reinforcement. Self-reinforcement.

Intrinsic religion. Religion that seeks a higher meaning and purpose in life and provides possible answers to the many mysteries that characterize human existence. Allport considered such religion to be healthy.

Introjected values. In Rogers's theory, conditions of worth that are internalized and become the basis for one's self-regard.

Introspection. Self-examination. Directing one's thoughts inward to discover the truth about one's self.

Introversion. Tendency to be internally oriented, quiet, subjective, and nonsocial.

Intuiting. Function of thought that makes hunches about objects or events when factual information is not available.

Irrational functions. Jung referred to sensing and intuiting as irrational functions because they do not involve logical thought processes.

Jackass theory of motivation. Kelly's description of his own theory because it claimed that motivation is inherent to human nature. Therefore, there is no need to postulate events that push or pull humans into action.

Jonah complex. In Maslow's theory, the fear of one's own potential greatness and the ambivalent feelings toward greatness in others.

Judiciousness. Ritualization characterizing Erikson's second stage of development. This involves the many ways that children learn right from wrong.

Kin altruism. Offering help to genetically related individuals. According to the sociobiologists, the closer the genetic relatedness, the stronger is the tendency to offer preferential treatment.

Kin selection. Increase in one's inclusive fitness that results from the preferential treatment of one's relatives.

L-data. Cattell's term for information about a person's everyday life. The *L* stands for life record.

Latency stage. In Freud's theory, psychosexual stage that lasts from about the sixth year to about the twelfth year of life. It is a time when sexual activity is repressed and an abundance of substitute activities are engaged in such as learning and athletics.

Latent content of a dream (Freud). Dream's true meaning that is disguised or distorted by dream work.

Learning (Dollard and Miller). The rearrangement of response probabilities that results when certain responses are reinforced and others are not.

Learning (Kelly). Any change in one's construct system.

Learning dilemma (Dollard and Miller). Contention that for learning to occur, both innate responses and previously learned responses must be ineffective in solving a problem. Therefore, learning is said to depend on failure.

Leash principle. Wilson's contention that the genes function to maintain a reasonable relationship between our culture and our biological makeup. If culture becomes too incompatible with our biological makeup, widespread deterioration of social behaviour is likely to lead to the extinction of the human species.

Legalism. Ritualism that can occur during Erikson's second stage of development. This involves a preoccupation with rules and regulations themselves instead of with what they were designed to accomplish.

Lexical hypothesis. The idea that all necessary information about personality is revealed in everyday language.

Libido (Freud). In Freud's earlier writings, libido was the psychic energy associated with the sexual instinct but later he expanded the concept of libido to include the energy associated with all the life instincts—for instance, hunger and thirst in addition to sex.

Libido (Jung).   According to Jung, the general life energy that can be directed to any problem that arises, be it biological or spiritual.

Lifestyle (Adler).   The primary means by which one attempts to attain his or her self-created or fictional goals in life.

Long-circuiting.   Indirect satisfaction of an erg. An example is a man developing athletic ability in order to be desirable to a woman who will satisfy his sexual desires.

Mand.   Verbal response that demands something and is reinforced when what is demanded is obtained.

Mandala.   Sanskrit word for circle. For Jung, the mandala is a symbol of wholeness, completeness, and perfection; that is, it symbolizes the self.

Manifest content of a dream.   What a dream appears to be about to the dreamer.

Masculine protest.   Attempting to become more powerful by being more masculine, and thereby less feminine. According to Adler's earlier theorizing, both men and women attempt to gain power by becoming more like the cultural ideal of the man.

Metaerg (Cattell and Eysenck).   Environmental-mould, dynamic source trait. Much the same as what other theorists called secondary or learned drives. (See also Attitude and Sentiment.)

Metamotives.   See Being values.

Metapathology (Maslow).   Psychological disorder that results when a being motive is not allowed proper expression.

Mind-body problem.   Problem of specifying how something mental (cognitive) can influence something physical, such as the body and vice versa.

Mistaken lifestyle.   According to Adler, any lifestyle that is not aimed at socially useful goals. In other words, any lifestyle that minimizes social interest.

Mitwelt.   World of human interactions.

Model.   Anything that conveys information to an observer.

Modulation corollary.   Statement that a construct system is more likely to change if the constructs contained in it are permeable. (See also Permeable construct.)

Monogamy.   Reproductive system whereby one male mates with one female.

Moral anxiety.   According to Freud, the guilt experienced when one either has or ponders doing or thinking something that violates the values of one's superego.

Motivational processes.   In social-cognitive theory, those processes that determine the circumstances under which learning is translated into behaviour. Such a translation will not occur unless the person has an adequate incentive.

Motor reproduction processes.   In social-cognitive theory, those processes that determine what behaviour a person is physically capable of performing.

Moving against people.   Adjustment to basic anxiety that uses the tendency to exploit other people and to gain power over them. Horney referred to the person using this adjustment technique as the hostile type. (See also Hostile type person.)

Moving away from people.   Adjustment to basic anxiety that uses the need to be self- sufficient. Horney referred to the person using this adjustment technique as the detached type. (See also Detached type person.)

Moving toward people.   Adjustment to basic anxiety that uses the need to be wanted, loved, and protected by other people. Horney referred to the person using this adjustment technique as the compliant type. (See also Compliant type person.)

Must conscience.   In Allport's theory, moral guide used by children based on the internalized values of authority figures such as the parents. The must conscience is similar to the superego postulated by Freud.

Myers-Briggs Type Indicator.   Paper-and-pencil inventory measuring psychological types similar to Jung's.

Nativism.   Contention that an attribute is determined by genetics rather than by experience.

Nativism-empiricism controversy (also called the nature-nurture controversy).   Argument concerning the extent to which an attribute, such as intelligence, is influenced by inheritance as opposed to experience.

Natural selection.   Fact that only organisms who possess adaptive traits in a given environment survive and reproduce.

Naturalistic fallacy.   Mistaken belief that what naturally *is* is also what *ought to be.*

Need for positive regard.   Need to receive warmth, sympathy, care, respect, and acceptance from the relevant people in one's life.

Need for self-regard.   Need a person develops to feel positively about himself or herself.

Need induction.   Creation of needs rather than their reduction. Allport believed the healthy human lives in accordance with long-term goals that create more problems than they solve. Thus his theory is said to emphasize need induction rather than need reduction.

Need reduction.   Satisfaction of a basic need. To many theorists, the elimination or reduction of needs is the primary goal in life. Allport did not agree.

Need-directed perception (also called *D-perception* or *D-cognition*).   Perception motivated by a search for objects or events that will satisfy a basic need; for example, a hungry person looks for food.

Negative correlation.   Condition that exists when, as values of one variable tend to increase, values of a second variable tend to decrease, and vice versa.

Negative identity (Erikson).   Identity contrary to the goals of society. Negative identities are all those roles that a child is warned *not* to assume.

Negative reinforcement.   Type of reinforcement that occurs when a response removes a primary or secondary negative reinforcer.

Nepotism.   Same as kin altruism.

Neurosis.   Condition that causes a person to function at less than maximal efficiency; according to psychoanalytic theory, this typically results from unconscious conflict that originated in early childhood.

Neurotic anxiety (Freud).   Caused by the fear that the impulses of the id will overwhelm the ego thereby causing the person to do something for which he or she will be punished.

Neurotic anxiety (May).   Anxiety that results from not being able to deal adequately with normal anxiety. For example, if a person conforms or develops inflexible values to avoid normal anxiety, the normal anxiety is converted into neurotic anxiety which causes a person to live life within narrow limits and inhibit various experiences that are necessary for healthy growth. (See also Anxiety and Normal anxiety.)

Neurotic guilt (May).   Guilt that arises when normal guilt is not recognized and dealt with constructively; it can overwhelm a person causing him or her to block out the very experiences conducive to personal growth.

Neurotic trends (Horney; also called *neurotic needs*). Ten strategies for minimizing basic anxiety.

Neuroticism (Eysenck).   The superfactor or type in Eysenck's theory that includes traits of anxiety, depression, guilt, low self-esteem, and shyness, to name a few.

Nomothetic method.   Research method that studies groups of individuals and therefore concentrates on average performance rather than on the performance of a single individual.

Nomothetic research.   Study of groups of individuals.

Noncontingent reinforcement.   Situation in which no relationship exists between an organism's behaviour and the availability of reinforcement.

Nondirective therapy.   Description of Rogers's first approach to therapy, in which the emphasis was on the client's ability to solve his or her problems.

Normal anxiety (May).   Anxiety that results from the revisions of one's value system and from the awareness of one's inevitable death. To grow as a person requires taking risks, which causes normal anxiety.

Normal guilt (May).   Feeling experienced when one recognizes the difference between what one is and what one could be. Because we can always be more than we are, normal guilt is unavoidable. (See also Guilt and Neurotic guilt.)

Numinous.   Ritualization characterizing Erikson's first stage of development. This involves the many culturally determined ways in which mother and infant interact.

Object-subject dichotomy.   May's term for the fact that as humans we are both the objects of experience and the interpreters, transformers, and originators of experience. (See also Human dilemma.)

Observational learning.   Learning that results from attending to something. Such learning is said to occur independently of reinforcement.

Oedipal conflict (May).   A struggle between dependence and independence.

Oedipus complex.   In Freudian theory, the situation in which a boy loves his mother and views his father as a dominant rival for her affection. The male Oedipal complex is resolved when he defensively identifies with his father thus completing the development of his superego. The female Oedipus complex begins when the girl discovers she lacks a penis and blames her mother for the deficiency. The female Oedipal complex

is partially resolved when she symbolically takes her father as a love object and desires a baby from him. This desire generalizes to other males, and the female Oedipal complex is more completely resolved only if she ultimately gives birth to a child, especially a male child.

Ontology.   Study of being. Within existentialism, ontological analysis is directed at understanding the essence of humans in general and of individuals in particular.

Operant behaviour.   Behaviour that cannot be linked to any known stimulus and therefore appears to be emitted rather than elicited.

Operant conditioning   (also called type R conditioning). Modification of response strength by manipulation of the consequences of the response. Responses that are followed by a reinforcer gain in strength; responses not followed by a reinforcer become weaker.

Operant level.   Frequency with which an operant response is made before it is systematically reinforced.

Oral stage.   In Freudian theory, the first psychosexual stage, which occurs during about the first year of life, at which time the mouth is the primary erogenous zone.

Oral-incorporative character (Freud).   Character type that results from a fixation at the early oral stage. Such a person spends considerable time engaged in activities such as eating, kissing, smoking, and listening.

Oral-sadistic character (Freud).   Character type that results from a fixation at the late oral stage. Such a person is orally aggressive and may be a fingernail biter and sarcastic.

Organ inferiority (Adler).   Condition that exists when some organ of the body does not develop normally. Such a condition can stimulate compensation or overcompensation, which is healthy, or can result in an inferiority complex, which is unhealthy. (See also Compensation and Overcompensation.)

Organismic valuing process (Rogers).   Frame of reference that allows an individual to know if his or her experiences are in accordance with his or her actualizing tendency.

Organization corollary.   States that constructs are arranged in a hierarchy from most general to most specific. (See also Superordinate construct and Subordinate construct.)

Ought conscience.   In Allport's theory, moral guide used by normal, healthy adults whereby their moral judgments are governed by their own personal values and propriate strivings.

Overcompensation (Adler).   Process by which, through considerable effort, a previous weakness is converted into a strength. An example is when a frail child works hard to become an athlete.

P-technique.   Type of factor analysis that studies how a single individual's traits change over time.

Paradigm.   Term used by Kuhn to describe a theoretical viewpoint shared by many researchers.

Parallelism.   Contention that an environmental event causes both mental and bodily reactions at the same time. According to this proposed answer to the mind-body question, bodily and mental phenomena run parallel to each other and are, therefore, not causally related.

Parapraxes.   Manifestations of repressed thoughts in everyday life such as slips of the tongue, "accidents," forgetfulness, and errors in writing and speaking.

Partial reinforcement effect (PRE).   Fact that a partially or intermittently reinforced response will take longer to extinguish than a response on a continuous or 100% schedule of reinforcement.

Partial reinforcement schedule.   Schedule of reinforcement that sometimes reinforces a desired response and sometimes does not. In other words, the response is maintained on a schedule of reinforcement somewhere between 100% and 0%.

Participant modelling.   Type of modelling that requires the observer to participate in the modelling experience. Typically, both the model and the observer engage in activities together that are anxiety-provoking to the observer. This type of modelling is generally found to be the most effective.

Peak experiences.   Mystical, oceanic experiences that are accompanied by a feeling of ecstasy or rapture. Such experiences were thought by Maslow to reach their full magnitude as B-values are fully embraced.

Penis envy.   Jealousy a female experiences because a male has a penis and she does not.

Perceived self-efficacy.   What a person *believes* he or she is capable of doing.

Performance standards.   Those standards that must be met or exceeded before one experiences self-reinforcement. If a person's performance does not meet or exceed a performance standard, he or she experiences self-punishment.

Permeable construct.   Construct that easily assimilates new experiences.

Perseverative functional autonomy.   Low-level habits retained even though they are no longer functional.

Person variables.   Variables contained within persons and thought to be responsible for their behaviour. Traits, habits, memories, information-processing mechanisms, and repressed early experiences exemplify person variables.

Person-centred stage.   Final stage in Rogers's thinking, in which the emphasis was on understanding the client not merely as a client but as a *total* person.

Persona.   Latin word meaning mask.

Persona (Jung).   Superficial aspect of the psyche that a person displays publicly. It includes the various roles one must play to function in a society.

Personal construct (Kelly).   Idea or thought that a person uses when construing personal experience. Sometimes simply called a construct.

Personal disposition.   Identical to an individual trait. The term *individual trait* was changed to personal disposition to avoid confusion with the term *common trait*.

Personal unconscious.   In Jung's theory, consists of material from one's lifetime that was once conscious and then repressed or material that was not vivid enough to make an initial conscious impression.

Personality (Allport).   The dynamic organization within the individual of those psychophysical systems that determine characteristic behaviour and thought.

Personality (Kelly).   A person's construct system.

Personality coefficient.   Mischel's quantification of the amount of consistency found in human behaviour. He found that the correlation of behaviour across time, across similar situations, and between personality questionnaires and behaviour was about 0.30. This weak correlation suggested that human behaviour was not nearly as consistent as it had been widely assumed to be.

Personality sphere (Cattell and Eysenck).   Universe of source traits in terms of which all humans can be compared. The number of source traits in this universe is as yet undetermined.

Phallic stage.   Freud's third psychosexual stage and the one that occurs from about the third to the fifth year of life, during which time the phallus is the primary erogenous zone. Because Freud believed the clitoris to be a small penis, he used the term phallic stage to describe the development of both male and female children.

Phenomenological field.   In Rogers's theory, that portion of experience of which an individual is aware. It is this subjective reality, rather than physical reality, that directs a person's behaviour.

Phenomenological reality.   In Rogers's theory, a person's private, subjective perception or interpretation of objective reality.

Phenomenologist.   One who studies intact, conscious experience.

Phenomenology.   Study of conscious experience as it exists for the person without any attempt to reduce, divide, or compartmentalize it in any way.

Philia.   Experience of friendship or companionship with one's loved one even when sex and eros are not involved. Simply liking to be with your loved one.

Phylogenetically inherited endowment.   According to Freud, images we inherit that reflect the consistent experiences of our ancestors. With his acceptance of such images Freud demonstrated his acceptance of Lamarck's theory of the inheritance of acquired characteristics.

Physical inferiority.   Actual physical weakness. (See also Organ inferiority.)

Physical monism (also called **materialism**).   Contention that no mind-body problem exists because no mind exists. No mental events occur, only physical events.

Physics envy.   Dismay expressed by many social scientists over the fact that physics is a rigorous science with a few highly heuristic explanatory principles and the social sciences are not.

Physiological needs.   Most basic cluster of needs in Maslow's hierarchy of needs. Included are the needs for water, food, oxygen, sleep, elimination, and sex.

Planning.   Use of cue-producing responses (thinking) in attempting to solve some future problem.

Pleasure principle.   In Freud's theory, hedonistic principle governing the id that demands the immediate reduction of any tension associated with an unsatisfied biological need.

Polyandry. Reproductive system whereby one female mates with more than one male.

Polygyny. Reproductive system whereby a male mates with more than one female.

Positive correlation. Condition that exists when the values of two variables tend to increase or decrease together.

Positive reinforcement. Type of reinforcement that occurs when a response makes available a primary or secondary positive reinforcer.

Posthypnotic amnesia. Inability to remember what one has done while hypnotized.

Posthypnotic suggestion. Phenomenon whereby a person performs an act while awake that he or she was instructed to perform while under hypnosis. Typically, the person is unaware of the reason for performing such an act.

Pre-emption phase. That phase of Kelly's CPC cycle in which people decide which construct to use to construe a novel situation.

Preconscious. According to Freud, state of information that is in the unconscious mind but has not been repressed. Such information enters consciousness easily when it is needed.

Prepared learning. Type of learning that occurs rapidly and with ease because it involves learning information and skills that enhance an organism's inclusive fitness.

Preverbal construct. In Kelly's theory, construct formulated early in one's life, before language was adequately developed. Although such a construct cannot be labelled verbally it can still be used to construe one's experiences.

Primal repression. In Freud's theory, repression of those anxiety-provoking thoughts that are innately part of the id and therefore independent of personal experience.

Primary generalization. Generalization that is determined by the physical properties of stimuli.

Primary negative reinforcer. Negative reinforcer that threatens an organism's survival—for example, pain or oxygen deprivation.

Primary positive reinforcer. Positive reinforcer that enhances an organism's survival—for example, food or water.

Primary processes. In Freud's theory, processes available to the id for satisfaction of needs. Those processes are reflex action and wish fulfillment (hallucinations). (See also Reflex action and Wish fulfillment.)

Primary reinforcer. Any stimulus that is positively or negatively related to an organism's survival.

Principle of conservation of energy. Principle stating that the amount of energy within a system remains constant. Although the amount of energy in a system cannot be increased or decreased, it can be rearranged and transformed freely within the system.

Principle of entropy. Second law of thermodynamics, which states that a constant tendency exists toward equalizing energy within a system.

Principle of equivalence. First law of thermodynamics, which states that the amount of energy in a system is fixed and, therefore, if some of it is removed from one part of the system, it must show up in another part.

Principle of falsifiability (also called principle of refutability). Popper's contention that a scientific theory must make risky predictions; that is, it must make predictions that could conceivably be false and, if so, would refute the theory.

Principle of mastery and competence. Principle stating that an innate need exists for humans to aspire to greater mastery and competence.

Principle of opposites. Contention that each component of the psyche has an opposite.

Principle of organizing energy level. Principle stating that energy that was once used for survival can be changed into concern for the future when survival is no longer an issue.

Principle of propriate patterning. Allport's principle stating that the proprium is the frame of reference that is used by a person in determining what is worth pursuing and what is not.

Principle of verification. The stipulation that scientific propositions must be capable of objective, empirical testing that is available to any interested person.

Projection. In Freudian theory, an ego-defence mechanism by which an anxiety-provoking thought is attributed to someone or something else instead of recognizing it as one's own.

Propositional construct. In Kelly's theory, construct that is cognitively tested as one that might be useful in construing a situation.

Propriate functional autonomy. Important motives around which one organizes one's life. Such motives are independent of the conditions that originally produced them.

Propriate striving. In Allport's theory, attribute that emerges during the seventh stage in the development of the proprium. At this stage, the adolescent becomes almost completely future oriented.

Proprium (Allport). All the facts about a person that make him or her unique.

Proximate causation. Immediate factors such as the organism's motivational state, the organism's previous experience in the situation, and various environmental events that are responsible for a particular response being made.

Psyche. Term that Jung equated with personality.

Psychic energy. More or less fixed amount of energy that Freud believed was available to drive the entire personality. According to Freud, psychic energy obeyed the principle of conservation of energy. (See also Principle of conservation of energy.)

Psychohistory. Term used to describe Erikson's use of his developmental theory of personality to analyze historical figures.

Psychosocial moratorium. Time during Erikson's fifth stage of development when the adolescent is searching for an identity.

Psychosocial stages of development. Erikson's eight stages of human development, so named to emphasize the importance of social experience to the resolution of the crises that characterize each stage.

Psychoticism. The superfactor or type in Eysenck's theory that includes traits of aggression, egocentricity, impulsiveness, and creativity, to name a few.

Pull theories of motivation. Those theories that emphasize terms such as *purpose, value,* or *need.* Kelly also called these carrot theories.

Punishment. Either removing a positive reinforcer or presenting a negative reinforcer.

Push theories of motivation. Those theories that emphasize terms such as *drive, motive,* and *stimulus.* Kelly also called these pitchfork theories.

Q-data. Information provided when people fill out a questionnaire on which they rate themselves on various characteristics. The *Q* stands for questionnaire.

Q-sort technique. Method Rogers used to determine how a client's self-image changed as a function of therapy. (See also Self-sort and Ideal-sort.)

R-technique. Type of factor analysis that studies many things about many people.

Range corollary. Statement that a construct is relevant to only a finite range of events. (See also Range of convenience and Focus of convenience.)

Range of convenience. Finite range of events to which a particular construct is relevant.

Rate of responding. Used by Skinner to demonstrate operant conditioning. If a response is followed by a reinforcer, the rate or frequency with which it is made will increase; if a response is not followed by a reinforcer, its rate or frequency will stay the same (if it is at its operant level) or will decrease.

Rational functions. Jung referred to thinking and feeling as rational functions because they involve making judgments and evaluations about experiences.

Rationalism. Belief that knowledge can be gained only by exercising the mind; for example, by thinking, deducing, or inferring.

Rationalization. Giving a rational, logical (but incorrect) excuse for behaviour or thoughts that otherwise would cause anxiety.

Reaction formation. Inhibition of an anxiety-provoking thought by exaggerating its opposite. For example, a person inclined toward pornography may become a censor.

Real self (Horney). Self that is healthy and conducive to positive growth. Although each person is born with a healthy real self, the view of this real self can be distorted by the basic evil.

Real self (Rogers). Client's description of how he or she currently views himself or herself.

Reality anxiety (Freud). Anxiety caused by real, objective sources of danger in the environment. It is the easiest type of anxiety to reduce or prevent.

Reality principle. In Freudian theory, principle governing the ego that causes it to do commerce with the environment in a way that satisfies both the id and the superego.

Reality testing. In Freudian theory, process by which the ego finds environmental experiences capable of satisfying the needs of the id or superego.

Reasoning. Attempted solution of an immediate problem through the use of cue-producing responses (thinking) rather than through overt trial and error.

Reciprocal altruism. Willingness to help genetically unrelated people, which is based on the understanding that those people (direct reciprocity) or other members of the community (indirect reciprocity) will help you when the need arises.

Reciprocal determinism. Contention that person variables, situation variables, and behaviour constantly interact with one another.

Reductive-analytic approach to science. Strategy of reducing an object of interest to its component parts in order to study and understand it.

Reflex action. Automatic reflexive response aimed at the removal of a source of irritation. Blinking to remove something from the eye is an example.

Regression. Returning to an earlier stage of development when stress is encountered.

Reinforcement (Hull). In Hull's theory of learning, drive reduction constitutes reinforcement.

Reinforcement (social cognitive theory). Within social cognitive theory, reinforcement (either direct or vicarious) provides information concerning what behaviour will be effective in a given situation. Also, reinforcement provides an incentive for translating learning into performance. (See also Vicarious reinforcement.)

Reinforcement theory. Any theory of learning which states that reinforcement must occur before learning can take place.

Reinforcer. In Hull's theory, a stimulus capable of reducing a drive.

Repression (Dollard and Miller). Learned response of not thinking an anxiety-provoking thought.

Repression (Freud). Ego-defence mechanism by which anxiety-provoking thoughts are held in the unconscious mind, thereby preventing a conscious awareness of them. (See also Primal repression and Repression proper.)

Repression proper (Freud). Repression of those anxiety-provoking thoughts that result from painful experiences in one's lifetime.

Reproductive imperative. According to Wallace, the biological mandate to reproduce and leave as many offspring as possible.

Reproductive value. Person's long-term ability to produce offspring. In general, a young person will have higher reproductive value than an older person because the younger person will be capable of reproducing over a longer period of time.

Resistance. Patient's unwillingness to ponder and report anxiety-producing thoughts during the therapeutic process. Freud believed that resistance was highly informative because it suggested what were troublesome topics for the patient.

Respondent behaviour. Behaviour that is elicited by a known stimulus.

Respondent conditioning (also called type S conditioning). Another term for classical or Pavlovian conditioning.

Resultant hierarchy of responses. Hierarchy of responses elicited by a cue after learning has taken place.

Retentional processes. Those processes that determine how experiences are encoded into memory for possible future use.

Risky predictions. Predictions that run the risk of being incorrect. According to Popper, for a theory to be considered scientific it must make risky predictions.

Ritualisms (Erikson). Distorted or exaggerated ritualizations.

Ritualizations (Erikson). Behaviours that reflect and thereby perpetuate the beliefs, customs, and values that are sanctioned by a particular culture.

Role (Kelly). Acting in accordance with another person's expectations.

Role confusion. The state produced by not acquiring an identity during Erikson's fifth stage of development. The state is characterized by an inability to choose a defining role in life and represents the negative resolution of the identity crisis.

Role construct (Kelly). Awareness of another person's expectations. In a sense, a role construct involves seeing the world through someone else's eyes.

Role Construct Repertory Test (Rep test). Test developed by Kelly to identify the constructs clients use to construe the relevant people in their lives.

Ruling-dominant type person (Adler). Person exhibiting the mistaken lifestyle that dominates and rules people. Such a person lacks adequate social interest.

Safeguarding strategies (Adler). Mechanisms neurotics use to preserve what little self- esteem and illusions of superiority a mistaken lifestyle can provide. (See also Aggression, Excuses, and Distancing.)

Safety needs. Second cluster of needs in Maslow's hierarchy of needs. Included is the need for order, security, and predictability.

Sapientism. Ritualism that can occur during Erikson's eighth stage of development. This involves the pretense of being wise.

Satellite relationships. Close relationship with individuals other than one's spouse.

Satisfaction. In Horney's theory, meeting of such physiological needs as those for water, food, and sleep required for a child's biological survival.

Science. Epistemological pursuit that combines the philosophical tools of empiricism and rationalism.

Scientific theory. Combination of the philosophical schools of rationalism and empiricism, with two major functions: (1) to synthesize (explain) many observations, and (2) to generate new information.

Second signal system. According to Pavlov, the verbal labels that symbolize environmental events.

Secondary dispositions. More specific than cardinal or central dispositions but still more general than habits and attitudes. A secondary disposition may be a person's preference for flamboyant clothing or for sweet food.

Secondary generalization. Generalization that is based on verbal labels (words), not on the physical similarity among stimuli.

Secondary negative reinforcer. Negative reinforcer that derives its reinforcing properties through its association with a primary negative reinforcer.

Secondary positive reinforcer. Positive reinforcer that derives its reinforcing properties through its association with a primary positive reinforcer.

Secondary processes. In Freud's theory, realistic processes by which the ego operates to bring about true need reduction as opposed to the temporary need reduction that results from the wish fulfillments of the id.

Secondary reinforcer. Objects or events that acquire reinforcing properties through their association with primary reinforcers.

Secondary revision (also called secondary elaboration). In Freud's theory, resynthesizing dream elements after they have been distorted by dream work. This resynthesizing gives the distorted dream elements enough meaning to be accepted into consciousness.

Seduction theory. Freud's early contention that hysteria results from an actual sexual seduction experienced during childhood. For reasons that are not entirely clear, Freud revised his theory to state that most seductions were imagined rather than real.

Self. Concept employed by several personality theorists to account for the facts that human behaviour is smooth-running, consistent, and well organized. The concept of self has also been used to explain why we are aware of ourselves as individuals.

Self (Jung). State of the psyche if the individuation process has been completely successful. When the various components of the psyche are harmonized, the self becomes the centre of all of the various opposing psychic forces.

Self (Rogers). That portion of the phenomenological field which becomes differentiated because of experiences involving terms such as *I, me,* and *mine.*

Self as knower. Attribute that emerges during Allport's eighth and final stage in the development of the proprium. At this stage, the proprium is aware of, unifies, and transcends the preceding seven aspects of the proprium.

Self as rational coper. Attribute that emerges during Allport's sixth stage in the development of the proprium. At this stage, the child begins to use complex mental operations (thinking) to solve problems.

Self-accusation. Form of neurotic aggression that involves wallowing in self-torture and guilt, the ultimate purpose of which is to hurt other people.

Self-actualization (Maslow). Highest level in Maslow's hierarchy of needs, which can be reached only if the preceding need levels have been adequately satisfied. The self-actualizing individual operates at full capacity and is B-motivated rather than D-motivated.

Self-actualization (Rogers). The goal of humans to enhance and maintain themselves, and the process of working toward this goal (see actualizing tendency).

Self-analysis. Process of self-help that Horney believed people could apply to themselves to solve life's problems and to minimize conflict.

Self-characterization. Sketch that Kelly sometimes had his clients write about themselves (in the third person) in order to learn what constructs they used to construe themselves and other people.

Self-control. Ability to tolerate a delay in gratification.

Self-efficacy. What a person is actually capable of doing.

Self-efficacy expectancy. Expectancy one has concerning one's ability to engage in effective behaviour. (See also Self-efficacy and Perceived self-efficacy.)

Self-esteem. Attribute that emerges during Allport's third stage in the development of the proprium. At this stage, the child develops a feeling of pride by doing things on his or her own.

Self-exonerating mechanisms. Cognitive mechanisms a person can employ to escape the self-contempt that ordinarily results when a person acts contrary to an internalized moral principle.

Self-extension. Attribute that emerges during Allport's fourth stage in the development of the proprium. At this stage, the child's self-identity generalizes to external objects.

Self-identity. Attribute that emerges during Allport's second stage in the development of the proprium. At this stage, the child develops a self-identity; for example, realizing that he or she is the same person although conditions change.

Self-image. Attribute that emerges during Allport's fifth stage in the development of the proprium. At this stage, the child develops a conscience and begins to formulate future goals.

Self-objectification (Allport). Honest appraisal of one's assets and liabilities that characterizes the healthy, mature adult. A person with self-objectification typically has a good sense of humour.

Self-realization (Horney). Innate tendency to strive for truthfulness, productivity, and harmonious relationships with fellow humans.

Self-realization (Jung). State of balance and harmony that is reached when the various components of the psyche are recognized and given expression.

Self-regulated behaviour. Behaviour governed by intrinsic reinforcement and punishment. Self-regulated behaviour is often directed at some major future goal that is approached through a series of subgoals. (See also Delay of gratification and Moral conduct.)

Self-regulatory systems and plans. Cognitive social learning person variable that determines the circumstances under which an individual experiences self-reinforcement and self-punishment. This variable also determines the setting of future goals and the formulation of plans (strategies) used in attaining those goals.

Self-relatedness. To be aware of one's existence as a being in the world who both has experiences and transforms them. To be conscious of the fact that one is both the object and subject of experience.

Self-sentiment. Concern for oneself that is a prerequisite to the pursuit of any goal in life.

Self-sort (Rogers). Statements chosen by a client as best describing the person as he or she actually is at the moment. Part of the Q-sort technique.

Sensing (Jung). Function of thought that detects the presence of objects.

Sentiment. Learned predisposition to respond to a class of objects or events in a certain way. A sentiment is one type of metaerg.

Shadow. In Jung's theory, deepest part of the collective unconscious, which contains all the animalistic urges that characterized our prehuman existence.

Shaping. Gradual development of a response that an organism does not normally make. Shaping requires differential reinforcement and successive approximations. (See also Differential reinforcement and Successive approximations).

Situation variables. Those variables found in the environment thought to be responsible for behaviour.

Skinner box. Small experimental chamber that Skinner invented to study operant conditioning.

Slot movements. The abrupt shifting from the use of one pole of a construct to its opposite, which is often precipitated by stress.

Social cognitive theory. Name given to Bandura and Mischel's theory because of its emphasis on the social and cognitive origins of human behaviour.

Social interest. Innate potential to live in harmony and friendship with others and to aspire to the development of a perfect society.

Sociality corollary. Statement that to engage in constructive social interaction with another person, one must first understand how that person construes his or her experiences. (See also Role.)

Socially useful type person. Person exhibiting a lifestyle containing a healthy amount of social interest. Such a lifestyle is not "mistaken."

Sociobiological theory of human nature. Contention that humans are born with tendencies to behave in ways that enhanced the fitness of our ancestors. For the sociobiologists, the human mind is well stocked with behavioural predispositions at birth and, therefore, is anything but blank.

Sociobiology. Systematic study of the biological basis of social behaviour, including that of humans.

Source traits. Traits that constitute a person's personality structure and are thus the ultimate causes of behaviour. Source traits are causally related to surface traits.

Stagnation. Lack of concern about the next generation that characterizes the person whose crisis during Erikson's seventh stage of development is resolved negatively.

Stimulus generalization. Tendency for stimuli other than the stimulus present in the learning process to elicit a learned response. The more similar these stimuli are to the one actually used in the learning process, the greater the probability is that they will elicit a learned response.

Stimulus-outcome expectancy. Belief that one environmental event will be followed by another specific event that has been consistently associated with the first event in the past.

Structuralism. American version of voluntarism. Like the voluntarists, the structuralists sought the basic elements of conscious thought, but they did not share the voluntarist's interest in the mind's creative ability.

Structured learning. Type of learning that results in rearranging one's personality traits. According to Cattell, this is the most important type of learning.

Struggle for survival. Competition for survival that results among members of a species when the number of organisms exceeds that which is sustainable by environmental resources.

Subception. Detection of an experience before it enters full awareness.

Subjective values. Cognitive social person variable that determines under what circumstances a person will translate what has been learned into behaviour. Subjective values determine what is worth having or aspiring for, and what is not.

Sublimation. In Freudian theory, displacement that results in a higher cultural achievement such as when an artistic or scientific activity is substituted for sexual activity.

Submergence. Situation in which one pole of a construct is used, but the other pole tends not to be. The unused pole is said to be submerged or unconscious.

Subordinate constructs. Constructs that are subsumed under a more general construct.

Subsidiation. In Cattell's theory, the hierarchy in which sentiments depend on ergs, and attitudes depend on sentiments.

Successive approximations. Situation in which only those responses that are increasingly similar to the one ultimately desired are reinforced.

Superego. In Freudian theory, moral component of the personality that has two parts: the conscience and the ego ideal. (See also Conscience and Ego ideal.)

Superfactor (also called type). In Eysenck's theory, a higher order factor that encompasses or explains a number of correlated traits or first-order factors.

Superiority complex. In Adler's theory, psychological condition that exists when a person concentrates too much on his or her own need to succeed while ignoring the needs of others. Such a person tends to be vain, domineering, and arrogant.

Superordinate construct. General construct that subsumes other constructs.

Superstitious behaviour. Behaviour that develops under noncontingent reinforcement in which the organism seems to believe that a relationship exists between its actions and reinforcement, when in fact no such relationship exists.

Suppression. Actively putting an anxiety-provoking thought out of one's mind. Suppression is reinforced by the escape from anxiety.

Surface traits. Outward manifestations of source traits. These are the characteristics of a person that can be directly observed and measured.

Survival of the fittest. Fact that only those organisms that possess adaptive traits survive and reproduce.

Suspension (Kelly). Situation in which an experience has low cognitive awareness because it is incompatible with one's current construct system. If one's construct system is changed so it can assimilate the experience, it (the experience) will enter full awareness; that is, it will no longer be suspended.

Symbolic modelling. Modelling involving something other than a live human, for instance, a film, television, instructions, reading material, or a demonstration.

Symbolization. Process by which an event enters an individual's awareness.

Synchronicity. Meaningful coincidence. When two independent events come together in a meaningful way.

Synergy. Working together. Individuals in a community characterized by synergy work in harmony and are not in conflict with their society.

Syntality. Description of the traits that characterize a group or a nation.

Synthesizing function of a theory. A theory's ability to organize and explain several otherwise disjointed observations.

Systematic desensitization. Therapeutic procedure whereby a client is asked to imagine a series of interrelated anxiety-provoking scenes until they no longer cause anxiety.

T-data. Information obtained about a person from performance on an objective test. The *T* stands for test.

Tact (Skinner). That part of verbal behaviour which accurately names objects and events in the environment.

Teleological behaviour. Purposive behaviour.

Teleology. Belief that a person's anticipations of the future must be considered if that person's personality is to be completely understood.

Temperament (Allport). One of the raw materials from which personality is shaped. Temperament is the emotional component of the personality.

Temperament (Cattell and Eysenck). Composite factors that describe the emotional, motivational, and cognitive aspects of behaviour. Temperament does not include intelligence or ability.

Temperament trait. Constitutional source trait that determines a person's emotionality and style of behaving.

Territory. Area or property that is perceived as one's own and is therefore defended if penetrated by an uninvited person or persons.

Thanatos. Name given to the death instinct. The source of aggression that Freud believed was self-destruction turned outward.

Thinking (Jung). Function of thought that names an object.

Third force psychology. Humanistic psychology, which was viewed by Maslow and others as an alternative to psychoanalysis and behaviourism.

Threat (Kelly).   Awareness that one or more important constructs will be invalidated thus requiring a major change in one's construct system. (See also Core structures.)

Threat (Rogers).   Anything that is thought to be incompatible with one's self-structure.

Thrownness (also called facticity, destiny, and ground of existence).   Those facts that characterize a person's life over which he or she has no control. Such facts include the biological, historical, and cultural events that characterize his or her life.

Time out from reinforcement.   A form of punishment by which an organism is denied access to positive reinforcers that are normally available in the situation for a specified interval of time

Token economies.   Example of Skinnerian behaviour therapy that usually occurs within an institutional setting such as a psychiatric hospital or a school. Within a token economy, desirable behaviour is reinforced by tokens (or sometimes points or cards) that can subsequently be traded for desirable objects or events such as food, cigarettes, privacy, or a choice of a television program.

Totalism.   Ritualism that can occur during Erikson's fifth stage of development. This involves embracing simplistic ideas mouthed by various "heroes" because those ideas may temporarily make life more tolerable.

Trait. (Cattell and Eysenck)   Refers either to a group of interrelated overt behaviours (surface trait) or to the deeper determinant of such interrelated behaviour (source traits). The main usefulness of surface traits is that they provide information about source traits.

Trait.   Mental structure that initiates and guides reactions and thus accounts for the consistency in one's behaviour.

Transference.   Phenomenon that sometimes occurs during therapy in which a patient begins to respond to the therapist as if he or she were an important person in the patient's life such as the patient's mother or father.

Transpersonal psychology (also called *fourth force psychology*).   Psychology that examines the human relationship to the cosmos or to something "bigger than we are" and the mystical, spiritual, or peak experiences that the realization of such a relationship produces.

Type (Allport).   Category into which one person can be placed by another person. To label a person as "an aggressive type" is to place him or her in a descriptive category based on behaviour.

Type (Cattell and Eysenck).   See Superfactor.

Type R conditioning   (also called operant conditioning).   Term Skinner used to describe the conditioning of operant or emitted behaviour to emphasize the importance of the response (R) to such conditioning.

Type S conditioning   (also called respondent conditioning).   Term Skinner used to describe classical conditioning to emphasize the importance of the stimulus (S) to such conditioning.

Tyranny of the should.   Horney's term for the condition in which one's idealized self is substituted for the real self and one's behaviour is governed by several unrealistic "shoulds."

Ultimate causation.   In sociobiological theory, those causes of an organism's behaviour that reflect the evolutionary history of the organism. Ultimate causes of behaviour reflect the behaviour's adaptive significance.

Umwelt.   Physical, objective world. The world that is studied by the physical and biological sciences.

Unconditional positive regard.   Experience of positive regard without conditions of worth. In other words, positive regard is not contingent on certain acts or thoughts.

Unconditioned response (UR).   Natural, automatic response elicited by an unconditioned stimulus (US).

Unconditioned stimulus (US).   Stimulus that elicits an automatic, natural response from an organism. Also called a primary reinforcer because conditioning ultimately depends on the presence of a US.

Unconscious (Kelly).   Constructs with low cognitive awareness. (See also Submergence and Suspension.)

Unconscious (May).   The experiences denied awareness because of inflexible values or because of the restrictive influence of neurotic anxiety and guilt.

Undoing.   An ego defence mechanism by which an attempt is made to atone for, or negate, an unacceptable act or thought by engaging in some form of ritualistic activity.

Unifying philosophy of life.   Unifying theme that holds together the life of a healthy, mature adult and gives it meaning. Such a theme is often religious in nature but, according to Allport, it does not need to be.

Validation.   Results when a construct or a construct system successfully anticipates an experience.

Value (Jung).   Varies as the amount of libidinal energy invested varies. Those components of the personality that have an abundance of libidinal energy invested in them are valued more than components with less energy invested in them.

Values.   Those categories of experience that are deemed most important to the person. Typically, values early in life involve the love, security, and nourishment provided by one's mother; later values include status and success. Mature values are future oriented, are arrived at independently, and are concerned with other humans.

Variable interval reinforcement schedule (VI).   Reinforcement schedule in which a certain average time interval must pass before a response will be reinforced. For example, the organism is reinforced on the average of every 30 seconds.

Variable ratio reinforcement schedule (VR).   Reinforcement schedule in which a certain average number of responses need to be made before reinforcement is obtained. For example, the organism is reinforced on the average of every fifth response (VR5).

Verbal behaviour.   Skinner's term for language.

Vicarious punishment.   Punishment that comes from observing the negative consequences of another person's behaviour.

Vicarious reinforcement.   Reinforcement that comes from observing the positive consequences of another person's behaviour.

Virtue (Erikson).   Ego strength that arises when the crisis dominating a stage of development is resolved positively.

Visceral brain (VB).   Eysenck's term for the limbic system, a subcortical brain system that influences the autonomic nervous system.

Vitalism.   Belief that life cannot be explained in terms of physical events and processes alone; rather, some nonphysical, vital force must be postulated.

Voluntarism.   Psychology's first school of thought. Founded in Germany, the main goals of voluntarism were to discover the elements of conscious thought through introspection, and to show how the mind could creatively arrange those elements.

Westermarck effect.   Tendency to avoid a sexual relationship later in life with someone with whom one had a close relationship as a young child.

Whisperings.   Barash's term for subtle, inherited behavioural predispositions.

Will (May).   Commitment to action.

Wish (May). Cognitive exploration of possible courses of action before actually committing oneself to one particular course.

Wish fulfillment.   The conjuring of an image of an object or event that is capable of satisfying a biological need.

Word-association test.   Research technique that Jung used to explore the complexes within the personal unconscious. It consisted of reading 100 words one at a time and having a person respond as quickly as possible with a word of his or her own.

Xenophobia.   Fear of strangers.

References

ACEVEDO, E. O., & HOLLANDER, D. B. (2000). Successful English Channel swimming: the peak experience. *Sport Psychologist, 14*(1), 1-16.

ADAMS, G. R., & FITCH, S. A. (1982). Ego stage and identity status development: A cross-sequential analysis. *Journal of Personality and Social Psychology, 43,* 547–583.

ADAMS, G. R., RYAN, J. H., HOFFMAN, J. J., DOBSON, W. R., & NIELSEN, E. C. (1985). Ego identity status, conformity behavior, and personality in late adolescence. *Journal of Personality and Social Psychology, 47,* 1091–1104.

ADAMS-WEBBER, J. R. (1979). *Personal construct theory: Concepts and applications.* New York: Wiley.

ADLER, A. (1917). *Study of organ inferiority and its physical compensation: A contribution to clinical medicine* (S. E. Jeliffe, Trans.). New York: Nervous and Mental Disease Publication. (Original work published 1907.)

ADLER, A. (1930). Individual psychology. In C. Murchison (Ed.), *Psychologies of 1930.* Worcester, MA: Clark University Press.

ADLER, A. (1956). *The individual psychology of Alfred Adler: A systematic presentation of selections from his writings.* H. L. Ansbacher & R. R. Ansbacher (Eds.). New York: Basic.

ADLER, A. (1956). Feeling unmanly as inferiority feeling. In H. L. Ansbacher & R. R. Ansbacher (Eds.), *The individual psychology of Alfred Adler.* New York: Basic. (Original work published 1910.)

ADLER, A. (1956). The use of heredity and environment. In H. L. Ansbacher & R. R. Ansbacher (Eds.), *The individual psychology of Alfred Adler.* New York: Basic. (Original work published 1935.)

ADLER, A. (1958). *What life should mean to you.* New York: Capricorn. (Original work published 1931.)

ADLER, A. (1964). *Problems of neurosis.* New York: Harper & Row. (Original work published 1929.)

ADLER, A. (1964). *Social interest: A challenge to mankind.* New York: Capricorn. (Original work published 1933.)

ADLER, A. (1979). The structure of neurosis. In H. L. Ansbacher & R. R. Ansbacher (Eds.), *Superiority and social interest: A collection of Alfred Adler's later writings.* New York: Norton. (Original work published 1932.)

AGNEW, J. (1985). Childhood disorders. In E. Button (Ed.), *Personal construct theory and mental health: Theory, research, and practice.* Beckenham, England: Croom Helm.

ALBERT, T. (1999). Apotropaic reading: Freud's "Medusa's Head." *Literature & Psychology, 45*(4), 1–30.

ALDERFER, C. P. (1972). *Existence, relatedness, and growth needs in organizational settings.* New York: Free Press.

ALLPORT, G. W. (1937). *Personality: A psychological interpretation.* New York: Holt, Rinehart and Winston.

ALLPORT, G. W. (1942). *The use of personal documents in psychological science.* Bulletin 49. New York: Social Science Research Council.

ALLPORT, G. W. (1950). *The individual and his religion.* New York: Macmillan.

ALLPORT, G. W. (1955). *Becoming: Basic considerations for a psychology of personality.* New Haven: Yale University Press.

ALLPORT, G. W. (1958). *The nature of prejudice.* Garden City, NY: Doubleday. (Original work published 1954.)

ALLPORT, G. W. (1958). What units shall we employ? In G. Lindzey (Ed.), *Assessment of human motives* (pp. 239–260). New York: Holt, Rinehart and Winston.

ALLPORT, G. W. (1960). *Personality and social encounter: Selected essays.* Boston: Beacon Press.

ALLPORT, G. W. (1961). *Pattern and growth in personality.* New York: Holt, Rinehart and Winston.

ALLPORT, G. W. (1962). The general and the unique in psychological science. *Journal of Personality, 30,* 405–422.

ALLPORT, G. W. (1965). *Letters from Jenny.* New York: Harcourt Brace Jovanovich.

ALLPORT, G. W. (1967). Autobiography. In E. G. Boring & G. Lindzey (Eds.), *A history of psychology in autobiography* (Vol. 5, pp. 1–25). New York: Appleton-Century-Crofts.

ALLPORT, G. W. (1968). *The person in psychology: Selected essays.* Boston, MA: Beacon Press.

ALLPORT, G. W. (1978). *Waiting for the Lord: 33 meditations on God and man.* New York: Macmillan.

ALLPORT, G. W., & ALLPORT, F. H. (1921). Personality traits: Their classification and measurement. *Journal of Abnormal and Social Psychology, 16,* 6–40.

ALLPORT, G. W., & CANTRIL, H. (1934). Judging personality from voice. *Journal of Social Psychology, 5,* 37–55.

ALLPORT, G. W., & ODBERT, H. S. (1936). Trait names: A psycholexical study. *Psychological Monographs, 47* (211), 1–171.

ALLPORT, G. W., & POSTMAN, L. (1947). *The psychology of rumor.* New York: Holt, Rinehart and Winston.

ALLPORT, G. W., & ROSS, J. M. (1967). Personal religious orientation and prejudice. *Journal of Personality and Social Psychology, 5,* 432–443.

ALLPORT, G. W., & VERNON, P. E. (1933). *Studies in expressive movement.* New York: Macmillan.

ALLPORT, G. W., VERNON, P. E., & LINDZEY, G. (1960). *A study of values* (3rd ed.). Boston: Houghton Mifflin.

ALTEMEYER, B., & HUNSBERGER, B. (1992). Authoritarianism, religious fundamentalism, question, and prejudice. *International Journal for the Psychology of Religion, 2,* 113–133.

ALTEMEYER, B., & HUNSBERGER, B. (1997). *Amazing conversions: Why some turn to faith & others abandon religion.* Amherst, NY: Prometheus.

ALTMAN, K. E. (1973). The relationship between social interest dimensions of early recollections and selected counselor variables. *Dissertation Abstracts International, 34,* 5613A. (University Microfilms No. 74-05, 364)

American Psychological Association approves FMSF as a sponsor of continuing education programs (1995, November-December) *False Memory Syndrome Foundation Newsletter* (e-mail edition).

American Psychologist. (1981). Awards for distinguished scientific contributions: 1980. *American Psychologist, 36,* 27–42.

American Psychologist. (1992). Citation for outstanding lifetime contribution to psychology. Presented to Neal E. Miller, August 16, 1991. *American Psychologist, 47,* 847.

ANGUS, L., KORMAN, Y., & LEVITT, H. (2000). A metaphor analysis in treatments of depression: Metaphor as a marker of change. *Counselling Psychology Quarterly, 13*(1), 23-35.

ANNIS, H. M. (1990). Relapse to substance abuse: Empirical findings within a cognitive-social learning approach. *Journal of Psychoactive Drugs, 22,* 117–124.

ANSBACHER, H. L. (1983). Individual psychology. In R. J. Corsini & A. J. Marsella (Eds.), *Personality theories, research, and assessment.* Itasca, IL: Peacock.

ANSBACHER, H. L. (1990). Alfred Adler's influence on the three leading cofounders of humanistic psychology. *Journal of Humanistic Psychology, 30,* 45–53.

ANSBACHER, H. L., & ANSBACHER, R. R. (Eds.). (1956). *The individual psychology of Alfred Adler.* New York: Basic.

ANSBACHER, H. L., & ANSBACHER, R. R. (Eds.). (1979). *Superiority and social interest.* New York: Norton.

APA Division of Clinical Psychology. *Division 12 News.* Citation for centennial award for distinguished contribution to clinical psychology. Presented to Hans J. Eysenck, August 9, 1996. *Division 12 News,* September, 1996 (e-mail edition).

ARAGONA, J., CASSADY, J., & DRABMAN, R. S. (1975). Treating overweight children through parental training and contingency management. *Journal of Applied Behavior Analysis, 8,* 269–278.

ASHTON, M. C., LEE, K., & SON, C. (2000). Honesty as the sixth factor of personality: Correlations with Machiavellianism, primary psychopathy, and social adroitness. *European Journal of Personality, 14,* 359–368.

ASPY, D. (1972). *Toward a technology for humanizing education.* Champaign, IL: Research Press.

ASPY, D., & ROEBUCK, F. (1974). From human ideas to humane technology and back again, many times. *Education, 95,* 163–171.

ATWOOD, G. E., & TOMKINS, S. (1976). On the subjectivity of personality theory. *Journal of the History of the Behavioral Sciences, 12,* 166–177.

AYLLON, T., & AZRIN, N. H. (1965). The measurement and reinforcement of behavior of psychotics. *Journal of the Experimental Analysis of Behavior, 8,* 357–383.

AYLLON, T., & AZRIN, N. H. (1968). *The token economy: A motivational system for therapy and rehabilitation.* New York: Appleton-Century-Crofts.

BAER, J. S., HOLT, C. S., & LICHTENSTEIN, E. (1986). Self-efficacy and smoking reexamined: Construct validity and clinical utility. *Journal of Consulting and Clinical Psychology, 54,* 846–852.

BALDWIN, A. C., CRITELLI, J. W., STEVENS, L. C., & RUSSELL, S. (1986). Androgyny and sex role measurement: A personal construct approach. *Journal of Personality and Social Psychology, 51,* 1081–1088.

BALDWIN, M. W., & WESLEY, R. (1996). Effects of existential anxiety and self-esteem on the perception of others. *Basic and Applied Social Psychology, 18,* 75–95.

BALMARY, M. (1979). *Psychoanalyzing psychoanalysis: Freud and the hidden fault of the father.* Baltimore: Johns Hopkins Press.

BANDURA, A. (1965). Influence of models' reinforcement contingencies on the acquisition of imitative responses. *Journal of Personality and Social Psychology, 1,* 589–595.

BANDURA, A. (1969). *Principles of behavior modification.* New York: Holt, Rinehart and Winston.

BANDURA, A. (1973). *Aggression: A social-learning analysis.* Englewood Cliffs, NJ: Prentice-Hall.

BANDURA, A. (1977). *Social learning theory.* Englewood Cliffs, NJ: Prentice-Hall.

BANDURA, A. (1978). The self system in reciprocal determinism. *American Psychologist, 33,* 344–358.

BANDURA, A. (1982). The psychology of chance encounters and life paths. *American Psychologist, 37,* 747–755.

BANDURA, A. (1986). *Social foundations of thought and action: A social cognitive theory.* Englewood Cliffs, NJ: Prentice-Hall.

BANDURA, A. (1989). Human agency in social cognitive theory. *American Psychologist, 44,* 1175–1184.

BANDURA, A. (1990a). Perceived self-efficacy in the exercise of control over AIDS infection. *Evaluation and Program Planning, 13,* 9–17.

BANDURA, A. (1990b). Mechanisms of moral disengagement. In W. Reich (Ed.), *Origins of terrorism: Psychologies, ideologies, states of mind* (pp. 161–191). New York: Cambridge University Press.

BANDURA, A. (1991). Social cognitive theory of self-regulation. *Organizational Behavior and Human Decision Processes, 50,* 248–287.

BANDURA, A. (Ed.). (1995). *Self-efficacy in changing societies.* New York: Cambridge University Press.

BANDURA, A. (1997). *Self-efficacy: The exercise of control.* New York: W. H. Freeman.

BANDURA, A., ADAMS, N. E., & BEYER, J. (1977). Cognition processes mediating behavioral change. *Journal of Personality and Social Psychology, 35,* 125–139.

BANDURA, A., ADAMS, N. E., HARDY, A. B., & HOWELLS, G. N. (1980). Tests of the generality of self-efficacy theory. *Cognitive Therapy and Research, 4,* 39–66.

BANDURA, A., BLANCHARD, E. B., & RITTER, B. (1969). Relative efficacy of desensitization and modeling approaches for inducing behavioral, affective, and attitudinal changes. *Journal of Personality and Social Psychology, 13,* 173–199.

BANDURA, A., CIOFFI, D., TAYLOR, C. B., BROUILLARD, M. E. (1988). Perceived self-efficacy in coping with cognitive stressors and opioid activation. *Journal of Personality and Social Psychology 55,* 479–488.

BANDURA, A., & JOURDEN, F. J. (1991). Self-regulatory mechanisms governing the impact of social comparison on complex decision making. *Journal of Personality and Social Psychology, 60,* 941–951.

BANDURA, A., & KUPERS, C. J. (1964). The transmission of patterns of self-reinforcement through modeling. *Journal of Abnormal and Social Psychology, 69,* 1–9.

BANDURA, A., & MISCHEL, W. (1965). Modification of self-imposed delay of reward through exposure to live and symbolic models. *Journal of Personality and Social Psychology, 2,* 698–705.

BANDURA, A., O'LEARY, A., TAYLOR, C. B., GAUTHIER, J., & GOSSARD, D. (1987). Perceived self-efficacy and pain control: Opioid and nonopioid mechanisms. *Journal of Personality and Social Psychology, 53,* 563–571.

BANDURA, A., REESE, L., & ADAMS, N. E. (1982). Microanalysis of action and fear arousal as a function of differential levels of perceived self-efficacy. *Journal of Personality and Social Psychology, 43,* 5–21.

BANDURA, A., & ROSENTHAL, T. L. (1966). Vicarious classical conditioning as a function of arousal level. *Journal of Personality and Social Psychology, 3,* 54–62.

BANDURA, A., ROSS, D., & ROSS, S. A. (1963). A comparative test of the status envy, social power, and secondary reinforcement theories of identificatory learning. *Journal of Abnormal and Social Psychology, 67,* 527–534.

BANDURA, A., TAYLOR, C. B., WILLIAMS, S. L., MEFFORD, I. N., & BARCHAS, J. D. (1985). Catecholamine secretion as a function of perceived coping self-efficacy. *Journal of Consulting and Clinical Psychology, 53,* 406–414.

BANDURA, A., & WALTERS, R. H. (1959). *Adolescent aggression.* New York: Ronald Press.

BANDURA, A., & WALTERS, R. H. (1963). *Social learning and personality development.* New York: Holt, Rinehart and Winston.

BANDURA, A., & WOOD, R. (1989). Effect of perceived controllability and performance standards on self-regulation of complex decision making. *Journal of Personality and Social Psychology, 56,* 805–814.

BANNISTER, D., & FRANSELLA, F. (1971). *Inquiring man: The theory of personal constructs.* New York: Penguin.

BANNISTER, D., & MAIR, J. M. M. (1968). *The evaluation of personal constructs.* New York: Academic Press.

BARASH, D. P. (1979). *The whisperings within: Evolution and the origin of human nature.* New York: Penguin.

BARASH, D. P. (1982). *Sociobiology and behavior* (2nd ed.). New York: Elsevier.

BARASH, D. P. (1986). *The hare and the tortoise: Culture, biology, and human nature.* New York: Penguin.

BARASH, D. P. (1987). *The arms race and nuclear war.* Belmont, CA: Wadsworth.

BARASH, D. P., & LIPTON, J. E. (1982). *Stop nuclear war! A handbook.* New York: Grove Press.

BARASH, D. P., & LIPTON, J. E. (1985). *The caveman and the bomb: Human nature, evolution, and nuclear war.* New York: McGraw-Hill.

BARTOL, C. R., & COSTELLO, N. (1976). Extraversion as a function of temporal duration of electrical shock: An exploratory study. *Perceptual and Motor Skills, 42,* 1174.

BAUDOUIN, R., & UHL, N. (1998). The relationship between Jungian type, academic and social integration, and persistence during the freshman year. *Journal of Psychological Type, 45,* 29–35.

BEATY, J. C. J. R., CLEVELAND, J. N., & MURPHY, K. R. (2001). The relation between personality and contextual performance in "strong" versus "weak" situations. *Human Performance, 14*(2), 125–148.

Becker, W., Madsen, C., Arnold, C., & Thomas, D. (1967). The contingent use of teacher attention and praising in reducing classroom behavior problems. *Journal of Special Education, 1,* 287–307.

Belmont, L., & Marolla, F. A. (1973). Birth order, family size, and intelligence. *Science, 182,* 1096–1101.

Bem, D. J., & Allen, A. (1974). On predicting some of the people some of the time: The search for cross-situational consistencies in behavior. *Psychological Review, 81,* 506–520.

Benitez, M. H., Ferrero, R. V., & Marco R. G. (1997). The personality factors and suicide attempts: A clinical psychometrical study. *Anales de Psiquiatrira, 13*(4), 149154.

Berger, S. M. (1962). Conditioning through vicarious instigation. *Psychological Review, 69,* 450–466.

Bergin, A. E., Masters, K. S., & Richards, P. S. (1987). Religiousness and mental health reconsidered: A study of an intrinsically religious sample. *Journal of Counseling Psychology, 34,* 197–204.

Berkowitz, L. (1989). Frustration-aggression hypothesis: An examination and reformulation. *Psychological Bulletin, 106,* 59–73.

Bernstein, D. M., & Belicki, K. (1996). On the psychometric properties of retrospective dream content questionnaires. *Imagination, Cognition, and Personality, 15,* 351364.

Bernstein, D. M., & Roberts, B. (1995). Assessing dreams through self-report questionnaires: Relations with past research and personality. *Dreaming, 5,* 13-27.

Betz, N. E., & Hackett, G. (1981). The relationship of career–related self-efficacy expectations to perceived career options in women and men. *Journal of Counseling Psychology, 28,* 399–410.

Bieri, J. (1955). Cognitive complexity-simplicity and predictive behavior. *Journal of Abnormal and Social Psychology, 51,* 61–66.

Black, M. E. A., Stein, K. F., & Loveland-Cherry, C. J. (2001). Older women and mammography screening behavior: Do possible selves contribute? *Health Education & Behavior. Special Issue, 28,* 200–216.

Blanchard, W. H. (1969). Psychodynamic aspects of the peak experience. *Psychoanalytic Review, 46,* 87–112.

Blatny, M., & Cermak, I. (1995). Personality indicators of aggression amd moral disengagement. *Studia Psychologica, 37*(3), 199–201.

Blechman, E. A., Taylor, C. J., & Schrader, S. M. (1981). Family problem solving versus home notes as early intervention with high-risk children. *Journal of Consulting and Clinical Psychology, 49,* 919–926.

Block, J. (1995). A contrarian view of the five-factor approach to personality description. *Psychological Bulletin, 117,* 187–215.

Bloomingdale, J. R., & Reinert, D. F. (2000). Spiritual experience, religous orientation and self-reported behavior. *International Journal for the Psychology of Religion, 10*(3), 173-180.

Blum, G. (1962). The Blacky test—sections II, IV, and VII. In R. Birney & R. Teevan (Eds.), *Measuring human motivation* (pp. 119–144). New York: Van Nostrand.

Bodden, J. C. (1970). Cognitive complexity as a factor in appropriate vocational choice. *Journal of Counseling Psychology, 17,* 364–368.

Bonett, R. M. (1994). Marital status and sex: Impact on career self-efficacy. *Journal of Counseling and Development, 73,* 187–190.

Bordages, J. W. (1989). Self-actualization and personal autonomy. *Psychological Reports, 64,* 1263–1266.

Bores-Rangel, E., Church, A. T., Szendre, D., & Reeves, C. (1990). Self-efficacy in relation to occupational consideration and academic performance in high school equivalency students. *Journal of Counseling Psychology, 37,* 407–418.

Borys, S., & Perlman, D. (1985). Gender differences in loneliness. *Personality and Social Psychology Bulletin, 11,* 63–74.

Boslough, J. (1972, December 24). Reformatory's incentive plan works. *Rocky Mountain News,* p. 13.

Bottome, P. (1957). *Alfred Adler: A portrait from life.* New York: Vanguard.

Bouchard, T. J., Jr. (1984). Twins reared together and apart: What they tell us about human diversity. In S. W. Fox (Ed.), *Individuality and determinism* (pp. 147–184). New York: Plenum Press.

Boudin, H. M. (1972). Contingency contracting as a therapeutic tool in the deceleration of amphetamine use. *Behavior Therapy, 3,* 604–608.

Bourne, E. (1978). The state of research on ego identity: A review and appraisal: I. *Journal of Youth and Adolescence, 7,* 223–251.

Bowers, K. S. (1973). Situationism in psychology: An analysis and a critique. *Psychological Review, 80,* 307–336.

Bradley, C. L., & Marcia, J. E. (1998). Generativity-stagnation: A five-category model. *Journal of Personality, 66,* 39–64.

Breland, H. M. (1974). Birth order, family constellation, and verbal achievement. *Child Development, 45,* 1011–1019.

Bringmann, M. W. (1992). Computer-based methods for the analysis and interpretation of personal construct systems. In R. A. Neimeyer & G. J. Neimeyer (Eds.), *Advances in personal construct psychology,* (pp. 57–90). Greenwich, CT: JAI Press.

BRONSON, W. C. (1966). Central orientations: A study of behavior organization from childhood to adolescence. *Child Development, 37,* 125–155.

BRONSON, W. C. (1967). Adult derivatives of emotional experiences and reactivity-control: Developmental continuities from childhood to adulthood. *Child Development, 38,* 801–878.

BRUNER, J. S. (1956). You are your constructs. *Contemporary Psychology, 1,* 355–357.

BUCKMASTER, L. R., & DAVIS, G. A. (1985). ROSE: A measure of self-actualization and its relationship to creativity. *Journal of Creative Behavior, 19,* 30–37.

BUGENTAL, J. F. T. (1996). Rollo May (1909–1994). *American Psychologist, 51,* 418–419.

BUSS, D. M. (1987). Sex differences in human mate selection criteria: An evolutionary perspective. In C. Crawford, M. Smith, & D. Krebs (Eds.), *Sociobiology and psychology: Ideas, issues, and applications* (pp. 335–351). Hillsdale, NJ: Erlbaum.

BUTLER, J. M., & HAIGH, G. V. (1954). Changes in the relation between self-concepts and ideal concepts consequent upon client-centered counseling. In C. R. Rogers & R. F. Dymond (Eds.), *Psychotherapy and personality change: Co-ordinated studies in the client-centered approach.* Chicago: University of Chicago Press.

BUTLER, P., CULP, A. M., HURLBUT, N. L., & JAMBUNATHAN, S. (1997). Adolescent mothers' self-esteem and role identity and their relationship to parenting skills knowledge. *Adolescence, 32*(127), 639-654.

BUTTLE, F. (1989). The social construction of needs. *Psychology and Marketing, 6,* 199–207.

CABRE, L. J. M., & CANDIOTI, A. G. (1996). The Brunhilde fantasy: Freud's countertransference in the analysis of Elma. *International Forum of Psychoanalysis, 5(3),* 191–202.

CAMPBELL, B. A., & CAMPBELL, E. H. (2000). Retention and extinction of learned fear in infant and adult rats. In C. Collier-Rovee & L. P. Lissitt (Eds.), *Progress in infancy research* (pp.1–15). Mahwah, NJ: Lawrence Erlbaum.

CANTOR, N., & MISCHEL, W. (1979). Prototypes in person perception. In L. Berkowitz (Ed.), *Advances in experimental social psychology* (Vol. 12, pp. 3–52). New York: Academic Press.

CANTOR, N. & ZIRKEL, S. (1990). Personality, cognition, and purposive behavior. In L. A. Pervin (Ed.), *Handbook of personality: Theory and research* (pp. 135–164). New York: Guilford Press.

CAPLAN, P. J. (1979). Erikson's concept of inner space: A data-based reevaluation. *American Journal of Orthopsychiatry, 49,* 100–108.

CARLSON, M., & MULAIK, S. A. (1993). Trait ratings from descriptions of behavior as mediated by components of meaning. *Multivariate Behavioral Research, 26,* 111–159.

CARTWRIGHT, D. S. (1956). Self-consistency as a factor affecting immediate recall. *Journal of Abnormal and Social Psychology, 52,* 212–218.

CATTELL, R. B. (1943). The description of personality: Basic traits resolved into clusters. *Journal of Personality and Social Psychology, 38,* 476–506.

CATTELL, R. B. (1944). *The culture free test of intelligence.* Champaign, IL: Institute for Personality and Ability Testing.

CATTELL, R. B. (1950). *Personality: A systematic, theoretical, and factual study.* New York: McGraw-Hill.

CATTELL, R. B. (1957). *Personality and motivation structure and measurement.* Yonkers, NY: World.

CATTELL, R. B. (1965). *The scientific analysis of personality.* Baltimore: Penguin.

CATTELL, R. B. (1972). *A new morality from science: Beyondism.* New York: Pergamon.

CATTELL, R. B. (1973). *Personality and mood by questionnaire.* San Francisco: Jossey-Bass.

CATTELL, R. B. (1975). Clinical analysis questionnaire (CAQ). Champaign, IL: Institute for Personality and Ability Testing.

CATTELL, R. B. (1979, 1980). *Personality and learning theory* (Vols. 1 & 2). New York: Springer.

CATTELL, R. B. (1987). *Beyondism: Religion from science.* New York: Praeger.

CATTELL, R. B., BRUEL, H., & HARTMAN, H. P. (1952). An attempt at a more refined definition of the cultural dimensions of syntality in modern nations. *American Sociological Review, 17,* 408–421.

CATTELL, R. B., EBER, H. W., & TATSUOKA, M. M. (1970). *Handbook for the 16 PF questionnaire.* Champaign, IL: Institute for Personality and Ability Testing.

CATTELL, R. B., & NESSELROADE, J. R. (1967). Likeness and completeness theories examined by sixteen personality factors measured by stably and unstably married couples. *Journal of Personality and Social Psychology, 7,* 351–361.

CATTELL, R. B., SAUNDERS, D. R., & STICE, G. F. (1950). *The 16 personality factor questionnaire.* Champaign, IL: Institute for Personality and Ability Testing.

CATTELL, R. B., SCHUERGER, J. M., & KLEIN, T. W. (1982). Heritabilities of ego strength (factor C), superego strength (factor G), and self-sentiment (factor Q_3) by multiple abstract variance analysis. *Journal of Clinical Psychology, 38,* 769–779.

CHAMOVE, A. S., EYSENCK, H. J., & HARLOW, H. F. (1972). Personality in monkeys: Factor analysis of rhesus social behaviour. *Quarterly Journal of Experimental Psychology, 24,* 496–504.

CHAPMAN, L. J., & CHAPMAN, J. P. (1969). Illusory correlation as an obstacle to the use of valid psychodiagnostic signs. *Journal of Abnormal Psychology, 74,* 271–280.

CHODORKOFF, B. (1954). Self-perception, perceptual defense, and adjustment. *Journal of Abnormal and Social Psychology, 49,* 508–512.

CHOMSKY, N. A. (1959). A review of verbal behavior by B. F. Skinner. *Language, 35,* 26–58.

CIACCIO, N. (1971). A test of Erikson's theory of ego epigenesis. *Developmental Psychology, 4,* 306–311.

CICCHETTI, D. V., LAOR, N., & WOLMER, L. (2001). The comprehensive assessment of defense style: Measuring defense mechanisms in children and adolescence. *Journal of Nervous & Mental Disease, 74*(2), 183–195.

CIOFFI, F. (1974). Was Freud a liar? *The Listener, 91,* 172–174.

CLARIDGE, G. S., DONALD, J. R., & BIRCHALL, P. (1981). Drug tolerance and personality: Some implications for Eysenck's theory. *Personality and Individual Differences, 2,* 153–166.

CLARIDGE, G. S., & ROSS, E. (1973). Sedative drug tolerance in twins. In G. S. Claridge, S. Carter, & W. I. Hume (Eds.), *Personality differences and biological variations.* Oxford: Pergamon.

COAN, R. W. (1966). Child personality and developmental psychology. In R. B. Cattell (Ed.), *Handbook of multivariate experimental psychology* (pp. 732–752). Chicago: Rand McNally.

COILE, D. C., & MILLER, N. E. (1984). How radical animal activists try to mislead humane people. *American Psychologist, 39,* 700–701.

COLLINS, K. M. T., & ONWUEGBUZIE, A. J. (2001). Writing apprehension and academic procrastination among graduate students. *Perceptual & Motor Skills, 92*(2), 560-562.

CONLEY, J. J. (1984). The hierarchy of consistency: A review and model of longitudinal findings on adult individual differences in intelligence, personality and self-opinion. *Personality and Individual Differences, 5,* 11–26.

CORDES, C. (1984). Easing toward perfection at Twin Oaks. *APA Monitor, 15* (11), 1, 30–31.

CORENBLUM, B., & STEPHAN, W. G. (2001). White fears and Native apprehensions: An integrated threat theory approach to intergroup attitudes. *Canadian Journal of Behavioural Science, 33,* 251–268.

COSTA, P. T., JR., & MCCRAE, R. R. (1980). Still stable after all these years: Personality as a key to some issues in adulthood and old age. In P. B. Baltes & O. G. Brim, Jr. (Eds.), *Life-span development and behavior* (Vol. 3). (pp. 65–102). New York: Academic Press.

COSTA, P. T., JR., & MCCRAE, R. R. (1985). *The NEO personality inventory manual.* Odessa, FL: Psychological Assessment Resources.

COTE, J. E., & LEVINE, C. (1983). Marcia and Erikson: The relationships among ego identity status, neuroticism, dogmatism, and purpose in life. *Journal of Youth and Adolescence, 12,* 43–53.

CRAIG, K. D., & WEINSTEIN, M. S. (1965). Conditioning vicarious affective arousal. *Psychological Reports, 17,* 955–963.

CRAIGHEAD, W. E., KAZDIN, A. E., & MAHONEY, M. J. (1976). *Behavior modification: Principles, issues, and applications.* Boston: Houghton Mifflin.

CRAMER, K. M., NICKELS, J. B., & GURAL, D. M. (1997). Uncertainty of outcomes, prediction of failure, and lack of control as factors explaining perceived helplessness. *Journal of Social Behaviour and Personality, 12,* 611–630.

CRAMER, P. (2001). Identification and its relation to identity development. *Journal of Personality, 69*(5), 667–688.

CRAMER, P. (2001). The unconscious status of defense mechanisms. *American Psychologist, 56*(9), 762–763.

CRANDALL, J. E. (1980). Adler's concept of social interest: Theory, measurement, and implications for adjustment. *Journal of Personality and Social Psychology, 39,* 481–495.

CRANDALL, J. E. (1981). *Theory and measurement of social interest: Empirical tests of Alfred Adler's concept.* New York: Columbia University Press.

CRANDALL, J. E. (1982). Social interest, extreme response style, and implications for adjustment. *Journal of Research in Personality, 16,* 82–89.

CRAWFORD, C. (1987). Sociobiology: Of what value to psychology? In C. Crawford, M. Smith, & D. Krebs (Eds.), *Sociobiology and psychology: Ideas, issues, and applications* (pp. 3–30). Hillsdale, NJ: Erlbaum.

CRAWFORD, C., SMITH, M., & KREBS, D. (Eds.). (1987). *Sociobiology and psychology: Ideas, issues, and applications.* Hillsdale, NJ: Erlbaum.

CROCKER, P. R. E., & ISAAK, K. (1997). Coping during competitions and training sessions: Are youth swimmers consistent? *International Journal of Sport Psychology, 28,* 355–369.

CROSS, H. J., & ALLEN, J. G. (1970). Ego identity status, adjustment, and academic achievement. *Journal of Consulting and Clinical Psychology, 34,* 288.

CRUMBAUGH, J. C. (1968). Cross-validation of Purpose-in-Life Test based on Frankl's concept. *Journal of Individual Psychology, 24,* 74–81.

CUTRONA, C. E. (1982). Transitions to college: Loneliness and the process of social adjustment. In L. A. Peplau & D. Perlman (Eds.), *Loneliness: A sourcebook of current theory, research and therapy,* (pp. 291-309). New York: Wiley.

DALY, M. (1989). Parent-offspring conflict and violence in evolutionary perspective. In R. W. Bell & N. J. Bell (Eds.), *Sociobiology and the social sciences* (pp. 25–43). Lubbock, TX: Texas Tech University Press.

DANDES, M. (1966). Psychological health and teaching effectiveness. *Journal of Teaching Education, 17,* 301–306.

DANIELS, M. (1988). The myth of self-actualization. *Journal of Humanistic Psychology, 28,* 7–38.

DARWIN, C. (1859). *The origin of species: By means of natural selection or the preservation of favoured races in the struggle for life.* New York: New American Library.

DAS, A. K. (1989). Beyond self-actualization. *International Journal for the Advancement of Counseling, 12,* 13–27.

DAVIS, S., THOMAS R., & WEAVER, M. (1982). Psychology's contemporary and all-time notables: Student, faculty, and chairperson viewpoints. *Bulletin of the Psychonomic Society, 20,* 3–6.

DAVIS-BERMAN, J. (1990). Physical self-efficacy, perceived physical status, and depressive symptomatology in older adults. *Journal of Psychology, 124,* 207–215.

DAVIS-SHARTS, J. (1986). An empirical test of Maslow's theory of need hierarchy using hologeistic comparison by statistical sampling. *Advances in Nursing Science, 9,* 58–72.

DAWES, A. (1985). Drug dependence. In E. Button (Ed.), *Personal construct theory and mental health: Theory, research, and practice.* Beckenham, England: Croom Helm.

DAWSON, K. A., & BRAWLEY, L. R. (2000). Examining the relationship between exercise goals, self-efficacy, and overt behavior with beginning exercisers. *Journal of Applied Social Psychology. Special Issue, 30,* 315–329.

DEANGELIS, T. (1994, July). Jung's theories keep pace and remain popular. *APA Monitor, 25,* 41.

DECARVALHO, R. J. (1990a). A history of the "third force" in psychology. *Journal of Humanistic Psychology, 30,* 22–44.

DECARVALHO, R. J. (1990b). The growth hypothesis and self-actualization: An existential alternative. *Humanistic Psychologist, 18,* 252–258.

DECARVALHO, R. J. (1991). Gordon Allport and humanistic psychology. *Journal of Humanistic Psychology, 31,* 8–13.

DE CATANZARO, D. (1987). Evolutionary pressures and limitations to self-preservation. In C. Crawford, M. Smith, & D. Krebs (Eds.), *Sociobiology and psychology: Ideas, issues, and applications* (pp. 311–333). Hillsdale, NJ: Erlbaum.

DE SWART, J. (2001). The biological conditions of consciousness: A review of Edelman and Tonini's *A Universe of Consciousness. Journal of Consciousness Studies, 8*(11), 91-96.

DEAL, J. E. (1996). Marital conflict and differential treatment of siblings. *Family Process, 35*(3), 333-346.

DEANNA, S., EVANS, N. J., & SALTER, D. W. (1997). Test-retest of the Myers-Briggs Type Indicator: An examination of dominant functioning. *Educational & Psychological Measurement, 57(4),* 590–597.

DIAMOND, M. J., & SHAPIRO, J. L. (1973). Changes in locus of control as a function of encounter group experiences: A study and replication. *Journal of Abnormal Psychology, 82,* 514–518.

DIGMAN, J. M. (1989). Five robust trait dimensions: Development, stability, and utility. *Journal of Personality, 57,* 195–214.

DIGMAN, J. M. (1996). The curious history of the five-factor model. In J. S. Wiggins (Ed.), *The five-factor model of personality.* New York: The Guilford Press.

DIGMAN, J., & TAKEMOTO-CHOCK, N. (1981). Factors in the natural language of personality: Reanalysis, comparison, and interpretation of six major studies. *Multivariate Behavioral Research, 16,* 149–170.

DIXON, T. M., & BAUMEISTER, R. F. (1991). Escaping the self: The moderating effect of self-complexity. *Personality and Social Psychology Bulletin, 17,* 363–368.

DOBSON, K. S., & BREITER, H. J. (1983). Cognitive assessment of depression: Reliability and validity of three measures. *Journal of Abnormal Psychology, 92,* 107–109.

DOLLARD, J. (1937). *Caste and class in a southern town.* New Haven: Yale University Press.

DOLLARD, J., DOOB, L. W., MILLER, N. E., MOWRER, O. H., & SEARS, R. R. (1939). *Frustration and aggression.* New Haven: YaleUniversity Press.

DOLLARD, J., & MILLER, N. E. (1950). *Personality and psychotherapy: An analysis in terms of learning, thinking and culture.* New York: McGraw-Hill.

DONAHUE, M. J. (1985). Intrinsic and extrinsic religiousness: Review and meta-analysis. *Journal of Personality and Social Psychology, 48,* 400–419.

DOSAMANTES-ALPERSON, E., & MERRILL, N. (1980). Growth effects of experiential movement psychotherapy. *Psychotherapy: Theory, research, and practice, 17,* 63–68.

DOUCET, C., & STELMACK, R. M. (1994). Movement time differentiates extraverts from introverts. *Personality and Individual Differences, 23,* 775–786.

DOUCET, C., & STELMACK, R. M. (2000). An event-related potential analysis of extraversion and individual differences in cognitive processing speed and response execution. *Journal of Personality and Social Psychology, 78,* 956–964.

DRAGUNS, J. G., KRYLOVA, A. V., MARTIN, T. A., ORYOL, V. E., & RUKAVISHNIKOV, A. A. (2000). Personality characteristics of the Nentsy in the Russian Arctic: A comparison with ethnic Russians by means of NEO-PR-R and POI. *American Behavioral Scientist, 44*(1), 126–140.

DRAYCOTT, S G., & KLINE, P. (1995). The big three or the big five—the EPQ-R vs the NEO-PI: A research note, replication, and elaboration. *Personality and Individual Differences, 18* (6) 801–804.

DREIKURS, R. (1957). *Psychology in the classroom.* New York: Harper & Row.

DREIKURS, R. (with Vicki Soltz). (1964). *Children: The challenge.* New York: Duell, Sloan and Pearce.

DU CAJU, M., FRAILE, J. C., GONZALEZ DE CHAVEZ, M., & GUTIERREZ, M. (2000). Comparative study of the therapeutic factors of group therapy in schizophrenic inpatients and outpatients. *Group Analysis, 33*(2), 251–264.

DUCK, S. W. (1979). The personal and interpersonal in construct theory: Social and individual aspects of relationships. In P. Stringer & D. Bannister (Eds.), *Constructs of sociality and individuality* (pp. 279–297). London: Academic Press.

DUFTON, B. D., & PERLMAN, D. (1986). Loneliness and religiosity: In the world but not of it. *Journal of Psychology and Theology, 14,* 135–145.

DUNN, J., & PLOMIN, R. (1990). *Separate lives: Why siblings are so different.* New York: Basic Books.

DUNNETTE, M. D. (1969). People feeling: Joy, more joy, and the "slough of despond." *Journal of Applied Behavioral Science, 5,* 25–44.

DWYER, A. L., & CUMMINGS, A. L. (2001). Stress, self-efficacy, social support, and coping strategies in university students. *Canadian Journal of Counselling. Special Issue, 35,* 208–220.

ECKSTEIN, D. (2000). Empirical studies indicating significant birth-order-related personality differences. *Journal of Individual Psychology, 6*(4), 481–494.

EIDELSON, R. J., & EPSTEIN, N. (1982). Cognition and relationship maladjustment: Development of a measure of dysfunctional relationship beliefs. *Journal of Consulting and Clinical Psychology, 50,* 715–720.

EISSLER, K. R. (2001). *Freud and seduction theory: A brief love affair.* Madison, CT, US: International Universities Press.

ELLENBERGER, H. (1970). *The discovery of the unconscious.* New York: Basic Books.

ELLIOTT, C. D. (1971). Noise tolerance and extraversion in children. *British Journal of Psychology, 62,* 375–380.

ELLIS, A. (1970). Tribute to Alfred Adler. *Journal of Individual Psychology, 26,* 11–12.

ELLIS, A., & GREIGER, R. (1977). *Handbook of rational emotive therapy.* New York: Julian Press.

ELMS, A. C. (1972). Allport, Freud, and the clean little boy. *The Psychoanalytic Review, 59,* 627–632.

ELMS, A. C. (1981). Skinner's dark year and *Walden Two. American Psychologist, 36,* 470–479.

ENDLER, N. S., SPEER, R. L., JOHNSON, J. M., & FLETT, G. L. (2001). General self-efficacy and control in relation to anxiety and cognitive performance. *Current Psychology: Developmental, Learning, Personality, Social. Special Issue, 20,* 36–52.

ENGELHARD, G. (1990). Gender differences in performance on mathematics items: Evidence from the United States and Thailand. *Contemporary Educational Psychology, 15,* 13–26.

EPTING, F. R., & LEITNER, L. M. (1992). Humanistic psychology and personal construct theory. *Humanistic Psychologist, 20,* 243–259.

ERIKSON, E. H. (1959). *Identity and the life cycle. Selected papers.* New York: International Universities Press.

ERIKSON, E. H. (1964). *Insight and responsibility.* New York: Norton.

ERIKSON, E. H. (1968). *Identity, youth, and crisis.* New York: Norton.

ERIKSON, E. H. (1969). *Gandhi's truth: On the origins of militant nonviolence.* New York: Norton.

ERIKSON, E. H. (1975a). Once more the inner space. In E. H. Erikson (Ed.), *Life history and the historical moment.* New York: Norton.

ERIKSON, E. H. (1975b). *Life history and the historical moment.* New York: Norton.

ERIKSON, E. H. (1977). *Toys and reasons: Stages in the ritualization of experience.* New York: Norton.

ERIKSON, E. H. (1985). *Childhood and society.* New York: Norton. (Original work published 1950.)

ERNST, C., & ANGST, J. (1983). *Birth order: Its influence on personality.* New York: Springer-Verlag.

ESTERSON, A. (1993). *Seductive mirage: An exploration of the work of Sigmund Freud.* La Salle, IL: Open Court.

ESTERSON, A. (1998). Jeffrey Masson and Freud's seduction theory: A new fable based on old myths. *History of the Human Sciences, 11,* 1–21.

EVANS, R. I. (1968). *B. F. Skinner: The man and his ideas.* New York: Dutton.

EVANS, R. I. (1976). *The making of psychology: Discussions with creative contributors.* New York: Knopf.

EVANS, R. I. (1981). *Dialogue with B. F. Skinner*. New York: Praeger.

EVANS, R. I. (1989). *Albert Bandura: The man and his ideas—A dialogue*. New York: Praeger.

EYSENCK, H. J. (1947). *Dimensions of personality*. London: Routledge & Kegan Paul.

EYSENCK, H. J. (1952). *The scientific study of personality*. London: Routledge & Kegan Paul.

EYSENCK, H. J. (1957). *The dynamics of anxiety and hysteria*. London: Routledge & Kegan Paul.

EYSENCK, H. J. (1965). Extraversion and the acquisition of eyeblink and GSR conditioned responses. *Psychological Bulletin, 63,* 258–279.

EYSENCK, H. J. (1967). *The biological basis of personality*. Springfield, IL: Charles C.Thomas.

EYSENCK, H. J. (1970). *The structure of human personality* (3rd ed.). London: Methuen.

EYSENCK, H. J. (1972). *Psychology is about people*. New York: Penguin Books.

EYSENCK, H. J. (1976). *Sex and personality*. London: Open Books.

EYSENCK, H. J. (1977). *Crime and personality* (3rd ed.). London: Routledge & Kegan Paul.

EYSENCK, H. J. (1980). Autobiograpical essay. In G. Lindzey (Ed.), *A history of psychology in autobiography* (Vol. VII). San Francisco: W. H. Freeman and Company.

EYSENCK, H. J. (1990a). Biological dimensions of personality. In L. A. Pervin (Ed.), *Handbook of personality: Theory and research*. New York: Guilford Press.

EYSENCK, H. J. (1990b). *Rebel with a cause*. London: W. H. Allen and Company.

EYSENCK, H. J. (1991). Dimensions of personality: 16, 5, or 3?—Criteria for a taxonomic paradigm. *Personality and Individual Differences, 12* (8) 773–790.

EYSENCK, H. J., & EYSENCK, M. W. (1985). *Personality and individual differences*. New York: Plenum Press.

EYSENCK, H. J., & LEVEY, A. (1972). Conditioning, introversion-extraversion and the strength of the nervous system. In V. D. Neblitsyn & J. A. Gray (Eds.), *Biological basis of individual behaviour*. London: Academic Press.

FABER, M. D. (1970). Allport's visit with Freud. *The Psychoanalytic Review, 57,* 60–64.

FALBO, T. (1981). Relationships between birth category, achievement, and interpersonal orientation. *Journal of Personality and Social Psychology, 41,* 121–131.

False Memory Syndrome Foundation (1992, November 5). Information needed in assessing allegations by adults of sex abuse in childhood. *False Memory Syndrome Foundation Newsletter*, p. 5.

FEIXAS, G., & VILLEGAS, M. (1991). Personal construct analysis of autobiographical texts: A method presentation and case illustration. *International Journal of Personal Construct Psychology, 4,* 51–83.

FERSTER, C. B., & SKINNER, B. F. (1957). *Schedules of reinforcement*. Englewood Cliffs, NJ: Prentice-Hall.

FIEBERT, M. S. (1997). In and out of Freud's shadow: A chronology of Adler's relationship with Freud. *Individual Psychology, 53,* 241–269.

FISHER, D. D. (1990). Emotional construing: A psycho-biological model. *International Journal of Personal Construct Psychology, 3,* 183–203.

FISHER, S., & GREENBERG, R. P. (1977). *The scientific credibility of Freud's theories and therapy*. New York: Basic.

FORD, K. M., & ADAMS-WEBBER, J. R. (1991). The structure of personal construct systems and the logic of confirmation. *International Journal of Personal Construct Psychology, 4,* 15–41.

FOREST, J. J. (1987). Effects on self-actualization of paperbacks about psychological self-help. *Psychological Reports, 60,* 1243–1246.

FOREST, J. J. (1988). Exploring more on the effects of psychological self-help paperbacks. *Psychological Reports, 63,* 891–894.

FOREST, J. J. (1991). Effects of attitudes and interests on personality change induced by psychological self-help books. *Psychological Reports, 68,* 587–592.

FOULDS, M. L. (1969). Self-actualization and the communication of facilitative conditions under counseling. *Journal of Counseling Psychology, 16,* 132–136.

FRANK, G. (2000). Transference revisited/transference revisioned. *Psychoanalysis & Contemporary Thought, 23*(4), 459-478.

FRANKL, V. E. (1970). Tribute to Alfred Adler. *Journal of Individual Psychology, 26,* 11–12, 146–147.

FRANKL, V. E. (1984). *Man's search for meaning* (Rev. ed.). New York: Washington Square Press. (Original work published as *Experiences in a concentration camp,* 1946.)

FRANKS, C. M., & LAVERTY, S. G. (1955). Sodium amytal and eyelid conditioning. *Journal of Mental Science, 101,* 654–663.

FRANKS, C. M., & TROUTON, D. (1958). Effects of amobarbital sodium and dexamphetamine sulfate on the conditioning of the eyeblink response. *Journal of Comparative and Physiological Psychology, 51,* 220–222.

FREDERIKSEN, L. W., JENKINS, J. O., & CARR, C. R. (1976). Indirect modification of adolescent drug abuse using contingency contracting. *Journal of Behavior Therapy and Experimental Psychiatry, 7,* 377–378.

FREUD, A. (1966). *The ego and the mechanisms of defense* (Rev. ed.). New York: International Universities Press. (Original work published 1936.)

FREUD, S. (1954). Project for a scientific psychology. In M. Bonaparte, A. Freud, & E. Kris (Eds.) and E. Mossbacher & J. Strachey (Trans.), *The origins of psychoanalysis, letters to Wilhelm Fliess, drafts, and notes: 1887–1902.* New York: Basic Books. (Original work published 1950.)

FREUD, S. (1955). A difficulty in the path of psychoanalysis. In J. Strachey (Ed. and Trans.), *The standard edition of the complete psychological works of Sigmund Freud* (Vol. 17, pp. 136–144). London: Hogarth Press. (Original work published 1917.)

FREUD, S. (1955). Beyond the pleasure principle. In J. Strachey (Ed. and Trans.), *The standard edition of the complete psychological works of Sigmund Freud* (Vol. 18). London: Hogarth Press. (Original work published 1920a.)

FREUD, S. (1955). A note on the prehistory of the technique of analysis. In J. Strachey (Ed. and Trans.), *The standard edition of the complete psychological works of Sigmund Freud* (Vol. 18). London: Hogarth Press. (Original work published 1920b.)

FREUD, S. (1958). Totem and taboo. In J. Strachey (Ed. and Trans.), *The standard edition of the complete psychological works of Sigmund Freud* (Vol. 13). London: Hogarth Press. (Original work published 1913.)

FREUD, S. (1960). Jokes and their relation to the unconscious. In J. Strachey (Ed. and Trans.), *The standard edition of the complete psychological works of Sigmund Freud* (Vol. 8). London: Hogarth Press. (Original work published 1905.)

FREUD, S. (1961). The ego and the id. In J. Strachey (Ed. and Trans.), *The standard edition of the complete psychological works of Sigmund Freud* (Vol. 19, pp. 3–59). London: Hogarth Press. (Original work published 1923.)

FREUD, S. (1961). *The future of an illusion.* New York: Norton. (Original work published 1927.)

FREUD, S. (1961). *Civilization and its discontents.* New York: Norton. (Original work published 1930.)

FREUD, S. (1964). *New introductory lectures on psychoanalysis.* New York: Norton. (Original work published 1933.)

FREUD, S. (1964). Moses and monotheism. In J. Strachey (Ed. and Trans.), *The standard edition of the complete psychological works of Sigmund Freud* (Vol. 23, pp. 3–137). London: Hogarth Press. (Original work published 1939.)

FREUD, S. (1965). *The interpretation of dreams.* New York: Norton. (Original work published 1900.)

FREUD, S. (1966). *On the history of the psycho-analytic movement.* New York: Norton. (Original work published 1914.)

FREUD, S. (1966). *Introductory lectures on psychoanalysis.* New York: Norton. (Original work published 1917.)

FREUD, S. (1966). *The complete introductory lectures on psychoanalysis* (J. Strachey, Ed. and Trans.). New York: Norton. (Original work published 1933.)

FRICK, W. B. (1989). *Humanistic psychology: Conversations with Abraham Maslow, Gardner Murphy, and Carl Rogers.* Bristol, IN: Wyndham Hall Press.

FROMM, E. (1941). *Escape from freedom.* New York: Henry Holt and Company.

FURNEAUX, W. D. (1957). Report to the Imperial College of Science and Technology. London.

GAGNON, J. H., & DAVISON, G. C. (1976). Asylums, the token economy and the merits of mental life. *Behavior Therapy, 7,* 528–534.

GALE, A. (1973). The psychophysiology of individual differences: Studies of extraversion and the EEG. In P. Kline (Ed.), *New approaches in psychological measurement.* New York: Wiley.

GALE, A. (1983). Electroencephalographic studies of extraversion-introversion: A case study in the psychophysiology of individual differences. *Personality and Individual Differences, 4,* 371–380.

GALTON, F. (1884). Measurement of character. *Fortnightly Review, 36,* 179–185.

GARCIA, M. E., SCHMITZ, J. M., & DOERFLER, L. A. (1990). A fine-grained analysis of the role of self-efficacy in self-initiated attempts to quit smoking. *Journal of Consulting and Clinical Psychology, 58,* 317–322.

GAY, P. (1988). *Freud: A life for our time.* New York: Norton.

GAYLOR, M., GIH, D., HARTUNG, P. J., & LEONG, F. T. L. (2001). Appraising birth order in career assessment: Linkages to Holland's and Super's models. *Journal of Career Assessment, 9*(1), 25–39.

GEEN, R. G., & QUANTY, M. B. (1977). The catharsis of aggression: An evaluation of a hypothesis. In L. Berkowitz (Ed.), *Advances in Experimental Social Psychology* (Vol. 10, pp. 1–37). New York: Academic Press.

GEEN, R. G., STONNER, D., & SHOPE, G. L. (1975). The facilitation of aggression by aggression: Evidence against the catharsis hypothesis. *Journal of Personality and Social Psychology, 31,* 721–726.

GEEN R. G., & THOMAS, S. L. (1986). The immediate effects of media violence on behavior. *Journal of Social Issues, 42* (3), 7–27.

GELFAND, T., & KERR, J. (Eds.). (1992). *Freud and the history of psychoanalysis.* Hillsdale, NJ: Analytic Press.

GENDLIN, E. T. (1988). Carl Rogers (1902–1987). *American Psychologist, 43,* 127–128.

GENDLIN, E. T., BEEBE, J., III, CASSENS, J., KLEIN, M., & OBERLANDER, M. (1968). Focusing ability in psychotherapy, personality, and creativity. In J. M. Schlien (Ed.), *Research in psychotherapy* (Vol. 3). Washington, DC: American Psychological Association.

GENDLIN, E. T., & TOMLINSON, T. M. (1967). The process conception and its measurement. In C. R. Rogers, E. T. Gendlin, D. J. Kiesler, & C. B. Truax (Eds.), *The psychotherapeutic relationship and its impact: A study of psychotherapy with schizophrenics.* Madison: University of Wisconsin Press.

GENIA, V. (1998). Religiousness and psychological adjustment in college students. *Journal of College Student Psychotherapy, 12*(3), 67–77.

GERSON, A. C., & PERLMAN, D. (1979). Lonelienss and expressive communication. *Journal of Abnormal Psychology, 88,* 258–261.

GEWIRTZ, J. L. (1971). Conditional responding as a paradigm for observational, imitative learning and vicarious imitative learning and vicarious reinforcement. In H. W. Reese (Ed.), *Advances in child development and behavior* (pp. 274–304). New York: Academic Press.

GIESE, H., & SCHMIDT, A. (1968). *Studenten Sexaulitat.* Hamburg: Rowohlt.

GIFFORD, R., & GALLAGHER, T. M. (1985). Sociability: Personality, social context, and physical setting. *Journal of Personality and Social Psychology, 48,* 1015–1023.

GIORGI, A. (1992). The idea of human science. *Humanistic Psychologist, 20,* 202–217.

GOLDBERG, L. R. (1981). Language and individual differences: The search for universals in personality lexicons. In L. Wheeler (Ed.), *Review of personality and social psychology* (pp. 141–165). Beverly Hills, CA: Sage.

GOLDBERG, L. R. (1990). An alternative "Description of personality": The big-five factor structure. *Journal of Personality and Social Psychology, 59,* 1216–1229.

GOLDBERG, L. R. (1993). The structure of phenotypic personality traits. *American Psychologist, 48,* 1, 26–34.

GOLDSTEIN, A. P., & MICHAELS, G. Y. (1985). *Empathy: Development training and consequences.* Hillsdale, NJ: Erlbaum.

GORDON, R. D. (1985). Dimensions of peak communication experiences: An exploratory study. *Psychological Reports, 57,* 824–826.

GOULD, D., HODGE, K., PETERSON, K., & GIANNINI, J. (1989). An exploratory examination of strategies used by elite coaches to enhance self-efficacy in athletes. *Journal of Sport and Exercise Psychology, 11,* 128–140.

GOULD, S. J. (1978). Sociobiology: The art of story telling. *New Scientist, 80,* 530–533.

GOULD, S. J., & LEWONTIN, R. C. (1979). The spandrels of San Marco and the Panglossian paradigm: A critique of the adaptationist programme. *Proceedings of the Royal Society of London, 205,* 581–598.

GRAHAM, W., & BALLOUN, J. (1973). An empirical test of Maslow's need hierarchy theory. *Journal of Humanistic Psychology, 13,* 97–108.

GREENSPOON, J. (1955). The reinforcing effect of two spoken sounds on the frequency of two responses. *American Journal of Psychology, 68,* 409–416.

GRIFFIN, P. W., & ROBAK, R. W. (2000). Purpose in life: What is its relationship to happiness, depression, and grieving? *North American Journal of Psychology, 2(*1*),* 113–119.

GRUENFELD, D. H. (1995). Status, ideology, and integrative complexity on the U.S. Supreme Court: Rethinking the politics of political decision making. *Journal of Personality and Social Psychology, 68,* 5–20.

GRUSEC, J., & MISCHEL, W. (1966). Model's characteristics as determinants of social learning. *Journal of Personality and Social Psychology, 4,* 211–215.

GUIGNON, C. (1984). Moods in Heidegger's being and time. In C. Calhoun & R. C. Solomon (Eds.), *What is an emotion? Classical readings in philosophical psychology* (pp. 230–243). New York: Oxford University Press.

GUPTA, B. S. (1973). The effects of stimulant and depressant drugs on verbal conditioning. *British Journal of Psychology, 64,* 553–557.

GURMAN, A. S. (1977). The patient's perception of therapeutic relationships. In A. S. Gurman & A. M. Razin (Eds.), *Effective psychotherapy: A handbook of research.* Oxford: Pergamon Press.

GUYDISH, J., JACKSON, T. T., MARKLEY, R. P., & ZELHART, P. F. (1985). George A. Kelly: Pioneer in rural school psychology. *Journal of School Psychology, 23,* 297–304.

HAFNER, J. F., FAKOURI, M. E., & LABRENTZ, H. L. (1982). First memories of "normal" and alcoholic individuals. *Individual Psychology, 38,* 238–244.

HALL, C. S., & LINDZEY, G. (1978). *Theories of personality* (3rd ed.). New York: Wiley.

HALL, C. S., & VAN DE CASTLE, R. L. (1965). An empirical investigation of the castration complex in dreams. *Journal of Personality, 33,* 20–29.

HALL, M. H. (1968, July). A conversation with Abraham Maslow. *Psychology Today,* pp. 35–37, 54–57.

HAMILTON, W. D. (1964). The genetical evolution of social behavior I & II. *Journal of Theoretical Biology, 7,* 1–52.

HANNAH, B. (1976). *Jung: His life and his work.* New York: Putnam's.

HARPER, R. G., WIENS, A. N., & MATARAZZO, J. D. (1978). *Nonverbal communication: The state of the art.* New York: Wiley.

HARREN, V. A., KASS, R. A., TINSLEY, H. E. A., & MORELAND, J. R. (1979). Influence of gender, sex-role attitudes, and cognitive complexity on gender-dominant career choices. *Journal of Counseling Psychology, 26,* 227–234.

HARRIS, J. A., VERNON, P. A., & JANG, K. L. (1998). A multivariate genetic analysis of correlations between intelligence and personality. *Developmental Neuropsychology, 14,* 127–142.

HARVEY, J. H. (1989). People's naive understandings of their close relationships: Attributional and personal construct perspectives. *International Journal of Personal Construct Psychology, 2,* 37–48.

HAWTON, H. (1948). *Philosophy for pleasure.* London: Watts.

HAYDEN, B., & NASBY, W. (1977). Interpersonal conceptual structures, predictive accuracy, and social adjustment of emotionally disturbed boys. *Journal of Abnormal Psychology, 86,* 315–320.

HAYDEN, T., & MISCHEL, W. (1976). Maintaining trait consistency in the resolution of behavioral inconsistency: The wolf in sheep's clothing? *Journal of Personality, 44,* 109–132.

HEILMAN, E. (1998). The struggle for self: Power and identity in adolescent girls. *Youth & Society, 30*(2), 182–208.

HEINE, S. J., & LEHMAN, D. R. (1997). The cultural construction of self-enhancement: An examination of group-serving biases. *Journal of Personality and Social Psychology, 72,* 1268–1283.

HEINE, S. J., & LEHMAN, D. R. (1999). Culture, self-discrepancies, and self-satisfaction. *Personality and Social Psychology Bulletin, 25,* 915–925.

HEINE, S. J., TAKATA, T., & LEHMAN, D. R. (2000). Beyond self-presentation: Evidence for self-criticism among Japanese. *Personality and Social Psychology Bulletin, 26,* 71–78.

HEPPNER, P. P., ROGERS, M. E., & LEE, L. A. (1984). Carl Rogers: Reflections on his life. *Journal of Counseling and Development, 63,* 14–20.

HERGENHAHN, B. R. (1974). *A self-directing introduction to psychological experimentation* (2nd ed.). Monterey, CA: Brooks/Cole.

HERGENHAHN, B. R. (1997). *An introduction to the history of psychology* (3rd ed.). Pacific Grove, CA: Brooks/Cole.

HERGENHAHN, B. R., & OLSON, M. H. (1997). *An introduction to theories of learning* (5th ed.). Upper Saddle River, NJ: Prentice-Hall.

HERMANS, H. J. M. (1988). On the integration of nomothetic and idiographic research in the study of personal meaning. *Journal of Personality, 56,* 785–812.

HEWITT, P. L., & FLETT, G. L. (1991). Perfectionism in the self and social contexts: Conceptualization, assessment, and association with psychopathology. *Journal of Personality and Social Psychology, 60,* 456–470.

HEWITT, P. L., FLETT, G. L., & EDIGER, E. (1996). Perfectionism and depression: Longitudinal assessment of a specific vulnerability hypothesis. *Journal of Abnormal Psychology, 105,* 276–280.

HIGGINS, N. C., & BHATT, G. (2001). Culture moderates the self-serving bias: Etic and emic features of causal attributions in India and in Canada. *Social Behaviour and Personality, 29,* 49–62.

HINDLEY, C. B., & GIUGANINO, B. M. (1982). Continuity of personality patterning from 3 to 15 years in a longitudinal sample. *Personality and Individual Differences, 3,* 127–144.

HOFFMAN, E. (1988). *The right to be human: A biography of Abraham Maslow.* Los Angeles: Jeremy P. Tarcher.

HOFFMAN, E. (1998). Peak experiences in childhood: An exploratory study. *Journal of Humanistic Psychology, 38*(1), 109–120.

HOLDEN, C. (1987, August). The genetics of personality. *Science, 237,* 598–601.

HOLDEN, G. W., MONCHER, M. S., SCHINKE, S. P., & BARKER, K. M. (1990). Self-efficacy of children and adolescents: A meta–analysis. *Psychological Reports, 66,* 1044–1046.

HOLDSTOCK, T. L., & ROGERS, C. R. (1977). Person-centered theory. In R. J. Corsini (Ed.), *Current personality theories.* Itasca, IL: Peacock.

HOMME, L. E., CSANYI, A., GONZALES, M., & RECHS, J. (1969). *How to use contingency contracting in the classroom.* Champaign, Il: Research Press.

HOOD, R. W., JR. (1970). Religious orientations and the report of religious experiences. *Journal for the Scientific Study of Religion, 9,* 285–291.

HOPKINS, R. J. (1995). Erik Homburger Erikson (1902–1994). *American Psychologist, 50,* 796–797.

HORLEY, J. (1991). Values and beliefs as personal constructs. *International Journal of Personal Construct Psychology, 4,* 1–14.

HORNEY, K. (1937). *The neurotic personality of our time.* New York: Norton.

HORNEY, K. (1939). *New ways in psychoanalysis.* New York: Norton.

HORNEY, K. (1942). *Self-analysis.* New York: Norton.

HORNEY, K. (1945). *Our inner conflicts.* New York: Norton.

HORNEY, K. (1950). *Neurosis and human growth: The struggle toward self-realization.* New York: Norton.

HORNEY, K. (1967). *Feminine psychology.* New York: Norton. (Original work published 1923–1937.)

HUESMANN, L. R., & MALAMUTH, N. M. (1986). Media violence and antisocial behavior. *Journal of Social Issues, 42(3),* 1–6.

HULL, C. L. (1943). *Principles of behavior.* New York: Appleton-Century-Crofts.

HUNDLEBY, J. D., PAWLIK, K., & CATTELL, R. B. (1965). *Personality factors in objective test devices: A critical integration of a quarter of a century's research.* San Diego: Knapp.

HUNSBERGER, B. (1985). Religion, age, life satisfaction, and perceived sources of religiousness: A study of older persons. *Journal of Gerontology, 40,* 615–620.

HUNSBERGER, B. (1992). Psychology of religion in Canada. *International Journal for the Psychology of Religion, 2,* 47–55.

HUNT, J. M. (1979). Psychological development: Early experience. *Annual Review of Psychology, 30,* 103–143.

HUNTLEY, C. W., & DAVIS, F. (1983). Undergraduate study of values scores as predictors of occupation twenty-five years later. *Journal of Personality and Social Psychology, 45,* 1148–1155.

ILARDI, R., & MAY, W. (1968). A reliability study of Shostrom's personal orientation inventory. *Journal of Humanistic Psychology, 8,* 68–72.

INGRAM, D. M. (2001). The Hofgeismar lectures: A contemporary overview of Horneyan psychoanalysis. *American Journal of Psychoanalysis, 60*(2), 113–141.

ISRAËLS, H., & SCHATZMAN, M. (1993). The seduction theory. *History of Psychiatry, 4,* 23–59.

JACOBSON, N. S. (1978). Specific and nonspecific factors in the effectiveness of a behavioral approach to the treatment of marital discord. *Journal of Consulting and Clinical Psychology, 46,* 442–452.

JAMES, W. (1956). The dilemma of determinism. In W. James, *The will to believe and other essays* (pp. 145–183). New York: Dover. (Original work published 1884.)

JANG, K. L., LIVESLEY, W. J., & VERNON, P. A. (1996). Heritability of the Big Five personality dimensions and their facets: A twin study. *Journal of Personality, 64,* 577–591.

JANKOWICZ, A. D. (1987). Whatever became of George Kelly? Applications and implications. *American Psychologist, 42,* 481–487.

JOHNSON, E. A. (1995). Self-deceptive responses to threat: Adaptive only in ambiguous contexts. *Journal of Personality, 63,* 759–791.

JOHNSON, E. A., VINCENT, N., & ROSS, L. (1997). Self-deception versus self-esteem in buffering the negative effects of failure. *Journal of Research in Personality, 31,* 385–405.

JONES, E. (1953,1955, 1957). *The life and work of Sigmund Freud* (Vols. 1–3). New York: Basic.

JONES, J. M., BENNET, S., OLMSTED, M. P., LAWSON, M. L., & RODIN, G. (2001). Disordered eating attitudes and behaviours in teenaged girls: A school-based study. *Canadian Medical Association Journal, 165,* 547–552.

JONES, J., EYSENCK, H. J., MARTIN, I., & LEVEY, A. B. (1981). Personality and the topography of the conditioned eyelid response. *Personality and Individual Differences, 2,* 61–84.

JOSEPHS, R., MARKUS, R., & TAFARODI, R. (1992). Gender and self-esteem. *Journal of Personality and Social Psychology, 63,* 391.

JOURARD, S. M. (1974). *Healthy personality: An approach from the viewpoint of humanistic psychology.* New York: Macmillan.

JUNG, C. (1921). *Psychologische typus.* Zurich: Rascher.

JUNG, C. G. (1928). *Contributions to analytical psychology.* New York: Harcourt Brace Jovanovich.

JUNG, C. G. (1953). The psychology of the unconscious. In *The collected works of C. G. Jung* (Vol. 7). Princeton, NJ: Princeton University Press. (Original work published 1912.)

JUNG, C. G. (1958). *The undiscovered self.* New York: Mentor.

JUNG, C. G. (1961). *Memories, dreams, reflections.* New York: Random House.

JUNG, C. G. (1961). The theory of psychoanalysis. In *The collected works of C. G. Jung* (Vol. 4). Princeton, NJ: Princeton University Press. (Original work published 1913.)

JUNG, C. G. (1961). Prefaces to "collected papers on analytical psychology." In *The collected works of C. G. Jung* (Vol. 4). Princeton, NJ: Princeton University Press. (Original work published 1916.)

JUNG, C. G. (1964). *Man and his symbols.* New York: Doubleday.

JUNG, C. G. (1966). Two essays on analytical psychology. In *The collected works of C. G. Jung* (Vol. 7). Princeton, NJ: Princeton University Press. (Original work published 1917.)

JUNG, C. G. (1968). *Analytical psychology: Its theory and practice.* (The Tavistock Lectures.) New York: Pantheon.

JUNG, C. G. (1969). The structure of the psyche. In *The collected works of C. G. Jung* (Vol. 8). Princeton, NJ: Princeton University Press. (Original work published 1931.)

JUNG, C. G. (1971). Psychological types. In *The collected works of C. G. Jung* (Vol. 6). Princeton, NJ: Princeton University Press. (Original work published 1921.)

JUNG, C. G. (1973). The psychological diagnosis of evidence. In *The collected works of C. G. Jung* (Vol. 2). Princeton, NJ: Princeton University Press. (Original work published 1909.)

JUNG, C. G. (1973). On the doctrine of complexes. In *The collected works of C. G. Jung* (Vol. 2). Princeton, NJ: Princeton University Press. (Original work published 1913.)

JUNG, C. G. (1978). On flying saucers. In *Flying saucers: A modern myth of things seen in the sky* (R. F. C. Hull, Trans.). New York: MJF Books. (Original work published 1954.)

KAGAN, J. (1994). *Galen's prophecy.* New York: Basic Books.

KAHN, M. (2002). *Basic Freud: Psychoanalytic thought for the 21st century.* New York : Basic Books.

KAHN, S., ZIMMERMAN, G., CSIKSZENTMIHALYI, M., & GETZELS, J. W. (1985). Relations between identity in young adulthood and intimacy at midlife. *Journal of Personality and Social Psychology, 49,* 1316–1322.

KANT, I. (1912). *Anthropologie in pragmatischer hinsicht.* Berlin: Bresser Cassiner (Original work published 1798.)

KARNER, T., KUBINGER, K. D., & MENGHIN, S. (1999). Multiple moderator effects on a testee's answer to personality questionnaire items. *Review of Psychology, 6*(1–2), 25–31.

KASSER, T., & SHELDON, K. M. (2001). Getting older, getting better? Personal strivings and psychological maturity across the life span. *Developmental Psychology, 37*(4), 491–501.

KAUFMAN, D. M., LAIDLAW, T. A., LANGILLE, D., SARGEANT, J., MACLEOD, H., (2001). Differences in medical students' attitudes and self-efficacy regarding patient-doctor communication. *Academic Medicine, 76,* 188–201.

KATZ, J. O. (1984). Personal construct theory and the emotions: An interpretation in terms of primitive constructs. *British Journal of Psychology, 75,* 315–327.

KAZDIN, A. E. (1977). *The token economy: A review and evaluation.* New York: Plenum Press.

KAZDIN, A. E. (1989). *Behavior modification in applied settings* (4th ed.). Pacific Grove, CA: Brooks/Cole.

KAZDIN, A. E., & BOOTZIN, R. R. (1972). The token economy: An evaluative review. *Journal of Applied Behavior Analysis, 5,* 343–372.

KAZDIN, A. E. & HERSEN, M. (1980). The current status of behavior therapy. *Behavior Modification, 4,* 283–302.

KELLEY, M. L., & STOKES, T. F. (1982). Contingency contracting with disadvantaged youths: Improving classroom performance. *Journal of Applied Behavior Analysis, 15,* 447–454.

KELLY, G. A. (1955). *The psychology of personal constructs* (2 vols.). New York: Norton.

KELLY, G. A. (1958). Man's construction of his alternatives. In G. Lindzey (Ed.), *Assessment of human motives.* New York: Holt, Rinehart and Winston.

KELLY, G. A. (1963). *A theory of personality: The psychology of personal constructs.* New York: Norton.

KELLY, G. A. (1964). The language of hypotheses: Man's psychological instrument. *Journal of Individual Psychology, 20,* 137–152.

KELLY, G. A. (1966). A brief introduction to personal construct theory. In D. Bannister (Ed.), *Perspectives in personal construct theory.* London: Academic Press.

KELLY, G. A. (1969). The autobiography of a theory. In B. Maher (Ed.), *Clinical psychology and personality: Selected papers of George Kelly* (pp. 40–65). New York: Wiley.

KELLY, G. A. (1970). A brief introduction to personal construct theory. In D. Bannister (Ed.), *Perspectives in personal construct theory.* New York: Academic Press.

KELLY, G. A. (1980). A psychology of the optimal man. In A. W. Landfield & L. M. Leitner (Eds.), *Personal construct psychology: Psychotherapy and personality.* New York: Wiley.

KEUTZER, C. S. (1978). Whatever turns you on: Triggers to transcendent experiences. *Journal of Humanistic Psychology, 18,* 77–80.

KIEL, J. M. (1999). Reshaping Maslow's hierarchy of needs to reflect today's educational and managerial philosophies. *Journal of Instructional Psychology, 26*(3), 167–168.

KIERKEGAARD, S. (1944). *The concept of dread* (W. Lowrie, Trans.). Princeton, NJ: Princeton University Press. (Original work published 1844 as *The concept of anxiety.*)

KINKADE, K. (1973). *A Walden Two experiment.* New York: Morrow.

KIRSCHENBAUM, H. (1979). *On becoming Carl Rogers.* New York: Dell.

KITAYAMA, S., & MARKUS, H. R. (1992, May). *Construal of self as cultural frame: Implications for internationalizing psychology.* Paper presented to Symposium on Internationalization and Higher Education, Ann Arbor, MI.

KLAVETTER, R., & MOGAR, R. (1967). Stability and internal consistency of a measure of self-actualization. *Psychological Reports, 21,* 422–424.

KLINE, B., & SAGGINO, A. (1996). The location of the Myers-Briggs Type Indicator in personality factor space. *Personality & Individual Differences, 21*(4), 591–597.

KLINE, P. (1966). Extraversion, neuroticism, and academic performance among Ghanaian university students. *British Journal of Educational Psychology, 36,* 92–94.

KLINE, P. (1972). *Fact and fantasy in Freudian theory.* London: Methuen.

KLUCKHOHN, C., & MURRAY, H. A. (1953). Personality formation: The determinants. In C. Kluckhohn, H. A. Murray, & D. M. Schneider (Eds.), *Personality in nature, society, and culture* (2nd ed.) (pp. 53–67). New York: Knopf.

KORN, J. H., DAVIS, R., & DAVIS, S. F. (1991). Historians' and chairpersons' judgments of eminence among psychologists. *American Psychologist, 46,* 789–792.

KOROTKOV, D., & HANNAH, T. E. (1994). Extraversion and emotionality as proposed superordinate stress moderators: A prospective analysis. *Personality and Individual Differences, 16,* 787–792.

KOWAZ, A. M., & MARCIA, J. E. (1991). Development and validation of a measure of Eriksonian industry. *Journal of Personality and Social Psychology, 60,* 390–397.

KRISHNAMOORTI, K. S., & SHAGASS, C. (1963). Some psychological test correlates of sedation threshold. In J. Wortis (Ed.), *Recent advances in biological psychiatry.* New York: Plenum Press.

KROGER, J. (2000). Ego identity status research in the new millennium. *International Journal of Behavioral Development, 24*(2), 145–148.

KUHN, T. S. (1973). *The structure of scientific revolutions* (2nd ed.). Chicago: University of Chicago Press.

LAMIELL, J. T. (1981). Toward an idiothetic psychology of personality. *American Psychologist, 36,* 276–289.

LANDFIELD, A. W., & EPTING, F. R. (1987). *Personal construct psychology: Clinical and personality assessment.* New York: Human Sciences Press.

LANDFIELD, A. W., & LEITNER, L. M. (Eds.). (1980). *Personal construct psychology: Psychotherapy and personality.* New York: Wiley.

LANE, J. A. S., MILLER, M. J., & WOEHR, D. J. (1998). The development and evaluation of a computer-administered measure of cognitive complexity. *Personality and Individual Differences, 25*(6), 1037–1049.

LANGLOIS, M. W., CRAMER, K. M., & MOHAGEN, R. G. Delineating the unique effects of predictability, controllability, and choice in perceptions of control. Manuscript under review.

LAVERTY, S. G. (1958). Sodium amytal and extraversion. *Journal of Neurology, Neurosurgery, and Psychiatry, 21,* 50–54.

LAWSON, K. D. (2000). Beyond corporeality: The virtual self in postmodern times. *Journal of Psychological Practice, 6*(1), 35–43.

LAY, C., FAIRLIE, P., JACKSON, S., RICCI, T., EISENBERG, J., SATO, T., TEEAAR, A., & MELAMUD, A. (1998). Domain-specific allocentrism-idiocentrism; A measure of family connectedness. *Journal of Cross-Cultural Psychology, 29,* 434–460.

LEAK, G. K., & CHRISTOPHER, S. B. (1982). Freudian psychoanalysis and sociobiology: A synthesis. *American Psychologist, 37,* 313–322.

LEFCOURT, H. M. (1973). The function of the illusion of control and freedom. *American Psychologist, 28,* 417–425.

LEFCOURT, H. M. (1991). Locus of control. In J. P. Robinson, P. R. Shaver, & L. S Wrightsman (Eds.), *Measures of personality and social psychological attitudes: Volume 1 of measures of social psychological attitudes.* San Diego, California: Academic Press.

LEFORT, S. M. (2000). A test of Braden's self-help model in adults with chronic pain. *Journal of Nursing Scholarship, 32,* 153–160.

LEITNER, L. (1984). The terrors of cognition. In D. Bannister (Ed.), *Further perspectives in personal construct theory.* New York: Academic Press.

LEITNER, L. M., & PFENNINGER, D. T. (1994). Sociality and optimal functioning. *Journal of Constructivist Psychology, 7,* 119–135.

LEMAY, M., & DAMM, V. (1968). The personal orientation inventory as a measure of self-actualization of underachievers. *Measurement and Evaluation in Guidance,* 110–114.

LENT, R. W., BROWN, S. D., & LARKIN, K. C. (1986). Self-efficacy in the prediction of academic performance and perceived career options. *Journal of Counseling Psychology, 33,* 265–269.

LEON, G. R., GILLENN, B., GILLENN, R. & GANZE, M. (1979). Personality, stability, and change over a 30–year period—middle age to old age. *Journal of Consulting and Clinical Psychology, 47,* 517–524.

LESTER, D., HVEZDA, J., SULLIVAN, S., & PLOURDE, R. (1983). Maslow's hierarchy of needs and psychological health. *Journal of General Psychology, 109,* 83–85.

LEVANT, R. F., & SCHLIEN, J. M. (Eds.). (1984). *Client-centered therapy and the person-centered approach: New directions in theory, research, and practice.* New York: Praeger.

LEWIN, K. (1935). *A dynamic theory of personality.* New York: McGraw-Hill.

LEWONTIN, R. C., ROSE, S., & KAMIN, L. J. (1984). *Not in our genes.* New York: Pantheon.

LINVILLE, P. W. (1985). Self-complexity and affective extremity: Don't put all of your eggs in one cognitive basket. *Social Cognition, 3,* 94–120.

LOFTUS, E. (1993). The reality of repressed memories. *American Psychologist, 48,* 518–537.

LOFTUS, E., & KETCHAM, K. (1994). *The myth of repressed memories and allegations of abuse.* New York: St. Martin's Press.

LOPREATO, J. (1989). The maximization principle: A cause in search of conditions. In R. W. Bell & N. J. Bell (Eds.), *Sociobiology an d the social sciences* (pp. 119–130). Lubbock, TX: Texas Tech University Press.

LOWRY, R. J. (Ed.). (1973). *Dominance, self-esteem, self-actualization: Germinal papers of A. H. Maslow.* Monterey, CA: Brooks/Cole.

LOWRY, R. J. (1979). *The journals of A. H. Maslow* (Vols. 1 & 2). Monterey, CA: Brooks/Cole.

LUDVIGH, E. J., & HAPP, D. (1974). Extraversion and preferred level of sensory stimulation. *British Journal of Psychology, 65,* 359–365.

LUMSDEN, C. J., & WILSON, E. O. (1981). *Genes, mind, and culture: The coevolutionary process.* Cambridge, MA: Harvard University Press.

LUMSDEN, C. J., & WILSON, E. O. (1983). *Promethean fire: Reflections on the origin of mind.* Cambridge, MA: Harvard University Press.

LUMSDEN, C. J., & WILSON, E. O. (1985). The relation between biological and cultural evolution. *Journal of Social and Biological Structures, 8,* 343–359.

LYNN, R. (1959). Two personality characteristics related to academic achievement. *British Journal of Educational Psychology, 29,* 213–216.

MACDONALD, D. A. (2000). Spirituality: Description, measurement, and relation to the Five Factor model of personality. *Journal of Personality, 68,* 153–197.

MADDI, S. R. (1996). *Personality theories: A comparative analysis.* Homewood, IL: Pacific Grove, CA: Brooks/Cole.

MAHONEY, J., & HARNETT, J. (1973). Self-actualization and self-ideal discrepancy. *Journal of Psychology, 85,* 37–42.

MALOTT, R. W., RITTERBY, K., & WOLF, E. L. C. (1973). *An introduction to behavior modification.* Kalamazoo, MI: Behaviordelia.

MANCUSO, J. C., & ADAMS-WEBBER, J. R. (Eds.). (1982). *The construing person.* New York: Praeger.

MANN, R. A. (1972). The behavior-therapeutic use of contingency contracting to control an adult behavior problem: Weight control. *Journal of Applied Behavior Analysis, 5,* 99–109.

MARCIA, J. (1966). Development and validation of ego identity status. *Journal of Personality and Social Psychology, 3,* 551–558.

MARCIA, J. E. (1993). The relational roots of identity. In J. Kroger (Ed.), *Discussions on ego identity* (pp. 101-120). Hillsdale, NJ: Lawrence Erlbaum.

MARCIA, J., & FRIEDMAN, M. L. (1970). Ego identity status in college women. *Journal of Personality, 38,* 249–263.

MARKUS, H. R., & KITAYAMA, S. (1991). Culture and the self: Implications for cognition, emotion, and motivation. *Psychological Reports, 98,* 224–253.

MARTIN, R. B., & SELLS, D. J. (2001). Gender modality differences in experiencing and emotional expression. *Canadian Journal of Counselling, 35*(2), 176–188.

MARUGAN, K. J. (1998). The erotic-homosexual nuance, in the Freud-Jung relation. *Clinica Y Analisis Grupal, 20*(2), 238-258.

MARROW, A. J., BOWERS, D. G., & SEASHORE, S. E. (1967). *Management by participation.* New York: Harper & Row.

MARX, M. H., & GOODSON, F. E. (Eds.). (1976). *Theories in contemporary psychology* (2nd ed.). New York: Macmillan.

MASLING, J. (Ed.). (1983). *Empirical studies of psychoanalytic theories.* Hillsdale, NJ: Analytic Press.

MASLOW, A. H. (1943a). A preface to motivation theory. *Psychosomatic Medicine, 5,* 85–92.

MASLOW, A. H. (1943b). A theory of human motivation. *Psychological Review, 50,* 370–396.

MASLOW, A. H. (1965). *Eupsychian management: A journal.* Homewood, IL: Irwin- Dorsey.

MASLOW, A. H. (1966). *The psychology of science: A reconnaissance.* New York: Harper & Row.

MASLOW, A. H. (1968). *Toward a psychology of being* (2nd ed.). New York: Van Nostrand.

MASLOW, A. H. (1971). *The farther reaches of human nature.* New York: Penguin.

MASLOW, A. H. (1987). *Motivation and personality* (3rd ed.). (Revised by R. Frager, J. Fadiman, C. McReynolds, & R. Cox). New York: Harper & Row. (Original work published 1954.)

MASSARIK, F. (1992). The humanistic core of humanistic/organizational psychology. *Humanist Psychologist, 20,* 389–396.

MASSON, J.M. (1984). *The assault on truth: Freud's suppression of the seduction theory.* New York: Farrar, Straus, and Giroux.

MASSON, J. M. (Trans. & Ed.). (1985). *The complete letters of Sigmund Freud to Wilhelm Fliess 1887–1904.* Cambridge, MA: Harvard University Press.

MASTERS, J. C., BURISH, T. G., HOLLON, S. D., & RIMM, D. C. (1987). *Behavior therapy: Techniques and empirical findings* (3rd ed.). Orlando, FL: Harcourt Brace Jovanovich.

MATHES, E. W., ZEVON, M. A., ROTER, P. M., & JOERGER, S. M. (1982). Peak experience tendencies: Scale development and theory testing. *Journal of Humanistic Psychology, 22,* 92–108.

MAU, W. (1997). Assessing the cognitive complexity of vocational value constructs using the career grid: A comparison of the expressed and supplied methods.

Measurement & Evaluation in Counseling & Development, 29(4), 202–214.

MAY, R. (1939). *The art of counseling: How to give and gain mental health.* Nashville, Abingdon-Cokesbury.

MAY, R. (1940). *The springs of creative living: A study of human nature and God.* New York: Abingdon-Cokesbury.

MAY, R. (1950). *The meaning of anxiety.* New York: Ronald Press.

MAY, R. (1953). *Man's search for himself.* New York: Norton.

MAY, R. (1967). *Psychology and the human dilemma.* New York: Van Nostrand.

MAY, R. (1969). *Love and will.* New York: Norton.

MAY, R. (1973). *Paulus: Reminiscences of a friendship.* New York: Harper & Row.

MAY, R. (1981). *Freedom and destiny.* New York: Norton.

MAY, R. (1982). The problem of evil: An open letter to Carl Rogers. *Journal of Humanistic Psychology, 22,* 10–21.

MAY, R. (1983). *The discovery of being: Writings in existential psychology.* New York: Norton.

MAY, R. (1985). *My quest for beauty.* Dallas, TX: Saybrook Publishing.

MAY, R. (1991). *The cry for myth.* New York: Norton.

MAY, R., ANGEL, E., & ELLENBERGER, H. F. (Eds.). (1958). *Existence: A new dimension in psychiatry and psychology.* New York: Basic.

McCANN, J. T., & BIAGGIO, M. K. (1989). Sexual satisfaction in marriage as a function of life meaning. *Archives of Sexual Behavior, 18,* 59–72.

McCOY, M. M. (1977). A reconstruction of emotion. In D. Bannister (Ed.), *New perspectives in personal construct theory* (pp. 93–124). London: Academic Press.

McCRAE, R. R., & COSTA, P. T., JR. (1985). Updating Norman's "Adequate taxonomy": Intelligence and personality dimensions in natural language and in questionnaires. *Journal of Personality and Social Psychology, 49,* 710–721.

McCRAE, R. R., & COSTA, P. T., JR. (1987). Validation of the five-factor model across instruments and observers. *Journal of Personality and Social Psychology, 52,* 81–90.

McCRAE, R. R. & COSTA, P. T., Jr. (1990). *Personality in Adulthood.* New York: The Guilford Press.

McCRAE, R. R., & COSTA, P. T., JR. (1996). Toward a new generation of personality theories: Theoretical contexts for the five-factor model. In J. S. Wiggins (Ed.), *The five-factor model of personality.* New York: Guildford Press.

McFARLAND, K. F., & RHODES, D. R. (2000). Purpose in life and self-actualization in agency-supported caregivers community. *Mental Health Journal, 36*(5), 513–521.

McGAW, W. H., RICE, C. P., & ROGERS, C. R. (1973). *The steel shutter.* LaJolla, CA: Film Center for Studies of the Person.

McGUIRE, W. (Ed.). (1974). *The Freud/Jung Letters.* Princeton, NJ: Princeton University Press.

McLAREN, L., GAUVIN, L., & WHITE, D. (2001). The role of perfectionism and excessive commitment to exercise in explaining dietary restraint: Replication and extension. *International Journal of Eating Disorders, 29,* 307–313.

McLEOD, C. R., & VODANOVICH, S. J. (1991). The relationship between self-actualization and boredom proneness. *Journal of Social Behavior and Personality, 6,* 137–146.

MEIER, S. T. (1983). Toward a theory of burnout. *Human Relations, 36,* 899–910.

MERCKELBACH, H., MURIS, P., & ROSSIN, E. (2000). Monitoring trait anxiety, and panic disorder symptomatology in normal subjects. *Journal of Behavior Therapy & Experimental Psychiatry, 31*(1), (21–28).

MIALL, D. S. (1989). Anticipating the self: Toward a personal construct model of emotion. *International Journal of Personal Construct Psychology, 2,* 185–198.

MILLER, G. A. (1965). Some preliminaries to psycholinguistics. *American Psychologist, 20,* 15–20.

MILLER, N. E. (1944). Experimental studies of conflict. In J. M. Hunt (Ed.), *Personality and the behavior disorders* (Vol. 1). New York: Ronald Press.

MILLER, N. E. (1948a). Studies of fear as an acquirable drive: I. Fear as motivation and fear reduction as reinforcement in the learning of new responses. *Journal of Experimental Psychology, 38,* 89–101.

MILLER, N. E. (1948b). Theory and experiment relating psychoanalytic displacement to stimulus response generalization. *Journal of Abnormal and Social Psychology, 43,* 155–178.

MILLER, N. E. (1959). Liberalization of basic S-R concepts: Extensions to conflict behavior, motivation and social learning. In S. Koch (Ed.), *Psychology: A study of a science* (Vol. 2). New York: McGraw-Hill.

MILLER, N. E. (1964). Some implications of modern behavior theory for personality change and psychotherapy. In P. Worchel & D. Bryne (Eds.), *Personality change.* New York: Wiley.

MILLER, N. E. (1982). Obituary: John Dollard (1900–1980). *American Psychologist, 37,* 587–588.

MILLER, N. E. (1983). Behavioral medicine: Symbiosis between laboratory and clinic. In M. R. Rosenzweig & L. W. Porter (Eds.), *Annual Review of Psychology, 34,* 1–31.

MILLER, N. E. (1984). *Bridges between laboratory and clinic.* New York: Praeger.

MILLER, N. E. (1985). The value of behavioral research on animals. *American Psychologist, 40,* 423–440.

MILLER, N. E. (1991). Commentary on Ulrich: Need to check truthfulness of statements by opponents of animal research. *Psychological Science, 2,* 422–423.

MILLER, N. E. (1992). Introducing and teaching much-needed understanding of the scientific process. *American Psychologist, 47,* 848–850.

MILLER, N. E., & DOLLARD, J. (1941). *Social learning and imitation.* New Haven: Yale University Press.

MILLER, P. M. (1972). The use of behavioral contracting in the treatment of alcoholism: A case report. *Behavior Therapy, 3,* 593–596.

MISCHEL, W. (1958). Preference for delayed reinforcement: An experimental study of cultural observation. *Journal of Abnormal and Social Psychology, 56,* 57–61.

MISCHEL, W. (1961a). Delay of gratification, need for achievement, and acquiesce in another culture. *Journal of Abnormal and Social Psychology, 62,* 543–552.

MISCHEL, W. (1961b). Preference for delayed reinforcement and social responsibility. *Journal of Abnormal and Social Psychology, 62,* 1–7.

MISCHEL, W. (1965). Predicting the success of peace corps volunteers in Nigeria. *Journal of Personality and Social Psychology, 1,* 510–517.

MISCHEL, W. (1968). *Personality and assessment.* New York: Wiley.

MISCHEL, W. (1969). Continuity and change in personality. *American Psychologist, 24,* 1012–1018.

MISCHEL, W. (1977). The interaction of person and situation. In D. Magnusson & N. S. Endler (Eds.), *Personality at the crossroads: Current issues in interactional psychology.* Hillsdale, NJ: Erlbaum.

MISCHEL, W. (1979). On the interface of cognition and personality. *American Psychologist, 34,* 740–754.

MISCHEL, W. (1984). Convergences and challenges in the search for consistency. *American Psychologist, 39,* 351–364.

MISCHEL, W. (1986). *Introduction to personality* (4th ed.). New York: Holt, Rinehart and Winston.

MISCHEL, W. (1990). Personality dispositions revisited and revised: A view after three decades. In L. A. Pervin (Ed.), *Handbook of personality theory and research* (pp. 111–134). New York: Guilford Press.

MISCHEL, W. (1993). *Introduction to personality* (5th ed.). Orlando, FL: Harcourt, Brace, Jovanovich.

MISCHEL, W., & BAKER, N. (1975). Cognitive appraisals and transformations in delay behavior. *Journal of Personality and Social Psychology, 31,* 254–261.

MISCHEL, W., & EBBESEN, E. B. (1970). Attention in delay of gratification. *Journal of Personality and Social Psychology, 16,* 329–337.

MISCHEL, W., EBBESEN, E. B., & ZEISS, A. R. (1972). Cognitive and attentional mechanisms in delay of gratification. *Journal of Personality and Social Psychology, 21,* 204–218.

MISCHEL, W., & LIEBERT, R. M. (1966). Effects of discrepancies between observed and imposed reward criteria on their acquisition and transmission. *Journal of Personality and Social Behavior, 3,* 45–53.

MISCHEL, W., & METZNER, R. (1962). Preference for delayed reward as a function of age, intelligence, and length of the delay interval. *Journal of Abnormal and Social Psychology, 64,* 425–431.

MISCHEL, W., & MOORE, B. (1973). Effects of attention to symbolically presented rewards upon self-control. *Journal of Personality and Social Psychology, 28,* 172–179.

MISCHEL, W., & MOORE, B. (1980). The role of ideation in voluntary delay for symbolically presented rewards. *Cognitive Therapy and Research, 4,* 211–221.

MISCHEL, W., & PEAKE, P. K. (1982). Beyond dÈja vu in the search for cross-situational consistency. *Psychological Review, 89,* 730–755.

MISCHEL, W., SHODA, Y., & PEAKE, P. K. (1988). The nature of adolescent competencies predicted by preschool delay of gratification. *Journal of Personality and Social Psychology, 54,* 687–696.

MISCHEL, W., SHODA, Y., & RODRIGUEZ, M. L. (1989). Delay of gratification in children. *Science, 244,* 933–938.

MITCHELL, C., & STUART, R. B. (1984). Effect of self-efficacy on dropout from obesity treatment. *Journal of Consulting and Clinical Psychology, 52,* 1100–1101.

MITCHELL, J. (1998). Neurosis and the historic quest for security. A social role analysis: Reply. *Philosophy, Psychiatry, & Psychology, 5*(4), 333–335.

MOORE, B., MISCHEL, W., & ZEISS, A. R. (1976). Comparative effects of the reward stimulus and its cognitive representation in voluntary delay. *Journal of Social Psychology, 34,* 419–424.

MOORE, M. K., & NEIMEYER, R. A. (1991). A confirmatory factor analysis of the Threat Index. *Journal of Personality and Social Psychology, 60,* 122–129.

MORIN, A. (1995). Preliminary data on a relation between self-talk and complexity of the self-concept. *Psychological Reports, 76,* 267–272.

MORIN, A. (1999). On a relation between inner speech and self-awareness: Additional evidence from brain studies. *Dynamical Psychology: An International, Interdisciplinary Journal of Complex Mental Processes* [On-line journal]. http://goertzel.org/dynapsyc/

MORIN, A., & CRAIG, L. (2000). Self-awareness, self-esteem, and alcohol use in famous and relatively well-known individuals. *Current Research in Social Psychology, 5,* 236-253.

MORIN, A., & EVERETT, J. (1990). Inner speech as a mediator of self-awareness, self-consciousness, and self-knowledge: An hypothesis. *New Ideas in Psychology, 8,* 337–356.

MORITZ, C. (Ed.). (1974). Miller, Neal, E(lgar). *Current biographical yearbook* (pp. 276–279). New York: W. H. Wilson.

MORUZZI, G., & MAGOUN, H. W. (1949). Brain stem reticular formation and activation of the EEG. *Electroencephalography and Clinical Neurophysiology, 1,* 455–473.

MULTON, K. D., BROWN, S. D., & LENT, R. W. (1991). Relation of self-efficacy beliefs to academic outcomes: A meta-analytic investigation. *Journal of Counseling Psychology, 38,* 30–38.

MURAN, J. C., SAMSTAG, L. W., SEGAL, Z. V., VENTUR, E. D., & WINSTON, A. (2001). A cognitive-interpersonal case study of a self. *Journal of Clinical Psychology, 57*(3), 307–330.

MURRAY, B. (1996a). Judges, courts get tough on spanking. *APA Monitor, 11,* 10.

MURRAY, B. (1996b). British case could set precedent. *APA Monitor, 11,* 10.

MUSSEN, P., EICHORN, D. H., HANZIK, M. P., BIEHER, S. L., & MEREDITH, W. (1980). Continuity and change in women's characteristics over four decades. *International Journal of Behavioral Development, 3,* 333–347.

MYERS, I. B. (1962). *The Myers–Briggs type indicator manual.* Palo Alto, CA: Consulting Psychologists Press.

MYERS, R. W. (2001). The Little Mermaid: Hans Christian Anderson's feminine identification. *Journal of Applied Psychoanalytic Studies, 3*(2), 149–159.

NADEAU, L., TRUCHON, M., & BIRON, C. (2000). High-risk sexual behaviors in a context of substance abuse: A focus group approach. *Journal of Substance Abuse Treatment, 19,* 319–328.

NEIMEYER, G. J. (1984). Cognitive complexity and marital satisfaction. *Journal of Social and Clinical Psychology, 2,* 258–263.

NEIMEYER, G. J. (1988). Cognitive integration and differentiation in vocational behavior. *Counseling Psychologist, 16,* 440–475.

NEIMEYER, G. J. (1992a). Personal constructs in career counseling and development. *Journal of Career Development, 18,* 163–173.

NEIMEYER, G. J. (1992b). Personal constructs and vocational structure. In R. A. Neimeyer and G. J. Neimeyer (Eds.), *Advances in personal construct psychology* (Vol. 2, pp. 91–120). Greenwich, CT: JAI Press.

NEIMEYER, G. J., & HALL, A. G. (1988). Personal identity in disturbed marital relationships. In F. Fransella & L. Thomas (Eds.), *Experimenting with personal construct theory* (pp. 297–307). London: Routledge & Kegan Paul.

NEIMEYER, G. J., & HUDSON, J. E. (1984). Couples' constructs: Personal systems in marital satisfaction. In D. Bannister (Ed.), *Further perspectives in personal construct theory.* New York: Academic Press.

NEIMEYER, G. J., & HUDSON, J. E. (1985). Couples' constructs: Personal systems in marital satisfaction. In D. Bannister (Ed.), *Issues and approaches in personal construct theory* (pp. 127–141). New York: Academic Press.

NEIMEYER, R. A. (1984). Toward a personal construct conceptualization of depression and suicide. In F. R. Epting and R. A. Neimeyer (Eds.), *Personal meanings of death: Applications of personal construct theory to clinical practice* (pp. 127–173). New York: Hemisphere/McGraw-Hill.

NEIMEYER, R. A. (1985). Personal constructs in clinical practice. In P. C. Kendall (Ed.), *Advances in cognitive-behavioral research and therapy* (Vol. 4, pp. 275–339). New York: Academic Press.

NEIMEYER, R. A. (1994). The role of client-generated narratives in psychotherapy. *International Journal of Personal Construct Psychology, 7,* 229–242.

NEIMEYER, R. A., MOORE, M. K., & BAGLEY, K. J. (1988). A preliminary factor structure for the Threat Index. *Death Studies, 12,* 217–225.

NEIMEYER, R. A., & NEIMEYER, G. J. (1985). Disturbed relationships: A personal construct view. In E. Button (Ed.), *Personal construct theory and mental health: Theory, research, and practice.* Beckenham, England: Croom Helm.

NEVILL, D. D., & SCHLECKER, D. I. (1988). The relation of self-efficacy and assertiveness to willingness to engage in traditional/nontraditional career activities. *Psychology of Women Quarterly, 12,* 91–98.

NICKELS, J. B., CRAMER, K. M., & GURAL, D. M. (1992). Toward unconfounding prediction and control: Predictionless control made possible. *Canadian Journal of Behavioural Sciences, 24,* 156–170.

NIEDENTHAL, P. M., SETTERLUND, M. B., & WHERRY, M. B. (1992). Possible self-complexity and affective reactions to goal-relevant evaluation. *Journal of Personality and Social Psychology, 63,* 5–16.

NORMAN, W. T. (1963). Toward an adequate taxonomy of personality attributes: Replicated factor structure in peer nomination personality ratings. *Journal of Abnormal and Social Psychology, 66,* 574–583.

NOUWEN, A., FREESTON, M. H., LABBE, R., & BOULET, L. P. (1999). Psychological factors associated with emergency room visits among asthmatic patients. *Behavior Modification, 23,* 217–233.

O'LEARY, A. (1992). Self-efficacy and health: Behavioral and stress-physiological mediation. *Cognitive Therapy and Research, 16,* 229–245.

OLSON, H. A. (Ed.). (1979). *Early recollections: Their use in diagnosis and psychotherapy.* Springfield, IL: Charles G. Thomas.

ORGLER, H. (1963). *Alfred Adler: The man and his work.* New York: Liveright.

OZER, E. M., & BANDURA, A. (1990). Mechanisms governing empowerment effects: A self-efficacy analysis. *Journal of Personality and Social Psychology, 58,* 472–486.

PAIGE, J. M. (1966). Letters from Jenny: An approach to the clinical analysis of personality structure by computer. In P. J. Stone (Ed.), *The general inquirer: A computer approach to content analysis.* Cambridge, MA: M.I.T. Press.

PALMER, E. C., & CARR, K. (1991). Dr. Rogers, meet Mr. Rogers: The theoretical and clinical similarities between Carl and Fred Rogers. *Social Behavior and Personality, 19,* 39–44.

PANCER, S. M., HUNSBERGER, B., PRATT, M. W., & ALISAT, S. (2000). Cognitive complexity of expectations and adjustment to university in the first year. *Journal of Adolescent Research, 15,* 38–57.

PANZARELLA, R. (1980). The phenomenology of aesthetic peak experiences. *Journal of Humanistic Psychology, 20*(1), 69–85.

PARIS, B. J. (1994). *Karen Horney: A psychoanalyst's search for self-understanding.* New Haven, CT: Yale University Press.

PARKER, A. (1981). The meaning of attempted suicide to young parasuicides: A repertory grid study. *British Journal of Psychiatry, 139,* 306–312.

PAULHUS, D. L., FRIDHANDLER, B., & HAYES, S. (1997). Psychological defense: Contemporary theory and research. In J. Johnson, R. Hogan, & S. R. Briggs (Eds.), *Handbook of personality psychology* (pp. 543–579). New York: Academic Press.

PAULHUS, D. L., & JOHN, O. P. (1998). Egoistic and moralistic biases in self-perception: The interplay of self-deceptive styles with basic traits and motives. *Journal of Personality, 66,* 1025–1060.

PAULHUS, D. L., & REID, D. B. (1991). Enhancement and denial in socially desirable responding. *Journal of Personality and Social Psychology, 60,* 307–317.

PAULHUS, D. L., TRAPNELL, P. D., & CHEN, D. (1999). Birth order effects on personality and achievement within families. *Psychological Science, 10,* 482–488.

PAUNONEN, S. V. (1998). Hierarchical organization of personality and prediction of behavior. *Journal of Personality and Social Psychology, 74,* 538–556.

PAUNONEN, S. V., & ASHTON, M. C. (1998). The structured assessment of personality across culture. *Journal of Cross-Cultural Psychology, 29,* 150–170.

PAUNONEN, S. V., ASHTON, M. C., & JACKSON, D. N. (2001). Nonverbal assessment of the Big Five personality factors. *European Journal of Personality, 15,* 3–18.

PAUNONEN, S. V., & JACKSON, D. N. (2000). What is beyond the Big Five? Plenty! *Journal of Personality, 68,* 821–835.

PAUNONEN, S. V., JACKSON, D. N., & KEINONEN, M. (1990). The structured nonverbal assessment of personality. *Journal of Personality, 58,* 481–502.

PAUNONEN, S. V., ZEIDNER, M., ENGVIK, H. A., OOSTERVELD, P., & MALIPHANT, R. (2000). The nonverbal assessment of personality in five cultures. *Journal of Cross Cultural Psychology, 31,* 220–239.

PAVLOV, I. P. (1928). *Lectures on conditioned reflexes* (Vol. 1). H. Gantt (Trans.). New York: International Publishers.

PAXTON, R. (1980). The effects of a deposit contract as a component in a behavioral programme for stopping smoking. *Behaviour Research and Therapy, 18,* 45–50.

PAXTON, R. (1981). Deposit contracts with smokers: Varying frequency and amount of repayments. *Behaviour Research and Therapy, 19,* 117–123.

PELHAM, B. W. (1993). The idiographic nature of human personality: Examples of the idiographic self-concept. *Journal of Personality and Social Psychology, 64,* 665–677.

PEPLAU, L. A., & PERLMAN, D. (1982). Perspective on loneliness. In L. A. Peplau & D. Perlman (Eds.), *Loneliness: A sourcebook of current theory, research and therapy,* (pp. 1–18). New York: Wiley.

PERLMAN, D. (1987). Further reflections on the present state of loneliness research. *Journal of Social Behaviour and Personality, 2,* 17–26.

PERLMAN, D. (1988). Loneliness: A life-span, family perspective. In R. M. Milardo (Ed.), *Families and social networks: New perspectives on family* (pp. 190-220). Thousand Oaks, CA: Sage Publications.

PERVIN, L. A.(1984). *Current controversies and issues in personality* (2nd ed.) New York: Wiley.

PERVIN, L. A. (1989). *Personality: Theory and research* (5th ed.). New York: Wiley.

PETERSON, C., MAIER, S. F., & SELIGMAN, M. E. P. (1993). *Learned helplessness: A theory for the age of personal control.* New York: Oxford University Press.

PETERSON, D. L., & PFOST, K. S. (1989). Influence of rock videos on attitudes of violence against women. *Psychological Reports, 64*, 319–322.

POLKINGHORNE, D. E. (1992). Research methodology in humanistic psychology. *Humanistic Psychologist, 20*, 218–242.

POOLE, M. E., & EVANS, G. T. (1989). Adolescents' self perceptions of competence in life skill areas. *Journal of Youth and Adolescence, 18*, 147–173.

POPPER, K. (1963). *Conjectures and refutations*. New York: Basic.

POWELL, R. A., & BOER, D. P. (1994). Did Freud mislead patients to confabulate memories of abuse? *Psychological Reports, 74*, 1283–1298.

POWER, T., & CHAPLESKI, M. (1986). Childrearing and impulse control in toddlers: A naturalistic investigation. *Developmental Psychology, 22*, 271–275.

PROCTER, H. G. (2001). Personal construct psychology and autism. *Journal of Constructivist Psychology, 14*, 107–126.

RABINOWITZ, F. E., GOOD, G., & COZAD, L. (1989). Rollo May: A man of meaning and myth. *Journal of Counseling and Development, 67*, 436–441.

RAMANAIAH, N. V., HEERBOTH, J. R., & JINKERSON, D. L. (1985). Personality and self-actualizing profiles of assertive people. *Journal of Personality Assessment, 49*, 440–443.

RATHUS, S. A., NEVID, J. S., & FICHNER-RATHUS, L. (1998). *Essentials of Human Sexuality*. Boston: Allyn and Bacon.

RAVIZZA, K. (1977). Peak experiences in sport. *Journal of Humanistic Psychology, 17*(4), 35–40.

REEVES, C. (1977). *The psychology of Rollo May*. San Francisco: Jossey-Bass.

RIGDON, M. A., & EPTING, F. R. (1983). A personal construct perspective on an obsessive client. In J. Adams-Webber & J. C. Mancuso (Eds.), *Applications of personal construct theory*. New York: Academic Press.

RIVERS, P., & LANDFIELD, A. W. (1985). Alcohol abuse. In E. Button (Ed.), *Personal construct theory and mental health: Theory, research, and practice*. Beckenham, England: Croom Helm.

ROAZEN, P. (1976). *Erik H. Erikson: The power and limits of a vision*. New York: Free Press.

ROAZEN, P. (1980). Erik H. Erikson's America: The political implications of ego psychology. *Journal of the History of the Behavioral Sciences, 16*, 333–341.

ROBINSON, D. N. (1985). *Philosophy of psychology*. New York: Columbia University Press.

ROBINSON, P. J., & WOOD, K. (1984). Fear of death and physical illness: A personal construct approach. In F. R. Epting & R. A. Neimeyer (Eds.), *Personal meanings of death: Applications of personal construct theory to clinical practice*. Washington, DC: Hemisphere.

RODGERS, W. M., & SULLIVAN, M. J. L. (2001). Task, coping, and scheduling self-efficacy in relation to frequency of physical activity. *Journal of Applied Social Psychology. Special Issue, 31*, 741–753.

ROGERS, C. R. (1939). *The clinical treatment of the problem child*. Boston: Houghton Mifflin.

ROGERS, C. R. (1942). *Counseling and psychotherapy: Newer concepts in practice*. Boston: Houghton Mifflin.

ROGERS, C. R. (1951). *Client-centered therapy: Its current practice, implications, and theory*. Boston: Houghton Mifflin.

ROGERS, C. R. (1955). Persons or science? A philosophical question. *American Psychologist, 10*, 267–278.

ROGERS, C. R. (1956a). Intellectualized psychotherapy. *Contemporary Psychology, 1*, 357–358.

ROGERS, C. R. (1956b). Some issues concerning the control of human behavior (Symposium with B. F. Skinner). *Science, 124*, 1057–1066.

ROGERS, C. R. (1956c, February). Implications of recent advances in prediction and control of behavior. *Teachers College Record, 57*, 316–322.

ROGERS, C. R. (1959). A theory of therapy, personality, and interpersonal relationships, as developed in the client-centered framework. In S. Koch (Ed.), *Psychology: A study of a science* (Vol. 3). New York: McGraw-Hill.

ROGERS, C. R. (1961). *On becoming a person: A therapist's view of psychotherapy*. Boston: Houghton Mifflin.

ROGERS, C. R. (1963). Actualizing tendency in relation to motives and to consciousness. In M. R. Jones (Ed.), *Nebraska Symposium on Motivation, 1963*. Lincoln: University of Nebraska Press.

ROGERS, C. R. (1966). Client-centered therapy. In S. Arieti (Ed.), *American handbook of psychiatry*. New York: Basic.

ROGERS, C. R. (1967). Autobiography. In E. G. Boring & G. Lindzey (Eds.), *A history of psychology in autobiography* (Vol. 5). New York: Appleton.

ROGERS, C. R. (1968). Graduate education in psychology: A passionate statement. In W. G. Bennis, E. H. Schein, F. I. Steele, & D. E. Berlew (Eds.), *Interpersonal Dynamics* (2nd ed., pp. 687–703). Homewood, IL: Dorsey Press.

ROGERS, C. R. (1969). *Freedom to learn*. Columbus, OH: Charles E. Merrill.

ROGERS, C. R. (1972a). My personal growth. In A. Burton (Ed.), *Twelve therapists*. San Francisco: Jossey-Bass.

ROGERS, C. R. (1972b). *Becoming partners: Marriage and its alternatives*. New York: Delacorte.

ROGERS, C. R. (1973). My philosophy of interpersonal relationships and how it grew. *Journal of Humanistic Psychology, 13,* 3–15.

ROGERS, C. R. (1974). In retrospect: Forty-six years. *American Psychologist, 29,* 115–123.

ROGERS, C. R. (1977). *Carl Rogers on personal power.* New York: Delacorte.

ROGERS, C. R. (1980). *A way of being.* Boston: Houghton Mifflin.

ROGERS, C. R. (1983). *Freedom to learn for the 80s.* Columbus, OH: Charles E. Merrill.

ROGERS, C. R. (1987). The underlying theory: Drawn from experience with individuals and groups. *Counseling and Values, 32,* 38–46.

ROGERS, C. R., & RYBACK, D. (1984). One alternative to nuclear planetary suicide. In R. F. Levant and J. M. Schlien (Eds.), *Client-centered therapy and the person-centered approach: New directions in theory, research, and practice.* New York: Praeger.

ROSATI, P. (1997). Psychological types of Canadian engineering students. *Journal of Psychological Type, 41,* 33–37.

ROSENBERG, L. A. (1962). Idealization of self and social adjustment. *Journal of Consulting Psychology, 26,* 487.

ROSENTHAL, D. A., GURNEY, R. M., & MOORE, S. M. (1981). From trust to intimacy: A new inventory for examining Erikson's stages of psychosocial development. *Journal of Youth and Adolescence, 10,* 525–537.

ROTENBERG, K. J. (1994). Loneliness and interpersonal trust. *Journal of Social and Clinical Psychology, 13,* 152–173.

ROTENBERG, K. J. (1998). Stigmatization of transitions in loneliness (1998). *Journal of Social and Personal Relationships, 15,* 565–576.

ROTENBERG, K. J., & FLOOD, D. (1999). Loneliness, dysphoria, dietary restraint, and eating behavior. *International Journal of Eating Disorders, 25,* 55–64.

ROTENBERG, K. J., & KMILL, J. (1992). Perception of lonely and nonlonely persons as a function of individual differences in loneliness. *Journal of Social and Personal Relationships, 9,* 325–330.

ROTENBERG, K. J., & MACKIE, J. (1999). Stigmatization of social and intimacy loneliness. *Psychological Reports, 84,* 147–148.

ROTENBERG, K. J., & MORRISON, J. (1993). Loneliness and college achievement: Do loneliness scale scores predict college drop-out? *Psychological Reports, 73,* 1283–1288.

ROWE, I., & MARCIA, J. E. (1980). Ego identity status, formal operations, and moral development. *Journal of Youth and Adolescence, 9,* 87–99.

RUBINS, J. L. (1978). *Karen Horney: Gentle rebel of psychoanalysis.* New York: Dial.

RULE, W. R. (1972). The relationship between early recollections and selected counselor and life style characteristics. *Dissertation Abstracts International, 33,* 1448A–1449A. (University Microfilms No. 72-25, 921).

RULE, W. R., & TRAVER, M. D. (1982). Early recollections and expected leisure activities. *Psychological Reports, 51,* 295–301.

RUNCO, M. A., EBERSOLE, P., & MRAZ, W. (1991). Creativity and self-actualization. *Journal of Social Behavior and Personality, 6,* 161–167.

RUNYAN, W. M. (1983). Idiographic goals and methods in the study of lives. *Journal of Personality, 51,* 413–437.

RYCHLAK, J. F. (1988). *The psychology of rigorous humanism* (2nd ed.). New York: New York University Press.

RYCHLAK, J. F. (1991). *Artificial intelligence and human reason: A teleological critique.* New York: Columbia University Press.

RYCHLAK, J. F. (1997). *In defense of human consciousness.* Washington, D.C.: American Psychological Association.

SACKETT, S. J. (1995). The application of Rogerian theory to literary study. *Journal of Humanistic Psychology, 35*(4), 140–157.

SAKS, A. M. (1995). Longitudinal field investigation of the moderating and mediating effects of self-efficacy on the relationship between training and newcomer adjustment. *Journal of Applied Psychology, 80,* 211–225.

SALMON, D., & LEHRER, R. (1989). School consultant's implicit theories of action. *Professional School Psychology, 4,* 173–187.

SANTOGROSSI, D., O'LEARY, K., ROMANCZYK, R., & KAUFMAN, K. (1973). Self-evaluation by adolescents in a psychiatric hospital school token program. *Journal of Applied Behavior Analysis, 6,* 277–287.

SAPER, Z., & FOREST, J. J. (1992). Effects of type of instruction on solution of psychological self-help problems. *Psychological Reports, 70,* 1095–1105.

SARTRE, J.-P. (1956). Existentialism. In W. Kaufmann (Ed.), *Existentialism from Dostoevsky to Sartre.* New York: Meridian.

SARTRE, J-P. (1957). *Existentialism and human emotions.* New York: Wisdom Library.

SATOPATHY, B. (2001). Getting the best out of your people: The Indian way. *Social Science International, 17*(2), 37–45.

SAUCIER, G., & GOLDBERG, L. R. (1998). What is beyond the Big Five? *Journal of Personality, 66,* 495–524.

SCHAEFER, H. H., & MARTIN, P. L. (1969). *Behavioral therapy.* New York: McGraw-Hill.

SCHALLER, M. (1997). The psychological consequences of fame: Three tests of the self-consciousness hypothesis. *Journal of Personality, 65,* 291–309.

SCHATZMAN, M. (1992, March 21). Freud: Who seduced whom? *New Scientist,* pp. 34–37.

SCHEIB, J. E. (1994). Sperm donor selection and the psychology of female mate choice. *Ethology and Sociobiology, 15,* 113–129.

SCHIAFFINO, K. M., & ZALESK, E. H. (2000). Religiosity and sexual risk-taking behavior during the transition to college. *Journal of Adolescence, 23*(2), 223–227.

SCHIEDEL, D. G., & MARCIA, J. E. (1985). Ego identity, intimacy, sex role orientation, and gender. *Journal of Personality and Social Psychology, 21,* 149–160.

SCHILL, T., MONROE, S., EVANS, R., & RAMANAIAH, N. (1978). The effects of self-verbalization on performance: A test of the rational-emotive position. *Psychotherapy: Theory, research, and practice, 15,* 2–7.

SCHOENBACH, C., & SCHOOLER, C. (1995). Social class, occupational status, occupational self-direction, and job income: A cross-national examination: *Errata. Sociological Forum, 10,* 193.

SCHOLZ, D. F., & FOREST, J. J. (1997). Effects of fictional, autobiographical, and self-help literature on personality measures. *Psychological Reports, 80,* 91–96.

SCHULTZ, G. S. (2000). The Taxonomy of Rights and educational objective attainment. *Journal of Developmental & Physical Disabilities, 12*(1), 61–71.

SCHUR, M. (1972). *Freud: Living and dying.* New York: International Universities Press.

SELIGMAN, M. E. P. (1975). *Learned helplessness: On depression, development, and death.* San Francisco: Freeman.

SENECAL, C., NOUWEN, A., & WHITE, D. (2000). Motivation and dietary self-care in adults with diabetes: Are self-efficacy and autonomous self-regulation complementary or competing constructs? *Health Psychology, 19,* 452–457.

SEPPA, N. (1997, June). Children's TV remains steeped in violence. *APA Monitor, 28,* 36.

SEWELL, K. W., ADAMS-WEBBER, J., MITTERER, J., & CROMWELL, R. L. (1992). Computerized repertory grids: Review of the literature. *International Journal of Personal Construct Psychology, 5,* 1–23.

SEXTON, T. L., & WHISTON, S. C. (1994). The status of the counseling relationship: An empirical review, theoretical implications, and research directions. *The Counseling Psychologist, 22,* 6–78.

SHAGASS, C., & JONES, A. L. (1958). A neurophysiological test for psychiatric diagnosis: Results in 750 patients. *American Journal of Psychiatry, 114,* 1002–1009.

SHEPHER, J. (1971). Mate selection among second generation kibbutz adolescents and adults: Incest avoidance and negative imprinting. *Archives of Sexual Behavior, 1,* 293–307.

SHEPHER, J. (1983). *Incest: a biosocial view.* Orlando, FL: Academic Press.

SHIOMI, K. (1978). Relations of pain threshold and pain tolerance in cold water with scores on Maudsley Personality Inventory and Manifest Anxiety Scale. *Perceptual and Motor Skills, 47,* 1155–1158.

SHODA, Y., MISCHEL, W., & PEAKE, P. K. (1990). Predicting adolescent cognitive and self-regulatory competencies from preschool delay of gratification: Identifying diagnostic conditions. *Developmental Psychology, 26,* 978–986.

SHOSTROM, E. L. (1963). *Personal orientation inventory.* San Diego: Educational and Industrial Testing Service.

SHOSTROM, E. L. (1964). An inventory for the measurement of self-actualization. *Educational and Psychological Measurement, 24,* 207–218.

SHOSTROM, E. L. (1966). *Manual for the personal orientation inventory (POI): An inventory for the measurement of self-actualization.* San Diego: Educational and Industrial Testing Service.

SHOSTROM, E. L. (1974). *Manual for the personal orientation inventory.* San Diego: Educational and Industrial Testing Service.

SHOSTROM, E. L., KNAPP, L. F., & KNAPP, R. R. (1976). *Actualizing therapy: Foundations for a scientific ethic.* San Diego: Educational and Industrial Testing Service.

SIGNELL, K. (1966). Cognitive complexity in person perception and nation perception: A developmental approach. *Journal of Personality, 34,* 517–537.

SILVERMAN, I. (1987). Race, race differences, and race relations: Perspectives from psychology and sociobiology. In C. Crawford, M. Smith, & D. Krebs (Eds.), *Sociobiology and psychology: Ideas, issues, and applications* (pp. 205–221). Hillsdale, NJ: Erlbaum.

SILVERMAN, L. (1976). Psychoanalytic theory: "The reports of my death are greatly exaggerated." *American Psychologist, 31,* 621–637.

SINGER, P. (1981). *The expanding circle: Ethics and sociobiology.* New York: Farrar, Straus and Giroux.

SKINNER, B. F. (1938). *The behavior of organisms: An experimental analysis.* Englewood Cliffs, NJ: Prentice-Hall.

SKINNER, B. F. (1948). *Walden Two.* New York: Macmillan.

SKINNER, B. F. (1950). Are theories of learning necessary? *Psychological Review, 57,* 193–216.

SKINNER, B. F. (1951). How to teach animals. *Scientific American, 185,* 26–29.

SKINNER, B. F. (1953). *Science and human behavior.* New York: Macmillan.

SKINNER, B. F. (1957). *Verbal behavior.* Englewood Cliffs, NJ: Prentice-Hall.

SKINNER, B. F. (1959). A case history in scientific method. In S. Koch (Ed.), *Psychology: A study of a science* (Vol. 2, pp. 359–379). New York: McGraw-Hill.

SKINNER, B. F. (1971). *Beyond freedom and dignity.* New York: Knopf.

SKINNER, B. F. (1974). *About behaviorism.* New York: Knopf.

SKINNER, B. F. (1976). *Particulars of my life.* New York: Knopf.

SKINNER, B. F. (1978). *Reflections on behaviorism and society.* Englewood Cliffs, NJ: Prentice-Hall.

SKINNER, B. F. (1983). *A matter of consequences.* New York: Knopf.

SKINNER, B. F. (1990). Can psychology be a science of mind? *American Psychologist, 45,* 1206–1210.

SKINNER, E. A., CHAPMAN, M., & BALTES, P. B. (1988). Control, means-ends, and agency beliefs: A new conceptualization and its measurement during childhood. *Journal of Personality and Social Psychology, 54,* 117–133.

SMITH, H. S., & COHEN, L. H. (1993). Self-complexity and reactions to a relationship breakup. *Journal of Social and Clinical Psychology, 12,* 367–384.

SMITH, J. E., STEFAN, C., KOVALESKI, M., & JOHNSON, G. (1991). Recidivism and dependency in a psychiatric population: An investigation with Kelly's dependency grid. *International Journal of Personal Construct Psychology, 4,* 157–173.

SMITH, M. S. (1987). Evolution and developmental psychology: Toward a sociobiology of human development. In C. Crawford, M. Smith, & D. Krebs (Eds.), *Sociobiology and psychology: Ideas, issues, and applications* (pp. 225–252). Hillsdale, NJ: Erlbaum.

SMITH, S. M., & DE MAN, A. F. (1996). Selected personality characteristics and attitudes toward feminism. *Social Behaviour and Personality, 24,* 273–278.

SMITH, T. W. (1983). Changes in irrational beliefs and the outcome of rational-emotive psychotherapy. *Journal of Consulting and Clinical Psychologists, 51,* 156–157.

SOMIT, A., ARWINE, A., & PETERSON, S. A. (1996). *Birth order and political behavior.* Lanham, MD: University Press of America.

SPELTZ, M. L., SHIMAMURA, J. W., & McREYNOLDS, W. T. (1982). Procedural variations in group contingencies. *Journal of Applied Behavior Analysis, 15,* 533–544.

SPRANGER, E. (1928). *Types of men: The psychology and ethics of personality* (5th ed.). (P. J. W. Pigors, Trans.). Halle: Niemeyer. (Original work published 1913.)

STALIKAS, A., & FITOPOULOS, L. (1998). The translation and standardization of the MBTI into the Greek language. *Journal of Psychological Type, 46,* 13–21.

STEELMAN, L. C., & POWELL, B. (1985). The social and academic consequences of birth order: Real, artificial, or both. *Journal of Marriage and the Family, 47,* 117–124.

STEIN, K. F. (1994). Complexity of self-schema and responses to disconfirming feedback. *Cognitive Therapy and Research, 18,* 161–178.

STELMACK, R. M. (1990). Biological bases of extraversion: Psychophysiological evidence. *Journal of Personality, 58,* 293–311.

STELMACK, R. M. (1997). The psychophysics and psychophysiology of extraversion and arousal. In H. Nyborg (ed.), *The scientific study of human nature: A tribute to Hans Eysenck at eighty* (pp. 388–403). Oxford, England: Pergamon Press.

STELMACK, R. M., ACHORN, E., & MICHAUD, A. (1977). Extraversion and individual differences in auditory evoked response. *Psychophysiology, 14,* 368–374.

STELMACK, R. M., & CAMPBELL, K. B. (1974). Extraversion and auditory sensitivity to high and low frequency tones. *Perceptual and Motor Skills, 38,* 875–879.

STELMACK, R. M., & GEEN, R. G. (1992). The psychophysiology of extraversion. In A. Gale & M. W. Eysenck (Eds.), *Handbook of individual differences: Biological perspectives* (pp. 227–254). Chichester: Wiley.

STELMACK, R. M., & PIVIK, T. R. (1996). Extraversion and the effects of exercise on spinal motoneutonal excitability. *Personality and Individual Differences, 21,* 69–76.

STELMACK, R. M., & WILSON, K. G. (1982). Extraversion and the effects of frequency and intensity on the auditory brainstem evoked response. *Personality and Individual Differences, 3,* 373–380.

STEPHENSON, W. (1953). *The study of behavior: Q-technique and its methodology.* Chicago: University of Chicago Press.

STERN, P. J. (1976). *C. G. Jung: The haunted prophet.* New York: Dell.

STEVENS, A. (1994). *Jung.* New York: Oxford University Press.

STEVENS, S. S. (1951). Psychology and the science of science. In M. H. Marx (Ed.), *Psychological therapy: Contemporary readings.* New York: Macmillan.

STEWART, A. J., FRANZ, C., & LAYTON, L. (1988). The changing self: Using personal documents to study lives. *Journal of Personality, 56,* 41–74.

STEWART, R. A. C. (1968). Academic performance and components of self-actualization. *Perceptual and Motor Skills, 26,* 918.

STEWART, V., & STEWART, A. (1982). *Business applications of repertory grid.* New York: McGraw-Hill.

STOLOROW, R. D., & ATWOOD, G. E. (1979). *Faces in a cloud: Subjectivity in personality theory.* New York: Aronson.

STUART, R. B., & LOTT, L. A. (1972). Behavioral contracting with delinquents: A cautionary note. *Journal Therapy and Experimental Psychiatry, 3,* 161–169.

STUMPHAUZER, J. S. (1972). Increased delay of gratification in young prison inmates through imitation of high delay peer models. *Journal of Personality and Social Psychology, 21,* 10–17.

SUINN, R. M., OSBORNE, D., & WINFREE, P. (1962). The self concept and accuracy of recall of inconsistent self-related information. *Journal of Clinical Psychology, 18,* 473–474.

SULLOWAY, F. J. (1979). *Freud, Biologist of the mind: Beyond the psychoanalytic legend.* New York: Basic.

SULLOWAY, F. J. (1996). *Born to rebel: Birth order, family dynamics, and creative lives.* New York: Pantheon.

SUTICH, A. (1976). The emergence of the transpersonal orientation: A personal account. *Journal of Transpersonal Psychology, 1,* 5–19.

SYMONS, D. (1987). If we're all Darwinians, what's the fuss about? In C. Crawford, M. Smith, & D. Krebs (Eds.), *Sociobiology and psychology: Ideas, issues, and applications* (pp. 121–146). Hillsdale, NJ: Erlbaum.

TAYLOR, A., & MACDONALD, D. A. (1999). Religion and the five factor model of personality: An exploratory investigation using a Canadian university sample. *Personality and Individual Differences, 27,* 1243–1259.

TEISMANN, M. W., & MOSHER, D. L. (1978). Jealous conflict in dating couples. *Psychological Reports, 42,* 1211–1216.

TELLEGEN, A., LYKKEN, D. T., BOUCHARD, T. J., JR., WILCOX, K. J., SEGAL, N. L., & RICH, S. (1988). Personality similarity in twins reared apart and together. *Journal of Personality and Social Psychology, 54,* 1031–1039.

TESCH, S. A., & WHITBOURNE, S. K. (1982). Intimacy status and identity status in young adults. *Journal of Personality and Social Psychology, 43,* 1041–1051.

TETI, D. M., & GELFAND, D. M. (1991). Behavioral competence among mothers of infants in the first year: The mediational role of maternal self-efficacy. *Child Development, 62,* 918–929.

THOMPSON, G. G. (1968). George Alexander Kelly (1905–1967). *Journal of General Psychology, 79:19–24.*

THOMPSON, T., & GRABOWSKI, J. (1972). *Reinforcement schedules and multi-operant analysis.* Englewood Cliffs, NJ: Prentice-Hall.

THOMPSON, T., & GRABOWSKI, J. (Eds.). (1977). *Behavior modification of the mentally retarded.* New York: Oxford University Press.

THORNE, F. C. (1975). The life style analysis. *Journal of Clinical Psychology, 31,* 236–240.

THORNE, F. C., & PISHKIN, V. (1973). The existential study. *Journal of Clinical Psychology, 29,* 387–410.

THORNHILL, N. W., & THORNHILL, R. (1987a). Evolutionary theory and rules of mating and marriage pertaining to relatives. In C. Crawford, M. Smith, & D. Krebs (Eds.), *Sociobiology and psychology: Ideas, issues, and applications* (pp. 373–400). Hillsdale, NJ: Erlbaum.

THORNHILL, R., & THORNHILL, N. W. (1983). Human rape: An evolutionary analysis. *Ethology and Socio-biology, 4,* 137–173.

THORNHILL, R., & THORNHILL, N. W. (1987b). Human rape: The strengths of the evolutionary perspective. In C. Crawford, M. Smith, & D. Krebs (Eds.), *Sociobiology and psychology: Ideas, issues, and applications* (pp. 269–291). Hillsdale, NJ: Erlbaum.

THURSTONE, L. L. (1934). The vectors of mind. *Psychological Review, 41,* 1–32.

TILLICH, P. (1952). *The courage to be.* New Haven: Yale University Press.

TRIGG, R. (1982). *The shaping of man: Philosophical aspects of sociobiology.* New York: Schocken.

TRIVERS, R. L. (1971). The evolution of reciprocal altruism. *Quarterly Review of Biology, 46,* 35–57.

TRUAX, C. B., & CARKHUFF, R. R. (1967). *Toward effective counseling and psychotherapy.* Chicago: Aldine.

TRUAX, C. B., & MITCHELL, K. M. (1971). Research on certain therapist interpersonal skills in relation to process and outcome. In A. E. Bergin & S. L. Garfield (Eds.), *Handbook of psychotherapy and behavior change.* New York: Wiley.

TUCKMAN, B. W. (1990). Group versus goal-setting effects on the self-regulated performance of students differing in self-efficacy. *Journal of Experimental Education, 58,* 291–298.

TUPES, E. C., & CHRISTAL, R. E. (1961). Recurrent personality factors based on trait ratings (USAF ASD Tech. Rep. No. 61–97). Lackland Air Force Base, TX: U.S. Air Force.

TURNER, C. W., HESSE, B. W., & PETERSON-LEWIS, S. (1986). Naturalistic studies of the long-term effects of television violence. *Journal of Social Issues, 42(3),* 51–73.

TURNER, R. H., & VANDERLIPPE, R. H. (1958). Self-ideal congruence as an index of adjustment. *Journal of Abnormal and Social Psychology, 57,* 202–206.

VACC, N. A., & GREENLEAF, W. (1975). Sequential development of cognitive complexity. *Perceptual and Motor Skills, 41,* 319–322.

VAN DEN BERGHE, P. L. (1987). Incest taboos and avoidance: Some African applications. In C. Crawford, M. Smith, & D. Krebs (Eds.), *Sociobiology and psychology: Ideas, issues, and applications* (pp. 353–371). Hillsdale, NJ: Erlbaum.

VAN DER POST, L. (1975). *Jung and the story of our time.* New York: Pantheon.

VAN HOOFF, J. (1971). *Aspects of social behaviour and communication in humans and higher nonhuman primates.* Rotterdam: Bronder.

VAN KAAM, A. (1966). *Existential foundations of psychology.* Pittsburgh: Duquesne University Press.

VERPLANCK, W. S. (1955). The operant, from rat to man: An introduction to some recent experiments on human behavior. *Transactions of the New York Academy of Science, 17,* 594–601.

VINEY, L. L. (1983). *Images of illness.* Miami: Krieger.

VINEY, L. L. (1984). Concerns about death among severely ill people. In F. R. Epting & R. A. Neimeyer (Eds.), *Personal meanings of death.* Washington, DC: Hemisphere.

VINEY, L.L., ALLWOOD, K., STILLSON, L., & WALMSLEY, R. (1992). Personal construct therapy for HIV and seropositivepatients. *Psychotherapy, 29:*430–427.

VYSE, S. A. (1990). Adapting a viewpoint: Psychology majors and psychological theory. *Teaching of Psychology, 17,* 227–230.

WALKER, B. M. (1990). Construing George Kelly's construing of the person-in-relation. *International Journal of Personal Construct Psychology, 3,* 41–50.

WALLACE, R. A. (1979). *The genesis factor.* New York: William Morrow.

WALLER, N. G., KOJETIN, B. A., BOUCHARD, T. J., JR., LYKKEN, D. T., & TELLEGEN, A. (1990). Genetic and environmental influences on religious interests, attitudes, and values. *Psychological Science, 1,* 138–142.

WATERMAN, A. S. (1982). Identity development from adolescence to adulthood: An extension of theory and a review of research. *Developmental Psychology, 18,* 341–358.

WATERMAN, A. S., GEARY, P. S., & WATERMAN, C. K. (1974). Longitudinal study of changes in ego identity status from the freshman to the senior year at college. *Developmental Psychology, 10,* 387–392.

WATERMAN, C. K., BUEBEL, M. E., & WATERMAN, A. S. (1970). Relationship between resolution of the identity crisis and outcomes of previous psychosocial crises. *Proceedings of the 78th Annual Convention of the American Psychological Convention, 5,* 467–468.

WATSON, J. B. (1926). Experimental studies on the growth of the emotions. In C. Murchison (Ed.), *Psychologies of 1925.* Worcester, MA: Clark University Press.

WATSON, P. J., MORRIS, R. J., & HOOD, R. W., JR. (1990). Extrinsic scale factors: Correlations and construction of religious orientation types. *Journal of Psychology and Christianity, 9,* 35–46.

WEBSTER, R. (1995). *Why Freud was wrong: Sin, science, and psychoanalysis.* New York: Basic Books.

WEHR, G. (1987). *Jung: A biography.* Boston: Shambhala.

WEINBERG, R. S., HUGHES, H. H., CRITELLI, J. W., ENGLAND, R., & JACKSON, A. (1984). Effects of preexisting and manipulated self–efficacy on weight loss in a self-control program. *Journal of Research in Personality, 18,* 352–358.

WEISS, R. L., BIRCHLER, G. R., & VINCENT, J. P. (1974). Contractual models for negotiation training in marital dyads. *Journal of Marriage and the Family, 36,* 321–330.

WEISSTEIN, N. (1975). Psychology constructs the female, or the fantasy life of the male psychologist (with some attention to the fantasies of his friends, the male biologist and the male anthropologist). In I. Cohen (Ed.), *Perspectives on psychology.* New York: Praeger.

WEST, S. (Ed.). (1983, September). Personality and prediction: Nomothetic and idiographic approaches [Special issue]. *Journal of Personality, 51,* (3).

WESTERMARCK, E. A. (1891). *The history of human marriage.* London: Macmillan.

WIEDENFELD, S. A., O'LEARY, A., BANDURA, A., BROWN, S., LEVINE, S., & RASKA, K. (1990). Impact of perceived self-efficacy in coping with stressors on components of the immune system. *Journal of Personality and Social Psychology, 59,* 1082–1094.

WIENER, D. N. (1996). *B. F. Skinner: Benign anarchist.* Needham Heights, MA: Allyn & Bacon.

WILCOCKS, R. (1994). *Maelzel's chess player: Sigmund Freud and the rhetoric of deceit.* Savage, MD: Rowand and Littlefield.

WILLET, R. A. (1960). Measures of learning and conditioning. In H. J. Eysenck (Ed.), *Experiments in personality* (Vol. 2). London: Routledge & Kegan Paul.

WILLIAMS, D. E., & PAGE, M. M. (1989). A multidimensional measure of Maslow's hierarchy of needs. *Journal of Research in Personality, 23,* 192–213.

WILSON, C. (1972). *New pathways in psychology: Maslow and the post-Freudian revolution.* New York: Taplinger.

WILSON, E. O. (1971). *The insect societies.* Cambridge, MA: Harvard University Press.

WILSON, E. O. (1975). *Sociobiology: The new synthesis.* Cambridge, MA: Harvard University Press.

WILSON, E. O. (1978). *On human nature.* New York: Bantam.

WILSON, E. O. (1980). Comparative social theory. *The Tanner lectures on human values.* Presented at the University of Michigan, Ann Arbor, MI.

WILSON, E. O. (1985). In the queendom of the ants: A brief autobiography. In Donald A. Dewsbury (Ed.), *Leaders in the study of animal behavior: Autobiographical perspectives* (pp. 464–484). Cranbury, NJ: Bucknell University Press.

WILSON, E.E. (1994). *Naturalist.* New York: Warner Books.

WILSON, E. O., & HÖLLDOBLER, B. (1990). *The ants.* Cambridge, MA: Harvard University Press.

WILSON, G. D. (1997). IN H. NYBORG (EDS.), *The scientific study of human nature: Tribute to Hans J. Eysenck at eighty* (pp.163-188). Amsterdam, Netherlands: Pergamon/Elsevier Science.

WILSON, M. (1989). Marital conflict and homicide in evolutionary perspective. In R. W. Bell & N. J. Bell (Eds.), *Sociobiology and the social sciences* (pp. 45–62). Lubbock, TX: Texas Tech University Press.

WILSON, S. R., & SPENCER, R. C. (1990). Intense personal experiences: Subjective effects, interpretations, and after-effects. *Journal of Clinical Psychology, 46,* 565–573.

WINTER, D. A. (1993). Slot rattling from law enforcement to lawbreaking: A personal construct theory exploration of police stress. *International Journal of Personal Construct Psychology, 6,* 253–267.

WITTELS, F. (1924). *Sigmund Freud: His personality, his teaching, and his school.* London: Allen and Unwin.

WOJCIK, J. V. (1988). Social learning predictors of the avoidance of smoking relapse. *Addictive Behaviors, 13,* 177–180.

WOLF, A. P., & HUANG, C. S. (1980). *Marriage and adoption in China, 1845–1945.* Stanford, CA: Stanford University Press.

WOLPE, J., & PLAUD, J. J. (1997). Pavlov's contributions to behavior therapy: The obvious and the not so obvious. *American Psychologist, 52,* 966–972.

WONG, P. T. P. (1992). Guest Editorial: Control is a double-edged sword. *Canadian Journal of Behaviour Science, 24,* 143–146.

WOOD, R., & BANDURA, A. (1989). Impact of conceptions of ability on self-regulatory mechanisms and complex decision making. *Journal of Personality and Social Psychology, 56,* 407–415.

WOOD, R., BANDURA, A., & BAILEY, T. (1990). Mechanisms governing organizational performance in complex decision-making environments. *Organizational Behavior and Human Decision Processes, 46,* 181–201.

WRIGHT, J. C., & MISCHEL, W. (1987). A conditional approach to dispositional contructs: The local predictability of social behavior. *Journal of Personality and Social Behavior, 53,* 1159–1177.

WRIGHTMAN, L. S. (1981). Personal documents as data in conceptualizing adult personality development. *Personality and Social Psychology Bulletin, 7,* 367–385.

WULFF, D. M. (1991). *Psychology and religion: Classic and contemporary views.* New York: Wiley.

WUNDT, W. (1903). *Grundzuge der physiologischen psychologie* (Vol. 3, 5th ed.). Leipzig: W. Engelmann.

YEAGLE, E. H., PRIVETTE, G., & DUNHAM, F. Y. (1989). Highest happiness: An analysis of artists' peak experience. *Psychological Reports, 65,* 523–530.

YIK, M. S. M., BOND, M. H., & PAULHUS, D. L. (1998). Do Chinese self-enhance or self-efface?: It's a matter of domain. *Journal of Research in Personality, 24,* 399–406.

YONGE, G. D. (1975). Time experiences, self-actualizing values, and creativity. *Journal of Personality Assessment, 39,* 601–606.

YOUNG-BRUEHL, E. (1990). *Freud on women: A reader.* New York: Norton.

ZAJONC, R. B., & MARKUS, G. B. (1975). Birth order and intellectual development. *Psychological Review, 82,* 74–88.

ZIMBARDO, P., & RUCH, F. (1977). *Psychology and life* (9th ed.). Glenview, IL: Scott, Foresman.

ZUCKERMAN, M. (1991). *Psychobiology of personality.* New York: Cambridge University Press.

ZUCKERMAN, M. (1995). Good and bad humors: Biochemical bases of personality and its disorders. *Psychological Science, 6,* 325–332.

ZUROFF, D. (1986). Was Gordon Allport a trait theorist? *Journal of Personality and Social Psychology, 51,* 993–1000.

Name Index

Subject Index

Credits

Photos

Chapter 2
Austrian National Tourist Office, 18; By permission of Sigmund Freud Copyrights, Wivenhoe, 18; Canadian Press/Fred Chartran, 24; BCTV, 32.

Chapter 3
Courtesy of Archives of the History of American Psychology—University of Akron and Clark University Archives and Special Collections, 51, 58; Canadian Press/Robert Galbraith, 60; Canadian Press/Jonathan Hayward, 69.

Chapter 4
UPI/Bettmann Newsphotos, 79; Canadian Press/Jon Murray, 82; Eyewire/Getty Images, 97.

Chapter 5
The Bettmann Archive, 104; Justin Pumfrey/Firstlight.ca, 108; Nancy Honey/Getty Images, 112.

Chapter 6
Jon Erikson, 128; Canadian Press/Fredericton Daily Gleaner/Stephen MacGillivray, 135; Richard Heinzen/SuperStock, 141.

Chapter 7
Dominique, 154; Al Harvey/The Slide Farm, 163; Canadian Press/Edmonton Sun/Brendan Dlouhy, 165.

Chapter 8
Raymond B. Cattell, 182; Hans J. Eysenck, 183; Canadian Press/The London Free Press/Dave Chidley, 196; Canadian Press/The Whig-Standard/Ian MacAlpine, 205.

Chapter 9
AP/Wide World Photos, 219; Corbis-Bettmann, 221; Pascal Crapet/Getty Images, 235.

Chapter 10
Yale University Library, 247; The Rockefeller University Archives, 247; Canadian Press/Mike Ridewood, 261.

Chapter 11
Photo by Joe Pineiro, Courtesy of David Eugene Smith Collection, Rare Book and Manuscript Library, Columbia University, 276; News and Publications Service, Stanford University, 276; Gerry Kahrman/Province, 284; AP/Wide World Photos, 292.

Chapter 12
Courtesy of Edward O. Wilson, 306; Courtesy of David P. Barash, 307; Canadian Press/Kevin Frayer, 332.

Chapter 13
Courtesy Brandeis University, 346; Canadian Press/Andrew Vaughn, 355.

Chapter 14
Carl Rogers Memorial Library at The Center for Students of the Person, La Jolla, CA., 375; Canstock, 381.

Chapter 15
Courtesy of Brooks/Cole Publishing Company, Pacific Grove, California, 401; City of Toronto Archives, Fonds 1244, item 1683, 408.

Chapter 16
Courtesy of Rollo Reese May, 429; Canadian Press/Andrew Vaughn, 432.

Excerpts

Chapter 3
Memories, Dreams, Reflections, by C. G. Jung, recorded and edited by Aniela Jaffe, translated by Richard and Clara Winston. Copyright © 1961, 1962, 1963 by Random House, Inc. Reprinted by permission of Pantheon Books, a division of Random House, Inc.

C. G. Jung, Two Essays on Analytical Psychology. In *The Collected Works of C. G. Jung* (Vol. 7). Princeton University Press, 1966. (Originally published 1917.)

Chapter 4
A. Adler, A. (1930). Individual Psychology. In C. Murchison (Ed.), *Psychologies of 1930.* Worcester, Mass.: Clark University Press, 1930.

H. L. Ansbacher, and R. R. Ansbacher (Eds.). (1956). *The Individual Psychology of Alfred Adler.* New York: Basic Books.

Figures 4–2 and 4–3 from Sulloway, F. J. (1996*). Born to rebel: Birth order, family dynamics, and creative lives.* New York: Pantheon.

Chapter 5
K. Horney. (1945). *Our Inner Conflicts.* New York: Norton.

Chapter 6

Reprinted from *Childhood and Society* (2nd ed.) by Erik H. Erikson, by permission of W. W. Norton & Company, Inc. Copyright renewed 1978, 1991 by Erik H. Erikson.

Chapter 7

Allport., G. W. (1955). *Becoming: Basic Considerations for a Psychology of Personality.* New Haven, CT: Yale University Press, 1955.

Allport, G. W. (1967). Autobiography. In E. G. Boring and G. Lindzey (Eds.), *A History of Psychology in Autobiography* (Vol. 5, pp. 1–25). New York: Appleton-Century-Crofts. Reprinted by permission Irvington Publishers.

Allport, G. W. (1961). *Pattern and Growth in Personality.* New York: Holt, Rinehart & Winston. Reprinted by permission of author's estate.

Allport. G. W. *The Nature of Prejudice,* Copyright © 1979 by Addison-Wesley Publishing Company, Inc. Reprinted with permission of the publisher.

Chapter 8

Cattell. R. B. (1965).*The Scientific Analysis of Personality.* Baltimore: Penguin.

Cattell, R. B. (1950). Personality: *A Systematic, Theoretical and Factual Study.* New York: McGraw-Hill.

Table 8–3 adopted from Cattell, R. B. *Personality and Learning Theory.* Copyright © 1979, 1980 Springer Publishing Company, Inc., New York. Used by permission.

Table 8–4 from McCrae, R. R. & Costa, P. T., Jr. (1990). *Personality in Adulthood.* New York: The Guilford Press.

Excerpts and Figures 8–5, 8–6, and 8–7 from Eysenck, H. J. & Eysenck, M. W. (1985). *Personality and Individual Differences: A Natural Science Approach.* New York: Plenum Press.

Chapter 9

Reprinted with permission of Macmillan Publishing Company from *Science and Human Behavior* by B. F. Skinner. Copyright © 1953 by Macmillan Publishing Company; copyright renewed 1981 by B. F. Skinner.

Skinner, B.F. *Beyond Freedom and Dignity.* Copyright © 1971 by B. F. Skinner. Reprinted by permission of Alfred A. Knopf, Inc.

Hergenhahn, B. R. & Olson, M. H. (1997). *An Introduction to Theories of Learning* (4th ed.). Englewood Cliffs, N.J.: Prentice Hall.

Chapter 10

Miller, N. E. & Dollard, J. (1941). *Social Learning and Imitation.* New Haven, CT: Yale University Press.

Dollard, J. and Miller, N. E. (1950). *Personality and Psychotherapy: An Analysis in Terms of Learning, Thinking and Culture.* New York: McGraw-Hill.

Chapter 11

Bandura, A. (1986). *Social Foundations of Thought and Action: A Social Cognitive Theory.* Copyright © 1986. Prentice Hall, Englewood Cliffs, N.J. Used with permission.

Table 11–1 from Mischel, W. (1993). *Introduction to personality* (5th ed.). Orlando, FL: Harcourt, Brace, Jovanovich.

Chapter 12

Crawford, C., Smith, M., & Krebs, D. (Eds.) (1987). *Sociobiology and Psychology: Ideas, Issues, and Applications.* Hillsdale, N.J.: Lawrence Erlbaum.

Symons D. (1987). If We're All Darwinians, What's the Fuss About? In C. Crawford, M. Smith, & D. Krebs (Eds.), *Sociobiology and Psychology: Ideas, Issues, and Applications* (pp. 121–146). Hillsdale, N.J.: Lawrence Erlbaum Associates.

Thornhill, R. & Thornhill, N. W. (1987). Human Rape: The Strengths of the Evolutionary Perspective (pp. 269–291); Thornhill, N. W. & Thornhill, R. (1987). Evolutionary Theory and Rules of Mating and Marriage Pertaining to Relatives. Both in C. Crawford, M. Smith, and D. Krebs (Eds.), *Sociobiology and Psychology: Ideas, Issues, and Applications.* Hillsdale, N.J.: Lawrence Erlbaum.

de Cantanzano, D. (1987). Evolutionary Pressures and Limitations to Self Preservation. In C. Crawford, M. Smith, and D. Krebs (Eds.), *Sociobiology and Psychology: Ideas, Issues, and Applications* (pp. 311–333). Hillsdale, N.J.: Lawrence Erlbaum.

Smith, M. S. (1987). Evolution and Developmental Psychology: Toward a Sociobiology of Human Development. In C. Crawford, M. Smith, and D. Krebs (Eds.) *Sociobiology and Psychology: Ideas, Issues, and Applications* (pp. 225–252). Hillsdale, N.J.: Lawrence Erlbaum.

van den Berghe, P. L. (1987). Incest Taboos and Avoidance: Some African Applications. In C. Crawford, M. Smith, and D. Krebs (Eds.) *Sociobiology and Psychology: Ideas, Issues, and Applications* (pp. 353–371). Hillsdale, N.J.: Lawrence Erlbaum.

Buss, D. M. (1987). Sex Differences in Human Mate Selection Criteria: An Evolutionary Perspective. In C. Crawford, M. Smith, and D. Krebs (Eds.) *Sociobiology and Psychology: Ideas, Issues, and Applications* (pp. 335–351). Hillsdale, N.J.: Lawrence Erlbaum.

The Hare and the Tortoise by David Barash. Copyright © David Barash, 1986. All rights reserved. Reprinted by permission of Viking Penguin, a division of Penguin Books USA, Inc.

Reprinted by permission of the publishers from *On Human Nature* by Edward O. Wilson, Cambridge, Mass.: Harvard University Press, Copyright © 1978 by the President and Fellows of Harvard College.

Excerpts from *The Whisperings Within* by David Barash. Copyright © 1979 by David P. Barash. Reprinted by permission of HarperCollins, Publishers, Inc.

Silverman, I. (1987). Race, Race Differences, and Race Relations: Perspectives from Psychology and Sociobiology. In C. Crawford, M. Smith, and D. Krebs (Eds.), *Sociobiology and Psychology: Ideas, Issues, and Applications* (pp. 205–221). Hillsdale, N.J.: Lawrence Erlbaum.

Chapter 13

Bannister, D. & Fransella, F. (1971). *Inquiring Man: The Theory of Personal Constructs.* New York: Penguin.

Kelly, G. A. (1955). *The Psychology of Personal Constructs: A Theory of Personality* (2 vols.). New York: Norton, 1955.

Figure 13–1 adopted from R. A. Neimeyer (1985) Personal Constructs in Clinical Practice. In P. C. Kendall (ed.) *Advances in Cognitive-Behavioral Research and Therapy* (Vol. 4, p. 281). New York: Academic Press. Used with permission.

Chapter 14

Rogers, C. R.. *On Becoming a Person.* Copyright © 1961 by Houghton Mifflin Company. Used with permission.

Rogers, C. R.. A Theory of Therapy, Personality, and Interpersonal Relationships, as Developed in the Client-Centered Framework. In S. Koch (Ed.), *Psychology: A Study of a Science* (Vol. 3). New York: McGraw-Hill, 1959.

Chapter 15

Excerpts from *Motivation and Personality,* Third Edition by Abraham H. Maslow, revised by Robert Frager, James Fadiman, Cynthia McReynolds, and Ruth Cox. Copyright 1954, 1987 by Harper & Row, Publishers, Inc., Copyright © 1970 by Abraham H. Maslow. Reprinted by permission of HarperCollins, Publishers, Inc.

Maslow, A. H. (1968). *Toward a Psychology of Being* (2nd ed.). New York: D. Van Nostrand.

Maslow, A. H. (1971). *The Farther Reaches of Human Nature.* New York: Viking.

Excerpts reprinted by permission of The Putnam Publishing Group from *The Right to be Human: A Biography of Abraham Maslow* (1988) by Edward Hoffman, Ph.D. Copyright © 1988 by Edward Hoffman.

Chapter 16

Reprinted from *Psychology and the Human Dilemma* by Rollo May, by permission of W. W. Norton & Company, Inc. Copyright © 1979 by Rollo May. Copyright © 1967 by W. W. Norton & Company, Inc.

Reprinted from *Love and Will* by Rollo May, by permission of W. W. Norton & Company, Inc. Copyright © 1969 by W. W. Norton & Company, Inc.